D0162773

CLIFFS NOTES

HARDBOUND LITERARY LIBRARIES

ENGLISH LITERATURE LIBRARY

Volume 3

Victorian Age

Part 1

11 Titles

ISBN 0-931013-09-7

Library distributors, hardbound editions:
Moonbeam Publications
18530 Mack Avenue
Grosse Pointe, MI 48236
(313) 884-5255

MOONBEAM PUBLICATIONS
Judith M.Tyler, President
Elizabeth Jones, Index Editor

FOREWORD

Moonbeam Publications has organized **CLIFFS NOTES,** the best-selling popular (trade) literary reference series, into a fully indexed hardbound series designed to offer a more permanent format for the series.

Hardbound volumes are available in a **BASIC LIBRARY,** a 24 volume series. The current softbound series (over 200 booklets) has been divided into five major literary libraries to help researchers, librarians, teachers, students and all readers use this series more effectively. The five major literary groupings are further subdivided into 17 literary periods or genres to enhance the use of this series as a more precise literary reference book.

Hardbound volumes are also available in an **AUTHORS LIBRARY,** a 13 volume series classified by author, covering 11 authors and over 70 Cliffs Notes titles. This series helps readers who prefer to study the works of a particular author, rather than an entire literary period.

**CLIFFS NOTES HARDBOUND
LITERARY LIBRARIES**
1990 by
Moonbeam Publications
18530 Mack Avenue
Grosse Pointe, MI   48236
(313) 884-5255

Basic Library - 24 Volume
ISBN 0-931013-24-0

Authors Library - 13 Volume
ISBN 0-931013-65-8

Bound In U.S.A.

ENGLISH LITERATURE LIBRARY

Volume 3

The Victorian Age,

Part 1

CONTENTS

Alice in Wonderland

ALICE IN WONDERLAND

NOTES

including
- *Life and Background*
- *List of Characters*
- *Introduction and Brief Synopsis*
- *Summaries and Commentaries*
- *Critical Analysis*
    Alice as a Character
    Abandonment/Loneliness
    The Child-Swain
    Children and Animals
    Death
    Nonsense
    Nature and Nurture
    Justice
    Time and Space
- *Essay Topics*
- *Selected Bibliography*

by
Carl Senna, M.F.A.
Visiting Scholar,
Brown University

Cliffs Notes
INCORPORATED
LINCOLN, NEBRASKA 68501

Editor

Gary Carey, M.A.
University of Colorado

Consulting Editor

James L. Roberts, Ph.D.
Department of English
University of Nebraska

ISBN 0-8220-0140-3
© Copyright 1984
by
C. K. Hillegass
All Rights Reserved
Printed in U.S.A.

1992 Printing

Cliffs Notes, Inc.   Lincoln, Nebraska

CONTENTS

ALICE IN WONDERLAND NOTES

LIFE AND BACKGROUND

Of all Lewis Carroll's major works, *Alice in Wonderland* has a unique standing in the category of whimsical, nonsense literature. Much has been written about how this novel contrasts with the vast amount of strict, extremely moralistic children's literature. This is true; *Alice* is quite different from all other Victorian children's literature. Yet, as odd as this story appears in relation to the other Victorian children's stories, this short novel is odder still because it was written by an extremely upright, ultra-conservative man – in short, a quintessential Victorian gentleman.

Lewis Carroll was born Charles Lutwidge Dodgson on January 27, 1832, in the parsonage of Daresbury, Cheshire, England, the third child and eldest son of eleven children of Reverend Charles Dodgson and his wife, Francis Jane Lutwidge. The parents were descended from two ancient and distinguished North Country families. From the Dodgsons, the son inherited a very old tradition of service to the Church and a tradition that he belonged to one of the most respected lineages in England – for example, family legend has it that King James I actually "knighted" either a loin of beef or mutton at the table of Sir Richard Houghton, one of Carroll's ancestors. This incident has been thought by some critics to have inspired the introductory lines in *Through the Looking Glass,* the sequel to *Alice in Wonderland*, when the Red Queen introduces the leg of mutton to Alice: "Alice – Mutton: Mutton – Alice."

For the sake of those who are curious about pen names and how authors choose one over another, "Lewis Carroll" is an interesting example. While teaching at Christ Church, Oxford, Charles Dodgson (Carroll) wrote comic literature and parodies for a humorous paper, *The Train.* The first of the several pieces submitted to *The Train* was signed "B. B." It was so popular that the editor asked Dodgson to use a proper nom de plume; at first, Dodgson proposed "Dares," after his birthplace, Daresbury. The editor thought that the name was too journalistic, so after struggling over a number of choices, Dodgson wrote to his editor and suggested a number of variations and anagrams, based on the letters of his actual name. "Lewis Carroll" was finally decided on, derived from a rearrangement of most of the letters in the name "Charles Lutwidge Dodgson." Clearly, Carroll was fascinated with anagrams, and he will use them throughout *Alice in Wonderland*; his interest in anagrams also explains much about the writings in his later life, and his mathematical works. Concerning Carroll, one cannot safely exclude any influence, least of all hereditary ones, but a good case can be made for the formative effect of Carroll's father on him. Those who knew Reverend Dodgson said that he was a pious and gloomy man, almost devoid of any sense of humor. Yet from his letters to his son, there is recorded evidence of a *remarkable* sense of fun. For example, in one letter to his son, he speaks of screaming in the middle of a street:

> "Iron-mongers-Iron-mongers—Six hundred men
> will rush out of their shops in a moment—fly, fly,
> in all directions—ring the bells, call the constables—
> set the town on fire. I will have a file & a screwdriver,
> & a ring, & if they are not brought directly, in forty
> seconds I will leave nothing but one small cat alive
> in the whole town of Leeds, & I shall only leave that
> because I shall not have time to kill it.

To a boy of eight, such correspondence from his father must have greatly heightened his later love for literary exaggeration; indeed, such fanciful letters may have been the genesis for Carroll's so-called nonsense books.

As we noted, Reverend Dodgson was said to be an austere, puritanical, and authoritarian Victorian man; Lewis Carroll's mother, however, was the essence of the Victorian "gentlewoman." As described by her son, she was "one of the sweetest and gentlest women that had ever lived, whom to know was to love." The childhood of Lewis Carroll was relatively pleasant, full of ideas and hobbies that contributed to his future creative works. His life at Daresbury was secluded, though, and his playmates were mostly his brothers and sisters. Class distinctions did not permit much socializing between children of the parsonage and the "lesser" parish children. Curiously, a number of the Dodgson children, including Carroll, stammered severely. More than one author has suggested that, at least in Carroll's case, his stammer may have arisen from his parents' attempts to correct his left-handedness. Isa Bowman, a childhood friend of Carroll's, has said that whenever adults approached them on their walks, Carroll's speech became extremely difficult to understand. Apparently, he panicked; his shyness and stammering always seemed worse when he was in the world of adults. This stammering made him into a bit of a "loner" and explains, somewhat, Carroll's longtime fascination with puzzles and anagrams, solitary games to amuse himself. It was as though the long suppressed, left-handed self endured in the fanciful, literary adult Carroll—in contrast to the very stern adult librarian, mathematics lecturer, deacon, dormitory master, and curator of the dining hall. Carroll was, seemingly, the archetype of the left-handed man in a right-handed world, like his own White Knight in *Through the Looking Glass* (the sequel to *Alice in Wonderland*).

"And now if ever by chance I put
My fingers into glue
Or madly squeeze a right-hand foot
Into a left-hand shoe . . ."

Carroll's fondness for games, language puzzles, and the world of the bizarre is further demonstrated in his flair for amusing his brothers and sisters—especially his sisters, which explains, perhaps, his lifelong attraction for little girls. In fact, a great deal of Carroll's childhood was spent taking care of his little sisters. At home, it was he who was in charge of these seven sisters, and his imagination was constantly being exercised in order to entertain them. In one of his fanciful story-games that he invented, he imagined a sort of "railway game," and as one of the rules of the game, at least *three* trains had to run over the passengers in order for the passengers to be attended to by physicians. Fortunately, though, rarely were Carroll's amusements cruel, and when the family moved to the Croft Rectory, Yorkshire, where Carroll's father assumed the Archdeaconry, Carroll wrote, directed, and performed light, gay plays, and he also manipulated puppets and marionettes for his family and friends.

In addition to the plays that Carroll wrote and the scripts that he composed for his puppet theater, he also wrote poems, stories, and humorous sketches for his own "magazines." In his "Useful and Instructive Poetry" magazine, for example, a volume that was composed for a younger brother and a sister, he satirized a copybook of stern, dogmatic maxims (a typical Victorian children's book), and in this poem, he alluded to his own handicap:

> "Learn well your grammar
> And never stammer . . . .
> Eat bread with butter;
> Once more, don't stutter."

Other poems in the volume focus on the theme of fairy tales, an interest which played a large part in the creation of *Alice.* An early poem of Carroll's, for instance, "My Fairy," suggests the contrariness of the creatures that Alice will meet in Wonderland:

> "I have a fairy by my side
> Which cried; it said, 'You must not weep.'
> If, full of mirth, I smile and grin,
> It says, 'You must not laugh,'
> When once I wished to drink some gin,
> It said, 'You must not quaff.'"

Similarly, in another early poem, "A Tale of a Tail," there is a drawing of a very long dog's tail, suggestive of the very slender, increasingly smaller mouse's tail in *Alice,* which coils across a single page in a sort of S-shape. Also, an early poem about someone falling off a wall anticipates Humpty Dumpty in *Through the Looking Glass,* and a "Morals" essay reminds one of the ridiculous conversations between the ugly Duchess and the evil Queen in *Alice.* It is difficult to ignore the writings of Carroll as a child in any analysis of his works, for in his childhood productions, we find conclusive evidence of early imitations, hints, allusions, suggestions, and actual elements of imaginary creatures, dreams, and visions that will appear in his later works.

EDUCATION

All his life, Carroll was a scholar; when he was not a student, he was a teacher, and until two years before his death, he was firmly imbedded in the life of Oxford University. Quite honestly, though, nothing very exciting ever happened in Carroll's life, apart from a trip to the Continent, including Russia. His vacations were all local ones, to his sister's home in Guildford, his aunt's home in Hastings, and to Eastbourne, the Lake Country, and Wales. He did not begin his formal schooling until the age of twelve, when he enrolled in Richmond Grammar School, ten miles from the Croft Rectory, but he had already received a thorough background in literature from the family library. Yet it was mathematics – and not English literature – that interested Carroll most. When he was very young, for example, Carroll implored his father to explain logarithms to him, presumably because he had already mastered arithmetic, algebra, and even most of Euclidian geometry.

Carroll entered Rugby in 1846, but the sensitive young child found the all-boys environment highly unpleasant; the bullying abuse, the flogging, and the caning was a daily part of school life. Nonetheless, Carroll was, despite his three years of unhappiness there, an exceedingly studious boy, and he won many prizes for academic excellence.

Carroll matriculated at Christ Church, Oxford, in 1851, and remained there for forty-seven years. But, two days after entering Oxford, he received word of his mother's death, something which deeply distressed him and seemed to have worsened his stammering. By all accounts, Carroll was not an outgoing student; with little money, and because of his stammer, his circle of friends always remained small. Yet in his academic work, he applied himself with the same energy and devotion that characterized his career at Rugby. He won scholarship prizes, honors in Classical exams, and also won a First Prize in Mathematics. His scholastic efforts were rewarded by a lifetime fellowship and a residency at Christ Church, so long as he remained unmarried and proceeded to take Holy Orders.

In 1854, the year Carroll took his B.A. degree, he began publishing poetry in the student magazines and in *The Whitby Gazette*. Carroll's writings had already established him as both a superb raconteur and humorist at Oxford, and in 1854, he began to seriously teach himself how to express his thoughts in proper literary form; it was at that time that his writings began to show some of the whimsy and fantasy that are contained in the *Alice* books.

In 1857, Carroll took his M.A. degree and was made "Master of the House." During those years, he immersed himself in literature, mathematics, and also in the London theater. He produced free-lance humorous prose pieces and verses for various periodicals, explored theories of dual identities, wrote satires, published mathematical and symbolic logic texts, invented word games and puzzles, and took up photography, a hobby that would make him famous as one of the best Victorian photographers. In short, Carroll became a sort of lesser English equivalent of Leonardo da Vinci. He invented the Nyctograph, a device for writing in the dark, and he also invented a method of remote control self-photography. Helmut Gernsheim, the author of *Lewis Carroll: Photographer,* calls Carroll's photographic achievements "astonishing"; in his estimation, Carroll "must not only rank as a pioneer of British amateur photography, but I would also unhesitatingly acclaim him as the most outstanding photographer of children in the nineteenth century."

CARROLL'S INTEREST IN LITTLE GIRLS

In every study of Carroll's life, one finds that Carroll had only the most formal encounters with mature women. There was seemingly no romantic interest in adult women. Some biographers have attributed this asexual interest to Carroll's stammering and his self-conscious shyness about it. On the other hand, Carroll's diaries and contemporary accounts about him are full of his encounters with children, nearly always with little girls. He obviously delighted in the company of little girls twelve years old and younger, and his diary records in great detail the aesthetic pleasure that he took in viewing "nice little children." Carroll's attractions for little girls were honorable and above reproach – at least we have, almost a century later, absolutely no evidence to the contrary.

Carroll's interest in discovering new little girls for his photographic studio seems to have amounted to his discovering hundreds, perhaps thousands, of girls in his lifetime. And in nearly every recorded case, Carroll produced a masterpiece of character study. His photographs are filled with unusually sensitive and candid "personalities" of the subjects. They caught the essence of human beings; they were not merely stiff, embalmed-like "objects." Occasionally, there is an extraordinary sense of straightforward eroticism – but it is straightforward; it is not murky or perverted. And in nearly every recorded case, Carroll had the full approbation of the child's parents, and invariably his work was chaperoned, at least indirectly. Had there been any intimacies between Carroll and his young female subjects, it would long ago have been ferreted out by the multitude of Freudian-oriented literary critics.

Today, we can understand why, occasionally, certain people thought Carroll's photographs to be erotic. Most people now, however, wouldn't consider them to be. His photographs are alluring; they look as if they almost could speak. They all have a provocative quality about them. But, they are "safe," and as we view them, they help us to understand Carroll's interest in seeing children as *his own* personal, private, peculiar *escape* from mature sex.

ALICE LIDDELL

In 1856, Carroll met Alice Liddell, the four-year-old daughter of Dean Henry George Liddell of Christ Church. Carroll had already established himself as a close friend of Alice's elder sister and cousin. But it is Alice who figures most prominently in Carroll's most famous creation, *Alice in Wonderland*.

On July 4, 1852, Carroll and a friend, Rev. Robinson Duckworth, took the Liddell children, Lorina (13), Alice (10), and Edith (8) on a boat ride (a row boat) up the Isis River (the local name for the Thames River). As they made their way upstream, Carroll began telling a story about the underground adventures of a little girl named Alice. According to Duckworth, the story "was actually composed and spoken over my shoulder for the benefit of Alice Liddell, who was acting as 'cox' of our gig. I remember turning around and saying, 'Dodgson, is this an extempore romance of yours?' And he replied, 'Yes, I'm inventing as we go along.'"

Upon disembarking, Alice asked Carroll to write out Alice's adventures for her, and Carroll promised to do so by the following Christmas, but the work was not completed until February 10, 1863. By that time, Alice was eleven, and Carroll was no longer seeing her with the regularity that he used to. Now he had made a new friend, the famous ingénue Ellen Terry, who was nearly seventeen. His interest in Ellen Terry is the closest relationship that Carroll had with an adult woman, apart from his family, of course.

From an initial length of 18,000 words, Carroll's manuscript expanded to 35,000 words, and the famous English illustrator John Tenniel read it and consented to draw illustrations for it. As Carroll searched for a publisher, he gave anxious thoughts to a perfect title. Various ones came to him: *Alice's Golden Hour, Alice's Hour in Elf-land, Alice Among the Elves, Alice's Doings in Elf-land,* and *Alice's Adventures Under Ground.* Finally, *Alice in Wonderland* was chosen, and Macmillan, the publishers for Oxford University, agreed to publish the book on a commission basis.

Alice was an immediate critical success when it appeared in 1865. *The Reader* magazine called it "a glorious artistic treasure . . . a book to put on one's shelf as an antidote to a fit of the blues." *The Pall Mall Gazette* wrote that "this delightful little book is a children's feast and a triumph of nonsense." About 180,000 copies of *Alice* in various editions were sold in England during Carroll's lifetime; by 1911, there were almost 700,000 copies in print. Since then, with the expiration of the original copyright in 1907, the book has been translated into every major language, and now it has become a perennial best-seller, ranking with the works of Shakespeare and the Bible in popular demand. In the words of the critic Derek Hudson: "The most remarkable thing about *Alice* is that, though it springs from the very heart of the Victorian period, it is timeless in its appeal. This is a characteristic that it shares with other classics – a small band – that have similarly conquered the world."

LIST OF CHARACTERS

Alice

The heroine and the dreamer of Wonderland; she is the principal character.

Alice's Sister

She reads the book "without pictures or conversations." Alice's boredom with her sister's book leads her to fall asleep and dream her adventures in Wonderland.

White Rabbit

The first creature that Alice sees in Wonderland. He leads Alice down the hole to Wonderland; he mistakes Alice for his servant, Mary Ann, and he orders her to fetch his gloves and fan. He is the Court Herald for the Knave of Hearts' trial.

Mouse

The first creature that Alice sees while she is floating in a pool of her own tears. The Mouse offers to dry all of the creatures by telling them about "dry" history. He tells Alice his own sad tale, and it is presented on the page in the shape of a mouse's tail.

Duck

One of the menagerie in the pool of tears. He argues with the Mouse over the meaning of "it."

Dodo

One of the animals in the pool of tears; he proposes the Caucus-race.

Lory (parrot)

Animal in the pool of tears. He argues with Alice over his authority and refuses to reveal his age.

Eaglet

Animal in the pool of tears.

Old Crab

Animal in the pool of tears.

Old Magpie

Another animal in the pool of tears.

Canary

Animal in the pool of tears. The Canary takes offense at Alice's describing her pet cat Dinah's appetite for birds.

Dinah

Alice's pet cat, who lives above-ground.

Pat

The White Rabbit's servant. He is ordered to evict Alice from the White Rabbit's house, but he gets Bill the Lizard to go into the house instead. Pat speaks with a brogue.

Young Bill the Lizard

The other servant of the White Rabbit; he makes an unsuccessful attempt to evict Alice from the White Rabbit's house.

Puppy

One of the nonpersonified or unanimated animals; he is of monstrous size (to Alice), and he almost crushes Alice in his playfulness after she flees from the White Rabbit's house.

Caterpillar

The water-pipe smoking character whom Alice finds on a mushroom. He is disagreeable and insulting to Alice. But he provides her with knowledge of the growth-altering mushroom.

Father William

An old man who is the subject of the misconceived poem that the Caterpillar asks Alice to recite. Instead of an ethical "model" for youths, Father William becomes, in Alice's recital of the moral poem, a corrupt figure.

Father William's Son

The inquiring son of Father William.

Pigeon

The pigeon hen attacks Alice because Alice's neck has been distorted by the mushroom into a serpent's shape. The pigeon's mis-identity of Alice is strengthened when she confesses to eating eggs when she was above-ground. The pigeon confuses a part of Alice (Alice's neck and her taste for eggs) for what he considers to be the "identifying quality" of a serpent.

Fish-Footman

Servant of the Queen of Hearts who delivers the Queen's invitation (for the croquet party) to the Duchess.

Frog-Footman

Doorman of the Duchess' house. He receives the Queen's croquet party invitation for the Duchess. He banters nonsense – with variations – to Alice.

Duchess

Mad human character of hideous physical aspect and perverse disposition. She abuses the pig/baby and throws it to Alice. Later, she moralizes with Alice at the croquet party. She flees the garden after offending the Queen of Hearts. Earlier, the Duchess was arrested and imprisoned, under an execution sentence, for having boxed the Queen's ears.

Cook

Duchess' cook. She throws pots and plates about, but doesn't hit anyone, although one plate grazes the Frog-Footman's nose. Her indiscriminate shaking of a pepper mill causes everyone in the Duchess' house to sneeze, especially the pig/baby, who screams and cries.

Cheshire-Cat

It first appears in the kitchen with the Duchess, the Cook, and the pig/baby. The Cat is always smiling. After leaving the Duchess' house, Alice finds the Cat on a tree limb. Alice tries to engage him in a serious conversation, but he replies to her in nonsense questions and answers. He vanishes and reappears, and sometimes only his head, or his enigmatic smile, is visible. In the next to the last chapter, he frustrates the Queen and the King of Hearts' order to execute him by making only his head visible – thus, there is no head to cut off. He directs Alice to the March Hare's Mad Tea-Party.

March Hare

Host of the Mad Tea-Party. He and another guest, the Mad Hatter, try to drown the third guest-resident, the Dormouse.

The Mad Hatter

Another guest-resident at the Mad Tea-Party. He explains to Alice why the tea-party is always held at six o'clock and why the time is *always* six o'clock. The Hatter and a personified Time have had a fight, and Time refuses to let the tea-party end. The Hatter is interrogated by the King at the Knave of Hearts' trial; he and the March Hare dunk the Dormouse in the teapot.

Dormouse

A hibernating guest-resident at the Mad Tea-Party. He tells anecdotes of three sisters who live in a treacle well and draw treacle. He is dunked in the teapot by the Mad Hatter and the March Hare. He is barely able to stay awake, but appears later at the Knave's trial.

Spade Gardeners

The Two, the Five, and the Seven of Spades; animated playing cards. They are "gardeners" for the Queen of Hearts. Alice finds them painting white roses red. Alice saves them from execution when the Queen orders them beheaded.

King of Hearts

He is the Queen's husband and also the judge at the trial of the Knave of Hearts.

Queen of Hearts

The furious queen of the enchanted garden. She is the real power behind Wonderland. Her violent and outrageous temper provokes Alice to overturn Wonderland and return to the world above-ground. The Queen introduces Alice to the Gryphon.

Knave of Hearts

The only "person" in Wonderland to evoke Alice's sympathy. He is accused of stealing tarts in the enchanted garden. Alice saves him from the queen's wrath and execution.

Three Sisters

Three little girls whom the Dormouse describes as living in the treacle well.

Mock Turtle

A sad "mock turtle" who used to be a tortoise; he regales Alice with accounts of his peculiar education. He recites the "Lobster-Quadrille." The Mock Turtle's name means "veal," a name that reflects the meaning of his lugubrious verse. He and the Gryphon are not overly hostile or rude to Alice.

Gryphon (Griffin)

A mythical creature who takes Alice to the Mock Turtle. He is introduced to Alice by the queen. He is polite to Alice and is never overtly hostile.

Guinea Pigs

Part of the inefficient jury at the Knave of Hearts' trial.

Pig/Baby

An "infant" whom Alice takes pity on when she sees it being cruelly tested by the Duchess. As Alice is escaping with it, it turns into a baby pig.

Mary Ann

Servant of the White Rabbit.

INTRODUCTION AND BRIEF SYNOPSIS

Alice was the work of a mathematician and logician who wrote as both a humorist and as a limerist. The story was in no sense intended to be didactic; its only purpose was to entertain. One may look for Freudian or Jungian interpretations if one chooses to do so, but in the final analysis, the story functions as comedy, with dialogue used largely for Carroll to play on words, mixing fantasy with burlesque actions.

The success of *Alice* (1865) enabled Carroll to forego his activities as a deacon. After the death of his deeply religious father in 1868, Carroll was able to propose a one-third cut in his salary as a mathematical lecturer. His most famous mathematical work, *Euclid and His Modern Rivals*, had been published the year before, and in 1881, he proposed to resign his academic post so that he could give full time to writing and pursuing mathematical studies. But in 1882, he was made Curator of the Common Room and was persuaded to remain there until 1892. He continued to write on mathematical topics and completed the first volume of his *Symbolic Logic*. By then, he was independently wealthy as a result of his many successful publications: *Phantasmagoria* appeared in 1869; in 1871, *Through the Looking Glass* came out; in 1876, *The Hunting of the Snark* appeared, and in 1883, *Rhyme and Reason* was published. Carroll's university responsibilities broadened in those years and from time to time he even accepted a request for a sermon. Though his authorship of the *Alice* books was well known, he absolutely shunned *all* publicity and refused to acknowledge any connection to "Lewis Carroll."

After leaving Oxford, Carroll settled into his sister's house in Guildford. And there he died in the afternoon of January 14, 1898. His memory is preserved in a perpetual endowment of a cot in the Children's Hospital, Great Ormond Street, London. In the long run, his books for children, especially the *Alice* books, have taken their place as books worthy of serious study of English literature. Thus, almost ironically, the so-called nonsense writer's achievements are timeless and unchallengeable, and the fame of *Alice* endures.

To fully appreciate *Alice*, one must keep in mind that the whole is simpler than its parts, and that although it was written originally for children, *Alice* has become a favorite adult piece of literature, a critical and philosophical work, rich in multiple meanings. More scholars (particularly economists and mathematicians) seem to allude to the *Alice* books with each passing day. The broad appeal of *Alice*, then, certainly lends substance to the notion that Alice and the novel are, ultimately, what you make of them. But there is some question as to whether children enjoy the puzzlement found in the story's episodes more than the story itself. In any case, children do not need critical information to appreciate *Alice*. The philosophical allusions and psychological implications are for adult tastes.

As a work of fiction, *Alice* lacks the conventional story line that we normally associate with a coherent, unified tale. Yet reading *Alice* does not leave us with a sense of incompleteness; *Alice* is far more than merely a series of disconnected episodes. In fact, *Alice* is told in the form of a dream; it is the story of Alice's dream, told in the third person point-of-view. Because Carroll chose a dream as the structure for his story, he was free to make fun of and satirize the multitudes of standard Victorian didactic maxims in children's literature. *Alice* lacks a "morally good" heroine and meaning; instead of Carroll's making an ethical point about each of her adventures (and showing how "good little girls" should behave in a situation just described), *Alice* parodies the instructive, solemn verse which filled Victorian children's books, verses which children were made to *memorize* and *recite*.

Alice, however, is not intended to *instruct* children in points of religion, morality, etiquette, and growing up to be mature, reasonable adults. In this novel, conventional "rationality" is replaced by the bizarre, fantastic irrationalities of a dream world. From episode to episode, Alice never progresses to any *rational* understanding or mental or psychological growth. Her adventures are *not* ordered; they are disordered. They are shifting and unpredictable, and there is always the menace of Gothic horror laced with the fantasies of Carroll's fairy tale. Indeed, Alice's dream sometimes has the aspects of a nightmare.

Wonderland is a world of wonders, a world where fairy or elf-like creatures and humans meet and talk with one another. Wonderland is a world where a baby is transformed into a pig; it is a place where a Cheshire-Cat keeps disappearing and reappearing, until only his grin remains—and even that suddenly disappears! Wonderland is a kingdom in which the Queen and King of Hearts have subjects who are a deck of cards, and where *all* the animals (except the pig/baby) have the nagging, whining, complaining, and peevish attitudes of adults. It is as though Carroll were trying to frustrate *logical* communication and trying to turn extraordinary events into what would seem like very ordinary events in Wonderland. The only laws in *Alice* seem to be the laws of chaos; all is nonsensical. Yet, one of the novel's key focuses is on the relationship between the development of a child's language and the physical growth of the child. In Wonderland, illogical and irrational Wonderland, sudden size change has a distorting psychological effect on Alice, and this is made even more mysterious by the verbal nonsense that accompanies it. This dream magic mesmerizes children, and it makes them laugh. Most adults do not. To break a law of logic is serious business to adults; children, however, love the wildly improbable.

In any case, most of the humor in *Alice* is due to the fact that the reader has the privileged knowledge that Alice is *dreaming*; thus, she *should not* assume that anything in Wonderland should function as it does in the real world. Wonderland is a sort of reverse utopia, a decadent, corrupted one.

Many years ago, Swiss child psychologist Jean Piaget demonstrated that children learn in stages and that before a certain mental age, a child will not be able to comprehend certain *abstract* relationships. Carroll seems to have already grasped this principle and is playing with the notion in this novel. Alice changes in size, but she *never matures*. The solemn adult creatures whom she meets speak to her, but what they say to her seems like absolute nonsense – that is, Carroll was satirizing the pseudo-intellectuality of adults in the Victorian world he saw all around him. And part of Alice's problem is that none of the nonsense *ever* makes sense; she never learns *anything*, even when she physically grows, or wanders through Wonderland's garden meeting people and creatures.

She grows nine feet tall after eating a cake in the opening chapter, yet she remains a child. Presumably, Alice would have continued to be baffled forever, so long as she remained in Wonderland. She is trapped in the midst of a vacuous condition, without beginning or end, without resolution.

The novel is composed of twelve brief chapters; it can be read in an afternoon. Each of the brief chapters, furthermore, is divided into small, individual, almost isolated episodes. And the story begins with Alice and her sister sitting on the bank of a river reading a book which has no pictures or dialogue in it. ". . . and what is the use of a book," thought Alice, "without pictures or conversations?" Thus, we find many pictures and read much dialogue (although very little of it makes sense) in *this* novel.

After introducing us to one of the creatures in Wonderland, the Gryphon, for instance, the narrator tells us, "If you don't know what a Gryphon is, look at the picture." As noted earlier, Wonderland is filled with strange animals, and Alice's encounters with these creatures, all of whom engage her in conversations, confuse her even more whenever she meets yet another inhabitant of this strange country.

Slowly losing interest in her sister's book, Alice catches sight of a white rabbit. However, he is not merely a rabbit; he will be the "White Rabbit," a major character in the novel. In this first paragraph, then, we learn about the protagonist, Alice, her age, her temperament, and the setting and the mood of the story. In a dream, Alice has escaped from the dull and boring and prosaic world of adulthood – a world of dull prose and pictureless experiences; she has entered what seems to be a confusing, but perpetual springtime of physical, if often terrifying, immediacy.

The White Rabbit wears a waistcoat, walks upright, speaks English, and is worrying over the time on his pocket watch. Alice follows him simply because she is very curious about him. And very soon she finds herself falling down a deep tunnel. For a few minutes, she is frightened; the experience of falling disorients her. Soon, however, she realizes that she is not falling fast; instead, she is falling in a slow, almost floating descent. As she falls, she notices that the tunnel walls are lined with cupboards, bookshelves, maps, and paintings. She takes a jar of orange marmalade off a shelf. But finding the jar empty, she replaces it on a lower shelf, as though she were trying to maintain a sense of some propriety – especially in this situation of absolute uncertainty. As she reflects on the marmalade jar, she says that had she dropped the jar, she might have killed someone below. Alice is clearly a self-reflective young girl – and she's also relatively calm; her thinking reveals a curiously mature mind at times. But like an ordinary little girl, she feels homesick for her cat, Dinah. In that respect, she is in sharp contrast with conventional child heroines of the time. Although Alice may be curious and sometimes bewildered, she is never *too* nice or *too* naughty. But she is always aware of her class-status as a "lady." At one point, she even fears that some of Wonderland's creatures have confused her for a servant, as when the White Rabbit thinks that she is his housekeeper, Mary Ann, and orders Alice to fetch his gloves and fan.

Thus, in Chapter I, Carroll prepares us for Alice's first major confrontation with absolute chaos. And note that Alice's literal-minded reaction to the *impossible* is always considered absurd here in Wonderland; it is laughable, yet it is her only way of coping. As she falls through the rabbit-hole, for instance, she wonders what latitude or longitude she has arrived at. This is humorous and ridiculous because such measurements – if one stops to think about it – are *meaningless* words to a seven-year-old girl, and they are certainly meaningless measurements of *anything* underground.

In Chapter II, Alice finds herself still in the long passageway, and the White Rabbit appears and goes off into a long, low hall full of locked doors. Behind one very small door, Alice remembers that there is "the loveliest garden you ever saw" (remember, she saw this in Chapter I), but now she has drunk a liquid that has made her too large to squeeze even her head through the doorway of the garden. She wishes that she could fold herself up like a telescope and enter. This wish becomes possible when she finds a shrinking potion and a key to the door. The potion reduces her to ten inches high, but she forgets to take the key with her (!) before shrinking, and now the table is too high for her to reach the key. To any young child, this is silly and something to be laughted at, but on another level, there's an element of fear; for children, the predictable proportions of things are important matters of survival. Yet here in Wonderland, things change – for no known reason – thus, logic has lost all its validity.

Then Alice eats a cake that she finds, and her neck shoots up until it resembles a giraffe's. Suddenly, she is a distorted nine feet tall! Clearly, her ability to change size has been a mixed blessing. In despair, she asks, "Who in the world am I?" This is a key question.

Meanwhile, the rapid, haphazard nature of Alice's physical and emotional changes have created a dangerous pool of tears that almost causes her to drown when she shrinks again. Why has she shrunk? She realizes that she has been holding the White Rabbit's lost white gloves and fan – therefore, it *must* be the magic of the fan that is causing her to shrink to almost nothingness. She saves herself by instantly dropping the fan. But now she is desperate; in vain, she searches her mind for something to make sense out of all this illogical chaos, something like arithmetic and geography, subjects that are solid, lasting, and rational. But even they seem to be confused because no matter how much she recites their rules, nothing helps. At the close of this chapter, she is swimming desperately in a pool of her own tears, alongside a mouse and other chattering creatures that have suddenly, somehow, appeared.

Alice in Wonderland is full of parody and satire. And in Chapter III, Victorian history is Carroll's target. The mouse offers to *dry* the other creatures and Alice by telling them a *very dry* history of England. Then, Carroll attacks politics: the Dodo organizes a Caucus-race, a special race in which every participant wins a prize. Alice then learns the mouse's sad tale as Carroll's editor narrates it on the page in the shape of a mouse's very narrow, S-shaped tail. The assembled, unearthly creatures cannot accept ordinary language, and so Alice experiences, again, absolute bafflement; this is linguistic and semantic disaster. Indeed, much of the humor of this chapter is based on Alice's reactions to the collapse of three above-ground assumptions: predictable growth, an absolute distinction between animals and humans, and an identity that remains constant. We might also add to the concept of a constancy of identity a conformity of word usage. But in Wonderland, Alice's previous identity and the very concept of a permanent identity has repeatedly been destroyed, just as the principles of above-ground are contradicted everywhere; here in Wonderland, such things as space, size, and even arithmetic are shown to have *no consistent laws.*

In Chapter IV, the confusion of identity continues. The White Rabbit insists that Alice fetch him his gloves and his fan. Somehow, he thinks that Alice is his servant, and Alice, instead of objecting to his confusion, passively accepts her new role, just as she would obey an adult ordering her about above-ground. On this day when everything has gone wrong, she feels absolutely defeated.

In the rabbit's house, Alice finds and drinks another growth potion. This time, however, she becomes so enormous that she fills up the room so entirely that she can't get out. These continuing changes in size illustrate her confused, rapid identity crisis and her continuous perplexity. After repulsing the rabbit's manservant, young Bill, a Lizard (who is trying to evict her), Alice notices that pebbles that are being thrown at her through a window are turning into *cakes*. Upon eating one of them, she shrinks until she is small enough to escape the rabbit's house and hide in a thick wood.

In Chapter V, "Advice From a Caterpillar," Alice meets a rude Caterpillar; pompously and dogmatically, he states that she must keep her temper—which is even more confusing to her for she is a little irritable because she simply cannot make any *sense* in this world of Wonderland. Alice then becomes more polite, but the Caterpillar only sharpens his already very short, brusque replies. In Wonderland, there are obviously no conventional rules of etiquette. Thus, Alice's attempt at politeness and the observance of social niceties are still frustrated attempts of hers to react as well as she can to very unconventional behavior – at least, it's certainly unconventional according to the rules that she learned above-ground.

Later, Alice suffers another bout of "giraffe's neck" from nibbling one side of the mushroom that the Caterpillar was sitting on. The effect of this spurt upward causes her to be mistaken for an egg-eating serpent by an angry, vicious pigeon.

In Chapters VI and VII, Alice meets the foul-tempered Duchess, a baby that slowly changes into a pig, the famous, grinning Cheshire-Cat, the March Hare, the Mad Hatter, and the very, very sleepy Dormouse. The latter three are literally trapped (although they don't know it) in a time-warp – trapped in a *perpetual* time when tea is being forever served. Life is one long tea-party, and this episode is Carroll's assault on the notion of time. At the tea-party, it is *always* teatime; the Mad Hatter's watch tells the *day* of the year, but not the *time* since it is *always* six o'clock. At this point, it is important that you notice a key aspect of Wonderland; here, *all* these creatures treat Alice (and her reactions) as though *she* is insane – and as though *they* are sane! In addition, when they are not condescending to her or severely criticizing her, the creatures continually contradict her. And Alice passively presumes the fault to be hers – in almost every case – because all of the creatures act as though their madness is normal and not at all unusual. It is the logical Alice who is the queer one. The chapter ends with Alice at last entering the garden by eating more of the mushroom that the Caterpillar was sitting on. Alice is now about a foot tall.

Chapters VIII to X introduce Alice to the most grimly evil and most irrational people (and actions) in the novel. Alice meets the sovereigns of Wonderland, who display a perversely hilarious rudeness not matched by anyone except possibly by the old screaming Duchess. The garden is inhabited by playing cards (with arms and legs and heads),who are ruled over by the barbarous Queen of Hearts. The Queen's constant refrain and response to seemingly *all* situations is: "Off with their heads!" This beautiful garden, Alice discovers, is the

Queen's private croquet ground, and the Queen matter-of-factly orders Alice to play croquet. Alice's confusion now turns to fear. Then she meets the ugly Duchess again, as well as the White Rabbit, the Cheshire-Cat, and a Gryphon introduces her to a Mock Turtle, who sings her a sad tale of his mock (empty) education; then the Mock Turtle teaches her and the Gryphon a dance called the "Lobster-Quadrille." Chapters XI and XII concern the trial of the Knave of Hearts. Here, Alice plays a heroic role at the trial, and she emerges from Wonderland and awakens to reality. The last two chapters represent the overthrow of Wonderland and Alice's triumphant rebellion against the mayhem and madness that she experienced while she was lost, for awhile, in the strange world of Wonderland.

This story is characterized, first of all, by Alice's unthinking, irrational, and heedless jumping down the rabbit-hole, an act which is at once superhuman and beyond human experience — but Alice does it. And once we accept this premise, we are ready for the rest of the absurdities of Wonderland and Alice's attempts to understand it and, finally, to escape from it. Confusion begins almost immediately because Alice tries to use her world of knowledge from the adult world above-ground in order to understand this new world. Wonderland, however, is a lawless world of deepest, bizarre dream unconsciousness, and Alice's journey through it is a metaphorical search for experience. What she discovers in her dream, though, is a more meaningful and terrifying world than most conscious acts of intelligence would ever lead her to. Hence, "Who in the world am I?" is Alice's constant, confused refrain, one which people "above-ground" ask themselves many, many times throughout their lifetimes.

Throughout the story, Alice is confronted with the problem of shifting identity, as well as being confronted with the anarchy and by the cruelty of Wonderland. When Alice physically shrinks in size, she is never really small enough to hide from the disagreeable creatures that she meets; yet when she grows to adult or to even larger size, she is still not large enough to command authority. "There are things in *Alice*," writes critic William Empson, "that would give Freud the creeps." Often we find poor Alice (and she is often described as being either "poor" or "curious") in tears over something that the adult reader finds comic. And "poor Alice" is on the verge of tears most of the time. When she rarely prepares to laugh, she is usually checked by the morbid, humorless types of creatures whom she encounters in Wonderland. Not even the smiling Cheshire-Cat is kind to her. Such a hostile breakdown of the ordinary world is *never* funny to the child, however comic it might appear to adults. But then Wonderland would not be so amusing to us except in terms of its sheer, unabated madness.

One of the central concerns of *Alice* is the subject of growing up – the anxieties and the mysteries of personal identity as one matures. When Alice finds her neck elongated, everything, in her words, becomes "queer"; again, *she is uncertain who she is.* As is the case with most children, Alice's identity depends upon her control of her body. Until now, Alice's life has been very structured; now her life shifts; it becomes fragmented until it ends with a nightmarish awakening. Throughout the novel, Alice is filled with unconscious feelings of morbidity, physical disgrace, unfairness, and bizarre feelings about bodily functions. Everywhere there is the absurd, unexplainable notion of death and the absolute meaninglessness of death and life.

Alice's final triumph occurs when she outgrows nonsense. In response to the Queen's cry at the Knave's trial: "sentence first – verdict afterward," Alice responds: "Stuff and nonsense! Who cares for *you*? You're nothing but a pack of cards!" At last, Alice takes control of her life and her growth toward maturity by shattering and scattering the absurdity of the playing cards and the silly little creatures who are less rational than she is. In waking from her nightmare, she realizes that reason *can* oppose nonsense, and that it can – and did – win. And now that the dream of chaos is over, she can say, from her distance above-ground, "It *was* a curious dream," but then she skips off thinking that – for a strange moment – what a wonderful dream it was.

SUMMARIES AND COMMENTARIES

CHAPTER I

"Down the Rabbit-Hole"

Alice in Wonderland begins as a pleasant fairy tale. Alice and her sister are reading a book that has neither pictures nor conversations. Alice finds the reading tedious; she is anxious for more vivid and direct forms of experience. Her boredom and anxiety cause her to withdraw from the "civilized pastime" of reading dull books and to fall to sleep, entering the world of dreams. At the edge of semi-sleep consciousness, she sees the form of a white rabbit scurrying toward a rabbit-hole. Immediately, Alice is curious and pursues him down the hole. The reason for Alice's pursuit is that she burns with curiosity; after all, the rabbit is wearing a waistcoat, talking to himself, walking upright, and he has a pocket watch; his image is thus unusual, suggesting romantic and fairy tale "people." The rabbit's hole functions like a large laundry chute, and, curiously, Alice "floats" down the hole in a slow descent. In her fall, she has fantasies relating to the absence of gravity, the quality of infinite space, the shape of her body, mass, and velocity. Her free, fanciful associations in the tunnel are in vivid contrast to her innocent, non-reflective curiosity that led her to leap down the hole in the first place.

In fact, her leap downward probably was unconscious. Not once did she hesitate for fear of what she might find or consider how she might get out. Her leap was a leap in a spirit of adventure, a reckless gamble done for fun.

On the other hand, Alice retains her belief in the world above-ground. There are shelves lining the walls of the tunnel, and on one shelf she finds a jar of orange marmalade. Things like the jar (which is empty) reaffirm her feelings that matters are not "too different" here, so she refuses to accept that her experience of floating down a rabbit-hole is unlike previous, curious adventures that she has had. This is just another adventure, and fancying that she might well be headed through the earth's center, she wonders how to determine her latitude and longitude. Note that it doesn't seem to matter to her that such terms do not apply *under* the earth's surface. Then, Alice considers the prospect of emerging head downward in New Zealand or Australia; her concern is almost a caricature of her childish belief in the impossible.

Strangely enough, there is no indication that she is truly disoriented; everything seems true to sense in spite of the absence of acceleration and gravity. Even her "sense of propriety" is functioning. She returns the empty marmalade jar to a lower shelf for fear that to drop it might injure someone below. Then, in an imaginary conversation with a woman whom she might meet on the other side of the world, she manages to curtsy in mid-air. Yet, already she is beginning to suffer nostalgia for her life in the conscious, above-ground world. The frightening possibility of being trapped in a dream occurs to her. Above-ground, her cat Dinah had an appetite for bats, and Alice is suddenly confronted by the thought that, possibly, *bats may also eat cats!* The age-old questions of eating, or being eaten, poses itself here in the context of an alien world while Alice is falling, falling . . . to heaven knows where.

Wonderland is one of the most spontaneous "places" in this novel. And suddenly Alice is in Wonderland! She has landed safely at the bottom of her long, slow fall. But, immediately, she hears the White Rabbit's anxious lament: "Oh, my ears and whiskers, how late it's getting!" Alice then loses sight of the rabbit in a hall that is paneled with doors. None of them, however, seems to be the right size for even a young girl of Alice's size; in fact, they are "strange doors." They seem to have a foreboding, funereal feeling about them. Thus, she does not attempt to open them.

On a glass table, though, she finds a tiny golden key, and this key opens a small, curtained door; but the entrance-way is small, rat-sized, in fact, and Alice cannot fit even her head through the doorway. And the door leads to a beautifully colorful, seemingly "enchanted garden." Alice wishes so very much that she could reduce her size and could explore the garden. Her wish that she could reverse her size is consistent with the logic of fantasy. Already, as the narrator observes, ". . . so many out-of-the-way things had happened lately, that Alice had begun to think that few things indeed were really impossible."

On the glass table, Alice finds a little bottle. It seems to have just magically appeared. The label on the bottle reads "DRINK ME." It is against her previous, proper English training to eat or drink strange foods, but curiosity (she *is* a child, after all) proves a stronger compulsion than doing the "right thing." So she drinks the liquid and is reduced immediately; now she can pass through the doorway leading to the garden! *But* she forgot to take the key before she drank the liquid, and now she has shrunk down to a tiny little girl. Disheartened that she can no longer reach the key, Alice begins to cry.

Then there is a curious change in her attitude. She stops herself from crying, as though her "selfish self" has been detached from her "proper self" and the latter is scolding her for crying. We almost hear her mother's voice: a desire for something *right now* is childish; it is "narcissistic"—selfish. It is naughty, and little girls shouldn't be selfish and want things *right now*. Thus, Alice restrains herself from crying.

Suddenly, a little glass box appears with a cake inside it (this is underneath the three-legged table). On the cake, there is a sign: "EAT ME." Alice eats the cake, but there is no *immediate* consequence. To her dismay, life is dull once again; it seems as though she has not really left the above-ground world at all. She feels that she is the same frustrated little girl that she was before. Except now there's an additional problem. When she was a normal-sized girl, she could not get out of the passageway, and now that she is too small, she has no means to escape. So there she sits, an enclosed soul, trapped in the traumatic nightmare of a prison cell. Already logic has begun to break down in this confusing, claustrophobic condition. Life is beginning to become exaggerated. Alice feels that she can't trust her sanity; curiosity seems to have taken its place. Thus, here in this introduction, rational expectations have taken Alice to an illogical and fantastic destination.

CHAPTER II

"The Pool of Tears"

As things turn out, the magic cake has a delayed effect. Suddenly, Alice's neck shoots up like a telescope, unfurling until her head touches the ceiling. "Curiouser and curiouser!" she exclaims. But that is all she says; she isn't angry, and her ungrammatical outburst is merely indicative of her being a surprised child. Her emotion is one of awe. That is all, and it shows her inherent self-control. However, she clearly realizes again that a serious problem is going to be her new *size*. And because *size* is related to what one eats or drinks, her concern is to eat and drink properly, but that seems almost impossible down here. One can't *trust* what one reads on little signs.

Note that the extension of Alice's neck has had an inverse effect on the other limbs of her body. Her arms now appear to be small stumps, her head seems miniscule, and, without relatively-sized shoulders or hips, her trunk resembles a frame minus any curves. In the John Tenniel illustrations (as many critics have noted), Alice appears almost phallic looking, much like a totem figure. But whatever the connotations imply about Lewis Carroll's fantasies, they are certainly unknown to Alice. Nothing in the story suggests that the pre-pubescent heroine has any self-consciousness about her oddly elongated, phallic-looking neck.

If Alice has any serious hangup at this point, it is related to food, because *food* always seems to produce trouble. Whenever Alice eats something, she becomes alienated from her body and her sense of who she is. After eating the cake, she wonders how amusing it will be to communicate by mail with her *feet*! Carroll is a master at reproducing the curiosity that can only surface in dreams. This is a child's world of the Absurd, and Alice is speculating on *possibilities*. Then, her Victorian training checks her whimsy: "Oh dear, what nonsense I'm talking!"

In despair again because the "proper" and rational side of her has come to the fore, Alice begins to cry, and again her "super-ego"—the voice of Authority—intervenes: "You ought to be ashamed of yourself, a great girl like you . . . to go on crying in this way! Stop this moment, I tell you!"

There is often this two-voiced sense of herself in Alice's soliloquies; there is the sense of propriety, as well as the voice of a separate child-self which keeps emerging, the latter growing stronger and stronger. It is the voice of a slowly, gradually maturing Alice as she becomes more adult, but note that she is very much "her own" adult as the story unfolds. At this point, of course, Alice is not aware that this shifting identity is a problem. That awareness will come later, after many more confrontations in Wonderland.

The humor that manifests itself in her talks to herself is mainly produced by her solemn attitude, when compared to her child's attitude and reaction to whatever queer situation she finds herself in. In spite of what has happened to Alice, she tries very hard to be totally serious about it and to *try* and make sense out of all this *nonsense*. Nonetheless, the laugh is on her, for the narrator's third-person voice always plays up Alice's child-like, comic aspects. He makes Alice's credibility at *trying* to be rational—despite her deep curiosity—ridiculous. This, of course, is the core of Carroll's humor in the novel.

One consequence of this two-voice structure is that Alice has no terribly strong emotions either way; her responses to the creatures in Wonderland seem totally cerebral. But she *tries*, as we have said, to deal with them as though they were logical and thinking beings—even though they are "creatures" and although they make no sense at all.

Alice forms no lasting relationships with any of them. In fact, in the climactic last chapter, she displays inflamed anger toward the Queen of Hearts; her only real expression of sympathy is for the Knave of Hearts.

As French philosopher Henri Bergson once observed, laughter and emotions are incompatible – which is perhaps why jokes by people who laugh while telling them are seldom as funny as jokes told without expression or those which are told with deadpan expressions. And inasmuch as the mad creatures of Wonderland never laugh or ever seem amused (not even, really, the Cheshire-Cat), the comic effect of Alice's dream becomes highly enhanced – that is, the story becomes funnier to the reader, even though at times it must seem scary to a child. But when the creatures are the saddest (the Mock Turtle, for example), or anxious (the White Rabbit), or enraged (the Queen of Hearts), or frightened (the gardeners), they seem all the more amusing and comic.

The parenthetical comments that the narrator sometimes inserts into the text greatly assist the graphic relationship between comedy and horror. The style and tone of the narrative is usually lucid, calm, a bit condescending, even snobbish at times, but it is also loving and indulgent. And then at other times, it is distant and hostile. The writing in *Alice in Wonderland*, you should note, is *always* on the edge of hysteria. So intense is it, that the split between man and nature is implicit in all of Alice's encounters with the creatures in Wonderland.

Part of the humor of cruelty – and the creatures of Wonderland are sometimes extremely cruel – is to maintain the balance between sadism and sentimentality. In this case, the split effect provides a proper tension and gives the writing a subtlety and a sober delicacy.

The double consciousness in the character of Alice is also a structural motif – a duality reflecting Alice's regression, at times, to a small child, and then a reversal, when she becomes a stern, Victorian moralist. At times, Alice's willfulness provides an escape from boredom. It irritates her to be corrected by creatures who sound irrational. Then, at other times, she wants to sink into the ground.

Here, Carroll sharpens the opposition of the two opposing impulses within Alice. Later, even Alice realizes that part of herself scolds and is very much like the critical creatures who live in Wonderland. Her search for true feeling and for some sanity in this strange world turns finally inward toward maturity, knowledge, and self-awareness, although she herself would (and will) not realize anything about herself unless it is involved in some sort of *external* experience. In order to know her true inner feelings, Alice will have to finally educate that other "scolding" Alice-voice which is confused by her estranged condition and trying always to cope with it *rationally.*

Alice cries until she is sitting in – what is to her – a gigantic pool of tears, even though in reality, the pool is only four inches deep. The White Rabbit reappears, bewailing his reception by the savage Duchess. Alice, with her long neck, startles him so that he drops his fan and gloves and scurries off.

Taking up the fan and gloves, Alice says: "Dear, dear! How queer everything is today!" Amid the fun, Alice is beginning to recognize something ominous; therefore, it is only natural that she tries to relate her present situation ("today") to the rigid, secure "order" of the past. She leapt down the rabbit-hole without any thought of how she would get out, and now her adventure has already begun to fragment her old structure of living a rather ordinary, boring, uninteresting day-to-day life. This disorientation is very much like a jarring fall – which she would have had if she had *actually* fallen down a truly deep hole. Her old world is collapsing fast. She must simultaneously attempt to discover how to begin to understand her dream while, at the same time, try to determine how it will *end.* She attempts to re-establish her identity by asking herself if she could have become *some other child.* But her sensibility as a proper Victorian little girl and also as an intelligent, educated middle-class girl make her dismiss any of the children who come to mind. "I'm sure I can't be Mabel, for I know all sorts of things, and she, oh, she knows such a very little." Nor is Alice helped in trying to figure out who she is by recalling logical certainties – such as arithmetic. When she attempts to establish who she is by reciting her multiplication tables from one to twenty, her uncertainty only deepens: "Let me see: four times five is twelve, and four times six is thirteen, and four times seven is – oh dear! I shall never get to twenty at that rate!"

Alice finds her distress unrelieved. She has no resources to help her. Wonderland is one enormous puzzle, and her solitude and alienation have now made her unsure whether or not *she* really exists as *Alice!* Her familiar, comforting world of facts and learning are no longer mentally true, and she wishes desperately for people whom she left behind to relieve her boredom. She knows that "It'll be no use their putting their heads down and saying 'Come up again, dear!' I shall only look up and say, 'Who am I, then? Tell me that first, and then, if I like being that person, I'll come up: if not, I'll stay down here till I'm somebody else.'"

The most crucial aspect of her sanity—her permanent self-identity—seems destroyed. But her lonely cry does express her horrible loneliness: "I do wish they *would* put their heads down! I am so very tired of being all alone here!"

All this while, Alice has been fanning herself and has put on one of the White Rabbit's gloves. Suddenly, she realizes that she has *shrunk*—and is *continuing to shrink!* In alarm, she drops the fan, and the shrinking stops. She realizes in horror that she might well have vanished into thin air if she had held the fan much longer.

As we have already noted, her trials have a serial nature, for no sooner has she stopped shrinking than she finds herself floating in the pool of her own tears. This is like a non-stop movie of horrors! In a single moment, she has passed from the threat of *vanishing,* and now she faces the prospect of *drowning.*

Some critics have interpreted her sea of tears as a symbolic evocation of a Lethean bath from which Alice will emerge "reborn." But Alice does not change. She swims and frolics until she is joined by a Mouse. His appearance enables Carroll to now parody one of the Victorians' favorite pastimes in which they educated their children: by rote learning.

In a soliloquy, Alice addresses the Mouse: "Oh Mouse," a phrase which reminds her instantly of a Latin grammar exercise in her brother's Latin textbook: *amo, amas, amat.* Then she recalls the English translation rather than the Latin conjugation of the verb for *love,* and what follows is a confusing of a *noun* declension: "A mouse—of a mouse—to a mouse—a mouse—O mouse!"

All of this is absolute nonsense to the Mouse, and Alice's attempt at further communication with the Mouse becomes further complicated when she tries to converse with the Mouse in French. Tactlessly, she chooses the phrase *"Ou est ma chatte?"* Of course, absurdly, the Mouse understands "cat" (*chatte*) in *any* language, and his initial apprehension of Alice quickly turns to fear and distrust. He swims away, very offended and very discomforted. Alice then realizes her blunder, but she keeps blathering away, describing her cat, Dinah. Alice is clearly out of control. And when she does fully realize the extent of her offense, she tries to switch the subject to *dogs*—as if dogs might make the Mouse feel any better. Her tactless bungling then becomes a predominating pattern. Nonetheless, the Mouse offers to tell her his history and why he dislikes cats *and* dogs, and he forgives her. Curiously, his maturity and politeness is in sharp contrast with Alice's unthinking, cruel lapse of manners. Alice is redeemed here only by the Mouse's having an adult sensibility. He forgives Alice because, as a child, she does not know any better. Chapter II concludes, then, with the pool of tears becoming suddenly filled with a strange menagerie of Wonderland creatures: a Duck, a Dodo, a Lory (a parrot), an Eaglet, and "several other curious creatures."

CHAPTER III

"A Caucus-Race and a Long Tale"

"How to dry off" is the central concern at the beginning of this chapter. Alice finds herself embroiled in a heated discussion with the Lory (the parrot) over who knows best how to dry off. The Lory cuts off the argument with the declaration that *he* is wiser than Alice because he is *older* than she is. In this dispute Alice becomes a child again—therefore, sort of an underdog—but her self-centered emotions indicate a mental maturity well beyond her chronological age. Still, in relation to the other animals, Alice seems altogether like the dependent child that she really is; but clearly the Lory's rude position reflects that although he *may* be more mature, *we* don't know that he is necessarily older than Alice. In any case, Alice will not let the Lory's response go unchallenged, and the scene turns hilarious when the Lory absolutely refuses to reveal his true age.

All along, the Mouse has seemed to assume himself to be the natural "authority figure" of this motley group, so he offers "to dry" the creatures by telling them a dry history. The Mouse states that ". . . the Patriotic Archbishop of Canterbury found it advisable . . ." but before he finishes, the Duck interrupts: "Found what?"

"Found it," the Mouse replies rather crossly, adding, "Of course you know what *it* means."

Wonderland certainly demands a strange "consistency" (one can't say 'logic') of its own—especially concerning language, for like the Eaglet's "Speak English!" the language of ordinary discourse is ambiguous. The Mouse's "it" could, of course, mean absolutely *anything*. At any rate, the dull, dry history of England does *not* help "dry" anyone. So the Dodo (an extinct bird) proposes a Caucus-race. Alice asks the Dodo to explain the Caucus-race, and he replies that "the best way to explain it is to do it." The Eaglet challenges him to "Speak English!" Thus, the Dodo explains that he is proposing that the creatures dry themselves in a race in which everyone starts and stops running when and where they please, and all win the race. For an extinct creature, the Dodo has a curious sport: natural selection, the cause of his extinction, is a race in which only the best win.

Alice thinks that the Caucus-race is absurd, but she participates in the running anyway. As an indication that the other animals recognize her superiority, she is selected to bestow the prizes (comfits, or candy, from her pockets). After the candy is distributed, however, *she* remains without a prize. The Dodo then suggests that she be rewarded with the only thing left in her pocket, an elegant thimble, which he gives to her as *her* prize.

The Caucus-race, of course, satirizes all political caucuses and the wheeling and dealing of politics in which, to win an election, a politician often has to ensure that even his opponents feel that they all have won *something* with the victor's win. Certainly a prize to everyone does lessen the rise of jealousies and rivalries, but Alice wants to laugh, and the gravity of the other creatures intimidates her. Her amusement reflects a Victorian Tory of the nineteenth century; political progress at that time was essentially random and circular, a sentiment best summarized in the French saying: *Plus ca change, plus c'est la même chose* (or in English: the more things change, the more they stay the same).

Having discovered that the Mouse has bitter memories of his enemies, Alice asks him to tell the history he promised. But rather than a personal autobiography, however, the Mouse's story is a genetic-racial memory. On the printed page, his "tale" resembles a sprawling, elongated (and the print becomes tinier and tinier) mouse's tail. It is a brutal story of an encounter between a mouse and a dog ("Fury") in a house. The story ends with the dog executing the mouse after a trial. The Mouse's sad tale prefigures the entire plot of *Alice in Wonderland*, for Alice will finally dispose of all of Wonderland because of her anger at the injustice of the Knave of Hearts' trial.

The calligrammatic tale/tail teaches Alice nothing about the Mouse's past experiences, so after the Mouse departs in a rage, Alice goofs again. This time, she offends the Canary and the Magpie by describing Dinah's appetite for birds. Leaving her judgment about "what *is* safe to talk about" in limbo, she abandons her basic sensitivity; it simply can't be trusted here in this strange world of Wonderland. Her existence here is certainly becoming "curiouser and curiouser" because she cannot identify with the other creatures and their natures. On the other hand, her subversive (so the creatures think) attempt at communication is collapsing into mad, slapstick kinds of verbal play. Not only does Wonderland's language have a false logic, but the very definition of terms rests upon inconsistencies. In fact, so consistent are the illogicalities that nonsense appears to be the "norm" and the basis of Wonderland.

CHAPTER IV

"The Rabbit Sends in a Little Bill"

In a dramatic, magical shift, Alice suddenly finds herself in the presence of the White Rabbit. But the glass table and the great hall have vanished. There is a clear contrast between the calmness of Alice and the nervous, agitated White Rabbit, looking frantically for his lost fan and gloves. Typically, however, the White Rabbit is *always* fretting over his appearance *and* the time, while Alice's problem concerns her physical size changes and her identity crisis. In a way, the two characters embody concerns of youth and age. For youth, the question is to establish an identity; for an older person, there is usually a constant wish to have the appearance, at least, of an identity, and there is usually a "fretting" about time, since one is more and more aware of the little time left for living as each day passes.

Alice's central problem in this chapter is accentuated very suddenly. The White Rabbit mistakes her for his house servant, Mary Ann, and he orders her to fetch a spare pair of gloves and fan at his house. His air of authority makes her obey him even though she resents her new status: "How queer it seems to be going on messages for a rabbit! I suppose Dinah'll be sending me on messages next!" Alice clearly knows the difference between herself and *servants*. But in Wonderland's bewildering anarchy, she is forever *trying* to make sense and order – in social status. It is her very Victorian class-consciousness that makes her reasonable, self-controlled and polite; yet her sense of class also makes her resent the creatures' nasty, insulting treatment. Class, in the end, distinguishes Alice from the eccentric creatures of Wonderland; whereas she always seems reserved, they seem ever at the mercy of their whims; and they are usually either ill-mannered, or grotesquely inept (the Mouse, for example).

At the White Rabbit's house, Alice finds the fan and the rabbit's gloves, and yet she is seemingly, uncontrollably drawn again to yet another bottle labeled "DRINK ME." She takes a nip of the liquid, and suddenly she is too large to leave the room; again, her curiosity and appetite have gotten her into trouble. However, this is no longer just "curious": growing too large is becoming a nightmarish theme; in this instance, Alice's growing larger – and then smaller – form a sort of internal rhythm that most children connect with time – that is, sometimes time *seems* long; sometimes, it seems short. Yet the consequences of eating or drinking the wrong things never result – in the real world – in one's becoming suddenly very wee or truly gigantic. Alice's size here brings her to regret her adventure: "It was much pleasanter at home," she thinks. Seemingly, she has "grown up," something she has long wanted to do; but now she laments the fact that growing up has not made her any more of an adult: "Shall I *never* get any older than I am now?" She's very big, but she's still a child. "Well, that'll be a comfort, one way – never to be an old woman – but then – always to have lessons to learn!"

The White Rabbit, meanwhile, has lost his patience and followed Alice to his house. He is in a furious mood, which frightens Alice, so she prevents him from entering the house. The humor here is due to the fact of Alice's being many, many times larger than the rabbit and, logically, she should have no reason at all to fear him. Nonetheless, the White Rabbit's angry, brusque orders are terribly intimidating to her because the White Rabbit *sounds* like an adult. For Alice (a well-trained child), no matter how impolite an adult is, an adult must be minded and must be feared. Adults may be a puzzle (and rude) but, to a child, their domination must be accepted *at all times*. Alice's real world society, then, is responsible for her behavior here and is further enforced by her class consciousness.

Prevented from entering his own house, the White Rabbit calls to his gardener, Pat. Here, note that whereas the White Rabbit speaks in standard, formal English, Pat has an Irish brogue (as does Bill the Lizard and the "card gardeners" in the "enchanted garden"). Pat recommends that "little" Bill (see chapter title) the Lizard enter the house through the chimney and evict Alice; because of his shape, Bill should have no trouble squeezing down the chimney. So Bill goes down the chimney, but Alice kicks him fiercely back *up* the chimney as soon as he reaches the fireplace.

Suddenly, there is a heavy, claustrophobic feeling within Alice, but she is by no means helpless. In contrast, it is the "tiny creatures" who are truly frustrated, and we see now a direct basis for Alice's disillusionment with "growing up." At last, she is physically large enough to control Wonderland's creatures, but she is unable to do so because her enormous size has her trapped in the rabbit's small house.

Without warning, the irate White Rabbit and his servants begin pelting Alice with small pebbles. More trouble! But as the pebbles land on the floor, they magically turn into *cakes!* Remembering that cakes had previously had an opposite effect to liquid, Alice eats a cake and is suddenly small again. Then, however, the creatures outside promptly attack her and chase her off.

Alice is now so small that she has to hide; all the creatures whom she sees are loathsome, especially a "monstrous" puppy, which nearly crushes her. In Alice's words, the puppy is "a dear little puppy" but because of his size, he might as well be "the villainous Fury" of the Mouse's tale. Alice does her best to escape from the puppy because since he is so big and she is so small, she is in just exactly the kind of jeopardy that the Mouse described. The puppy, friendly as he seems to large adults, is a brute to Alice, and the life of a tiny little Alice is certainly of no consequence to him. This impression is strengthened by the puppy's constant delight in almost trampling on her.

After she escapes from the puppy, Alice finds herself under a large mushroom, and on top of the mushroom sits a large blue caterpillar smoking a water-pipe (a "hookah").

CHAPTER V

"Advice from a Caterpillar"

Alice is well acquainted by now with the prime principle of Wonderland's chaos: illogic. Yet she continues—almost by instinct— to oppose the illogical context in which she continually finds herself.

Yet her experience so far should have prepared her for the possibility that the "pebble-cake" might *not* have reduced her size. But as eating cake *had* worked that way once before, she expected (logically) the same results. And, indeed, the cake produced the desired effect. Thus, it is the *reader* who is surprised!

Nothing has really changed, though. All of Alice's moral precepts – order, the idea and the use of logic, and precise language – have become turned upside-down; they are now either meaningless concepts, or cruel and twisted confusions for her. In her encounter with the blue Caterpillar, for example, the destruction of her identity and her belief in ordinary language, social manners, and human superiority to animals is intensified.

"Who are you?" the Caterpillar asks her. Alice replies in a negative, defensive, and tentative way: "I – I hardly know, Sir, just at present – at least I know who I *was* when I got up this morning, but I think I must have been changed several times since then."

The way that Alice responds to the Caterpillar is as significant as what she says. Compared to the other creatures that she has met, the Caterpillar is downright nasty. For him, all conventions of social etiquette have been cast away. Alice's attempts to display respect and politeness – by addressing him as "Sir" simply produce harsh derision and scorn. And he becomes even ruder – to the point of provocation. This is all becoming horribly frustrating! The conventions of social etiquette all seem to be working against Alice, and she has no recourse. She has no other set of standards or values. All of her training has conditioned her to simply bear impoliteness with politeness. It is *not* easy.

The crudity of the Caterpillar's first question is emphasized by the narrator's remark that such a question was not easy for Alice to answer. In the context of the dialogue, the narrator's voice reveals a wry touch of humor. But given what Alice has just been through, the haughty question is hardly a humorous one. The question "Who are you?" can be very hostile – especially when one is addressed by a *blue* Caterpillar. His cold and snide observations reduce Alice's feelings to a pathetic, suppressed anger. When he repeats his nasty question, she says in a grave, but exasperated voice: "I think you ought to tell me who you are first." In a devastating retort, the Caterpillar says: "Why?"

It is obvious that such an exchange imposes upon Alice simply more insecurity and feelings of guilt. Yet those kinds of feelings cannot be sustained for long; all too quickly they become hostile and negative. It is all Alice can do to contain her anger. The strength of her repressed feelings is a bit amusing to the reader. Her deliberate, determined restraint reveals the secret of much of the story's tension. Her self-control is remarkably exaggerated because Alice is a "proper little girl."

The Caterpillar's attitude has so frustrated her that Alice turns to leave him, but he pleads with her to come back, and after she reluctantly does, he says: "Keep your temper."

"Is that all?" asks Alice, more angry than ever.

The Caterpillar then further outrages her. He asks her how she thinks she has *changed*. Alice tells him that she can't remember things and that her size is *always* changing. Earlier, when she attempted to recite the very Victorian, very moralistic poem "How Doth the Little Busy Bee," for instance, "it all came different." In a deceptively simple form of mistranslation, Alice made a dutiful creature (the bee) become a slothful creature (a crocodile). The poem she mangles here is very much akin to what happened in Chapter II, for in that poem she kept saying: "How doth the little crocodile" – an animal who grins and eats little fish that swim into his mouth.

Carroll's parody of "proper" Victorian, didactic children's verses continues with the Caterpillar commanding her to recite "You Are Old, Father William." But the Father William poem comes out just as *immoral* and just as *altered* as the crocodile/bee poem. Each subject becomes the antithesis of the correct "moral" of the "correct verse." The Caterpillar tells Alice that her recitation is wrong because it is *totally* against the intent of "the true originals." Of course, it is – and that's what frustrates Alice so. Instead of being an old man of moderate pleasures, Father William is a lusty, scheming hedonist: he advises his son that the secret of longevity and health is an active, self-indulgent life – the very *opposite* of conventional wisdom on how to reach a ripe old, proper Victorian age.

At the conclusion of Alice's verse recital, the two mutually antagonistic temperaments move to a final clash. We almost see Alice gnashing her teeth in frustration as she tells the Caterpillar that she wishes she were larger than just *three* inches tall. Naturally, the Caterpillar is offended by the implication that there is something wrong with being three inches tall – since that is exactly *his height* when he is extended on his tail.

Thus, he explodes in anger and becomes viciously insulting. Then he abruptly crawls away in a huff. Once more, we are reminded of the unceasing antipathy between Alice and the creatures of Wonderland.

Oddly enough, in spite of the blue Caterpillar's anger, before he leaves Alice, he gives her the secret of realizing her wish. As he exits, he remarks: "One side [of the mushroom] will make you grow taller, and the other side will make you grow shorter." Perplexed, Alice asks *herself*: "One side of what?" The clairvoyant Caterpillar says: "Of the mushroom"—just as if she had asked the question aloud. Note that neither Alice nor the Caterpillar acts as though this act of mind-reading is anything extraordinary. Each of them seems to accept mind-reading as a matter of course. Alice has obviously been so thoroughly exasperated by the bizarre shrinkages and physical distortions inflicted upon her throughout the day that the Caterpillar's mental feat no longer impresses her. If she can converse at all with a Caterpillar, his mind-reading can't be much more extraordinary. But, remember, the creatures of Wonderland *never* behave as though they are abnormal.

The mushroom has predictable effects. This time, it leaves Alice with a curving, serpentine neck. There is a curious irony at play here: the Caterpillar again provides Alice with the means of changing her *size* rather than simply, psychologically, "growing up." Caterpillars, of course, emerge from a chrysalis as newborn butterflies or moths; they die, so to speak, to be reborn. Alice, however, never experiences a similar metamorphosis. In fact, she resents any notion that she is anyone other than who she has *always* been.

A good case here can be made that part of her objection to "growing up" is based on her fear of losing her identity. So long as she remains young Alice, she is innocent of good and evil. But with her neck suddenly slithering through the tree branches, she appears to be the embodiment of evil. In fact, a pigeon-hen immediately thinks that Alice is an egg-eating snake.

Thus, the Pigeon's attack on Alice changes Wonderland from a pastoral garden to a primal jungle of violence and death. Alice denies that she is a serpent. "I—I'm a little girl," she says, remembering the number of changes she has gone through during the day. "A likely story indeed!" smirks the Pigeon.

Alice is again unable to triumph at the cost of an "adult." On the contrary, she feels compelled to assume a role as it is defined for her by others, and the Pigeon, once more, reinforces Alice's problem of identity. Like her series of size changes, Alice's entire existence is one gigantic question mark. Her problem is that she truly sympathizes with the Pigeon's desire to protect the nest. Nevertheless, Alice fears that she won't be able to *prove* that she is, truly, just a little girl with an extremely long neck. And the Pigeon rejects Alice's claim – especially after she admits that Yes, she *has* eaten eggs. But her protests that she has no designs on these particular eggs come to nothing, and the Pigeon vehemently orders her away from the nest.

In a state of rejection, Alice desperately tries to reduce herself back to her previous size. She still has some of the Caterpillar's mushroom, so she nibbles at pieces of it, and by a process of trial and error, she begins to be able to control her size. Thus, her success in using the mushroom to obtain the desired height shows how well she is beginning to apply the logic of size reversibility.

CHAPTER VI

"Pig and Pepper"

The Caterpillar's nasty mood, even if he does *seem* nonchalant, is a subtle symbol of all the verbal chaos in Wonderland. Yet, here, in Chapter VI, that linguistic nonsense is replaced by random, violent, *physical disorder* in the action of the story.

Alice has come upon a house, just as a Fish-Footman delivers a letter to the Frog-Footman of the house. The letter is an invitation, which the Fish-Footman reads: "For the Duchess. An invitation from the Queen to play croquet." In a marvelous example of Wonderland's semantic, verbal fun, the Frog-Footman reverses the invitation: "From the Queen. An invitation for the Duchess to play croquet." In reality, it should *end* with "From the Queen."

When Alice attempts to enter the house, she finds herself further into the world of nonsense. The Frog-Footman is sitting before the door and is totally *un*cooperative as she knocks at the door. He replies to her every question in "absurd" reasoning – as if Alice had suddenly found herself in a Samuel Beckett play. With elegant precision, the Frog-Footman explains that her knocking on the door is useless because he can only answer the door from inside. Again, we see an illustration where the reply to a question is never addressed *to* the question, but to something else. Alice's knocking on the door is "useless," she is told, because the Frog-Footman, who opens the door from inside the house, is now *outside*; thus, he can't answer her; and, in any event, the noise from *inside* the house would prevent the Frog-Footman from hearing her knock *even if* he were inside. Truly, this *is* the World of the Absurd.

Yet, this kind of confusion is quite normal in Wonderland; *all* of reality here is viewed, so to speak, on a scale of values which are completely alien to the "normal" Victorian world of Alice.

A large plate suddenly comes flying out of the house and barely misses hitting the Frog-Footman's head. The Frog-Footman is totally oblivious to this. And his indifference to chaos is characteristic of Wonderland's creatures and indicates to Alice that there surely must be an underlying order here. Or perhaps it involves only a fatalistic indifference. For the Caterpillar and the Frog-Footman, things have *no purpose*. "I shall sit here," the Frog-Footman muses, "on and off for days and days."

"But what am I to do?" asks Alice.

"Anything you like," says the Frog-Footman.

The Frog-Footman's reply to Alice's question is idiotic nonsense, and with a child's simplicity, Alice finds the Frog-Footman's values totally illogical. Alice has been brought up to believe that things should be done and that they should be done with a purpose. In her world, there is order and there are schedules and tasks to be accomplished at certain times. Carroll's method in creating the tension between these two worlds is to increase the difference in the values "above-ground" and those of Wonderland. One is, therefore, not entirely correct in relating Wonderland's anarchy and nonsense to the creatures' irrational behavior. Alice, in fact, is making the assumption that there is—and *should be*—an order here; she is trying to make logic from illogic. Wonderland is a world of illogic, and Alice, as a proper little Victorian girl, keeps trying throughout the novel to relate, logically, to these creatures—who *seem* like adults and who, therefore, should be logical.

The creatures' acceptance of disorder may seem to be a parody of reality to the reader. Yet Wonderland's chaos is not altogether unreal. Our own reality, as a historical one, is impermanent and never without some degree of ambiguity. When we consider what has been accepted as "reality" throughout the ages regarding our world and its place in the Order of Things, we see how flimsy a word "logic" can be. Indeed, Alfred Einstein, the father of relativity, was deeply worried that God was "playing dice with the universe." If Alice fails to discover a correlation between her reality above-ground and her dream, it must be because she is "inside" her dream. To put it another way, one might even say that she is trapped in an unadjustable frame of meaning. For her, there is no scale of values except the one which she brings to Wonderland. She has a strong sense of being lost and abandoned; but the *creatures* know where *they* belong, and *none* of them identifies with her plight. Nor are the creatures able to befriend her. Note that Alice meets *no other children like herself* in Wonderland. And the creatures all speak to her on the inscrutable and mysterious level of adults. Unless they direct her to do something, their utterances are quite beyond her comprehension. In that sense, in Alice's dream, they are echoing memories of the many puzzling things that adults living above-ground have said, things that Alice did not understand.

Inside the house, Alice meets the Duchess, who nurses a crying baby. A cook, meanwhile, stirs a cauldron of soup and, indiscriminately, she shakes a pepper mill. The baby is crying, and it is sneezing, it seems, because of all the flying pepper. Next to the cook sits the Cheshire-Cat with his famous smile. The kitchen is in an absolute turmoil. But the Duchess ignores the sneezing, the crying, and the cook throwing pans. Alice watches silently as the Duchess brutally shakes and pounds the baby. The Duchess' rudeness and cruelty is the most extreme thus far in the story; even the cook is provoked to the point of directing her pans at the Duchess. Calmly, the Duchess ignores the others' reactions.

"If everybody minded their business," the Duchess says, "the world would go around a deal faster than it does."

"Which would not be an advantage," observes Alice.

"Talking of axes," says the Duchess, "Chop off her head!" The Duchess is abominable, and the baby bears the worst of her cruelty. While violently throwing the baby around, the Duchess sings a crude and savage lullaby:

> Speak roughly to your little boy,
> And beat him when he sneezes:
> He only does it to annoy,
> Because he knows it teases.

The cook and the baby then recite a chorus to each stanza:

"Wow! wow! wow!"

This verse, like the others before it, is another parody of a well-known poem in Carroll's time. Alice is rightly appalled at the lullaby's sentiments and the Duchess' cruelty. Every now and then, the Duchess calls the baby "Pig!" This is proof enough that the Duchess has a barbarous nature.

As the Duchess prepares to go play croquet with the Queen, she tosses the baby to Alice. Suddenly, Alice feels maternal and thinks that she must save the baby from the violent Duchess and from the crazy cook. But in the next moment, Alice finds that her sympathy is falsely placed. The baby struggles to get out of her embrace, and before Alice's very eyes, the baby is transformed into a grunting pig.

Confident that she *was* doing the right thing—despite the metamorphosis that is happening before her very eyes—Alice still finds her good intentions subverted by Wonderland's absurdities. Finally, she has no choice but to let the pig trot off, but she cannot let it go without a twinge of guilt. She considers it a handsome pig—but an *ugly baby*. Implicit in this observation is the assumption that "all things have a silver lining," a very Victorian type of thought. Alice remembers children who "might do well as pigs . . . if one only knew the right way to change them."

Alice has a new sense of self-satisfaction and superiority that has been reinforced by the contemptible behavior of the Duchess. She "saved" the pig/baby. Indeed, in the face of the rudeness she has experienced, Alice is finding that she doesn't have to struggle so hard to remain a "lady." All she has to do is *not* react to the crazy provocation that she meets. But even so, her moral superiority illustrates her painful isolation, and not even the smiling Cheshire-Cat enables her to relax for very long, for despite his wonderfully large smile, the cat has "long claws and a great many teeth."

Just after the pig trots away, Alice notices the Cheshire-Cat sitting on a bough in a tree. Whereas the Duchess is unpleasant and threatening, the friendly Cheshire-Cat treats Alice with a measure of respect—though he is no less maddening in his response to her questions. The Cat is neither didactic nor hostile; still, he is no less inconsistent. If he doesn't snap at her, he *still confuses* her. Seemingly, he is an honest cat, but Alice cannot make sense of his "honesty." For example, when Alice asks him which way to go, he responds: "That depends a good deal on where you want to get to." As Alice responds that she doesn't care, he replies: "Then it doesn't matter which way you go." He assures her that she will get somewhere if she only walks long enough; she is sure to reach the same destination regardless of the direction that she takes. Unlike the other creatures, the Cheshire-Cat *does* seem fair. However, he too creates frustration within Alice in exactly the very same illogical ways that adults have so often verbally confused Alice. And, in addition, his constant disappearances and reappearances are terribly distracting.

"How do you know I'm mad?" asks Alice.

"You must be or you wouldn't have come here," the cat says.

Alice then contradicts the cat when he claims to growl. "Call it what you like," he says. Then, in a clairvoyant moment, he casually mentions that he'll see Alice at the Queen's croquet game. At this point, Alice hasn't even been *invited* to the game, nor has she indicated any intention of going. But like the Frog-Footman, the Cheshire-Cat transfigures reality and anticipates events. He's not surprised that the baby became a pig; he's only uncertain whether Alice said "pig" or "fig." Ultimately, his smile is his most enduring and least confusing aspect. Alice complains that his vanishing and reappearing "so suddenly" make her dizzy. She asks him not to disappear; his response is to "slow down" his disappearance so that he appears to *dissolve*; in the end, only his grin remains, and then it too disappears. The Cheshire-Cat's smile is the embodiment of Wonderland's riddle; it is as famous and as enigmatic as Mona Lisa's smile.

Curiously, it is the Cheshire-Cat who offers Alice a "meaning" to Wonderland's chaos. Alice's curiosity has led her into a mad world, and she has begun to wonder if she herself is mad. She realizes that there is just a possibility that she may be mad! And the fact that Alice is, finally, *not* surprised at the cat's vanishing does indicate a kind of madness on her part. And after being told that the Mad Hatter and the March Hare are also mad, Alice *still* insists on meeting them. In her conversation with the cat, Alice tries to come to terms with madness, but it seems that she has no choice in the matter. All roads, as it were, lead to mad people, and she seems to be one of them. The cat's grin undermines her security in anything she hears because the connection between subject (cat) and attribute (grin) has been severed.

"Well," [Alice thought], "I've often seen a cat without a grin . . . but a grin without a cat! It's the most curious thing I ever saw in all my life."

Here is a smile without a face, without any substance—just a smile. The smile has become a nightmare of perplexity. Yet what the cat told Alice *is* logical; she *can* get somewhere by walking long enough in any direction. But it is not the answer to the question which Alice asked. Thus, the cat's responses to her inquiries are scaled to very different values than the values above-ground in Alice's familiar Victorian world. And looked at objectively, the Cheshire-Cat does not really accept Alice as an equal. He patronizes her gullibility as any adult might play with a child. In the end, Alice doesn't learn anything from him.

Soon, Alice finds the house of the March Hare. Since it is May, she reasons (a *wrong* thing to do in Wonderland), the Hare should be "mad" only in March. She nibbles at her mushroom until she becomes taller; increasing her size gives her more self-confidence, but she still has not learned that getting smaller or larger by such means will *not* enable her to deal with Wonderland any better.

CHAPTER VII

"A Mad Tea-Party"

Linguistic assaults are very much a part of the "polite bantering" in Wonderland. Often, traumatic and verbal violence seems just about to erupt all the time, breaking through the thin veneer of civilized behavior, but it rarely does. Alice reaches the March Hare's house in time for an outdoor tea-party. The tea-party turns out to be a *very mad* tea-party. In attendance are Alice, the March Hare, the Mad Hatter, and a Dormouse. All are indeed mad, except (perhaps) Alice and the sleepy Dormouse (who is only mad when he is awake). Alice has arrived just in time for tea, which is served at six o'clock. But it is *always* six o'clock, with no time to wash the dishes; thus, it is *always* tea time. In fact, the significant feature about this tea-party is that time has been frozen still. The idea of real, moving, passing time is non-existent.

The absense of time means that the Mad Tea-Party is trapped in a space without time. The world isn't turning, hands aren't moving around the clock, and the only "rotating" exists around the tea-party table. When the four have finished tea (although Alice gets none), they move to the next place-setting around the table. Dirty dishes accumulate, and there doesn't seem to be any substantive food. No one even seems to be taking tea. The Mad Hatter tells Alice that the Queen has accused him of murdering his friend Time; ever since the Mad Hatter and Time had a falling out, it has always been six o'clock. It's always tea time, and they have no time to wash the dishes between time for tea.

Alice typically does her best to cling to her *own* code of behavior (as always); she is *still* determined to "educate" the creatures to the rules of Victorian social etiquette. They protest her joining the party with cries of "No room! No room!" But Alice ignores them (she is larger now), and she sits down. The insanity of it all begins immediately when the March Hare offers her wine that doesn't exist. Alice complains, of course, about this lack of civility in offering her some non-existent wine. The March Hare counters that *she* was very rude to invite herself to their party. Her rules of etiquette completely fail her here. These creatures once again turn upside down all her principles of decorum.

"Your hair wants cutting," the Mad Hatter interrupts her at one point.

"You should learn not to make personal remarks," Alice says. "It's very rude."

Later, she violates her advice and impolitely interrupts the Mad Hatter. "Nobody asked *your* opinion," she says. "Who's making personal remarks now?" retorts the Mad Hatter.

Alice has been deflated and demoralized. The last above-ground rules of how to act and what to say seem to dissolve before her eyes. She *cannot* understand why they are acting this way!

Thus, the tea-party continues with endless cups of tea and a conversation of absolutely meaningless nonsense. Suddenly, the Mad Hatter asks Alice: "Why is a raven like a writing desk?"

At first glance, the riddle makes no sense as a logical question. And even the answer that Carroll provides elsewhere (the raven produces a few notes, all very flat, and it is never put the wrong end front) is nonsense. Presumably there should always be answers to any questions; at least, there were answers above-ground.

The Mad Tea-Party conversation repeats this miscommunication pattern like all the other absurd conversations that Alice has had with Wonderland creatures in previous chapters. She delightfully explains: "I'm glad they've begun asking riddles—I believe I can guess that."

"Do you mean that you think you can find out the answer to it?" asks the March Hare.

"Exactly so," says Alice.

"Then you should say what you mean," says the Hare.

Alice's confidence is shaken: "I do," she says, "at least—at least I mean what I say—that's the same thing you know."

But here, of course, Alice is speaking in the context of time's absence. There is no time. This is, even in Wonderland, "another world."

"Why," says the Hare, "you might just as well say that 'I see what I eat' is the same thing as 'I eat what I see!'" This is reverse logic— exactly right for Wonderland, but, of course, not correct above-ground.

Alice cannot make the creatures understand this, however, and finally she sighs. "I think you might do something better with time . . . than wasting it in asking riddles that have no answers." To this, the Hatter replies: "If you knew Time as well as I do . . . you wouldn't talk about wasting *it*. It's him."

Time is thus suddenly personified and becomes the source of much punning and comic relief. Alice participates in this nonsense in all seriousness, saying that she has to "beat time" when she learns music, even though she has "perhaps" never spoken to "him."

"Ah! That accounts for it," says the Mad Hatter. "He won't stand beating!"

Then the Mad Hatter launches into a satirical parody of another, famous children's verse: "Twinkle, twinkle little bat!" The bat is not the shining star of the Victorian poem, but a repulsive and morbid symbol of the ugly course of events about to begin. The Mad Hatter explains that his fight with Time and accusation of murder happened the last time that he was reciting that verse. So the disaster with Time is closely related to the Mad Hatter's distortion of the nursery rhyme. Filling his version with bats and flying tea-trays, the Mad Hatter's rhyme increases the comic personification of Time. The Mad Hatter has animated the inanimate star as a bat and has made an inanimate object *live*.

The Mad Tea-Party is filled with atrocious puns in conversation. The pun is determined by the coincidence of two words that sound so alike that relevant information is muddled. And here the play on words is a way of freeing meaning from conventional definition. The Dormouse, for instance, tells a story about three sisters who lived in a treacle well and were learning to "draw" treacle (molasses). Alice asks:

"But I don't understand. Where did they draw treacle from?"

"You can draw water out of a water-well," says the Mad Hatter, "so I should think you could draw treacle out of a treacle-well."

"But they were in the well," says Alice (very logically).

"Of course they were," says the Dormouse. "Well in."

The Dormouse's illogic continues to frustrate Alice. Playing on words that begin with the letter *M*, the Dormouse describes the sisters as *drawing* "all manner of things—everything that begins with an *M*, such as mousetraps, and the moon, and memory, and muchness— you know you say things are 'much of a muchness'—did you ever see such a thing as a drawing of a muchness!"

Alice stammers, and the Hatter cries, "Then you shouldn't talk."

With that rude remark, Alice storms away in disgust. She has *still* not succeeded in getting any closer to the reality she seeks. At the tea-party, she has not even received any tea *or* food. Her serving has been only a bitter course of verbal abuse and semantic teasing. Muchness indeed! The creatures are self-centered, argumentative and rude; they have violated all of the conventions of conversation that Alice has been taught to practice. All of these creatures in Wonderland have compounded the pain of Alice's psychological loss of place and time with their nonsense and cruel teasing.

As she leaves the table, Alice notices the other two attempting to drown the Dormouse in the teapot. His ritualistic death is, at least, a seemingly logical consequence of the Mad Hatter's ominous verse and Alice's departure. The Dormouse *should* have been hibernating instead of attending parties and telling anecdotes; dunking him seems to be sort of a realistic—if an absurd—way of forcing him back to "slumber." This will be, however, if they are successful, more than just a "slumber"; it will be death, "much of a muchness."

The Dormouse's fate serves as an appropriate conclusion to this chapter, for Alice enters another door and finds herself once again in the hallway with the glass table and the small doorway that leads to the beautiful garden. To try and reinforce the notion that Wonderland *must* have a hidden order, Alice first unlocks the door, and she then reduces her size by nibbling on a piece of the mushroom.

She has *finally* learned a lesson from her initial, frightening experience in Wonderland: she has been eating, drinking, and changing sizes, without thinking *first*.

CHAPTER VIII

"The Queen's Croquet-Ground"

At last, Alice finds herself in the garden that she has so long sought to explore. Far from being a wild Eden, though, the garden is well cultivated and tended. And now Alice meets a whole set of new creatures—this time, several animated playing cards. Immediately, she finds out that the Spades are, of course, the gardeners. And in spite of the Eden-like appearance, the garden has an aspect of "fear" in the air. Alice overhears three gardeners—the Two, the Five, and the Seven—talking about the Queen's threat to behead the Seven of Spades. They are painting the white roses red, an ominous color in view of their discussion.

Suddenly, the Queen and King of Hearts appear. They are followed by a suit of cards which represents the "royal retainers." The Clubs are the "police," the Diamonds are the "courtiers," and the Hearts make up the royal "peerage." The Queen sees Alice and the three Spade gardeners (who have thrown themselves flat on the ground so as to try and conceal their identity). The Queen asks Alice *who* the three cards are, and Alice replies tartly: "How should *I* know?"

This flippant answer throws the Queen into a rage; instantly she explodes with her infamous and beastly command: "Off with her head!"

"Nonsense," says Alice, very loudly.

The frequency and roaring of the Queen's threats reveal the terrible rule underlying the world of Wonderland. Execution, or the threat of execution, is indiscriminately announced—and canceled—in whimsical moments, with automatic reprieves. One may be sentenced to death without having committed a crime—indeed, without having received a verdict. In contradicting the Queen, Alice confronts the system of Wonderland *directly*, as a leading participant-actor; *she is no longer a detached observer.* Wonderland is now a world of cruelty, destruction, and annihilation, and Alice sees this, and already we can see the possibility of her emerging from it, smiling and unscathed.

The Queen orders the gardeners to be executed. Alice manages to save their lives, however, by hiding them in a flower pot. (Her fear seems to have been unfounded. The Gryphon tells her that nobody in Wonderland is ever executed.)

There is more humor in the subsequent scenes. Note, too, that Wonderland is a "Queendom," instead of a Kingdom because the King is subordinate to the Queen. Now, familiar characters like the White Rabbit, the Duchess, and the Cheshire-Cat enter the croquet-garden. The croquet game again reverses the real-world division between life and inanimate objects as hedgehogs form the balls, the flamingoes the mallets, and the card-soldiers the hoops. The White Rabbit apprises Alice of her inherent danger in a whispered conversation. Even the Duchess, he says, is in jail under a sentence of execution for having boxed the Queen's ears. Alice learns all this but she seems *not* to be intimidated. In the next scene, the Cheshire-Cat demonstrates the violently repressive regime of Wonderland.

Because the cat is impertinent to the King, it is sentenced to be beheaded. But only the cat's head has materialized so the decapitation cannot be performed. The failed execution marks the slow disintegration of Wonderland in Alice's estimation. Within the character of the cat, Alice recognizes a fair and open mind. But he is fair and open – only to a limited degree. She tries to explain to the cat that the croquet game doesn't make sense because the game has "no rules." The cat, however, replies in such non-sequiturs as "How do you like the Queen?" Clearly, the cat can no more understand a game with no rules than he can understand a world where cats could *not* disappear and reappear in thin air. Alice mistakes the Cheshire-Cat for a friend and someone with whom she can relate on a real-world, logical level. Her assumption is wrong.

CHAPTERS IX – XII

"The Mock Turtle's Story," "The 'Lobster-Quadrille,'" "Who Stole the Tarts?" and "Alice's Evidence"

Alice's major problem with Wonderland continues to be her inability to completely penetrate what she thinks exists – that is, its "logic."

The Queen has a soldier fetch the Duchess at the close of the last chapter, and Alice finds the Duchess in a surprisingly good mood. Alice attributes, logically, her previous ill-temper to the Cook's pepper. "Maybe it's always pepper that makes people hot-tempered," she thinks, very much pleased at having believed that she has discovered a "new kind of rule," a rule of logic that exists in this strange world of Wonderland.

The Duchess, very much in the mold of a proper Victorian, finds a rule in *everything*, but they are rules and precepts which are nothing more than improvised absurdities: ". . . flamingoes and mustard both bite. And the moral of that is – 'Birds of a feather flock together.' " As this conversation takes place, the Duchess has seductively dug her hideous chin into Alice's shoulder, but their silly dialogue underlines the fun – and the entire world of nonsense – in Wonderland's satire on the nature of all "rules."

The mad Queen appears, and her presence – just her *presence* – is intimidating. The Duchess cowers and flies away from the garden. This form of bullying is a humorous evocation of the world of power relations. The Duchess flees from the Queen – and at that moment, all the croquet players and hoops have been placed under custody and sentenced to death! Only Alice, the King and the Queen are left to play the insane croquet game. Presumably, the Duchess could challenge the Queen's power at this point. But the Duchess is like Alice; each of them respects rank. So the "more humane" Duchess yields to the Queen of Hearts.

Next, Alice meets two of the most incredible creatures in Wonderland; the Gryphon (Griffin) and the Mock Turtle (whose name comes from veal soup). The two creatures listen sympathetically to Alice's story of her adventures in Wonderland. The Gryphon finds her story merely curious, but the Mock Turtle thinks that her verse is "uncommon nonsense." Alice quickly finds out the false nature of their initial sympathy. The Gryphon's intense, selfish sorrow is revealed finally as being just a fancy, and the Mock Turtle's sensitivity is a reflection of his fearful name – a reminder of his eventual fate as something's or someone's meal.

Carroll's satire in Wonderland is once again brought into play in the Mock Turtle's education. As a "real tortoise," he studied such things as: "Reeling and Writhing . . . and the different branches of Arithmetic – Ambition, Distraction, Uglification and Derision . . . and

Mystery . . . Seaography; then Drawling – the Drawling-master was an old conger-eel, that used to come once a week: he taught us drawling, stretching and fainting in Coils." A classical teacher taught the Mock Turtle "Laughing and Grief." And finally lessons were called lessons "because they lessen from day to day."

Chapters IX and X, thus, break with the pattern of Wonderland. At last, Alice finds one character who displays an absence of hostility. The Gryphon, for instance, is often tart but his intentions are at least outwardly sympathetic. The Mock Turtle and the Gryphon seem to confirm Alice's sense of Wonderland's peculiar disorder, and in Chapter X, "The 'Lobster-Quadrille,'" we have another sad account of a meal and a dance, told in mock heroic couplets.

Chapter XI ("Who Stole the Tarts?") and Chapter XII ("Alice's Evidence") reduce the above-ground facsimile of justice to a travesty. The one constant factor in the "enchanted garden" – the Queen's furious demand for executions – turns out to have *always* been ignored, as Alice learns from the Gryphon. In Chapter XI, the Knave of Hearts is brought to trial and accused of stealing tarts. Eating again becomes the method of someone's downfall.

The Knave of Hearts' trial becomes a pointless formality as soon as we hear the Queen's directive: "Sentence first – verdict afterward." The White Rabbit serves as Herald of the Court, thus fulfilling the symbolic role which he plays in introducing the story. The members of the Mad Tea-Party and the Duchess' cook are all brought in to give evidence. But the trial is completely lacking – in *rules, evidence,* and *justice.* The trial becomes yet another humorous illustration of Wonderland's assault on real-world semantics and linguistic principles.

"Take off your hat," the King tells the Hatter.

"It isn't mine," the Hatter says.

"If that's all you know about it, you may step down," the King tells him.

"I can't go no lower," says the Mad Hatter, "I'm on the floor, as it is."

All during this time, Alice is beginning to grow to her original size. When she reveals this to the Dormouse, he replies: "You've no right to grow here." Part of the fun at this point is that Alice seems to know all about court proceedings and the names of things, although she has never been in a court of justice. The purpose of the narrator in letting us know this fact is that it prepares us for her discomfort at the absurdity and insanity of the court proceedings.

In the final chapter, ironically entitled "Alice's Evidence," it is Alice who gets all the evidence she needs to rebel against the cruelty of Wonderland's trial. After observing the jurymen scribble nonsense as they take testimony, she decides that the nonsense has gone far enough. (In one funny scene, she takes juryman Bill the Lizard's pencil away from him, but he continues to write with his finger.)

Alice dramatically demonstrates her new subversive attitude. The Queen asserts without any evidence that the Knave has been proven guilty by the "evidence." "It doesn't prove anything of the sort," replies Alice. The only thing offered in evidence for the prosecution is the White Rabbit's vague poem, which (as Alice observes) *no one understands.* The Queen makes her usual command: "Sentence first — verdict afterward." Alice retorts: "Stuff and Nonsense!" The Queen sentences Alice, but by then Alice has grown to her full height. "Who cares for *you?*" Alice says. "You're nothing but a pack of cards!"

This loud proclamation signals her flight from Wonderland's anarchy to the sanity of above-ground. Alice emerges finally from her confused doubts about this mixed-up world of Wonderland. She rebels, and she leaves the world underneath the ground for the world of common sense and consciousness. Her "lesson," if it can be called that, is that she learns what she has already known. That is, she imposes her order on chaos, and, in consequence, her world of wonderful but unreal and strange and fanciful, glorious things is destroyed. After all, one cannot live long in a dream world. Such things as identity, sanity, laws, logic, and self-preservation have a price. To sustain them, Alice had to reject endless, timeless "possibilities." Her dream, in effect, ends just before a nightmare begins.

The narrator concludes the Wonderland dream: "So Alice got up and ran off, thinking while she ran, as well she might, what a wonderful dream it had been."

Alice wakes up on the lap of her sister filled with the images of Wonderland from her "curious dream." Thus, fantasy is transformed into memory; and any memory can seem real, and it will seem real, in its own way, to Alice, always.

CRITICAL ANALYSIS

Alice as a Character

Alice is reasonable, well-trained, and polite. From the start, she is a miniature, middle-class Victorian "lady." Considered in this way, she is the perfect foil, or counterpoint, or contrast, for all the *un*social, bad-mannered eccentrics whom she meets in Wonderland. Alice's constant resource and strength is her courage. Time and again, her dignity, her directness, her conscientiousness, and her art of conversation *all* fail her. But when the chips are down, Alice reveals something to the Queen of Hearts—that is: spunk! Indeed, Alice has all the Victorian virtues, including a quaint capacity for rationalization; yet it is Alice's *common sense* that makes the quarrelsome Wonderland creatures seem perverse in spite of what they consider to be their "adult" identities.

Certainly, Alice fits no conventional stereotype; she is neither angel nor brat. She simply has an overwhelming curiosity, but it is matched by restraint and moderation. She is balanced in other ways, too. To control her growth and shrinking, she only "samples" the cake labeled "EAT ME." And never is there a hint that she would seek to use her size advantage to control her fate and set dictatorial rules of behavior for Wonderland. The Caterpillar takes offense when she complains of being three inches tall. And the Duchess is unreasonable, coarse, and brutal. But in each case, their veneer of "civility" is either irrational or transparent. The Caterpillar finds mirth in teasing Alice with his pointed, formal, verb games, and the rude Duchess mellows into a corrupt "set of silly rules." Yet, behind their playfulness, Alice senses resentment and rage. It is not so much that Alice is kept "simple" so as to throw into relief the monstrous aspects of Wonderland characters. Rather, it is that Alice, as she conceives of her personality in a dream, *sees herself* as simple, sweet, innocent, and confused.

Some critics feel that Alice's personality and her waking life are reflected in Wonderland; that may be the case. But the story itself is independent of Alice's "real world." Her personality, as it were, stands alone in the story, and it must be considered in terms of the Alice character in Wonderland.

A strong moral consciousness operates in all of Alice's responses to Wonderland, yet on the other hand, she exhibits a child's insensitivity in discussing her cat Dinah with the frightened Mouse in the pool of tears. Generally speaking, Alice's simplicity owes a great deal to Victorian feminine passivity and a repressive domestication. Slowly, in stages, Alice's reasonableness, her sense of responsibility, and her other good qualities will emerge in her journey through Wonderland

and, especially, in the trial scene. Her list of virtues is long: curiosity, courage, kindness, intelligence, courtesy, humor, dignity, and a sense of justice. She is even "maternal" with the pig/baby. But her constant and universal human characteristic is simple *wonder* – something with which all children (and the child that still lives in most adults) can easily identify with.

THEMES

Alice in Wonderland provides an inexhaustible mine of literary, philosophical, and scientific themes. Here are some general themes which the reader may find interesting and of some use in studying the work.

Abandonment/Loneliness

Alice's initial reaction after falling down the rabbit-hole is one of extreme loneliness. Her curiosity has led her into a kind of Never-Never Land, over the edge of Reality and into a lonely, very alien world. She is further lost when she cannot establish her identity. Physically, she is lost; psychologically, she also feels lost. She cannot get her recitations right, and she becomes even more confused when her arithmetic (a subject she believed to be unchanging and solid) fails her. Every attempt to establish a familiar basis of identity creates only the sense of being lost – absolutely lost. Alice becomes, to the reader, a mistreated, misunderstood, wandering waif. Trapped in solitude, she finds herself lapsing into soliloquies that reflect a divided, confused, and desperate self.

The Child-Swain

Alice is the most responsible "character" in the story; in fact, she is the only real person and the only "true" character. At most, the other creatures are antagonists, either a bit genial or cruel, depending on how they treat Alice at any given point in the story. Alice's innocence makes her a perfect vehicle of social criticism a la Candide. In her encounters, we see the charmingly pathetic ingénue – a child whose only purpose is to escape the afflictions around her. By implication, there is the view that a child's perception of the world is the only sane one. Conversely, to grow and mature leads to inevitable corruption, to sexuality, emotionalism, and adult hypocrisy. The child as an innocent, sympathetic object has obvious satirical utility, but only to the point that the child must extend sympathy herself – and Alice fails to do this when she describes her cat Dinah to the Mouse, and later when she confesses to having eaten eggs to the frightened mother pigeon.

Children and Animals

In an age such as our own, where philosophers earnestly debate the rights of animals, or whether machines can "think," we cannot escape the child's affinity for animals. And in Wonderland, except for the Gryphon, none of the animals are of a hostile nature that might lead Alice to any harm. (And the Gryphon is a mythical animal so he doesn't count as a "true" animal.) Most of the Wonderland animals are the kind one finds in middle-class homes, pet shops, and in children's cartoons. Although they may not seem so in behavior, most of them are, really, pets. Alice feels a natural identity with them, but her relationship ultimately turns on her viewing them as *adults*. So her identity with the animals has a lot to do with her size in relationship to adults. Alice emphasizes this point when she observes that some ugly children might be improved if they were pigs. In her observation lies the acceptance of a common condition of children and animals: each is personified to a degree. Thus, it is not surprising that in the world of the child, not only animals, but dolls, toys, plants, insects, and even playing cards have the potential to be personified by children (or adults).

Death

Growing up in Wonderland means the death of the child, and although Alice certainly remains a child through her physical changes in size – in other ways, death never seems to be far away in Wonderland. For example, death is symbolized by the White Rabbit's fan which causes Alice to *almost* vanish; death is implied in the discussion of the Caterpillar's metamorphosis. And death permeates the morbid atmosphere of the "enchanted garden." The Queen of Hearts seems to be the Goddess of Death, always yelling her single, barbarous, indiscriminate, "Off with their heads!"

Nonsense

One of the key characteristics of Carroll's story is his use of language. Much of the "nonsense" in *Alice* has to do with transpositions, either of mathematical scale (as in the scene where Alice multiplies incorrectly) or in the scrambled verse parodies (for example, the Father William poem). Much of the nonsense effect is also achieved by directing conversation to parts of speech rather than to the meaning of the speakers – to definitions rather than to indications. When Alice asks the Cheshire-Cat which way to go, he replies that she should, first, know where she's going. The Frog-Footman tells her not to knock on the door outside the Duchess' house; he can only open the door when he is inside (though Alice, of course, manages to open the door from the outside). And some of the nonsense in Wonderland is merely satirical, such as the Mock Turtle's education. But the nature of nonsense is much like chance, and rules to decipher it into logical meaning or sense patterns work against the principal intent of Carroll's purpose – that is, he wanted his nonsense to be random, senseless, unpredictable, and without rules.

Nature and Nurture

The structure of a dream does not lend itself to resolution. A dream simply is a very different kind of "experience." In this sense, Alice does not really evolve into a higher understanding of her adventure. She has the *memory* of Wonderland but she brings nothing "real" from Wonderland – only her memory of it. This is a powerful testament to the influence of her domestication. In Alice's case, good social breeding is more important than her natural disposition. But if Alice leaves Wonderland without acquiring any lasting, truly worthwhile knowledge, neither can she give any wisdom to the creatures whom she has met there. Nature, in each case, sets limits on the ability to assimilate experiences.

In the Caucus-race, for instance, the race depicts the absurdity of democracy. Yet, Alice's critical attitude – a product of her class education – is also satirized. The object of the race is to have everyone dry off; so it doesn't matter *who* wins or loses, and clearly the outcome of the race is irrelevant. To think otherwise, as Alice does, is absurd. The point of the running about is to dry off, which, incidentally, makes it equally absurd to call moving about for that purpose a "race."

Wonderland offers a peculiar view of Nature. For one thing, all the animals have obviously been educated. There is literally not a "stupid" one in the bunch (unless it is the puppy or the pig/baby). In general, the basic condition common to all the creatures is not ignorance – but madness, for which there seems to be no appropriate remedy. A Victorian reader must have wondered how the animals were "trained"; after all, the assumptions that Alice makes all rest on her "training." On this point, however, the reader can only speculate.

In Wonderland, much of the fun depends on the confusion of "training." Nature and natural feelings seem to more often than not mean danger or potential violence. (But except for the puppy and the pig/baby, there are no natural creatures, however much natural feelings are expressed.) The Duchess, for example, seems to be only the epitome of rage; she conveys a kind of sadistic delight in digging her chin into Alice's shoulder; anger even seems to motivate her didactic morals (that is, "Flamingoes and mustard both bite.").

Finally, nature seems superior to nurture in Wonderland, as the personification of beasts seems to be no improvement on the actual beasts themselves. The pig, for example, is a more content creature *as a pig,* for the baby was not happier when it was a *baby.*

Justice

Although there are plenty of "rules," the laws of Wonderland seem a parody of real justice. The Queen of Hearts, for example, thinks nothing of violating the law which protects people from illegal prosecution; she seeks the head of the Knave of Hearts for having been only *accused* of stealing the tarts. Thus, the Queen violates the spirit of the law against stealing to satisfy the logical necessity that *every* trial must have an execution. The spirit of the law is, so to speak, sacrificed to satisfy the reversibility of the symbolic letter of her logic. In the croquet game, anyone can be executed for reasons known *only* to the sovereign Queen, who acts as though she is a divinity with the power to take or give life. Under a monarchy, the monarchs are above the law. In Wonderland, however, the monarch's will is flaunted when the command is to execute someone. Ignoring the Queen's command to behead someone is a matter of survival as well as justice.

The trial of the Knave of Hearts satirizes both too much law and law by personal edict. Someone may have stolen the tarts, and it may well have been the Knave. But the offense is trivial, and the sentence is only a joke. One of the problems with the law in any context is its application. When the law ceases to promote harmony, then its purpose as a regulator of human affairs is subverted. In Wonderland, the idea of a law seems ridiculous because the *operative principle* of Wonderland is *chaos*. Injustice, then, is a logical consequence of living in Wonderland. The rule of the strongest person must be the law — that is, the law of anarchy. The trial of the Knave is proof of this woeful state of affairs. Fortunately, Alice is the strongest of the lot, and she overthrows the cruel Queen's sentence of execution and the savage kangaroo court. There is no way to change the law because no "law" exists. By her rebellion, Alice serves both the cause of sanity and justice.

Time and Space

Time, in the sense of duration, exists in Wonderland only in a psychological and artistic sense. When we ordinarily conceive of time, we think of units of duration — that is, hours, minutes, and seconds; or days, weeks, months, and years. We may also think of getting older and having lived from a certain date. We assume that the time reflected on a clock and our age are essentially the same kind of process. But a clock may repeat its measure of duration, whereas *we* have only *one* lifetime. Our age is therefore a function of an irreversible, psychological sense of duration. We live in the conscious knowledge that we can never return to a given point in the past, as we might adjust a clock for daylight savings time. Our personal, psychological time is absolute and irreversible. And that is the kind of time that creatures like the Mad Hatter employ in Wonderland. (We never know whether the White Rabbit uses a mechanistic time, only that he has a watch.)

When Alice looks at the Mad Hatter's watch, she sees a date, but she sees neither hours nor minutes. Because Time and the Mad Hatter do not get along, Time has "frozen" the tea-party at six o'clock. But it turns out that time is also reversed so that a year has the duration of an hour and vice versa. Reckoned in hour-lengths, the tea-party must go on for at least a year (unless Time and the Mad Hatter make up their quarrel). But because of psychological time, the creatures are able to leave and return to the tea-party. And because of psychological time, Wonderland's experience comes to an end, and just as our uniquely, individual lives will one day end, so will our nightmares and dreams.

ESSAY QUESTIONS

Long Essays

1. Relate aspects of enchantment to the nostalgia that Alice experiences in Wonderland. Why is Alice both fascinated and frustrated by her encounters below-ground?

2. Describe some of the ways that Carroll achieves humor at Alice's expense.

3. Give an analysis of the use of nonsense in *Alice*.

4. How does the question "Who am I?" relate to the wish to eat and the fear of being eaten in *Alice*?

Short Essays

1. Describe the White Rabbit's function in *Alice*.

2. What is the significance of the Cheshire-Cat in the Queen's Croquet-Ground scene?

3. Compare the Duchess' lullaby to the "You Are Old, Father William" verse.

4. Explain the sentiment of the Mouse's long tale, the Mock Turtle's story and the "Lobster-Quadrille."

SELECTED BIBLIOGRAPHY

AUDEN, W. H. "The Man Who Wrote Alice," *New York Times Book Review*, 28 February 1954, p. 4.

BERNADETTE, DORIS. "Alice Among the Professors," *Western Humanities Review*, V, (1950), 239-47.

BURPEE, LAWRENCE J. "Alice Joins the Immortals," *Dalhousie Review*, XXI (1941), 194-204.

CHESTERTON, G. K. "Lewis Carroll," in *A Handful of Authors*, New York, 1953, pp. 112-19.

DARTON, F. J. HARVEY. *Children's Books in England: Five Centuries of Social Life*, second edition, Cambridge, 1958.

FLESHER, JACQUELINE. "The Language of Nonsense in *Alice*," *Yale French Studies*, XLIII (1970), 128-44.

GREEN, ROGER LANCELYN. "The Real Lewis Carroll," *Quarterly Review*, CCXCII (1954), 85-97.

HUBBELL, GEORGE SHELTON. "The Sanity of Wonderland," *Sewanee Review*, XXXV (1927), 387-98.

HUDSON, DEREK. *Lewis Carroll*, London, 1954.

KENT, MURIEL. "The Art of Nonsense," *Cornhill*, CXLIX (1934), 478-87.

LENNON, FLORENCE BECKER. *Victoria Through the Looking Glass: The Life of Lewis Carroll*, revised edition, New York, 1962.

LEVIN, HARRY. "Wonderland Revisited," *Kenyon Review*, XXVII (1965), 591-616.

MacNEICE, LOUIS. "The Victorians," in *Varieties of Parable*, Cambridge, 1965.

MUIR, PERCY. *English Children's Books 1600-1900*, London, 1954.

PARTRIDGE, ERIC. "The Nonsense Words of Edward Lear and Lewis Carroll," in *Here, There and Everywhere*, London, 1950, pp. 162-88.

RACKIN, DONALD. "Corrective Laughter: Carroll's *Alice* and Popular Children's Literature of the Nineteenth Century," *Journal of Popular Culture,* I (1967), 243-55.

SEWELL, ELIZABETH. *The Field of Nonsense,* London, 1952.

THODY, PHILIP. "Lewis Carroll and the Surrealists," *Twentieth Century,* CLXIII (1958), 427-34.

WAUGH, EVELYN. "Carroll and Dodgson," *Spectator,* CLXIII (1939), 511.

WEAVER, WARREN. "Alice's Adventures in Wonderland: Its Origins and Its Author," *Princeton Library Chronicle,* XIII (1951), 1-17.

WHITE, ALISON. "Alice After a Hundred Years," *Michigan Quarterly Review,* IV (1965), 261-64.

WILSON, EDMUND. "C. L. Dodgson: The Poet-Logician," in *The Shores of Light,* New York, 1952, pp. 540-50.

WOOD, JAMES P. *The Snark Was a Boojum: A Life of Lewis Carroll,* New York, 1966.

WOOLF, VIRGINIA. "Lewis Carroll," in *The Moment, and Other Essays,* New York, 1949, pp. 81-83.

Bleak House

BLEAK HOUSE

NOTES

including
- *Life of the Author*
- *Introduction to the Novel*
- *List of Characters*
- *Brief Synopsis*
- *Summaries & Critical Commentaries*
- *Character Analyses*
- *Critical Essays*
- *Review Questions and Essay Topics*
- *Selected Bibliography*

by
Robert Beum
Memorial University of Newfoundland

NEW EDITION

INCORPORATED

LINCOLN, NEBRASKA 68501

Editor	Consulting Editor
Gary Carey, M.A.	*James L. Roberts, Ph.D.*
University of Colorado	*Department of English*
	University of Nebraska

ISBN 0-8220-0247-7
© Copyright 1991
by
C. K. Hillegass
All Rights Reserved
Printed in U.S.A.

1992 Printing

Cliffs Notes, Inc.   Lincoln, Nebraska

CONTENTS

BLEAK HOUSE
Notes

LIFE OF THE AUTHOR

Charles Dickens (February 7, 1812–June 9, 1870) was the second of eight children born to Elizabeth and John Dickens, improvident and irresponsible parents who (without deep regret, it seems) gave their offspring poor starts in the world. Without actually hating his parents, Dickens early saw them for what they were. He was particularly critical of his mother, a self-centered woman short on affection for Charles; for example, she wanted to prolong his stay at the shoe blacking warehouse where he had been sent, at the age of twelve, to help support the family. In later life, Charles' own generosity and sense of decency prompted him to assist his parents, who continued in their improvident ways.

Partly from natural inclination and partly by way of taking refuge from an irregular and problematical family life, the young boy immersed himself in the world of imagination. He read Shakespeare, Addison, Fielding, Goldsmith, and several other authors avidly. He was also fond of reciting, acting, and theatre-going, activities in which his father encouraged him. He also wandered happily along the Thames and through the towns and nearby countryside of Kent (England's warmest and most serene region), where the Dickenses resided from 1817 to 1822. Dickens' affection for Chatham, Rochester, and other towns in Kent ripened over the years, and his final novel, *The Mystery of Edwin Drood* (left unfinished), is set in Rochester and contains some of the author's most vivid and evocative writing.

Both his reading and his recitals, as well as his acting, served to educate Dickens for what would later become his career as a writer with a flair for the dramatic speech and dramatic incident. As most of his early reading was the works of eighteenth-century writers, it is not surprising that the values and attitudes expressed (by characters and author alike) in his own novels are essentially the same as those found in Fielding, Goldsmith, and Richardson. Those writers believed that human nature was essentially good and that this goodness was actually enhanced by the spontaneous and enthusiastic public expression of that very belief.

One day, as Charles and his father were walking just outside Rochester, his father pointed out the local mansion, Gad's Hill Place, and suggested that if the boy made the most of his talents he might someday be able to live in such a house. This is a classic example of a small, seemingly inconsequential moment that later proves to be highly significant. Gad's Hill Place became an ideal for the boy, and one that helped him associate talent with financial success. In 1856, when Dickens was forty-four, he was able to buy the house; he loved it and never moved again.

In 1822, John Dickens, then a senior clerk in the navy pay office, was transferred from Chatham to London. There, continuing to spend more than he earned, he soon became hopelessly insolvent. In 1824, Charles was taken out of school and sent to work, pasting labels on pots of shoe blacking. Two weeks later, John Dickens was jailed at Marshalsea, a debtors' prison. The humiliation and despair of 1824 left permanent emotional scars. However, what English literature was to gain from this experience when Dickens became a writer was an unprecedentedly vivid and varied presentation of childhood as vulnerability. In fact, Dickens must be credited as the first serious English novelist to deal extensively with the victimized child, a theme that has continued to produce masterpieces in fiction and film.

Bleak House centers around children and very young people, and, at the same time, around the law and its courts. Dickens went directly from childhood into the world of law. In 1827, he obtained employment as an office boy for Charles Molloy, a London solicitor; several weeks later, he was hired as a clerk for the law office of Ellis and Blackmore. Dissatisfied with these dull and low-paid jobs, he learned shorthand and, late in 1828, he became a shorthand writer for Doctors' Commons, another institution of the law. Intermittently, he also did law reporting for the Metropolitan Police Courts. In his spare time, he read widely and happily at the British Museum.

In 1829, Dickens fell in love with Maria Beadnell, an attractive and vivacious but rather snobbish and hard-hearted banker's daughter. To better his chance with her, he began looking for a better paying and more prestigious position. In 1832, he went strongly into journalism, becoming a Parliamentary reporter for the *Mirror of Parliament* and a general reporter for the *True Sun*. Maria Beadnell found Dickens somewhat interesting but never took him seriously as a suitor. After four years, Dickens gave up on her, but the loss was a crushing and long-enduring sorrow. Dickens' best biographer, Edgar Johnson, says that "All the imagination, romance, passion, and aspiration of his nature she had brought into flower and she would never be separated from." Knowing that his failure to win Maria was largely due to his low social standing and poor financial prospects, Dickens became more determined than ever to make a name for himself and a fortune to go with it.

Prospects brightened almost at once. He had been writing some sketches of London life, and several of these were accepted and published by the *Monthly Magazine* and the *Evening Chronicle*. In March 1834, Dickens landed a job as a reporter for the important Whig (liberal) newspaper, the *Morning Chronicle*.

Journalism kept him in practice with the written word and forced him to observe closely and report accurately; it was excellent training for a man who saw more and more clearly that he wanted to make his mark in literature. Early in 1836, Dickens' collected pieces were published as *Sketches by Boz*. The book was very favorably reviewed, sold well, and went through three editions by 1837.

A month after the appearance of this book, Dickens published the initial part of his first novel, *The Posthumous Papers of the Pickwick Club*. Immensely successful, *Pickwick* established Dickens at once as the most popular writer in England. He left the *Morning Chronicle* and became the editor of *Bentley's Miscellany*, a magazine in which *Oliver Twist* was published in installments beginning in February 1837.

On April 2, 1836, Dickens married Catherine Hogarth. Although the marriage produced ten children, it was never a love-match, and "Kate" never came close to meeting Dickens' ideal of romantic femininity. In Victorian England, divorce was difficult, scandalous, and often socially and financially ruinous. Eventually, however, Dickens did effect a permanent separation from Catherine. Quite early in the marriage, Dickens realized that it was Catherine's sister Mary who embodied his ideal: "so perfect a creature never breathed." Had Mary lived, it is virtually certain that Dickens would have become romantically involved with her. Her sudden death (apparently of unsuspected heart disease) at seventeen was the greatest loss that Dickens ever experienced. He made plans to be buried beside her and insisted that his first daughter be named Mary. Undoubtedly the loss of Mary Hogarth further strengthened Dickens' inclination to center much of his story material around the pathos of children or young adults who were caught up in emotional or physical suffering. Mary is the prototype of many of the young heroines of Dickens' novels. She is memorably portrayed by Lois Baxter in the British film *Dickens of London*, for which Wolf Mankowitz wrote the screenplay.

Oliver Twist was followed in 1839 by *Nicholas Nickleby*. This, Dickens' third novel, illustrates the continuing influence of theater on Dickens' approach to fiction. Individual scenes – usually of only minor importance – seem intended more for the stage than for the page and are so vivid and energetic that they often "steal the show," disrupting the unity of the book. Many of his other novels show the same tendency, and, in fact, Dickens created stage versions of several of his books and stories; these were usually quite popular and financially successful. As well as remaining an inveterate theatergoer, Dickens continued all his life to stage private theatricals, usually at Gad's Hill Place, for family and friends. A social art, theater appealed to the eminently sociable Dickens. A lover of energy, Dickens also found the vivacity, the dynamic projection of the stage irresistible.

Closely allied to his fondness for theater was his practice of giving highly dramatic readings from his works. These too were almost invariably well attended and highly remunerative. They began in 1853 and, from 1858, became very frequent. Unfortunately, they took a lot out of the author (he sometimes collapsed during or after a reading) and contributed to his premature aging.

His fourth novel, *The Old Curiosity Shop* (1841), was one of the most popular that Dickens ever penned. Its sales were spectacular, and it reached a world-wide audience. The story's heroine, Little Nell, has long remained the archetype of the angelically pure and self-sacrificing, but also game and intrepid, child. Mary Hogarth was Dickens' major inspiration.

Dickens perfectly illustrates the phenomenal energy and personal productivity seen in so many figures of the Victorian era. This novelist, playwright, theater habitué, socializer, charity benefit worker, lecturer, father of ten, and voluminous letter writer, was also the editor of several magazines. From 1841 onward, he had to meet deadlines, scout out talent, dream up projects, and promote sales – first for *Master Humphrey's Clock*, then for *Household Words*, and finally for *All the Year Round*. These periodicals printed his own sketches and short stories and serialized several of his novels.

Fairly early in his career, 1842, Dickens went on a reading tour of the United States, then undertook another in 1866. Both were very successful but neither had any particular influence on his work or ideas, possibly because he found American life to be, on the whole, vulgar and shallow. He recorded his first impressions in the highly readable *American Notes* (1842).

Dickens was a socially conscious Whig but could not be called a political activist. He was genuinely sympathetic to the working class and highly critical of both the idle among the nobility and the newly rich class that was created by industrialization. For the most part, however, his efforts on behalf of social reform were limited to charitable donations and benefit readings and to the social message implied in works of fiction, whose primary aim was to provide pleasure for the imagination. In his later years, Dickens became less optimistic about social improvement and dropped his criticism of the aristocracy; in 1865-1866, he defected from the liberals and supported a conservative cause backed by Tennyson, Freud, and Carlyle. Even in his earlier years, he was devoted to Queen Victoria and to British institutions and customs in general. He was an opponent of revolution and even of the right of workers to strike.

In 1857, Dickens met and became strongly attracted to Ellen Lawless Ternan, a young actress. In 1858, he separated from Catherine and took Ellen as his mistress. The two were as discreet as possible and never lived together, but met frequently. Dickens never regretted the break with Catherine or the choice of Ellen. Returning to London from a brief vacation in France, the two were survivors of the wreck of their train at Staplehurst on June 9, 1865. Dickens was able to help several of the injured passengers but the incident drained some of his own strength, perhaps permanently, and haunted him with nightmares for some time. He died five years to the day after the wreck. The crash inspired one of his best pieces of short fiction, "The Signal-Man." The only novel completed after the Staplehurst accident was the long and involved but impressive *Our Mutual Friend*. In rapidly deteriorating health in 1870, Dickens worked intensely on

The Mystery of Edwin Drood, but collapsed on June 8, leaving the work half finished. He died the following day.

Dickens' own favorite novel was his autobiographical *David Copperfield* (1850); it has remained one of posterity's favorites. In addition to *David Copperfield,* the novels that have stood up best under the scrutiny of the years are *Pickwick Papers* and several of the later books: *Bleak House* (1853), *Hard Times* (1854), *A Tale of Two Cities* (1859), *Great Expectations* (1861), and *Our Mutual Friend* (1865). Of Dickens' short fiction, "The Signal-Man" (1866), *The Cricket on the Hearth* (1845), and *A Christmas Carol* (1843) have remained the best known.

INTRODUCTION TO THE NOVEL

Bleak House is a long novel. This does not mean that Dickens' style is wordy or that the book could be abridged without losing the effects that Dickens wanted to achieve. None of Dickens' contemporaries thought that the book was too long. In fact, short novels were unusual in the Victorian era (1837–1901). The tempo of life was slower then. Most men, whether in cities or on the farms, lived close to their work: there was no daily massive rush of commuters. Most women were in the home all day and, as a rule, had more than enough time to do what needed to be done; this fact in itself kept the pace of domestic life slower than anything familiar to us today. People seldom traveled and, if they did, rarely did they go very far.

By today's standards, life was quiet in Dickens' era. Railways existed, but cars, trucks, planes, radio, movies, and television didn't exist. Most shops and places of public entertainment closed early. No crackling neon signs put any "buzz" in the night. At night, one could read or play cards—provided one could afford to burn the oil or candles; it was cheaper and easier to be inactive from sundown to sunup. On Sundays, everything was closed but the church doors and the park gates. Far fewer people were tyrannized by the deadlines that today's technology has made the rule of the workplace.

As a result of this slower pace of life, Victorian people generally had what contemporary psychologists call a "low threshold"—meaning that in order to feel pleasantly stimulated, they didn't require loud, gaudy, psychedelic, fast-moving, or ever-changing stimuli. Young people had, as always, their problems, but one of them was *not* a tendency to "burn out" early. In Victorian England, patience and easy-going ways were far more common than nerves and distractedness.

What this meant for literature is that proportionately more people had more time for reading, and, at the same time, they were psychologically well prepared for the art of reading. Reading is a quiet, completely unsensational activity, and it demands a certain patience. Time and patience are what the past, including the Victorian days, is all about.

Of course, there are other reasons why the Victorians read so assiduously. Dickens' era had a rapidly growing middle class, one that read and one that was large enough to ensure a constant demand for the printed word. The middle class was still trying to "prove itself" — to show the world that it was at least as fit to govern as the aristocracy. To establish and maintain its good name, this class had to show itself moral, sober, knowledgeable, responsible, and even, if possible, literate and refined like the lords and ladies. Knowledge and refinement were to be gained mostly from books, magazines, and other printed matter. To read was to gain, to become, to advance: such was the unconscious motto of a great part of the Victorian public. One should also note that most reading material was quite inexpensive in Dickens' London.

Victorians also read because they needed answers to new problems. The epoch was one of rapid and large-scale social change. Rampant industrialization and the enormous, largely unplanned growth of cities brought many difficulties. Urban crowding, child labor, the proliferation of slums, inadequate wages, unsafe and unsanitary working conditions, periodic widespread unemployment with little provision for the unemployed, vast increases in the incidence of alcoholism, venereal disease, and tuberculosis are only the most obvious ones. Controversy raged over what should be done about the situation.

The era was also a period of the breakup of traditional beliefs, of intense debate and confusion over values and concepts — moral, religious, scientific, and economic. New theories of biological and geological evolution were being proposed, and new approaches to the study of the Bible were vigorously challenging traditional interpretation. People wanted firm guidance on these and other issues. Those who could or might provide it were the writers. It was the public clamor for illumination that caused more and more poets, novelists and essayists to devote much of their time to thinking about — and speaking out upon – the issues of the day. Dickens himself began his writing career as an entertainer, a humorist – the comic *Sketches by Boz* and *Pickwick Papers* were his first books – but soon found himself caught up in the intense popular demand for clarification and advice. His third book, *Oliver Twist* (1838), began a series of social messages that ended only with his death.

Most of Dickens' readers had strong religious and ethical convictions. The Victorian middle class, at all levels, was heavily Protestant. Most of the "dissenting" churches (for example, Methodism and Congregationalism, those outside the established Church of England) were evangelical, and even the established church had been notably influenced by evangelical religion. Evangelicals emphasized, among other things, strict moral behavior; they felt a need to make such behavior highly, sometimes even aggressively visible. Their approach to temptation and evil was like the approach to a contagious disease; the unfortunates who had "fallen" were to be avoided and denounced. Generally, evangelicals wanted to be (at the very least, to seem) not just "good" people but models of goodness, exemplars of righteousness – and to live only amongst other such models. When it came to reading works of fiction, the evangelical in every Victorian wanted the author to offer characters whose purity made them paragons. For the sake of context and contrast, the author might provide distinctly wicked characters; these needed to be converted to virtuous ways, or punished, or both. Strongly evangelical habits of mind did not predispose readers either to understand or to identify with morally inbetween characters.

On the other hand, Dickens himself was a nominal Anglican rather than an "evangelical." He was not pious and not even a regular church-goer. Thus, by no means, does he represent an example of a Victorian author conforming unquestioningly to the expectations of religion or religiosity. He reserves the right to create morally inbetween characters (Richard Carstone is an obvious example), and when he wants to write pure entertainment – a ghost story or an adventure tale without any "edifying" value – he does so. Nevertheless, Dickens was determined, always, to remain popular and make money, and so his fiction does, on the whole, seek to ingratiate itself with the middle-class world. Most of his books and stories are well stocked with "pure," or at least admirable, characters. Villains are reformed or punished. Story endings are happy.

Though Dickens is known to have had no objection to the bawdy elements in his much-loved Fielding and in other eighteenth-century writers, he defers to the sexual puritanism that was conspicuous in Victorian society. He also shares the tendency of many in his audience to idealize and sentimentalize Woman. He was realistic enough to recognize that not all women were pleasant, and, in fact, some of the most monstrous characters in his books are females; but very often the good women (and girls) are Pure Goodness and, partly as a result of such exaggeration, not quite real or interesting. But such characters satisfied his own desire to contemplate an idealized femininity, and, of course, in his day, these characters helped sell the books.

Though Dickens deplored injustice and needless suffering and satirized, sometimes bitterly, anyone or anything that perpetrated them, he was by nature too much in love with life, too fun-loving and spontaneous, to be (or even to pose as) morally grave or cautionary or ethically obsessed. Like Shakespeare and Mozart, he personifies prolific creativity, and his first impulse is to celebrate. He probably could not have brought himself to stay with the theme of social reform if he hadn't been able to do so *creatively*—through exciting incidents and vivid characters that were fun to create, and through mocking tones, wry or hilarious cracks. One way he got around his evangelicized readers' desire for fictional characters who were paragons of virtue (and who, being so, are likely to be artistically uninteresting) was to concentrate, much of the time, on *child* characters. Children *might* be but aren't *expected* to be perfect, and being naive and inexperienced, they can more easily be indulged and forgiven than adults. Of course, Dickens had an imperative reason for creating so many child characters: his own childhood—especially its vicissitudes— haunted him.

* * * * * * *

Dickens ranks with Shakespeare, Moliere, and Aristophanes as one of the world's greatest masters of comedy. In his lifetime he enjoyed the greatest popularity any English author has ever known, and to this day, "Dickens" is an almost mythical name, conjuring up associations even for many people who have read little or none of his work. Obviously Dickens' comic art struck some perennially appealing note.

However, it is not comic achievement alone that accounts for Dickens' unprecedented popularity. In his childhood and early adult years, he experienced hardship and intense suffering. His own misfortunes gave him a keen sense of the harsh realities of life and developed in him a ready sympathy for people – especially children and young adults – beset with difficulties and sorrows. Thus, well before his writing career actually got going, he was accustomed to perceiving human experience in terms of its deeper, more complicated side, as well as its lighter side. In the mature Dickens, optimism and a zest for life – hence, a basically comic rather than tragic or pessimistic outlook – tended to prevail but were balanced by a desire to deal with serious and even painful themes. It is partly this balance, this wholeness, that prevented Dickens from being merely another amusing but rather superficial author.

In many of Dickens' novels, the comic element, or much of it, is actually in the service of a serious vision of life: the comedy does not exist simply for its own sake but is partly a means of presenting serious material in a way that makes for enjoyable reading. In Dickens' later novels, the comedy becomes subdued. As an example, note that *Bleak House*, which marks the end of Dickens' youthful ebullience, reflects his frustrations. He was by that time unhappy in marriage, and he thought that his work was having little or no effect on social conditions in England.

Nevertheless, despite its dreary atmospheres, dingy locales, and troubled characters, *Bleak House* remains with the genre (class) of comedy, in the sense that, by and large, all ends happily rather than tragically or pathetically. The book's principal villain, Tulkinghorn, is eliminated. Hortense, the killer, is brought to justice. Lady Dedlock lives long enough to be reunited with her daughter. Suffering brings out the best in Sir Leicester and George Rouncewell. The ending itself is supremely happy, and all along the way there are droll characters like Phil Squod and vibrantly laughing ones like Boythorn; and there is plenty of smiling amiability, as personified, for example, in Mr. and Mrs. Bagnet. Laughing – rather than bitter – satire is always cropping up. Nor should we overlook the comic contribution of Dickens' prose style. In it, irony abounds; the wry, amusing comment becomes standard fare.

Bleak House is generally regarded as one of Dickens' most impressive novels and a masterpiece of world literature, though not one of the greatest novels of all time. This acclaim does not mean that the book is flawless; it means that despite imperfections, *Bleak House* is still widely read and enjoyed. Some readers agree with G. K. Chesterton, who says that there is a certain monotony about the book: "the artistic . . . unity . . . is satisfying, almost suffocating. There is the *motif* and again the *motif.*" The book has also been faulted for having so many characters and lines of action (plots and subplots) that the intensity of the main action is diluted. Another charge is that none of the major characters is a fully developed, lifelike, and interesting figure. About such indictments, readers have to make up their own minds.

The book certainly has variety. Aside from diversified characters and plot lines, it combines romance and realism and resembles more than one fictional genre. In part, *Bleak House* is what the Germans call a **Bildungsroman** (literally, a formation novel), a story dealing with young people's initiation into the adult world. It is also partly a **romance** and partly a **murder mystery** (in fact, it is the first British novel in which a professional detective figures strongly). *Bleak House* is also a novel of **social criticism**. The main point of the novel is the needless suffering caused by the inefficiency and inhumanity of the law and, by extension, of all forms of institutionalized inhumanity.

Both the social criticism and the comic elements are typical of Dickens' novels. Typical also are several other features of *Bleak House*. As in almost all of Dickens' fiction, the main setting is the city. It is the city, not the country, that brings his imagination to its richest life, and, of course, it is in the city that the worst and the greatest number of social problems are manifested. As usual, too, there are many characters. Several are vivid – they "come alive" to our imagination. Most of the characters are distinctly "good" or "bad" rather than in-between. Few, if any, undergo a significant change (development). And, as is often the case, there is one character who is so benevolent (and well off) that he is able to reward the deserving and bring events to a conclusion that is at least typical of Dickens and of Victorian novels in general. No less characteristic is the abundance of highly dramatic (tense, high-pitched, or otherwise striking) incidents. There is the inevitable fascination with eccentrics and grotesque people and places – like Krook and his shop and Mr. Snagsby and the paupers cemetery. And, of course, there is the sympathetic portrayal of a beleaguered child – here, little Jo.

"Pure" – that is, virginal, incorruptible, and self-sacrificing – heroines like Esther Summerson and Ada Clare are as Dickensian as anything can be. So are happy endings, and though *Bleak House* presents undeserved sufferings and untimely deaths, the story does end happily for several of the principal characters, including John Jarndyce, Esther, Ada, and Allan Woodcourt.

Dickens' novels – especially those prior to *Bleak House* – are often marred by incoherence: sometimes the main point they start to make is abandoned; in other cases, no main point ever seems to develop. In this respect, *Bleak House* is atypical: no one can miss the insistent theme of the malaise and misfortune caused by "the law's delay." Untypical also is the emotional restraint. In earlier novels, Dickens often allows his characters (or himself as narrator) to express certain sentiments – especially pathos and gushy praise of "goodness" – in exaggerated terms and at length. Such effusions, acceptable to most readers in Dickens' era, seem sentimental or even maudlin today. *Bleak House* also breaks away from Dickens' earlier habit of relying heavily on coincidences that add drama and help the author out of plot difficulties but remain cheap and wildly implausible. In *Bleak House*, Dickens seldom seems to be "stretching things."

A common method of publishing novels in Victorian England was serialization in monthly magazines. Dickens published *Bleak House* in monthly installments in his own highly successful magazine *Household Words* between March 1852 and September 1853. Serialization affected *Bleak House* in various ways.

First, serialization meant that Dickens wrote as he went along: he did not outline the entire novel or even plan very far ahead – in fact, he was often so busy that he could barely meet the printer's monthly deadline for receiving the manuscript of the forthcoming installment. With some of Dickens' novels, this haste and extemporaneity resulted in some loose plot construction and in patches of writing that lacked polish. In *Bleak House*, Dickens managed to avoid these pitfalls of the serial method. The plot, though complicated, is tightly woven, and the prose style is consistently effective. Serialization may even have worked to Dickens' advantage, in this case at least. The magazine readers had a whole month to let their memory of the previous installment grow dim. The best way around this difficulty was for the writer to create really memorable scenes and characters. Thus, serialization may have prodded Dickens to offer striking material and suspenseful narration. It may have encouraged his already well developed taste for caricature – highly simplified but striking character portrayal – and for grotesquerie: both are inherently attention-getting, arresting. Unusual prose style itself is one way of producing a vivid impression. In *Bleak House* inventive wording, dynamic sentences, sustained, energetic irony, and present-tense narration contribute enormously to keeping the reader's interest.

LIST OF CHARACTERS

Mr. Bayham Badger

A London physician who provides training for Richard Carstone.

Mrs. Bayham Badger

His wife, who constantly talks about her three husbands.

Matthew Bagnet

The owner of a music shop; a former soldier who has kept up a friendship with George Rouncewell.

Mrs. Bagnet

Matthew's sensible, wholesome, good-natured wife.

Malta, Quebec, and Woolwich Bagnet.

The Bagnets' happy children.

Miss Barbary

Lady Dedlock's sister who raised Esther Summerson for a time and who was once Boythorn's beloved.

Lawrence Boythorn

The passionate, boisterous, but good-hearted friend of Mr. Jarndyce (modeled on the poet Walter Savage Landor, a friend of Dickens).

Inspector Bucket

A shrewd, relentless, but amiable and thoughtful detective.

Mrs. Bucket

The detective's keen-witted and helpful wife.

William Buffy, M.P.

A political friend of Sir Leicester Dedlock.

Richard Carstone

A cousin of Ada Clare; a restless, indecisive ward of Mr. Jarndyce.

The Reverend Mr. Chadband

A pompous, insincere preacher, the incarnation of religiosity.

Mrs. Chadband

Formerly Mrs. Rachael, who knew Esther Summerson as a child.

The Lord High Chancellor

The presiding official of the Chancery Court.

Ada Clare

A ward of Mr. Jarndyce and a close friend of Esther Summerson; like Esther, she is an ideally virtuous young woman.

Lady Honoria Dedlock

The charming, self-controlled wife of Sir Leicester and mother of Esther Summerson; the tragic protagonist of this novel.

Sir Leicester Dedlock

A proud, honorable aristocrat with an estate, Chesney Wold, in Lincolnshire.

Volumnia Dedlock

A somewhat giddy, elderly cousin of Sir Leicester and a frequent guest at Chesney Wold.

The Misses Donny

Twins who run Greenleaf, the boarding school where Esther Summerson spends some of her early years before going to Bleak House.

Miss Flite

A well-meaning, ineffectual old woman driven half mad by the Jarndyce and Jarndyce suit.

Mr. Gridley ("the man from Shropshire")

A man befriended by George Rouncewell and eventually driven to suicide by the frustrations of Jarndyce and Jarndyce.

William Guppy

A law clerk who twice proposes to Esther Summerson.

Guster

A maidservant of the Snagsbys, she often has "fits."

Captain Hawdon (Nemo)

A former army officer and, at the time of the story, an impoverished law writer (copyist); he is Esther Summerson's father.

Mademoiselle Hortense

A hot-tempered and vengeful French maid dismissed by Lady Dedlock; eventually she murders Tulkinghorn.

John Jarndyce

The benevolent owner of Bleak House and legal guardian of Esther Summerson, Richard Carstone, and Ada Clare.

Tom Jarndyce

John Jarndyce's cousin, made suicidal by the frustrations of the Jarndyce and Jarndyce suit.

Mrs. Jellyby

A woman obsessed with social activism and neglectful of her own family.

Mr. Jellyby

The long-suffering, mild-mannered husband of the neglectful Mrs. Jellyby.

Caddy (Carolyn) Jellyby

Mrs. Jellyby's eldest daughter; she becomes a close friend of Esther and marries Prince Turveydrop.

"Peepy" Jellyby

The sadly neglected youngest son of the Jellybys.

Jenny

The wife of a brickmaker in St. Albans.

Jo (Toughey)

A street-crossing sweeper in the Holborn district where the Chancery Court is located.

Jobling (Tony, Weevle)

A law-writer friend of William Guppy.

Mr. Kenge

A senior partner in the legal firm of Kenge and Carboy.

Mr. Krook

A grotesque old man who owns a rag-and-bottle shop and rents a room to Captain Hawdon.

Liz

A brickmaker's wife and a friend of Jenny.

Mercury

A footman in the household of Sir Leicester Dedlock.

Neckett ("Coavinses")

A sheriff's officer who arrests Harold Skimpole.

Charley (Charlotte) Neckett

Neckett's daughter who, after his death, become Esther's maid at Bleak House.

Mrs. Pardiggle

A busybody social worker who rules despotically over her six sons.

Rosa

Lady Dedlock's maid; she marries Watt Rouncewell.

Mrs. Rouncewell

The kindly old housekeeper for the Dedlocks at Chesney Wold.

Mr. Rouncewell

One of her sons, an iron master.

George Rouncewell (Mr. George)

Mrs. Rouncewell's other son, owner of a London shooting gallery.

Watt Rouncewell

Mrs. Rouncewell's grandson, betrothed to Rosa.

Harold Skimpole

A socially cheerful but irresponsible and parasitic man who is protected but eventually repudiated by John Jarndyce.

Grandfather Smallweed

A mean, greedy old invalid who personifies ruthless opportunism.

Grandmother Smallweed

The opportunist's childish wife.

Bartholomew Smallweed

The Smallweeds' grandson.

Judy Smallweed

The Smallweeds' granddaughter.

Mr. Snagsby

The rather timid owner of a store dealing in stationery supplies used in the law.

Mrs. Snagsby

A suspicious and jealous, if intelligent, woman who thinks that her husband may be the father of Jo.

Phil Squod

The droll, disfigured, loyal servant of George Rouncewell.

Hon. Bob Stables

A young, unemployed friend of the Dedlocks.

Esther Summerson

A ward of Mr. Jarndyce and daughter of Lady Dedlock; she narrates a large part of the story.

Little Swills

A comic vocalist.

Mr. Tangle

A lawyer in the Jarndyce and Jarndyce suit.

Mr. Tulkinghorn

Sir Leicester Dedlock's chief legal counsel; a secretive, arrogant, obscurely vindictive man determined to discover Lady Dedlock's secret.

Prince Turveydrop

A charming young dancing-master overworked by his father; he marries Caddy Jellyby.

Mr. Turveydrop

The founder of a dancing school, for which he takes all the credit while his son Prince does all the work.

Mr. Vholes

A jargon-speaking, unprincipled lawyer advising Richard Carstone.

Allan Woodcourt

A noble-hearted young doctor who marries Esther Summerson.

Mrs. Woodcourt

Allan's elderly mother, somewhat of an interfering old "biddy."

A BRIEF SYNOPSIS

Sir Leicester Dedlock, an idle, fashionable aristocrat, maintains his ancestral home in rural Lincolnshire and also a place in London. Lady Dedlock, his wife, "has beauty still" at or near fifty but is proud and vain. She keeps a secret unknown even to Sir Leicester. When she was young, she bore an illegitimate child, a girl, to her lover, Captain Hawdon. What she does not know, however, is that the child is still alive. This daughter, now an adult, was given the name Esther Summerson by the aunt who raised her. When the aunt (Miss Barbary) dies, kindly, retired John Jarndyce was appointed Esther's guardian.

At the time of the story, Esther is twenty and is traveling to Mr. Jarndyce's home, Bleak House (which is cheerful and happy—not bleak). On the journey, she has the companionship of his other two wards, Ada Clare and Richard Carstone. Ada, Richard, and Mr. Jarndyce are parties to a complicated, long-standing, and by now obscure legal suit called Jarndyce and Jarndyce. Various aspects of this entangled suit are heard from time to time in the High Court of Chancery in London. The issues involve, among other things, the apportionment of an inheritance.

At Bleak House, Esther notices that Richard Carstone has some weaknesses of character yet remains likeable; she forms a deep friendship with him as well as with the beautiful Ada. She also notices that the two young people rather soon find themselves in love.

One "muddy, murky afternoon," while looking at some legal documents, Lady Dedlock becomes curious about the handwriting on them. She asks Mr. Tulkinghorn, the Dedlocks' attorney, if he knows the hand. Tulkinghorn, a corrupt and self-serving but clever lawyer, does not, but eventually he discovers that the hand is that of a certain "Nemo." A pauper without friends, "Nemo" has been living in a dilapidated "rag-and-bottle" shop owned by an old merchant, Krook. Tulkinghorn finds "Nemo" dead, seemingly from too much opium. One person who knew the dead man is little Jo, an urchin street sweeper. At an inquest, Jo tells Tulkinghorn, "He [Nemo] wos wery good to me, he wos!"

Lady Dedlock knows that the handwriting is that of Captain Hawdon. So, disguised as her own maid (Mlle. Hortense), she finds Jo, who shows her where Hawdon is buried. Tulkinghorn, looking always to his own advantage, continues his keen interest in "Nemo" and is watchful of Lady Dedlock. The maid Hortense detests Lady Dedlock and helps Tulkinghorn ferret out the lady's secret. Tulkinghorn reveals to Lady Dedlock that he knows about her child and Captain Hawdon. He promises to keep his knowledge to himself, but later he tells her that he no longer feels bound to do so. Mlle. Hortense, feeling used by Tulkinghorn, turns against him. A short time later, Tulkinghorn is found shot to death. A detective, Mr. Bucket, is hired to investigate. The suspects include Lady Dedlock and George Rouncewell, son of the Dedlocks' housekeeper. Mr. Bucket tells Sir Leicester about Lady Dedlock's dealings with Tulkinghorn and says that she is a suspect. Sir Leicester has a stroke but is compassionate and fully forgiving of his wife. Bucket later discovers that the murderer is Mlle. Hortense.

Richard Carstone, insolvent, uncertain of his future, and temperamentally indecisive and insecure, futilely expends much time and energy on the Jarndyce and Jarndyce suit. He secretly marries Ada Clare as soon as she turns twenty-one. Meanwhile, Esther and young doctor Allan Woodcourt are attracted to each other but she accepts a marriage proposal from Mr. Jarndyce. The waif Jo contracts smallpox, and both Esther and her maid Charley catch it from him; Esther survives but with a scarred face. Shortly afterward, she learns that Lady Dedlock is her mother.

Feeling disgrace and remorse, Lady Dedlock dresses like an ordinary working woman and wanders away. After an intensive search, Esther and Detective Bucket find her lying dead in the snow at the gates of the paupers cemetery, where Captain Hawdon is buried. The case of Jarndyce and Jarndyce is concluded at last, but legal fees have consumed all the money that Richard Carstone would have inherited. He dies, and, soon afterward, Ada gives birth to a boy, whom she names Richard. John Jarndyce releases Esther from her engagement, and she marries Allan Woodcourt. Two daughters are born to them, and Allan tells his wife that she is "prettier than ever."

SUMMARIES & CRITICAL COMMENTARIES

CHAPTER 1 In Chancery

Summary

On a raw November afternoon, London is enshrouded in heavy fog made harsher by chimney smoke. The fog seems thickest in the vicinity of the High Court of Chancery. The court, now in session, is hearing an aspect of the case of Jarndyce and Jarndyce. A "little mad old woman" is, as always, one of the spectators. Two ruined men, one a "sallow prisoner," the other a man from Shropshire, appear before the court—to no avail. Toward the end of the sitting, the Lord High Chancellor announces that in the morning he will meet with "the two young people" and decide about making them wards of their cousin.

Commentary

This first chapter makes Dickens' social criticism explicit and introduces one of the book's principal themes: the ruin that the Chancery
Court has made and will continue to make of many people's lives.
Court costs and lawyers' fees have already exhausted all the inheritance money in Jarndyce and Jarndyce. The case has gone on for so
many years and has "become so complicated that no man alive knows
what it means." Rather than producing clarity and justice, the court –
like much of the workings of the law in general – produces a fog that
obscures, a fog that creates confusion and depression in which people
are lost. The "little mad old woman" is one of these; the prisoner and
the Shropshire man (Gridley) are others. The effect of presenting them
is to persuade us that Dickens is right: the High Court of Chancery
is an institutionalized abuse of the law.

Since "the two young people" (Ada Clare and Richard Carstone)
and their cousin (Mr. John Jarndyce) will soon figure prominently in
the story, Dickens prepares us for the eventual meeting. Their names
are not given here; they would mean nothing to us at this point, and
Dickens strengthens his attack on the court by implying that the
Chancellor, though he is "Lord" and "High," is, as usual, too negligent
and uninterested to be able to recall their names.

Chapter 1 moves ponderously, dramatizing the inaction of Chancery and the stagnation of the lives that wait for its decisions. There
is nothing here to satisfy a taste for fast-moving action. To stick with
Dickens, we have to adjust to his method, which is to offer a feast
in *description* and in *language*, rather than in a rapidly developing plot.

CHAPTER 2   In Fashion

Summary

"Bored to death" by the rainy weather of Lincolnshire, Lady
Dedlock has returned to the Dedlocks' home in London. She plans
to stay there a few days, then go on to Paris.

In middle age, Lady Dedlock retains her beauty and is always
attractively groomed. Her husband, the baronet Sir Leicester Dedlock,
loves her and does not complain that she brought to the marriage neither dowry nor prestige.

This afternoon she receives Mr. Tulkinghorn, a rich, close-lipped, and secretive solicitor (attorney) who represents her interests in Jarndyce and Jarndyce. Noticing some legal paper that Tulkinghorn has placed on a table next to her, she takes an interest in the handwriting and asks the lawyer whose it is. A few moments later, she feels faint and asks to be taken to her room. Sir Leicester is surprised but attributes her condition to the stress of the bad weather in Lincolnshire.

Commentary

Dickens now introduces two major characters (Lady Dedlock and Tulkinghorn) and a minor character, Sir Leicester (pronounced "Lester"). There is a continuity here with the first chapter: Dickens regards the world of the idle rich as comparable in futility to the world of Chancery Court, and, coincidentally, Lady Dedlock is involved in the Jarndyce and Jarndyce suit. Tulkinghorn is characterized as rather sinister, Sir Leicester as crotchety and self-satisfied but not vicious or depraved. About Lady Dedlock, we feel ambivalent. She seems rather empty, vain, and restless, but if Sir Leicester loves her, she may have some redeeming features that will be revealed later. The story's first bit of suspense appears when she half-faints.

CHAPTER 3   A Process

Summary

Esther Summerson, friendless and unloved, is raised at Windsor by her "godmother" (actually, her aunt), Miss Barbary. After the aunt's death, John Jarndyce, acting through his attorney Kenge, arranges to have Esther sent to Greenleaf, a boarding school at Reading. After six happy years as a student and teacher at Greenleaf, Esther is asked to serve in Bleak House, Mr. Jarndyce's household. At the Chancery Court, she meets and at once befriends Ada Clare and Richard Carstone. Like Esther, these two young people have been made wards of Mr. Jarndyce. As they leave Chancery, the three encounter a diminutive old lady (Miss Flite), who has been driven partly mad by the never-ending, convoluted Jarndyce and Jarndyce suit.

Commentary

This long chapter introduces and begins characterizations of the book's principal figures: Esther, Ada, and Richard. Curiosity about

Mr. Jarndyce is heightened: we wonder why he is so benevolent. To characterize Esther sympathetically, Dickens utilizes the principle of *contrast*: Esther's naturalness and goodheartedness are all the more impressive when set against the background of her aunt's dour, unbending puritanism. Implied in this chapter is Dickens' criticism of his society for its element of cold self-righteousness and its inexcusable harshness toward children.

CHAPTER 4 Telescopic Philanthropy

Summary

En route to Bleak House, Esther, Ada, and Richard spend the night at the Jellyby house. Mrs. Jellyby, a friend of John Jarndyce, neglects her house and children and is obsessed with projects designed to benefit Africa. Esther is affectionate and helpful to the Jellyby children, especially to the accident-prone Peepy and to the oldest daughter, Caddy. Serving as her mother's secretary, and badly overworked, Caddy is wretched.

Esther, Ada, and Richard continue to wonder what sort of person John Jarndyce is. Richard saw him briefly once but retains no distinct impression. Desperate in her impossible home and situation, a tearful Caddy finds solace in the compassionate Esther.

Commentary

Dickens maintained that people devoted to distant ("telescopic") philanthropy very often show a tendency to neglect the crying needs of those around them — and charity should begin at home. In this chapter, Dickens satirizes Mrs. Jellyby as a type of misguided "do-gooder." The chapter expertly blends satiric humor and effective pathos. The portrayal of the Jellyby children is another variation on one of Dickens' recurring themes: the vulnerability and suffering of children in a world mismanaged by adults. Caddy emerges as a memorable character, and the comfort she and the other children receive from Esther strengthens the reader's impression of Esther's beautiful spirit.

CHAPTER 5 A Morning Adventure

Summary

Before breakfast, Caddy Jellyby suggests to Esther that the two go for a morning walk. Ada and Richard join them, and, after walking a short distance, the four meet old Miss Flite. The somewhat daft but kindly old lady insists that they see her lodgings. These prove to be rooms rented above a grotesque "rag-and-bottle" shop owned by an aged eccentric, Mr. Krook. Krook speaks with the group and mentions the names Barbary, Clare, and Dedlock as figures in the Jarndyce and Jarndyce suit, and gives an account of Tom Jarndyce's shooting himself in a tavern after the suit had dragged on interminably.

After visiting briefly with Miss Flite, the young people walk back to the Jellyby house. Richard, already affected adversely by the unending Jarndyce and Jarndyce suit, nevertheless states that the suit "will work none of its bad influence on us" and (speaking particularly to Ada) says that it "can't divide us." Early that afternoon, the three wards leave in an open carriage, bound for Bleak House.

Commentary

Dickens creates Krook and his disordered, unproductive shop partly as macabre symbols of the legal system in general and the Lord High Chancellor and the Chancery Court in particular. The theme of the ruinous effects of Chancery is further developed through the presentation of the impoverished Miss Flite and the story of Tom Jarndyce's attempted suicide. Dickens prepares the reader for the story of "Nemo" by calling attention to the fact that Krook has another renter, a law copyist. Richard Carstone's attraction to Ada and his distress over the Jarndyce and Jarndyce suit foreshadow later developments.

CHAPTER 6 Quite at Home

Summary

Esther, Ada, and Richard arrive at Bleak House and meet the benevolent, self-effacing Mr. Jarndyce. Esther recognizes him as the kindly gentleman who shared a stagecoach with her six years ago. The young people find the old-fashioned house much to their liking. They meet Mr. Skimpole, a gracious but irresponsible dilettante whom John Jarndyce has taken under his protection. Under arrest for a small debt, Skimpole appeals to Richard and Esther; they combine their pocket money to save him from imprisonment. Learning of this incident, Mr. Jarndyce warns the young people never to advance any money whatever for Skimpole's debts. Esther looks forward cheerfully to her new role as housekeeper.

Commentary

Having presented the dreary, inhumane, and maddening world of Chancery and the equally intolerable world of the Jellybys, Dickens needs to put such disorder fully into perspective. He does so – again using sharp contrast: Bleak House and its owner symbolize the lively contentedness, hope, and creativity that prevail when human affairs are rightly ordered. Through the figure of Mr. Jarndyce, Dickens reinforces the optimistic message already implied in the portrayal of Esther: it is possible for goodness to triumph completely within the individual, and when it does, the individual will naturally seek to rescue and comfort those who are victimized by the operations of false values. To be effective – to make a difference in the world – human goodness requires a sense of responsibility and an active will. Mr. Skimpole, though effusively warm and vaguely good-natured, does not have these qualities; Mr. Jarndyce does. Harold Skimpole's irresponsibility is so extreme that it is dangerous; thus Chapter 6 is humorous, but it is also morally instructive.

CHAPTER 7   The Ghost's Walk

Summary

At Chesney Wold, the Dedlocks' estate in Lincolnshire, the rain continues. The old housekeeper, Mrs. Rouncewell, is assisted in her duties by Rosa, with whom Mrs. Rouncewell's grandson, Watt, is in love. Two visitors are admitted and given a tour of the house. One of them is Mr. Guppy, a law clerk at Kenge and Carboy. Mr. Guppy notices a portrait of Lady Dedlock and is sure that he has seen it before. When Guppy and his companion leave, Mrs. Rouncewell tells Watt and Rosa the story of The Ghost's Walk. In Oliver Cromwell's era (two centuries earlier), Sir Morbury Dedlock's wife once lamed some horses intended for the Cavaliers fighting against Cromwell. When her husband spied her slipping out to lame his favorite horse, they fought in the stall, and she suffered such a severe hip injury that she was painfully lame for the rest of her life.

One day, while limping on the terrace of the Dedlock estate, she fell and died, vowing to haunt the terrace until "the pride of this house is humbled." Mrs. Rouncewell tells Watt to start the tall French clock. He does so, but above its loud beat and the music it plays, he can *still* hear the footsteps of the ghost.

Commentary

The gloomy rain at Chesney Wold, the mystery of Guppy's reaction to Lady Dedlock's portrait, and the story of The Ghost's Walk enhance the reader's sense that misfortune is in store for the Dedlocks—and perhaps for others.

CHAPTER 8   Covering a Multitude of Sins

Summary

Esther is busy, proud, and happy in her role as housekeeper at Bleak House. She learns from Mr. Jarndyce that the suit in Chancery centers around a will which at one time involved a fortune but which is now essentially meaningless because court costs have consumed the fortune itself. She also learns that Tom Jarndyce, the former owner of Bleak House, tried unsuccessfully to disentangle the suit and, after many years of futile effort, shot himself.

Mrs. Pardiggle, accompanied by her five sons, pays a visit to Bleak House. A charity worker whose zeal unfortunately makes her own sons "ferocious with discontent," she describes her activities loudly and at great length. Reluctantly, Esther and Ada go with her to visit a poor bricklayer's family who live nearby. Shocked by the squalor of the bricklayer's home and disapproving of Mrs. Pardiggle's aggressiveness, the two young ladies try to remain as inconspicuous as possible. They stay behind when Mrs. Pardiggle leaves, as they want to inquire about a boy who has died in their presence. After making inquiries, they leave but return later to try to comfort the child's mother.

Commentary

This chapter helps maintain the book's continuity by returning to the theme of Jarndyce and Jarndyce, a legal suit which has been in abeyance for two chapters. The introduction of Mrs. Pardiggle thus strengthens Dickens' side-theme of satire against "do-gooders" who have never learned that their first obligation is to those closest to them. And once again Dickens contrasts the pretentiousness and emotional shallowness of the professional social activists with the genuine compassion and real assistance of the spontaneous and unassuming young women, as well as the poor neighbor woman.

CHAPTER 9   Signs and Tokens

Summary

Impractical, restless, and undirected, Richard Carstone is ill-prepared to obtain a position of any kind. To help him, Mr. Jarndyce writes to one of Richard's distant relatives, Sir Leicester Dedlock, but all prospects of help from him seem bleak. Esther, meanwhile, is convinced by unmistakable signs that Richard and Ada are in love.

Old Lawrence Boythorn (modeled very closely on one of Dickens' friends, the famous poet Walter Savage Landor) comes to Bleak House for a visit. He is an intense human being, a creature of extremes, but well-meaning and, in fact, lovable. A litigious person, he happens to be suing Sir Leicester, whom he dislikes; for Lady Dedlock, however, he has only affection and admiration.

In connection with Boythorn's legal action, Mr. Guppy arrives at Bleak House. While there, he shocks Esther by proposing to her. She rejects him firmly and he leaves greatly discouraged.

Commentary

The portrayal of Richard as unformed and somewhat irrational prepares us for his eventual failure. Boythorn contributes to the book's energy, humor, and variety in character. He also reinforces our tendency to be somewhat sympathetic toward Lady Dedlock despite her obvious limitations. Esther's response to Mr. Guppy's proposal of marriage confirms our impression of her good taste and sound judgment.

CHAPTERS 10 & 11   The Law Writer & Our Dead Brother

Summary

Not far from the Chancery Court stands a law stationery store, owned by Mr. Snagsby. Mild and timid, Snagsby is married to a shrill, vehement woman. Their one and only servant is Guster, a young woman often afflicted with "fits."

One afternoon, Mr. Tulkinghorn visits the stationery shop and asks Snagsby to identify the handwriting of certain Jarndyce and Jarndyce affidavits. Snagsby tells Tulkinghorn that the handwriting is that of a Mr. Nemo ("Nemo" is Latin for "no one"), who lives above the rag-and-bottle shop of Mr. Krook.

Tulkinghorn goes to Krook's place and finds Nemo dead, apparently of opium poisoning. Shortly thereafter, an inquest is held. From little Jo, the street crossing sweeper, Tulkinghorn learns that Nemo was a kind and considerate person. Nemo's death is ruled as accidental, and the obscure man is given a pauper's burial in a dismal, neglected churchyard.

CHAPTER 12   On the Watch

Summary

The Dedlocks return from Paris, prepare Chesney Wold for guests, and then entertain them. Still, however, Lady Dedlock is bored.

One evening Tulkinghorn brings news about Boythorn's legal action against Sir Leicester. While the lawyer is there, Lady Dedlock thanks him for sending her a message about the handwriting that caught her interest earlier. When she hears about Nemo's death, she insists on hearing the whole story. She pretends to be only "casually" interested, but Tulkinghorn sees this is only a deception.

Commentary

In the Snagsbys and their maid Guster, Dickens again shows his penchant for oddity, caricature, and the grotesque. Like other Victorian novelists, Dickens gives far more attention to such minor characters than is demanded by the plot. Such generosity in creation was more acceptable to Dickens' readers than to today's. The Victorian age, recall, was less hurried than ours and, in any event, it took more delight in reading.

The main plot develops further as Tulkinghorn intensifies his interest in the legal handwriting and in Lady Dedlock's curiosity about the copyist (Nemo). The ridiculously conducted inquest continues

Dickens' disdainful satire of legal institutions and procedures. The same satire is conveyed by the tone which Dickens adopts when he depicts the legal stationery items sold in Snagsby's shop.

CHAPTER 13   Esther's Narrative

Summary

Richard Carstone remains pathetically indecisive, unable to choose a career. Mr. Jarndyce attributes at least some of this irresoluteness to the influence of the Jarndyce and Jarndyce case, that "incomprehensible heap of uncertainty and procrastination." Esther believes that Richard's education, consisting mostly of learning to write Latin verse, has also been a factor—such training does nothing to prepare one for the work of the world. Among other professions, Mr. Jarndyce suggests that Richard might enjoy being a surgeon. Richard's reaction is immediate. Accepting the idea enthusiastically, he is soon a surgeon's apprentice in the house of Mr. Bayham Badger, where we learn that Mrs. Badger is a snobbish dilettante who has been married twice before (to "distinguished" men) and is forever talking about her husbands, past and present.

Esther has been attending various theatres and has noticed that Mr. Guppy follows her and always manages to have himself seen—wearing the downcast expression of a rejected suitor.

Richard and Ada now realize that they are in love, but Mr. Jarndyce advises them to postpone marriage because they are quite young and Richard needs to establish himself in his profession.

At a small dinner party given by the Badgers, Esther notices and seems attracted to one of the guests, a young surgeon of "dark complexion" (Allan Woodcourt).

Commentary

This chapter is devoted mostly to one of the subplots (the romance of Ada and Richard), but at the end, it surprises us and advances the main plot by indicating that Esther is attracted to a young surgeon. Even the subplot, however, reinforces Dickens' principal, explicit theme—that is, the pernicious influence of inhumane legal institutions and procedures. Dickens the social critic and sensible reformer is also evident in Esther's attitude towards training young men to write Latin verse. Dickens' abhorrence of unreal attitudes and behavior is again exemplified in the odd, insubstantial Mrs. Bayham Badger. This is the third exaggeratedly unreal wife thus far encountered (the earlier ones are Mrs. Jellyby and Mrs. Pardiggle); each is somewhat comic but also distinctly repugnant.

CHAPTER 14   Deportment

Summary

Esther's narrative continues. Embarking upon his new career, Richard leaves the Jarndyce household but remains foolishly hopeful of becoming rich from the Chancery suit.

From a surprise visit by Mrs. Jellby, Esther learns that Caddy, hoping to escape from her mother's tyranny, has become engaged to Prince Turveydrop, a dancing instructor in an academy of deportment run by Turveydrop senior. The old man, a "model of deportment," and nothing else, is completely useless and forces young Turveydrop to do all the work of the academy. Caddy has begun practicing "housekeeping" in old Miss Flite's lodging. Mr. Krook is trying to teach himself to read and write. His doctor, Allan Woodcourt, is invited to dinner at Bleak House.

Commentary

Dickens continues to tie his various characters more closely together: Caddy with Esther and Miss Flite, Krook with Dr. Woodcourt, and the latter with Mr. Jarndyce and Esther. One of the subplots, the adventures of Caddy Jellyby, is advanced, and Esther and Allan Woodcourt continue to move toward each other. Dickens' disgust with irresponsible do-gooders appears again, and the theme of parents tyrannizing their children is reinforced by the introduction of the arrogant and worthless (despite his being a model of deportment) old Mr. Turveydrop and his beleaguered son, Prince.

CHAPTER 15   Bell Yard

Summary

Here again, we see that Mr. Jarndyce is frequently distressed by the "philanthropists" with whom he associates. Harold Skimpole reveals that Coavinses (Neckett), the man who frequently arrested him for debt, has died. Mr. Jarndyce, Esther, and Ada go to Neckett's lodgings and find that the man left three destitute children – Charlotte (Charley), Tom, and eighteen-month-old Emma.

Mr. Gridley (a fellow boarder at Mrs. Blinder's), a bitter, truculent "man from Shropshire," is surprisingly kind and helpful to Neckett's children. He tells Mr. Jarndyce and his wards the cause of his bitterness: the delay of the Chancery Court has destroyed the inheritance that belonged to him and his brother.

Commentary

Harold Skimpole and the Chancery Court have something important in common: both seem unreal in attitude and both are quite irresponsible. Through the figure of Gridley, Dickens strengthens his criticism of Chancery. The unmerited and pathetic suffering of children, a recurring theme in much of Dickens' fiction, is portrayed again in the children made orphans by Neckett's death.

CHAPTER 16   Tom-all-Alone's

Summary

Sir Leicester Dedlock is abed, suffering with gout at Chesney Wold. Lady Dedlock, unsuccessfully disguised as a servant, goes to London and locates Jo, the crossing sweeper of a dilapidated street called Tom-all-Alone's. He takes her on a tour of the places mentioned in news accounts of Nemo's death and inquest, and she gives him a gold coin afterward. At Chesney Wold, Mrs. Rouncewell tells Rosa that the "step on the Ghost's Walk" has never been "more distinct than it is tonight."

Commentary

Suspense increases as readers wonder why Lady Dedlock is so intent upon learning all that she can about the deceased Mr. Nemo. In Jo and in the vivid descriptions of his street and Nemo's graveyard, Dickens creates a powerful image of the wretched folk of London and their grotesquely squalid environs.

CHAPTER 17   Esther's Narrative

Summary

From the Badgers, Esther and Ada learn that Richard is not taking his medical apprenticeship seriously. Later, Richard admits as much and says that he may abandon medicine and take up law. For Ada's sake, Esther and Mr. Jarndyce are alarmed.

Mr. Jarndyce tells Esther what he knows about her past. He had agreed to become her guardian if and when her aunt (Miss Barbary) died.

The next day, Allan Woodcourt, accompanied by his mother, comes to say goodbye. Allan is bound for the Orient as a ship's surgeon. The following morning, Caddy Jellyby delivers flowers that Allan left, seemingly on purpose, for Esther.

Commentary

Esther's quickening curiosity about her past parallels Lady Dedlock's pursuit of the facts about Nemo. To some readers, this parallel may suggest the possibility of a close connection between Esther and Lady Dedlock. There can no longer be any doubt that eventually Allan Woodcourt and Esther will be brought together.

CHAPTER 18   Lady Dedlock

Summary

Richard, not surprisingly, decides that he will drop his medical apprenticeship and begins a career in law, working in Mr. Kenge's office. Mr. Jarndyce, Esther, Ada, and Skimpole visit Boythorn at his place near Chesney Wold. At church, Esther is surprised at how much Lady Dedlock resembles Miss Barbary.

Later, by chance, Esther, Ada, and Mr. Jarndyce encounter Lady Dedlock in a gamekeeper's lodge, where they have all sought shelter from a fierce thunderstorm. Hearing Lady Dedlock speak, Esther's heart beats wildly, unexplainably: ". . . there arose before my mind innumerable pictures of myself." Lady Dedlock offends her French maid, Mlle. Hortense, by seeming to prefer Rosa, and, when it stops raining, Hortense walks home barefoot through the wet grass.

Commentary

This chapter tends to confirm the reader's surmise that strong connections exist, and will soon be revealed, between Esther, Lady Dedlock, and Miss Barbary. The portrayal of Hortense as a violently emotional person, offended by Lady Dedlock, prepares the reader for the revenge that the maid will take later in the novel.

CHAPTER 19   Moving On

Summary

It is now summer. The Snagsbys entertain their minister and his wife, Mr. and Mrs. Chadband. Outside the Snagsbys' house are Jo and a policeman who insists that the boy "move on." Jo maintains he has nowhere to move on to. As Mr. Guppy arrives on the scene, Jo is asked to explain the money found on his person. The boy says that it is the remains of a gold sovereign paid to him for showing a lady where Mr. Nemo lodged, worked, and was buried. Questioning Jo, Mr. Guppy learns the entire story. Mrs. Chadband says that in her younger years Guppy's firm (Kenge and Carboy) put her in charge of Esther Summerson, then a young child. The Snagsbys provide Jo with some food, after which he "moves on."

Commentary

Here the comic and the pathetic are intermingled – little Jo providing the pathos and the Chadbands the comedy. Mr. Chadband, whom Dickens satirizes, is one of the book's numerous eccentrics but is also a type: he represents the loud, voluble, but empty and rather hypocritical sermonizer, a species not rare in Dickens' era.

Dickens keeps two important threads running here: the mystery of Esther's identity and the mystery of Lady Dedlock's pursuit of the facts about Nemo. Little Jo's "moving on" from one nowhere to another nowhere continues the motif of childhood sorrow.

CHAPTERS 20 & 21   A New Lodger & The Smallweed Family

Summary

The only regular occupants of the office of Kenge and Carboy during the summer are Richard Carstone and Mr. Guppy. These two are visited by Bartholomew (Bart) Smallweed, a thin, precocious fifteen year old, and by Mr. Jobling, a law writer currently unemployed. Assisted by Guppy, Jobling finds work and takes the room at Krook's, formerly occupied by Nemo.

Chapter 21 introduces Bart Smallweed's grandparents and Bart's twin sister, Judy; also introduced is Charley (Charlotte) Neckett, who is badly treated as a servant girl in the Smallweed household. Grandfather Smallweed receives Mr. George Rouncewell, who comes to make a payment on a high-interest loan he contracted with the old man. Phil Squod, the attendant at George Rouncewell's shooting gallery, is depicted as an odd and misshapen but not unlikable man; he is intensely loyal to George.

Commentary

In these two chapters, minor characters who have appeared – or been mentioned – earlier are further characterized and begin now to be linked with the plot involving Lady Dedlock and Nemo. The Smallweeds are another of the numerous families dominated by its most disagreeable member and reeking with unhappiness.

CHAPTER 22   Mr. Bucket

Summary

Dining with Mr. Tulkinghorn, Snagsby tells him what Jo has said about the mysterious woman who was inquiring about Nemo. Mr. Bucket, a detective hired by Tulkinghorn, goes with Snagsby to search for Jo. Meanwhile, Lady Dedlock has fired her French maid, Mlle. Hortense.

When Jo is located, he is taken to Tulkinghorn's, where he identifies Hortense as the lady who gave him the gold coin. However, when he sees the woman's hands and hears her speak, he changes his mind. The detective is now certain that the disguised woman who asked Jo questions about Nemo is Lady Dedlock herself.

Commentary

The reader's revulsion to the crafty, secretive, self-seeking

Tulkinghorn increases as the lawyer is shown to be ever more intent upon prying into matters which are really none of his business. Hortense's ugly nature shows itself again as she seeks revenge upon Lady Dedlock. Lady Dedlock, despite her haughty shortcomings, appears to be of higher character than these people.

CHAPTER 23 Esther's Narrative

Summary

Mr. Jarndyce and his wards end their visit with Boythorn and return to Bleak House. Mademoiselle Hortense fails to persuade Esther to hire her. Richard wants to abandon law and enter the army (as an officer). Caddy Jellyby asks Esther to come to London and help her and Prince Turveydrop break the news of their engagement to Mrs. Jellyby and Turveydrop senior, both of whom consent. Mr. Jarndyce gives Charley Neckett to Esther as a helping maid.

Commentary

This chapter creates artistic unity by returning to several characters, themes, and subplots already established. Failing to find new employment, Hortense acquires further reasons for being upset and unbalanced. The theme of Richard's restlessness and irresponsibility appears once more. The subplot of Caddy's adventures is continued, and Dickens again brings Charley Neckett into view.

CHAPTER 24 An Appeal Case

Summary

Richard obtains a commission in the army and begins his training. Mr. Jarndyce, apprehensive about the young man's instability, asks him and Ada to break their engagement.

Richard takes fencing lessons from "Mr. George" (Rouncewell), the shooting gallery owner, who mentions that one of his customers is Gridley. Gridley is, in fact, a dying man who has taken refuge in the gallery. Mr. Bucket, disguised, arrives and tries to cheer Gridley, but to no avail. Exhausted and embittered, Gridley dies.

Commentary

Richard experiences the first real difficulties created by his instability and his leaving Ada parallels and foreshadows his early death. The episode focusing on Gridley is completed in such a way as to highlight the evils spawned by Chancery.

CHAPTER 25   Mrs. Snagsby Sees It All

Summary

Mrs. Snagsby suspects that her husband is keeping a secret from her. She concludes that he is the father of Jo, and she asks Mr. Chadband to interview Jo in Snagsby's presence. Soon she becomes convinced of her husband's guilt and falls into hysteria. Guster gives her supper to Jo and also gives him an affectionate pat on the back. Snagsby gives Jo a half-crown, unaware that Mrs. Snagsby is watching. After that, Mrs. Snagsby spies upon her husband relentlessly.

Commentary

Cold, jealous, emotionally weak women like Mrs. Snagsby create a character background against which the realized femininity of Esther and Ada is all the more impressive. The sharp contrasts also create a dramatic effect and, at the same time, give *Bleak House* the variety found in real life.

CHAPTER 26   Sharpshooters

Summary

During breakfast at the shooting gallery, Phil Squod reminisces about his early years and explains how he got to be so ugly. Unexpectedly, Grandfather Smallweed arrives, accompanied by Judy, his granddaughter. He mentions that Richard Carstone has an army commission. "Mr. George" (Rouncewell) suggests that Richard has no future in the army. The old man then asks George if he has a sample of the handwriting of Captain Hawdon (Hawdon borrowed money from Smallweed, who thinks that the captain may still be alive). A "friend in the city" has a document which he wants to compare with a specimen of Hawdon's handwriting. George agrees to accompany the old man to see the "friend" (Tulkinghorn) but will make no other promises until he learns more about the matter. He takes a paper from his cabinet and goes off with the old man and Judy to Lincoln's Inn Fields.

Commentary

This chapter draws George Rouncewell into the line of action involving Tulkinghorn's hounding of Lady Dedlock. The chapter is typical of Dickens' serio-comic art in general: it mixes Dickens' humorous treatment of Phil Squod with the ominous note sounded by Tulkinghorn's obsession.

CHAPTER 27   More Old Soldiers Than One

Summary

Tulkinghorn presents some papers to Mr. George and asks him to compare the handwriting with that of Captain Hawdon (Nemo). George refuses to cooperate and does not even admit that he possesses any of Hawdon's writing. He says that he has no head for business and that he wants to seek advice from a friend before he has anything more to do with the matter. He then goes to seek counsel of a former military comrade, Matthew Bagnet, owner of a musician's shop. Matthew, in turn, consults his wife, a personable and sensible woman; her advice is that George should avoid all involvement with people who are "too deep" for him. George then goes back to Tulkinghorn and refuses to give the lawyer any assistance. Angry, Tulkinghorn says that he wants nothing to do with the man who harbored Gridley, a "threatening, murderous, dangerous fellow." A clerk, passing by, hears this phrase and mistakenly supposes it applies to George himself.

Commentary

Readers are inclined to view George Rouncewell even more favorably now that he mistrusts and opposes the sinister Tulkinghorn and is a warm friend of the likable Bagnet family. Readers also sense that George's opposing the lawyer entails danger.

CHAPTER 28   The Ironmaster

Summary

Sir Leicester Dedlock has many poor relations and is at present entertaining several of them at Chesney Wold. They include the spinster Volumnia Dedlock and Bob Stables. Sir Leicester and Volumnia are appalled that Mr. Rouncewell, the ironmaster (a manufacturer of iron), has been considered suitable "to go into Parliament." Mr. Rouncewell confers with Lord and Lady Dedlock on the subject of the prospective engagement between Rosa, the maid, and Rouncewell's son, Watt. Sir Leicester is offended when Rouncewell says that if the engagement takes place, he wants to give Rosa two years of additional schooling (Sir Leicester thinks it foolish and dangerous to educate the lowly placed). Later, Lady Dedlocks seems to find comfort in Rosa and, at the same time, to become pensive or even distraught in her presence.

Commentary

In his portraits of Sir Leicester's poor but proud relatives, Dickens mildly satirizes those who use their rich "connection" as the basis for building unreal attitudes or expectations. Satirized also is Sir Leicester's immense pride. The man keeps his mind proudly closed on the subject of change, on class distinctions, and on most everything else. Yet Dickens does not present the upstart, middle-class ironmaster to be greatly admirable either. The motif of Lady Dedlock's melancholy and distraction is picked up again and is emphasized in such a way as to keep the reader's curiosity about her very much alive.

CHAPTER 29   The Young Man

Summary

At the approach of cold weather, the Dedlocks close Chesney Wold and move to their place in London. Their lawyer, Tulkinghorn, is a frequent visitor there, and, for Lady Dedlock, a discomfiting one. Guppy, the law clerk from Kenge and Carboy, has written her numerous letters requesting that he be allowed to visit her. Thus, one day she receives him, and he tells her that a long investigation has led him to believe that Lady Dedlock might have "a family interest" in knowing that the father of Esther Summerson (a name Lady Dedlock nervously admits knowing) was Captain Hawdon (Nemo).

After Guppy leaves, Lady Dedlock breaks into tears as she realizes that her daughter is alive. Her sister (Miss Barbary) lied about the child's having died shortly after birth.

Commentary

In this chapter, Lady Dedlock, one of the book's principal figures, learns a fact so momentous that all of her subsequent actions are bound to be highly significant. In this way, suspense is heightened.

CHAPTER 30   Esther's Narrative

Summary

Caddy Jellyby and Prince Turveydrop have a church wedding; Esther and Ada serve as bridesmaids. The newlyweds are to have a week's honeymoon at Gravesend (a seaport in southeast England). Allan Woodcourt's mother mentions to Esther that her son, Allan, has the "fault" of paying attention to girls in whom he has no real interest. The wedding guests include a Miss Wisk, a fanatic on the subject of women's emancipation.

Commentary

The "happy ending" for Caddy and Prince foreshadows the happy marriage later on of Esther and Allan Woodcourt. The mention of Allan prevents readers from forgetting about a character who will become more and more important but who is not now a part of the action.

A traditionalist on the subject of the family, and a critic of all fanaticism, Dickens takes the opportunity to satirize a proponent of women's liberation.

CHAPTER 31   Nurse and Patient

Summary

Seriously ill, Jo has left London and "moved on" to lodge at a brickmaker's house at St. Albans. The brickmakers' wives have sought assistance for Jo from city officials, but to no avail. They now come to Esther for help, and she has Jo placed in a loft of Mr. Jarndyce's stables. Skimpole warns Mr. Jarndyce that Jo has a dangerous, communicable disease. Charley Neckett attends Jo and contracts his disease shortly after the boy disappears. Esther then nurses Charley, but shortly after Charley recovers, Esther herself comes down with the disease and becomes temporarily blind.

Commentary

Pathos dominates the story at this point as Jo's suffering intensifies and Esther herself is stricken. Jo's disappearance and Esther's blindness are dramatic and seemingly important developments, and as such, they excite our interest in seeing how things will turn out. The illness contracted in turn by Jo, Charley, and Esther is almost certainly smallpox; it was rife in Dickens' era, as it had been in earlier times.

CHAPTER 32   The Appointed Time

Summary

Snagsby the law stationer, still spied upon by his wife, meets with Mr. Weevle (Jobling) near old Krook's house. When they go in, both men become aware of a strange odor like that of tainted and burned meat. Snagsby is so dismayed by it that he leaves. At about ten o'clock, Guppy arrives and goes upstairs with Weevle. At midnight the two are to meet Krook, who is supposed to bring letters written by Captain Hawdon.

They sit waiting, more and more uneasily, in the room where Hawdon (Nemo) was found dead. Greasy soot continually falls from the air, the smell of burnt fat persists, and finally the two men discover a horribly offensive yellow liquid on one of the window sills. Weevle goes to meet Krook, but he is unable to find him. In Krook's back room, the two find that the smell of burning originates there and that it seems to be Krook himself who has burned up—a victim of "spontaneous combustion." Incinerated with him, apparently, are the Hawdon letters. Horrified, Weevle and Guppy flee.

Commentary

These are among the grisliest pages in all of Dickens' work. The eerie atmosphere and the suspense are masterfully created. The chapter does little to advance the plot, but the sense of brooding and threatening evil enhances the story's theme of the appalling loss and destructiveness wrought by "the law's delay." Dickens believed in the possibility of death by "spontaneous combustion."

CHAPTER 33   Interlopers

Summary

Guppy and Jobling (Weevle) have gone to the Sol's Arms tavern adjoining Krook's shop. Alarmed or merely curious about what happened, numerous people of the area crowd into the tavern, many remaining awake all night. Snagsby comes in, is puzzled about the "combustion," and is soon confronted by his wife, who wants to know why he is there. Then the whole family of Smallweeds appears, and Grandfather Smallweed, whose wife turns out to be Krook's sister, lays claim to Krook's property.

The following night, Guppy visits Lady Dedlock and says that he will be unable to deliver the Hawdon letters he promised to bring her. As Guppy leaves, he sees Tulkinghorn; the old lawyer immediately becomes suspicious.

Commentary

Dickens strengthens artistic unity by establishing, through Krook, a relationship between the main plot and the subplot involving the Smallweeds. At the end of the chapter, the motif of Tulkinghorn's obsession with Lady Dedlock resumes.

CHAPTER 34   A Turn of the Screw

Summary

Mr. George (Rouncewell) and his co-signer Matthew Bagnet have borrowed about a hundred pounds from Grandfather Smallweed. The promissory note (which has been renewed several times) is now due but George and Matthew are unable to raise the cash. Smallweed is unmerciful and sends them to his lawyer, Tulkinghorn. Tulkinghorn too insists on immediate payment, but he relents when George gives him the specimen of Captain Hawdon's handwriting. The note is then renewed and Matthew is free from the contract. George goes to dine with the Bagnets and is cheered up by Mrs. Bagnet.

Commentary

George Rouncewell continues to come across as a likable personality. The plot advances as Tulkinghorn at last receives a sample of Captain Hawdon's handwriting. Clearly, from Tulkinghorn's reaction when he receives the sample of Hawdon's handwriting, he is planning mischief. Suspense is one of Dickens' key elements here.

CHAPTER 35   Esther's Narrative

Summary

After several weeks of serious illness, Esther recovers but is left with a scarred face. Richard has become hostile to Mr. Jarndyce, mistakenly suspecting that his guardian is somehow competing with him in the Jarndyce and Jarndyce suit. Esther wants a week in the country to grow more accustomed to her new appearance before she sees Ada. Boythorn has written to Mr. Jarndyce, insisting that Esther visit his estate at Chesney Wold. Before they leave for Boythorn's, Miss Flite visits them, tells much of her family history, and mentions that a veiled lady (Lady Dedlock) has visited Jenny (the brickmaker's wife), asked about Esther's condition, and that she took from the cottage the handkerchief Esther left. Esther believes that the veiled visitor was probably Caddy Jellyby. Miss Flite also tells Esther that Allan Woodcourt has heroically saved many lives in a shipwreck.

Commentary

Accepting her facial scarring without self-pity or bitterness, Esther becomes an even more likable heroine. Richard continues to make self-destructive moves. We are not allowed to lose sight of Allan Woodcourt or of Lady Dedlock's difficult situation.

CHAPTER 36   Chesney Wold

Summary

One day while Esther and Charley Neckett are in the park at Chesney Wold, Lady Dedlock appears, carrying the handkerchief she recently took from Jenny's cottage. She reveals herself as Esther's mother and asks the young woman to forgive her and keep her secret. She gives Esther a letter which is to be read and then destroyed; she also alerts Esther to the fact that Tulkinghorn is suspicious. Esther reads the letter, burns it, and then goes for a walk. Along the Ghost's Walk, she listens to the echoes of her own footsteps and realizes that her fate seems to be to bring "calamity upon the stately house" of Dedlock. The next afternoon, Ada arrives and both girls are overjoyed to be reunited.

Commentary

Joyful-tearful reunions are prevalent in Dickens' novels, and in this chapter there are two such. Today many readers find such scenes "overdone," "sentimental," or "unrealistic." But they pleased many readers in Victorian England, and Dickens sincerely believed that the expression of such sentiment, whether in fiction or in real life, served the useful purpose of promoting moral idealism and regard for others.

The plot advances somewhat as Esther realizes who she is and becomes aware of her mother's—and her own—difficult situation.

CHAPTER 37   Jarndyce and Jarndyce

Summary

One evening during the month-long visit at Boythorn's estate, Charley whispers to Esther, "You're wanted at the Dedlock Arms." At the inn, Esther finds Richard Carstone and Mr. Skimpole, whom Richard has come to admire: Skimpole, Richard says, is "worth . . . thrice his weight in gold." Esther realizes that "Richard could scarcely have found a worse friend." Richard, on leave from the army, is trying to bring his "Chancery interests" to a fruitful conclusion. Esther takes him to the house, where he and Ada meet again. Ada still loves Richard but Esther thinks he is too hostile to Mr. Jarndyce and too preoccupied with the Chancery suit to be genuinely in love with Ada. He asks Esther to tell Ada that he is still unable to see eye to eye with Mr. Jarndyce and is hopeful of good results at last from the suit in Chancery. By letter, Ada replies that the best thing he can do is to desist from building his future on the hope of an inheritance through the court. Skimpole has introduced Richard to Mr. Vholes, who now serves as Richard's adviser. Vholes is a venal and uninteresting person.

Commentary

The motif of Richard's course toward self-destruction continues. Dickens reinforces the reader's critical attitude toward Richard by having the young man befriend another foolish and totally irresponsible human being, Harold Skimpole.

CHAPTER 38   A Struggle

Summary

Soon after she returns to Bleak House, Esther decides to go to London to see Mr. Guppy. First, she visits Caddy and Prince Turveydrop. Taken aback by Esther's scarred face, Guppy emphatically retracts his former marriage proposal to Esther. Esther obtains from him a promise to "relinquish all idea of . . . serving me." She no longer needs Guppy's assistance in helping her learn her real identity, and Guppy's presence could possibly endanger her attempt to be secret about what she has learned from Lady Dedlock.

Commentary

Even more clearly than before, Guppy is seen to be an absurd and shallow human being. Esther once again demonstrates her prudence and resoluteness.

CHAPTER 39   Attorney and Client

Summary

Mr. Vholes, Richard's far-from-honest lawyer, asks Richard for an advance of twenty pounds. Observing Richard, Weevle says to Guppy that Richard's is a case of "smouldering" (rather than "spontaneous") combustion.

It occurs to Guppy that Captain Hawdon's papers may have survived the incineration of Krook. Grandfather Smallweed (in the company of Judy and Tulkinghorn, who is acting as Smallweed's solicitor) is already at Krook's place, searching through a litter of papers. No one finds anything of any value.

Commentary

By standing up to the vile but powerful Tulkinghorn, Guppy slightly redeems himself from the absurdity which he epitomized in the preceding chapter. Grandfather Smallweed's greed and Tulkinghorn's obsession remain prominent.

CHAPTER 40   National and Domestic

Summary

Toward the end of the elections, the guests and distant relatives of Sir Leicester arrive at Chesney Wold, where Mrs. Rouncewell (the housekeeper) has been preparing for them. Although Volumnia is sure that the election has gone Sir Leicester's way, Mr. Tulkinghorn dispels that illusion, announcing that the vote heavily favored the party of Mr. Rouncewell and his son. Tulkinghorn then does something to try to disconcert Lady Dedlock; without using names, he tells Sir Leicester the story of Esther, Captain Hawdon, and Lady Dedlock. Lady Dedlock shows no signs of being more than casually interested in this narrative.

Commentary

In its descriptions of the changing tones and moods of the Dedlock mansion as the day moves toward night, this chapter shows Dickens as a master of pictorial art. The satire of British party politics is not closely related to either the plot or the main themes, but it is rich and amusing. In his verbal torture of Lady Dedlock, Tulkinghorn's viciousness continues to manifest itself. The lady's self-control raises her in the reader's esteem.

CHAPTER 41   In Mr. Tulkinghorn's Room

Summary

Upstairs in Tulkinghorn's room, Lady Dedlock confronts the lawyer. She demands to know why he told her story to "so many persons." Tulkinghorn says that he wanted her to know that he was in on the secret. She indicates that she plans to leave Chesney Wold but wants to spare Sir Leicester any unnecessary pain. Tulkinghorn's "sole consideration in this unhappy case is Sir Leicester," but as he has not yet decided how to act upon his discovery of Lady Dedlock's secret, he says that at least for a while he will keep the matter to himself. Tulkinghorn goes to sleep; Lady Dedlock, distraught, paces for hours in her room. The next morning the Dedlock house is a place of bustling hospitality.

Commentary

Lady Dedlock makes a momentous decision: tragedy is fully upon her. Tulkinghorn's inflexibility and lack of affection and compassion are more impressive than ever. Dickens foreshadows the lawyer's imminent but unexpected death; the morning light finds Tulkinghorn "at his oldest; he looks as if the digger and the spade were both commissioned, and would soon be digging."

CHAPTER 42   In Mr. Tulkinghorn's Chambers

Summary

Returning to London, Tulkinghorn meets Snagsby; the latter complains of being harassed by Lady Dedlock's former servant Hortense. She is frantic to find Tulkinghorn. When she does locate him, she protests bitterly at having been used by him (she now sees that she was tricked into giving him information when, dressed as Lady Dedlock, she was presented to little Jo). She demands that the lawyer get her a new position – otherwise she will hound him "for ever" if necessary. He tells her he will have her imprisoned if she visits either him or Snagsby once more. Undaunted, she leaves. The lawyer enjoys a bottle of old wine, and now and then "as he throws his head back in the chair," he catches sight of a "pertinacious Roman pointing from the ceiling."

Commentary

Tulkinghorn's bitter encounter with Hortense makes the reader sense that "more will come" of this incident. This impression is reinforced by Dickens' use of foreshadowing. At the very end of the preceding chapter, Tulkinghorn is pictured complacent and then asleep — yet, somehow, looking very old and, in fact, not far from death. The present chapter closes with a Tulkinghorn who, though again complacent, catches sight of an arrow-wielding Roman painted on the ceiling.

CHAPTER 43   Esther's Narrative

Summary

For fear of increasing her mother's peril, Esther refrains from writing to her or trying to see her. Worried about Skimpole's influence on Richard, she and Ada discuss that situation with Mr. Jarndyce. Jarndyce says that in order to understand Skimpole better, the three of them should visit the "infant" in his home. This home, where Skimpole lives with this sickly wife and three daughters, is a dirty, dingy, dilapidated place. Mr. Jarndyce asks Skimpole to refrain from allowing Richard to give him any money or to buy anything for him. Skimpole introduces his daughters, who are much like their father, and he then accompanies Esther, Ada, and Mr. Jarndyce to Bleak House. They are there only a short time before Sir Leicester pays an unexpected visit. He has come to assure both Skimpole and Mr. Jarndyce that they are always welcome at the Dedlock mansion. Sir Leicester has reason to believe that Skimpole, not long ago, while examining some of the Dedlock family portraits, was inadvertently made to feel unwelcome. Esther, afraid that the subject of the family portraits might lead to some remark that might betray her mother, is greatly relieved when Sir Leicester leaves. Afterward, she talks in private with her guardian and tells him what she knows about her mother. In turn, she learns from Mr. Jarndyce that Boythorn was once in love with Lady Dedlock's sister, Miss Barbary, the woman who raised Esther. Miss Barbary broke her engagement in order to raise Esther.

Commentary

Here again is a microcosm of Dickens' serio-comic art. Most of the chapter is devoted to a comic portrait of Skimpole and his daughters, a subject almost completely irrelevant to the novel's main line of action. Yet present also are the important motifs of Lady

Dedlock's peril and of Richard's continuing irresponsibility about money and associations.

CHAPTER 44   The Letter and the Answer

Summary

Mr. Jarndyce promises to assist Esther and her mother in every way possible. He agrees that Tulkinghorn is a dangerous person. In the same conversation, Mr. Jarndyce tells Esther that one week later she should send Charley to his room for a letter, which he will have written by then.

The letter turns out to be a marriage proposal. Esther feels blessed to be chosen as the mistress of Bleak House. During the next several days, she expects Mr. Jarndyce to bring up the subject of the letter, but as he does not, she (a week after the proposal) takes the initiative and gives him the answer he has hoped for.

Commentary

Dickens and his readers seemed never to tire of doting upon the virtues of "good" characters like Esther and Mr. Jarndyce. Of romance or physical attraction, nothing is said here.

CHAPTER 45   In Trust

Summary

Vholes (Richard's attorney) appears unexpectedly at Bleak House one morning. The news he bears is that Richard is broke and may lose his army commission.

Esther goes to visit Richard at Deal, in Kent, taking Charley with her, as well as a letter in which Ada offers Richard her inheritance. Esther finds Richard almost unhinged. He wants to go to London with her and try once again to expedite the Chancery suit.

As they leave Kent, they accidentally meet Allan Woodcourt, who has just returned from India. Allan promises Esther that he will befriend Richard and try to be a good influence on him. Esther perceives that Allan is compassionate about her illness-ravaged face. Inwardly she welcomes his concern.

Commentary

Dickens knew that most of his readers would prefer to see some romance in Esther's life despite the many virtues of the aging John Jarndyce (and Dickens has hinted, all along, that Allan Woodcourt finds Esther much to his liking). Hence, to prevent a possible sag in his readers' interest, Dickens brings Allan onto the scene again immediately after Esther's acceptance of her guardian's proposal. Meanwhile, Richard moves closer and closer toward a bad end.

CHAPTER 46   Stop Him!

Summary

Walking in Tom-all-Alone's toward dawn, Allan Woodcourt sees a woman (Jenny, the brickmaker's wife from St. Albans) with a badly bruised forehead. She allows him to treat it. Continuing his walk, he catches a glimpse of a shabbily dressed boy (Jo), whom he vaguely remembers. A few moments later, he sees the boy being chased by Jenny. Thinking that Jo may have robbed her, Allan chases and finally catches the boy. Jenny, however, only wanted to talk to him. Earlier, she had bought medicine for him and nursed him when he was ill with the sickness that eventually infected Esther.

Jo tells his story. He ran away from the young Lady (Esther) who had taken charge of him during his fever and was then found by a man (Detective Bucket), who took him to a "horsepittle." The doctor tells Jo to come with him, and the two leave Tom-all-Alone's and emerge into "purer air."

Commentary

In encountering Jenny and Jo, Allan Woodcourt is drawn more closely into Esther's concerns. The chapter satisfies the reader's curiosity about the disappearance of Jo.

CHAPTER 47   Jo's Will

Summary

Allan and Jo continue to walk. At a breakfast stall, Jo, although he has become a starveling, is able to eat only a tiny amount. Examining the boy, Allan finds him quite ill and gives him a little wine, which helps. Jo is then able to eat, and as he does so, he tells the doctor "the adventure of the lady in the veil, with all its consequences." Uncertain of where to find a place of temporary refuge for the boy, Allan locates Miss Flite; she suggests George's shooting gallery. Jo's fear of Bucket is somewhat eased when George and Phil Squod volunteer to take care of the boy. George himself is preoccupied with the possibility that Tulkinghorn will close him down because of debts. Snagsby visits Jo and gives him four half-crowns. The child remains confused about the identities of Lady Dedlock, Esther, and Hortense. He knows no prayer and yet senses that "It's time fur me to go down to that there berryin ground." Allan begins to say the Lord's Prayer; Jo dies after repeating a few phrases of it.

Commentary

By what he learns from Jo, Allan Woodcourt is drawn more deeply into matters that most intensely concern Esther. Dickens' portrayals of the deaths of innocent children were favorably received by readers in his day. In the death of Jo, Dickens implies the callousness and improvision of the London world of 1853.

CHAPTER 48   Closing In

Summary

In the peril of her life, Lady Dedlock is resolved never to yield or droop. She continues to appear, as before, in high society and arranges for Rosa to leave. This latter action surprises and dismays Tulkinghorn, and he tells Lady Dedlock that their agreement is no longer in force. He will not, he says, reveal her secret past to Sir Leicester tonight, but he feels free to inform him at any time after this. Just before ten o'clock the same night, Tulkinghorn is found dead; he has been "shot through the heart."

Commentary

Without a confidant or a confessor, lonely Lady Dedlock nevertheless continues to show admirable strength of character. The demise of the vicious Tulkinghorn balances that of the likable Jo and provides some much-needed relief from what seems, through the book thus far, an almost uninterrupted triumph of gloom, trouble, and bad ends. Of course, the lawyer's death immediately causes the story to become, in part, a "murder mystery."

CHAPTER 49   Dutiful Friendship

Summary

Mr. Bagnet is preparing a birthday dinner for his wife. George Rouncewell has been invited; at *precisely* 4:30 in the afternoon he arrives, still somewhat distracted and depressed by the death of little Jo, but also delighted to be in the company of amiable old friends.

Unannounced and unexpected, Detective Bucket appears. Extremely congenial, he ingratiates himself with the whole group, including the children. He notices that George seems distracted. They leave together and Bucket arrests George on the charge of having murdered Tulkinghorn, who had, on one occasion, cried out "a threatening, murdering, dangerous fellow," words referring to Gridley but taken to refer to George. George is put in jail. Bucket collects the handsome reward offered by Sir Leicester for the capture of his lawyer's murderer.

Commentary

The plot continues to develop much like a detective story. Bucket's character becomes more distinct. However, there is no sense of climax here; the reader is virtually certain that George cannot be Tulkinghorn's killer.

CHAPTER 50   Esther's Narrative

Summary

Caddy and Prince Turveydrop have a baby girl, but Caddy is ill and feels sure that she will get better if Esther visits her. Esther makes three visits, and then Mr. Jarndyce suggests that it would be more convenient all around if he, Ada, and Esther all went to London for a protracted stay. He also makes arrangements for Allan Woodcourt to become Caddy's doctor.

Allan and Esther meet frequently. Eventually, Esther tells Ada and Caddy about Mr. Jarndyce's proposal of marriage. Caddy recovers her health. Allan seems "half inclined for another voyage." Esther notices a slight change—"a quiet sorrow"—in Ada's behavior, but cannot determine its cause.

Commentary

Caddy's illness becomes the means by which Esther and Allan get to know each other better. Our curiosity is aroused about the unexplained change in Ada.

CHAPTER 51   Enlightened

Summary

As soon as Allan Woodcourt arrived in London, he went to Mr. Vholes to get Richard's address. On that day, the pompous, wordy Vholes relentlessly pursues the theme that Richard needs money (as does Vholes, if he is to continue as Richard's legal counsel). Learning finally that Richard lives next door, upstairs, Allan visits him and finds the young man haggard and dejected—he has made no progress with his interests in the Chancery suit—but quite agreeable to receive advice and direction from Allan. When Esther suggests to Ada that they visit Richard, Ada is at first hesitant and acts strangely: she has "tears in her eyes and love in her face." When they do visit Richard, Ada reveals that she has been his wife for two months and will not be returning to Bleak House. Esther reveals the marriage to Mr. Jarndyce, and he accepts it calmly, but pities the two and twice remarks that "Bleak House is thinning fast."

Commentary

Dickens' further exposure of the mercenary and hypocritical Vholes enables him to continue his critique of the persons and institutions of the law. The marriage of Ada and Richard in such unpropitious circumstances darkens the story's atmosphere further, as it now seems inevitable that Richard's ominous future will also be Ada's.

CHAPTER 52   Obstinacy

Summary

Allan Woodcourt believes in George Rouncewell's innocence but

58

points out that circumstantial evidence is strongly against the accused. Esther, Allan, Mr. Jarndyce, and the Bagnets visit George in prison and are dismayed at his refusal to have a lawyer (he wants his own innocence, not legal maneuverings, to clear his name). He watches Esther closely as she leaves, then tells Mr. Jarndyce that on the night of the murder, a figure like hers went past him on the dark staircase. Mrs. Bagnet visits George's mother, hoping that she will be able to persuade her son to accept legal counsel.

Commentary

After an intermission of two chapters, Dickens the artist senses that continuity demands a return to the murder mystery. Drama is heightened by George's perilous obstinacy. A possible, major "piece of the puzzle" turns up when George remarks about the figure he saw but could not identify.

CHAPTERS 53 & 54   The Track & Springing a Mine

Summary

Bucket is an amiable man of good will but dogged in pursuit. At present he wanders far and wide, closely observing a multitude of people, places, and things.

At Tulkinghorn's funeral, he sits behind the lattice blinds of a carriage and scans the crowd that has gathered in Lincoln's Inn Fields. After the funeral, he visits the Dedlocks, where he is always welcome. His conversation with Sir Leicester, Volumnia, and others is mostly small talk, but as he leaves, he questions the footman (Mercury) about Lady Dedlock's habits. He learns that on the night of the murder, she took a lone walk.

The next morning, Bucket tells Sir Leicester that his wife is a suspect. Sir Leicester is dumbfounded when he learns of his wife's former lover, of her visit to his grave, and of the "bad blood" between her and Tulkinghorn.

The Smallweeds, Snagsbys, and Chadbands arrive and bear the news that love letters to Captain Hawdon from "Honoria" were discovered at Krook's shop, read by Grandfather Smallweed, and then turned over to Tulkinghorn. All of the new arrivals hope to make money, one way or another out of Lady Dedlock's troubles and Tulkinghorn's death. Bucket dismisses them and then arrests Mlle. Hortense. He summarizes her relationship with Tulkinghorn and her appearance, in Lady Dedlock's clothes, before little Jo. Bucket's wife kept watch on Hortense and can prove that the French woman wrote letters accusing Lady Dedlock. Both George Rouncewell and Lady Dedlock visited Tulkinghorn on the night of the murder but both were blameless. Hortense later threw the murder weapon in a small lake; Bucket recovered the gun by having the lake dragged. All this is such a shock for Sir Leicester that he suffers a stroke.

Commentary

At this point, the "detective story" aspect of the book reaches its completion. Still prompting the reader to read on, however, is (among other things) the unknown fate of Lady Dedlock. Bucket proves to be an intrepid sleuth, and though his main work is over, he will continue to play an active role in subsequent events. Both in defending his wife's honor and, afterward, in regarding her with compassion and without reproach, Sir Leicester shows hitherto unsuspected virtues, even as he succumbs to a stroke.

CHAPTER 55 Flight

Summary

Mrs. Bagnet brings Mrs. Rouncewell to George's prison cell, where mother and son are happily reunited after many years of separation. George consents to accept a defense lawyer.

When Mrs. Rouncewell goes to the Dedlock house, she tells Lady Dedlock that George is being held for Tulkinghorn's murder. She also shows Lady Dedlock a letter giving a printed (newspaper) account of the discovery of Tulkinghorn's body and bearing, under the account, Lady Dedlock's name and the word "murderess." Mr. Guppy arrives, warns her that Hawdon's letters, which he thought were destroyed, are now held by the Smallweeds, and he tells her further that Grandfather Smallweed will probably use them to try to extract money from her. (Guppy is protective of Lady Dedlock in accordance with the promise he made to Esther.)

When Guppy leaves, Lady Dedlock is seized with horror. Tulkinghorn, though dead, remains a menacing figure: even in death, he pursues her. She writes a brief letter to Sir Leicester explaining her own motives and movements on the night of Tulkinghorn's murder. She states that she is innocent of Tulkinghorn's murder, but that she is not innocent of anything else that "you have heard, or will hear." Then she "veils and dresses quickly, leaves all her jewels and her money" and exits the house.

Commentary

The reunion of George Rouncewell and his mother ties up one of the loose ends of a subplot and provides another occasion for Dickens to provide his early readers with something many of them delighted in: the effusive expression of virtuous domestic sentiment.

Once again Mr. Guppy, though still somewhat absurd, appears in a rather favorable light.

Lady Dedlock follows the pattern so often found in classical tragedy: because she lacks certain vital information (her husband's forgiveness, Hortense's arrest), she makes a fatal decision. Her character, however, is not sufficiently deep or noble to create the compelling effect of high tragedy; she is a figure of pathos.

CHAPTER 56   Pursuit

Summary

Not long after Lady Dedlock has left the house, Volumnia (a cousin in her sixties) discovers Sir Leicester unconscious on the floor of the library; he has had a stroke. Recovering somewhat but still unable to speak distinctly, he writes "My Lady" on a slate and is told that she has gone out. After reading her letter, he commissions Bucket to find her and give her his message: "Full forgiveness." The detective reassures old Mrs. Rouncewell that her son George is "discharged honourable," then he searches Lady Dedlock's room for clues that might help him locate her. He finds and keeps the signatured handkerchief that Esther left in the brickmaker's house, the one that Lady Dedlock discovered there. Bucket then goes to the shooting gallery and gets Esther's address from George. He then visits Mr. Jarndyce, explains his mission, and asks him to allow Esther to go with him in search of her mother. Meanwhile, Lady Dedlock is wandering in the area of the brickmakers' kilns in St. Albans.

Commentary

Bucket continues to be impressive as a skillful detective who is also a politic and warm-hearted human being. Sir Leicester continues to show only his better side. The story now turns into a worried, rather desperate rescue effort.

CHAPTER 57   Esther's Narrative

Summary

Bucket and Esther set out on their search. They stop first at a police station, where a detective gives a description of Lady Dedlock. They search far and wide through the dock area, then proceed to St. Albans. At a tea stop, Bucket learns that a figure like the one he seeks has gone on ahead. He explains to Esther that he himself removed Jo from St. Albans sometime ago to keep "this very matter of Lady Dedlock quiet." He also tells how he was assisted by Skimpole, who accepted a five-pound bribe.

Jenny, they learn, has gone to London, so, thinking that they might learn something from her, Bucket and Esther go back to the city.

Commentary

Dickens uses the search for Lady Dedlock partly as a way of giving a further display of his detective's shrewdness and persistence and partly as a way of clearing up the mystery of Jo's disappearance from St. Albans after Esther took charge of him. In any assessment of Skimpole's character, Bucket's comments about him would have to be taken in account.

CHAPTER 58   A Wintry Day and Night

Summary

While Sir Leicester lies ill at his town house, the high society in which the Dedlocks move is rife with rumors about them. Sir Leicester, though still seriously ill, waits expectantly for Bucket to return; he wants to be sure that the house is in cheerful readiness for Lady Dedlock. George Rouncewell and his mother discuss the absence of Lady Dedlock. The mother feels certain that Lady Dedlock "will never more set foot within these walls." The lady's "empty rooms, bereft of a familiar presence," seem oppressively dark and cold.

Sir Leicester wishes to see George. When George arrives, he lifts the stricken man up and puts him close to one of the windows so that he can have a better view of "the driving snow and sleet." Sir Leicester wants to make it clear to all that he remains "on unaltered terms" with his wife. Restless and wakeful throughout the night, he is watched over and cared for with tender devotion by the stalwart George.

Commentary

The portrayal of Sir Leicester as a touchingly regenerated personality continues. This chapter shows Dickens' masterful ability to modulate from one tone to a quite different one. The chapter commences on a note of sarcastic social satire but develops into scenes of atmospheric cold and foreboding and then into the expression of deeply realized — and this time unsentimentalized — human warmth and tenderness. Not very important in terms of plot, this chapter shows Dickens at the height of his powers in the rendering of atmosphere and feeling.

CHAPTER 59   Esther's Narrative

Summary

At 3 a.m., after a hard, hurried journey, Bucket and Esther reach London again. Searching through many shabby streets, Bucket eventually passes on to Chancery Lane where, by accident, they meet Allan Woodcourt, who has been attending Richard, described by Allan as not ill but "depressed and faint." Bucket drives the coach to Snagsby's place: he thinks that Guster, the servant, "has a letter somewhere" that will assist him in his search.

Guster is in one of her fits. Bucket assigns Allan the task of extracting the letter from her. In the meantime, the detective reproaches Mrs. Snagsby for the folly of being jealous of her husband. The doctor obtains the letter and passes it on to Bucket who, in turn, asks Esther to read it. It is a letter from her mother saying that she is on her way to the place where she has chosen to die. Guster confesses that she encountered a wretchedly dressed stranger who asked her how to find the paupers' burying ground. Bucket and Esther hurry to that place and find what seems to be the body of Jenny at the gate. Esther discovers, however, that the dead woman dressed in Jenny's clothes is not Jenny—it is Esther's mother, Lady Dedlock, "cold and dead."

Commentary

Here ends one of the book's central actions: the mystery of Lady Dedlock's secret. Dickens must now devote his attention, in the few chapters remaining, to bringing the other main lines of action to a close. Esther and Allan must be brought together and the fate of Richard and Ada remains to be clarified.

CHAPTER 60   Perspective

Summary

Esther falls ill and is attended by Allan. To keep her and himself closely in touch with Ada and Richard, Mr. Jarndyce decides to remain in London for an extended period of time and invite Allan's mother as a guest. Allan has decided to forego his projected long voyage. Mr. Jarndyce helps him secure an appointment in Yorkshire, where he will provide medical care for the poor.

Esther often visits Ada, whose love for Richard remains as strong as ever, despite his poverty and dismal prospects. Richard is languid, unkempt, and distracted. Esther surmises that he has lost faith in Vholes. Ada's greatest fear is that Richard will not live long enough to see the child she is now carrying.

Commentary

Dickens now prepares us for Richard's seemingly imminent demise. The constant presence of Allan Woodcourt also prepares us for another imminent event: his engagement to Esther.

CHAPTER 61   A Discovery

Summary

Esther now visits Ada every day and, "on two or three occasions," she finds Skimpole there. She thinks that it is likely that

Skimpole is continuing to help Richard spend money foolishly; she also senses that Skimpole's "careless gaiety" is vexing to Ada in her difficult situation.

Esther goes to see Skimpole and reproaches him for accepting a bribe to betray Jo's presence at Bleak House to Bucket. Skimpole defends himself with his usual perverse reasoning. Mr. Jarndyce becomes highly critical of Skimpole's behavior, and five years later, when Skimpole dies, the dilettante leaves a diary in which he says that Mr. Jarndyce, like "most other men I have known," is "the Incarnation of Selfishness."

As the months go by, Richard, still haunting the Chancery Court day after day, becomes more haggard and often sinks into an alarming lethargy of mind and body.

Allan Woodcourt walks Esther home one night and tells her that he loves her. Esther's first thought is, "Too late," but then she considers that thought to be "ungrateful" to Mr. Jarndyce. She tells Allan she is not free to think of his love. Allan is understanding, and the two part without unhappiness. Allan promises that he will continue to look after Richard.

Commentary

The story continues to hold the reader's interest because several lines of action remain to be resolved, among them the fate of Richard and Ada and the relationship between Esther and Allan. The fact that Esther has even a moment of regret about her prior commitment to Mr. Jarndyce makes her seem more lifelike. Readers are glad to see Skimpole exposed, at last, as the fraud and parasitic ingrate that he truly is.

CHAPTER 62 Another Discovery

Summary

The next morning, Esther tells Mr. Jarndyce, "I will be the mistress of Bleak House when you please." Mr. Jarndyce says, "Next month, then."

At that moment, Bucket and Grandfather Smallweed appear. Smallweed has discovered a signed will dated later than the wills already examined in the Jarndyce and Jarndyce suit. The new will reduces Mr. Jarndyce's interests considerably but advances those of Richard and Ada. Mr. Kenge, to whom the new document is given, is sure that it will carry much weight when, in a month's time, it is introduced in court.

Commentary

Even though Esther and Mr. Jarndyce have agreed to be married the following month, Dickens has made such a strong "case" for Allan Woodcourt that we suspect that some development yet to come will make it possible for Allan to triumph.

The newly discovered Jarndyce will intensifies our interest in the court case.

CHAPTER 63 Steel and Iron

Summary

George Rouncewell has given up the shooting gallery and is now a constant companion to Sir Leicester. One day, however, he rides north to "the iron country" and visits his brother. He also meets his nephew, Watt Rouncewell, and Watt's bride-to-be, Rosa. George is offered a job, turns it down, but agrees to give Rosa away at the wedding. Then he writes to Esther, telling her (in order to put her mind to rest) that the letter written to him long ago by Captain Hawdon, the one taken by Detective Bucket, was a note of no particular consequence.

Commentary

The Rouncewells, all good people, are being rewarded with "happy endings." The lines of action involving them are now drawing to a conclusion. One more glimpse of the capable, kind-hearted George will be gained.

CHAPTER 64 Esther's Narrative

Summary

Mr. Jarndyce has gone to Yorkshire to see Allan Woodcourt. Soon he invites Esther to join them. He has settled Allan in a "new

Bleak House" and releases Esther from her promise, having seen for some time that she will be far happier with Allan. Esther is astonished. She will still become "the mistress of Bleak House," but with Allan as her husband.

During their absence from St. Albans, Mr. Guppy has called three times. When they return, he calls again, accompanied by his mother and Jobling. Finding that the image of Esther still haunts him, he renews his proposal of marriage. Mr. Jarndyce, speaking for Esther, rejects the proposal. Guppy behaves well enough, but his mother is outraged, becomes insulting, and has to be forcibly removed by her son and Jobling.

Commentary

Here begins the happy ending for Esther and Allan — and even for Mr. Jarndyce, who becomes a Prospero figure (see Shakespeare's *The Tempest*), secretly pulling many strings to create a surprising and joyous culmination of events.

The visit by Guppy and his mother may be a superfluous addition to the story, though it does lend credibility to the fact that Esther's good looks are returning.

CHAPTERS 65 & 66   Beginning in the World & Down in Lincolnshire

Summary

The Jarndyce and Jarndyce case is finally ready to "come up," this time at Westminster Hall (in London). On their way to Westminster, Esther and Allan meet Caddy passing by in a carriage.

At Westminster Hall, they learn that legal costs have exhausted the entire worth of the estate. The shock is too much for the already ill Richard: though resolved to start life afresh — "to begin the world" — and reconciled at last with Mr. Jarndyce, he dies the same day. Miss Flite comes weeping to Esther. The "poor, crazed" woman has set her birds free.

Lady Dedlock has been buried unobtrusively in the family mausoleum at Chesney Wold. How she died is a mystery. Sir Leicester, riding on the estate with George Rouncewell, constantly honors her memory and her burial place. He and Boythorn still quarrel over the disputed thoroughfare, but in a way that gives satisfaction to both. George and

Phil Squod have a permanent residence in one of the lodges of the park. Chesney Wold, now headed only by an aging widower, settles into a "dull repose." Sir Leicester himself will live only a little longer. In the evenings, Volumnia reads political treatises to him. She discovers that she will inherit the estate.

Commentary

Things go according to Dickens' foreshadowing. Jarndyce and Jarndyce comes to nothing. Richard pays for his persistent folly. Sir Leicester remains firm in his dignity and touching in his devotion to Lady Dedlock. In the descriptions of a changed and subdued Chesney Wold, Dickens' art of creating atmosphere or mood by describing houses and grounds in changing light and seasons asserts itself triumphantly once more.

CHAPTER 67   The Close of Esther's Narrative

Summary

For "full seven happy years," Esther has been the mistress of the new Bleak House. She and Allan have two daughters. Ada's child, Richard, was born very shortly after his father's death. The boy and his mother "throve" and, in doing so, made Esther "the happiest of the happy." Mr. Jarndyce tells Ada that both Bleak Houses are her home but that "the older . . . claims priority."

Esther's maid, Charley Neckett, has married a miller; her younger sister Emma is now Esther's helper. Dissatisfied with the results of her efforts on behalf of Africa, Mrs. Jellyby has turned her energies in support of the right of women to sit in Parliament. Caddy is fresh and happy despite the fact that her husband, Prince, is lame and her child deaf and dumb. Peepy Jellyby "is in the Custom-House and doing extremely well." Old Mr. Turveydrop remains a Model of Deportment. Esther and Allan have built a "little Growlery" for Mr. Jarndyce's visits. Mr. Jarndyce is as helpful and happy as ever. Esther finds Ada "more beautiful than ever," and, according to Allan, Esther herself is prettier than ever before.

Commentary

A last look at several minor characters ties up all remaining loose

ends. Dickens' conclusion is written in such a way as to evoke poign-
antly the sense of time past linking up with time present; the final
note is that of the continuity and strength of the goodness that dominates in the survivors and successors and makes the future propitious.

CHARACTER ANALYSES

LADY DEDLOCK

Despite the obvious importance of Esther Summerson, Lady
Honoria Dedlock dominates *Bleak House*. She either initiates or
becomes the object of nearly all of the most interesting or exciting
actions in the story. Tulkinghorn's pursuit of her secret, her attempts
to evade his snares, her boldness and courage in seeking out Captain
Hawdon's burial place and in punishing herself by self-exile and what
amounts to suicide – all this is considerably more interesting than anything that happens to Esther.

The somewhat odd thing, experienced by some readers as a
weakness in the novel, is that Lady Dedlock's domination of the book
is not matched by her connection with the story's main theme. There
is a connection but it is not a strong one. To press his biggest point
(theme) home, Dickens should probably have made Lady Dedlock's
misfortunes the direct result of some aspect of the Jarndyce and Jarndyce court case or, in any event, of some action or inaction of the
Chancery court. Tulkinghorn is, of course, a Chancery court lawyer,
but he isn't restricted to that court, and corrupt or self-seeking lawyers are as likely to be found in one place as in another. It is a mere
accident – the noticing of some papers that Tulkinghorn happens to
spread on a table in the Dedlock house – that commences Lady
Dedlock's downfall. That initiating situation represents no meanness
or malevolence on the part of either Tulkinghorn or Chancery. Nor
does Lady Dedlock suffer because Jarndyce and Jarndyce has been
a fiasco; rich, secure, comfortable, she is in no way dependent on
the outcome of that suit even though she does have some slight
involvement in it. Lady Dedlock dominates the *story* but fails to dominate the *theme*. This is a clear example of artistic (or literary) disunity
and is perhaps the only serious instance of it in *Bleak House*.

Dickens also chooses not to give us an *intimate* portrait of the lady.
We see little of her inner life; the concrete details of her memories,

thoughts, feelings, moods, sensations are not presented. Such portraiture, barren of the concrete, of details, is called "externality" of characterization. Does it mean that Lady Dedlock remains, for us, unknown, unreal?

ESTHER SUMMERSON

In literature, as in life, troubles and suffering tend to be emotionally powerful and to arouse our interest and compassion – to some extent even when the sufferer is a far-from-admirable person or character.

We are not shown, in any detail, the inner suffering of Honoria Dedlock, but at least we know that her suffering exists. With Esther Summerson, even this source of interest in the character is mostly lacking. Except for her earliest years, when she was being raised by her rather unfeeling aunt (Miss Barbary), and during a short period of dismay and self-doubt after the scarring of her face by smallpox, Esther has lived a life far from rich in the drama of troubles and suffering. She dwells, throughout most of the story, in security and comfort and looks forward to a happy marriage with her guardian. Then she acquires even better prospects when her husband turns out to be Allan Woodcourt, who seems to be both dashing and solid. But the difficulty Esther experiences when she is trying to keep the identity of her mother a secret is not intense or long lasting.

Esther is also too uncomplicated to be one of the great heroines of literature. Complication makes for lifelikeness. It also challenges us intellectually – we are drawn into a deeper engagement as more and more of a character's complexity is presented to us, for the simple reason that we have to make some effort to understand it, to see the personality as a whole. And in reading, deeper engagement is another term for interest.

In her uncomplicated, unfailing goodness, Esther is more of an ideal than a "convincing" character, one that might have been based on a real-life individual. Matters are made worse by the fact that much of the story is narrated by Esther; we have the nagging feeling that much of what she observes and reports is more complicated – hence, more interesting – than her uncomplicated perspective allows us to see.

Most of the heroines (or female principals or protagonists) of Dickens' books are somewhat unsatisfying in this way. What may be virtuousness in life becomes faultiness in fiction: the ideal becomes the unreal.

But is there more to the matter? Is it possible that, at least to some extent, we dissociate Esther from all reference to real life and consciously or "instinctively" experience her *as* the ideal, *as* the Eternal Feminine, archetypal femininity, a Cinderella or Good Daughter or Beloved Bride figure? If so, then despite her limitations with regard to real-life women, she would affect us and not be a wholly wasted literary portrait.

JOHN JARNDYCE

Mr. Jarndyce is a "stock" character – that is, one seen repeatedly in literary works down through the ages and immediately recognizable. Such a character is sometimes a "rich uncle," sometimes a magnanimous aristocrat, sometimes a reformed miser like Dickens' Scrooge in *A Christmas Carol*. His mainspring is always generosity and the desire and ability to assist and protect anyone less fortunate than himself.

Stock or "type" characters can be quite interesting despite their familiarity. Shakespeare's big boastful fat man, Falstaff, is one of the most fascinating characters ever created even though he is a perfect type of the stock character known as the *miles gloriosus*, the braggart soldier, a type already familiar to playgoers in ancient Rome. Shakespeare, however, endows Falstaff with great individuality, making him a "round" character – that is, a highly developed stock character. Dickens makes no such endowment; as with Lady Dedlock, Tulkinghorn, Ada, Richard, and, in fact, virtually all of the characters in *Bleak House*, Mr. Jarndyce is viewed from the outside only. He is as obscurely benevolent as Tulkinghorn is obscurely malevolent. What made him so kindly and caring? Innate disposition? Circumstances? Something that happened to him at one particular time? We never learn. In fact, we learn considerably less about this individual in his concreteness than we do about Esther Summerson. And since he is even more purely, or at least more maturely, good than Esther is, we find ourselves nagged by another question: can any human being be as faultless, as sensible, capable, self-controlled, and completely benevolent as John Jarndyce? Perhaps he is not *quite* flawless, not completely godlike; he does, once in a great while, make a slight mistake, and sometimes he becomes worried or upset ("the wind is from the east"). Do these tiny humanizing touches make him a credible character after all? And do we at some level perceive and appreciate him as the archetypal Good Father?

MR. TULKINGHORN

Tulkinghorn, an extremely capable solicitor (a leading attorney) of the Chancery Court, is the main enemy, or antagonist, in this novel. He is an enigma which Dickens chooses not to solve.

As Sir Leicester's legal advisor, Tulkinghorn has a right, even a responsibility, to take notice of any action whatever that seems as if it might be detrimental to his client. Therefore, it is by no means unnatural or outrageous that he should wonder what his client's wife is up to when she begins to act strangely and make inquiries about the handwriting on a legal document. But Dickens himself neither makes this point not leaves it as an obvious inference. Tulkinghorn pursues the lady's secret so obsessively and ruthlessly that he gives the impression of desiring not so much protection of his client as power over the lady and the pleasure of inflicting pain.

Although a reader's rational sense might be better satisfied if Dickens had been more explicit about Tulkinghorn's motivations, we should remember that cruelly evil behavior is actually very hard to "explain." Should Dickens have indicated, at least, that somehow Lady Dedlock excited in the lawyer a compulsion to pursue and torture, a compulsion which he himself didn't understand? Or could one make a good case for the idea that the obscurity and irrationality of Tulkinghorn's behavior make it all the more mysterious and unpredictable and, therefore, all the more powerful in its impact on the reader?

Does Dickens mean for us to see Tulkinghorn as not only a *servant* of Chancery but a *symbol*, an extension or personification of it? If so, does he give that point sufficient emphasis that we can hardly miss it? When Tulkinghorn entraps Lady Dedlock, are we to think of Chancery as swallowing one more victim?

On one matter, many readers will agree: our not knowing what makes the unfathomable Tulkinghorn tick takes nothing away from his archetypal power as a Devil figure, the Sinister One.

RICHARD CARSTONE

Richard has the natural optimism and enthusiasm of youth but is also impractical, irresponsible, and congenitally restless. For these less desirable traits, the Chancery Court cannot be held responsible; the young man appears to have inherited them from his ancestors. Of course, these weaknesses make the *effects* of Chancery on Richard all the more credible. But they also raise a problem: having such defects, perhaps Richard would have turned out badly *anyway*. Would Dickens have made his point harder-hitting if he had shown us a quite solid young man being worn down and finally ruined by Chancery *despite* that solidity?

We view Richard only from the outside; his inner life is never revealed in its concreteness. If we are to *feel* the evils of the law as a symbol of, or at least a type of the "dead hand" of the past, we need to have someone who is sufficiently "real" to us so that we can feel strongly *for* him as those institutionalized evils progressively weaken and destroy him. Is Richard a sufficiently engaging and knowable character to be singled out by Dickens as the one who, more than anyone else, will drive the book's point home?

ADA CLARE

Ada Clare and Esther Summerson are *parallel characters* — that is, characters who are very much alike in many ways. Both are young, pretty, self-effacing, good-natured, sensible, responsible, and delicate; both are orphaned, then eventually stationed in the same household; they have similar values and expectations of life; young men are attracted to both of them. They are also mutual *confidants*; they confide in each other, and partly because they do, they reveal aspects of their characters to us.

We learn far less about Ada (a clear example of a "minor" character); she remains in the background most of the time, whereas Esther is often "on center stage." Even so, Ada is both close to Esther and, through Richard, strongly involved in Jarndyce and Jarndyce; therefore, she is a more important minor character than say, Jobling (Weevle) or Watt Rouncewell.

In relation to Richard, both Ada and Esther are *foil characters*, that is, characters who in some important way *contrast strongly* with some other character and, through that contrast, make the other's character more distinct. Mature, realistic, prudent, and steadfast, Ada is all that Richard is not. In fact, Ada (again, like Esther) expresses and represents normality and reality, the standards by which Dickens wants us to judge other characters. The strong sense of reality and normality with which Dickens endows both Ada and Esther gives these young women an important function in the story and prevents them from becoming mere figureheads – pretty but essentially useless objects of male desire and idealization.

Dickens emphasizes Ada's blonde, blue-eyed beauty. Might one make a plausible case for the idea that this emphasis, together with the fact that Ada remains, perhaps somewhat mysteriously and glamorously, in the background, gives to Ada, even more than to Esther, something of the power of the Archetypal or Eternal Feminine.

SIR LEICESTER DEDLOCK

Not tightly tied in with the book's main lines of action or its main themes, Sir Leicester nevertheless becomes one of the more interesting characters. Change tends to be interesting, and Sir Leicester changes; at least, later in the story we see aspects of his character that had not been clearly visible earlier. But from the very beginning, he seems more knowable and more complicated (if less ideal or admirable) than his wife, and somewhat more interesting than she or her daughter. Sir Leicester's very defects (they are relatively harmless ones) help make him, if satirical, also real. His eventual physical and spiritual sufferings are far out of proportion to his faults.

In the end, what seemed to be an idle and insulated aristocrat turns out to be a far from *spiritually idle* human being: he opens himself to the reality of continuing sorrow, bears his bereavement nobly, actively befriends George Rouncewell, and even more actively honors the memory of his dead wife. He becomes an even more poignant and haunting figure than he might otherwise have been because we perceive him as inseparable from his estate at Chesney Wold. We see him that way because Dickens describes the decline and the new melancholy of that estate with some of the most moving descriptive prose ever penned in English literature.

CRITICAL ESSAYS

CHARACTERIZATION

Like Shakespeare, another imaginatively fertile and vivacious writer, Dickens created dozens of characters who continue to delight readers today. His ability to invent such living characters was aided by his experience as a newspaper reporter: the job forced him to observe people's looks, words, and manner very closely and then record these observations accurately.

Of course, the disposition was already there. Even in childhood, Dickens was fascinated with images – the eternal features of things and people – and his talent for creating comic and grotesque characters manifested itself quite early. Aside from the generous amount of adventure in most of his novels, what draws readers to them year after year, through all the changes of fad and fashion, is the vitality of the characters and the fun – or drama – they give rise to in dynamic episodes.

Worth noting is the fact that characters in fiction do not actually have to be lifelike, in the sense of being complex and highly individualized, in order to be successful and memorable. Talking animals aren't at all lifelike, yet more than a few have achieved status as compelling characters. The Fool in *King Lear* has relatively few lines, some of them rather obscure, yet few minor characters have become more memorable. Claggart, the villain in *Billy Budd*, is barely characterized at all, but he haunts us. What adds a character to the permanent repertoire of our minds is not dependent on "realism" or even on complete credibility, but solely on the magic vitality that an author is able to endow from the depths and riches of spontaneous creativity. Dickens possessed both the vitality and the skill to find the words that conveyed it.

Dickens is very much a satirist and a comic entertainer, and very little of a depth-hunting "psychologist" with literary talent. Twentieth-century "psychological" novelists (for example, Virginia Woolf, James Joyce, May Sinclair) go minutely into the details of their characters' inner lives. *Inwardness*, in its wide range of sensations, formed and half-formed thoughts and feelings, transient images, and quickly changing shades of mood, is offered in all its concreteness or particularity. This is a sort of "realism" – psychological realism – and its writers give us the sense that they are trying not only to be "real," to "tell it like it is" without tidying or censoring, but also *complete*, as if they were scientists or clinicians attempting to construct a complete as well as a thoroughly accurate report. Such a method, despite its validity and success – it has produced a vast body of work, some of it highly successful – tends to have certain limitations of which its enthusiasts often seem oddly unaware. A reader may learn an immense amount of information about what goes on deeply with Character X and still not gain any *distinct and satisfying impression* of Character X as a person who might be encountered next door or at the grocery. Ultimately, each of us is *a whole*, a *personality*, and each of us *projects* that organic wholeness, or personality, which is perceived by those around us and experienced as distinct and unique. Because we are what we are, each of us carries a certain "aura," creates a certain *presence*, or *impression*. This is the visible self, the social self – the one that's seen by others and interacts with them. Characterization through "free association," "stream of consciousness," or "reverie" easily neglects this important *image reality* and *social reality* of us. In all the things we do as *social* beings – that is, as onlookers and participants, from working and talking to simply observing each other in passing – what we experience is *presences, impressions* having unity and uniqueness and immediacy. Hence, in the context of interacting individuals, Dickens' "external" or impressionistic method of characterization is in a sense actually more realistic, more true to what we experience in real life, than the seemingly more complete and "scientific" method of beginning from deep inside and then staying there. In any event, it was the image, the impression, the distinct presence and dramatic or graphic feature or manner, and at the same time delighting in the variety of human personalities, he tended to pack his books with greatly varying characters; the sheer number of his characters would in itself prevent him from drawing much upon the space-consuming method of characterization through deep inwardness. It has to be said that his achievement is creating a very large number of "living" characters by no means suffers in comparison with the work of the "stream of consciousness" and other deeply psychological authors.

Main characters (principals) have to be made interesting if only because they are "around" so much of the time. They are also tied to the book's serious themes, so we have to be able to take such important characters seriously: they dare not be trivial, monotonously simple and unchanging, or unreal.

For most readers, neither John Jarndyce nor Esther Summerson is completely real. They are characterized in such a way that they have dignity and seriousness, and they play crucial parts in the working out of Dickens' important themes. Therefore, they invite comparison with individuals like those found in real life. But when we make that comparison—and we do so spontaneously, unconsciously, as we read—we discover that both characters seem too good to be true: unreal.

Lady Dedlock, fortunately, is not marred by such pristine purity. She is a much more interesting character, and she illustrates Dickens' method when he creates "serious" characters—major or minor—in whom we become interested. The successful formula is to keep the characters human—keep perfection away—but make them good enough and likable enough to be "personable." Such characters tend to ingratiate themselves with us. Then, by inventing circumstances of danger or suffering for them, Dickens can make sure that we remain interested in their fates. (Incidentally, readers in 1853 seem to have found portraits of exemplary goodness—especially of benevolence and moral purity—more engaging than we do today.)

One of Dickens' specialties is **caricature**—that is, artistic distortion (as by exaggeration) designed to produce amusement but not contempt or indignation. Throughout Dickens' novels, scores upon scores of the minor characters are caricatures. One of the most obvious examples in *Bleak House* is the unnamed "debilitated cousin" of Sir Leicester; the fellow mangles words and sentences right out of intelligibility. Snagsby, with his mechanical cough and predictable repetitions, is another; Phil Squod, of droll speech and odd movement, is yet another.

A character who is also a caricature "sticks out"—is eminently noticeable—and also usually arouses our comic sense. Thus a caricature is exactly the kind of thing that appealed strongly to Dickens' own imagination: a conspicuous (therefore, arresting) **image**, and one that elicits goodnatured **humor**.

Obviously, when Dickens created caricatures, he did what came most naturally to him as a writer, and so it isn't surprising that his caricatures are often more successful than his ordinary characters. These many triumphs in caricature illustrate again the point made above, that characters highly stylized (artistically shaped and simplified) may have at least as much ability to capture and hold us as the characters of reportorial realism.

THEME

Like every sizeable work of fiction, *Bleak House* is built around several themes (also called motifs) – that is, insights, concepts, attitudes, or simply explorations of certain aspects of human experience. A novel built very strongly around a clearly formulated and debatable or controversial theme is sometimes called a **thesis novel** (a "propaganda novel" is one type of thesis novel). *Bleak House* has a strong and obvious theme whose point may, in fact, be more debatable than Dickens realized; yet the book is not a thesis novel, or at least not a clear example of one. Foremost, *Bleak House* is a romance – affairs of the heart for Esther, Ada, and Caddy figure very prominently – and it is a murder mystery, as well.

In an artistically sound (well-constructed) book, all of the major and minor themes, or motifs, should be closely related and thus enhance the book's unity. The most obvious (yet not necessarily the ultimate) theme in *Bleak House* is that of the undeserved suffering created by the High Court of Chancery, in particular, and by venal, self-serving lawyers (like Tulkinghorn), in general. An example of a minor theme (also called a side theme) is Dickens' implied criticism of people who might be well intentioned but who neglect their homes and families in order to be (or try to be) charitable to distant people about whom they know little.

This novel, like many other works of Dickens, balances themes of social criticism with motifs dealing with the truths of **personal experience**. Esther Summerson, one of the principal characters, is relatively little affected by the deplorable workings of the Chancery Court. In the main, her story centers around her initiation into life – her discovery of her own identity, and the development of her emotional relationships with Lady Dedlock, John Jarndyce, Allan Woodcourt, and others. The book's "happy ending" (happy for Esther, Ada, Allan, Mr. Jarndyce, and some others) is a theme itself. The ending implies that although the evil of the world is formidable, happiness remains a possibility, perhaps even a likelihood, especially for those who are both pure of heart and responsibly persevering. Another implied theme is that romance is important and is not necessarily an illusion or merely a momentary thing.

Dickens' ultimate attack is not on the Chancery Court. The workings (or misworkings) of Chancery do, as Dickens makes perfectly clear, constitute a major evil; Dickens savagely condemns that particular institution. But a larger issue is involved. Chancery itself – in fact, the whole system of Law – is also a **symbol**. Similarly, the fog is a symbol of Chancery and also of all similar institutions and operations; in other words, both Chancery and the fog symbolize the "dead hand" of the past — of custom and tradition. The dead hand of the past is a hand that continues to kill in the present. The point has never been better made than by Edgar Johnson in *Charles Dickens: His Tragedy and Triumph* (1952), which remains the greatest of all biographies of Dickens: ". . . both law and fog are fundamentally symbols of all the ponderous and murky forces that suffocate the creative energies of mankind. They prefigure in darkness visible the entanglements of vested interests and institutions and archaic traditions protecting greed, fettering generous action, obstructing men's movements, and beclouding their vision."

Dickens' task is to write in such a way that the reader *feels* that some issue larger than that of corrupt lawyers and a local London court is at stake. That Dickens succeeds in making us feel (rather than merely reason out) the ultimate theme, the destructive heaviness of the dead hand, is proved by the fact that *Bleak House* is still a "living" book.

About one point here, readers need to be perfectly clear. Though progressive-minded in various ways, Dickens is no past-hating revolutionary or social leveller. In attacking the dead hand of the past, Dickens is by no means rejecting *all* of the past, *all* of the British or Western tradition. We have to remember that Dickens had plenty of traditional, or "conservative," bones in his body. He rejoiced in many aspects of tradition — that is, of the past living on (if at the same time modifying) into the present. He understood the necessity of legal codes and institutions, he supported established religion, he celebrated the British monarchy, he delighted in the British tradition of cheerful politeness and in many other "inherited" features of British (and Continental) civilization. What he despises and rejects in *Bleak House* is the *dross* of the past, the institutionalized selfishness and coldness that survive *within* the tradition.

TECHNIQUE AND STYLE

Bleak House was written about a century and a half ago. Prose style, like almost everything else, has changed. Naturally today's reader may find Dickens' manner rather unfamiliar and in some ways a bit difficult. In order to see *Bleak House* in the right perspective, it is necessary to pursue this point.

Many people today are no longer well-practiced readers. Television and film are the preferred pastimes, and what people do read is more likely to be journalism (or the captions under pictures) than the prose of a literary artist like Dickens. Dickens wrote for an audience that loved to read and was unafraid to tackle a work of serious literature. Such a receptive and well prepared, or at least cooperative, audience freed Dickens to pitch his writing at a level that satisfied his artistic conscience.

In other words, Dickens was not forced to use only a very limited vocabulary or to forego subtleties of tone and emphasis; nor did he feel obliged to keep all his sentences short and simply constructed when emotion or the complexity of an idea cried out for longer or more complicated ones. He also knew that his readers were responsive to *playfulness* in words and hence would not insist that he keep coming bluntly to the point and "get on with things"; and so he was free to play one of his favorite roles: the entertainer – here a verbal entertainer, as elsewhere a mimic or theatrical entertainer (Dickens was an active public reader, actor, and practical joker as well as an author). In *Bleak House*, Dickens turns a "classical allusion" into a joke – but only because his readers, far more literate than today's readers, would recognize the allusion and therefore appreciate the twist.

When we read Dickens (or any nineteenth-century writer), we need to remember this fortunate, productive relationship between the author and the reading public. Despite their strong streak of puritanism and the limitations inherent in their middle-class outlook, Dickens' readers, far from demanding that the author write down to their level, were generally eager to have a book that helped them up to a higher level. They wanted guidance on the issues of the times and they also wanted to "progress" personally by becoming more knowledgeable (about sundry matters) and more skilled in language. Nineteenth-century society considered skill in writing and reading necessary for anyone who aspired to be genteel – or even civilized. In a great many households and throughout the educational system, the promotion of these skills had the power of moral force. In short, a writer in Dickens' era had great respect for his audience and a strong rapport with it – an exciting situation to be in!

Even in casual conversation, the characters in *Bleak House* (except for those at or near the very bottom of the social ladder, like Jo) speak rather elaborately. Their grammar (unless Dickens is making fun of some idiosyncrasy of expression) is flawless; they command a sophisticated vocabulary and tend to favor the formal word or phrase; their sentences can become quite involved without becoming unclear. It may be hard for us to believe that people ever really spoke that way. But they did. Correctness, in language as in manners, was a central concern for the typical middle-class person. Correctness and relative formality of expression were part and parcel of a society that was both stratified into classes and strongly influenced by classical education.

Bleak House has two oddities of technique — that is, the manner in which the story is presented. First, throughout the novel, there is an alternation in the point of view from which the story is being told. Second, there is a corresponding alternation between present tense and past tense.

Sustained use of present-tense narration is so unusual that, as we read, we hardly know what to expect from moment to moment. Thus there is a sort of suspense in the method itself as well as in the plot. It forces us to be enjoyably alert — and we've already had to become quite alert in order to catch Dickens' persistent **verbal irony** — that is, his saying one thing but actually meaning something else. This combination of continual irony and present-tense narration gives the writing great intensity.

By far the larger part of the story is narrated in this way by the "omniscient author." But, surprisingly, Dickens switches every now and then to "Esther's Narrative," allowing Esther Summerson to do some of the telling. This alternation strikes many people as an awkward and highly artificial technique because the reader remains aware that "Esther's Narrative" is still really Dickens' narrative. In other words, the alternation causes the point of view to call attention to itself for no good reason. The simultaneous change from present to past tense makes the awkwardness all the more conspicuous.

On the other hand, even if they "come at a price," Esther's narratives are a welcome relief. Present-tense narration is (as noted above) vivid and intense — it is the closest that fiction can get to the intensity of drama, where action is unfolded in the present, as one watches. But for this very reason, relief is needed. In an immensely long work like *Bleak House*, intensity can become fatiguing.

With the switch to the lower intensity of past tense comes an equally welcome change of **tone**. Dickens' "omniscient author" narration is almost consistently mocking or satiric in tone. It is a brilliant achievement but it is still basically monochromatic, or one-toned. Esther's narratives provide the contrast. Her outlook is as fresh and innocent as Dickens' is suavely jaded, and she has as many tones as she has responses.

Within the omniscient author portion of the book, Dickens makes his presentation as entertaining as possible, going out of his way to create variety and liveliness. He keeps us awake and amused by varying his tempo and the lengths and structures of his sentences; he uses racy colloquialisms, creates original figures of speech, forceful repetitions and parallel constructions, staccato-like fragments, and other attention-getting techniques.

PLOT

Dickens' taste in plot seems to have been influenced by the eighteenth-century novelist Henry Fielding (*Joseph Andrews*, 1742; *Tom Jones*, 1749) than by anyone else. In any event, the typical Dickens plot, like the plots of Fielding, is complicated, loosely constructed, and highly dramatic in the incidents that make it up. The main plot is usually interwoven with a number of subplots that involve numerous incidents and cover a period of several, or many, years. Such multiplicity militates against the possibility of feeling the story's unity distinctly – that is, of holding all the incidents in our mind at once and feeling their connectedness. Plot looseness (looseness of construction) can mean various things. Some of the subplots may not be related to the main plot; one or more of the subplots may be more tightly developed or inherently more interesting than the main plot; creaky devices of highly improbable coincidence may be brought in to get the author out of a jam created by lack of advance planning; or the main plot itself may consist of several self-contained episodes rather than of a central, developing, unified action. The main plot of *Bleak House* – the story of Lady Dedlock's past unfolding in the present and developing into a new situation that involves the book's other heroine, Esther Summerson – though complicated is artistically controlled, and the subplots are kept subordinate and, for the most part, are woven smoothly into it.

Plot, in the sense of meaningfully related mental and physical actions, implies directed **movement** and **change**. It therefore possesses inherent energy, dynamism. Dickens, an energetic, ambitious, relatively extroverted artist, a born entertainer and lover of vivacity, could be expected to put much of his novelistic stock in plot. This disposition alone would also explain the fact that Dickens' books feature highly dramatic – sometimes melodramatic – sentences. Dickens loved histrionic, action-crammed theatre. He haunted London's theatres, wrote and acted in several plays himself, and loved to give dramatic readings. It isn't surprising that he allowed theatre itself to influence his fiction.

In the twentieth century, the deliberately "plotless" novel has had a certain vogue. A number of talented and not-so-talented writers (Virginia Woolf, among the former) decided that since life itself from hour to hour and day to day is seldom dramatic and (worse yet!) sometimes not even noticeably meaningful, truly lifelike (realistic) fiction could forego the luxury of plot. Taking its cue from such writers and their admiring critics, classroom teaching of literature has shown a tendency to think that only bumpkins insist on plot. The same indifference to, or contempt for plot has been shown by writers who proffer, and critics and teachers who want, a social-political (ideological) message more than anything else. Finally, as the stock of writers' and critics' psychological or psychiatric probing of characters has gone up, the value of plot has gone correspondingly down.

It may be worthwhile to note that meaningful action, whether physical or mental, does have a certain charm. In fact, at least outside the English classroom and the critical essay, it is common knowledge that of all the kinds of material that may be presented to us, meaningful action is the kind most likely to hold our interest and generate excitement. Whatever literary critics "in the know" may claim, the fact is that the human species has an insatiable thirst for directed action, whether physical as at Wimbledon or mental as in Elsinore. It is also a fact that virtually all of the stories and plays that have come to be regarded as classics, from the *Iliad* to *Kim*, have been "full of plot."

SETTING

Most of the action of *Bleak House* takes place in or near London, around 1850. The London street scenes are in the Holborn district (on the north bank of the Thames and very close to the river). The depictions of neighborhoods, streets, buildings, working conditions, lighting, weather, dress and deportment of persons, etc., are completely authentic. The fog remains the most famous fog in all literature. Dense, long-lasting blankets of it, yellowish or yellow-brown with pollutants, were common in the coal-burning London of Dickens' time—and later. The descriptions of the goings-on at the Chancery Court are equally authentic, although Dickens provides only those details that support his point.

The Dedlocks' country estate at Chesney Wold is about 150 miles from London, in Lincolnshire, a large agricultural county in east-central England.

St. Albans, where John Jarndyce's Bleak House stands, is a small town; in 1850, it would have been about twenty miles from the northern outskirts of London.

Esther Summerson was born at Windsor (site of Windsor Palace), about twenty miles straight west of London.

Fifteen miles farther west is the much larger city of Reading (pronounced "Redding"), where Esther went to school.

Richard Carstone attended school at Winchester (famous for its huge, ancient cathedral), some fifty miles south of Reading and close to the English Channel.

The new Bleak House that Mr. Jarndyce builds for Esther and Allan Woodcourt is in Yorkshire (England's largest county), north of Lincolnshire. This new house would be 175-200 miles northeast of London.

There are several rural scenes, as Dickens enjoys England's "green and pleasant land," yet the countryside fails to kindle his imagination the way the city does. Hating city smoke as much as anyone, Dickens nevertheless lapses into conventionality when he breathes the country air.

THE FOG

A literary work does not necessarily become depressing or morbid simply because some of its subjects are gloomy, painful, or even grisly. Shakespeare's *Macbeth* gives us scene after scene of dark atmospheres, crime, natural and supernatural evil, horror, and insanity, yet the play has remained immensely popular for four centuries. Everything depends not on the subject itself but on the writer's *treatment* of it, meaning **technique** (manner of presenting the story) and **prose style** (choices in word, phrase, and sentence).

Heavy, persistent fog is not something that tends to lift spirits and brighten faces. In a story, such a fog may even serve as a symbol of institutional oppression and human confusion and misery. The fog that Dickens creates for *Bleak House* serves him in exactly that way. And yet it is not, after all, a real-life fog, but a verbal description of the real-life thing. *How* that depiction is managed – in other words, "expression" – becomes the crucial point, the real issue.

If, by plunging us again and again into the London fog, Dickens is trying to depress us, he is on shaky ground: all of us tend to seek pleasure and avoid pain. If the writing – taken up with an open mind and given a fair trial – really depresses us, we are quite likely to stop reading and declare Dickens an impossible, unreadable author.

But if we examine our actual response to the densely foggy and otherwise "implacable November weather" Dickens describes, we will find it to be something different from sheer depression or enervation. Our response – the one Dickens wants us to have – is probably complex and ambivalent. True, Dickens sees the foggy mire of the London streets as a nuisance, an unpleasantness, a source of vexation and dispiritedness. But he also finds such an extreme condition *interesting*: because they are rare or unusual, extremes in almost anything tend to generate interest. The fog is striking, piquant; it even has something of the glamour of the mysterious. In short, Dickens is an artist who delights in imagination and who is in charge of his material as he imagines and writes things down – he is enjoying the fog he creates, and that enjoyment is inevitably conveyed to us as we read. In fact, part of what Dickens delights in as he puts the fog together word by word is his very ability to *describe so interestingly*. We, in turn, admire (if only unconsciously) Dickens' mastery of the craft of writing – and admiration is a far from unpleasant thing for us to experience.

There are even more obvious elements of the positive in Dickens' clear paragraphs about the fog. There are witticisms and jesting figures of speech, as in the idea of meeting up with a "Megalosaurus" or of the soot being like snowflakes "gone into mourning . . . for the death of the sun."

In sum, though Dickens certainly does make his fog symbolize muddles and miseries, and thus tie it in with his themes of social criticism, that isn't the whole story. In the final analysis, our experience as we read is an experience not of fog itself, but of "expression"—of the words that create the fog. We find the fog not so much depressing as interesting and admirable. It's a vivid creation, and the sentences and phrases that create it crackle with imagination, alertness, and energy.

SYMBOLISM

Themes or motifs are often presented through **symbols**—that is, images used in such a way as to suggest a meaning beyond the physical facts of the images themselves.

Two quite effective symbols in *Bleak House* are the fog and "the Roman" who points down from Mr. Tulkinghorn's ceiling and symbolizes the theme of retribution, of evil ultimately bringing ruin upon itself.

Skillfully handled, symbolism adds both impact and unity to a literary work—or, for that matter, to any piece of writing. It has the impact (also called "power") of the **concrete**, and it helps unify because it repeats in a different form the motifs that are being presented through plot and character portrayal.

Symbolism is commonly called a "device" or "technique," but these terms are somewhat misleading because they imply **conscious manipulation** by the author and also imply that effective symbolism is external and might be learned by anyone in a classroom or from an instruction manual on how to write. At its best, symbolism comes straight out of the individual writer's unconscious artistry: it is instinctive and individual and often a mark of genius.

Symbols are often used to **foreshadow** later events in a story. In turn, the "technique" of foreshadowing lends unity to the story because it prepares us by dealing with things that will be developed later on. The *Bleak House* fog is a complex symbol that foreshadows several motifs of importance. Richard Carstone, for example, gradually becomes "lost," unable to "see," in the mental and spiritual fog generated by the High Court of Chancery.

REVIEW QUESTIONS AND ESSAY TOPICS

(1) Is it in any way a disadvantage that various chapters of *Bleak House* are narrated by Esther Summerson?

(2) Does Dickens' present-tense narration prevent him from doing certain things that are generally desirable in fiction?

(3) What prevents Lady Dedlock from coming across as a "round" (fully developed, very lifelike) character?

(4) Build a case for the position that the minor characters in *Bleak House* are generally more interesting than such major figures as Esther, John Jarndyce, and Lady Dedlock.

(5) Is *Bleak House* more interesting for its "atmosphere" than for its characters?

(6) Does Dickens make George Rouncewell's treatment of his mother convincing?

(7) Does Dickens adequately motivate Tulkinghorn's obsessive pursuit of Lady Dedlock's secret?

(8) Is Esther Summerson one of Dickens' "idealized and sentimentalized" heroines? Discuss.

(9) At what point in the story does Sir Leicester Dedlock demonstrate a certain depth of character? What is the nature of the change? Is it credible?

(10) Is Harold Skimpole a caricature, or is he rather a figure who might be drawn from real life?

(11) What is Skimpole's concept of "generosity" and how is it different from the usual understanding of the term?

(12) What (if any) advantage does the story gain from the fact that Boythorn is a rejected suitor of Miss Barbary?

(13) Does the very minor character Rosa contribute anything of value to *Bleak House*?

(14) Does Dickens make an artistic mistake when he has old Krook die of "spontaneous combustion"?

(15) Is *Bleak House* a stronger (or more interesting) book for its inclusion of the character William Guppy?

(16) If *Bleak House* is designed to be mainly a critique of the law and its practitioners in Dickens' time, why does Dickens give much prominence to the story of a woman—Lady Dedlock—whose problems stem mainly from matters other than those of the law?

(17) The end of *Bleak House* is a very happy one. Does such an ending detract from Dickens' purpose of creating a powerful critique of the Chancery Court and other aspects of the law?

SELECTED BIBLIOGRAPHY

ALTICK, RICHARD D. *Victorian People and Ideas.* New York: W.W. Norton & Co., 1973.

CECIL, DAVID. "Charles Dickens," in *Victorian Novelists: Essays in Revaluation*. New York: Bobbs-Merrill Co., 1935 (Phoenix Books Edition; Chicago: University of Chicago Press, 1958).

CHESTERTON, G.K. *Charles Dickens: The Last of the Great Men.* New York: The Press of the Readers Club, 1942 (originally published as *Charles Dickens: A Critical Study*. Dodd Mead & Co., 1906).

CHEW, SAMUEL C. AND ALTICK, RICHARD D. *The Nineteenth Century and After.* New York: Appleton-Century-Crofts, 1948, 1967.

CLARK, WILLIAM ROSS, ED. *Discussion of Charles Dickens*. Boston: D.C. Heath & Co., 1961.

CRUIKSHANK, ROBERT JAMES. *Charles Dickens and Early Victorian England* (Vol. II of the "Measure of the Ages" Series). New York: Chanticleer Press, 1949.

DALZIEL, MARGARET. *Popular Fiction 100 Years Ago*. London: Cohen & West, 1957.

DUPEE, F.W., ED. *The Selected Letters of Charles Dickens*. New York: Farrar, Straus & Cudahy, Inc., 1960.

FORSTER, JOHN. *The Life of Charles Dickens*. 3 vols. Bigelow, Brown and Co., 1902.

GISSING, GEORGE. *The Immortal Dickens*. London: Cecil Palmer, 1925.

HAYWARD, ARTHUR L. *The Dickens Encyclopaedia*. New York: E.F. Dutton, 1924.

HOLDSWORTH, WILLIAM S. *Charles Dickens as a Legal Historian*. New Haven: Yale University Press, 1929.

HOUSE, HUMPHRY. *The Dickens World*. London: Oxford University Press, 1941, 1960.

JOHNSON, EDGAR. *Charles Dickens, His Tragedy and Triumph*. 2 vols. New York: Simon & Schuster, 1952.

KAPLAN, FRED. *Dickens: A Biography*. New York: William Morrow & Co., Inc., 1988.

LEACOCK, STEPHEN. *Charles Dickens: His Life and Work*. Garden City, N.Y.: Doubleday, Doran & Co., 1934.

LONG, RICHARD W. (photographs by Adam Woolfitt). "The England of Charles Dickens," in *National Geographic*, Vol. 145, No. 4 (April 1974), pp. 443-83.

ORWELL, GEORGE. "Charles Dickens," in *Dickens, Dali, and Others: Studies in Popular Culture*. New York: Reynal & Hitchcock, 1946.

PEARSON, HESKETH. *Dickens: His Character, Comedy, and Career*. New York: Harper & Brothers, 1949.

SANTAYANA, GEORGE. "Dickens," in *Essays in Literary Criticism*, ed. Irving Singer. New York: Charles Scribner's Sons, 1956.

THOMSON, PATRICIA. *The Victorian Heroine: A Changing Ideal, 1837–1873*. London: Oxford University Press, 1956.

WAGENKNECHT, EDWARD. *The Man Charles Dickens.* Boston: Houghton Mifflin, 1929.

YOUNG, G.M. *Victorian Essays*, ed. W.D. Handcock. London: Oxford University Press, 1962.

NOTES

NOTES

NOTES

NOTES

NOTES

NOTES

NOTES

David Copperfield

DAVID COPPERFIELD

NOTES

including
- *Life of the Author*
- *Brief Synopsis of the Novel*
- *List of Characters*
- *Summaries and Commentaries*
- *Selected Bibliography*

by
J. M. Lybyer
Washington University

INCORPORATED

LINCOLN, NEBRASKA   68501

Editor

Gary Carey, M.A.
University of Colorado

Consulting Editor

James L. Roberts, Ph.D.
Department of English
University of Nebraska

ISBN 0-8220-0364-3
© Copyright 1980
by
C. K. Hillegass
All Rights Reserved
Printed in U.S.A.

1992 Printing

Cliffs Notes, Inc.   Lincoln, Nebraska

CONTENTS

DAVID COPPERFIELD NOTES

LIFE OF THE AUTHOR

Charles Dickens (1812-70) was born in Portsmouth, on the south coast of England, but his family moved to Chatham while he was still very young. His most pleasant childhood years were spent in Chatham, and re-creations of these scenes appear in a disguised form in many of his novels. His father, John Dickens, was a minor clerk in the Navy Pay Office and, like Mr. Micawber in *David Copperfield*, was constantly in debt.

In 1822, John Dickens was transferred to London, but debts continued to pile up, and the family was forced to sell household items in order to pay some of the creditors. Young Charles made frequent trips to the pawnshop, but eventually his father was arrested and sent to debtors' prison, and at the age of twelve, he was sent to work in a blacking warehouse, where he pasted labels on bottles for six shillings a week. This experience was degrading for the young boy, and Dickens later wrote: "No words can express the secret agony of my soul. I felt my early hopes of growing up to be a learned and distinguished man, crushed in my breast." The situation is an exact parallel to David Copperfield's plight at the wine warehouse. Even after his father was released from prison and the family inherited some money, his mother wanted him to continue with his job.

Later, for two and a half years, Dickens attended school at Wellington House Academy, and then in 1827, at the age of fifteen, he began work as a clerk in a law office and taught himself shorthand so he could report court debates. At the same time, he was learning about life in London and frequently attended the theater, even taking acting lessons for a short time.

Meanwhile, Dickens had fallen in love with Maria Beadnell, a frivolous young girl whose father objected to his daughter's being courted by a young reporter from a lower middle-class background. Nothing came of this relationship, but it probably intensified

Dickens' efforts to make something of himself. In 1832, he began working as a parliamentary reporter for two London newspapers, and two years later, he joined a new paper, the *Morning Chronicle*, where he was asked to write a series of sketches about London life. This request resulted in *Sketches by Boz*, which appeared in installments that were later, in 1836, published in book form. Dickens' career as an author was begun. This led to an offer to write a monthly newspaper series about a group of humorous English clubmen. These pieces became *The Posthumous Papers of the Pickwick Club*, and after they appeared, Dickens' reputation as a writer was assured.

He now felt financially secure and quit his job as a parliamentary reporter to devote all his time to writing. He married Catherine Hogarth in April, 1836; however, the marriage was never a happy one and Dickens separated from his wife twenty years later.

His writing output increased, and a number of novels, including *Oliver Twist* and *Nicholas Nickleby*, were published—first in monthly installments and then as novels. By the 1840s, Dickens was the most popular writer in England. In 1849, he began one of his most important novels, *David Copperfield*. His friend John Forster proposed that he tell the story in the first person, and this suggestion proved to be a perfect method for Dickens to fictionalize the background of his early life. David Copperfield became the "favorite child" of its author and in it Dickens transcribed his own experiences, producing not only a fine novel, but a disguised autobiography as well.

But the novel is not pure biography; rather, it is Dickens' experiences made into fiction. In the novel, David escapes from the warehouse to a sympathetic aunt, and he marries Dora after the "timely" death of her father. This did not happen in real life, and it is almost as though Dickens were reconstructing parts of his childhood the way he wished it had been. In the novel, too, Dickens shows his contempt for his parents (in the guise of the Murdstones) for sending him to the blacking factory, and, at the same time, his devotion to them (the Micawber family) as lovable eccentrics. Dora Spenlow becomes both Maria Beadnell and, later, the simple-minded Catherine Hogarth, his real wife. The novel, thus, is both fantasy and fact.

Little needs to be said about the humor in the novel; it is simply to be enjoyed. The scene at the inn where the waiter eats David's dinner, the night of revelry when David becomes drunk and falls down the stairs, the preposterous Micawber boarding the ship with a telescope under his arm—all are near-slapstick pieces of good fun, and it is easy to understand the continuing popularity of the novel.

After *David Copperfield*, Dickens wrote novels that were bitter and caustic. *Bleak House* is a brooding satire on the law courts, while both *Hard Times* and *Little Dorrit* suffer from uncontrolled social outrage. The wildly humorous characters of Sam Weller, of *The Pickwick Papers*, and Mr. Micawber give way to dark, sinister figures, and although the later novels perhaps show more craftsmanship, most readers feel that the "magic" had worn off.

During the last years of his life, Dickens traveled in England and America, giving public readings from his works. The strain weakened his health, and he died in 1870 at the age of fifty-eight. At the time of his death, he was working on a novel, *The Mystery of Edwin Drood*, and though many writers have attempted to supply an ending, the book remains unfinished.

BRIEF SYNOPSIS OF THE NOVEL

The novel traces the life of David Copperfield from the time of his birth to his mature manhood, when he is married and familiar with the vicissitudes of life. His early years are enjoyable with his mother—who was widowed shortly before his birth—and with her servant, Peggotty. Life is happy for David until his mother decides to marry Mr. Murdstone; afterward, life becomes unbearable for David. He is soon sent to a miserable school where he becomes friendly with James Steerforth, a fellow student.

When David's mother dies, he is taken from school and put to work by Mr. Murdstone in a London warehouse. Although David enjoys the company of the impoverished Micawber family, with whom he boards, his other associates and the work are intolerable, so, without money or property, he runs away to his Aunt Betsey Trotwood in Dover. Despite a stern exterior, Aunt Betsey treats him well, adopting him and sending him to a good school. While at school, he boards with a Mr. Wickfield and his daughter Agnes. (Throughout the novel, David retains a fond, sisterly affection for Agnes.) After graduation, David works in the law office of Spenlow & Jorkins and soon falls in love with Mr. Spenlow's daughter, Dora.

About this time, Em'ly, the Peggottys' beloved niece, runs off to marry Steerforth, whom David had innocently introduced to her while she was engaged to Ham, a nephew of the Peggottys. The family is saddened by this development, but Mr. Peggotty sets out to find her and bring her back. David uses his spare time doing clerical and literary work to help Aunt Betsey, who now finds herself without financial resources. He marries Dora, only to find that he has a "child-wife" who knows nothing of housekeeping and cannot accept any responsibility.

Meanwhile, Uriah Heep, an "umble" clerk in Mr. Wickfield's employ, whom David dislikes, has deceitfully worked his way into a partnership, aided by Mr. Wickfield's weakness for wine. In addition, David also discovers that his old friend Mr. Micawber has gone to work for Heep. David has remained fond of the Micawbers, and it troubles him that his old friend is working for a scoundrel. Eventually, however, Micawber has a grand moment of glory when he exposes Heep as a fraud, helping to save Mr. Wickfield and restoring some of Aunt Betsey's finances.

David's wife, Dora, becomes ill and dies, and David is troubled until Em'ly, the Peggottys' niece, returns to her uncle. David has felt guilty for some time for having introduced Em'ly to Steerforth. After a reconciliation is accomplished, Em'ly, along with some of the Peggottys, and the Micawbers leave for Australia to begin new lives. Before they leave, David witnesses a dramatic shipwreck in which Steerforth is killed, as is Ham in attempting to rescue him. Still saddened by the loss of his wife and other events, David goes abroad for three years. It is only after he returns that he realizes that Agnes Wickfield has been his true love all along, and their happy marriage takes place at last.

LIST OF CHARACTERS

MAJOR CHARACTERS

David Copperfield

He is the central character in the novel and tells the story of his life from birth to adulthood. David is a sensitive youth who first suffers under the cruel Murdstones and then is sent away to work in a wine warehouse. David first marries Dora Spenlow, an empty-headed young girl; afterward, he realizes how incompatible they really are. When Dora dies, he marries Agnes Wickfield and by the novel's end, he has matured into a successful writer and adult.

Clara Copperfield

David's mother. She is an attractive, tender person, but impractical and emotional and easily taken in by Mr. Murdstone, who marries her because he is interested in her annuity.

Clara Peggotty

The Copperfields' housekeeper, who also acts as David's nurse. She is a woman of intense loyalty and is David's only companion after his mother's death. Peggotty marries Barkis, the cart-driver, and continues throughout the novel to be David's friend.

Edward Murdstone

David's stepfather. A dark, handsome man who cruelly beats David and slowly drives David's mother to an early death.

Jane Murdstone

Mr. Murdstone's sister. She runs the Copperfield household and incessantly harasses David.

Mr. Barkis

The driver of the horse-cart that travels between Yarmouth and David's home. He is a shy, quiet man who uses David as a messenger in his courtship of Peggotty.

Mr. Chillip

The doctor who delivers David. He is an exceedingly mild-mannered, frightened little man who is especially afraid of David's aunt, Betsey Trotwood.

Daniel Peggotty

Clara Peggotty's brother and a Yarmouth fisherman. He is a warm-hearted man whose house is a refuge for anyone who needs help.

Ham Peggotty

Mr. Peggotty's orphaned nephew. Ham, like his uncle, is a considerate, kindly person. He is in love with Em'ly and waits patiently for her after she runs away. He finally dies in an attempt to save Steerforth, Emily's seducer.

Little Em'ly

Mr. Peggotty's orphaned niece. She is David's childhood sweetheart, but becomes engaged to Ham and later runs away with Steerforth. She is a quiet, compassionate young girl who wants to become a "lady," a desire that leads to unhappiness.

Mrs. Gummidge

The widow of Mr. Peggotty's partner. She constantly complains about her hardships, but when Em'ly runs away, she changes into a helpful, inspiring confidante of Mr. Peggotty.

Charles Mell

A schoolmaster at the Salem House boarding school. A gentle friend and teacher of David.

Mr. Creakle

The sadistic headmaster of the Salem House School. He is a fiery-faced man who enjoys flogging the boys with a cane. He later becomes a prison magistrate.

Mr. Tungay

The assistant and cruel companion of Mr. Creakle. He has a wooden leg and repeats everything that Creakle says.

James Steerforth

A spoiled young man whom David admires. He has a surface polish and the good manners that deceive people who do not know him. His true selfishness is shown when he deserts Em'ly, leaving her with his servant, Littimer. He is killed in a storm off Yarmouth along with Ham, who tries to save him.

Tommy Traddles

David's friend. Of all the boys at the Salem House School, Traddles receives the most punishment. He is a good-natured, loyal friend to both David and Mr. Micawber. Traddles is persistent, and this quality helps him rise from his humble background to become a judge.

Wilkins Micawber

A constantly impoverished, but always optimistic, gentleman who boards David during his stay in London. He is a broad comic character with a passion for writing flowery letters and uttering grandiloquent speeches. He finally accompanies Mr. Peggotty to Australia, where he becomes a successful magistrate.

Emma Micawber

Mr. Micawber's long-suffering wife. She stands by her husband through all his hardships, even joining him in debtors' prison.

Betsey Trotwood

David's great-aunt. She is unhappy that David was born a boy instead of a girl, but later she acts as his guardian and provider during his early years of schooling. Her formal, often brisk, nature is deceiving; she is basically a sympathetic person.

Richard Babley (Mr. Dick)

A lovable simpleton cared for by Betsey Trotwood. He is engaged in writing a long manuscript that he uses to paper a huge kite. Mr. Dick is devoted to David's aunt and becomes a great friend of David's.

Uriah Heep

A repulsive, scheming young man who attempts to marry Agnes Wickfield and gain control of her father's law practice. He pretends to be humble and uses this as a means to gain vindictive revenge on people he believes have snubbed him. He is exposed by Mr. Micawber and ends up in prison.

Mr. Wickfield

A solicitor and the widowed father of Agnes Wickfield. He is a proud man, but his excessive drinking allows Uriah Heep to take advantage of him.

Agnes Wickfield

The daughter of Mr. Wickfield; David's second wife. She is a dutiful companion and housekeeper to her father and a sisterly friend to David while he stays at the Wickfield house. She proves to be a perfect wife and an inspiration to David in his writing.

Dr. Strong

The headmaster of the school which David attends in Canterbury. He is a scholarly, trusting gentleman who is married to a girl much younger than himself. Although his wife is accused of infidelity, he maintains his faith in her.

Annie Strong

Dr. Strong's youthful wife. She is a beautiful, affectionate girl whose family exploits her husband.

Jack Maldon

Annie Strong's cousin. He is a lazy, vain young man who tries to compromise Mrs. Strong, but is repulsed.

Mrs. Markleham

Annie Strong's mother. A forceful, selfish woman, she always takes Jack Maldon's part and unwittingly helps cause the misunderstanding between her daughter and Dr. Strong.

Mrs. Steerforth

James Steerforth's mother. A possessive woman who has spoiled her son by over-indulgence and a smothering affection; she lapses into a semi-invalid state when she hears of her son's death.

Rosa Dartle

Mrs. Steerforth's companion. She is a neurotic, quick-tempered young woman with a consuming love for Steerforth.

Littimer

Steerforth's personal manservant. He is a formal, haughty person who has an air of respectability, yet he aids Steerforth in his seduction of Em'ly. He is trapped by Miss Mowcher and is sent to Creakle's prison.

Miss Mowcher

A middle-aged dwarf who is a hairdresser for wealthy families. She is upset when she realizes that she was duped into helping Steerforth run off with Em'ly, and is instrumental in the capture of Littimer, who aided Steerforth.

Martha Endell

Em'ly's friend. She is a suffering woman who is forced to go to London to hide her shame. Martha redeems herself by saving Em'ly from a similar life and finds happiness in her own life after she arrives in Australia.

Mr. Spenlow

A proctor and partner in a law firm in Doctor's Commons. He is a pompous, aristocratic lawyer who objects to David's plans to marry his daughter.

Dora Spenlow

David's first wife. She is an impractical, empty-headed girl who cannot cook or manage a household. Although she is a poor selection as a wife, David is so taken by her childlike beauty that he overlooks her faults and marries her. Their marriage is a comedy of mismanagement until Dora dies, leaving David free to marry the domestically perfect Agnes.

MINOR CHARACTERS

Mr. Omer

The Yarmouth undertaker and dealer in funeral clothes.

Minnie Omer

Mr. Omer's daughter and Em'ly's working companion.

Joram

Minnie Omer's sweetheart and eventually her husband, and finally, Mr. Omer's business partner.

Mr. Quinion

A business associate of Mr. Murdstone.

Janet

Betsey Trotwood's housekeeper. She assists Miss Trotwood in chasing donkey riders off the lawn.

Mr. Jorkins

Mr. Spenlow's seldom-seen partner. He is reputed to be a strict businessman, but he is really a mild-mannered individual whose name is used to frighten new employees.

Julia Mills

Dora's girl friend. She is a romantic person who advises David in his courtship with Dora.

Mrs. Crupp

David's landlady. She is a lazy woman who drinks David's brandy and feuds with Aunt Betsey.

Sophy Crewler

Traddles' sweetheart. A patient girl from a large family, she marries Traddles and assists him in his work as a lawyer.

SUMMARIES AND COMMENTARIES

CHAPTERS 1-2

Summary

David was born in the "Rookery," in Blunderstone, Suffolk, England, on a Friday just as the clock began to strike midnight. This was thought to be an unlucky omen by some women of the neighborhood and by the nurse who attended his birth. A few hours before David's birth, however, Mrs. Copperfield is unexpectedly visited by Miss Betsey Trotwood, an aunt of David's father whom Mrs. Copperfield has never met. Miss Trotwood, "the principal magnate of our family," is a domineering woman who immediately takes charge of the household and insists that the expected child will be a girl; she declares that the new baby *girl* will be named Betsey Trotwood Copperfield. "There must be no mistakes in life with *this* Betsey Trotwood," she says. "I must make that *my* care."

Already agitated by the impending birth of this new baby, and by the death of David's father six months before, Mrs. Copperfield is further troubled by the abrupt appearance and manner of Miss Trotwood. She becomes ill with labor pains, and Ham, the nephew of the servant, Peggotty, is sent to get the doctor, Mr. Chillip. The mild-mannered Chillip is astonished, as is everyone else, by the brusqueness of Miss Trotwood. Later, when he tells her the baby is a *boy*, she silently but swiftly puts on her bonnet, walks out of the house, and vanishes "like a discontented fairy."

In Chapter 2, David recalls his home and its vast and mysterious passageways, the churchyard where his father is buried, Sundays in church, and his early life with his youthful, pretty mother and the kindly, capable Peggotty.

One night, after David learned to read, he is reading a story to Peggotty, and he asks, "if you marry a person, and the person dies, why then you may marry another person, mayn't you?" Almost immediately afterward, his mother enters the house with a bearded man whom David resents at once. After the stranger's departure, David hears an argument between his mother and Peggotty about the man. Peggotty insists that the man, Mr. Murdstone, is not an acceptable suitor.

About two months later, Peggotty invites David to spend a fortnight with her at her brother's place at Yarmouth. David is eager to go, but he asks what his mother will say. "She can't live by herself, you know," he insists. Young as he is, he does not realize that he is being sent away deliberately. His mother has a tearful farewell with him. As David and Peggotty drive off in a cart, David looks back. He sees Mr. Murdstone come up to his mother and apparently scold her for being so emotional.

Commentary

The first chapter is typical of the Victorian novelistic style, especially its long sentences and frequent digressions. The second paragraph is a long single sentence containing eighty-nine words (many sentences are longer). This chapter, and indeed the entire novel, frequently wanders from the main story line. The fourth paragraph of the book is a long digression on David's being born with a caul (a membrane that covers the head of a new-born child and was thought to bring good luck) and on his family's attempt to dispose of it profitably. After a lengthy detour, David pulls himself back to his narrative with an admonition to himself not to "meander." These stylistic features were the result of the publishing practices prevalant at Dickens' time. Books were first published serially in magazines and writers were paid by the word; hence, they included as many words as possible, even if the story became rambling and excessively wordy.

The first chapter also illustrates Dickens' handling of characterization. Dickens is often criticized for creating caricatures rather than characters in his works, of producing people who are one-dimensional and unreal. Both Miss Trotwood and the doctor are described extravagantly, but it must be remembered that this burlesque produces a humorous effect, and most readers of the time accepted the "overdone" quality, preferring entertainment to realism. David's mother and the servant girl, Peggotty, are described with greater restraint.

The character of Mr. Murdstone is strongly caught in Chapter 2. His name itself, compounded of "murder" and "stone," is typical of Dickens' device of creating an artificial name to reflect a person's character. As this chapter ends, the lines are drawn—David and Peggotty are hostile to Mr. Murdstone; Mrs. Copperfield, on the other hand, flattered and naive, is grateful for his attentions.

Summary

Ham, Peggotty's nephew who was present at David's birth, is waiting for them at a Yarmouth public-house and leads them to the hulk of an old ship drawn up on land; it has been renovated into a sort of "real home" and that is where the Peggotty family lives. Although everything has a strong odor of fish, the boat is clean, and David's room (in the stern of the barge) is the "most desirable bedroom ever seen."

David is introduced to Mr. Peggotty, a bachelor brother who is the head of the house. David is puzzled about the relationship of Ham and of Em'ly (a young girl who lives there and is a little younger than David); he learns from Peggotty that they are both orphan children of relatives who died at sea.

The next morning before breakfast, David and Em'ly play on the beach and Em'ly tells him about her fear of the sea because it has taken so many of her relatives. She runs out on a timber jutting from the side of the pier where the water is deepest and David becomes alarmed that she will fall in. He comments much later that he has never forgotten this episode, and he wonders if it might not have been better if she had drowned while she was young and innocent. They return from the beach with shells that they have collected, and they exchange an innocent kiss before going to eat. David feels certain that he is in love.

The holiday ends, and David and Peggotty return home by the same carrier's cart. David is sad at having to leave Yarmouth, but he looks forward to seeing his mother once more. He is not met by his mother, however; he is met by a strange servant, and for a minute David is afraid something has happened to his mother. Peggotty takes David to the kitchen and admits that she should have told him earlier what has happened—David's mother has remarried; David has a new "Pa." He is then led into the parlor to meet Mr. Murdstone.

In Chapter 4, Dickens focuses on David's unhappiness. David thinks of little Em'ly and cries himself to sleep. In the morning, Peggotty and David's mother come to his room, and his mother accuses Peggotty of prejudicing the boy against her and her new husband. Mr. Murdstone appears and cautions his wife about the need for "firmness" in handling David. He sends both women from the room, but not before scolding Peggotty for addressing her mistress by her *former* name. "She has taken *my* name," he says, "Will you remember that?" Mr. Murdstone says further that unless David's manner improves he will be whipped with a strap.

After dinner, a coach arrives; Miss Murdstone, the sister of David's stepfather, has come to stay with the family. She is as hard and as austere a person as her brother, and she promptly informs everyone that *she* doesn't like *boys*. She observes that David *obviously* needs training with his manners, then immediately pre-empts the household keys and assumes all authority for running the household affairs. By degrees, she and her brother begin to intimidate David's mother until she becomes virtually an outsider in her own home.

One morning when David reports for his lessons, Mr. Murdstone is already there—with a cane, which he "poised and switched in the air." When the lesson goes badly, David is paraded upstairs, and his stepfather beats him, but not before David is able to literally bite the hand that feeds him (and in this case, restrains him). David is confined to his room for five days like a prisoner, and he is allowed out only for morning exercises and evening prayers. On the fifth day, Peggotty steals up to the room and speaks to David through the keyhole, informing him that tomorrow he is to be sent to a school near London.

The next morning David is sent away to school in the familiar horse-drawn cart. His grieving mother first implores him to "pray to be better," and then she blurts out, "I forgive you, my dear boy. God bless you!"

Commentary

The stay at Peggotty's home is one of the most idyllic experiences in David's life. The simple warmth of the poor family is in contrast to the coldness that David will encounter in his own home. Mr Peggotty is a friendly man who sums himself up with his introductory phrase to David: "You'll find us rough, sir, but you'll find us ready." He is contrasted with Mrs. Gummidge, who lives there, and her often-repeated complaint: "I am a lone lorn creetur' and everythink goes contrairy with me." Dickens' characters invariably have one pet saying that, along with their names, indicates their personalities. Mrs. Gummidge later shows another side of her personality.

Note in Chapter 3 that Dickens foreshadows coming events when he says that it might have been "better for little Em'ly to have had the waters close above her head that morning. . . ." This effect is overly melodramatic perhaps, but it is a common technique of Victorian novelists to sustain reader interest over the course of a long narrative.

CHAPTERS 5-6

Summary

Before the cart goes half a mile it stops, and Peggotty appears from behind a hedgerow. Without saying a word, she hugs David and gives him some cakes to eat and a purse containing money, the coins wrapped in a note in his mother's handwriting, saying, "For Davy. With my love."

Mr. Barkis, the cart driver (who is as slow moving as the horse he drives), consoles David, and during the ride David offers him one of the cakes which Barkis eats "at one gulp exactly like an elephant." Mr. Barkis shyly inquires about Peggotty's cooking and asks if she has any "sweethearts." When David replies that she does not, the cart driver asks David to inform Peggotty that "Barkis is willin' "—a message David does not understand. (Later, David includes this unusual marriage proposal from Barkis in a letter to Peggotty.)

David sleeps in the cart until they reach Yarmouth, the first stage on his journey to London. Mr. Barkis drops David at an inn where eating arrangements have been made for him under the name of "Murdstone." He is served dinner, but the waiter tells him frightening stories about the food and then proceeds to eat most of David's meal himself.

The trip continues all night, but David is unable to sleep in the crowded coach. In the morning they reach London, "fuller of wonders and wickedness than all the cities of the earth," but no one is there to meet him. David, who is only "between eight and nine" years old, worries if he has been deliberately deserted. But some time later, a gaunt and shabby young man (Mr. Mell), one of the school's masters, calls for him. After David buys something to eat, they go to an alms-house (a poor house) where the schoolmaster visits his poverty-stricken mother.

This short visit over, they complete the journey to Salem House, David's new school. It is a dilapidated old structure with "ink splashed about it" and a general odor of decay. David is admitted by a brutish man with a wooden leg; then he learns that he has been sent to school early as a punishment because the other boys are home for the holidays. He reads the names of the students carved on an old door in the schoolyard and speculates on what they will be like.

A month passes before David is introduced to the sadistic Mr. Creakle, a former hop-dealer and now the proprietor of Salem House. He is a balding man who can only whisper when he speaks and is usually accompanied by the man with the wooden leg, acting "with his strong voice, as Mr. Creakle's interpreter to the boys." Mr. Creakle pinches David's ear, calls him the "young gentleman whose teeth are to be filed" (because of a misunderstanding, he believes that David bites other people), and informs David that he has "the happiness of knowing" David's stepfather.

Mr. Sharp, another schoolmaster and superior to Mr. Mell, returns the next morning, along with Tommy Traddles, a boy whose name David had read carved on the playground door. David is made fun of by the other boys as they arrive, but it is not as bad as he had expected, due largely to Traddles' help. David meets J. Steerforth, one of the senior boys and the acknowledged student leader, who states that David's punishment is a "jolly shame." Steerforth and David are in the same dormitory, and they become friends, primarily because David allows Steerforth to keep his money for him. Steerforth buys some wine and biscuits for them out of the money, and they dine on them as a treat in the evening. The other boys attend the "royal spread," and David enjoys talking about the school with them.

Commentary

David's naiveté at the inn, in Chapter 5, is the first of many similar experiences which he will encounter in the world outside of Blunderstone Rookery. He becomes the butt of jokes both during the journey and at the school. He is homesick for Peggotty and his mother, and on his trip from Yarmouth, he observes children in the streets and wonders "whether their fathers were alive, and whether they were happy at home." David himself is unhappy and he looks forward to the opening of school with apprehension.

In Chapter 6, we are concerned with Steerforth's leadership—a quality implied in his name; his suave manner so impresses the naive David that he is unable to see that Steerforth is using David's money to feed the entire "bedroom." A foreshadowing of future action in this chapter occurs when Steerforth asks David if he has a sister, stating that if David has one, he would like to know her. Although David has no sister, we think of little Em'ly, who is very much like David, and we should remember that Steerforth has complimented David on the very qualities that he and Em'ly share.

CHAPTERS 7-8

Summary

Mr. Creakle opens school the next day by switching a good number of the boys, including David, with a cane; "Half the establishment was writhing and crying before the day's work began," Dickens comments. The beatings are David's most vivid recollection of the school, along with the abuse suffered by poor Traddles who was "caned every day that half-year. . . ."

The classes themselves are conducted within an atmosphere of noise and "sheer cruelty" in which boys are "too much troubled and knocked about to learn." One day the usually gentle Mr. Mell (to whom David is sympathetic) is conducting class and calls for silence in the room, particularly from Steerforth.

Steerforth begins to insult the schoolmaster, calling him a "beggar" and encouraging the other students to join the abuse. Mr. Creakle enters the room and takes Steerforth's side, adding further insult to the poor teacher. Steerforth tells everyone that Mr. Mell's mother is boarded in an alms-house (information which David had innocently told his friend). After further harassment, Mr. Creakle fires the schoolmaster on the spot.

One day, Mr. Peggotty and Ham visit David, bringing him an assortment of seafood and information about the health of the Peggotty household. David asks about little Em'ly, whom Mr. Peggotty describes as "getting to be a woman." Steerforth appears, and Mr. Peggotty and Ham invite him to visit them if he should ever come to Yarmouth.

The half-year passes, with summer days changing to frosty fall mornings, and David looks forward to the holidays when he can return home. Finally school is out, and David begins the long coach trip home to see his mother.

David spends the first night of his return journey at an inn in Yarmouth, where Mr. Barkis calls for him the next morning in his carrier. David tells the driver that he sent Peggotty the message that was requested, but Mr. Barkis replies that "nothing come of it." He asks David to repeat the message to her and to say that he is "a-waiting for an answer." David still does not realize that this is a marriage proposal.

When David arrives home, he finds his mother in the parlor. He is surprised to find her holding an infant, which she introduces as his new brother.

The Murdstones being out on a visit, Peggotty, David, and his mother have supper together and spend a happy evening. David relates Barkis's message again and learns its meaning for the first time.

David's mother implores Peggotty to stay with her, and Peggotty vows that she will. David notices his mother's failing health—"her hand . . . so thin and white"—and her changed manner, "anxious and fluttered." But the familiar scene lulls away his anxiety, and he launches into stories about all that has happened.

The Murdstones return late that evening, and in the morning David apologizes to his stepfather for having been so disrespectful as to bite his hand during their last meeting. Later, however, David is set upon by Miss Murdstone for picking up his baby brother, and his mother is reprimanded for comparing the appearance of her two boys. David feels that he makes everyone, even his mother, uncomfortable with his presence, so he begins spending his evenings with Peggotty in the kitchen. However, he is told sternly "not to associate with servants" and not to retreat to his room during the day. In this way the holidays "lagged away," and David is not sorry when it is time to leave again for school. He will never see his mother again.

Commentary

Chapter 7 further delineates the character of Steerforth, whom David admires, but who, in reality, is a rogue who uses other people for his own ends. David does not tell him about Em'ly, being "too much afraid of his laughing at me"; yet they will meet and Steerforth will bring about her destruction. Steerforth's superficial, polished, and handsome appearance are weapons which he uses on people. Ham and Mr. Peggotty, like David, believe that he is a cultured gentleman. The unlucky Traddles, in all his misfortune, proves to be the most humane of all the boys.

The wretchedness of the school headed by the cruel Mr. Creakle is Dickens' protest against many schools of that period. Dickens attended Wellington Academy in North London, and this is probably a disguised account of his own schooling.

In Chapter 8, the main emphasis is on the fact that David is deeply torn between his love for his mother and the desire to be near her, and his terrible dislike for the Murdstones. The Murdstones completely dominate David's mother and have such control over her that she ends up defending the Murdstones in an argument with Peggotty. David's realization that the gulf between him and his mother cannot be bridged under these conditions is a stage in his slowly developing maturity.

CHAPTERS 9-10

Summary

David's tenth birthday falls on a foggy school day during March, and he is called into Mr. Creakle's parlour, happily anticipating a basket from Peggotty. Instead he is told by the proprietor's wife that his mother has died. "If ever child were stricken with sincere grief, I was," says David, as he prepares to return home by night-coach the next afternoon, not imagining that he is "never to return" to Salem House.

David is met in Yarmouth by Mr. Omer who, along with his three daughters, makes a living preparing funeral arrangements. David is fitted for a funeral suit, and over tea he learns from the funeral arranger that his infant brother has also died and "is in his mother's arms."

Peggotty meets David at the door and ushers him into a silent house, where even the Murdstones don't speak to one another. Miss Murdstone sits imperturbably at her desk each day, writing; Mr. Murdstone alternately sits and paces silently. A day or two before the funeral, Peggotty takes David to his mother's room to see her laid out.

After the funeral, Miss Murdstone gives Peggotty a month's notice and hints that David will not be returning to school. David's presence in the house is almost ignored by the Murdstones, and once more he is able to visit in the kitchen with Peggotty. She tells him that she will return to Yarmouth to live, and that perhaps (the Murdstones approving), David can come and stay with her for a short time. Permission is given by Miss Murdstone, and at the end of the month, Barkis calls to take them on a journey.

After a bumpy ride, during which Barkis quizzes Peggotty about her "situation," they arrive in Yarmouth and are welcomed by Ham and Mr. Peggotty. On the way, Peggotty tells David that she intends to marry Barkis unless "my Davy . . . [is] . . . anyways against it." David says that he is happy for her.

The household is much the same as David remembers, although little Em'ly has grown more beautiful and has become the family favorite. Mr. Peggotty inquires about Steerforth, and David launches into a long description of Steerforth's noble character while little Em'ly listens intently. David prays that evening that he "might grow up to marry little Em'ly."

Each evening Barkis courts Peggotty by calling at the house with a gift and sits silently in the parlour while Peggotty sews. One day, just before the end of his visit, David, little Em'ly, Peggotty, and Mr. Barkis take a holiday trip together. Mr. Barkis stops the coach at a church, and he and Peggotty go inside. Alone with Em'ly, David professes his love for her, and Em'ly allows him to kiss her. When the couple returns from the church, David learns that Mr. Barkis and Peggotty have just been married.

David returns to the Murdstones and is neglected again. Most of his days are spent reading or daydreaming, with an occasional visit to Mr. Chillip, the family doctor who presided at David's birth. Peggotty comes once a week to see David, and on one trip, she indicates that Mr. Barkis is "something of a miser."

One day, Mr. Murdstone tells David that educating him serves no purpose; what David needs is a fight with the world—and "the sooner . . . the better." Mr. Quinion, the manager of Murdstone and Grinby, wine merchants, has been summoned to escort David to London, where he will work to provide his "eating, drinking, and pocket-money." David realizes that the Murdstones simply want to get rid of him.

Commentary

The sentimentality of Chapter 9 is partially balanced by the realistic psychological behavior of David, who, finding that he is the center of attention by his schoolmates on that last day, makes the most of it and receives a "kind of satisfaction" which makes him feel very "distinguished." This is parallelled by the attitude of Mr. Omer's daughter and her boyfriend, who, although surrounded by a coffin, mourning clothes, etc., continue their courtship, oblivious of the surroundings. Life continues, Dickens seems to say in this chapter; people seek enjoyment even in the face of unhappiness.

In Chapter 10, David's association with the Peggotty household is strengthened, suggesting a continuing relationship. His glowing account of the virtues of Steerforth suggests that he too will be heard of again, and little Em'ly's wide-eyed interest in David's eulogy hints at future developments.

The description of David's life after his return to the Murdstones is one of Dickens' classic themes—*the cruel neglect of children*—worse, in his own view, than physical abuse. "What would I have given to have been sent to the hardest school that ever was kept!" says David.

CHAPTERS 11-12

Summary

Murdstone and Grinby's warehouse is on a wharf; the entire building is overrun with rats and "discoloured with the dirt and smoke of a hundred years." David's job, along with three or four other boys his age, is to wash bottles and paste on new labels. David is introduced to Mr. Micawber, with whom he is to live, and then he is put to work. At eight o'clock, Mr. Micawber returns to take David to his lodgings, where the young lad is introduced to Mrs. Micawber and her small children.

David learns that the family has been forced to take in a lodger because of Mr. Micawber's debts, and later David notices that creditors appear at the house at all hours of the day. However, Mr.

Micawber, with his implicit faith that "something will turn up," seems unperturbed by their demands for money.

David offers to help the family with the loan of his wages, but instead, Mrs. Micawber asks him to pawn household goods for them so that the family can buy food. This suffices for awhile, but at last Mr. Micawber is arrested and taken to debtors' prison, where his family soon joins him; here David observes that "they live more comfortably . . . than they had lived for a long while . . . ." (English jails at that time allowed family members to live with the imprisoned debtor.)

David rents a small room near the prison and continues his solitary existence. The work at Murdstone and Grinby's warehouse is degrading, and the other boys employed there are a lowly group of urchins.

Mr. Micawber holds a dinner party at the prison in celebration of his impending release, and Mrs. Micawber vows to David that she "will never desert Mr. Micawber" no matter how difficult things become. Upon his release, the Micawbers decide to move to Plymouth, where Mr. Micawber can "exert his talents in the country." This influences David to end his "weary days at Murdstone and Grinby's" and run away to Miss Betsey Trotwood, his only relation and a person who he thinks might be sympathetic to his plight.

David writes Peggotty for Miss Betsey's address and the loan of a half-guinea for travelling expenses. When this arrives, he hires a young man with a cart to transport his trunk to the coach office, but the stranger steals his half-guinea and rides off with the trunk. David is alone in London without luggage or funds.

Commentary

Dickens' own childhood forms a good deal of the background of Chapter 11, and Mr. Micawber is a brilliant caricature of Dickens' father. The degradation that David feels at Murdstone and Grinby's is an exact account of the author's feelings about his early life. At the age of nine, Dickens' father, along with the rest of his family, was sent to debtors' prison and Charles became an apprentice in a blacking factory, pasting labels on bottles. His parents appeared to show little concern for Charles' situation, especially the boy's education. Although the Micawbers are treated humorously in the novel, Dickens never forgave his own parents and always thought that his upbringing was no better than an orphan's.

Chapter 12 develops the characters of the Micawbers, who were introduced in the previous chapter as David's landlords. The mutual good feeling between David and the family suggests that their relationship will ripen into deep friendship.

In addition, David's escape from drudgery leads him into deeper troubles as he sets out for Miss Betsey's. This is an example of Dickens' protest against the exposure of children to hardships, a protest that is found in so much of his writing.

CHAPTERS 13-14

Summary

Determined to reach Miss Betsey's home in Dover, David sets out on foot. He passes a small second-hand clothing store, sells his waistcoat for a small sum, and then spends the night in a haystack near Salem House School.

David, "a dusty, sunburnt, half-clothed figure," arrives in Dover after six days of traveling and inquires about his aunt. After several unsuccessful inquiries, he is directed to Miss Trotwood's cottage. Miss Trotwood, seeing the ragged urchin in her garden, sternly bids him, "Go away! Go along! No boys here!" But when David tells her who he is and what an unhappy life he has led since his mother's death, she takes charge of him with vigor, but it should be added, with abruptness.

Janet, the Trotwood housekeeper, is directed to prepare a bath for David; in the meantime, his aunt feeds him some broth. After David naps, he is fed a large supper while Miss Trotwood comments on the folly of marriage. The conversation is interrupted with her cry, "Janet! Donkeys!" Suddenly Miss Trotwood and the housekeeper rush outside to chase the donkey-riders off the lawn. This is a frequent occurrence at the cottage.

The household consists of Miss Trotwood, the housekeeper, and Mr. Dick, a congenial simpleton whom Miss Trotwood has befriended. They are all kindly people, and David feels fortunate to be there.

At breakfast the next morning, Miss Trotwood tells David that she has written to his stepfather. David implores her not to send him back, but she is noncommittal in her reply.

David visits with Mr. Dick (actually, his name is Mr. Richard Babley, but he detests the name), who is writing a long "Memorial" to the Lord Chancellor. When a part of the manuscript is finished, Mr. Dick uses it to paper a huge kite. In this way Mr. Dick circulates his "facts a long way." David thinks him quite mad, but a harmless, friendly fellow nonetheless.

A reply to Miss Trotwood's letter arrives, stating that the Murdstones are coming to speak to her about David. David is terrified at the prospect of this visit. When the Murdstones arrive the next day, they immediately incur the wrath of Miss Trotwood by guiding their donkeys across the front lawn. Finally, the Murdstones enter the house, and David's stepfather tells about the many difficulties he has had with the rebellious boy. Miss Trotwood counters by saying that David's interests, particularly his annuity, has not been looked after and that his mother was ill-used. Exasperated, Mr. Murdstone states that if David does not return, "my doors are shut against him. . . ."

Miss Trotwood asks David if he wishes to return, and he replies that he does not; she then asks Mr. Dick what she should do with the boy and after a bit of thought, he replies, "Have him measured for a suit of clothes directly." She thanks Mr. Dick for his good sense, and with some final caustic remarks, she ushers the Murdstones out of the house. David now has a new set of guardians and his aunt decrees that he shall now be known as "Trotwood Cooperfield." And so David begins a new life.

Commentary

In Chapter 13, Dickens uses elements of the popular picaresque, or adventure story. This type of novel was well established in Dickens' time and consisted of the wandering journey of a hero through a series of thrilling, unconnected incidents. The hero is forced to live by his wits as he encounters different people (usually of low station) who attempt to cheat him or otherwise use him for their own ends. Because the hero sees all levels of society, the author is able to give a panoramic picture of life during a particular time.

The delineation of Miss Trotwood's true character in Chapter 14 is Dickens' way of revealing that behind the brusque exterior shown in the first chapter lies a compassionate nature. Note, too, her concern, as evidenced in her guardianship of Mr. Dick and her instinctive rejection of the Murdstones.

Summary

It is decided that David will attend school in Canterbury, and the next day Miss Trotwood escorts David on his journey. In Canterbury they stop at the office of Mr. Wickfield, a lawyer, and are welcomed at the door by a Mr. Uriah Heep, a red-haired clerk about fifteen years old. Miss Trotwood has come for advice on which school to enroll David in. Mr. Wickfield takes Miss Trotwood to visit "the best we have," while David observes Uriah Heep, whose eyes look "like two red suns."

Miss Trotwood likes the school, but none of the available boarding houses suit her, so it is decided that David will board with Mr. Wickfield. David meets Mr. Wickfield's daughter, Agnes, a girl of David's age, and he is then shown his room. David's aunt tells him to "be a credit to yourself, to me, and Mr. Dick," embraces him, and then departs.

After supper that evening, David notices that Mr. Wickfield drinks a great deal of wine. Just before bedtime, David sees Uriah Heep closing up the office, and after a brief conversation, David says goodnight and shakes Uriah's hand. "But oh, what a clammy hand his was! as ghostly to the touch as to the sight. I rubbed mine afterwards, to warm it, *and to rub his off.*"

David begins school the next day and is introduced to his new schoolmaster, Doctor Strong, a carelessly dressed man with a "lustreless eye," whose life's project is the writing of an immense never-to-be-completed dictionary. With Dr. Strong is his pretty wife, Annie, who is much younger than her husband. In a conversation between Wickfield and Strong, David hears about one of Annie's cousins, a Mr. Jack Maldon, apparently a loafer, for whom Mr. Wickfield is trying to find some suitable provision.

Although school is very pleasant, it has been so long since David has mingled with boys his own age that he is apprehensive about how he will get on with his classmates. He has such an initial fear of his new situation that he hurries back to Mr. Wickfield's at the close of the first day of classes to avoid meeting any of the students.

After dinner that evening, Mr. Wickfield has his usual large portion of wine. David enjoys Agnes' company; however, he reassures himself that he loves Em'ly—but yet he feels "there are goodness, peace, and truth, wherever Agnes is."

When it is time for bed, David notices Uriah Heep is still in the office, poring over a huge book. Heep is studying law, but he contends that he is far too "umble" ever to become Mr. Wickfield's partner. Instead, Uriah suggests that David might "come into the business," but David protests that he has "no views of that sort."

David learns more about Doctor Strong from some of the boys that board at his house. The old Doctor has been married to the pretty young Annie for less than a year, and during that time he has had to support a host of her relatives. Among them is Mrs. Markleham (known to the boys as the Old Soldier), who is Annie Strong's mother.

One night, a small party is held for Jack Maldon, who is leaving for India "as a cadet, or something of that kind, Mr. Wickfield having at length arranged the business." It is also Doctor Strong's birthday. Mrs. Markleham, in wishing him "many, many, many happy returns," thanks him for what he has done for her family, but she does it in such a way that her self-centeredness is clearly revealed. She also mentions that she remembers when Jack Maldon was "a little creature, a head shorter than Master Copperfield, making baby love to Annie. . . ."

Throughout the evening, Mrs. Strong seems ill at ease. Although she is "a very pretty singer," she is unable to begin a duet with her cousin, Jack Maldon, and when she tries to sing by herself, her voice dies away and she is left "with her head hanging down over the keys."

As Maldon departs, David notices that he is carrying "something cherry-coloured in his hand." Shortly afterward, Annie is found in a swoon, and her mother notices that her bow, a "cherry-coloured ribbon," is missing. Annie says that she thinks she had it safe, a little while ago.

Commentary

In Chapter 15, we first meet one of the notable villains of all of English literature—Uriah Heep. His future activities will play an important part in the lives of several of the characters. As yet he is only a boy, and it is doubtful that his ambitions are formed, although they are perhaps already in the making. Dickens has managed to make Uriah Heep so unpleasant physically that he is repulsive to David.

Although Mr. Wickfield is obviously a good man, we should already detect a weakness in his character—if only in the fact that he feels that he has to drink a great quantity of wine each night before going to bed. He is devoted to his daughter, whom he calls his "little housekeeper," and she is equally devoted to him.

We see in Chapter 16 that after an initial period of adjustment, David is happy in Doctor Strong's school, and he has every reason to be. It is "an excellent school, as different from Mr. Creakle's as good is from evil." There is "an appeal, in everything, to the honour and good faith of the boys," and the boys feel that they have "a part in the management of the place, and in sustaining its character and dignity." Such a school was virtually unknown in Dickens' day, indicating that he had educational views that were *far ahead* of their time.

CHAPTERS 17-18

Summary

David, in corresponding with Peggotty, returns the half guinea she loaned him, and he learns from her that the Murdstones have moved from the house in Blunderstone, leaving it "shut up, to be let or sold."

At school, David is visited, occasionally, by his aunt and also by Mr. Dick on alternate Wednesdays. On one of Mr. Dick's visits, he tells David about a strange man who has been hanging around the Trotwood house frightening Aunt Betsey and causing her to faint. Unaccountably, Mr. Dick has seen her give *money* to the strange man.

Uriah Heep asks David to have tea with him and his mother, if their "umbleness" doesn't prevent him. David accepts the invitation, and that evening he meets Mrs. Heep, "the dead image of Uriah, only short." Although there has been a considerable lapse of time since Mr. Heep's death, Mrs. Heep is still wearing "weeds" (black mourning dresses).

Mrs. Heep and her son proceed to "worm things out" of David, first about his past life, and then about Mr. Wickfield and Agnes. David has begun to feel "a little uncomfortable" and to wish himself "well out of the visit," when Mr. Micawber suddenly appears. He has been walking down the street and through the open door, he spied David. David introduces Micawber to Uriah and his mother.

The next evening, David looks out of the windows and is surprised to see Mr. Micawber and Uriah Heep "walk past, arm in arm." He learns, the next day when he dines with the Micawbers, that Mr. Micawber went home with Uriah and drank brandy and water at Mrs. Heep's. Micawber is much impressed with Uriah and says that if he had known him when his "difficulties came to a crisis . . . my creditors would have been a great deal better managed" than they were.

The next morning, David receives a note from Mr. Micawber saying that there is no hope of receiving the money from London, and indicating that Micawber will soon be returning to debtors' prison. David, on his way to school, hurries toward the hotel "to soothe Mr. Micawber with a word of comfort." However, he meets "the London coach with Mr. and Mrs. Micawber up behind, Mr. Micawber the very picture of tranquil enjoyment." David is both relieved and sorry at their going.

David reminisces about his school days. He remembers being in love with Miss Shepherd, "a little girl . . . with a round face and curly flaxen hair," and how "all was over" when she made a face and laughed at him one day. He also remembers the boys at Doctor Strong's school and how the Doctor "waylaid the smaller boys to punch their unprotected heads.'

In time, David becomes the head-boy at the school, and he feels that the boy he was when he first came to the school is no longer part of him. "That boy is gone"; also gone is the little girl he "saw on that first day at Mr. Wickfield's. . . . In her stead, the perfect likeness of [her mother's] picture—a child-likeness no more—moves about the house, and Agnes . . . is quite a woman."

Again David is in love, this time with Miss Larkins, a woman of about thirty. Although she has many officers as admirers, David dreams of winning her. He dances with her at a ball, and for several days afterward, he is lost "in rapturous reflections." One day Agnes tells him that Miss Larkins is to be married to an elderly hop-grower, Mr. Chestle. David is "terribly dejected for about a week or two." He is now seventeen.

Commentary

In Chapter 17, we have the first of several far-fetched *coincidences* that appear in the novel. The possibility of Mr. Micawber's just happening by at a time when David is an awkward position, and wishes to escape, is very remote. It may be argued that such things *do* indeed happen now and then in real life, but they happen so rarely that when a coincidence is used in a novel—just to further the plot—it does seem artificial, especially to today's readers.

Also artificial (for today's readers) is Dickens' use of a *mysterious stranger*, whose identity is not revealed for some time (although it is not impossible to guess at once who he is). The stranger was used by Dickens to heighten reader interest and to add an element of suspense to the story; the novel, remember, was originally published in serial form and many of the conventions that you are reading here were original with Dickens and were borrowed by many lesser and later writers.

With Chapter 18, we are now at the end of what many readers believe is the finest part of the novel—David's childhood and school days. We have watched him grow from babyhood to the age of seventeen, and he has become, through Dickens' great sympathy for him, a truly believable character. In fact, David may well be the only *truly* believable character in the novel; most of the others merely possess exaggerations of the traits we meet every day.

CHAPTERS 19-20

Summary

Unsure of what he wishes to do in the world, David is encouraged by Aunt Betsey to visit Peggotty so that he may have "a little change" and "thereby form a cooler judgment." His aunt gives him a "handsome purse of money, and a portmanteau" (a suitcase), and he sets out.

David first stops at Canterbury to say goodbye to Agnes and Mr. Wickfield. While he is there, Agnes tells David that she is worried about her father's condition. David says that he has become concerned over Mr. Wickfield's increased drinking, that whenever Mr. Wickfield "is least like himself," he is most certain to be wanted on "some business" by Uriah Heep.

Later at Dr. Strong's, David observes another domestic problem. A letter has arrived from Jack Maldon in which he states that he is ill and wants to return. Mrs. Markleham succeeds in getting Dr. Strong to let Maldon come over while Annie "never once spoke or lifted up her eyes." David senses trouble ahead.

Arriving in London, David registers at a hotel and is given a small room over a stable. After a dinner during which he tries to give an impression of worldly maturity, he attends a performance of *Julius Caesar* at Covent Garden. When he returns to the hotel, he is overjoyed to run into James Steerforth, now an Oxford student; he is on his way home to visit his mother. Steerforth admonishes one of the hotel's employees for giving David such a poor room, and David is immediately given a much better room.

The next morning at breakfast, Steerforth invites David to come home with him and meet his mother. David accepts the invitation, and at dusk they arrive by stagecoach at an old brick house in Highgate, a suburb of London. Steerforth's mother is elderly and rather formal. Her companion is Rosa Dartle, a thin, black-haired lady of about thirty. Miss Dartle has a scar on her lip, which Steerforth tells David he caused. "I was a young boy, and she exasperated me, and I threw a hammer at her."

David invites Steerforth to go with him to visit the Peggotty family, and Steerforth is interested but condescending. He expresses pleasure at the chance "to see that sort of people"; he tells Miss Dartle that "there's a pretty wide separation between them and us. . . . They are wonderfully virtuous, I dare say. . . . But they have not very fine natures, and they may be thankful that, like their coarse rough skins, they are not easily wounded."

Commentary

Throughout Chapter 19, we see David trying to find his place in a mature world—adopting manners which he associates with maturity but which seem rather amusing to the reader. David is finding it hard to assert himself, and it is easier for him to stand by quietly rather than risk taking a stand that might expose his immaturity. In contrast, Steerforth is a man of the world. He demands what he wants when he wants it. And he is imperious enough to get it.

Jack Maldon's imminent return from India suggests that an interesting subplot is building up in the Strong household. As yet it is not clear just what feelings may remain from childhood days, when Annie was Maldon's sweetheart.

In Chapter 20, during the time that David spends with the Steerforth family, Dickens' main emphasis is on the intense love that Mrs. Steerforth feels for her son. He is the very center of her existence, and she no doubt values anything if it has a relationship to her son. For example, it is obvious to us that her *only* interest in David is the fact that he, too, is devoted to Steerforth.

Of interest in this chapter, also, is Rosa Dartle; she has a peculiar, indirect way of seeking information from others, hinting rather than speaking outright. Steerforth sums her up nicely: "She brings everything to a grindstone and sharpens it, as she has sharpened her own face and figure these years past. . . . She is all edge."

CHAPTERS 21-22

Summary

During his stay at the Steerforth home, David is much impressed with Littimer, a servant there. "He surrounded himself with an atmosphere of respectability, and walked secure in it. It would have been next to impossible to suspect him of anything wrong, he was so thoroughly respectable," David says of Littimer.

Finally, David and Steerforth leave for Yarmouth and, arriving late, spend the night at an inn. The next morning, David goes alone to visit Mr. Barkis and Peggotty. On the way he comes to Mr. Omer's shop, which is now listed as OMER AND JORAM. David goes inside and talks to Mr. Omer, who tells him that Little Em'ly works in his shop as a seamstress and that she mixes well with the other girls—apparently because of her rare beauty and her dream of becoming a "lady."

David calls on Peggotty, who at first fails to recognize him. She takes David upstairs to see Mr. Barkis, now a rheumatic invalid confined to bed. Steerforth arrives a little later, and after dinner, he and David set out for the Peggotty houseboat. As they walk along the shore, Steerforth comments that "the sea roars as if it were hungry" for them.

They arrive just as the engagement between little Em'ly and Ham is being announced. The family is overjoyed, and the jubilant

Mr. Peggotty exclaims that "no wrong can touch my Em'ly." David and Steerforth are welcomed into the celebration, and when Steerforth leaves the Peggotty home, he remarks that Ham is "rather a chuckle-headed fellow for the girl, isn't he?" David feels a shock in this unexpected and cold comment. But, "seeing a laugh in his eyes," he thinks that Steerforth must be joking. "Ah, Steerforth! . . . When I see how perfectly you understand them . . . I know that there is not a joy or sorrow, not an emotion, of such people that can be indifferent to you."

Steerforth replies, "I believe you are in earnest, and are good. I wish we all were!"

During the visit, which lasts for more than two weeks, Steerforth spends a great deal of time boating with Mr. Peggotty, while David visits his old home at Blunderstone. The old neighbors have moved and his parents' graves have been cared for by Peggotty; David feels "a singular jumble of sadness and pleasure" about his early years here.

One evening, David is surprised to find Steerforth in a despondent mood. He does not tell David what is bothering him, but says only that he wishes "with all my soul I could guide myself better." The mood is only momentary, however, and he soon improves his spirits and tells David that he has bought a used boat, renaming it the *Little Em'ly*. Mr. Peggotty will be the "captain" in Steerforth's absence. David believes this to be evidence of his friend's charity toward Mr. Peggotty.

Later, Steerforth's austere and respectable servant, Littimer, arrives with a letter from Steerforth's mother. Then there is another arrival—Miss Mowcher, a fat, middle-aged dwarf, who is a hairdresser for wealthy families. Steerforth describes Little Em'ly to the dwarf as "The prettiest and most engaging little fairy in the world. . . . I swear she was born to be a lady."

Later, David walks back to the Barkis house and finds Ham waiting outside for Em'ly. She is in the house talking to Martha Endell, a girl who once worked with her at Mr. Omer's. Ham explains to David that Martha Endell is a "fallen woman," and because Mr. Peggotty would not want Em'ly to speak to her, she earlier gave the girl a note telling her to meet her at the Barkis cottage. Ham gives Martha some money so that she can go to London, where she is not known. After Martha leaves, little Em'ly sobs, "I am not as good a girl as I ought to be! Not near! Not near!"

Commentary

Sometimes Dickens' chapters tend to ramble; this is not the case, however, with Chapter 21. Here, he pulls together two strands of David's story—his old friends at Yarmouth and his old school friend Steerforth. Dickens takes the opportunity here to point up the *simple goodness* of the Yarmouth people, and he once again hints at character flaws in Steerforth.

Chapter 22, in contrast to Chapter 21, is more ambiguous. Although it is not explicitly stated, there seems to be an indication that little Em'ly has entered upon a secret relationship with Steerforth. Steerforth shows some remorse over his behavior, as evidenced by his brooding, but it is short-lived. Em'ly, perhaps seeing in the fate of Martha Endell something of her own possible fate, sobs as Martha leaves. She tells Ham, "Oh, my dear, it might have been a better fortune for you if you had been fond of someone else—of someone steadier and much worthier than me."

There is also an interesting new facet of Steerforth revealed in this chapter when Steerforth tells David that it might have been better for him (Steerforth) if he "had had a steadfast and judicious father." We have seen in Chapter 20 the excessively motherly devotion that Mrs. Steerforth has lavished upon her son; thus, by now, we should be beginning to suspect that Steerforth is *not* the paragon that everyone in the story believes him to be.

CHAPTERS 23-24

Summary

Steerforth and David depart by coach the next morning, leaving Littimer behind to do "what he has to do," as Steerforth cryptically comments. During the journey, David tells Steerforth about the previous night's encounter with Martha Endell, the "fallen woman." David seeks Steerforth's advice about which profession he should pursue. He inquires about being a proctor, a job suggested to him in a recent letter from his aunt, but Steerforth comments that it is a dull job; David would be "a sort of monkish attorney at Doctors' Commons."

David meets Aunt Betsey in London and tells her that he would be happy to be a proctor. However, when he learns that it will cost his aunt a thousand pounds to place him with a firm, David asks if she can afford it. Her reply is that she has "*no* other claim upon my means—and you are my adopted child."

The next day they set out for the office of Messrs. Spenlow and Jorkins, in Doctors' Commons, where David is to learn his new profession. On the way, an "ill-dressed man" approaches them, and for a moment Aunt Betsey is terrified. However, to David's great astonishment, she tells him to wait for her, and she drives off in a coach with the strange man. When Aunt Betsey returns a half hour later, she tells David, "Never ask me what it was, and don't refer to it." Significantly, David notices that all the guineas are gone from her purse when she gives it to him to pay the driver of the coach.

At the law office, David meets Mr. Spenlow, a well-dressed little man, who explains that his partner, Mr. Jorkins, is a ruthless taskmaster (Later David finds him to be a mild man and learns that his image as a tyrant is a ruse to pressure people). Arrangements are made for David to begin a month's probation, and after everything is arranged, David is lodged at the home of Mrs. Crupp, who immediately takes a motherly interest in him. The next day his aunt leaves for Dover, and David is ready to begin his career in law.

At first David is pleased with his living quarters, but he soon becomes lonely and wonders why Steerforth has not come to visit. When Steerforth turns up, David invites him and two of his Oxford friends to dinner, and he tries to arrange with Mrs. Crupp to cook the meal. However, Mrs. Crupp is unable to prepare the food, and it must be ordered from the pastry cook.

During dinner, everyone consumes a great deal of wine, and David soon becomes "singularly cheerful and light-hearted" and even tries smoking for the first time. It is suggested that they attend the theater, and on the way out, David is conscious of someone falling down the stairs. He is surprised to find that it is he.

The theater is very hot, and to David "the whole building looked . . . as if it were learning to swim." They go downstairs to where the ladies were; there, the boisterous David becomes the center of attention. He discovers Agnes at the theater with some friends and tries to talk to her. She is embarrassed and asks him to leave. Steerforth helps David return home. The next morning David is plagued with remorse and shame—and with a headache.

Commentary

In Chapter 23, David is launched on a career through his aunt's benevolence. But a disturbing element in her life (a life seemingly so mysteriously free of any past) is introduced, suggesting that there is something or someone in her past to account for the belligerent, withdrawn character we first knew her as. For example, we should ask ourselves at this point: who is the mysterious stranger who so greatly terrifies Aunt Betsey?

Chapter 24 is one of Dickens' most entertaining chapters in this novel. Young David's becoming intoxicated and making a fool of himself is underplayed just enough to make the scene realistic yet comic. His attempts to talk to Agnes and his abrupt "Goori" (goodnight) when he is told to leave, are examples of classic Dickens humor.

CHAPTERS 25-26

Summary

Two mornings after the dinner party, just as David is about to leave his room, a messenger arrives with a letter from Agnes, asking him to meet her at the home of Mr. Waterbrook, her father's London agent. When David meets Agnes, he reproaches himself for his conduct at the theatre. Agnes is forgiving, and David calls her his "good Angel." She warns David against Steerforth, his "bad Angel," but David insists that Steerforth is a good and loyal friend.

Agnes then relates her growing fears about Uriah Heep, who seems to be gaining more and more power over her father. In fact, Agnes believes that Uriah is going to enter the firm as a partner. David is indignant about this and tells Agnes that she must prevent it. Agnes, however, asks David to be congenial to Uriah for her father's sake.

The next day David attends a dinner party at Mr. Waterbrook's and encounters Uriah Heep again. While David is with Agnes, he senses Uriah's "shadowless eyes and cadaverous face, to be looking gauntly down . . . from behind." David is pleased to find Tommy Traddles, his old schoolmate, at the party. He learns that Traddles is preparing for the bar and, at the same time, working for the pompous Mr. Waterbrook. After the party, David suddenly remembers

Agnes' plea to be kind to Uriah Heep, and so he invites him to his room for coffee. There, Uriah reveals his increasing sense of power and even confides that he loves Agnes and hopes to marry her. David is appalled at this prospect. Uriah asks if he can spend the night, and in the morning, after Uriah leaves, David asks Mrs. Crupp to "leave the windows open, that my sitting-room might be aired and purged" of his presence.

When Agnes leaves to return to Canterbury, Uriah Heep appears and boards the same coach. David is uneasy and fears that Uriah may succeed in his desire to marry Agnes. In addition, Steerforth is now at Oxford, and although letters pass between them, David remembers Agnes' warning and harbors "some lurking distrust" of him.

David begins his apprenticeship with the firm of Spenlow and Jorkins. One day, Mr. Spenlow invites David to come for a visit to his house at Norwood to meet his daughter, who has been attending school in Paris. When Mr. Spenlow and David arrive at the house, David is introduced to Dora Spenlow and is immediately overcome with her loveliness. "All was over in a moment. I had fulfilled my destiny. I was a captive and a slave. I loved Dora Spenlow to distraction!"

David is understandably startled to find Miss Murdstone at the Spenlow home; she is serving as a hired companion and protecter for Dora. David at first fears that Miss Murdstone will disparage him to Dora, but he and Miss Murdstone, when they are alone, agree to keep their past relationship a secret. David learns that Dora does not like Miss Murdstone; her closest friend is her dog, Jip.

Back in London, David lives in a dream about Dora and buys sumptuous waistcoats, "not for myself; *I* had no pride in them, for Dora."

Commentary

Chapter 25 is important primarily because it introduces Agnes Wickfield; she is the first person in the book to sense the true character of Steerforth. Everyone else, including David, has been dazzled by his charms. However, Dickens has already suggested to the *reader* that Steerforth's seeming perfection hides weak self-indulgence (for which his mother is largely responsible). We suspect that he is furthering an interest in little Em'ly, despite her engagement to Ham.

When Dickens relates the discussion at the dinner party in this chapter, note how carefully he portrays the shallowness of human feeling as he describes the "upper classes." Here, the conversation centers around the "terribly" great importance of "blood"—meaning that only families of the aristocracy are of any concern.

David's feelings for Dora, in contrast, are handled realistically; in fact, most critics believe that they are based on Dickens' own life. When Dickens was about eighteen, he fell in love with Maria Beadnell, but her father sent her away to Paris so that she could not see the young suitor and Dickens saw very little of her after that.

CHAPTERS 27-28

Summary

David goes to visit Tommy Traddles, who lives in a very poor section of Camden Town, where garbage and junk clutter the streets. David finds Traddles' apartment house, whose "genteel air" reminds him of the days he spent with Mr. and Mrs. Micawber. They discuss their school days and Traddles' life since leaving school. He explains to David that he went to his uncle's household to live, but his uncle didn't like him. After his uncle's death, Traddles began to copy law writings for a living and then to "state cases" and make abstracts. This led him to the study of law, which exhausted his limited funds. He then found jobs with a couple of other offices, including Mr. Waterbrook's, as well as with a firm that was preparing to publish an encyclopaedia. Finally, he "managed to scrape up" the hundred pounds necessary for him to be "articled." Traddles also reveals that he is engaged to be married to one of the ten daughters of a curate in Devonshire. He expects it to be a long engagement, but they have made a beginning by buying two small pieces of furniture.

David is surprised and delighted to learn that Traddles' landlord is Mr. Micawber, who is still patiently waiting for something to turn up. David talks with Mr. and Mrs. Micawber and learns that they are expecting another child. He is invited to dinner but declines the invitation; instead, he asks them to dine with him at a later date.

David makes arrangements about the dinner party which he plans for the Micawbers and Tommy Traddles, but he has to compromise with Mrs. Crupp by agreeing to eat out for the next two weeks; otherwise, she will not cook the meal. When his guests arrive, Mr. Micawber becomes involved in preparing the punch, while Mrs. Micawber sits at the dressing table and gets herself ready for the party.

As they all sit around eating the mutton, Littimer arrives and asks David if he has seen Steerforth. When David says that he hasn't, Littimer says that Steerforth will probably be coming up from Oxford tomorrow. He insists that David be seated, and he then takes over the task of preparing the remainder of the mutton. During Littimer's presence, everyone is uncomfortable, and it is only when the servant leaves that they seem "to breathe more freely." Before Littimer goes, David asks him if he remained long at Yarmouth. Littimer says that he stayed to see the boat completed but he does not know if Steerforth has seen it yet.

The conversation turns to Mr. Micawber's employment. It is agreed that the corn business, in which Micawber is employed, is not very profitable and that Mr. Micawber should advertise his talents in the papers—"throw down the gauntlet" to society, as it were—to see what will turn up. The cost of this advertising will be met by a promissory note. Before the party adjourns, David warns Traddles not to act as co-signer for any bills, but Traddles says that he has already done so.

Shortly afterward, Steerforth appears. David, as a result of Agnes' warning, has been feeling a slight uneasiness about him. However, he is now so overjoyed at seeing his friend that he feels "confounded and ashamed" at having doubted him. Steerforth has just come from Yarmouth, and he gives David a letter from Peggotty, which says that Barkis is gravely ill. David decides to visit Peggotty, but Steerforth persuades David to spend the next day with him at his home before going to Yarmouth.

Commentary

In the opening of Chapter 27, David is reminded of the Micawbers. This may lead readers familiar with Dickens to believe that, before the chapter ends, Mr. Micawber will put in an appearance. Dickens does not disappoint these readers. This is another unlikely *coincidence*, but something one has to understand is part of Dickens' technique, just as was his having Miss Murdstone show up in Chapter 26, as an employee in the Spenlow household. The possibility of this happening in real life is very remote, but it helped lace together Dickens' intricate network of plots and subplots.

When we get to Chapter 28, we see that David has matured from the time he first knew Mr. Micawber, and he now realizes that his old friend is a failure. This is clearly shown when he warns Traddles not to co-sign any bill with Micawber.

Steerforth, while discussing the approaching death of Barkis, reveals a ruthlessness in his nature. "It's a bad job . . . but the sun sets every day, and people die every minute, and we mustn't be scared by the common lot. No! Ride on! Roughshod if need be, smooth-shod if that will do, but ride on! Ride over all obstacles and win the race!"

David shows the first indication of his having matured in regard to Steerforth when, after leaving him, he remembers what his friend said about riding over *all* obstacles and winning the race. David finds himself wishing, for the first time, that Steerforth "had some worthy race to run."

CHAPTERS 29-30

Summary

David is cordially received at the Steerforth residence, especially by Rosa Dartle, who begins asking him questions about Steerforth's activities. She blames David for keeping Steerforth away from home longer than usual, and she hints that something may cause a quarrel between Steerforth and his mother.

Steerforth flatters Miss Dartle into playing the harp and singing for them, and David comments that her song is the most "unearthly" he has ever heard. When Miss Dartle finishes playing, Steerforth laughingly puts his arm around her and says, "Come, Rosa, for the future we will love each other very much!" Miss Dartle promptly strikes him and angrily leaves the room. David asks why she did this, but Steerforth says he does not know, but that she is "always dangerous."

Before retiring for bed, Steerforth tells David that should something ever separate them, "think of me at my best." Before leaving the next morning, David looks in at Steerforth sleeping peacefully in his bed. In retrospect, he realizes he would never see Steerforth again as a friend. "Never more, oh God forgive you, Steerforth! to touch that passive hand in love and friendship. Never, never more!"

David arrives in Yarmouth and takes a room in the village inn because he feels that the spare room at Peggotty's is probably taken by "the great Visitor—Death." He meets Mr. Omer in his shop and is told that Mr. Barkis is dying. He inquires about Em'ly, and Mr. Omer says that she has become "unsettled" recently and that he will be relieved when she's married. Word arrives that Barkis is unconscious and beyond help, and David rushes to the house.

At the house, everyone thanks David for being kind enough to come. Em'ly appears and seems shaken and chilled; she turns away from Ham to cling to Mr. Peggotty. Mr. Peggotty explains that it is her youth which causes her to take the dying of Barkis so hard; however, David is puzzled by her actions. David is then taken in to see Barkis, who is propped up and just barely conscious. Peggotty assures David that he will not die until the tide is out (an old superstition of English fishermen). Barkis opens his eyes for the last time and sees David. With a pleasant smile he says, "Barkis is willin' " and goes "out with the tide."

Commentary

It is obvious in Chapter 29 that Rosa Dartle is in love with Steerforth, despite the fact that she is some years older than he. But it is a neurotic sort of love, mixed with much bitterness and perhaps even hatred. It is doubtful that such a woman could love openly, for she has hidden her emotions behind an attempt to be self-effacing; furthermore, she resents all that stands between her and Steerforth —his mother, even Steerforth himself, and, more recently, David. Steerforth, of course, probably has never known for sure of Miss Dartle's love for him, but he has, of course, sensed it, and he has idly played with it in his self-indulgent way.

Miss Dartle, in implying that something may come between Steerforth and his mother, has shrewdly guessed that Steerforth is involved in some possible scandal. But she does not know any details. She believes that David does and she questions him, but he knows nothing, as yet, about Steerforth's secret activities.

By the time we finish Chapter 30, we are almost half-way through the novel. Dickens has introduced scores of characters, major and minor. With the death of Barkis we begin to see how Dickens disposes of them—to clear the way for further development, to provide drama and pathos, and to pick up loose ends.

CHAPTERS 31-32

Summary

David is entrusted with the will of the deceased Mr. Barkis, and he prides himself on his ability to read the document and distribute the items in the proper manner. David has found the will in the mysterious box which Barkis carried with him religiously all these years. Along with the will, the box contains "miniature cups and saucers, a horseshoe, a polished oyster shell . . . and almost three thousand pounds." Peggotty is provided for in the will, as is Mr. Peggotty, with David and Em'ly as minor heirs.

Only Peggotty, Mr. Peggotty, and David attend the funeral. That evening David goes to Mr. Peggotty's houseboat. Everyone tries to cheer up Peggotty by telling her that she did her "dooty by the departed, and the departed know'd it." Mr. Peggotty lights the candle for Em'ly (as he has done for so many years) and places it in the window. He vows that even after Em'ly is married he will continue to put the candle in the window, "pretending I'm expecting of her, like I'm a-doing now." Ham arrives at the house, but without Em'ly. He draws David, alone, out of the house and weeps as he tells him that Em'ly has run away with her lover. The others, too, learn of the situation, and David reads to them a farewell note she left for Ham. Mr. Peggotty asks who the man is, and Ham cries, "Mas'r Davy, it ain't no fault of yourn—and I am far from laying of it to you—but his name is Steerforth, and he's a damned villain."

Mr. Peggotty announces, "I'm a-going to find my poor niece in her shame, and bring her back. No one stop me! I tell you I'm a-going to seek my niece!" Mrs. Gummidge collects her wits, stops feeling sorry for herself, and, for the first time, takes a mature, forceful interest in handling affairs by talking Mr. Peggotty out of leaving the house that very night. David hears him crying and tells us that "I cried too."

Even though Steerforth has run off with Em'ly, David still thinks of all the favorable things about him; he chooses to think of Steerforth as "a cherished friend, who was dead." Late one night, David is interrupted by the unexpected visit of a tearful and agitated Miss Mowcher, who reveals her part in the plot. She had been tricked into sending communications between Em'ly and Steerforth through Littimer. Now, "suspecting something wrong," she has returned from London. Miss Mowcher believes that Em'ly and Steerforth have gone abroad and vows revenge. "Littimer had better have a bloodhound at his back than little Mowcher," she vows.

The next morning, Mr. Peggotty, Peggotty, and David leave for London, where they decide to visit Mrs. Steerforth. Mrs. Steerforth is quite unmoved by Em'ly's letter and her wish to return a "lady." She states emphatically that her son's marriage to Em'ly is "impossible." If Steerforth returns without Em'ly, she will forgive him; otherwise "he never shall come near me."

Mr. Peggotty takes a little money from his sister to begin his search. "If any hurt should come to me, remember that the last word I left for her was, 'My unchanged love is with my darling child, and I forgive her!' "

Commentary

Clearly in Chapter 31, David's maturity is becoming more and more evident. In the simple matter of the reading of the will, David feels "supreme satisfaction" that he is the only one able to do this. Yet, at the end of the chapter, he weeps because, for the first time, he is fully aware of the evil nature of the clever Steerforth.

The death of Barkis in the preceding chapter was handled with restraint, but with this "greater loss," Dickens pulls out all the stops with his description of the night, the rain, and the feelings of the family as they realize that Em'ly is gone. This is the climax of the Em'ly-Steerforth plot, or subplot.

Chapter 32 is yet one more example of Dickens' depicting the upper classes as heartless and cruel. The forgiving nature of Mr. Peggotty is diametrically opposed to the cold aloofness at the

Steerforth house, where Miss Dartle calls the Peggotty group a "depraved, worthless set." Dickens, probably because of his upbringing, felt that only "simple people" had the capacity to feel deeply and to be sentimental about things.

CHAPTERS 33-34

Summary

David reveals how much he loves Dora Spenlow; thoughts of her continually enter his mind and he despises any man who does not realize how wonderful Dora is. In the meantime, he manages Peggotty's affairs, "proving the will" and putting all her business in an orderly fashion. After the legal matters are settled, David takes Peggotty to the "Commons office" to pay her bill and is startled to meet Mr. Murdstone in Mr. Spenlow's company. The conversation between Mr. Murdstone, David, and Peggotty is very strained, as David still remembers the heartaches this man caused. Mr. Murdstone is in the law office to obtain a marriage license so that he can wed a girl who has just come of age.

David and Mr. Spenlow go into court to settle a divorce case and afterwards they engage in a lengthy conversation about the law. David feels that many aspects of the law are in need of reform and suggests some changes in the workings at the law office, but the conservative Mr. Spenlow considers it "the principle of a gentleman to take things as he found them." Mr. Spenlow forgets about his personal reform movement.

On the day of the picnic David hires a "gallant grey" horse, buys a bouquet of flowers, and rides to the Spenlow home. Dora is in the garden with a friend, Miss Julia Mills, and with Jip, her dog. They all leave for the picnic, and David stares at the beautiful Dora the entire trip. He is so absorbed that he is surprised to find other people are at the picnic too. His jealousy is aroused by a red-whiskered gentleman who competes with him throughout the day for Dora's company, and David tries his best to forget his feelings by flirting with another girl at the celebration and even contemplates leaving. As the picnic ends, Julia Mills tells David that Dora will be staying at her home for a few days, and she invites him to come to call on them. David is elated once more.

Three days after the picnic, David goes to visit Dora; he plans to declare his great passion for her. After much timidness, he finally bursts forth with his feelings and they become engaged, but they decide to keep the betrothal a secret for the time being. David, however, goes to a jeweler and buys a ring to seal the engagement. Within a week, they have their first quarrel, but Miss Mills is able to bring the couple back together.

David writes to Agnes informing her of his engagement to Dora and about the circumstances of Em'ly's flight. He is anxious to impress Agnes with his sincere love for Dora. Traddles comes up to David's room, and they exchange conversation about their fiancées before Traddles asks a favor of David. He explains that Mr. Micawber is still having financial problems and, consequently, has changed his name to Mr. Mortimer, has taken to wearing glasses, and only goes out at night in order to avoid his creditors. Traddles adds that he has signed his name for only one of Mr. Micawber's recent debts. His own difficulty is that he has had some of his personal possessions seized by the pawnbroker who lent money to Mr. Micawber; now the pawnbroker raises the prices whenever Traddles attempts to buy them back. Peggotty and David buy back Traddles' things and return to David's apartment. There, they find visitors: Aunt Betsey is sitting on her luggage and Mr. Dick is holding a huge kite. His aunt tells him that she has lost all her wealth and is ruined. "All I have in the world is in this room, except the cottage," she says, and *that* must be put up for rent. The old lady is undaunted, however, and she reminds David that "We must meet reverses boldly, and not suffer them to frighten us. . . . We must live misfortune down."

Commentary

Early in his life, Dickens worked as a lawyer's clerk and then as a parliamentary reporter for a newspaper. Here in Chapter 33, he trades in on that experience to flesh out the reality of this episode. Through his experiences, he developed a deep suspicion of the law and its workings. In this chapter, more than perhaps anywhere else in the novel, Dickens satirizes governmental officials who have large comfortable offices while whose who do the real work are shut up in cold, dark rooms.

After the critical attack on petty officials in the preceding chapter, Dickens turns to a warmer tone in Chapter 34. Aunt Betsey, who was once David's sole means of support, is the focus here; she is financially unable to provide for herself now and must even stay the night with David in order to save expenses. David is called upon to be "firm and self-reliant" so that he can help the person who befriended him when *he* was in trouble. David's maturity soon will stand its greatest test.

CHAPTERS 35-36

Summary

After David gets his aunt settled, he has a long discussion with Mr. Dick about her poverty. When Mr. Dick begins to cry, David has to cheer him up. Peggotty and Mr. Dick then leave for the night, and David and his aunt talk about Dora, his new-found love. Miss Trotwood implies that the girl is "light-headed" and "silly"; however, she does not interfere with the relationship. She then expresses her approval of Peggotty (she renames her "Barkis") even though "the . . . ridiculous creature . . . has been begging and praying about handing over some of her money" to Miss Trotwood. Finally David and his aunt retire, but David is too upset to sleep well. He has continuous dreams of poverty the rest of the night.

The next morning, David goes to the law office of Spenlow and Jorkins to "cancel his articles" and recover a portion of his aunt's thousand pounds which had been put up for his tuition. He is refused, however, and is forced to return home empty-handed. As David leaves the law office, he meets Agnes Wickfield, who is on her way to see Miss Trotwood. Agnes has come to London with her father and Uriah Heep, and she tells David that Mr. Heep (and his mother) live with them now and that Uriah has become a full partner in the firm, exerting an overpowering influence on her father.

David and Agnes return to the house and surprise Miss Trotwood. She is very happy to see Agnes and tells them both how she came to lose her fortune: Agnes' father had taken care of her money and all her affairs, but after he teamed up with Uriah Heep, she decided to invest the money herself, "and a very bad market it turned out to be." Agnes tries to help by suggesting that David can find extra work as a secretary to Dr. Strong; without hesitation, David resolves to see Dr. Strong about the position.

In high spirits, David sets out to prove himself worthy of his aunt's faith and Dora's love. He goes to Highgate to see Dr. Strong and succeeds in gaining part-time employment. The arrangement stipulates that David must work every morning and every evening, five days a week for seventy pounds a year, allowing him to pursue his studies for the rest of the day. The primary drawback of this job is the necessity of overcoming the "efforts" of Jack Maldon, who has returned from India and has been "helping" the doctor; for example, he complicated one of the doctor's manuscripts by making numerous mistakes and obscuring it with various sketches.

Impatient to do even more odd jobs, David goes to see Traddles. His purpose is to inquire about earning more money by reporting the debates in Parliament for a newspaper. Even though Traddles tells him about the extreme difficulty of mastering "the mystery of shorthand writing and reading," David decides to start work on it immediately. Next, Mr. Dick's problem is considered. Upset by Miss Trotwood's reverses, Mr. Dick constantly frets about having nothing useful to do. His dilemma prompts Traddles to find him work copying legal documents. The first week's earnings for this work give Mr. Dick such joy and satisfaction that he confides to David that he is *sure* that he will be able to provide for Miss Trotwood.

Traddles, excited by Mr. Dick's success, nearly forgets about a letter which Mr. Micawber sent to David by him. In the letter which Mr. Micawber has sent, he tells of his intention of moving away to accept another position and he invites his two friends to a small celebration on the eve of the departure. Arriving at the Micawbers, David learns that "the Micawbers are going to Canterbury, where Mr. Micawber is to be the confidential clerk of Uriah Heep!"

Commentary

In Chapter 35, Dickens reveals to us that Miss Betsey has reservations about David's sweetheart, Dora. She feels that David needs someone to "sustain him and improve him," and she chides him that, when it comes to love, he is "blind, blind, blind." Agnes acts as a captive audience for David's recital of his love for Dora. At the end of the chapter, as David leaves for his rooms, he hears a blind beggar call "Blind! Blind! Blind!" and it reminds him (and us) of what his aunt has said.

David's sudden acceptance of new responsibilities and his extreme determination to prove his worth highlight Chapter 36. His determination to master shorthand so that he can report debates in Parliament is partially boyish enthusiasm (it will take several years of study), the rest resolution "to turn the painful discipline of my younger days to account, by going to work with a resolute and steady heart." Further evidence of David's maturity is evident if he is compared to other characters who, although older than he, do not have such a determined and levelheaded approach.

CHAPTERS 37-38

Summary

Mrs. Crupp attempts to intimidate Miss Trotwood as she tried to intimidate Peggotty but David's Aunt Betsey proves too strong a character for her, and David observes that Mrs. Crupp "subsided into her own kitchen, under the impression that my aunt was mad." David is very comfortable in his aunt's care.

Although David loves Dora, he has not told her about his being poor and he decides that he must. At first, she refuses to understand and then she begins to cry. David tries to explain that he deeply loves her, but she tells him, "Don't talk about being poor, and working hard." She is more concerned about whether or not her dog, Jip, will have a daily mutton-chop! David explains that it would help if Dora would try to learn something about housekeeping and cooking, but this causes Dora to become almost hysterical and she faints. Finally, Miss Mills enters the room and calms Dora. Later Miss Mills tells David that Dora "is a favorite child of nature" and that practical responsibilities are beyond her scope.

David discovers that learning shorthand is very difficult, but because he is stimulated by his love for Dora and aided by Traddles' advice and assistance, he becomes rather confident of his skill. Finally, David experiments by trying to record one of the speakers in the Commons. Unfortunately, he discovers that he needs much more practice.

Going to the Commons one day, David is called into the upstairs room of a neighboring coffeehouse by Mr. Spenlow, Dora's father; there, he is confronted by Miss Murdstone, holding all of his letters to Dora. It seems that Dora's dog, Jip, was playing with one of the letters and Miss Murdstone found it. Mr. Spenlow is *very* angry, and when David states that he and Dora are engaged, Mr. Spenlow is determined to protect his daughter from the "consequences of any foolish step in the way of marriage," even to the extent of threatening to change his will if necessary. Mr. Spenlow says that he will forget the matter if David, in turn, will forget about marrying Dora. When David refuses, Mr. Spenlow gives him a week to reconsider, and if David decides not to, he will send Dora abroad again.

During the week, David consults Miss Mills, but this only makes him feel more miserable and depressed than before.

The next Saturday, David appears at the Commons and learns that Mr. Spenlow died mysteriously the night before. A few days later, Mr. Jorkins, David, and an office clerk search Mr. Spenlow's desk for a will, but none is found; rather, it is discovered that his records are out of order, that he has lived beyond his income, and that Dora will be left with very little money. She is sent to live with two maiden aunts, and the only news David hears of her is by way of a journal kept by Miss Mills, his "sole companion of this period."

Commentary

Chapter 37 deals foremost with the matter of David's being deeply in love and not quite comprehending what *we* clearly see: Dora, in her present state, will prove little more than a hindrance to him. He would be far better off with the sisterly Agnes.

The key episode in Chapter 38 parallels Dickens' own love affair with Maria Beadnell. Mr. Spenlow hints that Dora might be shipped off to Paris to prevent her marriage; Mr. Beadnell did that very thing. In the novel, Mr. Spenlow dies, and David is able to marry his sweetheart, but in real life Dickens was not so fortunate to have had this happen.

CHAPTERS 39-40

Summary

Aunt Betsey sends David to Dover to supervise the renting of her cottage, the only possession she has left; she hopes that this responsibility will lift David out of his depression.

David rapidly concludes the business in Dover and continues on to Canterbury to visit Mr. Wickfield and Agnes. At Mr. Wickfield's house, David talks to Mr. Micawber (now Uriah's clerk) about his new job. David finds that Mr. Micawber is pleased with his new employer and thinks that his work is a "great pursuit." David, however, senses an "uneasy change" in him.

David talks to Agnes about his troubles and how much he misses her advice on matters. He says that he finds it difficult to confide in Dora in the same way because she is so "easily disturbed and frightened." Agnes suggests to David that he write to Dora's aunts and seek permission to visit Dora.

After leaving Agnes, David goes downstairs to see Uriah Heep and Mr. Wickfield. Mrs. Heep is also living there, and David thinks of the Heeps as "two great bats hanging over the whole house and darkening it with their ugly forms." Next day, David takes a walk. He is followed by Uriah, who confides that he fears that David might be a rival for Agnes. David reluctantly tells Uriah that he is "engaged to another young lady," which obviously relieves Uriah. Reassured, Uriah tells David about his education in the London charity schools, where he learned to eat "umble pie with an appetite." Now Uriah is proud to note that he has "a little power."

At dinner, David sees Uriah use this power by suggesting that he hopes to marry Agnes. Mr. Wickfield becomes furious, and David tries to calm him. Uriah becomes frightened that Mr. Wickfield, in his anger, will "say something . . . he'll be sorry to have said afterwards," and tries to return to his "umbleness" again. Wickfield expresses to David his shame over his downward path in life and slowly starts to sob. Agnes comes in and comforts her father, and they leave the room together. Later that night David makes her promise that she will "never sacrifice herself" for a "mistaken sense of duty." Next morning, as David leaves, Uriah admits that perhaps he has "plucked a pear before it was ripe." But, says the sinister Uriah, "It'll ripen yet! I can wait!"

One snowy night, on his way home from Dr. Strong's, David passes a woman on the street whom he recognizes but cannot recall; seconds later, as he meets Mr. Peggotty, he realizes the woman whom he passed was none other than Martha Endell, the "fallen woman" whom Em'ly had once helped. The chance meeting with

Mr. Peggotty takes place on the steps of St. Martin's Church, on a route David took only because of the storm.

Mr. Peggotty shows David various letters which he received from Em'ly, in which she asks for understanding and forgiveness, and indicating clearly that she will never return. The letters also contain money, obviously originating from Steerforth, but Mr. Peggotty vows that he will return every cent of the money if he has to go "ten thousand miles." The last note received bears the postmark of a town on the Upper Rhine, and Mr. Peggotty declares that he is going there now in search of Em'ly. Throughout Mr. Peggotty's story, David sees Martha Endell listening at the inn door. After awhile they part, and the grieving uncle "resumes his solitary journey."

Commentary

Finally in Chapter 39 Uriah Heep is beginning to show his true colors. His protestations of "umbleness" are now as many as ever, but his account of his early days in the charity school reveals that his "false humility" is an educated policy rather than his personal philosophy. Heep has Mr. Wickfield in his control and intends to keep secret the source of his control.

The pathetic journey in Chapter 40 of the good and noble Mr. Peggotty was the type of scene which Victorian readers loved. Undaunted by hardships, getting along the best way he can, the loving "father" seeks his wayward child to the far corners of the earth. Martha Endell, the tainted symbolic "sister," will be instrumental in saving Em'ly just as she is about to become a prostitute. In this chapter, Dickens once again uses *coincidence* (fortuitous meetings) to further the intricacies of plot and subplot.

CHAPTERS 41-42

Summary

David receives a reply to his letter to Dora's aunts, Miss Lavinia and Miss Clarissa Spenlow, stating that he may call upon them—accompanied by a "confidential friend" if they so desire. David asks Traddles to go with him, and during the trip Traddles passes the time with the story of his own engagement to Sophy and the objections he encountered from her family. This makes David even more nervous.

The Spenlow sisters are dressed in black and remind David of two birds, "having a sharp, brisk, sudden manner . . . like canaries." David's anxiety is not helped when they address Traddles as Mr. Copperfield. As the conversation advances, David finds that the decision about David's courtship will be made by Miss Lavinia, the younger of the two sisters. After a period of questioning, answering and lecturing, it is decided that David "may court" Dora.

In time, Aunt Betsey becomes acquainted with the Spenlows, and everyone adjusts quite well to the circumstances, except Jip, the dog. David notices that the aunts treat Dora like a child; however, when he mentions this to Dora, she starts to cry, so he drops the subject. He also attempts to teach Dora something about becoming a housewife; he brings her a "cookery book" and begins to instruct her on how to keep account books. Dora soon becomes disgusted when the columns do not add up for her and she starts to draw pictures all over the books. David does not make any progress and decides just to enjoy her company.

After Agnes arrives with her father on a visit of a fortnight to the Doctor's, Uriah corners David in the Doctor's garden. He hints that he is in love with Agnes, and then he expresses hatred for Annie, Doctor Strong's young wife, because he feels that she stands between Agnes and him. He goes on to imply a relationship between Annie and Jack Maldon.

On the next evening, David takes Agnes to meet Dora. Since David is anxious that "Agnes should like her," he is pleased to find that they become very friendly. In fact, Dora considers Agnes so clever that she wonders why David fell in love with her rather than with Agnes.

After David leaves Agnes at Dr. Strong's house, he sees a light in the Doctor's study and enters to find Mr. Wickfield, Doctor Strong, and Uriah Heep in a troubled state. Uriah tells David that he has just informed Dr. Strong of the "goings-on" between Annie and Jack Maldon. Mr. Wickfield admits that he himself thought Annie may have married the Doctor for "worldly considerations only." Dr. Strong, however, criticizes himself for the situation because his wife is so much younger than he, and he cannot help but regard Annie as the "wronged" partner.

After the Doctor and Mr. Wickfield leave the room, David argues with Uriah over "entrapping me into your schemes" and becomes so angry that he slaps Uriah on the cheek.

David later notices that the Doctor exhibits a "gentle compassion" toward his wife and urges her to spend more time with her mother, Mrs. Markleham, "to relieve the dull monotony of her life." Annie is unhappy over this estrangement from her husband, and David often notices her "with her eyes full of tears." Only Mr. Dick serves as "a link between them."

David receives a letter from Mrs. Micawber. She says that "Mr. Micawber is entirely changed. . . . He is secret." She tells David that she is having difficulty obtaining even the barest of expense money from him, and she asks for David's advice.

Commentary

In Chapter 41, Dickens gives us another clear picture of Dora, showing her as the shallow, impractical child or "pretty toy," unable to face anything requiring even a slight measure of self-discipline. She is a lovable person, if a simple one; however, the reader can only wonder at David's deep love for her and be dubious about the possibility of success in the marriage now planned.

In Chapter 42, Dickens focuses on yet another woman: the innocent Annie as she is being slandered by Uriah. Here, David comes to the rescue and strikes him, but he is unable to combat the schemes of the villainous clerk. In all of the subplots in the latter part of this long novel, David is merely an observer of the action, for the main part, and is powerless to intercede.

CHAPTERS 43-44

Summary

David reminisces about his life and remembers how his love for Dora continued to grow. He is now twenty-one and has "tamed that savage stenographic mystery [shorthand]" and reports the debates in Parliament for "a morning newspaper." He is also writing for magazines with some success and says, "Altogether, I am well off." His greatest happiness, however, is due to his coming marriage.

Miss Lavinia and Miss Clarissa, Dora's aunts, have given their consent to the marriage and are now in a state of frenzy trying to make the bride's wardrobe. Aunt Betsey helps by hunting for furniture in the London stores while Peggotty cleans and recleans the cottage where David and his new wife will live. Tommy Traddles attends the wedding. Sophy, Traddles' fiancée, and Agnes Wickfield are bridesmaids.

After David reaches the church door, "The rest is all a more or less incoherent dream." However, after the wedding breakfast, David and Dora drive away together, and he awakens from the dream to realize, "It is my dear, dear, little wife beside me, whom I love so well!"

The glamour of the wedding wears off almost at once. Their servant, Mary Anne Paragon, is a poor cook. David tells Dora to talk to her about the preparation of meals, but Dora's only recourse is to cry. David asks his aunt to explain housekeeping to his wife, but she refuses and tells David that he must have patience with "Little Blossom" and to "estimate her . . . by the qualities she has, and not by the qualities she may not have." She goes on to say, "This is marriage, Trot; and Heaven bless you both in it, for a pair of babes in the wood as you are!"

A line of incompetent servants comes and goes at the cottage. When David and Dora go shopping, the merchants cheat them. One night Traddles comes to dinner, but the house is so cluttered that David wonders if there is enough room for Traddles to use his knife and fork. Jip walks on the table, "putting his foot in the salt or the melted butter." The mutton is barely cooked, and the oysters that Dora bought cannot be opened. When Traddles leaves, Dora says she is sorry, but David confesses, "I am as bad as you, love." Later, David is "assisted" in his writing by his "child-wife," who sits beside him and holds the pens while he writes.

Commentary

The first part of Chapter 43 draws upon Dickens' own beginnings as a writer. He became a parliamentary reporter for the *London Morning Chronicle*, and during this time his first articles about London life were published in magazines. Shortly after this, in 1836, he married Catherine Hogarth, although he apparently cared more for Mary Hogarth, his wife's sister. This relationship is somewhat paralleled in *David Copperfield* by that between David and Agnes, whom David loves here as a sister.

Dickens' description of the wedding no doubt pleased Victorian audiences, but his method of presenting it as a mere backward glance severely underplays the action so that the description seems quaint and artificial, like a faded photograph.

Chapter 44 continues with this same sort of autobiographical paralleling. Although the circumstances of David's courtship are based largely on Dickens' involvement with Maria Beadnell, the incompetence of Dora reflects Dickens' attitude toward his own wife, Catherine Hogarth. It is interesting also to note the similarity in the names of Maria Beadnell and Martha Endell, which may indicate another subconscious reference by the author.

CHAPTERS 45-46

Summary

David frequently sees Dr. Strong and observes that his marriage is becoming more troubled. Mrs. Markleham, the "Old Soldier," drags Annie around to operas, concerts, and other forms of entertainment, even though Annie would prefer to stay at home. Although Dr. Strong encourages Annie to get out more, the selfish Mrs. Markleham widens the gap between the couple. Mr. Dick becomes disturbed over this because both Dr. Strong and Annie are his friends. Aunt Betsey, while speaking with David, predicts that Mr. Dick will soon "distinguish himself in some extraordinary manner."

One night Mr. Dick visits David in his parlour. Mr. Dick expresses his concern over the marital drift between the Doctor and his wife. He asks if the Doctor is angry with her, and David replies, "No. Devoted to her." "Then I've got it, boy!" Mr. Dick replies. Then one evening in the autumn, David and his aunt visit Dr. Strong. Mrs. Markleham is at the house and says that she has just overheard the Doctor making out a will in which he leaves everything to Annie. Mrs. Markleham is pleased about this and thinks that it is only right. Everyone goes into the study, where David notices Mr. Dick standing in the shadow of the room. Annie glides into the room "pale and trembling." Mr. Dick supports her on his arm and lays the other hand upon the Doctor's arm. Annie kneels in front of her husband and begs him "to break this long silence." Dr. Strong will only say that it is not her fault. It is left up to David to explain the suspicion that Uriah Heep has aroused in her husband. Annie then dispels the suspicion that she married the Doctor for his money and exposes her *mother* as the opportunist. Annie admits that before she married the Doctor she had liked Jack Maldon "very much . . . very much." She also says that they had been "little lovers once" and that she might have come to "persuade" herself that she really loved him and might have married him and "been most wretched." She then assures her husband, ". . . in my lightest thought I have never wronged you—never wavered in the love and fidelity I owe you!" Afterward, the two are reunited, and after the reunion, Aunt Betsey attributes the success of the affair to Mr. Dick. "You are a very remarkable man, Dick!"

David has been married almost a year and is becoming more and more successful in his writing. One night, as he is walking home and thinking about the novel he is writing, he passes the Steerforth house. He is stopped by Mrs. Steerforth's maid, who tells him that Rosa Dartle wishes to speak with him.

Miss Dartle asks David if Em'ly has been found, and when David answers that he knows nothing about her, Miss Dartle sadistically suggests, "She may be dead." Miss Dartle calls Littimer into the room to give a report. Littimer explains that he and a Mr. James traveled all over Europe with Em'ly and that she was admired wherever they went. He says that Em'ly, however, was often depressed, and that she and Steerforth frequently quarreled until finally Steerforth left her. Before departing, Steerforth implied that she should marry Littimer. Littimer says that Em'ly was so upset that he had to watch her constantly so that she wouldn't kill herself. He then says that Em'ly escaped from him and has not been seen since. Once again Miss Dartle expresses the hope that Em'ly ("this low girl") may be dead.

The next evening, David goes to Hungerford Market in London to find Mr. Peggotty. David informs him of what he has learned from Littimer, and they agree that the best chance of finding Em'ly would be through Martha Endell, Em'ly's friend, who has been living in London; before they leave to find Martha, Mr. Peggotty sets out a candle and also lays out one of Em'ly's dresses. By coincidence, David and Mr. Peggotty come upon Martha and follow her until they reach an appropriate place to talk.

Commentary

Poetic justice takes its turn in Chapter 45. Mrs. Markleham is exposed for the selfish person that she is. The "devoted" Doctor and his unwavering wife are reunited, and one of Dickens' subplots has run its course. Dickens also shows himself to a bit of the "champion of the underdog" in this chapter by allowing the weak-minded Mr. Dick to succeed in reuniting the couple.

Dickens slows his narrative in Chapter 46 by allowing Littimer to comment at length on his travels with Em'ly. He states that she speaks different languages and "wouldn't have been known for the same country person . . . her merits really attracted general notice." However, her greatest pleasures seem to be sitting on the beach and talking to the boatmen's wives and children. David is able to picture her "sitting on the far-off shore, among the children like herself when she was innocent, listening to the little voices such as might have called her Mother had she been a poor man's wife." When Em'ly first met David, she feared the sea and wanted to be a "lady," choosing Steerforth over Ham because Steerforth represented to her a chance of escaping the fishing town and becoming a "lady." This episode foreshadows Em'ly's eventually forsaking her selfish ambitions. The attempt to realize an ambition by selfishly ignoring the feelings of others is, according to Dickens, a tragic character flaw that can only end in unhappiness.

CHAPTERS 47-48

Summary

David and Mr. Peggotty catch up with Martha just as she approaches the bank of a river (probably the Thames). David realizes she is about to commit suicide, and, with the help of Mr. Peggotty, he pulls her back from the edge of the water. Martha begins to sob that it would be best if she jumped in the river because her life is so miserable. Martha blames herself for Em'ly's disappearance and is beside herself with grief because Em'ly had been so kind to her. David explains that she is not to blame and that they are there to ask her to help them find the missing girl. Martha now has a reason to live and vows never to give up until Em'ly is found.

David returns to his aunt's home and observes that the mysterious stranger who had so upset Aunt Betsey is in the garden. His aunt comes out of the house and gives the man some money and the man leaves. David asks his aunt who this man is, and she confides that it is her *husband*. She explains that she has been separated from him for many years and that he has become a gambler and a cheat. She says that she still gives him money out of nostalgia for their past love but that it embarrasses her to have him turn up at her home. She then asks David to keep the subject a secret.

While working for the newspaper, David has managed to complete a novel, which becomes a success. Surprisingly, he is not "stunned by the praise." He does, however, decide to give up reporting.

David has been married for a year and a half, and he and Dora still have little luck with housekeeping. They employ a page, but this man constantly fights with the cook and steals food from them. He finally ends up in jail for stealing Dora's watch. David then decides that he should "form Dora's mind," so she can become more responsible in household management. He begins by reading Shakespeare to her and by giving out "little scraps of useful information, or sound opinion." This fails, and David begins to think about Agnes and to wonder what things would have been like if he hadn't met Dora.

David hopes that their expected baby will change his "child-wife" into a woman, but the baby dies shortly after birth and Dora's health begins to fade. One night Aunt Betsey bids goodnight to "Little Blossom," and David cries to think, ". . . Oh what a fatal name it was, and how the blossom withered in its bloom upon the tree!"

Commentary

Two important themes of Dickens are highlighted in Chapter 47; these are the disciplined heart and wise prudence. Although Dickens has portrayed Aunt Betsey as a woman whom David admires, or whom Dickens himself admires, even *she* has a weakness, for she reveals to David that her husband is still alive, and that it is he to whom she has been giving considerable sums of money. She recalls the time "when she loved him [her husband] . . . right well . . . [but] he repaid her by breaking her fortune and nearly breaking her heart." Yet she still gives him money, "sooner than have him punished for his offences." It is only in Agnes that Dickens comes close to his "perfect" human being. Agnes has both admirable emotional control and the prudence to wait for David, who returns her unexpressed love by loving her as a sister.

Dora's death is clearly foreshadowed in Chapter 48 by David's comparing Dora with a withering blossom. It is also foretold by the condition of Jip, the dog. The dialogue concerning Jip is also indicative of Dora's impending death. Dora comments, "He is getting quite slow," and Aunt Betsey immediately replies, "I suspect . . . he has a worse disorder than that." After the baby dies, Dora becomes so weak that David must carry her up and down the stairs. Clearly we can anticipate another deathbed scene.

CHAPTERS 49-50

Summary

David receives a long, flowery letter addressed to him at Doctors' Commons from Mr. Micawber in which he tells David that he wants to meet with him and Traddles at King's Bench Prison. The letter is perplexing, and David reads it several times to unscramble its meaning.

David and Traddles meet Mr. Micawber at the designated place and they sense that much is on his mind. David asks about Uriah Heep, and Mr. Micawber says that he is sorry for anyone who knows such a man. Finally, they board a coach and go to Aunt Betsey's house, where they can talk. Both Aunt Betsey and Mr. Dick are present. They ask Mr. Micawber to make some of his wonderful punch, but he is so upset that he forgets what he is doing and ruins the drink. Mr. Micawber eventually reveals the name of the person who is the cause of his emotional upset: "Villainy is the matter . . . and the name of the whole atrocious mass is—HEEP!" Mr. Micawber calls him a "detestable serpent" and vows that he will crush the "hypocrite and perjurer." Micawber makes some mention of the Wickfields, but, before explaining what Heep has done to them, he rushes from the house. As he leaves, he mentions a future meeting at which he plans to "expose [this] intolerable ruffian— HEEP!" David later receives a "pastoral note" from Mr. Micawber, asking them to be present at an inn in Canterbury one week from now for this purpose.

David fears that Em'ly must be dead, but Mr. Peggotty still believes that she is safe and will be returned to him. During this time, Mr. Peggotty has been a frequent visitor at David's house, and both Dora and David admire the man for his abiding faith.

One night Martha visits David and tells him they must journey to London immediately; she has left a note for Mr. Peggotty to follow as soon as possible, yet she says nothing of what to expect. When they arrive in London, David is taken to a shabby rooming house where he and Martha observe Rosa Dartle entering Martha's apartment just ahead of them. David and Martha listen through a side door, and David recognizes Em'ly's voice. They hear Miss Dartle blaming Em'ly for Steerforth's going away, as she hurls insults at the poor girl. Em'ly pleads for mercy, but Miss Dartle continues her vindictive abuse. "If you live here tomorrow, I'll have your story and your character proclaimed on the common stair." David is frequently tempted to interrupt the scene, but he decides to wait for Mr. Peggotty.

Miss Dartle hurries out of the room and down the stairs, brushing past the onrushing Mr. Peggotty. Em'ly cries "Uncle" and faints in Mr. Peggotty's arms; he tenderly carries her motionless body down the stairs.

Commentary

In Chapter 49, Dickens turns to autobiography again as he expresses the oratorical mannerisms of his own father in Micawber's penchant for writing flowery letters; also, the childlike impulses that characterized Dickens' father are illustrated in Micawber. He is unwilling to reveal the problem that is causing him so much agony, for example, until he is asked to make his favorite punch and is cajoled into talking by the others.

Chapter 50 is often said to be a bit too melodramatic for most people's tastes. Em'ly is still the innocent young girl who can muster only a frail defense when Miss Dartle shames her. Em'ly pleads for forgiveness and explains how much she has suffered because of her passion for Steerforth.

CHAPTERS 51-52

Summary

The next morning, Mr. Peggotty tells David and his aunt about Em'ly's escape from Littimer. Em'ly had run along the beach until she fell down with exhaustion, and when she awoke, there was a woman leaning over her. The woman recognized Em'ly and took her home, where she cared for her and arranged for Em'ly to sail to France.

In France, Em'ly "took service to wait on travelling ladies at an inn," but one day she saw "that snake" (either Steerforth or Littimer), and she immediately left for England. She had wanted to go directly to Yarmouth, but she was afraid that Mr. Peggotty had not forgiven her, so she went to London. Here she met a woman whom she thought was a friend but who was really about to lead Em'ly into a life of prostitution. Before Em'ly could be harmed, Martha found her and "brought her safe out."

Mr. Peggotty makes plans to go to Australia with Em'ly to begin a new life. The next morning, Mr. Peggotty and David go to Yarmouth to prepare for the departure, and David visits Mr. Omer at his shop. The old tailor is paralyzed and is in a wheelchair, but is in the best of spirits. He says that he has read David's book and tells him how proud he is to have known him and his family.

David continues on to the Peggotty house where Mr. Peggotty is packing for the voyage. Ham asks David to write to Em'ly for him and to tell her to forgive him for pressing his affections upon her. Ham feels that, if he had not had her promise to marry him, she might have confided her troubles to him and that then he could have saved her.

Before Mr. Peggotty locks the door on the old boat for the last time, Mrs. Gummidge begs him to let her go with him and Em'ly on their trip. Mr. Peggotty gives in to her request, and the next morning, they leave for London to begin the long journey to Australia.

David and Mr. Dick prepare to leave for Canterbury for the mysterious meeting arranged by Mr. Micawber. Dora insists that she can manage quite well until their return and that Miss Betsey should go with them. Tommy Traddles also accompanies them on the trip. Micawber tells them to call at the office of Wickfield and Heep and ask for Miss Wickfield.

The somewhat confused group proceeds to the office as directed and asks to see Agnes Wickfield. Mr. Micawber leads them into Mr. Wickfield's former office and they meet Mr. Heep, who is surprised at their presence. Despite his usual nervous, slimy manner, Uriah attempts to play the "gracious" host; however, when Agnes joins them, Mr. Micawber begins to berate the clerk for his trickery. Micawber, in a grandiose manner, proceeds to expose Uriah Heep by reading a detailed account of his crimes against the firm, Mr. Wickfield, and Micawber himself. The proof is quite substantial (a notebook that Uriah thought he had destroyed), yet the cowardly villain admits nothing and merely utters counterthreats hoping to deter the proceedings. Mrs. Heep keeps telling her son to be "umble," but Uriah realizes that this will no longer work. In fact, Uriah is quite beside himself when his mother, quite unwittingly, substantiates several of the charges.

When all the facts are made known, Miss Trotwood joins the attack. She seizes Heep by the collar and demands that money which she invested be returned to her (she had previously blamed herself for the loss because she didn't want to hurt Mr. Wickfield's feelings, but now she realizes Uriah was "the consummate villain"). Once David succeeds in calming his aunt, Traddles takes over the matter and tells Uriah that he must make reparations for all his dishonest dealings or be sent to prison.

Quite satisfied with his brilliant performance, Micawber is even further delighted to be reunited with his family. Again he is hopeful that "something will turn up" and he is thrilled when Miss Trotwood suggests that she can "loan" him the funds necessary for him and his family to accompany Mr. Peggotty to Australia. Micawber is certain that it will be just the thing and that "something of an extraordinary nature will turn up on that shore."

Commentary

In Chapter 50, Dickens turns to Em'ly's redemption; this can only be realized when she rejects the last symbol of sophistication—that is, her knowledge of foreign languages. Littimer told David that Em'ly picked up the language quite well and had become, to all appearances, a "lady." But now Mr. Peggotty says that "the language of that country was quite gone from her." He says that finally the child of the woman with whom she was staying called her a "fisherman's daughter," and that Em'ly understood and began to cry. Only then was Em'ly able to begin her journey back home—cured of her "illness."

Dora's illness in Chapter 42, in contrast, is treated lightly, although it is obvious that David is deeply troubled about it.

In contrast to the collapse of Uriah Heep, two other characters reach their peak. Mr. Micawber reveals a serious side by his efforts to collect evidence, and a nobleness of character by his willingness to accept poverty rather than continue to live in the deceitful web spun by Uriah Heep. He even succeeds in putting his flowery eloquence to good use in the composition and the delivery of his letter. Traddles is also outstanding in the affair. David is sorry that he didn't recognize his former classmate's true character and capabilities before this.

CHAPTERS 53-54

Summary

David remembers back to the time of his wife's death after Dora had been ill for some time. In fact, David cannot remember when she was *not* sick. David noticed that Jip, Dora's dog, had become quite old and pathetically feeble, just like his mistress. Dora tells David to write a letter to Agnes asking her to come, and David does so. One night shortly after Agnes' arrival, Dora tells David that she was too young to marry and that perhaps it might have been better if she and David had "loved each other as a boy and girl, and forgotten it." She sends David downstairs and bids farewell by saying, "It is much better as it is."

David sits in his chair beside the fireplace while Jip lies on the floor beside him. David's thoughts wander to what Dora has said, and he cannot help thinking that perhaps Dora was correct in her remark. At that moment, Jip comes to him and whines to go upstairs. David tells the dog: "Not to-night, Jip . . . it may be never again." Thereupon, Jip lies down and "with a plaintive cry is dead." At this exact moment, Agnes comes downstairs, "full of pity and . . . grief." David knows that Dora, too, is dead.

David is very distressed over Dora's death, and Agnes suggests that he go abroad in order to forget his unhappiness. She makes all the arrangements, but David must wait until after "the final pulverization of Heep" and until the emigrants leave.

The emigration of the Micawber family is to be financed by Miss Trotwood, who has regained her money. Traddles explains that he went over the Wickfield accounts and found that the business was not short of funds and that Miss Betsey's money would be returned, except for two thousand pounds that she had withdrawn some years before. Miss Betsey informs David that she didn't tell him about this nest egg because she wanted to see if he could get along without her financial help. Miss Betsey also agrees to pay Mr. Micawber's IOU's as they are now due, and Mr. Micawber can repay her after he makes good in Australia. Agnes decides to open a school so she can take care of her father now that his business has been liquidated. Traddles reports that Uriah embezzled the money because of his hatred for David, and that now Heep and his mother have gone to London, but that "if he could do us, or any of us, any injury or annoyance, no doubt he would."

Miss Trotwood is distressed by something all this time, but David doesn't know what it is. Finally, his aunt asks him to go for a ride in the morning, and she will tell him the reason. They drive to a London hospital where a hearse is waiting with the body of her missing husband. He died a few days before, and Miss Betsey notes that "Six-and-thirty years ago, this day, my dear . . . I was married. God forgive us all."

Commentary

Dickens has often been taken to task by the critics for the very overdone scene which is the key focus of Chapter 53; neither the death of David's mother nor that of Barkis contains as much pathos, but it must be said in Dickens' defense that Dora shows more maturity and practicality than she has ever shown before. Her analysis of their inept marriage is accurate, and she exhibits a deep understanding of David's inclinations by inviting Agnes to be with her at the end.

In Chapter 54, Dickens begins to tie up the threads of his far-flung plots. Heep is disgraced and removed to London; the Micawbers and Mr. Peggotty are removed even further, to Australia; and Miss Betsey's fortune is saved and her husband buried. The minor characters are being dispensed with so that David's life will again become the focus of the reader's attention.

CHAPTERS 55-56

Summary

David has written to Em'ly at Ham's request and in the return letter, she asks him to thank Ham for his kindness and bid him farewell. David decides that since he has a few days before the emigrants' ship leaves, he will go to Yarmouth and deliver the note to Ham personally. On the way to Yarmouth a great storm begins to break. He spends the night at the old inn in Yarmouth and during the night the rain and wind grow stronger. David joins the townspeople as they watch the raging sea and then he goes to find Ham, but discovers that Ham is out repairing someone's ship. David returns to the inn and after a fitful night he is awakened by shouts from someone outside his door that a ship is wrecked down on the beach. He rushes to the scene and sees the schooner being battered to destruction by the wind and waves. One mast is broken off and the sailors onboard are trying to cut that part away. Several of the seamen are washed overboard to their death and only a single, curly-haired man remains alive on the foundering vessel. David then sees Ham running through the crowd on shore and knows that he is going to try to reach the ship. David attempts to restrain him, but Ham has some men tie rope around him and he swims out to the wreck. Ham never makes it aboard, however, for a huge wave breaks up the ship. When they draw in the rope, Ham is dead. Ham's body is carried to a nearby house, and David stays there until a fisherman comes and tells him to look at the other body that has washed ashore. It is that of Steerforth. "I saw him lying with his head upon his arm, as I had often seen him lie at school."

David realizes that his feelings for his friend have never really changed; he has always loved and admired Steerforth no matter what he has done. David knows that it is his responsibility to tell Mrs. Steerforth of her son's death and to return the body for burial. It is some time before Mrs. Steerforth realizes that David is reporting her son's death. Rosa Dartle then launches a vehement attack on Mrs. Steerforth, blaming her for the misfortune, and proclaiming her own love for Steerforth. Mrs. Steerforth goes into a state of shock, and Miss Dartle begins to cry and tenderly tries to comfort her.

Commentary

The most outlandish coincidence of all occurs in this chapter, but the description of the storm overshadows everything else, and one almost forgets the improbability of Steerforth's appearance because the climax is so startling. In Chapter 56, Dickens resolves the entire Steerforth story—Steerforth is dead, not as a direct result of his dissolute habits, but as if Nature had taken a hand in exacting payment for the harm he has done; Rosa Dartle is revealed as an embittered, rejected worshipper of Steerforth, whom she had continued to love unrecognized and unrequited ever since their childhood; Mrs. Steerforth, already an invalid, is reduced to shock by the news of her son's death—another instance of Dickens' penchant for visiting poetic justice on undeserving characters.

CHAPTERS 57-58

Summary

David decides to keep the news of Steerforth's tragic death from Mr. Peggotty and Em'ly. He enlists the aid of Mr. Micawber, who agrees (with characteristic flourish and oratory) to keep newspaper reports from reaching the group before they sail. David wants Mr. Peggotty and Em'ly to depart "in happy ignorance" for their new life in Australia.

David, his aunt, Agnes, and Clara Peggotty see them off, and David joyfully discovers that Martha Endell will accompany the group to Australia. Mrs. Micawber rounds up her children and recites her promise never to desert her husband. The ship begins to move and David waves goodbye to Em'ly and Mr. Peggotty standing arm-in-arm as the ship pulls away.

David then leaves England and spends three years traveling around the world. His sorrow over the loss of his wife increases daily, unrelieved by his journeys to different countries.

David receives a packet of letters from Agnes while he is in Switzerland in which she tells David that his sorrow must be his strength so that he can turn "affliction to good." David intensely returns to his writing and sends a story to Traddles, who acts as an agent for David. David's fame continues to grow, and he finally begins his third work of fiction. His mind begins to clear and his health improves. He decides to return to England.

Commentary

Chapter 57 provides a welcome relief from the sadness and the pathos of the preceding sections. Dickens provides the reader with emotional variety and also shows that life goes on in the face of tragedy.

The shipboard scene is very effective. The ship's passengers, like the Micawbers and the Peggottys, are all seeking a new start. This optimism on the part of downtrodden, weary, and dispossessed people helps end the chapter on a happy note and conveys Dickens' firm belief in the inevitable triumph of good.

In Chapter 58, we see that David's special thoughts are still about Agnes. He realizes that he loves her, but he thinks that they will never be able to marry because of the brother-sister relationship that exists between them. These thoughts plague David's mind as he prepares to return home.

CHAPTERS 59-60

Summary

David returns to London on a wintry autumn evening and he plans to surprise his friends, who do not expect him until Christmas. At Gray's Inn Coffee-house, David asks a waiter about "Mr. Traddles' . . . reputation among the lawyers," but the waiter doesn't seem to know Tommy's name, and David begins to worry about his friend's position.

Eventually, David finds Traddles' apartment and discovers that he is now married to Sophy, whom he courted for so long. Sophy's five sisters are living with them, but the family seems happy, and David is convinced that Traddles will succeed in his law practice.

David returns to the coffee house and notices Mr. Chillip, the old family doctor, seated in a corner. Mr. Chillip doesn't recognize him at first, but after David reintroduces himself they talk about Mr. Murdstone (now Mr. Chillip's neighbor) and how he has driven his second wife "all but melancholy mad." When David talks about Miss Betsey Trotwood, the doctor hurries off to bed "as if he were not quite safe anywhere else." (Clearly, he remembers, in David's words, the "Dragon.")

When David arrives at Miss Trotwood's cottage, he is "received with open arms" by his aunt, Mr. Dick, and their new housekeeper—Peggotty. The happy group is together once more.

David and his aunt stay up very late and talk, primarily about Agnes. David asks if she has acquired any suitors, and Miss Betsey replies that she could have married twenty times but she seems to have a special "attachment." His aunt will tell him no more because it is only a suspicion on her part.

In the morning, David travels by horseback to Canterbury to see Agnes. At the house, David and Agnes are joyfully reunited. David finds that he cannot tell Agnes of his great love for her, and she proceeds to talk about her school and her quiet life with her father. When David asks about her "attachment," she becomes evasive, and David lets the topic drop. Mr. Wickfield relates the story of his marriage and the mistakes he has made in his past; however, he praises Agnes and compares her affectionate and gentle heart to her mother's broken one. Later, David is able to tell Agnes of his gratefulness to her for all her help.

When David rides back at night, all his memories go with him. He fears that Agnes is unhappy . . . and he knows in his heart that he is too.

Commentary

Very little happens to David in Chapter 59. Dickens uses the device of having David be told about the happenings of various characters. Very quickly the various loose ends of the story are being picked up and tucked away in these last few chapters. Agnes, perhaps, is the only person who has remained unchanged throughout the course of the novel. Her blend of sense, sympathy, and motherly affection are enduring qualities that transcend the physical existence of things.

CHAPTERS 61-62

Summary

David receives such a large volume of mail because of his writing that he decides to have Traddles manage his correspondence from London. In particular, David and Traddles discuss a letter that has arrived from Mr. Creakle, the former Salem House proprietor. He is now a magistrate who runs a model prison and the two young men decide to visit him. As Traddles and David are escorted through the building, Mr. Creakle explains that each prisoner is isolated so that they may all be restored to a "wholesome state of mind, leading to sincere contrition and repentance." Mr. Creakle is very proud of two of his model prisoners, Numbers Twenty-Seven and Twenty-eight. David is amazed to find that they are *Uriah Heep* and *Littimer*! Uriah is in jail for fraud, forgery, and conspiracy, and when he sees David he sanctimoniously "forgives" David for being "violent" to him and warns him to mend his ways. Littimer was imprisoned for robbing his master, and David learns that he would have escaped had it not been for Miss Mowcher, the dwarf hairdresser.

David frequently visits Agnes to read her parts of his novel-in-progress. All the time he is with Agnes, he thinks of how much he loves her and what a perfect wife she would be.

Shortly after Christmas, Aunt Betsey tells David that Agnes is about to be married. This rouses David to action, and he rides out to see Agnes to break down the barrier "with a determined hand." Agnes is very reluctant to talk about her "attachment" and she begins to cry. David hesitantly professes his intentions and Agnes tells him that he is the only person she has ever loved. Two weeks later they are married.

The wedding is a very simple affair and the only guests are Traddles, Sophy, and Dr. Strong and his wife. After the ceremony, Agnes tells David that the night Dora died, she told Agnes that only she should "occupy this vacant place."

Commentary

Chapter 61 offers a brief interlude from David's romantic problems, and it gives Dickens a chance to comment on prison reform. Although Dickens did not believe in excessive brutality, neither did he condone "soft" treatment for inmates. David, you should note, is *very* cynical about the "model" prison.

At long last, the long "blind-man's-bluff" romance between Agnes and David is finally resolved in Chapter 62. David finally realizes who it is that he *really* loves; this is a coup for Dickens; his main character realizes what the reader has hoped for all along.

CHAPTERS 63-64

Summary

David and Agnes have been married for ten years when one night an old man calls on them. It is Mr. Peggotty, who has now returned to England for a brief visit. He tells David how his little band of emigrants have prospered in Australia by raising livestock. Em'ly has had many chances to marry but she has refused them all and is content to stay with her uncle. Martha Endell is married, and even Mrs. Gummidge could have married, but she rejected her suitor rather firmly by hitting him with a bucket. Mr. Micawber has become a noted District Magistrate, and David reads a news account of a dinner in his honor in which the toastmaster was none other than Doctor Mell, David's former teacher.

Mr. Peggotty stays with David for nearly a month and before he leaves he visits Ham's grave. He asks David to copy the plain inscription on the tablet and then he gathers up a tuft of grass from the grave, and a little earth, "for Em'ly."

David looks back on his life and tells the reader about his old friends—almost like a theater curtain call. Aunt Betsey is older, but unchanged, and is cared for by Peggotty. Mr. Dick continues to work on his writing and to fly his kites. Mrs. Steerforth and Rosa Dartle still live together and grieve over their loss. Julia Mills, Dora's old friend, is married to a wealthy Scot and is unhappy. Traddles is a Magistrate and he and Sophy have two boys who are being educated at the best schools and are distinguishing themselves as scholars. Dr. Strong labors on his Dictionary (somewhere around the letter "D"), and Jack Maldon sneers at the world and thinks Doctor Strong "charmingly antique." Justice has won out.

The happiest of all is David. His love for Agnes is complete. "The dear presence, without which I were nothing, bears me company." His only wish is that she will continue to live with him and that when he dies, she will be near him, "pointing upward."

74

Commentary

These final two chapters are often called in today's vernacular, the author's anticlimactic "mopping-up" operation. Dickens disposes of all the remaining characters, and we see that his faith remains in the superiority of good and its eventual triumph over evil. This was a dictum that Dickens inserted into every one of his novels.

SELECTED BIBLIOGRAPHY

CHESTERTON, GILBERT KEITH. *Charles Dickens.* New York: Schocken Books, 1965.

FIELDING, K. J. *Charles Dickens: A Critical Introduction.* New York: David McKay Co., 1958.

FORSTER, JOHN. *The Life of Charles Dickens,* 2 vols. New York: E. P. Dutton, 1928.

HOUSE, HUMPHRY. *The Dickens World,* 2nd ed. New York: Oxford University Press, 1960.

JOHNSON, EDGAR. *Charles Dickens: His Tragedy and Triumph.* New York: Simon and Schuster, 1953.

LEY, J. W. T. *The Dickens Circle.* London: Chapman and Hall, 1919.

MILLER, J. HILLIS. *Charles Dickens: The World of His Novels.* Cambridge, Massachusetts: Harvard University Press, 1959.

NISBET, ADA. *Dickens and Ellen Ternan.* Berkeley: University of California Press, 1952.

ORWELL, GEORGE. *Dickens, Dali, and Others.* New York: Harcourt, Brace, 1946.

PEARSON, HESKETH. *Dickens: His Character, Comedy, and Career.* New York: Harper and Brothers, 1949.

VAN GHENT, DOROTHY. *The English Novel: Form and Function.* New York: Holt, Rinehart and Winston, 1953.

NOTES

NOTES

NOTES

NOTES

NOTES

NOTES

Dr. Jekyll & Mr. Hyde

DR. JEKYLL AND MR. HYDE

NOTES

including
- *Life of the Author*
- *General Plot Summary*
- *List of Characters*
- *Summaries and Critical Commentaries*
- *Character Analyses*
- *Questions for Review*
- *Essay Topics*
- *Select Bibliography*

by
James L. Roberts, Ph.D.
Department of English
University of Nebraska

Cliffs Notes

INCORPORATED

LINCOLN, NEBRASKA 68501

Editor

Gary Carey, M.A.
University of Colorado

Consulting Editor

James L. Roberts, Ph.D.
Department of English
University of Nebraska

Cliffs Notes, Inc.   Lincoln, Nebraska

CONTENTS

DR. JEKYLL AND MR. HYDE
Notes

LIFE OF THE AUTHOR

Robert Louis Balfour Stevenson was born at Edinburgh, Scotland, on November 13, 1850. He was a sickly youth, and an only son, for whom his parents had high hopes. When at last Stevenson was able to attend school, he did extremely well and entered the university at sixteen. His family expected him to become a lighthouse engineer, a family profession, but Stevenson agreed, as a compromise, to study law instead. He was a young rebel; he thought that his parents' religion was an abomination, and he soon became known as a bohemian, ranting about bourgeois hypocrisy.

When he was twenty-three, Stevenson developed a severe respiratory illness and was sent to the French Riviera to recuperate. This was the first of his many travels abroad, usually to France. In fact, many of his best-known writings use voyages and travels as their framework – *Treasure Island* and *Kidnapped,* for example – and Stevenson would travel for the rest of his life. He was always restless and curious about the world, and he never put down roots for long in any single location.

While Stevenson was staying at Fontainebleau, in France, in 1876 (he was twenty-six), he met Fanny Osbourne, an American woman who was separated from her husband. He fell in love with her, and much to the horror of his parents, he courted her for two years. In 1878, Mrs. Osbourne returned to California, and the elder Stevensons felt that perhaps their son would come to his senses and forget the "loose" American woman. They were wrong. Robert decided to follow Fanny to California. He arrived there in 1879, very ill and very poor. It was not an easy time for the young lovers. Stevenson barely managed to eke out a living and was ill much of the time. They were married early in 1880 and honeymooned on the site of an abandoned silver mine. It was not long, however, before they received a telegram from Stevenson's father, relenting and offering them financial support. Soon afterward, the couple sailed for Scotland.

For some time, the Stevensons lived in Switzerland because of Robert's bad health, but still he continued to suffer from bouts of severe respiratory illness; he returned to the Scottish Highlands, but became critically ill with a lung hemorrhage. He tried living in England, but the climate there was also bad for him. All this time, however, he continued to write and publish. His best-known novels, *Treasure Island* and *Kidnapped,* are both products of this period, as is *The Strange Case of Dr. Jekyll and Mr. Hyde* (1886), more commonly referred to as *Dr. Jekyll and Mr. Hyde*.

In August 1887, Stevenson and his family sailed for America, where he found himself famous. Thus, he chartered a yacht and sailed for the South Seas. He lived there for the rest of his life, writing novels, essays, and poetry and traveling among the islands. *In the South Seas* (1896) and *A Footnote to History* (1892) are records of his fascination with the exotic new peoples and the countries he encountered. Finally, when Stevenson was forty, he decided to make his home in Samoa, and he lived there, with his wife, his mother, and his wife's two children, for four years. He died very suddenly early in December, 1894; surprisingly, his death was due to a cerebral hemorrhage and not to the long-feared tuberculosis which had plagued him so relentlessly throughout his life.

GENERAL PLOT SUMMARY

Every Sunday, Mr. Utterson, a prominent London lawyer, and his distant kinsman, Mr. Richard Enfield, take a stroll through the city of London. Even though to a stranger's eyes, these two gentlemen seem to be complete opposites, both look forward to, and enjoy, their weekly stroll with one another.

One Sunday, they pass a certain house with a door unlike those in the rest of the neighborhood. The door reminds Mr. Enfield of a previous incident in which he witnessed an extremely unpleasant man trampling upon a small, screaming girl while the strange man was in flight from something, or to somewhere. The screams from the small girl brought a large crowd, and various bystanders became incensed with the indifference of the stranger, whose name they discovered to be Mr. Edward Hyde. Enfield can recall the man only with extreme distaste and utter revulsion. The crowd forced the man to make retribution in the form of money, and they were all surprised when he returned from inside the "strange door" with ten pounds in gold and a check for ninety pounds. They held him until the banks opened to make certain that the check was valid because it was signed by the well-known Dr. Henry Jekyll, and they suspected that it was a forgery. To their amazement, the check was valid.

That evening, in his apartment, Mr. Utterson has further reason to be interested in Mr. Hyde because Dr. Jekyll's will has an unusual clause that stipulates that Edward Hyde is to be the sole beneficiary of all of Jekyll's wealth and property. Utterson goes, therefore, to visit an old friend, Dr. Lanyon, who tells him that some ten years ago, he and Dr. Jekyll became estranged because of a professional matter. Utterson decides to seek out Hyde, and he posts himself as a sentinel outside the mysterious door previously mentioned by Enfield. After some time, Utterson encounters the man Hyde entering the door, and he initiates a conversation with him. Hyde suddenly becomes highly suspicious of Utterson's interest in him and quickly retreats inside the door. Utterson walks around the block and knocks at the front door of Dr. Jekyll's house. Upon questioning the butler, Poole, Utterson discovers that Edward Hyde has complete access to Jekyll's house.

About a fortnight later, Utterson is invited to one of Jekyll's dinner parties and remains after the other guests have left so that he can question Jekyll about his will and about his beneficiary, Edward Hyde. Jekyll is unhappy discussing Edward Hyde and insists that his wishes—that Mr. Hyde be the recipient of his property—be honored.

About a year later, an upstairs maid witnesses the vicious murder of a kindly and distinguished old gentleman, the prominent Sir Danvers Carew, M.P. (Member of Parliament). But the assailant escapes before he can be apprehended. The maid, however, is able to positively identify the murderer as Edward Hyde. Mr. Utterson and the police go to Hyde's apartment, but the housekeeper informs them that he is gone. When Utterson confronts Jekyll about the whereabouts of Hyde, Jekyll shows the lawyer a letter which Hyde wrote saying that he was disappearing forever. Jekyll maintains that he himself is completely through with him.

After the disappearance of Hyde, Jekyll comes out of his seclusion and begins a new life, for a time. But at about the same time, Utterson is dining with his friend, Dr. Lanyon, and he notes that Dr. Lanyon seems to be on the verge of a complete physical collapse; Lanyon dies three weeks later. Among his papers is an envelope addressed to Utterson, and inside is an inner envelope, sealed with instructions that this envelope should not be opened until after Jekyll's death or disappearance. Utterson strongly feels that the contents of the envelope contain information about Edward Hyde.

On another Sunday walk, Utterson and Enfield pass along the street where Enfield saw Hyde trampling on the young girl. They step around the corner into the courtyard and see Dr. Jekyll in an upstairs window. Utterson invites Jekyll to accompany them on a walk, but suddenly Jekyll's face is covered with abject terror and, after a grimace of horrible pain, he suddenly closes the window and disappears. Utterson and Enfield are horrified by what they have seen.

Some time later, Utterson receives a visit from Poole, Dr. Jekyll's man servant. Poole suspects that foul play is associated with his employer; Dr. Jekyll, he says, has confined himself to his laboratory for over a week, has ordered all of his meals to be sent in, and has sent Poole on frantic searches to various chemists for a mysterious drug. Poole is now convinced that his employer has been murdered and that the murderer is still hiding in Jekyll's laboratory.

Utterson is sufficiently convinced that he returns to Jekyll's house, where he and Poole break into the laboratory. There, they discover that the mysterious figure in the laboratory has just committed suicide by drinking a vial of poison. The body is that of Edward Hyde. They search the entire building for signs of Jekyll and can find nothing, except a note addressed to Utterson.

The note informs Utterson that he should go home and read, first, the letter from Dr. Lanyon and then the enclosed document, which is the "confession" of Dr. Henry Jekyll.

Dr. Lanyon's narrative reveals that Dr. Jekyll had written to him, in the name of their old friendship, and had requested him to follow precise instructions: go to Jekyll's laboratory, secure certain items, bring them back to his house, and at twelve o'clock that night, a person whom Lanyon would not recognize would call for these things. Lanyon writes that he followed the instructions precisely and at exactly twelve o'clock, a horribly disagreeable, misbegotten "creature" appeared at the laboratory to claim the items for Dr. Jekyll. Before leaving, he asked for a "graduated glass," proceeded to mix the powders and liquids, and then drank the potion. To Dr. Lanyon's horror, the figure transformed before his eyes into that of Dr. Henry Jekyll. Lanyon closes his letter by pointing out that the man who stepped into the house that night to claim Jekyll's items was the man known as Edward Hyde.

The final chapter gives a fully detailed narration of Dr. Jekyll's double life. Jekyll had been born wealthy and had grown up handsome, honorable, and distinguished, and yet, he committed secret acts of which he was thoroughly ashamed; intellectually, he evaluted the differences between his private life and his public life and, ultimately, he became obsessed with the idea that at least two different entities, or perhaps even more, occupy a person's body. His reflections and his scientific knowledge led him to contemplate the possibility of scientifically isolating these two separate components. With this in mind, he began to experiment with various chemical combinations. Having ultimately compounded a certain mixture, he then drank it, and his body, under great pain, was transformed into an ugly, repugnant, repulsive "being," representing the "pure evil" that existed within him. Afterward, by drinking the same potion, he could then be transformed back into his original self.

His evil self became Edward Hyde, and in this disguise, he was able to practice whatever shameful depravities he wished, without feeling the shame that Dr. Jekyll would feel. Recognizing his two "selves," Jekyll felt the need of providing for, and protecting, Edward Hyde. Therefore, he furnished a house in Soho, hired a discreet and unscrupulous housekeeper, and announced to his servants that Mr. Hyde was to have full access and liberty of Jekyll's residence and, finally, he drew up a will leaving all of his inheritance to Edward Hyde. Thus, this double life continued until the murder of Sir Danvers Carew by Edward Hyde.

This horrible revelation caused Jekyll to make a serious attempt to cast off his evil side – that is, Edward Hyde – and for some time, he sought out the companionship of his old friends. However, the Edward Hyde side of his nature kept struggling to be recognized, and one sunny day while sitting in Regent's Park, he was suddenly transformed into Edward Hyde. It was at this time that he sought the help of his friend Dr. Lanyon. He hid in a hotel and wrote a letter asking Dr. Lanyon to go to the laboratory in his house and fetch certain drugs to Lanyon's house. There, Hyde drank the potion described in Lanyon's letter. The drug caused him to change to Dr. Jekyll, while Dr. Lanyon watched the transformation in utter horror.

After awhile, Edward Hyde almost totally occupied Jekyll's nature, and the original drug was no longer effective to return Hyde to Jekyll. After having Poole search throughout London for the necessary "powder," Jekyll realized that his original compound must have possessed some impurity which cannot now be duplicated. In despair at being forced to live the rest of his life as Hyde, he commits suicide at the moment that Utterson and Poole are breaking down the laboratory door.

LIST OF CHARACTERS

Mr. Gabriel John Utterson

The central character of the novel, who narrates most of the story, either directly or through documents which come into his possession. He is also the counsel for, and close friend to, both Dr. Jekyll and Dr. Lanyon.

Mr. Richard Enfield

A distant kinsman of Mr. Utterson, he is a well-known man about town and is the complete opposite of Mr. Utterson; yet they seem to thoroughly enjoy their weekly Sunday walks together.

Dr. Henry (Harry) Jekyll

A prominent physician in London; very handsome, distinguished, and generally respected; he has alienated some of his close professional friends because of his experiments concerning the dual nature of mankind.

Edward Hyde

As the name indicates, Hyde is the fleshy (or "sinful," according to Victorian standards) manifestation of Dr. Jekyll's personality; he is guilty of committing atrocious acts throughout the novel. The search to determine who Edward Hyde is constitutes the first half of the novel.

Dr. Hastie Lanyon

Dr. Jekyll's closest friend of many years; Lanyon broke with Jekyll concerning how much evil can be found within a person. Dr. Lanyon's narration in Chapter 9 reveals the true nature of Jekyll's and Hyde's relationship.

Poole

He is Dr. Jekyll's man servant, chief butler, and all-around manager of the house; he has been in Dr. Jekyll's service for so long that he knows every footstep and motion associated with his employer; he is, therefore, able to report to Mr. Utterson that the man in seclusion is not Dr. Jekyll.

Bradshaw

Dr. Jekyll's footman and man-about-the-house, who goes around to the back entry of Jekyll's laboratory to guard the back door, while Poole and Utterson break in through the front door.

Mr. Guest

Mr. Utterson's secretary, who is "a great student and critic of handwriting." He finds something amazingly similar between Dr. Jekyll's and Mr. Hyde's handwriting.

Sir Danvers Carew

A distinguished M.P. (Member of Parliament), who does not appear in the work, but whose unprovoked and vicious murder by Edward Hyde causes a turning point in the novel.

Inspector Newcomen of Scotland Yard

The officer who accompanies Utterson on a search of Hyde's house in Soho after the murder of Sir Danvers Carew.

SUMMARIES AND COMMENTARIES

CHAPTER 1

"Story of the Door"

When the novel opens, Mr. Utterson (a lawyer) and his friend Richard Enfield (a distant kinsman) are out for their customary Sunday stroll in London. People who know both men find it puzzling that the men are friends; seemingly, they have nothing in common. Yet both men look forward to their weekly Sunday walk as if it were "the chief jewel of each week." Mr. Utterson, the lawyer, is a cold man, very tall and lean, and has a face "never lighted by a smile." Enfield is much more outgoing and curious about life, and it is on this particular Sunday walk that he raises his cane and indicates a peculiar-looking door. He asks Utterson if he's ever noticed the door. With a slight change in his voice, Utterson says that he has, and then Enfield continues; the door, he tells Utterson, has "a very odd story."

Enfield says that at about 3 A.M. on a black winter morning, he was coming home and because the street was deserted, he had a vague sense of discomfort. Suddenly, he saw two figures, a man and a girl about eight years old. They ran into each other, and the man "trampled calmly over the child's body and left her screaming on the ground." He cannot forget the "hellish" scene.

He tells Utterson that he collared the man, brought him back, and by that time, a crowd had gathered. Like Enfield, they all seemed to instantly loathe the very sight of the sadistic man, who was, in contrast to the others, very calm and very cool. He said simply that he wanted to avoid a scene, and he offered to pay a generous sum to the child's family. Then he took out a key, opened the strange door, and disappeared behind it. He emerged shortly with ten pounds in gold and a check for ninety pounds. Enfield can't remember the precise signature on the check, but he does remember that it belonged to a well-known man. He tells his friend that he finds it extremely strange that this satanic man would just suddenly take out a key and open "the strange door," then walk out "with another man's check" for nearly one hundred pounds. Of course, Enfield says, he immediately thought that the check was forged, but the man agreed to wait until the banks opened, and when a teller was questioned, the check proved to be genuine. Enfield surmises that perhaps blackmail was involved, and ever since that winter morning, he has referred to that house as the "Black Mail House." He has "studied the place," and there seems to be no other door, and no one ever comes in or out, except, occasionally, the villainous man who ran down the child.

But Enfield feels strongly that someone else *must* live there, and yet the houses in that block are built so oddly and so compactly that he cannot ascertain where one house ends and the next house begins.

Utterson, the lawyer, tells his friend Enfield that sometimes it's best to mind one's own business, but he does want to know the name of the man who ran down the child. Enfield tells him that "it was a man of the name of Hyde." Asked to describe Hyde, Enfield finds it difficult because the man had "something wrong with his appearance, something displeasing, something downright detestable."

Utterson then asks a very lawyer-like question: "You are quite sure that he used a key?" He explains that he already knows the name of the other party involved in Enfield's story, and he wants Enfield to be as exact as possible. Enfield swears that everything he has said has been true: "The fellow had a key." And then he adds, "What's more, he has it still. I saw him use it, not a week ago."

Utterson sighs, and the two men make a pact never to speak of the horrible incident again, shaking hands to seal their agreement.

Commentary

The story of Dr. Jekyll and Mr. Hyde is perhaps one of the most familiar tales in all of literature. In fact, it is so familiar that many people assume that the tale has been in existence for longer than it actually has been. It is also familiar because the terminology (that is, the names of *Jekyll* and *Hyde*) is now a part of our common language and can be found in any dictionary. In fact, many people who have never heard of the name Robert Louis Stevenson can offer a reasonably acceptable meaning for the term "Jekyll and Hyde," and their explanation would not vary far from those found in selected or random dictionary definitions such as:

(1) "One who has quasi-schizophrenic, alternating phases of pleasantness and unpleasantness."

(2) "A person having a split personality, one side of which is good and the other evil."

(3) "This phrase refers to a person who alternates between charming demeanor and extremely unpleasant behavior."

In fact, the names of *Jekyll* and *Hyde* have even been used in alcoholism manuals to describe the behavior of a sober person who is kind and gentle but who unexpectedly changes into a vicious, cruel person when drunk. The contrast in the behavior of a drunk and sober person is therefore commonly referred to as the "Jekyll and Hyde Syndrome."

All of the general views or above definitions of a "Jekyll and Hyde" personality come almost entirely from the last two chapters of the novel. Until then, the novel is presented as a closely knit mystery story.

Another concept to keep in mind while reading this novel is that the above definitions and all of the assumptions made about Jekyll and Hyde are postulated on the assumption that man is made up of only two parts—one good and one evil. This is not necessarily Stevenson's intent, as stated later by Dr. Jekyll, who thought that man's personality *might be* composed of many different facets, and that man's evil nature was only a small portion of his total makeup. Consequently, when the transformation from Jekyll to Hyde occurs, Hyde cannot wear Jekyll's clothes because they are much too big for him—that is, the evil part of Dr. Jekyll's total being, depicted through Hyde, is represented as being much smaller than Jekyll. Thus, man is not necessarily *equal* parts of good and evil; instead, the evil portion will often express itself more forcefully and powerfully than do the other aspects. However, for the sake of discussion, and since Dr. Jekyll himself admitted that he could detect only two sides of himself, we will most often refer to Hyde as Jekyll's evil "double."

The entire nineteenth century was often concerned with the concept of man's double self, often referred to as a *Doppelgänger,* a term taken from German literary criticism. This nineteenth-century genre began with a story about a type of double, when Dr. Frankenstein created his monster in 1818 (and due to popularizations of this story, most people think that Frankenstein is the name of the monster instead of the scientist), and later, Sigmund Freud and others before Stevenson wrote about man's contrasting natures—it was, however, Stevenson's story of Jekyll and Hyde that has so completely held the attention of readers throughout the decades. And as noted, the popularizations of a story will often distort parts of that story. For example, Stevenson intended the main character's name to be pronounced Je (the French word for "I") *Kill* (Je-*Kill* = I kill), meaning that the doctor wanted to isolate the evil portion of himself, appropriately named "Hyde," meaning low and vulgar hide or flesh which must *hide* from civilization. The character's name in the movies, however, was pronounced with the accent on the first syllable and it has remained so.

The *double* is also represented in even simpler ways in this novel. For example, Utterson and his kinsman, Richard Enfield, are so completely different from each other that people who know them are totally puzzled by their frequent walks together. Yet, as with the *double,* man is often drawn to someone totally opposite from himself.

Utterson, we discover, possesses those qualities that make him the perfectly reliable literary narrator. He is intellectual, objective, and tolerant; he is also reluctant to judge and is inclined to help people rather than to condemn them. And even though he is undemonstrative, he has won the deep trust of many important friends who confide in him and appoint him the executor of their estates. Consequently, Utterson makes the very best type of narrator since he is privy to the secrets of powerful men but is also discreet enough not to violate any trust.

In contrast, it is Enfield's vivacity, directness, and curiosity about life which involves us in the story as he narrates with gusto and enthusiasm his first horrible encounter with Edward Hyde. Thus, the reader's introduction to Hyde is through a "well-known man about town" who delights in entertaining people with strange and unusual stories. After this chapter, however, Enfield, as a narrator, is disposed of, and we will rely upon a more solid, restrained narrator such as Utterson.

The ultimate purpose of this novel (or tale) will be to demonstrate Dr. Jekyll's view of Hyde; yet this, as noted, is only the last portion of the novel. Before then, Stevenson will use several narrators and devices to present a number of opinions about Hyde. But, by using Enfield as the initial narrator, we get our first opinion about Hyde through Enfield, "the well-known man about town," and in describing his first encounter with Hyde, Enfield also gives us the views of all of the others gathered about when Hyde tramples the young girl underfoot. If we remember that Enfield is the type of person who prides himself on being a connoisseur of the beautiful, it might at first seem natural that he would over-exaggerate his own personal loathing for Hyde, especially since Enfield cannot specify any single deformity or any single distortion in Hyde's physique; rather, Enfield has simply a general sense of nausea and extreme distaste, so extreme that he senses that there is something unnatural about Hyde: "There was something wrong with his appearance; something displeasing, something downright detestable. I never saw a man I so disliked." But if we do not completely trust Enfield's sensibilities, then there are the reactions of the crowd of people which gathers at the scene and remains there to make sure that Hyde does not escape. For example, the women, upon looking at Hyde, suddenly seem to be "as wild as Harpies," and then the apothecary who is "as emotional as a bagpipe" turns sick upon seeing Hyde and has a strong desire to kill the man. Others, including the child's family, all possess this intense loathing for Hyde, accompanied with a desire to kill him.

This first chapter, then, presents not only Enfield's view of Hyde, but also the views of several others and, consequently, the reader is entranced about a person who can evoke such horrible responses in such differing types of people. And we should also note that Dr. Jekyll is not even mentioned – in fact, this part of London is built so strangely that it is not until quite some time later that we are able to discern that the particular door which evoked Enfield's narration is, in reality, the back door to Dr. Jekyll's laboratory. The novel begins, therefore, as a type of mystery story, in spite of the fact that there is probably no modern reader who can come to the novel without a previous knowledge that Hyde is really a part of Dr. Jekyll; but for the original audience, each of the subsequent chapters involved an attempt to discover the identity of Hyde and how he was blackmailing, or framing, or using Dr. Jekyll in some evil and probably obscene, horrible way.

CHAPTER 2

"Search for Mr. Hyde"

That evening, instead of coming home and ending the day with supper and "a volume of some dry divinity," Mr. Utterson (the lawyer) eats, and then he takes a candle and goes into his business room.

There, he opens a safe and takes out the will of Dr. Henry Jekyll. He ponders over it for a long time. The terms of the will stipulate that all of the doctor's possessions are "to pass into the hands of his friend and benefactor Edward Hyde" in case of – and this phrase, in particular, troubles Utterson – "Dr. Jekyll's 'disappearance or unexplained absence.'" Utterson realizes that, in essence, the will allows Edward Hyde to, in theory, "step into Dr. Jekyll's shoes . . . free from any burden or obligation." Utterson feels troubled and uneasy. The terms of the will offend his sense of propriety; he is "a lover of the sane and customary sides of life." Until now, Dr. Jekyll's will has seemed merely irregular and fanciful. Since Utterson's talk with Enfield, however, the name of Edward Hyde has taken on new and ominous connotations. Blowing out his candle, Utterson puts on his greatcoat and sets out for the home of a well-known London physician, Dr. Lanyon. Perhaps Lanyon can explain Dr. Jekyll's relationship to this fiendish Hyde person.

Dr. Lanyon is having a glass of wine when Utterson arrives, and he greets his old friend warmly; the two men have been close ever since they were in school and college together. They talk easily for awhile, and then Utterson remarks that Lanyon and he are probably "the two oldest friends that Henry Jekyll has." Lanyon replies that he himself hasn't seen much of Jekyll for ten years, ever since Jekyll "became too fanciful . . . wrong in mind." Utterson inquires about Edward Hyde, but Lanyon has never heard of the man. Thus, Utterson returns home, but he is uneasy; his dreams that night are more like nightmares, inhabited by Hyde's sense of evil and by a screaming, crushed child. Why, he frets, would Jekyll have such a man as Hyde as his beneficiary?

Utterson begins watching "the door" in the mornings, at noon, at night, and "at all hours of solitude." He must see this detestable man for himself. At last, Mr. Hyde appears. Utterson hears "odd, light footsteps drawing near," and when Hyde rounds the corner, Utterson steps up and, just as Hyde is inserting his key, Utterson asks, "Mr. Hyde, I think?"

Hyde shrinks back with a "hissing intake of breath." Then he collects his cool veneer: "That is my name. What do you want?" Utterson explains that he is an old friend of Dr. Jekyll's, and Hyde coldly tells him that Jekyll is away. Utterson asks to see Hyde's face clearly, and Hyde consents if Utterson will explain how he knew him. "We have common friends," Utterson says. Hyde is not convinced, and with a snarling, savage laugh, he accuses Utterson of lying. Then, with a sudden jerk, he unlocks the door and disappears inside.

The lawyer is stunned by Hyde's behavior. Enfield was right; Hyde *does* have a sense of "deformity . . . a sort of murderous mixture of timidity and boldness." Utterson realizes that until now he has never felt such loathing; the man seemed "hardly human." He fears for the life of his old friend Dr. Jekyll because he feels sure that he has read "Satan's signature on the face of Edward Hyde."

Sadly, Utterson goes around the corner and knocks at the second house in the block. The door is opened by Poole, Dr. Jekyll's elderly servant, who takes the lawyer in to wait by the fire. Utterson surveys the room, "the pleasantest room in London." But the face of Hyde poisons his thoughts, and he is suddenly filled with nausea and uneasiness. Poole returns and says that Jekyll is out. Utterson questions him about Hyde's having a key to "the old dissecting room." Poole replies that nothing is amiss: "Mr. Hyde has a key." Furthermore, he says, "we have all orders to obey him."

After Utterson leaves, he is stunned; he is absolutely convinced that his old friend Jekyll "is in deep waters"; perhaps the doctor is being haunted by "the ghost of some old sin, the cancer of some concealed disgrace." His thoughts return again to Mr. Hyde; he is positive that Hyde has "secrets of his own – black secrets." He must warn Jekyll; he feels that if Hyde knew the contents of Jekyll's will, he would not hesitate to murder the good doctor.

Commentary

At the end of Chapter 1, Stevenson suggests that Utterson knows more about Enfield's story than he is willing to admit. Remember that one of Utterson's qualities is his ability to keep strict confidences and remain always an honorable gentleman, even when indiscretion (such as opening Lanyon's letter prematurely) seems wise.

Now, in Chapter 2, we are given Utterson's own private narration, in which we discover that he is not only a close friend to Dr. Henry Jekyll, but he is also the executor of Jekyll's will. Thus, when Utterson returns once again to Jekyll's strange will and finds that *all* of his property under *any* circumstance is to be left to Edward Hyde, we now realize why Utterson was so fascinated with Enfield's narration.

In the first chapter, we were only distantly involved with Hyde. But now that we know that Hyde will be the sole inheritor of Dr. Jekyll's large estate, and as Utterson's fears increase, so do ours. In such a mystery story, the reader is expected to wonder about the possibility of Hyde's blackmailing Dr. Jekyll. Since we trust Utterson, who has a great fear for Jekyll, our own fears are also heightened.

When Utterson visits Hastie Lanyon, who was once Jekyll's closest friend (along with Utterson), and we hear that Lanyon has not seen Jekyll since Jekyll first advanced some very strange and "unscientific" theories, we then have our first hint that the mysterious Dr. Jekyll is involved in some sort of unacceptable or advanced medical practice – at least from the viewpoint of such a traditionalist as Lanyon. The exact nature of Jekyll's practice will not be revealed until the final chapter.

The most important scene in this chapter is Mr. Utterson's direct encounter with Edward Hyde. Note that even the staid Utterson will pun on Hyde's name: "If he be Mr. Hyde . . . I shall be Mr. Seek." And throughout the novel, the upright Mr. Utterson will seek to discover Mr. Hyde, who is the hidden, evil part of Dr. Jekyll. This chapter begins the search because it was only with great effort and great diligence (standing watch by "the door" day and night until Hyde finally appeared) and at a sacrifice of his other duties, that Utterson was able to talk with Hyde. This must show both an affection for Jekyll and a fear of Hyde.

Beginning with the previous chapter and at the end of this chapter, when Utterson is so deeply troubled, he begins to suspect Hyde of all sorts of things. And since Utterson speaks for the readers, we also begin to suspect Hyde of many things. Among the possibilities that Mr. Utterson entertains is the possibility that Hyde is blackmailing Jekyll. And before we know who Hyde really is, we suspect that he is doing all sorts of evil things: he might be a blackmailer, a forger, a potential murderer (and later, an actual murderer), a sadist, a man capable of committing any act of violence, a man of all sorts of unmentionable, unscrupulous conduct – in other words, a *thoroughly evil* man. In fact, Hyde is *all* of these, but what we never suspect is that he is also *a part of Dr. Jekyll.*

Mr. Utterson's opinion of Hyde conforms essentially to Enfield's view of Hyde. Utterson also sees him as "dwarfish," and he says that Hyde "gave an impression of deformity without any nameable malformation." For some unexplained reason, Utterson regards Hyde with a "hitherto unknown disgust, loathing, and fear." It is as though he is able "to read Satan's signature upon a face." Later that night, the *thought* of Hyde causes a "nausea and distaste of life."

If we now examine the actions of Hyde, we will see that in the first chapter, he knocked a girl down without any twinge of guilt. He made no deliberate attempt to harm the girl – there was no deliberate maliciousness or cruelty. Stevenson uses the phrase "like a Juggernaut," a word which suggests that Hyde's action was one of complete indifference – not an evil-conceived, satanic act. In fact, Hyde stood by and took (or assumed) complete responsibility for his actions and made recompense fully commensurate with his cruel act.

Yet, however, his very presence and appearance arouse a sense of absolute evil in the beholder. In other words, Hyde is the type of person who evokes the worst in the beholder and causes the beholder to want to commit some type of horrible crime – even murder. Stevenson seems to be saying that Hyde is a part of *all* people, and the very sight of Hyde brings out the worst in us; therefore, we want to kill and reject that evil part of our nature, as Dr. Jekyll will attempt to do. As we will see later, the mere sight of Hyde and the realization of the evil he represents will kill Lanyon, and we must assume that before Utterson knows who Hyde really is, that the man has the most disturbing effect on Utterson's life of anything he has ever encountered. And remember that the first chapter announced that Utterson was one who was given to tolerance; he was a person slow to judge other people for their vices. But just as Jekyll will find out that he cannot reject a part of himself, Stevenson seems to suggest that his readers, while being repulsed by Hyde, can never fully reject the Hyde aspect of their natures.

CHAPTER 3

"Dr. Jekyll was Quite at Ease"

Two weeks later, Dr. Jekyll gives a small dinner party, for which, we gather, he is well known, for the narrator refers to it as being "one of his pleasant dinners." Five or six of Dr. Jekyll's old cronies are invited, and among them is Mr. Utterson. As usual, the food is superb, the wine good, and Utterson manages to be the last guest to leave.

Utterson has often been one of the last guests to leave Jekyll's dinner parties, so Jekyll thinks nothing of Utterson's lingering behind. In fact, Jekyll is pleased, for he likes Utterson very much. Often, after his guests have departed, he and Utterson have sat and talked together, quietly relaxing after the noisy chatter of the dinner party.

Tonight, as they sit beside a crackling fire, Jekyll, a large man of perhaps fifty, warmly smiles at Utterson, and the lawyer answers Jekyll's smile with a question. He asks Jekyll about his will.

At this point, the narrator speaks to us directly; he says that "a close observer" might have detected that the topic was "distasteful" to Jekyll, but that Jekyll very carefully controlled his reactions to Utterson's question. Assuming a feigned, light-hearted and rather condescending tone, Jekyll chides Utterson for being so concerned about the will. He compares Utterson's anxiety to Dr. Lanyon's "hide-bound" stuffiness. Now, we realize that Dr. Lanyon did not reveal to Utterson his real reason for being so disappointed in Jekyll. Jekyll, however, unknowingly reveals more to us—and to Utterson—about Dr. Lanyon's distaste for Jekyll's scientific interests, interests which Dr. Lanyon told Jekyll were "scientific heresies."

Jekyll says that he still likes Lanyon, but that as a scientist, Dr. Lanyon is limited—too old-fashioned and conservative, too much of a "hide-bound pedant." Then Jekyll becomes more emotional. Dr. Lanyon, he says, is "an ignorant, blatant pedant. I was never more disappointed in any man than Lanyon."

Utterson, however, is firm about the subject at hand. He returns to the original subject of Dr. Jekyll's will. He says again that he strongly disapproves of the terms of Jekyll's will. In answer, Jekyll says that he knows that Utterson disapproves of the will. Utterson will not drop the subject. He tells Jekyll that he disapproves of the will more strongly now than ever because of some new information that he has concerning Edward Hyde.

When Jekyll hears the name of Hyde, the narrator tells us, "the large, handsome face of Dr. Jekyll" grows pale. Jekyll says that he wants to hear no more. But Utterson insists: "What I heard was abominable."

Jekyll becomes confused; he stammers. Concerning Hyde, Jekyll says that Utterson will never understand. His relationship with Hyde is "painful . . . a very strange one." Jekyll says that his relationship with Hyde is "one of those affairs that cannot be mended by talking."

Utterson pleads with his old friend to "make a clean breast"; he will keep everything confidential. He promises that, if he can, he will get Jekyll out of this "painful relationship." But Jekyll's mind is resolute. He says that he knows Utterson means well, and that of all his friends, he would trust Utterson to help him most, but that "it is not so bad as that." He says that he can, at any moment he chooses, "be rid of Hyde." He profusely thanks Utterson for his concern, and then asks him to look on the subject as a private matter and "let it sleep."

Utterson is silent; he gazes into the fire, then gets to his feet. Jekyll says that he hopes that the two of them will never talk about "poor Hyde" again. He says that he has "a very great interest in Hyde," and that if he is "taken away," he wants Utterson to promise him that Hyde will get everything entitled to him in Jekyll's will.

Utterson is blunt; he is sure that he can *never* like Hyde. Jekyll says that he doesn't ask Utterson to *like* Hyde; he merely asks Utterson to promise that he will give Hyde, as beneficiary, all of Jekyll's estate: "I only ask for justice . . . when I am no longer here." Heaving a sigh, Utterson agrees: "I promise."

Commentary

This chapter presents another side of Utterson; for example, we discover that "where Utterson was liked, he was well liked. Hosts loved to detain the dry lawyer." This quality in Utterson, therefore, allows him to linger after Jekyll's party so as to be able to discuss Jekyll's will with him.

And thus, for the first time in the novel, we meet the other character in the novel's title. And the most immediately noticeable thing about him is that he is an extremely handsome man. This, of course, contrasts with the other part of himself – that is, Hyde, who is extremely loathsome. Also, Jekyll is a well proportioned, large man, as contrasted to the dwarfish Hyde. Symbolically, then, Hyde, the evil part of Dr. Jekyll, represents only a small portion of the total makeup of Dr. Jekyll. Also, Hyde is much younger than Jekyll, suggesting that the evil portion of Jekyll has not existed as long as has the "total" Dr. Jekyll, and later in Jekyll's "confession," he does speak of his youthful indiscretions, which occurred probably in, or around, his twenties.

The contrast between Dr. Jekyll and Dr. Lanyon was presented in the last chapter by Dr. Lanyon, who thought that Jekyll was "too fanciful" or too metaphysical, and he, therefore, rejected Dr. Jekyll's theories. Now we see that Dr. Jekyll views Lanyon as a "hidebound pedant" who is too distressed to investigate new and startling concepts. Ultimately, Dr. Jekyll refers to Lanyon as "an ignorant, blatant pedant."

When the two men discuss Dr. Jekyll's will, Utterson feels a professional obligation to advise his friend to change his will. In fact, Utterson tries to get Jekyll to confess what horrible sin or crime aligns him with this "abominable" Mr. Hyde: "Make a clean breast of this in confidence; and I make no doubt I can get you out of it." When Utterson confesses that he can never "like" this abominable man, Jekyll is also aware of this: "I don't ask that . . . I only ask for justice; I only ask you to help him for my sake, when I am no longer here." The irony, of course, is that while Utterson is so adamantly opposed to Hyde, he does not know that he is attacking a part of Jekyll to Jekyll's face.

This chapter occurs early in the Jekyll/Hyde relationship, and Jekyll is able to assure Utterson that "the moment I choose, I can be rid of Mr. Hyde. I give you my hand upon that." But it is Jekyll's choice to keep Hyde around—for awhile. Originally, the ultimate aim of Dr. Jekyll's experiment was to discover his evil nature and isolate or reject it. But he became fascinated with this evil side of his nature. And as we will later see, Jekyll will reach a point where he can't control Hyde, who will begin to appear unexpectedly and begin to rule Jekyll's life.

CHAPTER 4

"The Carew Murder Case"

This chapter begins almost a year later and recounts the details of the murder of Sir Danvers Carew, a well-known and highly respected London gentleman. Carew was murdered near midnight on a foggy, full-moon night in October, and his murder was witnessed by a maid who worked and lived in a house not far from the Thames. That night, she went upstairs to bed about eleven o'clock and, because the night was so mysteriously romantic, she sat gazing out of her bedroom window for a time, "in a dream of musing." Never, she tells the police, had she felt happier and more at peace with the world.

Ironically, her mood of languid revery is broken, for as she gazes down beneath her window, she recognizes the "small" figure of Mr. Hyde, a man who had once visited her master and for whom she had *immediately* taken an instant dislike. From her window that October night, the woman saw the detestable Mr. Hyde meet "an aged and beautiful gentleman with white hair"; then suddenly, after a few words, Mr. Hyde lifted his heavy walking stick and clubbed the old gentleman to death. Indeed, the blows which he struck were so thunderous that "bones were audibly shattered," and then, "with ape-like fury," Hyde trampled the old gentleman underfoot. At the horror of what she saw, the maid suddenly fainted.

When the police arrive on the scene, they find no identification on the body, and they are puzzled that neither the victim's gold watch nor his wallet was taken. The only bit of evidence they discover concerning the man's identity is a sealed envelope addressed to Mr. Utterson. Thus, they call Utterson, and he is able to identify the corpse. The police are visibly stunned. "This will make a deal of noise," they comment, meaning that the case will draw a lot of publicity because Sir Danvers was such a well-known figure in London society and politics.

When Utterson is shown the murder weapon, he recognizes it immediately. It is the battered half of a walking cane which he gave Dr. Jekyll many years ago. He reflects for a moment and then tells the police officer to come with him; he can lead them to the murderer's quarters.

On the way to Hyde's apartment, the narrator describes in much detail the "chocolate-colored wreaths" of fog that they drive through on their way to "the dismal quarter" where Hyde lives. This district, says the narrator, seems "like a district of some city in a nightmare." Yet this is where Edward Hyde, heir to Jekyll's quarter of a million pounds, lives.

The woman who answers their knock tells them that Hyde is not at home; in fact, last night was the first night that he had been home in nearly two months; "his habits were very irregular." When Utterson introduces the officer as being from Scotland Yard, he is sure that the old silver-haired woman seems almost to relish the prospect of Hyde's being in trouble. They search Hyde's apartment and immediately see that Hyde left in a hurry. Clothes are thrown here and there, drawers are pulled out, and on the hearth is a pile of grey ashes.

The inspector stirs the embers and finds half of a checkbook. Behind a door, he also discovers the other half of the murder weapon, the heavy walking stick.

Delighted with what he has found, the inspector and Utterson visit Hyde's bank and ascertain that Hyde's account contains several thousand pounds. The officer is sure that Hyde can be captured now because "money's life to the man." All he has to do now, he says, is post handbills with Hyde's picture and a description of the man. However, this proves to be an almost impossible task because Hyde has no family, and seemingly, he was never photographed. Moreover, of those who have seen him, no one has seen him more than two times. The only thing that everyone agrees on is that Hyde carries "a haunting sense of unexpressed deformity."

Commentary

Since a year has elapsed since the last chapter, we can never know what Hyde has been doing, what atrocities he has committed and what degradations he has stooped to. Apparently, they have been many and numerous because he has moved from being a creature who tramples on a child in the first chapter to this chapter, where he commits an unprovoked murder. In other words, Hyde's capacity for evil is increasing.

The crime, a murder of a distinguished, well-known social and political figure, is committed by the light of the full moon. Here, Stevenson is using the full moon so that from a practical point-of-view, the upstairs maid can clearly see and describe the encounter between Hyde and Sir Danvers, but also, the full moon, in terms of superstition, is the time when evil beings, often in the shape of deformed men or werewolves, commit their most heinous acts.

The crime seems to be without motivation. Yet Stevenson is careful to describe Hyde's reaction to Sir Danvers. Sir Danvers is described as "an aged and beautiful gentleman with white hair." He also seemed to "breathe . . . an innocent and old-world kindness of disposition"; in addition, he was also noble and high-minded. If, therefore, Hyde represents pure evil, he would naturally detest meeting such a "good" gentleman, one who is the direct opposite of Hyde's loathsome self. And in murdering the innocent and noble Sir Danvers, Hyde is described as having an "ape-like fury," one who is maddened with rage to the point of committing the most unspeakable horror against innocence. It is as though Hyde was not content to simply murder the distinguished man – he had to completely destroy him; he even mangled the dead body so that the bones were audibly shattered and even then, he was not yet content – he had to trample upon his victim. It is as though the goodness of Sir Danvers brings out the most intense evil in Hyde.

Utterson is unexpectedly drawn into the case since Sir Danvers was another of his distinguished clients, again suggesting the ultimate importance and influence of Utterson. This seeming coincidence then allows Utterson to be in on the investigation of Sir Danvers' death and to report accurately all of the findings.

When the body is definitely identified as being that of Sir Danvers, Inspector Newcomen of Scotland Yard is immediately appalled, suggesting, therefore, the public fame connected with the murdered man. Thus, this is not just a murder, but the murder of a renowned man of government, and his murder affects the entire nation more than would, say, the murder of a common citizen; the murder of a high public official directly interferes with the smooth and safe operation of the government.

When Utterson takes the inspector to Hyde's address, he, of course, takes him to the address in Soho, not to Dr. Jekyll's "back door." There, they are met by Hyde's housekeeper, a woman with an "evil face, smoothed by hypocrisy." This type of housekeeper would be appropriate for Hyde since she would be closed-mouthed about Hyde's evil doings, but even this evil housekeeper seems to take delight in the fact that Hyde has gotten into trouble. Again, apparently Hyde's propensity for evil has increased over the past year.

When the inspector has the murderer identified and discovers that the murderer has several thousands of pounds (in today's monetary spending capacity, this would be more than fifty thousand dollars), he is sure that he will be able to apprehend the criminal. Yet, as he wants to prepare a description of Hyde and publish a photo of him, he can find only a few people who can describe him, but no photograph of Hyde exists. It is as though Hyde doesn't exist – as indeed he *doesn't*, except in terms of Dr. Jekyll.

CHAPTER 5

"Incident of the Letter"

Mr. Utterson goes immediately to Dr. Jekyll's residence and is admitted by Poole, who takes him out of the house and across a former garden to the "dissecting rooms." They enter, climb a flight of stairs, enter a door covered with imitation red felt and, at last, Utterson sees Dr. Jekyll, "looking deadly sick." He is alone and sitting beside a fireplace in a dim, dusty-windowed room. Utterson asks him if he has heard the news about Sir Danvers. Jekyll says that he heard the paperboys yelling about it earlier. Utterson is firm. He asks only one question of the doctor: surely his old friend has not been "mad enough" to have hidden Hyde. Jekyll assures Utterson that he will never again set eyes on Hyde, that Hyde is "quite safe," and that he will never be heard of again. Utterson is concerned, however, and betrays his anxiety for his old friend Jekyll. At this, Jekyll takes out a note and asks Utterson to study it and keep it for him. Utterson opens the note. It is from Hyde, assuring Jekyll that he should not worry about Hyde's safety, for he, Hyde, has a sure means of escape. Utterson asks Jekyll bluntly if Hyde dictated the terms of Jekyll's will, particularly the clause that contains the words, "the possibility of Jekyll's disappearance." When Jekyll is seized with "a qualm of faintness," Utterson's mouth grows tight. He was sure of Hyde's part in making the terms of the doctor's will. He asks Jekyll if there was an envelope for the note, and the doctor tells him that there was, but that he burned the envelope. It bore no postmark, however. Utterson tells the doctor that he has had a narrow escape, for Hyde obviously meant to murder the doctor. Jekyll covers his face with his hands, moaning about the horrible lesson he has learned.

As Utterson is leaving, he questions Poole about the note that Jekyll gave him: what sort of messenger delivered it? Poole tells the lawyer that there has been no messenger. Furthermore, nothing came in the mail except some circulars. This news alarms Utterson. Clearly, the note came from Hyde. Thus, Hyde must have given it to Jekyll in the dissecting rooms.

Utterson leaves amidst the shouting of newsboys, still hawking papers about the murder of Sir Danvers. When he is at last at home, alone except for his head clerk, Mr. Guest, Utterson sits pondering the details of the case. And then, "insensibly," according to the narrator, the lawyer asks Guest, who happens to be a "great student and critic of handwriting," if he will study the note which Jekyll gave him and if he will comment on it. As the clerk is studying the note, he comments that the man who wrote it is "not mad" (earlier, Guest had commented that Sir Danvers' murderer was certainly mad), but that the note is written in "an odd hand." Just then, a servant enters, carrying an invitation from Jekyll to Utterson, asking the lawyer to dinner. Guest asks Utterson if he may see the invitation and compare the handwriting to the handwriting on the note.

After a pause, Utterson asks why Guest is comparing the two specimens of handwriting. Guest tells him that "there's a rather singular resemblance; the two hands are in many points identical; only differently sloped."

When Utterson is alone, he locks the note in his safe. He is horrified. Henry Jekyll, he is sure, forged the note that was supposedly written by Edward Hyde, the murderer of Sir Danvers. His old friend, the doctor, forged a note to cover up for a murderer!

Commentary

At the beginning of this chapter, when Utterson goes to visit Dr. Jekyll, he is admitted to Jekyll's laboratory for the first time. In fact, he was not even aware of the existence of this part of the property (and the three "dusty windows barred with iron" will later be the windows where Utterson and Enfield will see Dr. Jekyll sitting, in Chapter 7). Note that when Utterson meets Dr. Jekyll here, he is aware that an immense change has taken place in the doctor: Dr. Jekyll looked "deadly sick." He did not rise to meet his visitor, but held out a cold hand and "bade him welcome in a changed voice." Dr. Jekyll's sickness, of course, symbolically represents his sick conscience that is shocked that such a horrible murder could take place, for he, of course, knows that he (or a part of him) is responsible for the crime.

It is likewise ironic that when Utterson asks Jekyll directly, "You have not been mad enough to *hide* this fellow," the pun on *hide* is challenging, because the reason for the creation of Hyde was so that Dr. Jekyll could indeed hide his own debaucheries behind Hyde and still live his own respectable life as Dr. Jekyll. And when the doctor assures Utterson that "I swear to God I will never set eyes on him again. I bind my honor to you that I am done with him in this world," we assume (along with Utterson) that Dr. Jekyll is speaking the truth; however, this is an oath that will be impossible to keep because Hyde has too much of a grasp on Dr. Jekyll, who will indeed, as in the next chapter, hide Hyde for awhile, but eventually Hyde will emerge on his own terms.

When Utterson again points out to Dr. Jekyll the possibility that he and his name would be dragged through a trial if Hyde is ever caught, Dr. Jekyll again insists that "I am quite done with him." Again, the point is that since his early youth, Dr. Jekyll has tried to outwardly live an exemplary life, and his creation of Hyde was done out of scientific curiosity and also so that Dr. Jekyll could participate in debaucheries without danger of detection; therefore, now, the fear of scandal makes the doctor resolve to never see Hyde again. As Dr. Jekyll says, "I was thinking of my own character, which this hateful business has rather exposed." And too, he has always feared that his distinguished reputation would be stained by his secret, dubious activities.

We should also note that when Dr. Jekyll's servant, Poole, assures Utterson that no letter was delivered by a messenger, we assume along with Utterson that Hyde *must* have delivered it by the laboratory door – the door which Enfield had observed in Chapter 1. It is, after all, fitting that such a person as Hyde would use only the *back* door.

While Utterson functions as the central intelligence of the first part of the novel, we should always be aware that much of the information by which we formulate our opinions concerning Jekyll/Hyde come from different sources. For example, written documents, such as Dr. Jekyll's will, tell us a great deal, but we also rely upon Utterson to theorize about it. And we should also note that Utterson's theories or conjectures will always be *wrong* – because his knowledge does not include the workings of an actual separation of a Jekyll/Hyde phenomenon. For example, in this chapter, after the murder, he will confront Dr. Jekyll and ask him directly if it wasn't Hyde who forced him to make certain concessions in the will. Dr. Jekyll admits (by a nod) that it was. This, of course, is misleading, but – at this point – we accept Utterson's analysis. Likewise in this chapter, we have another document – the letter in which Hyde writes that he is disappearing forever. Again, we are misled when Utterson's trusted, confidential clerk, an expert on handwriting, reads the letter and offers the proposition that both Hyde's letter and the invitation which Utterson has just received from Dr. Jekyll were written by the same person, only with a slightly different slope in the handwriting. Immediately, Utterson is alarmed, thinking that once again, Dr. Jekyll has forged the letter to cover up for the evil Mr. Hyde. And again, we accept Utterson's theory, but what is ironic is the fact that since Dr. Jekyll and Mr. Hyde are one person, Utterson is, of course, right, but in a way that neither the reader nor Utterson could ever suspect.

CHAPTER 6

"Remarkable Incident of Doctor Lanyon"

Despite the fact that thousands of pounds are offered for Sir Danvers' murderer, Scotland Yard receives no information. Seemingly, Hyde has vanished. Yet, if the man himself has disappeared, past stories about him continue to surface. More tales about his past acts of cruelty are uncovered, and a general sense of Hyde's vile and violent life remains. But, as for the man Hyde, it is as though Jekyll was right: Hyde seems to have permanently left his quarters in Soho (then, a down-and-out, bohemian section of London) and escaped—never to be heard of again.

Coincidentally, just as the disappearance of Hyde seems to be a matter of fact, Jekyll's sanity and his sense of good health return. The doctor comes out of his self-imposed seclusion and begins giving dinner parties again. He is seen often in public, and people take note of how happy and healthy he looks. For two months, it seems as though Dr. Jekyll immensely enjoys life once more.

Yet, on January 8, Utterson dined with Jekyll, and only four days after this festive and merry dinner party, Utterson goes to see his old friend and is turned away by Poole. Likewise, he is turned away several more times. Utterson becomes concerned. He had come to believe that both Jekyll's mental and physical health had returned to him. But now it seems that Jekyll has lapsed into a grave illness that threatens both his body and his soul. For that reason, Utterson hurries off to see Dr. Lanyon.

He is relieved to find that the doctor is at home, but when he sees Lanyon, he is stunned to discover that his old friend is terribly ill. Lanyon "had his death-warrant written legibly upon his face."

Utterson senses that Lanyon, however, is not dying of physical decay; it seems as though he is a victim of some "deep-seated terror" within his mind. Utterson cannot help himself; he remarks on how very ill Lanyon looks, and the doctor admits that indeed, he is seriously ill. "I have had a shock," he tells Utterson, and when Utterson mentions their friend Jekyll's similar illness, Lanyon's face changes. He says that he never wishes to see or talk about Dr. Jekyll. He is vehement: he is done with the doctor; from now on, he will regard Jekyll as being already dead.

Utterson protests at such a display of hatred, but Lanyon is firm. He never wants to see Jekyll again. He tells Utterson that perhaps someday Utterson will learn about the "right and wrong of this." The phrase "of this" eludes Utterson; he cannot fathom what Lanyon is referring to, but whatever "this" may be, it is sufficient to cause Lanyon to tell Utterson that if he cannot talk about a subject other than Jekyll, he must leave.

When Utterson returns home, he sits down and writes a letter to Jekyll, asking straightforwardly for an answer about why he and Lanyon have quarreled. The following day, he receives Jekyll's answer. But after reading the doctor's letter, Utterson knows no more than he did formerly.

Jekyll shares Lanyon's view that the two old friends must never meet again. As for himself, Jekyll says that he intends to lead a very secluded life from now on. However, he pleads with Utterson to believe in Jekyll's genuine friendship for him, but he asks Utterson to trust him to know what is best for all concerned. "I have to go my own dark way," Jekyll says, and it is a way that Utterson must not try and follow. He says further that he has brought a terrible punishment and a danger on himself; he never imagined that he could, or would, become "the chief of sinners," or that the earth contained such "sufferings and terrors"; he begs Utterson to respect his fervent wish for absolute privacy and solitude.

The lawyer's worst fears are confirmed. The old "dark influence" has returned and enveloped Jekyll; only a few weeks ago, it seemed impossible — Jekyll had seemed to be healthy and cheerful. Now, all that has changed, and what is more, Jekyll has condemned himself to a living hell. Utterson is tempted to diagnose the malady as simply madness, but because of Lanyon's frenzied condemnation of Dr. Jekyll and because of his ambiguity about his reasons for hating Jekyll so thoroughly, surely it is more than simple madness which now consumes Jekyll. There must be something else.

Less than three weeks later, Lanyon is dead. After the funeral, Utterson returns home and goes to his business office; there, by candlelight, he takes out a sealed envelope and studies it. Written on the outside of the envelope is: "PRIVATE: for the hands of G. J. Utterson Alone, and in case of his predecease to be *destroyed unread.*" The emphasis on these last two words puzzles Utterson. Reluctantly, he decides to open the envelope. Within, there is another envelope, also sealed, with instructions "*not* to be opened till the death or disappearance of Dr. Henry Jekyll."

Utterson's mind reels; the same phrase that he read in Jekyll's will, "death or disappearance," confronts him anew, flooding him with black, sinister waves of revulsion for Edward Hyde. Without a doubt, Lanyon's writing is on both envelopes, and thus the mystery concerning Hyde, Jekyll, and Lanyon mounts, and as much as Utterson longs to solve the mystery once and for all, he cannot betray his old friend's honor and faith. Thus, he replaces the inner envelope into the outer envelope and replaces both of them in his safe once again. Then he goes to Jekyll's apartment, but Poole has unpleasant news. The doctor, he says, lives almost continually alone in the single, small room over the laboratory; he does not read, and he says very little. Something terrible seems to be preying on his mind.

Utterson continues to return to Jekyll's quarters, but each time, Poole has the same melancholy news: Jekyll is living alone above the laboratory and seeing no one. Thus, Utterson's futile visits become fewer and fewer.

Commentary

At the opening of the chapter, when the police are investigating Hyde's life and deeds, and we hear about the numerous vile practices he has committed, we now realize that during the year that elapses between Chapters 3 and 4, Hyde had apparently practiced every type of vile and violent deed and "had collected a multitude of enemies." This causes Utterson to utter "the death of Sir Danvers was . . . more than paid for by the disappearance of Mr. Hyde." This is not a callous statement when we realize the extreme extent of the evil practiced by Hyde. Utterson is the type who would gladly sacrifice a single life if it insured the riddance of a universal evil which Hyde now appears to be.

It is also symbolic that once Dr. Jekyll has rejected Hyde, Jekyll changes completely. In medical terms, he has purged himself of some deep disease that was eating away at him. With Hyde gone, for some time (Sir Danvers was murdered by Hyde in October, and it is now early January), Jekyll has changed back into his old social self and has been a delightful host. Thus, it is even more puzzling when Jekyll suddenly reverts to his old secretive self. The explanation for this episode is not given until Chapter 10, when Jekyll explains that he was sitting in Regent's Park, when suddenly, to his horror, he became Edward Hyde and found himself clad in the over-sized clothes of Dr. Jekyll. The shock of this transformation occurring without the use of his potion causes the doctor to totally isolate himself.

During Utterson's visit to Dr. Lanyon, he discovers the man to be the victim of some unknown terror which has literally announced his doom—he will be dead in three weeks. What Utterson or the reader does not know is that by the chronological time of Utterson's conversation with Lanyon, Dr. Lanyon has already been exposed to the events narrated in his document that we will read in Chapter 9. That is, on the 8th of January, Utterson had dined with Dr. Jekyll and yet it is only two days later when Lanyon received the letter from Jekyll, dated January 10th, begging for help, and it was then that Lanyon was exposed to the fact that Jekyll and Hyde are the same. We do not know this until later, but the novel is already looking forward to that knowledge, and we can now understand Dr. Lanyon's total collapse.

The cause of Lanyon's death—the horror—is not fully clear until the entire novel is considered. It must be remembered that both men had once been very close friends and that both men are eminent in their professions. Likewise, we ultimately know that Dr. Lanyon has disapproved of Dr. Jekyll on professional grounds—that Jekyll's *metaphysical* speculations about human behavior transcend the true limits of physical medicine, that Dr. Jekyll's ideas are "too fanciful" for him, and thus they broke company. However, no matter how metaphysical or fanciful Dr. Jekyll's *ideas* are, when Dr. Lanyon was exposed to the *reality* of the speculations in the person of Hyde, who before Lanyon's eyes became Jekyll, it horrifies him. The actual horror of the discovery that Jekyll and Hyde are one person lies *not* in the discovery itself, but in the full realization concerning the nature of evil in *all men*. The effect of Lanyon's being exposed directly to EVIL INCARNATE is simply too monstrous for Dr. Lanyon to absorb, admit, or handle because this would mean that every person, including Dr. Lanyon, is partly evil. The shock of this realization therefore kills him. A similar type of idea is found earlier in the century in Nathaniel Hawthorne's story "Young Goodman Brown"; Brown went forth into the forest, where he had a vision of evil, in which he saw all of the good ministers and goodwomen and even his wife, Faith, in secret conspiracy with the Devil. After that night, Young Goodman Brown was forever a changed and gloomy man. A direct confrontation with the personification of evil in the person of Edward Hyde and his transformation back into Jekyll was simply more than the good Dr. Lanyon could handle.

Utterson's character is put to a test in this chapter. Upon Dr. Lanyon's death and the receipt of the envelope with the instructions "not to be opened till the death or disappearance of Dr. Henry Jekyll," Utterson is sore put *not* to obey his friend's request.

Having lost one friend, Dr. Lanyon, and fearing the loss of Dr. Jekyll because of the strange wording "death or disappearance"—the same words Jekyll used in his will—all of these things combine to tempt Utterson to violate Lanyon's trust and open the envelope, especially since it might contain some information which might help save Dr. Jekyll. But "professional honor and faith to his dead friend" restrain him from opening the envelope, which he locks away in his safe.

CHAPTER 7

"Incident at the Window"

Mr. Utterson and Mr. Enfield are taking one of their customary Sunday strolls and, by chance, their path takes them past "that door," the door that they agreed never to speak of again. They pause now and look at it. Enfield thinks that Mr. Hyde will never be heard of again, and Utterson is quick to agree. He then asks Enfield if he ever told his old friend that he actually saw Hyde, and, furthermore, that when he saw the man, he was filled with a fierce feeling of revulsion. Enfield remarks that it's impossible to see Hyde and not feel nauseated.

Utterson suggests that they step into the courtyard for a look at the windows, and as they do, he reveals his uneasiness about Dr. Jekyll's health. Ominously, he says that perhaps just "the presence of a friend" outside, in the court, might strengthen the poor man.

The two men survey the windows of Jekyll's quarters, and their eyes are drawn to one window in particular. It is half-open and sitting close beside it, looking like a prisoner in solitary confinement, is Dr. Jekyll. Unhesitatingly, Utterson calls out to the doctor, "Jekyll, I trust you are better."

Jekyll's reply is dreary: he feels low, very low, and fears that he "will not last long, thank God." Trying to cheer his old friend, Utterson urges Jekyll to get out – "whip up the circulation" – and he invites Jekyll to join him and Enfield.

Jekyll sighs. He says that Utterson is a good man for suggesting a stroll together, but he cannot join them; he dare not. Yet, he stresses that he is very glad to see Utterson, and he would like to invite the two men up, but "the place is really not fit." Utterson suggests then that they converse where they are, and the suggestion causes Jekyll to turn and smile at them. But suddenly his features convulse and freeze in an expression of "abject terror and despair." The narrator tells us that the change in Jekyll's expression was so instantaneous and so horrible that it "froze the very blood of the two gentlemen below."

Jekyll's window is jerked down so viciously that, without a word, Utterson and Enfield turn and leave the courtyard. They do not speak to one another until they reach a neighboring thoroughfare, where there are "still some stirrings of life." Both men are so pale that when they look at one another, there is "an answering horror in their eyes."

Utterson speaks softly, "God forgive us, God forgive us." Enfield nods, and the two men walk on once more in silence.

Commentary

Chapter 7 is obviously the shortest chapter in the novel, only about two pages long, but it contains a key scene: during the walk that Utterson and Enfield take, they find themselves before that same door which prompted Enfield to relate the story of his encounter with Hyde in Chapter 1. Likewise, here are the three windows that were half-open in Jekyll's laboratory, described in Chapter 5. Now the reader is fully aware of the significance of the *front* of Jekyll's house with its great facade and its elegant interior, as contrasted to the *back* entrance (Hyde's entrance), with its dilapidated structure.

Some readers and students feel cheated that Stevenson does not fully reveal what Utterson saw at the window in Jekyll's face just before Jekyll slams the window down and disappears. We must only assume that suddenly Jekyll takes on some of Hyde's traits, and that now both Utterson and Enfield have had a glimpse of the duality of man, of the evil that resides in the soul of man. But whereas Lanyon was a man who could not tolerate such an insight, Utterson and Enfield both belong to a different world. Enfield is "that man about town" who has theoretically seen many sorts of things, and Utterson, from the first pages, is a man who is not quick to judge his fellow man. Yet each of these men, upon seeing something in Dr. Jekyll's face, feel "abject terror and despair" and what they see freezes "the very blood of the two gentlemen."

CHAPTER 8

"The Last Night"

One evening after dinner, Utterson is sitting peacefully beside his fireplace when he receives a visit by a very agitated and upset Mr. Poole. He offers Poole a glass of wine to calm him, and although Poole accepts it, he neglects to drink it as he hesitatingly tells Utterson about his fears concerning Dr. Jekyll. Poole is terribly afraid. He fears that there has been "foul play," the nature of which he "daren't say." At this, Utterson grabs up his hat and his greatcoat, and the two men set forth in the wild, cold March night for Jekyll's house. When they arrive at Jekyll's quarters, a servant opens the door very guardedly, asking, "Is that you, Poole?" Once inside, Utterson finds all of Jekyll's servants "huddled together like a flock of sheep," and when they see Utterson, one maid breaks into "hysterical whimpering." This matter is far more serious than Utterson ever imagined. Several of the servants try to speak up, but Poole silences them and leads Utterson through the back garden, warning the lawyer that if "by any chance" Jekyll asks him into his private room, "don't go." This advice, along with Poole's barely controlled terror, unnerves Utterson.

The two men go to Dr. Jekyll's cabinet door in the laboratory.

Poole calls out that Utterson is here, asking to see the doctor. A strange voice within states that Jekyll will see no one. Politely, Poole says, "Thank you." Then, back in the kitchen, he asks Utterson, "Was that my master's voice?" Utterson grows pale. "It seems much changed," he says, trying to conceal his own fears. Poole is blunt. "Changed," he says, is hardly the word for "Jekyll's" voice. Poole says that he has worked for Jekyll for twenty years. The voice which they heard was *not* Dr. Jekyll's voice. Eight days ago, Poole says, he heard Jekyll cry out the name of God.

It is Poole's opinion that Dr. Jekyll was "made away with" at that time, and whoever is in the room now is "a thing known only to heaven."

Utterson tries his best to be rational about the mystery. Logically, he says, if someone *had* murdered Jekyll, why would he still be in there? Poole then explains more about whoever is in the room. "Whatever *it* is," he says, it "has been crying night after night for some sort of medicine." Earlier, Jekyll used to cry out for certain medicines and would write his orders on a sheet of paper and throw the paper on the stairs. For a week, there's been more papers on the stairs, a closed door, and whimpering. Poole has done his best to find the exact medicine, but no matter what he has brought back, it has not been "the right stuff." "It" always says that Poole has brought something that is "not pure" and, therefore, Poole has continued to receive orders to go on yet another errand to yet another store. "The drug is wanted bitter bad," Poole tells Utterson.

Utterson asks for some of these notes, and Poole is able to find one, crumpled up in one of his pockets. At first glance, the note seems to be merely a formal request—nothing amiss—asking that the pharmacist search for the drug "with the most sedulous care." Expense is no consideration, the note stresses, and there is a sense of urgency: "The importance of this to Dr. Jekyll can hardly be exaggerated." And then in a scribbled postscript, there is: "For God's sake, find me some of the old [drug]."

Utterson finally has to admit that this is indeed murky business. More than murky, says Poole: "I've seen *him*," he adds, referring to whoever lurks behind Jekyll's door. One day, Poole says, he came into the large room just below Jekyll's private room and there, digging among some crates, was a creature who was so startled at seeing Poole that he cried out "and whipped upstairs." If that *were* Jekyll, why did it run? Why did it "cry out like a rat"? And why did it wear a mask?

Ever the rational lawyer-sleuth, Utterson tries to explain to Poole that, to him, it seems as though Jekyll has been "seized with one of those maladies that both torture and deform the sufferer." The frantically sought-after drug, he hopes, is proof that Jekyll believes that "ultimate recovery" is possible.

Despite Utterson's rational explanations, Poole is not convinced: "That thing was not my master. . . . this was more of a dwarf. . . . do you think I do not know my master? . . . that thing was never Doctor Jekyll—God knows what it was, but it was never Doctor Jekyll." He is adamant: "In the belief of my heart . . . murder was done."

Utterson says that if Poole is convinced, then Utterson has no alternative: he considers it his duty to break down Jekyll's door, and Poole can use an ax which is in the surgery room, while Utterson will use the fireplace poker. Before they commence, though, they confess to one another that they both believe that *Hyde* is in the room and that it was he who killed Jekyll. They call Bradshaw, one of Jekyll's servants and tell him and a boy to watch the laboratory on the other side of the square. Then they set their watches. In ten minutes, they will assault the red blaize door of Dr. Jekyll's private room.

As the minutes pass, Jekyll's room grows quiet until all they can hear are soft, light footfalls, very different from Jekyll's heavy creaking tread, pacing to and fro. "An ill-conscience," Poole whispers, "there's blood foully shed." When ten minutes are up, a candle is set on the nearest table to give them more light. Then Utterson cries out: "Jekyll, I demand to see you."

The voice that answers Utterson pleads, "For God's sake, have mercy!" Utterson is stunned: the voice is *not* Jekyll's. *It belongs to Hyde.* Instantly, he calls out to Poole: "Down with the door!"

Poole crashes his ax four times against the sturdy red door, and each time, dismal, animal-like screeches are heard inside. On the fifth time, the lock bursts open, and the door falls inward. The scene inside is strange and incongruous. A quiet fire is flickering in the hearth, a tea kettle is singing, papers are neatly placed on the business table, and things are laid out for tea. Yet in the midst of this cozy scene, the body of a man is lying face down, terribly contorted and still twitching. The body is indeed dwarf-like, dressed in clothes far too large for him, clothes that would have fit Jekyll's large stature. Clearly, all life is gone, despite the fact that the muscles continue to twitch involuntarily. In one hand are the remains of a crushed vial. To Utterson, it seems to be a clear case of suicide. Sternly, he tells Poole that they have come too late to save or punish Hyde. Only one task remains now: they must find Jekyll's body.

They search the entire wing but find nothing: "nowhere was there any trace of Henry Jekyll, dead or alive." They go to the dissecting room and find Hyde's key, broken in half and rusty. The mystery remains. Once more they go up and view Hyde's dead body, then begin examining Jekyll's chemical equipment. Poole points out to Utterson the heaps of "white salt" that Jekyll had sent him on errands for.

The teapot suddenly boils over and startles them; Utterson picks up a pious work of literature and is aghast at the blasphemies written in the margin. The "cheval," the full-length mirror, puzzles both men. "This glass has seen some strange things," Poole whispers.

Examining Jekyll's business table, Utterson spies a large envelope with his name on it and unseals it; several enclosures fall to the floor. The first thing he reads is a will, a will very similar to the one which Jekyll left with Utterson earlier. However, this time, Utterson – and not Hyde – is designated as Jekyll's beneficiary. For a moment, Utterson is dazed. *Why* would Jekyll make out a new will? Utterson knows that he has nagged and reprimanded Jekyll excessively in the past. Surely Jekyll was angry at Utterson for being so demanding. Yet why did Jekyll make Utterson his beneficiary?

Utterson then examines another piece of paper. Shouting at Poole, he is delighted to recognize the doctor's handwriting and the date at the top of the note: Jekyll "was alive and here this day," he cries. Surely, Utterson thinks, the doctor must *still* be alive; perhaps he has fled. With great anxiety, he decides to read the next enclosure.

The message is brief. Jekyll has disappeared, under circumstances that he had the "penetration to foresee." However, his end, he fears, is certain. He asks Utterson to read Dr. Lanyon's note first, for Lanyon has told Jekyll that his note is now in Utterson's possession. If after reading Lanyon's narrative, there are still unanswered questions, Utterson is then to read the large, sealed packet containing Jekyll's "confession."

Utterson turns to Poole and asks him to say nothing of this sealed packet; perhaps they can yet save Jekyll's reputation. Glancing at a clock, he sees that it is ten o'clock. He will go home, read the documents, return before midnight, and then they will send for the police.

Commentary

Chapter 8 functions as perhaps the most traditional narrative chapter in the novel. Most of the other chapters present *incidents*: "Story [or Incident] of the Door," "Incident of the Letter," "Remarkable Incident of Dr. Lanyon," and "Incident at the Window"; the other chapters, similarly, give accounts of wills, what is reported in the newspapers, Dr. Lanyon's "Account," and finally Dr. Jekyll's own "Statement." In contrast, this chapter flies along in its narrative sequences with such varied activities as the gathering of forces within Jekyll's house (and note how frightened all the servants are: some, like the maid, succumb to hysterics; likewise, all stand "huddled together like a flock of sheep"). They are terrified of what Mr. Hyde stands for and are afraid that he might appear. Then, in swift succession, there is the breaking down of Jekyll's door, the discovery of the dead body of Edward Hyde, the frantic search for Dr. Jekyll, the discovery of the new will, the new note, and Dr. Jekyll's final statement. In other words, whereas many of the other chapters concern themselves with only one single incident, this chapter is crowded with *many* incidents.

The beginning of the chapter is rather slow because the distraught Poole is not educated enough to convince Utterson of the seriousness of the strange events occurring in Dr. Jekyll's laboratory. We should note the long, laborious method by which Utterson is finally convinced. That is, each time Poole offers some information, Utterson is able to offer some rational explanation; he sees the faithful Poole as merely a superstitious servant.

Utterson is not yet ready to act, but when Poole exposes Utterson to the sound of the voice behind the door, Utterson acknowledges that a change has indeed occurred. Then, when Utterson is told about Poole's hearing a cry of despair eight days ago, about the continual crying night and day, about the desperate need for some chemicals and some drugs, about the glimpse of the strange man in the laboratory, about the weeping of a seemingly lost soul, and about the dwarfish figure that Poole believes to be that of Edward Hyde, Utterson is at last ready to act.

After breaking the door down and upon seeing the dead person (a suicide) in the laboratory, Utterson and we, the readers, still think that the dead person is Edward Hyde, even though the "clothes were far too large for him, clothes of the doctor's bigness." In addition, Utterson's puzzlement over why such an evil person would commit suicide adds to the mystery. Then the mystery of the duality is increased by Utterson's assumption that Hyde has murdered Dr. Jekyll. The search for Jekyll's body still leaves the reader in suspense over the Jekyll/Hyde dichotomy or duality, especially when the search for Dr. Jekyll's body is, of course, futile: "Nowhere was there any trace of Henry Jekyll, dead or alive."

The discovery of the broken key and the rusty "fractures" (door or key openings) suggests that Jekyll's rational actions have allowed him to arrange his living accommodations so that Hyde has been prevented from going out the back door. He could not leave by the front door because since the murder of Sir Danvers, he would have been apprehended by, or at least reported by, the servants. Thus, even at the most insane end of his life, Jekyll retains enough of his old rational self to keep Hyde in bounds.

As Utterson and Poole examine Dr. Jekyll's laboratory quarters, more evidence of the Jekyll/Hyde duality is found. For example, they find a pious book which Jekyll had held in great esteem, "annotated in his own hand with startling blasphemies." But, of course, Utterson is misled here. Had he remembered his assistant's, Mr. Guest's, analysis of handwriting—that Hyde's and Jekyll's handwriting was virtually the same except for a slightly different slope—then he would have realized that the vulgar and blasphemous annotations were made by Hyde—not Jekyll—and yet they are the same, thus emphasizing, ironically, the duality of man.

The entire mystery reaches its apex at the end of this chapter with the discovery of Dr. Jekyll's new will, making Gabriel John Utterson Jekyll's sole beneficiary. The name of Edward Hyde is struck out. Utterson's confusion is that the vile, evil Hyde was obviously there in the laboratory, saw the change in the will, and yet did nothing. Furthermore, by the date of the brief note—dated that day—Utterson is totally confused, because of the realization that earlier in the day, Jekyll was still alive. Finally, in the note which Jekyll left to Utterson, the word "disappeared" appears again: "When this shall fall into your hands, I shall have disappeared." This same word appeared in Jekyll's original will, as well as in Dr. Lanyon's instructions to Utterson, and now it appears again in this letter. Therefore, Utterson is utterly confused. And since the final two chapters are "documents," and we neither see nor hear anymore from Utterson, we can only speculate as to how this strange information from his two closest friends will affect him.

CHAPTER 9

"Doctor Lanyon's Narrative"

On the night of January 9, Lanyon writes, I received a registered letter. Immediately, I recognized the handwriting of my old school-companion Henry Jekyll on the envelope. This surprised me. Henry and I weren't in the habit of corresponding; after all, we both live in London and I had just seen him the night before at one of his dinner parties. Whatever could be the reason for such a formality as sending a registered letter? My curiosity was high.

Dear Lanyon [writes Jekyll],

Despite the fact that we have differed on scientific matters in the past, you are one of my oldest friends, and that is why I am asking you to do a favor for me. It is a favor on which my honor rests. If you fail me, I am lost.

Please help me. Take a cab to my house, Poole will let you in, and then go to my room. If the door is locked, force it open. Open the drawer marked "E" (force the lock if necessary), and take out all its contents – some powders, a vial, and a paper book. Take everything home with you. Then, at midnight, a man will arrive at your house, ordered to do so by me. Give him the drawer you took from my room. That is all. If you do this, you will have earned my complete gratitude. I know that what I am asking borders on the fantastic, but if you fail to carry it out, either my death or my madness will be on your conscience. I tremble at the thought that you might fail me. If you do this, however, my troubles will be over.

Your friend,

H. J.

P.S. If the postoffice fails to deliver this on schedule, do as I ask anyway. Expect my messenger at midnight. It may be too late; I cannot say. If it is, you will have seen the last of Henry Jekyll.

After I finished reading Jekyll's letter, I reflected on the possibility that Dr. Jekyll was insane. Yet until that was proved, I felt bound to do what my old friend asked me to do. Thus, I went immediately to Jekyll's house; a locksmith had been called and after two hours, the door to Jekyll's private study was opened. I took out the drawer described in Jekyll's letter, tied it carefully in a sheet, and returned home with it. There, I examined it carefully. What I found whetted my curiosity, but it told me little that was definite. There was a simple-looking sort of salt, a vial half-full of blood-red, highly pungent liquor, and the notebcok contained little – a series of dates, covering a period of many years, which ceased quite abruptly nearly a year go. A few brief remarks were beside the dates; the word "double" occurred perhaps six times in a total of several hundred entries and once, very early in the list, were the words, "total failure," followed by several exclamation marks. For the life of me, I couldn't imagine how any of this could affect the honor, the sanity, or the life of my old friend Dr. Jekyll. And why all the secrecy? The more I thought about it, I wondered if Jekyll might not be suffering from some sort of cerebral disease. Yet I was determined to do as he asked – but not before loading my old revolver.

At midnight, the knocker on my door sounded very gently. Outside was a small man crouching against one of the porch pillars. I asked him if he was Jekyll's agent. He gestured a tortured "yes" and, looking furtively behind him, slipped inside. Keeping a hand on my revolver, I took a close look at the small man. I had never seen him before. He was certainly a distasteful creature; his face jerked in convulsions, he seemed physically ill, and as a doctor, I wondered about these symptoms. His clothes, which were obviously expensive, were much too large for him. His trousers were rolled up ridiculously, and the waist of his coat fell below his hips. Under other circumstances, I would have laughed at his clown-like appearance, but this man was clearly abnormal, disgustingly so. Again, as a medical man, I couldn't help being curious about his origin, his life, and his livelihood.

The strange little man was unusually excited, asking again and again if I had "it." I tried to calm him, but he seemed to be on the verge of hysteria, so I pointed to where it lay, on the floor behind a table. Instantly, he sprang on it, then laid his hand on his heart, and I could hear his teeth grate and his jaws convulse. Then he began mixing the powders with the liquid, which changed colors before my eyes. I was fascinated, and he noted this and asked, "Will you be wise? Will you be guided? I can take this glass and leave. Or I can swallow it before you and show you a new land of knowledge, new paths to fame. What you see will stagger the Devil himself."

I confess that my curiosity again got the best of me. I asked him to continue. He agreed but reminded me of my professional vows and of my deep-rooted belief in traditional medicine, for what I was about to see would be a wonder from the realm of *transcendental* medicine.

Then he drank the potion in one long swallow and cried out, reeled, staggered, clutched at the table, and suddenly his face became black, his features began to melt, and in the next moment, Henry Jekyll stood before me.

What he told me during the next hour, I cannot bring myself to put on paper. I can only relate what I saw and how my soul was sickened. I ask myself if I believe it, and I cannot answer. Terror haunts me constantly. My faith in medicine and mankind has been sundered. I feel my days are numbered. Only one thing remains to be said. That "creature" who came on an errand for Jekyll, by Jekyll's own admission, was none other than Edward Hyde, the murderer of Sir Danvers Carew!

Commentary

In terms of the narrative structure of the novel, finally and for the first time, the reader comes to the astounding realization that (1) Dr. Jekyll and Mr. Hyde are one and the same person; or (2) Dr. Jekyll and Mr. Hyde are two parts of the same person, one evil and the other good; or (3) Mr. Hyde is a part of Dr. Jekyll, that diminished part that represents the evil in all of us. There could be other options in addition to the above, but these are the most traditional.

Likewise, in terms of the narrative structure, this information comes to us in the form of a long narrative set forth by Dr. Lanyon, but we should also be aware that Dr. Lanyon does not tell us *everything*: when Hyde has drunk the potion and has again become Jekyll, the two "old friends" apparently talked for an hour, but Dr. Lanyon writes, "What he [Jekyll] told me in the next hour, I cannot bring my mind to set on paper." Therefore, the reader does not yet have the complete story, because the timid, shocked, and horrified Dr. Lanyon is too stricken by the implications of Jekyll's story to even write it down.

We should remember from Chapter 6 that on the 8th of January, Lanyon, along with Utterson and others, dined at Dr. Jekyll's house; then on the 9th of January, Dr. Lanyon received the note from Dr. Jekyll (dated the 10th of December, an error of consistency on Stevenson's part), a note in which Jekyll, in the person of Hyde, pleads with his old friend for help; now we realize this will be a type of help which will finally bring Lanyon into direct contact with Jekyll's theories, which Lanyon has so long rejected. The direct confrontation will be in the person of Edward Hyde, with his sinister and evil ways. And true to form, Lanyon's initial reaction to Hyde is the same as the reaction of others—"There was something abnormal and misbegotten in the very essence of the creature."

When Hyde has received the chemicals from Dr. Lanyon and has mixed the infamous potion, he taunts Lanyon with a challenge: shall he (Hyde) leave now, with Lanyon still in ignorance, or does Lanyon have "the greed of curiosity"? If Hyde stays, then "a new province of knowledge and new avenues to fame and power shall be laid open to you, here, in this room, upon the instant; and your sight shall be blasted by a prodigy to stagger the unbelief of Satan." We must first question how this revelation will open up new avenues of "fame and power" to Lanyon—especially since the same knowledge has destroyed Jekyll. But we must remember that it is *not Jekyll* who is offering Lanyon this awful challenge—it is, ironically, *Hyde*, and he wants revenge for the many times that Lanyon has ridiculed Jekyll for being "too fanciful" and "too metaphysical" and for being interested in such "unscientific balderdash." Finally, Lanyon is to see with his own eyes what he has so long rejected and ridiculed. The entire person of Jekyll/ Hyde would, of course, not taunt the good Dr. Lanyon, but the evil, malicious, and vindictive Hyde takes great, perverse pleasure in taunting Lanyon.

Lanyon assents, and Hyde drinks the potion. What happens to Hyde is a delightful challenge to filmmakers and is vividly described by Stevenson: "A cry followed: he reeled, staggered, clutched at the table, and held on, staring with injected eyes, gasping with open mouth. . . . He seemed to swell – his face became suddenly black and the features seem to melt and alter." The effect of this scene destroys Lanyon, for as we saw in Chapter 6, Dr. Lanyon is dead three weeks after this scene. Observing the metamorphosis, Lanyon can only scream, "Oh God . . . Oh God" again and again as he watches Hyde become Jekyll. Thus Hyde and, ultimately, Jekyll both have their revenge.

The horror of the transformation is not, we assume, the only thing that kills Lanyon. After the transformation, Jekyll talks to Lanyon for an hour, and we must assume that he tells Lanyon everything that we hear in Chapter 10. The point is that Lanyon cannot tolerate the idea that man has an evil nature, and yet he has just been exposed to the incontrovertible proof that man does indeed possess an actual evil nature which *can* be isolated from his dual-natured self. As we noted earlier, the actual horror of the discovery that Jekyll and Hyde are one and the same person lies not in the transformation itself but in the full realization concerning the nature of evil found in all men because Hyde has stood before Lanyon as EVIL INCARNATE. And this is followed by Jekyll's long explanation which Lanyon "cannot bring [his] mind to set on paper." For upon hearing Jekyll's story, Lanyon's "soul sickened. . . . My life was shaken to its roots; sleep has left me; the deadliest terror sits by me at all hours. . . . I feel that I must die." Thus, the deadliest terror that Lanyon fears must be the fear that *his own* evil nature will emerge, and for a prominent man who has lived an exemplary, mild, and meek life while attaining fame, this possibility is simply too much; it destroys him. But before it destroys him, he completely rejects not just Hyde, but Jekyll also – in his entirety. As Lanyon said in Chapter 6, "I wish to see or hear no more of Dr. Jekyll. . . . I am quite done with that person; and I beg that you will spare me any allusions to one whom I regard as dead." Thus, we now know that the horror of the discovery that Jekyll and Hyde are one person results in the discovery that Lanyon himself is also part evil. To escape thinking further about this self-realization, Lanyon therefore rejects Dr. Jekyll – as well as himself – because he has not the strength to struggle with evil. The knowledge of this phenomenon simply kills him.

CHAPTER 10

"Jekyll's Full Statement"

I was born [writes Jekyll] to a wealthy family and, after a good education, I gained the respect of all who knew me. I seemed to be guaranteed an honorable and distinguished future. If I had any single, serious flaw, it was that I was perhaps inclined to be a bit too spirited. Other people admired my light-hearted good nature, but personally, I was annoyed by it. I preferred to present an unchanging seriousness to the public. For that reason, I willfully decided to conceal *all* my pleasures. Now, years later, I realize that my life has been an admirable one, but it has certainly been a fraudulent one. No one but me knows my true nature. All these years, the public has seen only a veneer of my real self. No one could guess what degrading things I have done secretly, things which I must say in all honesty, I enjoyed very much. And yet I do *not* consider myself a hypocrite, for man has a dual nature. The professional, respectable side of my character is as much a part of me as is the side that has enjoyed to the fullest my secret "irregularities."

Because I knew, first-hand, about my own – and man's – dual nature, my medical studies began to increasingly focus on the origins and dimensions of this phenomenon of duality. This investigation, of course, bordered on the mystical and the transcendental, but only these disciplines could help me better understand myself and the duality of all human beings.

What I hoped to do, eventually, was to separate these two sides of a person's character. I reasoned with myself that if I could do this, then I could eradicate the unhappiness that exists in the "darker self," the self that so often makes life seem unbearable. I saw my quest as humanistic, for if I achieved my goal, man might walk more securely "on the upward path" and no longer be exposed to the disgrace of evil.

To me, the curse of mankind seemed to be that man should have two separate natures within himself, forces which were continually struggling with one another. Thus, I began to speculate that our so-called "solid" body might not be so solid, after all. If one could find the physical or psychic membrane that bound our duality, it would be possible to sever it. But because I attempted to rid man of "the bad seed" that resides in him, I find now to my sorrow that such a task is impossible. My discovery remains incomplete. I feel now that man is doomed to lead a life which will always be a life of burden.

However, I tell myself, I *tried* to remove that burden, and I *was* able to discover a drug that could extract the "lower elements" of myself. Moreover, I was able to look upon this "self" and see that it, while ignoble, was a part of myself, therefore "natural."

I want you to know that I did nothing rashly. I attempted my experiment only after much consideration, for I knew that I was risking death by using so potent a drug as I had devised. But it was my extreme scientific curiosity that tempted me to try and reach into the unknown and shatter the theory that man was indivisible. I was sure that human beings had at least two distinct entities—a good self and an evil self. My task was to use my body for my experiment and try to extract my "evil" self.

I well remember the night I took the potion. I had bought a large quantity of a particular salt that I knew would be the key catalyst; I mixed it with the other ingredients and watched them boil and smoke and then, summoning up all the courage I had, I drank the potion. It began working almost immediately: a grinding tore at my bones, I was racked with deadly nausea, and when my mind cleared, I felt strangely younger, lighter, and happier. I felt newborn, and, above all, absolutely free! I had no conscience. I was evil and wicked with no constraints.

I stretched my hands out in joy and was suddenly aware that not only had I changed inwardly, but that I had changed physically. I had become stunted. Desperately, I sought a mirror and dashed from the laboratory, ran across the courtyard and into my bedroom, where there was a mirror. There, for the first time, I saw my evil side, Edward Hyde, sickly and deformed, despite the fact that I seemingly felt younger and happier. I realized, of course, that my "professional" self had been rigorously trained. This "side" of myself which I now saw had been kept secret for many, many years in the dark cellar of my soul. No wonder it looked sickly and less developed. Studying

Hyde's face in the mirror, I was horrified to recall the aura of "goodness" that continually emanated from Jekyll's face, whereas evil positively colored the entire countenance of Edward Hyde. Yet I was not entirely repelled by what I saw, for this was me, or at least a part of me. What I saw in the mirror seemed natural and human.

I did not linger at the mirror. I had to complete my experiment. Therefore, I rushed to my laboratory, prepared the potion again, and regained the self known to the world as Henry Jekyll, a dual-natured man, wholly unlike the one-dimensional, wholly evil man whom I had been only moments earlier. It occurred to me then that the evil within me was, or might be, stronger than the good, but I dismissed the thought. After all, my potion was neutral. Had I wished to release my pure, wholly saint-like qualities, I could have. But I chose, instead, to extract the evil side of my nature and I had, in the process, given birth to the wholly evil Edward Hyde.

My discovery, though, was dangerous because now, I was growing old. I *liked* feeling young and free. Thus, I was increasingly tempted to drink the potion and drop the dull body of the aging Dr. Jekyll and become, instead, the lithe, young Edward Hyde. In fact, I liked Hyde so much that I furnished a house and hired a discreet but unscrupulous housekeeper for him. Then I announced to my servants that Mr. Hyde was to have free liberty and power in my house. It was a queer, perverse sort of joy to call at my own home in the body of Hyde and watch the reactions of the servants. My next task was to make Hyde my beneficiary in case anything should happen, accidentally, to Jekyll during one of the experiments.

Hyde was a rare luxury. Other men had to hire professional villains to carry out their crimes and also risk a bad conscience afterward, in addition to blackmail. I was safe. Edward Hyde could enjoy all my wicked pleasures and execute all of my angry, vengeful, irrational wishes – and he would be free from shame, for he was free from conscience. He was truly evil. *I*, Jekyll, however, did have a sense of objectivity, and often I was awed at the utter depravity of Hyde. Yet even if I was aghast at Hyde's sensual debauchery, his acts were beyond all "natural" laws, as was I. Thus, my conscience relaxed. It was Hyde, not I, who was guilty. Jekyll's good qualities remained fresh and intact each morning after Hyde had spent an entire night in drunken, bestial orgies of lust and violence. And then, finally, my own conscience – that is, Jekyll's – did not merely "relax"; it slept.

I will not go into the details of Hyde's depravity, except to mention that one night he accidentally ran headlong into a child, and the mishap drew a crowd. Coincidentally, Utterson, among the people who gathered was a kinsman of yours. For the first time, I feared for my life, and in order to pacify the child's family, I had no alternative but to open the door to the dissecting room, go inside, and write a check on Jekyll's account. Later, I prudently set up a separate checking account for Hyde and had him use a backhand script when necessary. I thought that I had taken sufficient precautions to furnish safety for Hyde, but some two months before Sir Danvers Carew was murdered, a terrifying thing occurred. I awoke and realized that I was not Jekyll. I thought that I had gone to bed in my own body in my own room, but I could not be sure, for I realized that I had awakened in the small, misshapen body of Hyde.

I rushed to the mirror in absolute terror. It was Hyde whom I saw. Somehow, during the night, my body chemistry had reversed itself, and the evil Hyde had taken possession of me. I had no alternative but to dash through the courtyard and the corridors and see one of my servants look in wonder at Hyde's appearance in my house at such an early hour.

Ten minutes later, I was Jekyll again. I made a pretense of eating breakfast, but I was not hungry. I feared that I was losing the power to choose when I wished to change myself into Hyde. Hyde was now making that decision. Accordingly, it became necessary for me to double, then triple, the dosage of the drug in order to keep Hyde in check. And not knowing what side effects the drug might have, I knew that I was risking death. But I had no choice. *I* had to control Hyde. My "better" self was losing not only the power to return to its former self, but I realized that I, Jekyll, was losing the *will* to do so. Soon I was faced with a dilemma. Which person did I want to be ? The free, conscience-less Hyde? Or the "good," suppressed Doctor Jekyll? If I remained Jekyll forever, I could never more enjoy the depravities that Hyde gorged himself on. I would be, once more, a good man, but I would be a sterile shell of a man, constantly fighting the fires of temptation because I had tasted—and reveled in—sin, with no remorse or shame.

Rationally, I chose to remain Jekyll, and I said farewell, I thought, to the secret pleasures of the free soul, Edward Hyde. But my decision wasn't one of total commitment. I didn't do away with Hyde's apartment or his clothes – despite the fact that for two months, I led an exemplary life. Then, without warning one day, I was tortured with throbbing knots of lust and depravity. Hyde was struggling to be released. And in a moment of weakness, I gave him his freedom. I drank the potion and once more, Edward Hyde was freed. He had been caged for so long that he came out roaring, and one of his first acts was to savagely murder Sir Danvers Carew.

When I was able to transform myself once more into Jekyll, I broke Hyde's key to the dissecting room and stamped it under my heel. I was finished with Hyde. Yet one day while I was in Regent's Park enjoying the sun, I began to feel my body change of its own will. I became Hyde. The only solution was to flee to a hotel and write a letter to Lanyon and one to Poole in order to obtain the ingredients for the potion so that I could become Jekyll once more.

I was able to accomplish this, but Lanyon of course was horrified to see Hyde change into the body of Jekyll before his eyes. Yet his horror did not match my own horror later, for Hyde increasingly began to take possession of me. If I slept or dozed, I awoke as Hyde and I was doomed. I was no longer able to control Hyde.

Today, Hyde still controls me. And he despises me. He fears the gallows and so he must dash back into Jekyll's body for safety, but he does so resentfully, and he takes out his raging hate by scribbling blasphemies in the margins of my books. He even destroyed the portrait of my father. But how can I kill Hyde? He loves his freedom so. I no longer have the old powders for the potion. Poole has been unable to obtain any that are effective. Whatever I used originally must have had an unknown impurity that allowed me to release Hyde. Thus, I now must end my narrative – as Jekyll. Yet if while writing this, Hyde surfaces, he will tear it to pieces. Hopefully, I can finish and save it for you, Utterson, so that you can begin to understand my strange history. Will Hyde die on the gallows? I no longer have the power to control or foresee either my own destiny or Hyde's. This is truly my hour of death!

Commentary

In Chapter 8, Henry Jekyll referred to his document which constitutes the entirety of Chapter 10 as "the *confession* of your unworthy and unhappy friend – Henry Jekyll," yet this final chapter refers to the document as a "full statement." This statement, then, gives us an account of Dr. Jekyll's experiments and along with the preceding chapter, it constitutes what the average person considers as the entire Jekyll/Hyde story.

In giving us his background, Jekyll constantly emphasizes the excellence of his background which commands the respect of all; his honorable conduct is exemplary to the world, when contrasted with the "blazon irregularities" which he hid with a morbid sense of shame. Thus, early in Jekyll's life, he recognized a "profound duplicity of life . . . so profound a *double* dealer." He also recognized early "that man is not truly one, but truly two," and then he acknowledged "the thorough and primitive duality of man." Also, very early, he saw the need to hide the shameful part of himself from the world, and the necessity to try and separate the two selves.

Note here that many critics are not content to interpret the novel as a conflict between good (Jekyll) and evil (Hyde), but, instead, the novel points out, according to them, that evil (represented by Hyde) is only a small portion of man, a portion represented by Hyde's diminutive and dwarfish size. Certainly, Dr. Jekyll implies this when he theorizes that "man will be ultimately known for a mere polity of multifarious, incongruous, and independent denizens"—that is, evil and good and many other qualities will ultimately be found to make up the entire man. However, Jekyll and his experiments can only prove at the present moment that man's existence has two parts— one good and one evil. Jekyll's experiment, which Lanyon found so horrifying, was an attempt to separate the two components, and when he discovered the correct formula and drank it, Jekyll was approaching a robust fifty years of age; yet after his transformation into Edward Hyde, he felt younger, lighter, and more sensual. He knew from the beginning that he was "tenfold more wicked [and] evil."

As often noted in the above commentaries, after the transformation to Hyde, Jekyll "had lost in stature." He was much smaller as "the evil side of [his] nature . . . was less robust and less developed than the good." This observation obviously contradicts the critics who see Jekyll/Hyde as being ½ good and ½ evil. Hyde, therefore, as the evil part of man, is *less* than the total man, but he is nevertheless an important part of the total man. This is represented in the scene when Hyde looks in the mirror and sees himself as "natural and human": he was "conscious of no repugnance, rather a leap of welcome." This is, of course, because Jekyll sees Hyde as a part of himself. And yet, from Chapter 1 onward, everyone who encounters Hyde is utterly horrified and repulsed by his pure evil. Ultimately, Jekyll himself will come to look upon Hyde as his "errant son" who must be punished.

As Hyde, then, all sorts of pleasures were indulged in. It is never mentioned what the exact nature of all the secret, depraved, disreputable acts was, but most people (perhaps because of the movie versions of this novel) consider these "vulgar" acts to have something to do with sex. In the minds of the late Victorians (late nineteenth century), evil and sex were synonymous, and certainly to such a highly respectable and eminent man as Dr. Jekyll, it would have been extremely disgraceful if he were to have been discovered in some sort of illicit sex. Of course, we know that, as Hyde, he did murder Sir Danvers without provocation, but no other crimes were ever attributed to him; after the murder, however, all sorts of tales surfaced concerning his disreputable life and his vile actions. Therefore, since he was never charged with any other specific crime, most readers do assume that his vileness, vulgarity, and villainy were associated with sexual matters—matters which a dignified and respectable scientist could not be associated with, but activities which he, as Jekyll, had pursued in his early youth and now could once more enjoy in the person of Hyde, while the respectable Jekyll remained perfectly safe from detection. Even after the murder of Sir Danvers, and Jekyll vows to give up the "liberty, the comparative youth, the light step, leaping impulses, and secret pleasures that I had *enjoyed* in the disguise of Hyde," the extreme enjoyment he receives as Hyde is ultimately why Jekyll cannot put Hyde aside. Jekyll thoroughly enjoys, vicariously, the multifarious, decadent activities performed by his double.

Thus, Jekyll's enjoyment of Hyde's activities allows Hyde to grow in stature, and of the two men, Hyde is slowly gaining the ascendancy over Jekyll. The mere fact that Jekyll never gave up the house in Soho (rented for Hyde) nor destroyed Hyde's clothes is proof to us that the vow he made to Utterson in Chapter 5, after the murder of Sir Danvers ("I swear to God I will never set eyes on him again. I bind my honor to you that I am done with him"), was indeed a hypocritical or empty vow. Even though Jekyll did try for two months to lead a "life of such severity," the Hyde in Jekyll was constantly struggling for release. Repressed for so long, when Hyde emerged, he "came out roaring." Jekyll now has to contend with his "lust of evil," with the "damned horrors of the evenings," and with"the ugly face of iniquity" which stared into his soul. Hyde is not to be denied because, secretly, Jekyll still desires his presence and his activities. But he also knows that if he lets "Hyde peep out an instant . . . the hands of all men would be raised to take and slay him." Therefore, Hyde is trapped by his own evil ways and is confined to the laboratory.

However, when Jekyll is sitting peacefully one day in Regent's Park, in broad daylight, he feels all of the symptoms of Hyde emerging without the aid of the chemical potion. Hyde appears because Jekyll, who has so long tried to deny and suppress him, subconsciously desires that he appear again. But the appearance must be concealed, and so Jekyll/Hyde – by now, it is difficult to separate the two – conceive of a plan to get their revenge on Dr. Lanyon, who has so often ridiculed Dr. Jekyll and has refused to even contemplate the possibility of an evil side of his nature existing. Thus, the elaborate scheme involving Lanyon – the letter written by Hyde, but in Jekyll's handwriting – allows Jekyll/Hyde to achieve their revenge against Dr. Lanyon.

From this point on, until Utterson and Poole break down the door, Jekyll/Hyde have an even stranger relationship with each other. Jekyll hates Hyde for the ascendancy that Hyde has over him, and Hyde hates Jekyll both because of Jekyll's hatred, but more importantly because Hyde knows that Jekyll can destroy him (Hyde) by committing suicide as Jekyll. The final irony is that Jekyll is the one who commits suicide (the evil Hyde, of course, would never do this), but during the act of Jekyll's dying, Hyde regains the ascendancy so that Utterson and Poole find not the body of Jekyll, but that of Hyde.

CHARACTER ANALYSES

Dr. Henry (Harry) Jekyll

A prominent, popular London scientist, who is well known for his dinner parties, Jekyll is a large, handsome man of perhaps fifty. He owns a large estate and has recently drawn up his will, leaving his immense fortune to a man whom Jekyll's lawyer, Utterson, thoroughly disapproves of.

Jekyll's own story of his life is recorded in his "Statement," which comprises the entirety of Chapter 10. He was born to a good family, had a good education, and was respected by all who knew him. As a youth, he thinks that perhaps he was too light-hearted. He confesses to many youthful indiscretions, which he says that he enjoyed very much — indiscretions which he was very careful to keep secret. However, there came a time when he realized that his professional career could be ruined if one of these indiscretions were to be exposed, and so he repressed them.

Now, however, that he is middle-aged, he has been fascinated with the theory that man has a "good" side and a "bad" side, and he has decided to investigate the theory. His investigations were successful; he compounded a potion that could release the "evil" in a person in the form of an entirely different physical person, one who would take over one's own body and soul. Then one could commit acts of evil and feel no guilt; furthermore, one could drink the same potion and be transformed back into one's original self.

Jekyll's evil dimension took the form of Edward Hyde, a man who committed any number of crimes and performed acts of sexual perversion; seemingly, his most serious crime is the vicious murder of Sir Danvers Carew, a Member of Parliament.

Jekyll's fascination with his "other" self became so obsessive that he was finally no longer able to control the metamorphosis process, and Edward Hyde began appearing whenever *he* wanted to — and not at the command of Dr. Jekyll. Jekyll became, therefore, a frightened recluse, trying desperately to control Hyde, but successively failing, especially whenever he would doze off. Finally, crazed by anxiety and a lack of sleep, he hears Utterson and Poole, his butler, breaking down his private study door and, in desperation, he commits suicide, but just as he loses consciousness, Hyde appears, and it is the writhing body of the dying Hyde which Utterson and Poole discover.

Edward Hyde

Hyde, as his name indicates, represents the fleshy (sexual) aspect of man which the Victorians felt the need to "hide" — as Utterson once punned on his name: "Well, if he is Mr. Hyde, I will be Mr. Seek."

Hyde actually comes to represent the embodiment of pure evil merely for the sake of evil. When he is first extracted and in our first encounter with him, he is seen running over a young girl, simply trampling on her. He does not do this out of spite — or intentionally; it is simply an amoral act. He does make reparations. But even in this first encounter, he raises a fear, an antagonism, and a deep loathing in other people. The reaction of others to him is one of horror, partly because while looking at him, others feel a deep desire to strike out at him and kill him. In other words, his mere physical appearance brings out the very worst evil in other people.

Since Hyde represents the purely evil in man (or in Dr. Jekyll), he is, therefore, symbolically represented as being much smaller than Dr. Jekyll—Jekyll's clothes are far too large for him—and Hyde is also many years younger than Jekyll, symbolically suggesting that the evil side of Jekyll did not develop until years after he was born.

Hyde also creates terror; the servants are extremely frightened of him. When they think he is around the house, the servants cringe in horror, and some go into hysterics.

As the novel progresses, Hyde's evil becomes more and more pronounced. He bludgeons Sir Danvers Carew to death for absolutely no reason other than the fact that Sir Danvers appeared to be a good and kindly man—and pure evil detests pure goodness.

Since Hyde represents the evil or perverse side of Jekyll, and since Jekyll does, vicariously, enjoy the degradations which Hyde commits, Hyde gradually begins to take the ascendancy over the good Dr. Jekyll.

A conflict between them erupts, as though the older Dr. Jekyll is a father to the errant and prodigal son. He wants to punish this son, but at the same time, he recognizes that Hyde is an intimate part of himself. Ultimately, when Jekyll commits suicide in order to get rid of Hyde (suicide is an evil act in the eyes of the church), this allows Hyde to become the dominant evil figure, and the dying Jekyll becomes Hyde in the final death throes.

Gabriel John Utterson

Except for the last two chapters, most of the rest of the novel is seen through the eyes of Mr. Utterson, who functions as the "eyes" of "conscience" through which we, the readers, evaluate most of the novel. Therefore, if Utterson is deceived in his opinion of some event, then the reader is likewise deceived. This is because Utterson is such a fine, objective narrator who represents a highly moral and upright person; thus, we believe all that he says, and since he is a man of such prominence and integrity, we cannot doubt his explanation or his view of any event.

Utterson is a strange case of opposites. We first hear that he has a fondness for wine but mortifies himself with gin instead. This, at first, sounds weird for a moral narrator, but then we are told that he is not censorious – that is, he is not anxious to judge and condemn his fellow man. This allows many people of differing degrees to come to him to seek advice, and it allows him to be privy to the secrets of the great and the less great. Yet, he also possesses an intense loyalty to his friends and is constantly concerned for their welfare. This attribute allows him to be deeply distressed over Dr. Jekyll's relationship with Mr. Edward Hyde. That is, Utterson is a shrewd judge of character, and he sees in Edward Hyde an immoral and evil person, and he is deeply concerned for his friend's (Dr. Jekyll's) well-being.

For example, when he is convinced that Edward Hyde has injured Dr. Jekyll, he is quick to take action and break down the door to the laboratory in order to come to his friend's aid.

Utterson is also the type of person who inspires trust – and deservedly so. When his friend Dr. Lanyon leaves a note not to be opened until Dr. Jekyll's death or disappearance, he is tempted to read it in order to see if there is any information which will assist Dr. Jekyll. Yet his honor forces him to store the document away without reading it.

Ultimately, we do not know how Utterson is affected by the revelation found in Dr. Lanyon's and Dr. Jekyll's confessions, but from the horror of seeing Dr. Jekyll at the window, when Dr. Jekyll apparently began changing into Hyde, we can assume that Utterson was deeply affected, but due to his objective control over life and its vicissitudes – as a lawyer he has seen all types of criminals – we can assume that, unlike Dr. Lanyon, Utterson was able to survive.

Dr. Hastie Lanyon

In contrast to Jekyll, the "metaphysical" scientist and his interest in releasing "evil" spirits which become physically alive, taking over the body and soul of their owner and embodying it in their own misshapen representations, Lanyon is a "traditional" scientist – completely uninterested in "the other world." Once, Lanyon and Jekyll were fast friends, but when Jekyll became too fascinated with delving into the darker aspects of science, Lanyon broke off their friendship—about ten years before the novel begins.

Lanyon is questioned keenly by Utterson about Jekyll, but Lanyon will say nothing definite, just that Jekyll is interested in the perverse aspects of science, and for that reason, he is no longer friends with him.

Finally, Jekyll/Hyde decide to take their revenge on Lanyon for his prudish denunciations of Jekyll; Hyde arranges a metamorphosis to occur before the good doctor Lanyon. Lanyon is so horrified that Jekyll has been successful in releasing his own evil that Lanyon cannot face the thought that there resides a similar Edward Hyde within him; three weeks after Hyde's contrived baiting of Lanyon's curiosity, the meek doctor is dead of shock.

QUESTIONS FOR REVIEW

1. What is the nature of the relationship between Mr. Utterson and Mr. Enfield?

2. How is Jekyll's house and laboratory physically situated so as to suggest a symbolic significance to the arrangement?

3. After reading the first chapter, how do you account for the reader's intense interest in such an evil man as Edward Hyde?

4. Describe the basic physical appearance of Henry Jekyll, and then describe the physical appearance of Edward Hyde.

5. What qualities does Mr. Utterson possess that make him such an excellent narrator, or the "central intelligence," or "consciousness" through which most of the novel is presented?

6. Discuss the significance of the names of Utterson, Jekyll and Hyde.

7. Discuss Jekyll's and Lanyon's relationship with one another.

8. Justify Utterson's reluctance to read Lanyon's statement until after "the death or disappearance" of Jekyll.

9. What, in your opinion, did Utterson and Enfield see in Jekyll's face that so astounded or horrified them?

10. Could Dr. Jekyll's entire confession be written by Hyde? Explain.

ESSAY TOPICS

1. At the beginning of the novel, Dr. Jekyll is in total control of Mr. Hyde, yet at the end of the novel, Mr. Hyde is in control of Dr. Jekyll. Show how this reversal came about.

2. Utterson as a narrator is objective and honest, and yet he often comes to the wrong conclusion about matters such as forgery, Hyde's existence, Jekyll's motives, and other matters. Discuss the character of Utterson and how he is so often misled in his opinions.

3. Contrast Dr. Jekyll and Dr. Lanyon in their basic responses to scientific medicine, to metaphysics, to the basic nature of evil itself, and to man's duality.

4. Discuss this novel as a "mystery story" and demonstrate how there are many clues that lead the reader to solve the "mystery" before the solution is revealed to us in the final chapters.

5. Using this novel as your basis, discuss the nature of "good" and "evil," or "the double" and the duality of man's nature, as presented in this novel.

6. What qualities does Utterson possess that allow so many prominent men (Jekyll, Lanyon, Sir Danvers, etc.) to trust him so completely?

7. Why is the novel more effective by having all the main characters – Utterson, Jekyll, Lanyon (and maybe Enfield and Sir Danvers) – be prominent, well known, respected men?

8. There are many narrators – among them, Enfield, Utterson, Poole, Lanyon, and Jekyll – in this novel. Discuss what each narrator contributes to the novel.

SELECT BIBLIOGRAPHY

CHESTERTON, G. K. *Robert Louis Stevenson.* London, 1927.

DONAN, DOYLE, A. *Through the Magic Door.* London, 1907.

COOPER, LETTICE. *Robert Louis Stevenson.* Edinburgh and London, 1899.

DAICHES, DAVID. *Robert Louis Stevenson.* Glasgow, 1947.

EIGNER, EDWIN M. *Robert Louis Stevenson and Romantic Tradition.* Princeton, 1966.

ELWIN, MALCOLM. *The Strange Case of Robert Louis Stevenson.* London, 1950.

FIEDLER, LESLIE. *No! in Thunder.* London, 1963.

GROSS, JOHN. *The Rise and Fall of the Man of Letters.* London, 1969.

GUTHRIE, CHARLES. *Robert Louis Stevenson.* Edinburgh, 1920.

HELLMAN, GEORGE. "The Stevenson Myth," *Century Magazine,* December 1922.

HINKLEY, LAURA. *The Stevensons: Louis and Fanny.* New York, 1950.

OSBOURNE, LLOYD. *An Intimate Portrait of R. L. S.* New York, 1924.

SMITH, JANET ADAM. *Henry James and Robert Louis Stevenson.* London, 1948.

STEPHEN, LESLIE. *Robert Louis Stevenson.* London, 1903.

NOTES

NOTES

NOTES

Dracula

DRACULA

NOTES

including
- *Life of the Author*
- *General Plot Summary*
- *List of Characters*
- *Summaries & Critical Commentaries*
- *German Expressionism and the*
  American Horror Film
- *Selected Filmography*
- *Topics for Discussion*
- *Selected Bibliography*

by
Samuel J. Umland, Ph.D.
University of Nebraska

Cliffs Notes

INCORPORATED

LINCOLN, NEBRASKA 68501

Editor

Gary Carey, M.A.
University of Colorado

Consulting Editor

James L. Roberts, Ph.D.
Department of English
University of Nebraska

ISBN 0-8220-0417-8
© Copyright 1983
by
C. K. Hillegass
All Rights Reserved
Printed in U.S.A.

1992 Printing

Cliffs Notes, Inc.   Lincoln, Nebraska

CONTENTS

DRACULA NOTES

LIFE OF THE AUTHOR

Many of the events of Bram Stoker's life are still a mystery and are open to speculation. Most biographers have had to rely on public records to determine the interests and life of the author, thus prompting Daniel Farson, Stoker's grandnephew and also one of his biographers, to write: "Stoker has long remained one of the least known authors of one of the best-known books ever written."

We know that Bram Stoker was born in Dublin, Ireland, on November 8, 1847, the third son of seven children. Sickly and bedridden as a child, Stoker eventually grew to well over six feet in height and became athletic and muscular, crowned with a head of thick, red hair. He is referred to by biographer Farson as a "red-haired giant." As a student at Trinity College in Dublin, Stoker graduated with honors in science, and he later returned to the college for an M.A. degree.

It appears that Stoker was always interested in writing because, for a time, he worked as a drama critic; additionally, the author whom he most admired was Walt Whitman, whose controversial book of poetry, *Leaves of Grass*, Stoker publicly defended. After years of correspondence, Stoker finally met Whitman in 1884, and he met him again a few more times, the last time in 1887. Stoker also worked for the Irish civil service, much like his father had done.

In 1876, when Stoker was twenty-nine years old, he met the famous and talented actor Henry Irving, a meeting which became of great value to both men. Of course, Stoker had seen Irving many times before this, witnessing with awe Irving's considerable dramatic talent. Stoker and Irving became close friends, and Stoker soon became the actor-manager of Irving's theater. Stoker appears to have enjoyed the life of the theater for he held the position for twenty-seven years, beginning in 1878, until Irving's death in October of 1905.

In 1878, Stoker married Florence Balcombe, who had had the choice of marrying either Bram Stoker or Oscar Wilde. At the time, Stoker was thirty-one years old, Wilde only twenty-four. Stoker and Wilde remained friends, however, and Stoker was admitted into Wilde's literary circle. During his life Bram Stoker met many leading artistic and prominent figures of his day; in addition to Oscar Wilde, he entertained Arthur Conan Doyle, Alfred Lord Tennyson, Mark Twain, and once he even met Theodore Roosevelt. Bram Stoker's son and only child, Noel, was born in 1879, and in 1882 Stoker published his first substantial literary effort, *Under the Sunset*, a collection of tales for children.

Evidently, Stoker was a man of considerable energy and talent. As well as being acting manager of Irving's theater, he delivered lectures, traveled extensively, toured with Irving's acting company, and he wrote several novels, as well as several works of non-fiction. His first novel, a romance entitled *The Snake's Pass*, was published in 1890. Then, written over a period of several years, beginning in 1890, Stoker's masterpiece, *Dracula*, was published by Archibald Constable in 1897. The book has continued to grip the public's imagination ever since, and it has never been out of print since its publication. Upon the publication of *Dracula*, Charlotte Stoker, the author's mother, felt the book would bring Bram immediate success, and she personally liked the book very much.

Stoker dedicated *Dracula* to one of his close friends, Hall Caine, who was also a novelist; in fact, few people know that the "dear friend Hommy-Beg" of the dedication is Hall Caine. "Hommy-Beg" is an affectionate childhood nickname for Caine, which means "little Tommy."

During his recovery from a stroke which occurred soon after Irving's death, Stoker wrote a book of non-fiction which he called *Personal Reminiscences of Henry Irving* (1906), a volume about both the famous English actor and Stoker himself. Meanwhile, Stoker had earlier published *The Mystery of the Sea*, in 1902, and he produced another romantic novel, *The Man*, in 1905. Both novels are interesting reading, primarily for their examination of the roles of women in society, as well as for Stoker's characterization of women.

Stoker did not cease to write stories of horror and mystery after he finished *Dracula*. After *Dracula*, his novels of mystery and horror include *The Jewel of Seven Stars* (1903), a compelling Rider Haggard-like tale of adventure and romance set in Egypt, *The Lady of the*

Shroud (1909), and *The Lair of the White Worm* (1911), both of which are interesting novels and deserve more than a passing glance, though they are not near the achievement that *Dracula* is. Some of Stoker's short tales of horror, particularly "Dracula's Guest," an episode cut from the final version of *Dracula*, as well as the Poe-like "The Judge's House," are very good and well worth reading.

Regardless of which novel Stoker himself considered his best, *Dracula* remains his most popular work, and it has spawned countless adaptations and spin-offs in plays, novels, and movies, as well as comic books. Critical analyses and psychological interpretations of *Dracula* abound.

In his last years, Stoker's health declined rapidly, and the cause of his death, though clouded by mystery, has generated some substantial amount of discussion. His biographers have been reticent to discuss it. Recently, though, Daniel Farson, Stoker's grandnephew, in his biography, cites Stoker's death certificate, which has as the cause of death the medical phrase *Locomotor Ataxy* – also called *Tabes Dorsalis* – known in those days as general paralysis of the insane, which implies, therefore, that Stoker had contracted syphilis, presumably around the turn of the century, and died of it. If Stoker died of syphilis, it will probably remain only speculation, since the truth of the matter hinges on whether or not *Locomotor Ataxy* can be construed as being syphilis.

Stoker's literary efforts certainly hold some degree of achievement, and these efforts probably represent those things by which he should be remembered. Stoker died on April 20, 1912, at the age of sixty-four.

GENERAL PLOT SUMMARY

Sometime in the late nineteenth century, Jonathan Harker, a young English lawyer, is traveling to the Castle Dracula, which is located in Transylvania, in order to finalize a transfer of real estate in England to Count Dracula. Harker becomes extremely nervous when all of the local peasants react in fear after they hear of his destination; nevertheless, he continues on to the castle until he meets an emissary of the Count in the Borgo Pass. The mysterious coach driver continues on to the castle, arriving in pitch darkness, to the accompaniment of howling wolves.

Even though his accomodations are comfortable, Harker finds Count Dracula to be a pale, gaunt, thin man, rather strange, and Harker is mortified when, after accidentally cutting himself shaving, the Count lunges at Harker's throat in "demoniac fury." Harker soon finds himself imprisoned within the castle and assailed by three seductive female vampires, whom he can barely stave off. Harker also discovers the Count's secret – that is, the Count survives by drinking the blood of human beings – and, now, he is intent on killing Harker. The Count escapes Jonathan's attempt to kill him, and he swiftly leaves the castle with fifty boxes of earth, bound for England. The last we hear of Jonathan Harker, he is weak and sick, left alone with no visible means of escape from the castle.

The novel then shifts to England, where Harker's fiancée, Mina Murray, is visiting her friend Lucy Westenra, who has accepted the marriage proposal of Arthur Holmwood, while rejecting the proposals of Dr. John Seward, head of a lunatic asylum, and Quincey Morris, an American from Texas, currently visiting Holmwood. Mina's two main concerns are that Lucy has taken up her old habit of sleepwalking, and that it is a long time since she has heard from her own fiancé, Jonathan.

One night while the two women are out walking, they witness the approach of a strange ship. When the ship is wrecked on the beach, the only creature which survives is a huge dog, which quickly disappears. We soon discover that the wrecked ship is carrying fifty boxes of earth from the Castle Dracula.

Soon after the shipwreck, late one night, Mina discovers that Lucy is sleepwalking again. In her search, Mina discovers Lucy on the ladies' favorite seat, near the graveyard overlooking the town. Mina is shocked to see hovering over Lucy a tall, thin, black shape, but when she arrives at Lucy's side the shape has disappeared. When awakened, Lucy remembers nothing of what has happened, except that she is chilled. In wrapping Lucy against the cold, Mina assumes that she inadvertently pricked Lucy with a pin, for she sees two tiny red marks on Lucy's neck. On later, successive nights, Lucy is often found standing at the women's bedroom window; next to her is a creature which appears to be a large bird, but it is, in fact, a bat. Lucy's health declines over the next few weeks, and because of this Mina refuses to tell Lucy about Lucy's mother's sickness. Meanwhile, Dr. Seward, Lucy's former suitor, is unable to ascertain the cause of Lucy's decline.

Soon, Mina hears from Jonathan, and so she leaves Lucy and goes to nurse him. Almost immediately, Lucy's condition deteriorates, and Dr. Seward finds it necessary to wire for his old friend and mentor, Dr. Abraham Van Helsing, who offers another medical opinion. Van Helsing is particularly disturbed by the two tiny spots on Lucy's throat and her apparent but unexplainable loss of blood since there are no signs of hemorrhage.

It becomes necessary to give Lucy numerous blood transfusions, and after each one she improves significantly, only to deteriorate quickly in the next couple of days. Van Helsing finally deems it necessary to drape Lucy's room, as well as her neck, with garlic, a technique, we learn later, which is used to ward off vampires. Eventually, however, the vampire manages to evade the spells against him, and he attacks Lucy again. One significant night, an escaped wolf is used to smash the window of Lucy's room. The wolf's attack so frightens Lucy's mother that she dies of shock, and Lucy, left helpless, is again attacked by the vampire.

Van Helsing, knowing that Lucy is near death, summons her fiancé, Arthur Holmwood, to her side. Holmwood himself comes from the deathbed of his father. As Holmwood bends to kiss Lucy good-bye, Lucy, whose canine teeth have become strangely lengthened, attempts to attack Arthur. As Van Helsing throws Arthur back from her, Lucy dies.

After Lucy's death, the papers report the strange appearance of a person whom the village children label as "the Bloofer Lady," a creature who has been attacking young children in the area. Van Helsing, shaken by the reports, summons Dr. Seward to attend him in an examination of Lucy's coffin. After Seward's initial shock, he agrees, albeit with reservations, to open Lucy's coffin.

In the meantime, Mina and Jonathan have been married, and they return to England. Mina has transcribed Jonathan's diary of his journey in Transylvania, and soon afterward Van Helsing reads it. Van Helsing then calls all of Lucy's ex-suitors together, and he explains to them his belief that Lucy has been bitten by a vampire and has become one herself. The only way to save her soul, he says, is to drive a wooden stake through her heart, cut off her head and stuff it with garlic. Eventually Van Helsing convinces them of the truth of his claims, and the "service" is performed on Lucy.

Now the protagonists begin a search for the Count and also for the fifty boxes of earth which he brought with him to England; these six people – Jonathan, Mina, Dr. Seward, Van Helsing, Holmwood, and Quincey Morris – vow to confront the vampire. Soon after the search begins, Van Helsing realizes that a dreadful change is taking place in Mina. One horrific night, Van Helsing and Seward break into Mina's room, find Jonathan unconscious, and Mina being forced to suck blood from a deep slash across Dracula's chest. In a twinkling, Dracula disappears.

They finally discover and destroy all of the fifty boxes except one, which they learn has been sent by ship back to Dracula's castle. Using various methods, including the hypnosis of Mina, they follow Dracula all the way to the Borgo Pass in Transylvania, where they find the last remaining box being transported to Castle Dracula by a group of gypsies. They overcome the gypsies, throw the box to the ground, tear open its lid, and discover the body of the Count. With a huge thrust, Jonathan cuts off the vampire's head, while Morris drives his knife into the Count's heart. The Count himself crumbles into dust, and Quincey Morris, having been wounded by the gypsies in an attempt to retrieve the box, dies of a mortal wound, and so the novel ends.

LIST OF CHARACTERS

Dracula

He is the vampire who has been "Un-Dead" for several hundred years and keeps his vitality by sucking blood from live victims. He is the Transylvanian Count for whom the book is named. Despite the fact that he is actually seen on only a few of the approximately four hundred pages of the novel, his presence constantly pervades the entire work; of note is the fact that his desire to move from the barren and desolate Transylvania, which is sparsely populated, to the more populous England, is the initiating point of the novel since someone from England must make the trip to Castle Dracula to complete the transactions. In appearance, Count Dracula is described as being a "tall old man, clean shaven, save for a long white mustache and clad in black from head to foot, without a single speck of color about him anywhere." Contrary to popular understanding, Stoker has his Dracula sporting a large, bushy Victorian mustache and having a profuse head of dense, curly hair, massive eyebrows, and peculiarly sharp white teeth, especially the canine teeth. Dracula also possesses astonishing vitality, as is witnessed every time that he appears in a difficult situation.

Jonathan Harker

The young London solicitor who is sent to Transylvania to finalize the transfer of real estate in England to Count Dracula. His journals record the essential facts of his journey from Bistritz to the Borgo Pass, where he is met by Count Dracula's carriage, as well as recording the facts of his arrival and stay at the Castle Dracula. Harker is engaged to a young schoolmistress named Mina Murray.

Miss Mina (Wilhelmina) Murray

The fiancée of Jonathan Harker; she will become a "persecuted maiden" during the latter part of the story. She is quite young, and her job is that of an assistant schoolmistress. She is also an orphan. She will later become Mina Harker and will assist in tracking down Count Dracula.

Miss Lucy Westenra

Mina Murray's closest friend. She is a young woman of nineteen who becomes engaged to Arthur Holmwood. Her penchant for sleep-walking allows her to become Dracula's first victim, and after her "death," she will become one of the "Un-Dead."

Mrs. Westenra

Lucy's mother, who is dying of a heart ailment; she becomes another victim of the vampire.

Arthur Holmwood

A vigorous man, twenty-nine years old, the only son of Lord Godalming; Holmwood will later inherit this title after the death of his father. His engagement to Lucy and the necessity of driving a stake through Lucy's heart after she is one of the "Un-Dead" motivates Holmwood to join in tracking down and exterminating Dracula.

Dr. John Seward

The head of a lunatic asylum, Seward is roughly the same age as Holmwood and is one of Lucy Westenra's suitors. He is an intelligent and determined man.

Quincey P. Morris

Another of Lucy's suitors. Morris is an American from Texas. His great wealth allows him to pay many of the expenses incurred in tracking down Dracula.

Dr. Abraham Van Helsing

An M.D., a Ph.D., and a D.Litt., as well as an attorney. He is a lonely, unmarried old bachelor who is both kindly and fatherly. He is from Amsterdam, and his profound knowledge of medicine, folklore, and the occult allows him to take complete charge of Lucy's illness, which he identifies immediately as vampirism. He is also chiefly in charge of the strategy of tracking down Count Dracula.

R. M. Renfield

A huge, lumbering, fifty-nine-year-old madman who is a patient of Dr. Seward; he also comes under the influence of Dracula.

Mr. Swales

An old man who befriends Lucy and Mina at Whitby, site of the landing of Count Dracula's ship. He is an archetypal figure, the one person who senses and articulates the approaching horror of Dracula, but, Cassandra-like, he is not believed.

CRITICAL COMMENTARIES

CHAPTER 1

Summary

This novel is not told in a straightforward, chronological, omniscient manner, like many nineteenth-century novels. Instead, it is composed of a collage of letters, journal entries and diary jottings, in addition to a portion of a ship's log, various newspaper clippings, and even a "phonograph diary." Since the story is basically a mystery, this technique is highly effective in sustaining suspense, for there are literally dozens of narrative pieces for readers to fit together before they can see the complexity of the novel resolved and the entirety of Stoker's pattern. Stoker most likely borrowed this approach to his novel from Wilkie Collins, who used the same technique in his "detective" novel *The Woman in White* (1860).

Jonathan Harker's journal entries begin on May 3, sometime in the late nineteenth century. The young London lawyer has been traveling by train across Europe and is currently in Budapest, in route to Count Dracula's estate, located somewhere in the Carpathian Mountains of Transylvania — the "land beyond the forest." Harker has been sent by his London law firm to complete the final transactions for a transfer of real estate, which the Count has recently purchased in England, and thus far, Harker is very pleased with his trip. He is favorably impressed with Budapest, and he remarks that already he can tell that he is leaving the Western world behind him and that he is "entering the East," a section of Europe whose peoples and customs will be, for the most part, strange and unfamiliar.

At the beginning of his journey, the tenor of his narrative is low-key — that is, Harker records what he contemplates, what he sees, and what he eats (in regard to the latter, he jots off a couple of reminders to himself to obtain certain recipes for his fiancée, Mina Murray).

As his journal entries continue, Harker continues to record the details of the exotically spiced meals which he dines on, plus descriptions of the many old castles which he sees perched atop steep hills in the distance. The train dawdles on through the countryside, and Harker continues to describe the colorfully costumed peasants whom he sees; he is especially fascinated by the local garb of the swarthy, rather fierce looking men of the region, for they remind him of bandits, but he says that he has been assured that they are quite harmless.

At the eve of twilight, when Harker's train reaches Bistritz, not far from the infamous Borgo Pass, Harker disembarks and checks into the "delightful . . . old fashioned" Golden Krone Hotel (Count Dracula has instructed him to stay here). Before retiring for the night, Harker reads a note of cordial welcome from Count Dracula, then he records some of the local stories about the Pass, as well as some of the other local beliefs and superstitions. For example, the Borgo Pass marks the entry into Bukovina, and the Pass itself has been the scene of great fires and centuries of massacres, famine, and disease. Coincidentally, Harker's arrival at Bistritz is on the eve of St. George's Day, a night when "evil things in the world . . . have full sway." At first, Harker is unconcerned about these local superstitions, but after he witnesses an old peasant woman's fearful awe of the name "Dracula," and after he realizes the extent of her fear for his safety, and after he finally accepts her gift of a rosary to ward off evil spirits, Harker begins to become a bit uneasy about setting off the next day for the Borgo Pass, despite the fact that Dracula's carriage will be waiting for him when he arrives late on the eve of St. George's Day.

The morning of the departure does not bode well: a considerable crowd of peasants has gathered around the coach, muttering polyglot words which all seem to be variants of the word *vampire*; then, almost as if it happens en mass, the crowd makes the sign of the cross and points two fingers at him (a superstitious sign of blessing for a good, safe journey). The coach is off, and in contrast to the rugged road and the feverish haste of the horses, the countryside seems happy, bright, and colorful. But the forest trail, Harker notes, begins to rise ever upward, and soon they begin ascending the lofty, steep terrain of the Carpathian Mountains. The country peasants, as the coach dashes by them, all kneel and cross themselves, and Harker notes that the hills soon pass into a misty and cold gloom. Evening arrives, and soon they are passing beneath ghost-like clouds, as the coach careens alongside late-lying snows. Harker asks to walk, but his request is denied; foot travel is impossible because of the large number of fierce wild dogs in the woods. Meanwhile, the driver lashes his horses onward at an ever faster and more furious speed until at last the coach enters the Borgo Pass.

The passengers disembark, the horses neigh and snort violently, and the peasants suddenly begin screaming. Simultaneously, a horse-drawn caleche drives up, and the driver instructs Harker that he will take him to Count Dracula. Once inside the caleche, Harker collapses in the close darkness, feeling like a child, cowering within the eerie loneliness. Glancing at his watch, he notices in alarm that it is midnight. A wild howling commences, the horses strain and rear, and wolves begin to gather from all sides as fine, powdery snow begins to fall. Harker falls asleep, probably from psychological strain and also from physical weariness; when he awakens, the caleche is stopped and the driver is gone. A ring of wolves "with white teeth and lolling red tongues" surrounds Harker. He feels "a sort of paralysis of fear." The ring of terror is unbearable; he shouts and beats on the side of the caleche. There seems to be no one around. Then without warning, the driver reappears, signals the wolves to disperse, and he drives onward, ascending again, ever higher, until at last they are in the courtyard of a vast ruined castle, the castle of Count Dracula.

Commentary

From what we read in Harker's journal, it is clear that the young lawyer is a very logical, organized sort of man. Clearly, Stoker is setting up his protagonist as a very rational individual; in this way, the horror of the melodrama which will occur later will be encountered by a man who will try to combat it with common sense and logic. As a result, the terror of Stoker's narrative will become heightened and will seem more believable and less excessively hysterical. Had Stoker chosen a nervous, emotional type of man for his hero, his gothic melodrama would have become, or could have become, laughable and ludicrous. This is not the case, however; because of the carefully calculated way in which Stoker indicates and unravels the mystery of Count Dracula, he achieves a mastery over his subject matter that mitigates the raw horror and, instead, intensifies each chapter's sense of anxiety and portentous dread.

One of the first devices that Stoker uses to let us know that Harker is sensible and rational (in addition to the fact that he is a lawyer) is by having Harker recall in his journal that he spent quite a bit of time prior to his journey in the British Museum; there, he read as much as he could about the provinces through which he would be traveling (provinces originally occupied by Attila and the Huns); Harker tried his best to locate the exact locality of Castle Dracula, but unfortunately, he was not able to pinpoint the location precisely, because the castle is located in one of the "wildest and least known portions of Europe." Yet even this ominously mysterious fact does not worry Harker unduly; because he is able to use his smattering of German, he is enjoying his adventuresome trip – thus far – and his notes become more minutely descriptive and confessional as he continues; the purpose for recording as much as he can, he says, is so that he can later refresh his memory when he is telling his fiancée, Mina, about the journey.

One of the first clues in Harker's journal that suggests to us something about the terror that will soon commence concerns Harker's reaction to Transylvania itself. He notes that "every known superstition in the world is gathered into the horseshoe of the Carpathians"; he also records, again matter-of-factly, the minor annoyance of his having had "all sorts of queer dreams" recently; in addition, he heard a "dog howling all night under [his] window." He wonders, rather naively, if perhaps it was the excessive paprika in the chicken casserole which he ate for dinner that could have been responsible for his bad dreams.

CHAPTERS 2-4

Summary

Dracula's castle is described, like almost everything else, in precise detail. Harker notes the castle's great round arches, the immense iron-studded stone doors, the rattling chains, and the clanking of massive bolts, and he compares the scene with a nightmare. Dracula himself is as mysterious as his castle is. He is an old man and is clean shaven, except for a long white Victorian moustache, and he is clad all in black without "a single speck of color about him anywhere." He speaks in perfect English and welcomes Harker inside, shaking his hand with an ice-cold, vice-like grip. His house, as he guides Harker forward, is seen to be filled with long passageways and heavy doors; finally they come to a room in which a table is laid for dinner, set beside a roaring fire. The Count's greeting is so warm that Harker forgets his fears and gives Dracula the details of the real estate transfer. Dracula explains that, at present, because of gout, he will not be able to make the journey to England himself, but that one of his trusted servants will accompany Harker back to London.

After supper, Harker enjoys a cigar (Dracula does not smoke), and he studies his host: Dracula's face is strong; his high, thin nose is aquiline, and his nostrils seem to arch peculiarly; his shaggy brows almost meet, and his bushy hair seems to curl in profusion. His mouth, thick and white, covers "sharp white teeth which protrude over the lips." His ears are pale and pointed, and his cheeks are firm but extremely thin. His breath is fetid and rank. "The general effect is one of extraordinary pallor."

Both of the men hear wolves howling from far off, and Dracula is the first to speak: "The children of the night," he says, "what music they make!" Shortly, thereafter, the two men retire, and Harker records a final entry for the day: "I think strange things which I dare not confess to my own soul. God keep me, if only for the sake of those dear to me."

As Harker explores the Count's castle the next day, he notices a number of unusual, intriguing things: a meal is already prepared and is ready for him—and no servant is present. The table service is made of gold, the curtains and upholstery are made of costly fabrics, seemingly centuries old, and *nowhere* is there a mirror. To his joy, however, Harker at last discovers a vast library, and he is in the midst of perusing one of the volumes when the Count appears. Dracula tells Harker that he may go anywhere he wishes in the castle, except where the doors are locked. Then he changes the subject and reveals that he greatly fears his proposed journey to England. He feels that his mastery of the English language is insufficient. In addition, he has grown so accustomed to being a master in his own land that he dreads going to England and suddenly being a nobody. For that reason, he wants Harker to remain in the castle as long as possible in order to perfect Dracula's English pronunciation. Harker immediately agrees to do so, and thus they talk further—first, about inconsequential things, and then Dracula explains about the evil spirits in Transylvania that sometimes hold sway. There is "hardly a foot of soil" in all this region, says the Count, "that has not been enriched by the blood of men, patriots, or invaders.

Afterward, their conversation turns to England, and while it is evident that the Count is concerned that he shall, for the most part, be alone in his new surroundings, he is immensely pleased by the description of his new estate: it is surrounded by high walls, made of heavy stone, is in need of repair, but contains massive, old iron gates; it is surrounded by dense trees, and the only building in the nearby vicinity is a private lunatic asylum. "I love the shade and the shadow," Dracula says; "I am no longer young; and my heart, through years of mourning over the dead, is not attuned to mirth."

The two men talk throughout the night, and at the coming of dawn, when the cock crows, Dracula leaps up excitedly and excuses himself. Harker feels nothing tangibly amiss, but he confesses in his diary that he feels uneasy; he wishes that he were home and that he had never journeyed to Transylvania.

Next morning as Harker is shaving, his host's voice startles him, and he cuts himself. Then two unexplainable, horrible things occur. Harker realizes that, first, there is no reflection of Count Dracula in the shaving mirror; and second, when the Count sees Harker's fresh blood trickling from his chin, his eyes blaze up "with a sudden demoniac fury," and he lunges for Harker's throat. Instinctively, Harker touches his crucifix, and Dracula's fury vanishes. He counsels Harker to take care how he cuts himself in this country; then Dracula flings the shaving glass onto the courtyard stones below, where it shatters into a thousand pieces. Dracula vanishes, and Harker ponders about what has happened. He also wonders about the fact that he has never seen the Count eat or drink. Harker then explores the castle farther and finally concludes that no matter how many beautiful vistas which he is able to see from the battlements, the castle is a veritable prison, and he is its prisoner.

After Harker realizes that he is indeed a prisoner in Dracula's castle, he succumbs to panic and feelings of helplessness; momentarily, he believes that he is going mad, but he recovers almost instantly and tries to rationally analyze what he must do to escape and survive. More than anything else, Harker realizes that he will "need all [his] brains to get through." Ironically, since Harker is not a religious man, he is grateful for the crucifix which was given to him; it is "a comfort and a strength."

A good night's sleep is virtually impossible for Harker, despite the fact that he has placed the crucifix over the head of the bed; thus, he paces throughout the night, looks out of his windows, and by accident, he sees Dracula, on two separate occasions, emerge from his room on the floor below, slither out, head downward, in lizard fashion, with his cloak spread out "around him like great wings." It is shortly afterward that Harker records in his diary that he fears for his sanity; he hopes that he does not go mad. His diary is his only solace; he turns to it "for repose."

One of Harker's favorite rooms in the castle is one that he feels was probably a woman's room; romantically, he likes to imagine that in this room "ladies sat and sung and lived sweet lives whilst their gentle breasts were sad for their menfolk away in the midst of remorseless wars." It is during one moonlight night in this room that three women appear before Harker — and whether or not this is a dream, we cannot be sure. Harker's horror, however, is quite real, and that concerns us most. Two of the women are dark, and both of them have vivid, glowing red eyes; the other woman is fair. All have "brilliant white teeth," and all of them cause a burning, sexual desire within Harker. Unexplainably, Harker finds himself allowing the fair woman to bend over him until he can feel her hot breath on his neck. As two sharp teeth touch his neck, and as he closes [his] eyes "in languorous ecstasy," waiting "with beating heart," Count Dracula suddenly sweeps in and orders the women out. But before they go, Harker notices that they grab a small bag with "some living thing within it"; with horror, Harker is sure that he hears a low wail, like that "of a half-smothered child." Then he sinks into unconsciousness.

Significantly, Harker awakens in his own bed. Perhaps the women and the gruesome bag were only part of a bad dream. Thus he steels himself for others "who are — waiting to suck [his] blood." Harker waits, and while he does so, he notices gypsies who are driving wagons filled with large, square, empty boxes. Later, he hears the muffled sounds of digging, and again, he sees the Count slither down the side of the castle, lizard-fashion, wearing Harker's clothes and carrying "the terrible bag." A howling dog cries far below in the valley. The horror overcomes Harker; locked in his prison, he sits down and cries.

It is then that he hears a woman below, crying out for her child, tearing her hair, beating her breasts, and "beating her naked hands against the door." Within moments, a pack of wolves pour "like a pent-up dam" into the courtyard. Then they stream away, "licking their lips."

Harker has no choice; he must try to encounter Dracula during daylight. Therefore, he crawls out his window and descends, perilously, until he reaches the Count's room. Oddly, it is empty, and it seems "to have never been used"; everything is covered with dust, including a "great heap of gold in one corner." Seeing an open door, Harker follows a circular stairway down through dark, tunnel-like passages; with every step, he becomes more aware of a "deathly, sickly odour, the odour of old earth newly turned."

In the vaults below, Harker discovers fifty boxes, and in one of them, he finds the Count, apparently asleep, even though his eyes are "open and strong." Horrified, he flees to his room and tries to decide what he must do.

On June 29th, he reveals the full extent of his terror. He is terribly afraid; if he had a gun, he would try to kill the Count, but at this point, he believes that the Count is supernatural and that bullets would have no effect on him. Yet when the Count appears, he bids Harker goodbye, assuring him that a carriage will take him to the Borgo Pass and from there, he will be able to return to England.

Later, Harker opens his door and sees "the three terrible women licking their lips." He throws himself on the floor, imploring heaven to save him until he can escape the following day.

Not surprisingly, Harker wakes early, scales down the wall, and once more he finds the Count laid out in one of the large wooden boxes. Curiously, the old man looks "as if his youth [had] been half renewed." The reason is clear. He has been renewed by blood. On his lips are thick blotches of fresh blood which trickle from the corners of his mouth and run over his chin and neck. Dracula is gorged with blood, "like a filthy leech." The thought of Harker's assisting this monster to travel to England and satiate his lust on unsuspecting English men and women so horrifies Harker that he seizes a shovel and slashes madly at the Count's "hateful face." The Count's mad eyes so paralyze Harker, however, that the blow only grazes the Count's forehead. Hearing voices, Harker flees to the Count's room, where he hears the boxes below being filled with earth and the covers nailed shut. Then he hears the sound of wheels in the driveway, the crack of whips, and a chorus of gypsies. Now Harker is convinced that he is absolutely alone, a prisoner, and Dracula is off for England to wreak his evil. Yet Harker is still determined to at least try and escape and take some of the gold with him. He is sure that this castle is a nest for the "devil and his children," and he cannot remain in it a moment longer. The precipice which he must confront is steep and high, but he must attempt it at all costs. The last entry in his journal, at this point, is desperate: "Good-bye, all! Mina!"

Commentary

These three chapters set the tone for all subsequent treatments of the Dracula legend. That is, whereas many works based on Count Dracula will alter the story significantly, most of the subsequent treatments of this legend will have some of the incidents found in these chapters. They include (1) an emissary (sometimes the pattern includes unsuspecting travelers) who is in a foreign land to contact the mysterious Count Dracula, who has bought some property in England. The young man, therefore, has come to finalize the arrangements with Dracula. (2) The setting is always someplace in Transylvania, a land sparsely populated and filled with howling wolves. It is also often remote and strange and unfamiliar, with no main roads to enter or depart by. (3) Everything is strange, even the language, which prevents the emissary from communicating with the natives (The natives are always of peasant stock and extremely superstitious and often xenophobic). (4) The representative usually stops in some remote inn, without such modern conveniences as telephones, where a carriage with an inscrutable driver will take him to the Borgo Pass. (5) The peasants will offer him various charms to ward off *vampires*, a word that strikes fear into the peasants. (6) The Borgo Pass is well known for mysterious happenings and the emissary usually arrives about midnight, a time when evil spirits have free reign in the world. (7) The emissary is met by someone working for the Count and is taken to the Count's castle. (8) The castle is a decaying edifice, located at the top of a tall mountain amid a desolate area, where one can gain access to the castle only by a steep, narrow road. The castle is a landmark, but few people tour the place. (9) Everything is old and musty in the castle. (10) Count Dracula is seen only at nighttime, and the emissary never sees him eat anything even though there is plenty of freshly prepared food. (11) The narrator usually sees Count Dracula performing some act which would be considered supernatural, such as slithering down the sheer precipice of the castle in a "bat-like" manner. (12) Often there is the presence of a female vampire (or vampires), who will attempt to seduce the narrator. (13) Usually the emissary is imprisoned in the castle and must effect his own escape.

Other factors of a lesser nature can be included, factors such as the narrator's explorations of the castle and his discovery of many coffins or boxes of dirt or the proliferation of bats about the castle, the eerie noises, and the mysterious absence of mirrors (since vampires do not cast a reflection in a mirror), and sometimes there are the cries of young babies and the presence of blood at unexpected places. Therefore, the individual writer can utilize as many of the above archetypical patterns as he or she so chooses.

CHAPTERS 5 & 6

Summary

The scene abruptly shifts from Transylvania to London, and the story of Mina Murray (later Mina Harker) and Lucy Westenra is introduced. The story in the following few chapters is presented through a series of letters between Mina Murray and Lucy Westenra, and also through journal entries of various characters, as well as by newspaper articles and even a ship's log. In these chapters we are also introduced to Dr. John Seward whom Lucy describes as "one of the most resolute men" she ever saw, "yet the most calm"; Arthur Holmwood, whom Lucy chooses to marry; and Quincey P. Morris, a Texan, a friend of Arthur Holmwood; and Dr. Seward, director of a lunatic asylum. All of these characters will figure prominently in the story.

Mina Murray, an assistant "schoolmistress," is engaged to Jonathan Harker. In Mina's letter to her dear friend Lucy, she tells of Jonathan's recent letters from Transylvania which assure her that he is well and will soon be returning home. (These are early letters from Jonathan, of course.) Mina's first letter is dated a few days after Jonathan's arrival at Castle Dracula.

Lucy's reply reveals that she is in love with a Mr. Arthur Holmwood, a "tall, curly haired man." She also mentions a doctor whom she would like Mina to meet. The doctor, John Seward, is "handsome" and "really clever," twenty-nine years old, and the administrator of a lunatic asylum. At the conclusion of Lucy's letter, we learn that Mina and Lucy have been friends since childhood and that each depends on the other for happiness.

In Lucy's next letter to Mina, Lucy reveals to us that she will be twenty years old in three months. On this particular day (the 24th of May), she has had no less than *three* marriage proposals, and she is ecstatic. The first proposal was from Dr. Seward, whom she turned down. The second proposal came from the American, Quincey P. Morris. She finds the American to be gallant and romantic, yet she feels that she must turn him down as well. The third proposal came from Arthur Holmwood, whose proposal she accepted.

Following the exchange of letters between Mina and Lucy, we have an excerpt from Dr. Seward's diary (kept on a phonograph) from the 25th of May, the day following his proposal to Lucy. Dr. Seward reveals his depression over Lucy's rejection, but he will resign himself to his vocation. Dr. Seward also mentions, most importantly, his curiosity about one of his patients. This patient's name is R. M. Renfield, who is fifty-nine years old and a man of "great physical strength." Dr. Seward notes that Renfield is "morbidly excitable" and has "periods of gloom ending in some fixed idea" which the doctor is unable to determine. Seward concludes the entry by stating that he believes Renfield to be potentially dangerous.

Following Seward's entry is a letter from the American, Quincey P. Morris, to Arthur Holmwood, dated May 25th. In the letter, Quincey asks Arthur to drink with him to drown his sorrows over a woman's rejection – and also, he proposes to drink to Arthur's happiness. Quincey also reveals the name of another fellow who will be present, one who also happens to wish to drown his sorrows – Dr. Seward.

Mina's journal of the 24th of July comes from Whitby, a town located in northeast England, on the seacoast; her description of Whitby would pass for one in a travel guide. Of special note is Mina's description of the ruins of Whitby Abbey: Mina says that it is a "most noble ruin . . . full of beautiful and romantic bits," and she mentions the legend of a "white lady" who is seen in one of the Abbey's windows. She also mentions a large graveyard which lies above the town and has a "full view of the harbor."

Of the friends whom Mina makes at Whitby, she is most charmed by a "funny old man" named Mr. Swales. Mr. Swales is very old, for Mina tells us that his face is "all gnarled and twisted like the bark of a tree," and that Swales brags that he is almost one hundred years old. He is a skeptical person and scoffs at the legend of the "white lady" of Whitby Abbey.

A week later, Mina and Lucy are on the hillside above Whitby talking to old Mr. Swales. Lucy playfully refers to him as the "Sir Oracle" of the area. Mina mentions Lucy's robust health and her happy spirits since coming to Whitby. On this day, Mr. Swales refuses to tell Mina and Lucy about a legend which he scoffs at. The legend involves and maintains that many of the graves in the yard are actually empty. This notion is, of course, preposterous to Mr. Swales, and he tells the ladies that they should not believe the silly superstitions of the area.

Mina reports that Lucy and Arthur are preparing for their wedding and that she still hasn't heard from Jonathan for a month;

interestingly, the date of this entry is also the date of the last entry that Jonathan Harker made in the journal that he kept in Count Dracula's castle in Transylvania.

Dr. Seward, meanwhile, reports that the case of Renfield is becoming more and more curious. Seward reports that Renfield has developed qualities of selfishness, secrecy, and dubiousness; in addition, Renfield has pets of odd sorts; presently, Renfield's hobby is catching flies, and he has a large number of them. When Seward demands that Renfield get rid of them, Renfield asks for a delay of three days. Two weeks later, Seward reports that Renfield has become interested in spiders and has "several very big fellows in a box." Evidently, Renfield is feeding the flies to the spiders and also munching on the flies himself. About ten days later, Seward reports that the spiders are becoming a great nuisance and that he has ordered Renfield to get rid of them. As Seward is issuing this demand, a fly buzzes into the room and Renfield catches it and "exultantly" eats it. Renfield keeps a notebook in which whole pages are filled with masses of numbers, as if it is an account book; we can assume that he is totaling up the number of flies that he has eaten.

A week later, Seward discovers that Renfield also has a pet sparrow and that Renfield's supply of spiders has diminished; it would seem that Renfield also maintains a supply of flies for the spiders by tempting them with pieces of food. About ten days later, Seward reports that Renfield has "a whole colony of sparrows" and that the supply of flies and spiders is almost depleted.

Fawning like a dog, Renfield begs Seward for a nice little kitten which he can "feed – and feed – and feed." Seward refuses Renfield's request, and Renfield immediately becomes hostile and threatening. Seward fears that Renfield is an "undeveloped homicidal maniac." Upon returning to Renfield's cell a few hours later, Seward discovers Renfield in the corner, "gnawing his fingers." Renfield immediately begs for a kitten again. The next day, Renfield is spreading sugar on the window sill, evidently trying to catch flies again. Seward is surprised that the room is empty of birds, and when Renfield is asked where they are, he responds that they have all flown away. Seward is disconcerted, however, when he sees a few feathers and some blood on Renfield's pillow. A few hours later, an attendant tells Seward that Renfield vomited and disgorged a large quantity of feathers. That evening, Seward orders that Renfield be given a strong opiate to make him sleep. Seward decides to classify Renfield as a "zoöphagous [life eating] maniac." Seward defines this phenomenon as a person who tries "to absorb as many lives as he can," one who has laid himself out to achieve it in a cumulative way. Seward is thrilled with the possibility that he might advance this branch of science and, thus, become famous.

The novel now shifts back to Mina Murray's journal, July 26th, about a week after Seward's last entry. Mina voices concern about not hearing from Jonathan Harker and also, curiously, about Lucy. Additionally, Mina is confused as to why she hasn't heard from Jonathan because yesterday, Jonathan's employer, Mr. Hawkins, sent her a letter from Jonathan, a letter that was written at Count Dracula's castle. The letter consists of only one line, a statement that he is starting home. Mina notes that this extreme brevity is totally unlike Jonathan.

Mina is also concerned about Lucy because Lucy has once again "taken to her old habit of walking in her sleep." In a late entry of the 6th of August, Mina notes that the fishermen claim that a harsh storm is approaching. Old Mr. Swales tells her that he has never felt closer to death and that he is tired of fighting it. He also senses approaching calamity and doom: "There is something in that wind . . . that sounds, and looks, and tastes, and smells like death." At the end of the entry, she reports sighting a strange ship which old Mr. Swales says is a Russian ship.

Commentary

Stoker continues with his epistolary style, continuing in the tradition of having two young, naive ladies corresponding about love and life. These innocent girls will very soon become involved in the horror which Dracula brings. Stoker contrasts their innocence with the approaching plague of horror and evil, a typically gothic pattern of narrative; it would not be dramatically effective to have depraved characters confront the evil menace.

The setting is a typical one for the gothic novel. We leave the hustle and bustle of a metropolitan city and journey to an isolated city, replete with legends of empty graves, sepulchral old natives, and legends of dead people who haunt huge old houses. Furthermore, any type of ghost story should be set in some place far from civilization, and here at Whitby, where there are rambling old houses, sleepwalking, and graveyards, we have a perfect gothic setting.

The story of Renfield foreshadows the social disruption and insanity which will accompany Dracula's descent upon England. This is further symbolized by Renfield's desire for blood and the sucking of fresh blood, which will be Dracula's, or the vampire's, goal. Renfield can be seen as an archetype of "the predecessor" (such as John the Baptist) because Renfield prepares us for the imminent arrival of his "lord" and "master," Dracula. Stoker will continue to pervert Christian myths throughout the novel. Dracula is a satanic figure, and the horrors of Renfield are maudlin, compared to the greater horror which is Dracula himself.

Lucy's sleepwalking also prefigures the arrival of Count Dracula. As it happens, the day that she begins sleepwalking will closely correspond to the day that Dracula's ship crosses the straits of Gibraltar into Western civilization. And it will be because of her sleepwalking that she will become a member of the "Un-Dead."

Old Mr. Swales is the archetypal prophetic figure, one who senses and can articulate the approaching doom and horror, yet one whose exhortations and prophesies are ignored or remain misunderstood by the populace.

CHAPTERS 7 & 8

Summary

Utilizing the narrative device of a newspaper clipping (dated August 8th), the story of the landing of Count Dracula's ship is presented. The report indicates that the recent storm, one of the worst storms on record, was responsible for the shipwreck of a strange Russian vessel. The article also mentions several observations which indicate the vessel's strange method of navigation; we learn that observers feel that the captain had to be mad because in the midst of the storm the ship's sails were wholly unfurled.

Many people who witnessed the approach of the strange vessel were gathered on one of Whitby's piers to await the ship's arrival. By the light of a spotlight, witnesses noticed that "lashed to the helm was a corpse, with drooping head, which swung horribly to and fro" as the ship rocked. As the vessel violently ran aground, "an immense dog sprang up on deck from below," jumped from the ship, and ran off. Upon closer inspection, it was discovered that the man lashed to the wheel (the helm) had a crucifix clutched in his hand. According to a local doctor, the man had been dead for at least two days. Coast Guard officials discovered a bottle in the dead man's pocket, carefully sealed, which contained a roll of paper.

In a newspaper article the next day, it is revealed that the ship, a schooner, was a Russian vessel, one from Varna, called the *Demeter*. The only cargo on board was a "ballast of silver sand" and "a number of great wooden boxes filled with mould." It is revealed that the cargo was consigned to a Whitby solicitor, Mr. S. F. Billington, who has claimed the boxes. The bizarre circumstances of the ship's arrival have been the talk about town for the last few days, and there has also been some interest as to the whereabouts of the big dog which jumped ashore on the first night. The dog has disappeared, and some citizens are worried that the dog may be dangerous. Reportedly, a half-breed mastiff was found dead, its throat torn out and its belly split open.

The narrative continues with excerpts from the *Demeter*'s log. The log begins on the 6th of July, which would be a week after Jonathan Harker's last entry in his journal. According to the log entries, all is calm aboard the ship for several days. On the 16th of July, however, one crew member is found missing, and the log indicates that all the sailors are downcast and anxious. The next day, the 17th of July, a sailor reports seeing a "tall, thin man, who was not like any of the crew, come up the companionway, and go along the deck forward and disappear." Yet no one, upon inspection of the ship, is to be found.

Five days later, on the 22nd of July, the ship passes Gibraltar and sails out through the Straits with apparently no further problems. Two days later, however, another man is reported lost, and the remaining men grow panicky and frightened. Five days later, another sailor is missing. On the 30th of July, only the captain, his mate, and two crew members are left. On the 2nd of August, another crew member disappears. At midnight on the next night, the remaining deck hand disappears, and the captain and the mate are the only remaining men aboard. The captain reports that the mate is haggard and close to madness. In a panic, the mate, a Roumanian, hisses, "*It* is here." The mate thinks that "it" is in the hold, perhaps "in one of the boxes." The mate descends into the hold, only to come flying from the hold moments later, screaming in terror, telling the captain, "He is there.

I know the secret now." In despair, the mate throws himself over-board, preferring drowning to a confrontation with "the thing." Since the captain feels that it is his duty to remain with the ship, he vows to tie his hands to the wheel and take the ship to port. At this point, the log ends.

The log of the *Demeter* stirs up a great deal of controversy, and most of the townsfolk regard the captain as a hero. The reporter ends his narration by stating that the great dog has not yet been found.

The narrative shifts then to Mina's journal (August 8th), the day of the great storm. Lucy is still sleepwalking, and Mina has yet to hear from Jonathan.

On the 10th of August, Mina indicates that the burial of the sea captain was on this day and that Lucy is very upset about the events of the last few days. In a shocking revelation, we learn that old Mr. Swales was found dead this morning, near the graveyard, at the seat where Lucy and Mina would often visit with him. According to the doctor, the old man must have "fallen back in the seat in some sort of fright" because his neck was broken.

Mina's journal for the 10th of August concludes with the obser-vation that Lucy is happy and seems better in body and in spirit than she has for quite some time. The next entry is a few hours later; at 3 A.M., Mina awakened with a horrible sense of fear and discovered that Lucy's bed was empty. After satisfying herself that Lucy was nowhere to be found inside the house, she threw a heavy shawl about herself and headed outdoors to search for Lucy. While searching, it occurred to Mina that Lucy might have gone to their favorite place, the seat on the hill where old Mr. Swales was found. She looked towards the hill where the seat was located and, under the light of a "beautiful moon," she saw on the seat a half-reclining figure, "snowy white." Above the figure, "something dark" was bending over the reclining figure. Mina raced to the spot. When she approached the seat, Mina saw something "long and black" bent over the half reclin-ing figure. Mina called to Lucy in fright, and "the thing raised a head." Mina could see "a white face and red, gleaming eyes." By the time Mina reached the seat, the moonlight was so brilliant that Mina could see that Lucy was alone. It appeared that Lucy was merely asleep, but her breathing was hesitant and coming in long, heavy gasps; then Lucy shuddered and covered her throat with her hand. Mina threw her shawl over Lucy to warm her, and Lucy pulled the shawl up about her neck as though she were cold. Mina accounts for the two puncture wounds in Lucy's throat as the result of pin pricks caused when Mina was trying to pin a shawl around Lucy's exposed neck. Mina then escorts Lucy back home and puts her back to bed. Just before falling asleep, Lucy begs Mina not to tell anyone of the incident.

That morning (August 11th) Lucy looks better to Mina than she has for weeks. Mina berates herself for wounding Lucy with the safety pin, for again she notices the two little red pin pricks on Lucy's neck, "and on the band of her nightdress was a drop of blood." Lucy casually laughs off Mina's concern. The rest of the day is spent happily, and Mina expects a restful night.

In her journal entry of the next day, however, Mina indicates that her expectations were wrong. Twice that night Mina discovered that Lucy was awake and trying to leave the room. Yet, the next morning, Lucy was, seemingly, the picture of health to Mina.

The 13th of August is a quiet day, yet that night Mina discovers Lucy sitting up in bed in a dazed sleep, "pointing to the window." Mina goes to the window, and in the brilliant moonlight she notices "a great bat" flitting about in circles. Evidently the bat is frightened by the sudden appearance of Mina at the window and flies off.

The next day at sunset, Mina indicates that she and Lucy spent the day at a favorite spot on the East Cliff, and, at sunset, Lucy made a most unusual remark: "His red eyes again! They are just the same." At the moment when Lucy utters this phrase, Mina notices that Lucy's eyes are directed towards their favorite seat, "whereon was a dark figure seated alone." To Mina, the stranger's eyes appeared for a moment "like burning flames." Later, the two return home and say no more about the incident.

After seeing Lucy to bed that night, Mina decided to go for a short stroll. Coming home in the bright moonlight, she glanced up at their bedroom window and noticed Lucy's head leaning out. Mina thought that Lucy was looking for her, but she was not – Lucy did not even notice Mina. She appeared, in fact, to be fast asleep. Curiously, seated on the window sill next to her was something that looked like a "good sized bird." Running upstairs to the bedroom in a panic, Mina discovered that Lucy was now back in her bed – asleep, but holding her hand to her throat as if chilled. Mina chooses not to awaken her, yet she notices, much to her dismay, that Lucy looks pale and haggard. Mina attributes this to Lucy's fretting about something.

On the next day (15th of August), Mina notices that Lucy is "languid and tired" and that she slept later than normal. Mina receives a bit of unexpected and shocking news from Mrs. Westenra, Lucy's mother. Mrs. Westenra's doctor has informed her that she has only a few months to live because of a heart condition.

Two days later, Mina is despondent. She has had no news from Jonathan yet, and Lucy seems to be growing weaker and weaker by the day. Mina cannot understand Lucy's decline, for she eats well and sleeps well and gets plenty of exercise. Yet at night, Mina has heard her awaken as if gasping for air, and just last night, she found Lucy leaning out of the open window again; Lucy was incredibly weak and her breath came with much difficulty. Inspecting Lucy's throat as she lay asleep, Mina noticed that the puncture wounds had not healed; if anything, they were larger than before and the edges were pale and faintly puckered. "They were like little white dots with red centers."

In a letter dated the 17th of August, Mr. S. F. Billington (to whom the boxes from the *Demeter* were consigned) orders the boxes to be delivered to Carfax, near Purfleet, in London.

Mina's journal (August 18th) records that Lucy is looking better and slept well the last night. Lucy seems to have come to terms with the night when she was found sleepwalking. Lucy spends most of her time thinking of her fiancé, Arthur. Lucy feels that the recent events are like a dream, yet she has a "vague memory of something long and dark with red eyes . . . and something very sweet and very bitter all around . . . sinking into deep green water." Her "soul seemed to go out from [her] body and float about in the air." She tells Mina there was suddenly "a sort of agonizing feeling." And then Mina woke her.

On the 19th of August, Mina receives news of Jonathan — he is in a hospital in Budapest. Mina intends to leave the next morning to go to Budapest to be with him; Jonathan apparently has been hospitalized because of brain fever. In a letter from a Sister Agatha, Mina is warned that she should be prepared to spend some time at the hospital, for Jonathan's illness is very serious.

The narrative shifts then to Dr. Seward's diary. Renfield, it seems, has had a swift and drastic change in personality. He has periods of excitement, and he acts as if he were a caged animal. He had been respectful, but recently, he has become quite "haughty." He has told Seward that "the Master is at hand." Dr. Seward attributes Renfield's condition to a "religious mania." Renfield's pets (the spiders, flies, and sparrows) are no longer important to him. Later that night, Renfield escapes. Dr. Seward and several attendants follow Renfield to Carfax (the destination of the fifty boxes of earth belonging to Count Dracula). Following him onto the grounds, Seward finds Renfield "pressed close against the old iron-bound oak door of the chapel," apparently talking to someone. Renfield is apparently addressing someone whom he calls "Master"; Renfield seems to consider himself a slave. Dr. Seward and the attendants put a restraint on Renfield and return him to his cell. There, Renfield says that he "shall be patient, Master."

Commentary

Once again Stoker relies on clever stylistic devices to add verisimilitude to his story. By using newspaper clippings, the ship's log, the medical journal, excerpts from telegrams and diaries, he builds a cumulative picture of events as though they might really have happened and, thus, he gives greater credence to this improbable story.

The ship that was sighted at the end of Chapter 6 has turned out to be the ship which was carrying the loads of dirt from Count Dracula's estate, the cargo that Jonathan Harker saw being loaded on wagons in Transylvania. Apparently, Count Dracula himself is "residing" in one of these boxes. The storm, the howling dogs, and the mysterious disappearance of the sailors—all are symbolic of the approaching evil which is represented by Count Dracula. It is clear that Dracula is a harbinger of the natural catastrophes which are occurring. His evil presence is felt by old Mr. Swales, who at his advanced age cannot withstand the horrors represented by the arrival of Dracula and is found dead, murdered to make it seem as though he were killed accidentally. It can be assumed that the mysterious dog that came from the ship was Dracula himself in one of his guises, and that it was responsible for knocking the old man down and causing his death. Many supernatural things, like Mr. Swales' death, are never fully explained by Stoker, leaving all the events surrounded by an aura of superstition and mystery.

The calm Victorian life, filled with all of the amenities of life, is being penetrated by everything which Dracula represents, and the disruption is seen mainly in the manner in which he "penetrates" a young virgin's (Lucy's) neck, sucking both life and blood from her.

32

The illness of Arthur Holmwood's father (only slightly mentioned), as well as the approaching death of Lucy's mother, seem cabalistically linked to the approach and arrival of Count Dracula, and, thus, by the end of the novel we will see that both Lucy and her mother have become victims of the intruding spectre of horror. Dracula is more than just a vampire, more than just a satanic presence affecting only a few; he is also a symbol of total social disruption and chaos. If not stopped, he will destroy all of Victorian society. Count Dracula's appearance and his satanic presence – his black clothes, his fiery red eyes, and his pale features – are a total contrast to the winsome, innocent, and virginal presence of the two ladies (Lucy and Mina) who represent purity.

Once again, Stoker inverts the traditional Christian myth when Renfield anticipates and looks forward to the arrival of his "lord and master" in the person of Count Dracula. Stoker, in an interesting choice of phraseology, considers Renfield's behavior at Carfax as though Renfield is experiencing a "Real Presence," as though Dracula were the (perverted) Holy Ghost. The entire scene is a perversion of the Catholic communion, wherein the Real Presence of the Holy Ghost is present each time that the Eucharist is administered.

In terms of the narrative structure so far, we don't know *why* Count Dracula left Transylvania to come to England – rather than go somewhere else, or even why he had to leave his native country. However, in these chapters, we find out that Jonathan Harker *did* escape, but his method of escape will never be revealed to us; remember that when we last saw him, he was a prisoner in Dracula's castle, surrounded by wolves and supernatural beings. Yet suddenly, without explanation, he appears in Budapest, where he is cared for by nurses.

CHAPTERS 9 & 10

Summary

In a letter from Budapest, Mina tells Lucy that she has arrived safely and that she has found Jonathan Harker greatly changed. He is only a shadow of his former self, and he remembers very little of what has happened to him; he suffered a terrible shock, and his brain has a mental block against whatever caused his present condition.

Sister Agatha, who has attended him, has told Mina that he raved and ranted about dreadful and unspeakable things, so dreadful that she often had "to cross herself." Sister Agatha maintains that "his fear is of great and horrible things, which no mortal can think of." Mina notices a notebook and wonders if she could look through it for some clue as to what happened; Jonathan tells her that he has had brain fever, and he thinks that the cause of the brain fever *might* be recorded in the notebook. However, he does *not* ever want to read the contents of the book *himself*. Thus he gives the journal to Mina and says that if she wants to read it she may, but he never wants to read it lest it cause some horror in their married life.

Mina informs Lucy that she and Jonathan have decided to get married immediately, and, that very afternoon, the marriage ceremony was performed. As a wedding gift, Mina took the notebook, wrapped it, tied it, and sealed it in wax, using her wedding ring as the seal, saying that she would *never* open it unless it were for his — Jonathan's — sake. After reading her friend's letter, Lucy sends Mina a letter of congratulations, telling her that she herself is feeling quite healthy.

Dr. Seward records in his diary that Renfield has now grown very quiet and often murmurs to himself, "Now I can wait, now I can wait." He does not speak to anyone, even when he is offered a kitten or a full grown cat as a pet. He responds, "I don't take any stock in cats. I have more to think of now."

This has happened for three nights; now, Seward plans to arrange a way for Renfield to escape so that they can follow him. At an unexpected moment, however, Renfield escapes. The attendant follows him to Carfax, where he is again pressed against the old chapel door.

When Renfield sees Dr. Seward, he tries to attack him, but is restrained. Renfield grows strangely calm, and Dr. Seward becomes aware that Renfield is staring at something in the moonlit sky. Upon following his gaze, Seward can see nothing, however, but an exceptionally large bat.

Lucy Westenra, (on the 24th of August) records in her diary that she has been dreaming, as she did earlier at Whitby (she is now at Hillingham, another of the houses which her family owns). Also, she notes that her mother's health is declining. On the night of the 25th, she writes that she awoke around midnight to the sound of something scratching and flapping at the window. When she awoke in the morning, she was pale, and her throat pained her severely.

Arthur Holmwood writes to Dr. Seward on the 31st of August, asking him to visit Lucy and examine her. Then, the next day, he telegrams Dr. Seward to inform him that he has been called to his father's bedside, where he wants Dr. Seward to contact him.

On the 2nd of September, Dr. Seward writes to Arthur Holmwood that Lucy's health does not conform to any malady that he knows of, and that Lucy is somewhat reluctant to have him examine her completely. Dr. Seward is concerned about her "somewhat bloodless condition" because there are no signs of anemia. Lucy complains of difficulty in breathing, lethargic sleep, and dreams that frighten her. Dr. Seward is so concerned that he has sent for his old friend and master, the famous Professor Van Helsing of Amsterdam. The doctor is a profound philosopher, a metaphysician, and one of the most advanced scientists of his day.

In a letter of response, Dr. Van Helsing tells Dr. Seward that his affairs will allow him to come immediately, and that he is happy to do Dr. Seward a favor since Dr. Seward once saved his life. Consequently, Dr. Seward is able to write to Arthur Holmwood on the 3rd of September that Dr. Van Helsing has already seen Lucy and that he too is concerned about her condition, yet he has not said what is wrong with Lucy, except that there is no apparent functional cause of her illness. However, Dr. Van Helsing insists that a telegram be sent to him every day in Amsterdam letting him know about Lucy's condition.

In his diary, Dr. Seward notes that Renfield is often becoming violent at the stroke of noon and that he often howls like a wolf, disturbing the other patients. Later, the same day, he seems very contented, "catching flies and eating them." He has more sugar now and is reaping quite a harvest of flies, keeping them in a box as he did earlier. He asks for more sugar, which Dr. Seward promises to get for him. At midnight, Dr. Seward records another change in the patient. Visiting Renfield at sunset, he witnesses Renfield trying "to grab the sun" just as it sinks; then Renfield sinks to the floor. Rising, Renfield dusts the sugar and crumbs from his ledge, tosses all his flies out the window, and says, "I'm sick of all that rubbish." Dr. Seward wonders if the sun (or the moon) has any influence on Renfield's "paroxysms of sudden passion."

Dr. Seward sends telegrams on the 4th, 5th, and 6th of September to Dr. Van Helsing, the final one being a desperate plea for Dr.

Van Helsing to visit Lucy, for her condition has become much worse. Seward then sends a letter to Arthur, telling him that Lucy's condition is worse and that Van Helsing is coming to attend her. Seward cannot tell Lucy's mother about the problem because of the old woman's heart condition.

In his diary, Dr. Seward says that when Van Helsing arrived he was admonished to keep everything about this case a secret until they are certain about what is going on. Dr. Seward is anxious to know as much as possible about the case, but Van Helsing thinks that it is too premature to discuss it. When they reach Lucy's room, Dr. Seward is horrified by Lucy's ghastly pale, white face, the prominence of her bones, and her painful breathing. Observing Lucy's condition, Van Helsing frantically realizes that she must be given an immediate blood transfusion or she will die. Dr. Seward is prepared to give blood himself when Arthur suddenly arrives, volunteering that he will give "the last drop of blood in my body for her."

While Dr. Van Helsing is administering the transfer of blood from Arthur to Lucy, he gives Lucy a narcotic to allow her to sleep. After awhile, the transfusion restores color to Lucy's face, while Arthur, meanwhile, grows paler and paler. During the transfusion, the scarf around Lucy's throat falls away, and Dr. Seward notices the red marks on Lucy's throat. Later, Van Helsing asks Seward what he thinks about the marks. As they examine the wounds, they notice that they occur "just over the external jugular vein . . . two punctures, not large, but not wholesome looking." There is no sign of disease, and Seward wonders if this is not how the blood is lost. Van Helsing has to leave, and so he orders Seward to stay all night and watch over Lucy. The next morning (September 8th), Seward thinks Lucy looks better. He recalls the conversation of the evening before, when Lucy told him she did not like to go to sleep because "all that weakness comes to me in sleep." However, when Seward promised to stay with her all night, she slept soundly.

Next day, Dr. Seward had to work all day at the asylum, and that night, the 9th of September, he was extremely exhausted by work and the lack of sleep. Therefore, when Lucy showed him a room next to hers, a room with a sofa, he instinctively stretched out and fell asleep. That night, Lucy recorded in her diary how safe she feels with Dr. Seward sleeping close by.

Dr. Seward records in his diary that early on the morning of September 10th, he was awakened by the gentle hand of Dr. Van Helsing, and together they went to visit Lucy. They found her — horribly white, with shrunken gums, lips pale and blue, and looking as though she were a corpse. Immediately, they realized that another transfusion would be essential. This time, Dr. Seward is the only person available for giving blood, and he does so, "for the woman he loved." Van Helsing reminds Seward that nothing is to be said of this. Again they examine the little punctures in her throat; the wounds now have a "ragged, exhausted appearance at their edges."

In the afternoon, Van Helsing is with Lucy when the professor opens a large bundle. He opens it, hands Lucy the contents, and instructs Lucy to wear the flowers around her neck; Lucy, recognizing that "the flowers" are common garlic, thinks that he is joking. Van Helsing tells her that he is *not* joking; he says that the garlic is a special garlic, coming all the way from Haarlem (a town in Holland). Dr. Seward skeptically observes all of this, wondering if Van Helsing is "working some spell to keep out an evil spirit." Van Helsing places other bits of garlic around the room, and when they leave he tells Dr. Seward that he will be able to sleep peacefully tonight since all is well.

Commentary

Jonathan Harker's journal ended on the 30th of June, and it is still with him in the hospital, sealed and to be opened and transcribed later by Mina. The entire novel, then, is, to a large degree, held together by Harker's journal, and his observations become instrumental in resolving the mystery of Dracula. Throughout these two chapters, Lucy's health declines and improves, only to decline again. Constant emphasis is given to the two small wounds on her neck, and the reader must assume, although the author does not state it, that the expansion of the wounds and the decline of Lucy's health is a result of the vampire's repeated bloodsucking.

In addition to focusing on bloodsucking, these chapters include other examples of the Vampire-Gothic tradition. There is Renfield, who howls at noon (Dracula's powers are weakest then), yet Renfield is calm at sunset. There is also the presence of bats, as well as other mysterious "noises." Mainly, however, these chapters are concerned with the transfusion of blood into Lucy. Of course, Stoker is playing on the notion of a *lover's life's blood*. Recall that Arthur declares, "My life is hers, and I would give the last drop of blood in my body for her." The same thing, in a perverted sense, can be said for Lucy's blood, which is given to her "demon lover," the vampire. The same thing is happening when Dr. Seward gives *his* blood to his beloved Lucy, and finally, in future chapters, Van Helsing, who has learned to love Lucy as a daughter, will gladly give *his* blood to save her. Each time, Van Helsing points out that the blood is from a strong, powerful, virile young man, yet he is continually vexed as to how the lady's strength disappears. Of note here is the fact that it was dangerous to give such transfusions, because if the blood wasn't of a matching type, it could have possibly killed her. In emergencies, however, any blood is usually given to a patient if a transfusion will, hopefully, save a life.

CHAPTERS 11-13

Summary

On the 12th of September, Lucy is perplexed by the presence of the garlic flowers, but she has such trust in Van Helsing that she is not frightened to fall asleep that night.

In Dr. Seward's diary, we learn that he picked up Van Helsing and went to see Lucy the next day. They met Mrs. Westenra in the hall and discovered that she had checked on Lucy, found the room very "stuffy," and, thus, she removed those "horrible, strong smelling flowers" from around Lucy's neck and from here and there in the room, and then opened the windows in order for the room to air out. Van Helsing was very restrained in the presence of Mrs. Westenra, but as soon as she had left, Dr. Seward saw Van Helsing break down and begin to "sob with loud, dry sobs, that seemed to come from the very wracking of his heart." He feels that they are "sore beset" by some pagan fate. He recovers, and then he rushes to Lucy's room. Lucy is on the verge of death, and Seward knows that she must have another transfusion immediately, or she will die. This time, Van Helsing must be the donor since Seward has given blood to her so recently. Later, Van Helsing gently warns Mrs. Westenra that she must *never* remove anything from Lucy's room because the "flowers" and other objects have medicinal value.

Four days later, Lucy records that she is feeling much better. Even the bats flapping at her window, the harsh voices, and the distant sounds do not bother her any more.

At this point, the story is interrupted with a newspaper article about an "escaped wolf." The article tells about a curious incident a few nights earlier. It seems that when the moon was shining one night, all of the wolves of the zoo began to howl and a "big grey dog was seen coming close to the cages where the wolves were." When the zoo keeper checked the cells at midnight, he found one of the wolves missing. Suddenly the big wolf, Bersicker, returned home, docile and peaceful, except that his head was peppered with broken glass.

Dr. Seward's diary records how, on the 17th of September, he was attacked by Renfield in his office. Renfield grabbed a knife, cut Seward's wrist rather severely, and a puddle of blood formed on the floor; Renfield then began "licking it up like a dog," murmuring over and over to himself, "The blood is life."

Van Helsing telegraphs Seward, telling him to meet him at Lucy's house that night. The telegram, however, doesn't arrive until almost morning, and Seward leaves immediately for Lucy's—on the 18th of September. On the 17th of September, at nighttime, Lucy records everything she can remember in a memorandum: she was awakened by a flapping at the window and was frightened because no one was in the house; she tried to stay awake and heard something like the howl of a dog, but it was more fierce and frightening. She looked out the window, but could see only a big bat flapping its wings. Disturbed by the noise, her mother came into the room and got into bed with her. The flapping continued, and Lucy tried to calm her mother. Suddenly there was a low howl, broken glass was flying into the room, and in the window was seen "the head of a great, gaunt, grey wolf." Lucy's mother, frightened, clutched at the wreath of garlic and tore it from Lucy's neck in fright. When the wolf drew its head back, there seemed to be a "whole myriad of little specks . . . wheeling and circling around like a pillar of dust." Lucy found her mother lying lifeless, and then Lucy lost consciousness. Upon regaining consciousness a short time later, the four household maids came in and were so frightened at the sight of Mrs. Westenra's body that Lucy instructed them to go into the dining room to fetch a glass of wine. Later, when Lucy checked on them, she found them all unconscious, and upon examining the decanter, she discovered that it reeked of laudanum (an opium and alcohol mixture used as a painkiller). Lucy realizes that she is alone in the house, and she wonders where she can hide her memorandum so that someone can find it next day.

In his diary (September 18th), Dr. Seward records that he arrives at Lucy's house but isn't admitted inside. A moment later, Van Helsing arrives, and he learns that Seward did not get the telegram instructing him to stay the night. They go to the rear of the house, break in and discover the four servant women's bodies. Running to Lucy's room, they see a horror indescribable to them. Lucy's mother is dead, partly covered with a white sheet. Lucy herself is unconscious, her throat bare, the two white wounds horribly mangled, and Lucy lifeless as a corpse. Before a transfusion can be considered, however, they must warm Lucy. They revive the maids and order them to heat water, towels, and sheets. As they are wondering how to proceed next, since neither of them can give blood at the moment, and the maids are too superstitious to be relied upon, Quincey Morris arrives. He reminds them that *he also* loved Lucy, and he will give his blood to save her. While the transfusion is taking place, Van Helsing hands Seward a piece of paper that dropped from Lucy's nightgown as they carried her to the bath. Seward reads it and is vexed by its contents. He asks Van Helsing about it. The grim reality confronting them immediately, however, is to get a certificate of death filled out for Mrs. Westenra.

Later, Quincey questions Dr. Seward about Lucy's illness; he wonders where all of the blood which she received from Arthur, Seward, and Van Helsing has gone. He is reminded of a time "on the Pampas . . . [when] one of those big bats that they call vampires" attacked one of his prize mares, and the mare had to be shot.

When Lucy awakens late in the afternoon, she feels her breast for the note (which Dr. Van Helsing returned); she finds it and tears it to pieces. That night, Lucy sleeps peacefully, but her mouth "show[s] pale gums drawn back from the teeth," which look sharper and longer than usual.

That night (September 19th) Arthur Holmwood arrives to stay with Lucy. Dr. Seward's entry for September 20th notes that he is despondent and depressed. Arthur's father's death, along with the death of Mrs. Westenra, has disheartened him, and, it seems, Lucy's condition is worsening. Arthur, Dr. Seward, and Van Helsing take turns looking over her. Van Helsing has placed garlic all around the room, as well as around Lucy's neck, and he has covered the wounds on her neck with a silk handkerchief. Lucy's canine teeth appear longer and sharper than the rest. Around midnight, Seward hears a noise outside Lucy's window, and he sees a great bat flying around. When he checks on Lucy, he discovers that she has removed the garlic from around her neck. Seward also notices that she seems to be fluctuating between two states—when she is conscious, she clutches the flowers close to her neck, but when she is unconscious, she pushes the garlic from her, as though it were abhorrent. At 6 o'clock on the morning of the 20th, when Van Helsing examines Lucy, he is shocked and calls for light. The wounds on Lucy's throat have disappeared. He announces that she will soon be dead. Arthur is awakened so that he can be with her at the end, and when he comes to her, she revives. As Arthur stoops to kiss her, Van Helsing notes that Lucy's teeth seem as though they are about to fasten onto Arthur's throat. He stops Arthur and tells him to simply hold Lucy's hand, for it will comfort her more. Seward again notices that Lucy's teeth look longer and sharper than before, and suddenly Lucy opens her eyes and says to Arthur "in a soft voluptuous voice" that Seward has never heard before, "Arthur, Oh my love, I am so glad you have come! Kiss me." As Arthur bends to kiss her, Van Helsing, in a fury of strength, flings Arthur across the room, saying, "Not for your living soul, and hers!" He then instructs Arthur to come and kiss her on the forehead, only once. Suddenly, Lucy is dead! And in death, Lucy seems to regain some of the beauty that she had in life. Seward remarks, "It is the end!" but Van Helsing replies, "Not so. It is only the beginning. We can do nothing as yet. Wait and see."

Chapter 13 begins with a continuation of Dr. Seward's diary, where we read that arrangements are made for Lucy and her mother to be buried at the same time. Meanwhile, Arthur must return to bury his father. Van Helsing, who is also a lawyer, looks through Lucy's papers and retrieves all those documents which he feels might give him a clue about her death.

That night, Seward is confused by Van Helsing's actions. Van Helsing once again takes a handful of wild garlic and places the garlic all around the room and around Lucy's coffin, and then he takes a small gold crucifix and places it over Lucy's mouth. Then he makes an astonishing request to Seward. Tomorrow, he wants Seward to help him cut off Lucy's head, take out her heart, and, as we later learn, stuff her mouth with garlic. They will have to do it after the coffin has been sealed so that Arthur and others will not see the mutilated body. Seward is confused about the need for mutilating the poor girl's body, but Van Helsing tells him to be patient about an explanation; then he reminds him of that moment when Lucy was dying, when she reached up to kiss Arthur. At that moment Lucy gained consciousness enough to thank the good doctor for his actions. He reminds Seward that "there are strange and terrible days before us."

After a good sleep, Van Helsing awakens Seward with perplexing news – someone has stolen the crucifix from Lucy's mouth during the night. Now they must wait to see what happens.

When Arthur returns, he tries to explain his total despair to Seward – he has lost his fiancée, his father, and, now, his fiancée's mother, all in the matter of just a few days. He looks at Lucy's corpse and doubts that she is really dead. That night, Van Helsing asks Arthur if he can have Lucy's personal papers, assuring him that he will examine them only to determine the cause of Lucy's death. Arthur agrees with Van Helsing's request.

Mina Harker records in her journal (September 22nd) that she and Jonathan are on the train to Exeter. They arrive soon in London and then take a bus to Hyde Park. While strolling about, Mina is alarmed when Jonathan suddenly has another "nervous fit." She follows Jonathan's gaze to discover Jonathan is staring in terror at a "tall, thin man, with a beaky nose and black moustache and pointed beard." Jonathan exclaims "It is the man himself!" In a few minutes, the man hails a carriage and leaves. Jonathan is convinced that it is Count Dracula. That night, Mina receives a telegram from Van Helsing, who informs her that Mrs. Westenra and Lucy have died.

The chapter concludes with an excerpt from the Westminster Gazette (September 25th), three days after the funeral. According to the article, the area surrounding Hampstead Hill, the area where Lucy was buried, has been terrorized by a mysterious woman whom the local children refer to as "the Bloofer Lady."

Commentary

These chapters include some of the more traditional treatments for handling or warding off the presence of vampires. Van Helsing, who is the only one knowledgeable about demonology and in particular about vampire lore, sends for garlic and hangs Lucy's entire room, especially the windows, with it; then he makes a wreath of garlic to drape around Lucy's neck, and he also places a crucifix around her neck. The garlic and the crucifix are two traditional agents that have become associated with the devices that can be used to ward off vampires.

In these chapters, it is clear that evil spirits can accomplish their aims in devious sorts of ways, as attested to by sixteenth-century legends concerning Faust. For example, even though Lucy is locked in her room and protected from the vampire by the profusion of garlic, the evil spirit of the Un-Dead is able to summon a wolf from his cage in a zoo, have him smash in a window, and thereby enable the vampire to enter the room. The smashing of the window and the wolf's horrible and terrifying attempt to enter the room cause Lucy's mother to panic and to rip the garlic away from Lucy's throat, leaving Lucy vulnerable to attack. The evil presence of the vampire manages to "materialize" inside Lucy's room, where it drugs the four household maids, thus preventing their aiding Lucy.

It is interesting to note that at this point, while we have been using the term "vampire" off-handedly, Quincey Morris's discussion of the vampire bat is the first time that the term "vampire" has actually been used in the novel. Stoker is careful to point out, or to detail, the lengthening of Lucy's canine teeth so that they resemble the archetypical vampire teeth, the teeth that the vampire uses to suck blood from its victim.

As a sidenote, it is interesting to consider that within a week we have witnessed the deaths of four people intimately associated with either Lucy or Mina: Lucy's mother, Mr. Hawkins (Jonathan's employer), and Arthur's father (Lord Godalming) have died (thus causing Arthur Holmwood to inherit the title), and, of course, Lucy herself has died.

Early in Chapter 11, when Van Helsing finds out that Lucy's mother took the garlic out of Lucy's room, Van Helsing, for the first time in his life, breaks down, loses his composure, and sobs bitterly. This is a dramatic device, used to indicate the magnitude of the evil which he is facing.

In this novel and other similar stories, Van Helsing represents those powers for good combating the powers of evil which are so dimly known and which so few people believe; thus, the deaths and Van Helsing's dejected state illustrate how completely the evil of Dracula has affected society.

As we will discover, Lucy is, in fact, the Bloofer Lady. Recall that she died on September 20th, and the first appearance of the Bloofer Lady occurred after Lucy's burial on the 22nd; thus, Lucy has risen from the dead after three days – in a dreadful perversion of the Christian Resurrection.

CHAPTERS 14-16

Summary

Mina decides to transcribe the journal which Jonathan kept at the Castle Dracula in Transylvania. On the 24th of September, she receives a letter from Dr. Van Helsing asking her if he may discuss Lucy's illness with her. Mina agrees to see him and, that day, Van Helsing arrives. This is the first time that Mina has met Van Helsing, and she gives him Jonathan's journal, which she has finished transcribing. Later that day, Mina receives a note from Van Helsing in which he expresses an intense desire to meet Jonathan. Mina suggests that Van Helsing come for breakfast on the next day.

For the first time in several months, Jonathan Harker begins another diary (or journal). In the new journal, he writes that he is sure that Count Dracula has reached London; in fact, it was the Count whom he saw in Hyde Park. That day Jonathan meets Van Helsing, and the two discuss Jonathan's trip to Transylvania. Just before Van Helsing leaves, he notices an article in the local paper, and he becomes visibly shaken.

Dr. Seward also begins keeping a diary again, even though earlier he had resolved never to do so again. In his diary, Seward notes that Renfield is his same old self – that is, Renfield is back to counting flies and spiders. Seward notes that Arthur seems to be doing well and that Quincey Morris is with him. That very day, in fact, Van Helsing shows him the article in the paper concerning the Bloofer Lady. Van Helsing points out that the injuries to the children are similar to Lucy's neck injury; therefore, the incidents have something in common. Seward is skeptical that there is any connection between the injuries, but Van Helsing berates him, asking him, "Do you not think that there are things that you cannot understand and yet which are; that some people see things that others cannot?" Van Helsing continues to urge Seward to believe in things supernatural, to believe in things which, heretofore, he did not believe in. In desperation, Van Helsing finally tells Seward that the marks on the children "were made by Miss Lucy" (Chapter 15). For awhile, Seward has to struggle to master his anger against Van Helsing, and he questions the sanity of the good doctor. Van Helsing points out that he knows how difficult it is to believe something horrible, particularly about one so beloved as Lucy, but he offers to prove his accusation that very night.

The two men have a mutual acquaintance (Dr. Vincent), who is in charge of one of the children who was injured by the Bloofer Lady. They plan to visit the child and then to visit Lucy's grave.

The child is awake when Van Helsing and Seward arrive, and Dr. Vincent removes the bandages from around the child's neck, exposing the puncture wounds, which are identical to those which were on Lucy's throat. Dr. Vincent attributes the marks to some animal, perhaps a bat.

When they leave the hospital, it is already dark, and they go immediately to the cemetery and find the Westenra tomb. They enter the tomb and light a candle. To Seward's dismay, Van Helsing begins to open the coffin. Seward expects a rush of gas from the week-old corpse, but when the coffin is finally opened, they discover it to be empty.

Seward, despite what he sees, is not convinced; he believes a body-snatcher may have stolen the corpse. The two leave the tomb, and Van Helsing and Seward take up vigils in the cemetery near the Westenra tomb. After some hours, Seward sees "something like a white streak" and, then, at the same time, he sees something move near Van Helsing. When he approaches Van Helsing, he discovers that Van Helsing is holding a small child in his arms. Still, this is not proof enough for Seward. They take the child where a policeman will be sure to find it, and they then head home, planning to meet at noontime the next day.

The next day (September 27th), they return to the cemetery, and as soon as possible, they reenter the Westenra tomb and reopen the coffin again. To Seward's shock and dismay, there lies the lovely Lucy, "more radiantly beautiful than ever." Still, Seward is not convinced; again, he wonders if someone might not have placed her there, but he cannot understand why she looks so beautiful after being dead an entire week. Van Helsing then tells Seward that a horrible thing *must* be done: they must cut off Lucy's head, fill her mouth with garlic, and drive a stake through her heart. Yet before doing it, Van Helsing has second thoughts. He feels that he cannot perform the act without Arthur's and Quincey's knowing about it, since they both loved her and gave their blood for her.

That night, Van Helsing informs Seward that he intends to watch the Westenra tomb and try to prevent Lucy's prowling about by blocking the tomb's door with garlic and a crucifix. He leaves Seward a set of instructions which he is to follow if something should happen to him.

The following night (September 28th) Arthur and Quincey come to Van Helsing's room. After the two are convinced of Van Helsing's good intentions and have his trust, Van Helsing informs them of the things which he intends to do. First, he will open the coffin (which Arthur strongly objects to – until Van Helsing explains that Lucy might be one of the "Un-Dead"), then he will perform the necessary "service." Arthur, however, will not consent to *any* mutilation of Lucy's body. Van Helsing pleads that he *must* do these things for Lucy's sake, so that her soul will rest peacefully. A few hours later, the four men go to the cemetery. In the tomb, the coffin lid is removed, and they all see that the coffin is empty. Van Helsing asks for Seward's confirmation that the body was in the coffin yesterday; Seward, of course, concurs with Van Helsing. Van Helsing then begins an intricate ceremony: from his bag he removes a "thin, wafer-like biscuit" and crumbles it to a fine powder; then, he mixes the crumbs with a doughy substance and begins to roll the material into the crevices between the door jam and the mausoleum door. Van Helsing informs them that he is sealing the tomb so that the "Un-Dead may not enter." He informs them that the wafer was "the host" which he brought with him from Amsterdam. The four men hide among some trees near the tomb and begin waiting. Soon, by the light of the moon, the men see a ghostly white figure moving through the cemetery. As it nears them, it becomes all too apparent that the creature is, indeed, Lucy Westenra. According to Seward's diary entry, her "sweetness was turned to adamantine . . . and the purity to voluptuous wantonness." The four men surround her before the tomb. Lucy's lips are covered with fresh blood, and her burial gown is stained with blood. Upon learning that she is surrounded, Lucy reacts like a cornered animal. The child which she holds is tossed to the ground, and she moves towards Arthur saying, "Come, my husband, come." Arthur's love turns to hate and disgust, yet he is also petrified with fear. Just as Lucy is about to attack him, Van Helsing repels her with a crucifix. Dashing towards the tomb, she is prevented from entry by the host, which Van Helsing placed earlier around the door. Asking Arthur if he is to proceed with his duty, Arthur responds: "Do as you will. . . . There can be no horror ever any more." Advancing on the tomb, Van Helsing removes the seal around the door, and immediately, the ghostly body passes through the interstices and vanishes inside. After witnessing this, the men return home for a night's rest.

The next night (September 29th), the four men return to the Westenra tomb and perform the necessary ceremonies which destroy the vampire. Arthur himself must drive the stake through his finacée's heart. Before parting ways that evening, they vow to join together and seek out "the author of all this our sorrow" (Count Dracula) and destroy him.

Commentary

In these chapters, even though we have heard earlier that Jonathan Harker's journal was to be sealed as a bond of faith between Jonathan and Mina, we now discover that Mina has not only read it but transcribed it because Dr. Van Helsing thinks that something in it might provide a clue about the mystery of Lucy's death. Thus, as the novel began with Jonathan Harker's journal and then progressed for many chapters without his narration, now Mina and Harker are again both drawn back into the main story.

This novel has set the course for all subsequent vampire lore — for example, the belief that a wooden stake must be driven through the vampire's heart and that the head must be removed and the mouth stuffed with garlic. All of the numerous, subsequent treatments of the vampire legend depend on these factors. Furthermore, in Chapter 16, the term *nosferatu* is used. Stoker tells us that it is an Eastern European term and that it means the "Un-Dead"; this is the first time that all of the protagonists are privy to all of the information that Van Helsing has so far withheld. As a point of historical fact, *Nosferatu* is the title of two German films that deal with the Dracula legend (See the section on Filmography). Furthermore, the translation of "nosferatu" as the "Un-Dead" has now become standard usage.

It is interesting that the love which Arthur, Quincey, and Seward had for Lucy has been basely transfigured into hate at the sight of

Lucy; moreover, it is somewhat surprising that these lusty men are disgusted at the abundant sensuality of Lucy, now that she is a vampire. When she approaches Arthur in her vampire form, it is with a sensual embrace. Instead of arousing passion, however, there is only a feeling of repulsion and disgust. It is clear that in her vampire form, Lucy's *carnal* aspect is highlighted and emphasized. The ceremony which kills her "Un-Dead" self frees her pure spirit from the sinful, carnal nature of her body and is a rite of purification, as symbolized by the sudden return of *innocent* beauty to her face at the conclusion of the ceremony.

CHAPTERS 17-19

Summary

Dr. Seward's diary continues sometime later, and he details for us his first meeting with Mina Harker. Mina, he says, will travel with Seward to Seward's asylum, where she will stay as a guest. In *her* journal, Mina details the discussion which she and Seward had concerning Lucy's death. Mina agrees to type out Seward's diary, which has heretofore been kept on a phonograph. Seward is horror-struck that Mina may discover the true nature of Lucy's death, but Mina, through her persistence, convinces Seward to allow her to listen to the phonograph cylinders. Later, both Seward and Mina express their dismay at the stories which they read in each other's respective diaries.

The next day (September 30th), Jonathan arrives, and Seward expresses his admiration for Jonathan's courage. For the first time, Seward realizes that Count Dracula might be next door, at the estate at Carfax. Seward concludes his diary, noting that Renfield has been calm for several days. Seward assumes that Renfield's outbreak was due to Dracula's proximity.

Jonathan Harker discovers from his journey to Whitby that the "fifty cases of common earth" which arrived on Dracula's ship have been sent to the old chapel at Carfax. While Jonathan assumes that all fifty cases are still at Carfax, we later learn that Count Dracula has had them sent to various locations in and around London.

Mina is both pleased and inspired by the resolute, determined energy which she now sees in Jonathan; he now seems cured of his illness, full "of life and hope and determination." Later on the 30th,

Arthur Holmwood – now referred to as Lord Godalming – and Quincey Morris arrive. Lord Godalming is still physically shaken by the deaths of his father, Mrs. Westenra, and Lucy. Unable to restrain himself any longer, he breaks down and cries like a baby on Mina's breast.

In Chapter 18, Dr. Seward notes that Mina Harker wishes to see Renfield. He takes her to Renfield's room, and Renfield, curiously, asks them to wait until he tidies things up. "His method of tidying was peculiar. He simply swallowed all the flies and spiders in the boxes . . . ." Renfield is extremely polite to Mina and seems to respond in a most sane way to her inquiries. Van Helsing arrives and is pleased to discover that all the records – diaries, journals, etc. – are in order and that all those intimate with the Count now are to be presented with the facts surrounding the case.

Mina Harker, in her journal (September 30th), recalls in detail many of the things known about vampires, a subject which prior to this time she has been ignorant of. Van Helsing presents many conclusions about the *nosferatu* (or the "Un-Dead"): (1) They do not die; (2) can be as strong as twenty men; (3) can direct the elements – storms, fog, thunder, etc.; (4) can command the rat, the owl, the bat, the wolf, the fox, and the dog; (5) can grow large or become small at will; (6) can, at times, vanish and "become unknown"; and (7) can appear at will in different forms. The problem which the vampire's adversary must overcome is how to deal successfully with all of these obstacles. They all make a pact to work together in order to see how "the general powers arrayed against us can be controlled and to consider the limitations of the vampire." Van Helsing points out that the vampire has been known in all lands all over the world. From the world's information about vampires, it is known that: (1) the vampire cannot die due to the passing of time; (2) the vampire flourishes on the blood of human beings; (3) the vampire grows younger after feeding on blood; (4) its physical strength and vital faculties are refreshed by blood; (5) it cannot survive without blood; (6) it can survive for great lengths of time without any nourishment; (7) it throws no shadow; (8) it makes no reflection in a mirror; (9) it has the strength of many; (10) it can control wild packs of wolves and can become a wolf (as the Count did when his ship arrived at Whitby); (11) the vampire can transform itself into a bat; (12) it can appear in a mist, which it itself can create; (13) the vampire can travel on moonlight rays as elemental dust; (14) it can become so small and transparent that it can pass through the tiniest crevices; and (15) it can see perfectly in the dark. Its limitations are as follows: (1) it cannot enter a household unless it is summoned *first*; (2) its power ceases at daylight; (3) in whatever form it is in when daylight comes, it will remain in that form until sunset; (4) the vampire must always return to the unhallowed earth of its coffin, which *restores its strength* (this, of course, is the purpose of the fifty cases of earth); (5) garlic is abhorrent to a vampire; (6) the crucifix, holy water, and holy wafers (the host) are anathemas; (7) it is rendered inactive if a wild rose is placed over it; and (8) death occurs when a wooden stake is driven through the heart, the head cut off, and garlic stuffed in the mouth.

As Van Helsing concludes his lecture, Quincey Morris leaves the room, and a shot is heard outside. Morris explains that he saw a bat and fired at it.

On October 1st, early in the morning, Dr. Seward records that as they were about to leave the asylum, he received an urgent message from Renfield. The others ask if they may attend the meeting with Renfield, and they are astonished at the brilliance and lucidity of Renfield's plea to be released immediately. His scholarly logic and perfect elocution are that of a totally sane man. His request is denied.

In Chapter 19, in his journal, Jonathan Harker records that Seward believes Renfield's erratic behavior to be directly influenced by the immediate proximity of Count Dracula. Later, as they are about to enter Dracula's Carfax residence, Van Helsing distributes objects which will protect each of them from the vampire. The house, they discover, is musty, dusty, and malodorous. They immediately search out the chapel and, to their horror, they can find only twenty-nine of the original fifty boxes of earth. Suddenly, the chapel is filled by a mass of rats.

Towards noon, Seward records that Van Helsing is deeply fascinated by Renfield. On the same day, Mina feels strange to be left out of Jonathan's confidence, because she has no idea what happened last night, but she does remember that just before falling asleep, she heard unusual sounds and noises outside her window, and she felt as if she were in the grip of a strange lethargy. She thought that she saw a poor man "with some passionate entreaty on his part" who wanted inside. She put on her clothes, but she must have fallen asleep or gone into a trance, accompanied by strange dreams. When she awakened she noticed that the window of her bedroom was open, and she was certain that she closed it before she went to sleep. Things became confused in her mind, but she recalls seeing two red eyes which alarmed her extremely.

On the second of October, she records that she slept but felt very weak that day and asked for an opiate to help her sleep. The chapter closes as Mina feels sleep coming upon her.

Commentary

Chapter 17 is the first time in the novel when all of the protagonists are finally together. These six people – Mina, Jonathan, Dr. Van Helsing, Dr. Seward, Lord Godalming (Arthur), and Quincey Morris – will confront the evil represented by Count Dracula. They must undertake the task by themselves since no authority or outsider would possibly believe their story. These six people, of course, have positive proof of the existence of vampires. In fact, Jonathan feels rejuvenated in health now that he is confronting the evil Count head-on. Stoker is dependent on the tradition that only a few people are privy to information which exposes them to the dangerous forces of the supernatural, thus isolating them from the general populace. This is a standard device of many a thriller and gothic romance.

Chapter 18 is a key chapter of the novel, because for the first time Stoker defines the vampire and its supernatural powers, strengths, and the means by which the vampire can be entrapped. In all subsequent stories concerning vampires or Dracula himself, Stoker's parameters have been used – the garlic, the crucifix, the wooden stake, the holy wafers, etc. This chapter, then, defines the very essence of what constitutes vampire literature. Other authors may vary or slightly redefine these parameters, but the more traditional material concerning vampires is presented here.

The later portions of Chapter 19 present us with the first clue, however slight, that Mina Harker is to become the vampire's next victim. It is not by accident that he chooses Mina as his next victim; she is the wife of Jonathan Harker, whom the vampire encountered in Transylvania, and she was the closest friend of his last victim, Lucy Westenra. It is interesting that we are made aware of the Count's visit by the impressionistic writing of Mina herself. For example, she records things in her journal which she does not fully understand or associate with vampirism, but the reader, through dramatic irony, is fully aware of what is transpiring. There is a curious ambiguity presented in this chapter, as to how the vampire gains entrance to Mina's room. Recall that Van Helsing stated that vampires cannot enter a place without first being invited. The reader, at this point, does not have any idea as to how the vampire entered the room, unless it was because of the actions of Mina herself.

CHAPTERS 20-23

Summary

Jonathan, through his persistent investigations, discovers the whereabouts of twelve more of the boxes of earth: two groups of six were deposited at two different places in London. Jonathan assumes that it is the Count's plan to scatter the boxes throughout all of London. We should recall that there were twenty-nine boxes in the chapel and, added to the twelve which Jonathan discovered, they have now accounted for forty-one of the original fifty boxes. On the evening of October 2nd, Jonathan receives a note which informs him of the whereabouts of the remaining nine boxes. He also notes that Mina is lethargic and pale, but he puts it out of his mind.

That evening, all of the men meet to determine the course of action for retrieving the remaining nine boxes. Once again, Jonathan notes that Mina is very tired and pale.

Dr. Seward notes again that Renfield is remarkably lucid and, what is more, that Renfield seems to be a literate and learned man. Renfield scoffs at the notion of collecting flies and spiders. Later, however, Renfield reverts to his old ways. That night, Seward orders an attendant to stand guard outside Renfield's cell to note any aberrant behavior. Later that night there is a scream from Renfield's cell. Upon rushing to investigate, Seward discovers that Renfield has been seriously hurt—his face has been brutally beaten, there is a pool of blood on the cell floor, and his back is apparently broken.

Seward knows Renfield himself could not have administered the wounds to his own face—especially with his back broken. Dr. Van Helsing arrives, and they determine that Renfield is slipping fast; thus, they decide to operate immediately. Renfield, realizing that he is dying, tells them in an agony of despair what happened. Apparently, without identifying who it was, he says that *he* "came up to the window in the mist . . . but he was solid then . . . I wouldn't ask him to come in . . . ." He maintains that it was "he" who used to send the flies and spiders and the rats and dogs, promising that he would give Renfield everything that lives: ". . . all red blood, with years of life in it." Renfield refers to 'him' as "Lord and Master." Last night, Renfield says, "he" slid through the window. Renfield then says that after Mrs. Harker came to see him, he knew she wasn't the same and knew that "*he* had been taking the life out of her." Renfield tried to attack "him," but he was "burned," and his strength became "like water." Van Helsing realizes that "he is here and we know his purpose."

They rush to Mina's door immediately, leaving Renfield, and begin to arm themselves against the vampire. Van Helsing tries to open the door, which is locked, and when they finally break the door down, the sight which greets them is appalling. Jonathan Harker is lying unconscious on the bed and, kneeling on the edge of the bed, is the "white clad" Mina. Beside her is a tall thin man, clad in black—Count Dracula himself. His right hand is behind Mina's head, and he is forcing her to suck the blood from a cut in his bare chest. When the Count raises his head to greet them, his eyes are blood-red, his nostrils white, and they see "white sharp teeth, behind the full lips of the blood-dripping mouth, clamped together like those of a wild beast." The Count begins to attack them, but is repelled by the sacred wafer which is wielded as a weapon by Van Helsing. The lights go out, and when they come on again they see nothing but a faint vapor escaping under the door. Suddenly, Mina Harker recovers and emits an ear-piercing scream, filled with despair and disgust. Her face is "ghastly . . . from the blood which smeared her lips and cheeks and chin." From her throat trickles a thin stream of blood.

They have difficulty awakening Jonathan, and soon all traces of the vampire are lost. Mina feels unclean and untouchable. Lord Godalming examines the house and discovers that the Count has apparently destroyed all of their records and that Renfield is dead.

In spite of the horror that the story might cause, they ask Mina to recount the entire episode as best she can remember it. She recalls the first time she saw the thin, black clad man with the strange teeth when Lucy was alive, and how he subsequently came to her in her room and placed "his reeking lips" upon her throat. Mina would swoon and not know how long Dracula was overpowering her. He told her, "You are now to me flesh of my flesh . . . when my brain says 'Come,' you shall come." With that, he opened his shirt, and with a sharp nail he cut himself across his breast and pressed Mina's mouth to the wound, so that she either had to suffocate or drink the blood.

In Chapter 22, Jonathan Harker states that he feels compelled to either write in his journal or go mad after hearing Mina's story. Jonathan wants to stay with his wife, but since it is daylight, he knows that there is no danger to her. They go to Carfax and "sterilize" all of the boxes by placing a holy wafer within each of them. They then find a way to enter into the Count's most recent abode in Piccadilly (a prominent London square). Before they leave the asylum, they make sure that Mina is appropriately armed. As Van Helsing touches her forehead with a sacred wafer, Mina lets out a fearful scream because the wafer has seared and burned her forehead. Mina realizes that she is "unclean" and pleads with the men to kill her if she becomes a vampire.

Dracula's house in Piccadilly is as malodorous as the one at Carfax. Expecting to find nine boxes of earth, they are astonished to find only *eight* boxes. They do find keys to all of the other houses belonging to the Count, however, and then Quincey and Lord Godalming go off to destroy the boxes of earth in those houses.

Chapter 23 begins with Van Helsing, Harker, and Seward waiting for the return of Lord Godalming and Quincey Morris. Van Helsing, in an attempt to draw Jonathan's mind from Mina's condition, informs them of his resolution that Dracula must be killed, because, he says, Dracula is expanding his circle of power in order to harm innocent people; he cites Dracula's using Renfield to gain access to Mina. While waiting, they receive a note from Mina informing them that Dracula has left Carfax and is heading south, presumably to spend the evening in one of his other houses.

Lord Godalming and Quincey Morris return with the news that they have "sterilized" Dracula's remaining boxes, and Van Helsing suddenly realizes that Dracula will be forced to come to the house at Piccadilly soon. A short time later, they hear a key inserted into the door, and with a gigantic "panther-like" leap, Count Dracula enters and eludes their ambush. Through his diabolical quickness, the Count dodges their attempts to kill him, yet with a powerful thrust of a knife, Jonathan manages to rip open the Count's vestments, scattering banknotes and gold. As they corner the Count, he suddenly dodges away from them; then he retrieves a handful of money from the floor and throws himself out a window. As he flees, he taunts the men, reminding them that his revenge has just begun. All of them return to Seward's house, where Mina is awaiting them. Before they retire, Van Helsing prepares Mina's room against the vampire's entry.

In Jonathan Harker's journal, early on the morning of the 4th of October, he records how Mina asked him to call Van Helsing in order to hypnotize her. Under hypnosis, Mina is able to enter into the spirit of Dracula, and she becomes aware of flapping sails, the lapping of water, and the creaking of an anchor chain. Van Helsing concludes that Dracula is on board a ship that is now ready to sail. He now understands why Dracula so desperately tried to retrieve the gold coins – he needed ready cash to pay for his passage out of the country. Once again, they all renew their pledge to follow Dracula and destroy him.

Commentary

The two central incidents of these chapters involve Mina's encounter with Dracula and her coming under his evil influence. Second, these chapters are also concerned with the discovery and "sterilization" of the fifty boxes of earth which Dracula brought with him.

Since we earlier heard that a vampire can only enter an establishment if invited, we are at first surprised that he has been able to enter Mina's room, and we are inclined to wonder if *she* invited him in. Later, however, we learn that Dracula had used the "zoöphagous" patient Renfield to invite Dracula into the house. It is now clear why Stoker has been using the patient in the novel and also why all the principal characters are visitors in Seward's house. Later, Van Helsing uses the fate of Renfield to prove that Dracula is expanding his sphere of influence and is using innocent people to accomplish his aims – therefore, Dracula must be searched out and destroyed.

It becomes clear in these chapters that Dracula has some kind of mind control over his victims – that is, he can induce them to open windows, for example, in order to let him enter the home. Evidently Stoker was interested in hypnosis or "animal magnetism," since Van Helsing, through hypnotizing Mina, is able to learn of Dracula's whereabouts. Dracula, too, can hypnotize and, indeed, he is an individual of great personal magnetism. It is in these chapters that we learn that Stoker was, in fact, creating a gothic villain which would be similar to many gothic villains in earlier literature. Among other things, Count Dracula is a member of the corrupt aristocracy. The gothic villain/aristocrat was probably derived from Richardson's novels *Pamela* (1740) and *Clarissa* (1747), in which the villain's persecution of the innocent maiden dramatized for middle-class audiences the exaggerated nature of the class struggle.

It is important for the reader to understand the dramatic and philosophical importance of the villain's aristocratic heritage; if Dracula were a peasant, the story would hardly be as dramatic.

CHAPTERS 24 & 25

Summary

Van Helsing thinks that Jonathan Harker should stay in England with his wife, since he now knows that Dracula is returning to Transylvania. Jonathan Harker expresses in his journal how happy Mina is that Dracula is returning to Transylvania, but when Harker looks at the terrible mark on Mina's forehead (a sign of the evil "infection" that was caused by Dracula's blood), he is reminded of the reality of the vampire.

In her journal Mina Harker records the various reports concerning Dracula's departure. In the investigations, it was discovered that Dracula boarded a ship headed for Varna, a seaport on the Black Sea, near the mouth of the Danube River, the same place he had left from three months earlier. Evidently, Van Helsing has deduced the reason why Dracula came to England: Dracula's own country is so "barren of people" that he came to England, a place where life is rich and flourishing; he is now returning to his native soil to escape discovery.

Seward recalls his fear concerning Mina Harker, and in a short time, Van Helsing confirms his views: Mina is changing. Characteristics of the vampire are beginning to show in her face – that is, her teeth are longer, and her eyes are colder. He now fears that the Count could, by hypnosis, even over long distances, discover their plans, so they must keep Mina ignorant of their plans so that the Count cannot discover their whereabouts through her. They determine how long it will take the ship to reach Varna by sea, and they set a date for their own departure so that they will be in Varna before Count Dracula arrives. Then Mina surprises them by telling them that she should accompany them on the journey, since through hypnotizing her they can discover the whereabouts and intentions of Count Dracula. Everyone agrees with her, so it is settled: Mina will accompany them.

Chapter 25 begins with Dr. Seward's journal, written on the evening of October 11th. While Mina Harker is pleased that they are going to take her with them, she makes them repeat their promise *to kill her* if she is ever so totally changed into a vampire form that they cannot save her. All of them swear to do so, and Seward is pleased that the word "euthanasia" exists, because it euphemistically disguises the nature of her request. Mina makes one seemingly unusual request—in case she has to be killed, she would like to hear the "burial service" read to her immediately this very night.

Four days later, on the 15th of October, the six people arrive at Varna via the Orient Express, and when they arrive, they place Mina under hypnosis, during which she reports that she still senses the lapping of water against the ship. Van Helsing expresses his desire for them to board the ship as soon as it arrives at Varna. If they can board the ship before Dracula's coffin is removed, they will have him trapped, for one of the limitations of vampires is that they cannot cross running water. On the 17th, Jonathan notes in his journal that Van Helsing has secured admittance for the group to board Dracula's ship as soon as it arrives, so that they may more easily carry out the extermination of the vampire.

A week later, they receive a telegram from London reporting that the ship was sighted at the Dardanelles. Dr. Seward, therefore, assumes that it will arrive the next day. While waiting, Dr. Seward and Van Helsing are concerned about Mina's lethargy and her general state of weakness. They wait for two days and still the ship does not arrive. On the 28th of October they receive a telegram reporting that the ship has arrived at the port of Galatz, a city on the coast, near Varna.

Van Helsing offers a theory that when Mina was weak, the Count had pulled her spirit to him; now, the Count knows of their presence, as well as their efforts to trap and exterminate him. At present, however, Mina is feeling free and healthy, and she and Van Helsing use their knowledge of criminology to deduce that the Count is a "criminal type"—hence, he will act as a criminal, and therefore, his main purpose will be to escape his pursuers.

Commentary

It is only now, this late in the novel, that we learn the real reason why Dracula has come to England: his country is "barren of peoples," and England is teeming with numbers of new victims. Since Count Dracula brought with him fifty boxes of earth, one can assume that he was intending to stay in England quite some time.

The central incident of these chapters is the infection of Mina: she has a mark on her forehead, a sign that she is "unclean," that she is "infected" with vampirism. Her teeth have grown noticeably longer and her eyes have grown colder. We are also led to believe, in the course of these chapters, that the pursuers are in perfect control because they remember to arm themselves with all kinds of weapons—even Winchesters for the wolves. In theory, they will be able to track down Dracula's destination as far as Varna. However, in the next chapter, we discover that the Count deliberately misled them, and that instead of Varna, he had his box of earth sent on to Galatz, thus bypassing the awaiting pursuers.

The idea of hypnosis is continued throughout these chapters, as well as in the two remaining chapters, in order to track down Dracula, and once again Mina extracts a promise that if she begins to change into a vampire, she wants to be killed. In preparation she has the Church's burial service read to her. The notion of "euthanasia" would have been a shocking notion to Victorian readers.

CHAPTERS 26 & 27 and NOTE

Summary

On the 29th day of October, Dr. Seward records that Mina, under hypnosis, can hear and distinguish very little, and that the things which she does hear—such as the lowing of cattle—indicate that Dracula's coffin is now being moved up-river. Jonathan Harker records on October 30th that the captain of the ship which brought Dracula told of the unusual journey which they made from London to Galatz—that is, many of the Roumanians on board ship wanted him to throw the box overboard, but the captain felt obligated to deliver the box to the person to whom it was assigned. We find out, then, that one Immanuel Hildesheim received the box, and that the box was given to a Slovak, Petrof Skinsky. Skinsky was found dead in a churchyard, his throat apparently torn open by some wild animal. On that same day, Mina, having read all of the journal entries, and after consulting maps for waterways and roads, concludes that the Count would have had to take the river to Sereth, which is then joined to the Bristriza, which leads then to the Borgo Pass, where Jonathan Harker stopped at the beginning of the novel. They choose to separate and head for the pass: Van Helsing and Mina by train; Lord Godalming and Jonathan Harker by a steam launch (steamboat); Quincey Morris and Seward by horseback.

Harker and Godalming, in questioning various captains of other boats along the river, hear of a large launch with a double crew traveling ahead of them. They keep up the pursuit during the first three days of November. Meanwhile, Mina and Van Helsing arrive at Veresti on the 31st of October, where Van Helsing hires a horse and carriage for the last seventy miles of the journey.

Chapter 27 begins with a continuation of Mina Harker's journal. She records that she and Van Helsing traveled all day by carriage on the first of November. She remarks that she thinks the countryside is beautiful, yet the people are "very, very superstitious." In one house where the two of them stop, a woman noticed the red mark on Mina's forehead and crossed herself and pointed two fingers at Mina "to keep off the evil eye." That evening, Van Helsing hypnotizes Mina, and they learn that Dracula is still on board ship. On the 2nd of November, they again travel all day towards the Borgo Pass, hoping to arrive on the morning of the 3rd of November. They arrive at the Borgo Pass, and Van Helsing again hypnotizes Mina. They discover that the Count is still on board ship; after Mina awakens from the trance, she is full of energy and zeal, and she miraculously knows the way towards the Count's castle; she also "knows" the location of an unused side road, a road which is unmarked. They choose to take that path. That day Mina sleeps considerably and seems incredibly weak and lethargic. When Van Helsing attempts to hypnotize her again, he discovers that he can no longer do it. He has lost his power to hypnotize.

They spend the night in a wild forest east of the Borgo Pass, and Van Helsing builds a fire. Then, using a holy wafer, he places Mina in a protective circle. Later that night, the three female vampires which accosted Jonathan materialize near their campfire and tempt Van Helsing with their teeming sexuality. They also tempt Mina to come with them. The horses evidently die of terror, and Van Helsing's only weapon against the three female vampires is the fire and the holy wafer. At dawn, the sunlight drives away the three female vampires.

On the afternoon of the 5th of November, Van Helsing and Mina arrive by foot at Count Dracula's castle. Using a heavy blacksmith's hammer, Van Helsing knocks the castle door off its hinges and enters Dracula's demesnes. Recalling the description in Jonathan's journal, Van Helsing finds his way to the old chapel where Dracula lies during his non-active times. In his search of the old chapel, Van Helsing discovers the three graves of the three female vampires. He performs the purification ritual and puts an end to the female vampires. The female vampires' voluptuous beauty dissolves into dust upon the driving of a stake through their hearts. Van Helsing then finds a large tomb "more lordly than all the rest," upon which is one word: DRACULA. Van Helsing crushes a holy wafer and lays it within the tomb "and so vanished him from it, Un-Dead, forever." Before he leaves the castle, Van Helsing places holy material around the entrance so that the Count can never enter the castle again.

The novel ends with a passage from Mina Harker's journal, an entry that begins on the late afternoon of the 6th of November, a date some six months since the novel began. Mina and Van Helsing are on foot, traveling east in the midst of a heavy snowfall. The howling of wolves seems perilously close. On a high mountain road, utilizing his field glasses, Van Helsing notices in the distance a group of men; they seem to be gypsies around a cart. Van Helsing knows instinctively that the cart is carrying a box of un-holy dirt containing the Count and that they must reach the box before sunset, which is quickly approaching. The two men who are riding toward the North, Van Helsing assumes, must be Quincey Morris and Dr. Seward. This would mean that from the other direction, Jonathan and Lord Godalming must not be far away. Simultaneously, the six people converge on the wagon and the gypsies. The sun continues to set.

Jonathan and Lord Godalming stop the gypsies by using their Winchesters, just as Morris and Seward arrive, wielding their guns. With an almost superhuman effort, Jonathan eludes the defenders, leaps upon the cart, and throws the box to the ground. Quincey, wielding his knife, slashes his way through the gypsies and gains access to the box, but not before he is stabbed by one of the gypsies. Regardless of the wounds, Quincey, along with Jonathan, rips the lid from the box. Inside is the dreaded Count Dracula, covered with the un-holy dirt which has been jostled all over him. As the six of them stare into the coffin, Dracula's eyes look toward the setting sun, "and the look of hate in them turned to triumph." Then, at the very last moment of sunlight, Jonathan, wielding a great knife, chops off Count Dracula's head, while Quincey Morris's bowie knife plunges into the Count's heart, "and almost in the drawing of a breath," writes Mina, "the whole body crumbled into dust and passed from sight." Mina notices that even at the moment of death, within such a horrid face and image, she sees a look of peace. The gypsies, seeing the body disintegrate, withdraw in abject fright. Sadly, Quincey Morris has been fatally wounded; before he dies, however, he is able to note that the curse on Mina's forehead is gone. Quincey dies "a gallant gentleman."

In a Note attached to the end of the novel (reportedly from Jonathan Harker), we learn that it is seven years later; he and Mina have a son whom they named Quincey. Lord Godalming and Dr. Seward are both happily married. In a final note of irony, Jonathan reports that of all the material of which "the record" is made, "there is hardly one authentic document"; the only remaining notes are those which have been transcribed on a typewriter: "Therefore, we could hardly ask anyone . . . to accept these as proofs of so wild a story."

Commentary

The closing chapters of the novel suggest a type of chase novel, with the "good guys" chasing the evil person, who seems to be able to constantly elude them. Even at the end of the novel, it seems as though the Count will escape into the sinking sunset before the "rituals" can be performed upon him. Actually, for most readers, the last half of the novel becomes somewhat long and drawn out, but this novel was written at the end of the Victorian period when the reading public expected novels to last a long time. The killing of Dracula, of course, represents the social victory of middle-class morality over the corrupt morality of the aristocracy. The latent virtue of the Count is revealed in Mina's account, however, for as the Count is freed from the influence of the vampire form, his face contains a look of peace.

That the events really happened is now questioned by the final Note, which announces that all of the original documents have been lost and what we have read has been no more than the typewritten, transcribed notes of the originals, notes which cannot be used as absolute proof of the horrible things which have transpired.

In spite of the flaws of this novel, it has been an unlimited source of stories, plays, novels, and movies, as well as a source for assorted psychological theories. This novel is an example of a type of literature in which the germ, or kernel, idea far transcends the execution.

THE AMERICAN HORROR FILM AND THE INFLUENCE OF GERMAN EXPRESSIONISM

What exactly is a "horror film," or, more specifically, what exactly is *horror*? In what ways are our expectations different when we go to see a horror film than when we go to see a "western film" or a "science fiction film"? What is it that we hope to experience when we go to see a "horror film"?

Certainly, we expect to be "terrified," whatever that may be, or at least we are prepared to be "frightened" in some way; we expect the hair to rise on the back of our necks. But what is it that terrifies us, or "frightens" us, or, essentially, incites in us a sense of *horror*? Is it the presence of "horrible creatures" – however we may imagine them? Or is it the presence of ghosts, or other kinds of supernatural creatures, that frightens us? Certainly, the supernatural is present in all these experiences, and human beings generally fear the supernatural because things supernatural are considered hostile to human life. The fact that human beings fear the supernatural can be observed every Sunday; priests and ministers, for example, often exhort us to *fear* God. Yet God, ideally, is *not* hostile to human life.

Thus, some consideration of what horror is may help us to arrive at some tentative conclusion about the nature of horror. Tentatively, perhaps we can consider what horror does: *horror reaffirms the sacred, or Holy, through a formulaic plot in which human beings encounter the demonic, or Un-Holy*. If there *are* Un-Holy beings, by implication, there are Holy beings. To test this tentative hypothesis, perhaps an application of it to classic horror stories would be helpful.

This hypothesis is certainly applicable to *Dracula*. The Count has a terrifying sense of the demonic about him, suggested superficially by his appearance. Yet *religious* artifacts such as the cross affect the Count (in fact, it has become a popular cultural cliche that to ward off a vampire, all one has to do is brandish a cross – even if the "cross" is no more than crossed forefingers).

Horror has an interesting history. Essentially, the Cthulhu Mythos of H. P. Lovecraft posits the existence of a race of supernatural beings which are hostile to human life, eagerly awaiting their chance to reclaim the earth and rid it of human beings. Lovecraft, especially in such stories as "The Colour Out of Space," "The Shadow over Innsmouth," and "The Rats in the Walls," was perhaps the first Western author to write exclusively in the horror genre, and he quickly learned how to manipulate the intuitive revulsion that human beings have towards tentacled and clawed creatures. And, in addition, Lovecraft's creatures, besides being hideously and abnormally ugly, *reek* horribly.

Of course, there are other works of horror which do not precisely conform to the tentative definition of horror, such as Robert Louis Stevenson's *Dr. Jekyll and Mr. Hyde* or Joseph Conrad's *Heart of Darkness*. Yet what these works posit is that if there *is* anything demonic or Un-Holy that exists, it consists of those obscure motivations and desires which lurk within the *human mind*. These works conform to what we can label "modern horror," as opposed to "classic horror."

Concerning "classic horror," one of the first great horror films, *The Cabinet of Dr. Caligari* (1919), certainly subscribes to the "modern horror" genre also. What is ostensibly a tale of insane authority becomes the musings of a madman. In fact, the influence of German Expressionism on Hollywood films of the Thirties and Forties was tremendous. As an art form, Expressionism is generally considered to be best represented by the works of Van Gogh, Cézanne, and Edward Munch. In painting, Expressionistic art is characterized by a sense of imbalance in the pictorial arrangements in order to achieve distortion; the use of oblique angles and sharp curves; a distortion of line and color, where primary colors are generally used in violent contrast; and a subjective vision of the exterior world. Expressionism also usually incorporates the style of *grisaille*, painting in grey monotone in which objects are often seen only with a suggestion of form and outline without attention to precise detail. The content of Expressionistic art is characterized by its grotesqueness and implausibility. It is a revolt against both Naturalism and Impressionism and has similar counterparts in literature and sculpture.

The enormously creative German cinema in the 1920s was influenced, on the one hand, by the theater of Max Reinhardt, an innovative stage director, and, on the other, it was influenced by Expressionistic art. The advances in lighting techniques, pioneered by Reinhardt, coupled with the rise of Expressionism, was of supreme importance to the experimental film-makers in post World War I Germany. Most of the actors in the early Expressionistic films were members of Reinhardt's acting company; later, some of them became film directors themselves.

The first great Expressionistic masterpiece in film is *The Cabinet of Dr. Caligari* (1919), written by Hans Janowitz and Carl Mayer, and directed by Robert Wiene. Janowitz was deeply impressed by the work of Paul Wegener, a member of Reinhardt's acting troupe, who had directed the influential *Student of Prague* (1913), in collaboration with the Dane Stellan Rye, and *The Golem* (1915), remade in 1920.

Many of the Expressionistic film-makers in Germany during the Twenties eventually came to the United States. *Caligari* screenwriter Carl Mayer did, as well as Conrad Veidt, the actor who played the somnambulist Cesare in *Caligari.* (Veidt, interestingly enough, was also a member of Reinhardt's acting company.) In addition to these men, the great German film director F. W. Murnau, who directed the first "vampire" film, *Nosferatu* (1922), also went to Hollywood and directed several important films. The innovative Expressionistic cinematographer Karl Freund, who had photographed Wegener's 1920 version of *The Golem* and Fritz Lang's science-fiction classic, *Metropolis* (1927), became one of the most in-demand cinematographers in Hollywood. Freund was the cinematographer of *Dracula* (1931), and he also became an accomplished film director. He directed such horror film masterpieces as *The Mummy* (1932, the first of the series) and *Mad Love* (1934). *Mad Love* starred the now famous, late actor Peter Lorre, who achieved stardom with his powerful portrayal of the child murderer in Fritz Lang's *M* (1931). Fritz Lang, director of *Metropolis* (1927), was the first scheduled director of *The Cabinet of Dr. Caligari*, but he was committed to finish an earlier project. The Expressionist Paul Leni, a set designer for Max Reinhardt, came to the United States in 1927 and directed Conrad Veidt in *The Man Who Laughs* (1928), a silent film produced by Universal Pictures. Leni is important because he singlehandedly developed a new genre of the horror film, juxtaposing scenes which utilized carefully designed and lighted sets and uniquely focused cameras against scenes intended as comic interludes. Leni's unique approach was certainly an influence on James Whale, the director of the first two *Frankenstein* films. Leni's influence can also be found in the work of Whale's art director for the first two Universal *Frankenstein* pictures – Charles D. Hall, who was the art director for Leni's *The Man Who Laughs* (1928), *The Cat and the Canary* (1927), and *The Last Warning* (1929). Although Leni's output was slight (he died in Hollywood in 1929), he was an important link between the German and American cinemas.

Thus, the influence of German Expressionism on early Hollywood films is profound and readily evident. Most directors truly concerned about film art knew of the German Expressionistic films and learned from them. Upon close examination of the classic horror films of the Thirties, it is discovered that these films are not simply idle "crowd-pleasers," but serious attempts by concerned individuals at producing art.

FILMS INFLUENTIAL ON THE PRODUCTION OF *DRACULA* FILMS

The following selected filmography does not attempt to be, nor does it wish to be, exhaustive or complete. Nevertheless, the listing does present the more interesting and noteworthy "vampire" films. Every attempt has been made to include those films which possibly can be seen by contemporary audiences. Unfortunately, some films have disappeared or have been lost; therefore, no attempt has been made to include those films. In addition, most foreign productions have been excluded. Of the foreign productions, only those films which possibly can be seen by American audiences have been included. The notes and annotations on the films produced by Hammer Studios of Great Britain are dependent largely on *A Heritage of Horror: The English Gothic Cinema 1946-72*, by David Pirie (London: Gordon Fraser, 1973).

SELECTED FILMOGRAPHY
Rating Scale

***** A film that is a "must-see"; both artistically brilliant and influential in the history of cinema.

**** An excellent film, distinguished by its innovation on the genre because of its technical brilliance, yet artistically insubstantial in some way.

*** A good film, which, due either to negligence in production or to technical incompetence, resulted in no special distinction; most likely, a work which is exploitive of the genre; nevertheless, a film that is valuable.

** Mediocre. Technically competent, nostalgically interesting, yet it carries no special distinction whatsoever.

* Poor. A film in which, in addition to the producer's irresponsibility, the directorial integrity is in question.

Nosferatu (or, A Symphony of Horror) (1922). ***** Directed by the acclaimed German Expressionist F. W. Murnau and photographed by the brilliant Fritz Arno Wagner (*M*), this is one of the most critically acclaimed horror films. Max Schreck's appearance in the film is perhaps one of the most memorable in all of cinema history: pale and thin, his version of a vampire has a shaved head with two elongated front teeth, sunken cheeks, wide bulging eyes, and fingernails which are extremely long, curved, and pointed like claws. Because Murnau did not have the literary rights to Bram Stoker's *Dracula*, he changed the setting, altered the plot slightly and changed the vampire's name to Count Orlock. *Nosferatu* can be considered the first vampire film in much the same way that Stoker's *Dracula* is the first vampire novel; every subsequent artistic attempt must measure itself against both this film and the novel.

London After Midnight (1927) *** This silent film was directed by Tod Browning (who would eventually direct *Dracula* for Universal). It starred Lon Chaney as Inspector Edmund Burke, alias "Mooney," a fake vampire. The story was based on Browning's own novel, entitled *The Hypnotist*. *London After Midnight* may be, in fact, the first full-length American vampire film. Murnau's *Nosferatu* did not reach the United States until 1929, when it was released as *Nosferatu, the Vampire*. Curiously, Chaney's make-up is similar, though not identical, to Max Schreck's in *Nosferatu*.

Dracula (1931) * * * Directed by the "Edgar Allan Poe of the Cinema," Tod Browning, and photographed by the Expressionist cinematographer Karl Freund, this film is the first vampire *sound* film and is still one of the most popular vampire films. Its popularity is probably due to Bela Lugosi's Dracula, who, with his authentic Hungarian accent and satanic appearance, captured the popular culture's imagination as an authentic vampire. The script for the film was not based on Stoker's *Dracula*, however. Instead, it was based on a popular play by John Balderston and Hamilton Deane. Lugosi, in fact, recreated his stage role for the movie. While this original movie is a popular film, it is not a great film. Browning's direction is adequate but not compelling; it does not match the energy of his earlier films—such as *The Unholy Three* (1925), or *The Unknown* (1927), which are more lavish and carefully directed; nor does it approach the genuinely grotesque horror of his next film, *Freaks* (1932). Freund's photography is rather lackluster; his next effort, *Murders in the Rue Morgue* (1932), made with Robert Florey, is a more appropriate example of Freund's innovative technique. Still, *Dracula*, like the novel, has managed to capture the public's imagination ever since its release.

Vampyr (1932) * * * * * This film is one of Carl Theodore Dreyer's best movies, a film which relies on suggested rather than visible horror. It has a remarkably gloomy sense of atmosphere; every shot is as carefully composed as the finest photograph. It is probably one of the most artistically crafted of any vampire film, perhaps of all horror films—with the exception of *The Cabinet of Dr. Caligari* (1919) and *Nosferatu* (1922).

The Vampire Bat (1933). * * A rather run-of-the-mill horror picture which has a superb cast: Lionel Atwill, Fay Wray, and Dwight Frye (who played the role of Renfield in Browning's *Dracula*, as well as the hunchbacked laboratory assistant of Dr. Frankenstein in *Frankenstein* (1931). The story takes place in a remote Balkan village, where a "mad" doctor tries to conceal his bizarre experiments by creating a vampire "scare."

The Mark of the Vampire (1935). * * * Made in 1935, but not released until 1972, the film is a re-make by Tod Browning of his earlier silent film *London After Midnight*. Browning expanded the original story by adding a seductive female ghoul (played by Carol Borland). The movie is memorable because it was the last of Tod Browning's horror films—four years later, in 1939, Browning retired from filmmaking altogether.

Dracula's Daughter (1936). ** This film was directed by Lambert Hillyer for Universal. Hillyer was a prolific director, responsible for directing dozens of "B-grade" westerns. The story is based on a short story by Bram Stoker entitled "Dracula's Ghost," which was originally part of *Dracula*, but extracted just before the novel's release. Thus, one can see how derivative vampire films were becoming. The direction was increasingly hackneyed, and the writers were desperately lacking in inspiration. Universal did the same thing with the *Frankenstein* series; they produced countless spin-offs of the original, and each subsequent film was representative of uninspired artistic conviction.

The Vampire Bat (1940). ** In this film, vampire bats are bred for instruments of revenge by a "mad" scientist (Bela Lugosi). A rather uninspired film which exploited both the audience's attraction to vampirism and Lugosi's cult personality.

Spooks Run Wild (1941). * Another film which exploits the cult of personality surrounding Lugosi; in this case, he plays Nardo, a magician suspected of being a vampire. It is a rather shoddy attempt to adapt the plot of *The Cabinet of Dr. Caligari* to a vampire story.

Son of Dracula (1943). * Written by Curt Siodmak (creator of the original script for *The Wolf Man* (1941), a true classic of the horror film genre), the premise is hardly original. It is, basically, the plot of *Dracula* all over again: the son of the Count emigrates to England in search of new victims, except that his name isn't Dracula, but, instead, it is Alucard—Dracula spelled backwards. This kind of comic book gimmick is indicative of the inspiration for this banal film. Moreover, casting Lon Chaney, Jr., an actor capable of eliciting a great deal of sympathy for his (often) confused and misunderstood 'Beastman' was a serious mistake.

Return of the Vampire (1943). * The plot of *Dracula* again, except adapted to World War II England. Instead of searching for new victims, the screenwriters suggest that the vampire (named Armand Tesla) is in England seeking revenge against those who tried to kill him.

House of Frankenstein (1944). * As the popularity of the *Frankenstein* series declined, Universal (which produced every American *Frankenstein* picture until 1948) attempted to capture an audience by tossing into the plot every "monster" popular at the time — the Wolf Man, Dracula, Frankenstein, and even the ever-present "mad" scientist. A predictably silly and banal film.

House of Dracula (1945). *** Directed by Erle C. Kenton, *House of Dracula* contains an acting performance by Onslow Stevens (as Dr. Edelmann) which approaches the sublimity of Ernest Thesiger's in *The Bride of Frankenstein* (1935), possibly the best horror film ever made. Edelmann discovers the Frankenstein monster and is prompted to revive it, but is convinced by his beautiful, yet hunchbacked laboratory assistant (played by Jane Adams) to forsake his attempt to revive the monster. Eventually, Edelmann, who has become infected by a vampire's blood, chooses to revive the monster. The material, however, is never quite under control by director Kenton; the film stumbles and plods along at its own unique pace, while the preposterousness of the action proves to be the very reason why the film works. Despite its B-movie status and its illogical plotting, the film is ultimately both humane and moral.

Isle of the Dead (1945). * This RKO-Radio production, directed by Mark Robson and produced by the phenomenal "boy wonder" producer Val Lewton, promises much and produces almost nothing. The story centers around a group of people stranded on an island and menaced by a malevolent force, and the situation seems insolvable. In other words, the plot is as banal as an exhausted horror genre can make it. When plague breaks out among the group, an old peasant woman suspects the presence of "vorvolakas," demons which "drain all the life and joy from

from those who want to live." *Isle of the Dead* is essentially a poorly done "stalk and slash" movie and has no vampire *per se*.

The Vampire's Ghost (1945). * * * A film notable for the script and story by Leigh Brackett (1915-78), one of the best of the American screenwriters (she wrote the script for Howard Hawks's *The Big Sleep* (1946) along with William Faulkner and Jules Furthman, as well as the screenplay for Robert Altman's *The Long Goodbye* (1973), among others). The film has a disturbingly oppressive atmosphere and concerns a vampire terrorizing a small African village.

The Thing (1951). * * *The Thing* is memorable for several reasons: as a piece of popular culture trivia (James Arness was ' The Thing'; as the first science fiction film which utilizes the vampire figure; and as one of the few science fiction films of which critics are fond). Yet, *The Thing* neither merits the lavish critical acclaim it has received, nor does it truly deserve to be forgotten. The plot of *The Thing* is stereotypical horror: a group of victims are stranded and isolated in a remote location and are stalked by a hostile presence.

Plan Nine from Outer Space (1966). * A 1-star rating for this film was given reluctantly. The film is so badly done that it must be seen to be believed. Its alternative title gives one a clue to its plot: *Grave Robbers from Outer Space*. It is Bela Lugosi's last film. In fact, Lugosi died during production of the film, and he was replaced by a look-alike who always kept his cape up around his face so that the audience (presumably) wouldn't know that the actor wasn't Lugosi. Essentially, the plot concerns a group of aliens from outer space who intend to implement "Plan Nine"—the revival of corpses which will be used as troops against living human beings.

The Horror of Dracula (1957). * * * * * This is the first of Great Britain's Hammer Studios' vampire films, and it is a true classic of the genre. It was directed by Terence Fischer and was written by Jimmy Sangster, who based the film on Stoker's novel.

Sangster managed to return the Count to the tradition of the English gothic villain: he is a charming and intelligent aristocrat who transforms his female victims into carnal, lascivious creatures. The death of the Count is similar to the death of the vampire in Murnau's *Nosferatu*: he is tricked into staying out until daybreak, and then he is exposed to sunlight, which causes him to crumble away into dust. Not only does the villain's demise allow special effects, but it culminates the hero's ritualistic chase of the villain to his castle.

Blood of the Vampire (1957). *** An interesting film which revolves around a prison warden who is also a vampire and supplies himself with blood from his prisoners. Prints of this film are rare.

The Brides of Dracula (1960) **** *Brides* was Hammer's sequel to *The Horror of Dracula*, and it features the same writer and director as the previous effort. This film also has a climactic chase scene and a sufficiently bombastic demise of the vampire.

Black Sunday (1960). **** Based on a short story by Nikolai Gogol entitled "The Viy," *Black Sunday* (also known as *Revenge of the Vampire*) was labeled by critic Carlos Clemens as a "relentless nightmare," and it has been said of cinematographer Ubaldo Terzoni's photography that it was "the best black and white photography to enhance a horror movie in the past two decades." Directed by Mario Bava, the film depicts a witch/vampire's vengeance on the descendants of the people who ritualistically killed her in the seventeenth century. Virtually unknown outside of the horror film, the film stars Barbara Steele, who has become, curiously, a cult figure.

Kiss of the Vampire (1962). *** Hammer Studios eventually found it difficult to continue resurrecting the Count, but this film, directed by Don Sharp, features a clever script about a young couple seduced into depravity while on their honeymoon in Bavaria.

Devils of Darkness (1964). ** Interesting only as trivia, this was the first of the British vampire films in a modern setting—that of "swinging London."

The Last Man on Earth (1964). *** Based on Richard Matheson's classic science fiction novel *I Am Legend*, in which the sole survivor of a horrible plague is a man who wanders around in a grim, deserted world and is relentlessly stalked at night by a group of vampires. Shot in black and white, the film is quite unrelenting in its vision of terror. Vincent Price plays the title role. The story was later re-made in the United States (this production was Italian), and it was entitled *The Omega Man* (1971).

Dracula—Prince of Darkness (1965). **** Directed by veteran director Terence Fischer, this film is a true gem of the vampire cinema. A group of bored and provincial Victorian couples are stranded in a remote castle, where a lone, devoted follower of the Count murders one of them and uses the victim's blood to resurrect the Count by pouring it over his ashes. Unfortunately, the Count had degenerated into a one-dimensional character: he is just menacing; no longer is he charming or refined or even rapaciously seductive. The Van Helsing figure in the novel is replaced in this film by a priest—Father Sandor, who stalks the vampire to his castle and brings about his demise.

Billy the Kid vs. Dracula (1966). * Perhaps the worst horror film— if one can call it that—ever made, along with *Jesse James Meets Frankenstein's Daughter* (1965); both were directed by William Beaudine. The most amazing thing about this film is why—and how—it ever got produced.

The Fearless Vampire Killers (1967). *** This is Roman Polanski's much over-praised vampire film, an attempt to parody the genre, a task easily enough accomplished given the trivialized state of the contemporary genre. At least, however, Polanski got the mythology right, but the humor is rather juvenile, and his attempts at eroticism are adolescent.

A Taste of Blood (1967). ** A run-of-the-mill horror film about an American who is infected with the vampire blood of one of his ancestors. Its form is that of the "stalk and slash" movie—the absolute bottom-of-the-barrel stereotypical formula.

Dracula Has Risen from the Grave (1968). ** A Hammer Studios' film in which, as the title implies, the plot is banal and the writer's inspiration is sorely lacking.

Taste the Blood of Dracula (1970). **** Hammer Studios hired Hungarian-born Peter Sasdy to direct this sequel to 1968's *Dracula Has Risen from the Grave*, using a script by John Elder (Anthony Hinds). Coupled with Arthur Grant's superb photography, Hammer achieved its best effort since 1957's *Horror of Dracula*. In this picture, the Dracula presence is explicitly associated with the disintegration of the family, coming much closer in spirit to Stoker's novel. Certainly one of the best vampire films Hammer ever made.

The Scars of Dracula (1970). * Produced immediately after *Taste the Blood of Dracula* and directed by Roy Ward Baker, this film is one of the most seriously flawed vampire films which Hammer ever attempted. A vicious, unbelievably cruel film.

Count Yorga, Vampire (1970). ** Directed by Bob Kelljan, this production features a vampire in the tradition of the English gothic villain. Courteous and refined, Count Yorga seeks the blood of Southern California teenage girls. Unfortunately, the situations have become stereotyped, and the plot is absolutely predictable.

Daughters of Darkness (1970). * Harry Kümel's film is concerned with the sexuality of vampirism. This film features bisexual female vampires and lots of self-consciously "arty" scenes composed of red, black, and white colors. This kind of sophomoric symbolism is indicative of the artistic pretensions of this silly little soft-core film. The film did well, however, when it premiered in the United States in May of 1971.

House of Dark Shadows (1970). *Another of the bumper crop of vampire films made in 1970 which exploits the teenage fascination with *Dark Shadows*, a gothic soap opera of the late '60's. The vampire in this film and in the TV series was played by Jonathan Frid.

The 'Karnstein Trilogy': *The Vampire Lovers* (1970) ** directed by Roy Ward Baker; *Lust for a Vampire* (1970) **½ directed by Jimmy Sangster; and *Countess Dracula* (1970) ** directed by Peter Sasdy. These films are based on Joseph Sheridan Le Fanu's short story "Carmilla" (1871), a story of vampirism with lesbian overtones. Thus, these films exploit the sexuality of vampirism — specifically, a female vampire whose favorite victims are the daughters of nobility. Most of the action of these films centers around Karnstein castle. All of the films feature wonderfully stylized sets and (self-consciously) "arty" photography, creating a rather dream-like atmosphere. *The Vampire Lovers*, the first of the series, was a huge commercial success, and thus inspired Hammer to produce more of the same. The second film, *Lust for a Vampire*, is probably the best of the trilogy, although it too exults in lots of free-flowing blood. *Countess Dracula* features a vampire who bathes in the blood of her victims in order to restore her youth and beauty. All of these films are blatant "soft-core" pornography and were extremely popular with American teenage audiences.

The Omega Man (1971). *** A competent film adaptation of Matheson's *I Am Legend* (see *The Last Man on Earth*, 1964) starring Charleton Heston in the title role. This film has rather stylized production values, though its symbols — such as that of Heston's crucifixion at the end of the film — is rather blatant and heavy-handed. Nevertheless, a thoroughly competent and delightful film.

Twins of Evil (1971). ** This film was a further attempt by Hammer Studios to exploit Le Fanu's "Carmilla," with predictable results.

Dracula, A.D. 1972 (1971) * and **Dracula Is Dead (1972).** * Both of these films were directed by Alan Gibson and scripted by Don Houghton. The second of the above films is a sequel to the first. These films represent Hammer's attempt to set the story of Dracula in modern London. The results are wretched. In both films, Christopher Lee played the vampire while Peter Cushing played the protagonist.

Vampire Circus (1971). *** Directed by Robert Young, this film is one of Hammer's plethora of films during the 1970-71 period which have any merit at all and is well worth seeing.

The Return of Count Yorga (1971). **** With the aid of Yvonne Wilder on the script, who also plays a featured role in the film as a Cassandra-like mute, Bob Kelljan was able to surpass his mediocre *Count Yorga, Vampire* and create something close to a classic of the genre – albeit, for the most part, forgotten. With the aid of cinematographer Bill Butler (*Jaws, One Flew Over the Cuckoo's Nest*), Kelljan was able to create a film with an overpowering sense of menace and pervasive horror. The presence of the vampire is similar to Stoker's – an indication of growing social disruption. Count Yorga and followers completely disrupt an orphanage and pervert all relationships. The ending of the film is one of the best of the vampire cinema. Butler unleashed his visual pyrotechnics; it was filmed in slow motion freeze frame for optimum effect.

Blacula (1973). *** Shakespearian actor William Marshall played the role of the vampire in this picture, which is neither one of the great vampire films nor a "blackploitation" film. The film has a spirit of fun which wasn't present in any vampire films of the previous decade.

Scream, Blacula, Scream (1973). ** Director Bob Kelljan was not able to achieve the merits of the original *Blacula* (directed by William Crain), much less approach the artistry of his best film, *The Return of Count Yorga*, with this picture.

Andy Warhol's Dracula (1975). **** Released a few months after *Andy Warhol's Frankenstein* (May, 1974), this film, like its predecessor, evaluates its particular genre, in this case the vampire cinema, and it views it as one which exploits the subliminal psycho-sexual fears of its audience. Of course, the assumption of the film-makers is that these audiences are awaiting some kind of ludicrous confirmation of those subliminal fears through ritual enactment and formulaic plot. Thus, the proceedings of *Andy Warhol's Dracula* are predictably ludicrous and necessarily silly. They are also, paradoxically, quite disturbing.

Old Dracula (1975). * An American International release – in the worst sense of that infamous genre. This film, which stars David Niven as the vampire, is a prolonged practical joke at the audience's expense.

Dracula (1979). ** Directed by John Badham (*Saturday Night Fever*), this production attempts to be quite stylized and original. The script is based on a popular Broadway play of the same title, and Frank Langella re-created his stage role for the film. The film focuses on Dracula's seductive charms, and it features him as an archetypal Byronic lover. The premise is not so clever (or original) as the film-makers thought. The plot is predictably stereotyped.

Nosferatu (1979). ** The nature of this film is the natural result when a world-acclaimed artistic director sees fit to give his stamp of approval to a genre which has undergone pop culture trivializing. This is Werner Herzog's re-make (called homage by the director) of Murnau's classic. The film was, predictably, self-consciously "arty" and did not transcend the genre to any large degree whatsoever.

Love at First Bite (1980). ** Premise: Dracula is kicked out of his Transylvanian castle by local officials and comes to America, where he falls in love (with a beautiful woman) for the first time in his life. As a Dracula "spoof," it exhibits some degree of comic sophistication, thus rendering the film pleasantly innocuous.

TOPICS FOR DISCUSSION

1. Discuss the supernatural powers of the vampire and the limitations imposed upon the vampire.

2. Trace the gothic elements found in *Dracula*.

3. While at first Renfield seems extraneous to the plot, how does he ultimately serve a definite function?

4. Discuss the peculiar inversion of Christian values found in the novel.

5. Discuss the techniques which Stoker uses to give a sense of verisimilitude to the novel.

6. Discuss the importance of having the vampire be a member of the aristocracy and prey upon refined young ladies rather than upon "ladies of the street."

7. Discuss the various sexual implications found in vampirism — say, for example, seduction through the neck.

8. Discuss the implication that Dracula is merely an evil presence rather than a real character.

SELECTED BIBLIOGRAPHY

BATE, WALTER JACKSON. *From Classic to Romantic*, (1946). A study of the development of gothic fiction.

BAXTER, JOHN. *Hollywood in the Thirties*, (1968).

BENTLEY, C. F. "The Monster in the Bedroom: Sexual Symbolism in Bram Stoker's *Dracula.*" *Literature and Psychology.* 22 (1972). Pp. 27-34.

BIRKHEAD, EDITH. *The Tale of Terror*, (1921).

BURKE, EDMUND. *On the Sublime,* (1757). Burke's influential essay emphasized the value of terror and pathos in order to produce a reader's active involvement.

CARTER, HUNTLY. *The Theater of Max Reinhardt,* (1914).

EISNER, LOTTE H. *The Haunted Screen,* (1952, rev. 1965).

FARSON, DANIEL. *The Man Who Wrote* Dracula*: A Biography of Bram Stoker,* (1976).

FLORESCU, RADU AND RAYMOND T. MCNALLY. *Dracula: A Biography of Vlad the Impaler, 1431-1476,* (1973).

LUDLAM, HARRY. *A Biography of Dracula: The Life Story of Bram Stoker,* (1962).

MCNALLY, RAYMOND T. and RADU FLORESCU. *In Search of Dracula: A True History of Dracula and Vampire Legends,* (1972).

PRAZ, MARIO. *The Romantic Agony,* (1933). A study of the history of particular neurotic strains in Romantic literature.

RAILO, EINO. *The Haunted Castle,* (1927). Examines the important motifs of gothic fiction.

SUMMERS, MONTAGUE. *The Gothic Quest,* (1939). An intensive study of the genre up to 1800.

_____. *The Vampire: His Kith and Kin,* (1928).

_____. *The Vampire in Europe,* (1929).

WOLF, LEONARD, ed. *The Annotated Dracula,* (1975). Provides the original text of *Dracula* and includes extensive annotations.

VARMA, P. DAVENDRA. *The Gothic Flame,* (1956). The best recent study.

NOTES

NOTES

Far from the Madding Crowd

FAR FROM THE MADDING CROWD

NOTES

including
- *Life and Background*
- *General Synopsis*
- *List of Characters*
- *Summaries and Commentaries*
- *Hardy's Philosophy and Ideas*
- *Essay Questions*
- *Bibliography*

by
R. E. Jonsson, Ph.D.

INCORPORATED

LINCOLN, NEBRASKA 68501

Editor

Gary Carey, M.A.
University of Colorado

Consulting Editor

James L. Roberts, Ph.D.
Department of English
University of Nebraska

ISBN 0-8220-0465-8
© Copyright 1973
by
C. K. Hillegass
All Rights Reserved
Printed in U.S.A.

1992 Printing

Cliffs Notes, Inc.   Lincoln, Nebraska

CONTENTS

Far from the Madding Crowd Notes

LIFE AND BACKGROUND

"It is the office of good literature, the distinction of classical literature, to give form in every age to the age's human mind." Thus critic Lionel Johnson appraised the works of Thomas Hardy, "the English novelist who continues the high tradition of the art, is faithful to the spirit of his age, but faithful also to the spirit of his country." True indeed to his land, Hardy attempted to give form to a small sector of his native southwest England, which he dubbed Wessex. Mindful of changes wrought by nature and the progress of history, and wishing to perpetuate the old customs of his land, he systematically used adjacent sections of Dorset County as the locale for each Wessex novel. These novels are the backbone of Hardy's prose writing.

Thomas Hardy was born on June 2, 1840, in Brockhampton, Dorset, England. At the time of his birth, the old family of le Hardy, as it was once called, was poor and barely above the status of the laboring class. Hardy was the eldest of four children. Too frail for school attendance, he was taught first by his mother, then in the private school of the lady of the manor. At eight, he was strong enough to enter the village school, whose master was competent and beloved. Regular church attendance, family participation in singing and playing musical instruments at church services and village functions, and inveterate walking and reading taught literary, biblical, and local lore to a child sensitive enough to receive and store it.

At sixteen, Hardy was apprenticed to an architect in Dorchester. At twenty-one, he was employed by a prominent ecclesiastical architect in London. His scope as an architect was thereby widened, as were his intellectual horizons. He spent his lunch hours in London's museums. He attended concerts, lectures, and plays, and he continued the study of the classics which he had begun in Dorchester, and also studied French. At this time, too,

Hardy began to write poetry. His first novel, *Desperate Remedies*, was published anonymously in 1871. This and his two succeeding novels, *Under the Greenwood Tree* (1872) and *A Pair of Blue Eyes* (1873), although not popular successes, were favorably reviewed by the critics.

The editor of *Cornhill Magazine* requested that Hardy write a serialized novel. At this point Hardy was harboring the germ of a new idea: he thought of making it a pastoral tale with the title *Far from the Madding Crowd*—and the chief characters would probably be a young woman who farmed, a shepherd, and a sergeant of the cavalry. Loss of another writer's manuscript precipitated the magazine editor's acceptance of Hardy's material merely on the strength of an outline for the first two months of a year's installments. The novel, published in 1874, became Hardy's first popular and financial success.

Success enabled Hardy to discontinue his work as an architect, to marry Emma Lavinia Gifford (in 1874), and to spend the next quarter of a century writing novels. Although there were annual stays of a month or two in London and occasional trips to the Continent, the Hardys spent the major portion of their time in Dorset, called Wessex in his novels. Here Hardy designed and built Max Gate, which remained his home until his death at eighty-seven in January, 1928.

Hardy made many friends in the world of literature and learning, and played an active social role in the London seasons. He wrote assiduously; when he was ill, he dictated his material to his wife. Those of his novels which he placed in the category of "Character and Environment" became best known: *The Return of the Native* (1878), *The Mayor of Casterbridge* (1886), *Tess of the D'Urbervilles* (1891), and *Jude the Obscure* (1896). On the brink of a new literary era, Hardy broached topics and themes with greater frankness and starkness than some Victorian readers liked; consequently, he lived through a period of outraged criticism. Today we wonder at the furor.

Later in his career, Hardy gradually turned again to the poetry he really preferred and, following *Jude,* he worked primarily in this medium. One of his greatest works is the mammoth verse drama *The Dynasts* (1904-8), which is about the Napoleonic wars.

The first Mrs. Hardy died in November, 1912; the couple had no children. Hardy married for a second time in 1914 (at the age of seventy-four). His second wife, Florence Emily Dugdale, had long been a friend of both Hardy and his first wife and had worked as his secretary. After Hardy's death, she published a biography of Hardy which includes his own notes, letters, and comments. Some critics maintain that this biography is essentially an autobiography which Hardy wrote himself.

Hardy was given the Order of Merit in 1910 by King Edward VII. He enjoyed the veneration proffered him, the honors and awards and the visits to Max Gate by the famous. His death in 1928 was an occasion of national mourning. Though Hardy had wished to lie in the family vault at Dorset, the nation wished to honor him with burial in the Poets' Corner of Westminster Abbey. A compromise was effected; as an eminent group of public and literary figures saw Dorset earth sprinkled on the casket of Thomas Hardy in the Abbey, his brother saw the heart of Thomas Hardy interred in the village graveyard at Dorset.

Recognition of Hardy's talents was widespread in his own time and has proved enduring. Translations of his works began right after 1874 with *Far from the Madding Crowd;* there were also early Braille editions. Today the average American bookshop carries more than one edition of Hardy's major works. The motion picture industry, too, has recognized Hardy, and *Far from the Madding Crowd* has been made into a movie.

GENERAL SYNOPSIS

Bathsheba Everdene has the enviable problem of coping with three suitors simultaneously. The first to appear is Gabriel Oak, a farmer as ordinary, stable, and sturdy as his name suggests. Perceiving her beauty, he proposes to her and is promptly rejected. He vows not to ask again.

Oak's flock of sheep is tragically destroyed, and he is obliged to seek employment. Chance has it that in the search he spies a serious fire, hastens to aid in extinguishing it, and manages to obtain employment on the estate. Bathsheba inherits her uncle's farm, and it is she who employs Gabriel as a shepherd. She intends to manage the farm by herself. Her farmhands have reservations about the abilities of this woman, whom they think is a bit vain and capricious.

Indeed, it is caprice which prompts her to send an anonymous valentine to a neighboring landowner, Mr. Boldwood, a middle-aged bachelor. His curiosity and, subsequently, his emotions are seriously aroused, and he becomes Bathsheba's second suitor. She rejects him, too, but he vows to pursue her until she consents to marry him.

The vicissitudes of country life and the emergencies of farming, coupled with Bathsheba's temperament, cause Gabriel to be alternately fired and rehired. He has made himself indispensable. He does his work, gives advice when asked, and usually withholds it when not consulted.

But it is her third suitor, Sergeant Francis Troy, who, with his flattery, insouciance, and scarlet uniform, finally captures the interest of Bathsheba. Troy, who does not believe in promises, and laments with some truth that "women will be the death of me," has wronged a young serving maid. After a misunderstanding about the time and place where they were to be married, he left her. This fickle soldier marries Bathsheba and becomes an arrogant landlord. Months later, Fanny, his abandoned victim, dies in childbirth. Troy is stunned—and so is Bathsheba, when she learns the truth. She feels indirectly responsible for the tragedy and knows that her marriage is over.

Bathsheba is remorseful but somewhat relieved when Troy disappears. His clothes are found on the shore of a bay where there is a strong current. People accept the circumstantial evidence of his death, but Bathsheba knows intuitively that he is alive. Troy does return, over a year later, just as Boldwood, almost mad, is trying to exact Bathsheba's promise that she will marry him six years hence, when the law can declare her legally widowed. Troy interrupts the Christmas party which Boldwood is giving. The infuriated Boldwood shoots him. Troy is buried beside Fanny, his wronged love. Because of his insanity, Boldwood's sentence is eventually commuted to internment at Her Majesty's pleasure.

Gabriel, who has served Bathsheba patiently and loyally all this time, marries her at the story's conclusion. The augury is that, having lived through tragedy together, the pair will now find happiness.

LIST OF CHARACTERS

Bathsheba Everdene

Spirited young mistress of a large farm.

Gabriel Oak

Patient, reliable shepherd; suitor of Bathsheba.

Mr. Boldwood

Gentleman farmer enamored of Bathsheba.

Francis Troy

Lover and, later, husband of Bathsheba.

Fanny Robin

Runaway maid.

Mrs. Hurst

Bathsheba's aunt.

Liddy Smallbury

Bathsheba's maid.

Maryann Money

Bathsheba's charwoman.

Mrs. Coggan

Employed by Bathsheba.

Cainy Ball

Young under-shepherd to Gabriel.

Benjy Pennyways

Bathsheba's ex-bailiff.

Bill Smallbury
Henery Fray
Jacob Smallbury   } Some of Bathsheba's farmhands.
Labal Tall

SUMMARIES AND COMMENTARIES

CHAPTER 1

Summary

Twenty-eight-year-old Gabriel Oak was surveying his fields one mild December morning. From behind a hedge, he watched a yellow wagon come down the highway, the wagoner walking beside it. When the wagoner retraced his path to retrieve a lost tailboard, the horses halted. This delay permitted Oak to view the wagon's motley array of household goods, complete with plants and pots. Enthroned atop everything sat a pretty, dark-haired young woman in a crimson jacket. Looking to make sure the wagoner was out of sight, she took out a mirror. Her smile, tentative at first, widened at her satisfying reflection. She flushed as "she simply observed herself as a fair product of Nature in the feminine kind." Hearing the wagoner return, she replaced the glass.

After the two resumed their journey, Gabriel left his "point of espial" and followed them down the road. At the tollgate, the wagon was stopped. Unimpressed by the wagoner's protest that the girl refused to pay an additional twopence, the gatekeeper would not let the wagon pass. Stepping forward, Gabriel handed twopence to the keeper, saying, "Let the young woman pass." The girl glanced carelessly at him. "She might have looked her thanks to Gabriel on a minute scale, but she did not speak them; more probably, she felt none."

Gabriel did not disagree with the gamekeeper's comment on the attractiveness of the retreating girl. But, perhaps irked by her snub, he maintained that she had her faults, the greatest of them being "what it is always. . . . Vanity."

Commentary

"Far from the madding crowd" was how Thomas Hardy wished us to view his beloved native country and the types who inhabited it. Thus isolation furnished both the theme and the title of the novel. *Far from the Madding Crowd* might well entitle his whole series of Wessex novels.

In the first paragraph, the friendly face of Gabriel Oak smiles at us. His features are average, his clothes ordinary, and his "moral color was a kind of pepper-and-salt mixture." Even his idiosyncrasy is a mild one: he wears a large watch with a faulty hour hand. Undismayed, he checks the time by peering into neighbors' windows or by referring to the position of the stars. Unconcerned with time's passing, he leisurely continues to do what he thinks is right. He cares for his fellow beings and is capable of judging them.

Hardy, with the eye of the artist, loved the color and line of the landscape. Thus he personalized nature. His horses were "sensible," his cat "with half-closed eyes" viewed birds "affectionately." His delineation of people was part caricature, as with Gabriel, and part portraiture, as with the young woman whom Hardy shows through Gabriel's eyes. Hardy's first picture of these two young people will be counterbalanced by a well-illuminated, mellowed portrait in the final chapter, when both have matured.

Critics credit Hardy's first profession, that of architecture, with responsibility for his sense of form, both literary and aesthetic. This, his first successful novel, was designed to appear serially; one result of this is the inclusion of a bit of suspense at the close of each installment to keep the reader eager for the next one.

CHAPTER 2

Summary

Swirling winds blew over Norcombe Hill one St. Thomas' Eve. "The trees on the right and the trees on the left wailed or chaunted to each other in the regular antiphonies of a cathedral choir." Mingling with the wintry midnight sounds came the sounds of a flute. They issued from a small, arklike structure on wheels, of the type shepherds dragged about the fields to shelter themselves as they attended to their ewes at lambing time.

Gabriel was keeping vigil. After less than a year "as master and not as man," he now owned (but had not yet paid for) two hundred ewes, which he kept on leased land. With his lantern, he made the rounds of the straw-thatched hurdles around which the ewes stood. Cradling a fragile, newborn lamb, he hastened back to his hut and placed it on some hay before the bit of fire. The hut's furnishings were meager: they consisted of a small stove, a bed of corn sacks, a few medications and ointments, some food, and the flute. Not stopping to adjust the two round ventilating holes, Oak instantly fell asleep on his cornshuck bed. Soon the warmth restored the lamb, which began to bleat. Gabriel roused instantly and carried it back to its mother. The stars told him, his timepiece having failed as usual, that scarcely an hour had passed.

Perceiving a faint light on the horizon, Gabriel went to the edge of the plantation to check. The light came from a hut built into the slope. As he looked through the chinks in the roof, the light illuminated two women tending an ailing cow, and a second cow just delivered of a calf. The older woman was glad the cow was improving; the younger lamented that there was no man to do these heavy chores and that she had lost her hat. All the same, she volunteered to ride to town to fetch cereals in the morning.

As the enshrouding cloak fell from her head, Gabriel discerned the dark tresses and red jacket of the girl he had seen in the wagon.

Commentary

One cannot be unaware of Hardy's sense of the unity of man with nature: the eternal hills of his Wessex, the sounds of wind and weather, the ever-circling constellations, the light at different times of day and different seasons, the growth of vegetation, and the behavior of living creatures. His characters convey a general feeling of being a part of the universe; his narrative captures its rhythms. Far from the madding crowd, he seems to say, man comes into his own. Gabriel is so perfectly attuned to nature that he does his tasks, at whatever hour, faithfully and unquestioningly.

The notes of Gabriel's flute, "a sequence which was to be found nowhere in nature," remind us of Hardy's own participation in a church choir and his playing in an orchestra in his youth; there is an obvious musical dimension to his art appreciation.

Hardy notes that a limited view causes our imagination to fill in the outlines "according to the wants within us." And so it is with Gabriel: "Having for some time known the want of a satisfactory form to fill an increasing void within him, his position moreover affording the widest scope for his fancy, he painted her a beauty." This statement shows us another side of Gabriel. He has a romantic as well as a practical sensibility.

CHAPTER 3

Summary

Next morning, Gabriel heard the girl's pony coming up the hill. Guessing that she had come to look for her hat, he hurriedly searched for it and found it in a ditch. Returning to his hut, he watched the girl approach. To avoid low branches, she lay flat on the pony, her face to the sky. No proper Victorian lady would ride thus, but "the tall lank pony seemed used to such doings, and ambled along unconcerned. Thus she passed under the level boughs."

On the girl's return to the cattle shed, a farm boy exchanged a milking pail for the bags of cereal she brought. When she emerged from the hut with the pail full of milk, Gabriel approached to return the hat. They exchanged a few civilities, which ceased when the girl realized from Gabriel's clumsy speech that he had witnessed her unconventional riding performance. This blunder "was succeeded in the girl by a nettled palpitation, and that by a hot face." Considerately, Gabriel turned away from her blushes. When a slight sound made him turn back, she had gone. Crestfallen, he returned to his work.

Five days later, on a freezing day, the fatigued Gabriel came from his rounds into the hut. Putting extra fuel in his stove, he promised himself that he would adjust the ventilator, but he fell asleep before he did so. When he came to, his wet head was lying in the girl's lap. She explained that his dog, barking frantically, had fetched her from the milking shed and brought her to the hut. Finding no water, she had revived him with the milk. She reprimanded him for his carelessness but smiled when Gabriel tried to express his thanks and told her his name. The girl became a bit coquettish as he tried to shake her hand, but his ineptness and lack of sophistication in not trying to kiss it irked her once again. She left, her name still unknown to him.

Commentary

By having Oak continue to observe from a distance the object of his infatuation, Hardy is able to elaborate upon his description of the girl and her character. Her riding antics furnish a bit of comedy and also warn us that she is not a conventional young Victorian lady. There is a matter-of-factness in the girl's rescue of Oak and in her tart ridicule of his lack of judgment. Her coquettish behavior in the latter part of the chapter contrasts with her earlier hoydenism.

CHAPTER 4

Summary

Gabriel ascertained in town that the young woman was Bathsheba Everdene. "This well-favoured and comely girl soon made appreciable inroads upon the emotional constitution of young Farmer Oak." He waited to watch her each day at the milking and dreaded the time when the cow should go dry and Bathsheba would no longer come to the shed. He constantly repeated her name. "I'll make her my wife, or upon my soul I shall be good for nothing!"

Seeking an excuse to visit her, Gabriel decided to take as a gift a tiny lamb whose mother had died. He groomed himself with care and set forth, accompanied by his faithful dog, George. From behind a hedge near her house he heard a feminine voice calming a frightened cat. He called out that his dog was "as mild as milk," but nobody answered.

Once inside the house, Gabriel told the girl's aunt, Mrs. Hurst, of his desire to marry and inquired whether Bathsheba had suitors. Hoping to make a match, the aunt assured him that Bathsheba had many. Abashed, her would-be wooer replied, "That's unfortunate. . . . I'm only an everyday sort of man, and my only chance was in being the first comer." Forlorn, he walked away but was pursued by the tomboy calls of Bathsheba, who regretted having been away when he visited. Naively, she assured him that there were no other suitors. " 'Really and truly I am glad to hear that!' said Farmer Oak, smiling . . . and blushing with gladness."

Earnestly, Gabriel promised her all manner of things, including a piano. Hesitating over some of the items, Bathsheba said at last, "I've tried hard all the time I've been thinking; for a marriage would be very nice in one sense. People would talk about me and think I had won my battle, and I should feel triumphant, and all that. But a husband—." Finally Bathsheba admitted that she did not love Gabriel, and although the farmer said he would be happy if she just liked him, Bathsheba replied, "You'd get to despise me." Gabriel vehemently asserted, "Never. . . . I shall . . . *keep wanting you* till I die." He asked if he could come calling. She laughingly replied that that would be ridiculous, considering his feelings. " 'Very well,' said Oak firmly. . . . 'Then I'll ask you no more.' "

Commentary

With pronounced humor, Hardy gives the details of Gabriel's courtship of Bathsheba. He spruces up for his visit, polishing the silver chain of his watch and cutting himself a new walking stick. Auntie's boasts of numerous suitors for Bathsheba; Gabriel's offers of a piano, newspaper notices, and cucumber frames; Bathsheba's eagerness to be a bride unencumbered by a husband— these are all amusing and convincing bits of life. The scene also gives us a chance to see more of Bathsheba's vanity and an aspect of Gabriel we had not yet observed—pride.

CHAPTER 5

Summary

"The more emphatic the renunciation, the less absolute its character." This Gabriel learned when he heard that Bathsheba had gone to Weatherbury. Why or for how long she had gone, he did not know. His affection mounted, but he maintained his even temper.

The lambing phase of the sheepfarming over, he returned home for the luxury of sleeping in a real bed. He called the dogs, but only George responded. The younger dog, George's son, completely unlike his sire, was probably still eating a lamb carcass, a rare treat. George was competent and imbued with a sense of his responsibilities. The younger dog still lacked comprehension of what was expected of him.

Gabriel was roused from a sound sleep by the violent ringing of sheep bells. He rushed out, following the sound until he came to a broken rail at the edge of a chalk pit. Young George, evidently inspired by his meal, had zealously chased the sheep, driving them over the brink. Gabriel looked into the deep chasm. There, dead and dying, lay two hundred ewes, all heavy with an equal number of prospective young. There also lay all his hopes for a farm of his own. Gabriel's "first feeling . . . was one of pity for the untimely fate of these gentle ewes and their unborn lambs." Later, without rancor, he did his duty: he destroyed the dog.

Gabriel calculated that selling all his belongings and utensils would just cover the claims of the dealer who had staked him to his first independent venture. The debt was paid, "leaving himself a free man with the clothes he stood up in, and nothing more."

Commentary

Similar to Hardy's use of color to portray external appearance is his philosophy as to the sensitivity of men and animals.

Each creature has a sense of its purpose in life, to a greater or lesser degree. Thus, George's son must be destroyed to prevent further destruction, since he lacks all instinct for his trusted position.

CHAPTER 6

Summary

Casterbridge was holding its February hiring fair. A few hundred hearty workers stood about, each showing the symbol of his trade: carters, a bit of whipcord on their hats; thatchers, straw; shepherds, their crooks. One young fellow's "superiority was marked enough to lead several ruddy peasants standing by to speak to him inquiringly, as to a farmer, and to use 'Sir' as a finishing word. His answer always was, — 'I am looking for a place myself — a bailiff's.'"

No one seemed to need bailiffs. Toward the end of the day, Gabriel went to have a shepherd's crook fashioned, and he also exchanged his overcoat for a regulation smock. Now, ironically, bailiffs were in demand; yet prospective employers seemed to edge away when Gabriel said he'd lost his farm.

Watching the evening's merriment, Gabriel felt his flute in his pocket. "Here was an opportunity for putting his dearly bought wisdom into practice." His tunes were so well received that soon he had earned enough pence to feel more secure. There was another fair in Shottsford the next day. Hearing that this town lay beyond Weatherbury, Gabriel thought of Bathsheba and resolved to go to the fair via Weatherbury. After going about four miles in that direction, he saw a haywagon without horses beside the road and lay down in it for a rest. After dark he wakened to find the wagon in motion. He eavesdropped on the conversation of the two men in front and conjectured that the vain woman whom they were discussing was Bathsheba. Dismissing the thought, since the woman under discussion seemed to be the owner of a large farm, he slipped out of the wagon unseen.

Suddenly Gabriel saw a fire in the distance. As he ran toward it, he realized that the fire was in a rickyard. His familiarity with the nature of burning hay drove him to hurry to save it before it enveloped the piled-up corn. Others were converging on the fire, too. In the general confusion, Gabriel stood out as one who naturally takes command.

To one side stood two veiled women. They identified Gabriel as a shepherd, for he was wielding a crook, but no one seemed to know him. Finally the fire was extinguished. One of the women sent the other, her maid, to thank Gabriel. The maid told Gabriel that the other woman owned the farm. Gabriel approached her, saying, "Do you happen to want a shepherd, ma'am?" Silently, the astonished Bathsheba lifted her veil. Gabriel mechanically repeated his question.

Commentary

This long chapter abounds with architectural terminology and with evidence of Hardy's skills as an artist and a writer. We view masses of people in motion, but from the immense canvas detailed individual figures emerge as well. Hardy portrays many facets of the fair—speech, customs, costumes, indigenous trades, a sergeant, and a recruiter.

Gabriel continues his service as an on-the-spot observer for Hardy. The farmer has been matured by the reverses he has experienced and is learning to compromise. Even as the workers are "waiting on Chance," so is Gabriel. In Hardy's works, many such evidences of belief in fate and fortune exist. Oak's effort to "help" the fates by changing his costume is unavailing. When he decides to continue to Shottsford in his search for employment, the motivation is not too farfetched, for there are not many roads to choose; he is poor and cannot afford an inn. His rest in the wagon and the overheard conversation give Hardy an opportunity to introduce more dialect and to further characterize the Wessex folk.

The animation of the fire scene is a dramatization of country life and of some of the hazards encountered in the seemingly serene landscape.

CHAPTER 7

Summary

"Bathsheba. . . . scarcely knew whether most to be amused at the singularity of the meeting, or to be concerned at its awkwardness." The other firefighters enthusiastically endorsed Gabriel, and so she sent him to her bailiff. All the helpers were to be rewarded with refreshments at Warren's Malthouse. The bailiff, an unfriendly individual, hired Gabriel but could not, or would not, suggest lodgings. He referred Oak to the malthouse, where someone might know where he could stay.

As Gabriel plodded along the road, he came upon a young woman standing by a tree. She furnished him with directions to Warren's. But when in turn she asked the way to Buck's Head, Gabriel could not tell her. She realized he was a stranger and said awkwardly, "Only a shepherd—and you seem almost a farmer by your ways." She asked that he not tell of meeting her. Gabriel perceived her agitation, saw her shiver with the cold, and hesitatingly offered her a shilling, saying, "It is all I have to spare." She accepted it gratefully. He sensed that she was actually trembling. As he went on his way, "he fancied that he had felt himself in the penumbra of a very deep sadness."

Commentary

Hardy is fond of contrasts and antitheses in his phrases and uses these principles in presenting opposing situations and people. Gabriel's generosity and humility are repeatedly contrasted with Bathsheba's selfishness and vanity. Bathsheba's newly aggrandized position is contrasted with Gabriel's recent fall to poverty. The nasty bailiff, "moving past Oak as a Christian edges past an offertory-plate when he does not mean to contribute," is the direct antithesis to the warm and generous Gabriel who gives his last coins to the trembling girl.

CHAPTER 8

Summary

The malthouse was "inwrapped with ivy" and had a cupola on the roof and one window, which formed a small square in the door. Inside, the room glowed with light from the hearth. "The stone-flag floor was worn into a path from the doorway to the kiln, and into undulations everywhere." At one side were a curved settle and a small bedstead. The fragrance of malt filled the room. As Gabriel entered, everyone turned to look at him. An old maltster recognized Gabriel's name; he had known Oak's father and grandfather, and he launched into a garrulous account of them. This made Gabriel seem less of a stranger. He was offered a drink from the "God-forgive-me," a tall, two-handled mug standing among the coals. Gabriel rejected an offer to get him a cleaner cup, and, thus, drinking with the group, he was accepted by them.

There were many country types present, including men of all sorts—the old and decrepit, the scroungers, the cheerful, the shy, and the aggressive. They recalled other drinking bouts and discussed Miss Everdene's family. Her late uncle, who had left her the farm, and her father, a "celebrated bankrupt," fickle and romantic, were properly gone over. Bathsheba had become a beauty, they thought. And her bailiff was dishonest. Gossip was rampant, and all was punctuated by the reminiscences of the ancient maltster.

Gabriel's flute showed from his pocket, and the men asked for a tune. He obliged, confessing that he was down on his luck and the flute had served to earn him a little money. When the men began leaving, Gabriel went off with Jan Coggan, who had offered him a room.

Shortly, a man came running in with the news that Miss Everdene had caught her bailiff stealing and had dismissed him, and that Fanny Robin, the mistress's youngest employee, had disappeared. Bathsheba sent word that she would like to talk with one or two of the men, and those who were left in the malt-house went to see her. On their arrival, she spoke to them from an upper window, instructing them to make inquiries about Fanny the next day in the neighboring villages. Someone reported that Fanny had a soldier friend in Casterbridge.

Gabriel, in a bed at last, lay awake thinking of Bathsheba, delighted to have seen her again. He resolved to fetch his belongings, which consisted mostly of the few books which "constituted his library; and though a limited series, it was one from which he had acquired more sound information by diligent perusal than many a man of opportunities has done from a furlong of laden shelves."

Commentary

The malthouse chapter is important to Hardy's project of depicting his Wessex world. Besides offering some fine sketches of local figures, Hardy presents the atmosphere of the old malt-house, showing us country customs and affording us a general insight into the variety of characters composing this "simple" world. There is a veritable gallery of personality types, all speaking variations of the local dialect, and all charming in their idiosyncrasies. They serve as foils for each other and also as the medium for disseminating background information. Most important, together they function as a collective commentator on country life and current events.

CHAPTER 9

Summary

Bathsheba's home, which "presented itself as a hoary building, of the early stage of Classic Renaissance," was once the manorial hall of a small estate. Ornate stone pilasters, finials, and other Gothic features adorned it. All the outlines were softened by a mossy growth. The entire complex of buildings was mellowed, and its new function, as a farmhouse, seemed to have turned it front to rear, reversing its focus.

Within, the floors, at present uncarpeted, creaked and sagged. Bathsheba and her maid-companion, Liddy, were in one of the upper rooms, sorting the belongings of the former owner. Liddy was the old maltster's great-granddaughter, and "her face was a prominent advertisement of the light-hearted English country girl." Maryann Money could be heard scrubbing, and Mrs. Coggan was busy in the kitchen. A horse tramped up the footpath, and the women were thrown into confusion when they saw that the rider was a gentleman. He knocked, and the responsibility for answering the door was delegated from one to another. Eventually Mrs. Coggan, flour-covered, opened it and announced Mr. Boldwood. Bathsheba could not see him, said Mrs. Coggan, for she was "dusting bottles sir, and is quite a object." Boldwood explained that he was merely inquiring as to whether Fanny had been found.

Later, the girls told Bathsheba that Boldwood was a gentleman farmer, a forty-year-old bachelor. He had befriended Fanny and had sent her to school. Then he had gotten her the position with Bathsheba's uncle. Boldwood, they agreed, was kind, but "never was such a hopeless man for a woman!" He had resisted all female attempts to ensnare him.

Bathsheba, in a petulant mood, told Maryann that she should long since have been married off. The girl agreed: "But what between the poor men I won't have, and the rich men who won't have me, I stand as a pelican in the wilderness!" To Liddy's question, "Did anybody ever want to marry you, miss?" Bathsheba answered, "A man wanted to once." But "he wasn't quite good enough" for her. At this point, a file of employees was seen arriving.

Commentary

To describe the manor house, Hardy draws on the terminology of architecture, with which he is professionally conversant. He adds the mellowed tones of a painter's appreciation and creates the venerable, musty atmosphere of the estate.

This is our first meeting with the gossiping female servants; they are as absorbing as their male counterparts in the previous chapter. Into this preserve comes the very masculine Boldwood. Through conversation with busybody Liddy, Bathsheba learns about him. He is fond of children (he rewards the little gatekeeper), but impervious to womanly charms and wiles.

CHAPTER 10

Summary

After a short wait, Bathsheba granted the men an audience. They had settled on benches at the foot of the hall. Bathsheba opened the time book and the canvas moneybag. Liddy sat beside her "with the air of a privileged person."

Bathsheba announced her dismissal of the bailiff and her intention to manage the farm herself. "The men breathed an audible breath of amazement." Then she called the roster, asking each employee about himself. The men were awkward; some joked, and each seized the opportunity to draw the attention of the crowd for a moment. Young Cainy Ball was made undershepherd to Gabriel, who spoke to Bathsheba with confidence.

Bathsheba asked for news of Fanny and learned that Boldwood had had the pond dragged, but to no avail. Then Smallbury arrived from Casterbridge, stamping snow from his boots. The soldiers had left the town, and Fanny with them; rumor had it that her friend "was higher in rank than a private." Bathsheba suggested that someone inform Boldwood.

Before dismissing the help, Bathsheba promised, "If you serve me well, so shall I serve you." She would arise early and be watching. "In short, I shall astonish you all."

Commentary

Critics consider this chapter representative of Hardy's work in its character delineation and its humor: Bathsheba is mistress of the situation; Gabriel loses none of his stature, although he is properly humble; Liddy is comical with the sense of her own importance; and the idiosyncratic characteristics of the staff members are developed further. The story has received a push forward.

CHAPTER 11

Summary

Hours later, in snow and darkness, a figure appeared on the public path which was bordered by a river. In the background could be heard the constant gurgling of water. The figure was counting out the windows of a barracks. Stopping at the fifth, it threw a small snowball which "smacked against the wall at a point several yards from its mark. The throw was the idea of a man conjoined with the execution of a woman. No man . . . could possibly have thrown with such utter imbecility as was shown here." After many efforts, the girl finally struck the proper window.

The window opened and a man's voice asked who was there. The girl identified herself as Fanny Robin. She regarded herself as Sergeant Troy's wife because of his frequent promises, and she wished to publish their marriage banns. They agreed to meet the next day. Then she went away, amid the guffaws of Troy's companions.

Commentary

Hardy lets the weather serve to show the interrelation between atmospheric conditions and mood. The approach of winter is well portrayed, and the bleakness of the barracks territory reflects Fanny's dismal situation. The tall "verticality" of the barracks wall is dramatically contrasted with the smallness of the little waif; her credulity is contrasted with Troy's blustering. Using nature to mirror mood or situation is a common device in Hardy. Note the seasons in which major events occur throughout the book. Spring is often a time of happiness and renewal; winter, a time of death and despair.

CHAPTER 12

Summary

Bathsheba followed up her decision to be a good farmer by attending the corn market at Casterbridge the next day. She saw how the men bargained, using facial contortions and gesticulations, manipulating their sticks as props or as prods for livestock as if they were extensions of their hands. She stood out, completely feminine, moving between them "as a chaise among carts." She first approached farmers whom she knew and, as her confidence grew, gathered courage to address others. She had brought her sample bags of corn and was soon pouring grains into her hand with professional skill.

The impression was conveyed that she was learning her business rapidly, despite her femininity. "Strange to say of a woman in full bloom and vigour, she always allowed her interlocutors to finish their statements before rejoining with hers." But she stood firm on her pricings. The men were interested because of her pluck and admired her as much for that as for her appearance.

Only one man seemed aloof—a dignified, striking man of about forty. Because he ignored her, Bathsheba was convinced that he was unmarried. She was intrigued, and on the way home with Liddy she commented on him. Liddy did not know whom she meant. Just then a low carriage passed by with the mystery man in it, and Liddy identified him as Farmer Boldwood, whom Bathsheba had earlier refused to see. He didn't turn in greeting but rode indifferently by. The rest of the girls' trip was spent in conjecture as to the reason for his standoffishness. Had he been jilted? Was it merely that his nature was reserved? For each possibility Bathsheba offered, Liddy parroted agreement.

Commentary

Obviously Hardy attended many country markets, appreciatively noting the mannerisms of the participants. Here he has preserved a bit of Wessexiana just on the verge of change.

Bathsheba's character is developing. Shy in her appearance among so many unknown men, she nonetheless stands her ground for the furtherance of her farm and makes progress in achieving the respect of her competitors.

Though it has been suggested that Hardy is somewhat anti-feminist, the paragraph he devotes to Bathsheba's managerial techniques does not seem grudging. She lets the men talk, but "in arguing on prices she held to her own firmly, as was natural in a dealer, and reduced theirs persistently, as was inevitable in a woman. But there was an elasticity in her firmness which removed it from obstinacy, as there was a *naïveté* in her cheapening which saved it from meanness."

CHAPTER 13

Summary

To while away Sunday afternoon, Bathsheba and the chatterbox Liddy, who, "like a little brook, though shallow was always rippling," practice an old superstition: divining one's future husband by consulting the Bible with a key. Bathsheba turned to the Book of Ruth and, reading, she was a bit abashed. "It was Wisdom in the abstract facing Folly in the concrete." After they went through the ritual with the key and Bible, Liddy asked of whom Bathsheba had been thinking, surmising that her mistress's mind might have been on Boldwood, as her own had been. She was sure that everyone in the church had focused attention on Bathsheba except Boldwood, who sat in the same line of pews. Bathsheba seemed unperturbed by this. As the girls chatted, she recalled having bought a valentine for little Teddy Coggan and proceeded to inscribe it with a verse. Liddy prodded her into sending it to Boldwood instead. Whatever her reason, Bathsheba did address it to the farmer, and from her supply of seals she selected one that said, "Marry me."

"So very idly and unreflectingly was this deed done. Of love as a spectacle Bathsheba had a fair knowledge; but of love subjectively she knew nothing."

Commentary

In four short pages, two giddy girls carry out a silly act which will avalanche into a tragedy. Liddy ("her presence had not so much weight as to tax thought, and yet enough to exercise it") misleads Bathsheba, while her mistress, "bounding from her seat with that total disregard of consistency which can be indulged in towards a dependent," acted on her maid's idle suggestion. Hardy has, in addition, shown us old country customs and, not for the first time, has suggested that women can be guilty of somewhat unpredictable behavior.

CHAPTER 14

Summary

Boldwood sat in his living room, "where the atmosphere was that of a Puritan Sunday lasting all the week." He was increasingly fascinated by the anonymous valentine, which "must have had an origin and a motive." In spite of himself, Boldwood kept reverting to the mystery. He tried to visualize the sender. Sticking the letter in the corner of his mirror, he was conscious of it through the night. He slept badly and rose to watch the sunrise. Unearthly colors played on the glazed fields.

When the mailman came in his cart and proffered him an envelope, "Boldwood seized and opened it, expecting another anonymous one — so greatly are people's ideas of probability a mere sense that precedent will repeat itself." The mailman pointed out that the letter was for the new shepherd, and Boldwood realized that it was intended for Gabriel Oak. Recognizing a distant figure across the field, followed by a dog, Boldwood left to take the letter to Gabriel and to apologize for having opened it.

Commentary

Hardy has furthered the plot by introducing the matter of the anonymous valentine and following it with another letter handed to Boldwood. Additional facets of Boldwood's character are revealed. Boldwood's complexities are here contrasted with Bathsheba's lack of sophistication; her frivolity is set alongside the brooding nature of the farmer. Oblivious to the effect of her whim, Bathsheba has undoubtedly slept the night through.

One is struck by the abundance of figures of speech in this chapter. These are stock in trade for any writer, but they are expertly handled by Hardy. As has been mentioned, Hardy drew his images from many sources—visual, physical, historical, natural, and mythological.

CHAPTER 15

Summary

After a few hours of sleep, the maltster made himself a breakfast of bread and bacon which "was eaten on the plateless system" and flavored with a "mustard plaster." Although he was toothless, his hardened gums functioned efficiently.

Warren's Malthouse served as a sort of clubhouse, an alternative to the inn. Henery appeared, followed by several carters, and expressed the opinion that Bathsheba would not manage the farm successfully. All viewed the prospect of her management negatively. They also disapproved of Bathsheba's new piano and other new furnishings. Henery longed to be bailiff. He felt God had cheated him. A religious discussion followed.

Oak arrived with some newborn lambs to be warmed, for the fields here had no shepherd's hut. When he heard that the men had been discussing Bathsheba, he grew angry and threatened anyone maligning the mistress. The men sought to appease him, flattering him a bit and changing the subject. Joseph now became the victim of taunts directed at his lesser farming skills. Oak admitted that he, too, wished to be bailiff.

Soon Boldwood appeared with Gabriel's letter. It was from Fanny Robin, thanking Gabriel for his help and returning his shilling. She asked again for secrecy and explained that she would be marrying Sergeant Troy. Gabriel showed Boldwood the letter, for he knew that the farmer had been kind to Fanny. Bold-wood was doubtful of her marriage plans, for he knew Troy to be unreliable.

Little Cainy broke in, coughing from running, with the news that there were more twin lambs. Gabriel branded the revived ones with Bathsheba's initials. As he left, Boldwood asked Gabriel to identify the handwriting of the mystery valentine. Learning it was Bathsheba's, Boldwood was troubled.

Commentary

In this chapter we see further evidence of Gabriel's stead-fastness and loyalty and his unhurried manner of doing what needs to be done. We meet the gossipmongers again. Another link is added to the Fanny Robin matter. Boldwood fears for Fanny and also broods about the reason for Bathsheba's sending the valentine.

Bill Smallbury's remark, "Your lot is your lot, and the Scrip-ture is nothing; for if you do good you don't get rewarded accord-ing to your works, but he cheated in some mean way out of your recompense," is a passing comment on what later became one of Hardy's main themes, the indifference of God to man.

CHAPTER 16

Summary

A small congregation at All Saints' Church was startled by the clash of spurs at the close of a weekday service. A cavalry soldier strode into the chapel and spoke to the curate. "'Tis a wedding!" murmured one of the women, brightening. "Let's wait!"

Through the open door from the vestry they heard the creak-ing mechanism of the clock indicating half-past eleven. No one appeared, and there was tittering and giggling. So again at the three-quarter hour. "I wonder where the woman is," a voice whispered. This was repeated at the full hour. As the angry sergeant was about to leave, Fanny arrived, breathless, to explain that she had been waiting at All Souls', which she had mistaken for All Saints'. She suggested that they meet again the next day, but Troy refused to go through such a performance a second time. Fanny, trembling, asked when the wedding would be. "'Ah, when? God knows!' he said, with a light irony, and turning from her, walked rapidly away."

Commentary

Troy is infuriated by his humiliation before the old women and takes out his rage on poor, confused Fanny. Her reaction to his anger is near terror. Though we have seen little of Troy, Fanny's actions do provide some clues to his nature.

CHAPTER 17

Summary

On Saturday at the market, Boldwood saw Bathsheba. "Adam had awakened from his deep sleep, and behold! there was Eve. . . . and for the first time he really looked at her." He found her beautiful, but, unaccustomed to judging women, "he furtively said to a neighbor, 'Is Miss Everdene considered handsome?'" The neighbor assured him that she was. Boldwood was overcome by jealousy as he watched her talking with a young farmer.

Bathsheba was aware of having made an impression and regretted her capriciousness. "She that day nearly formed the intention of begging his pardon. . . . The worst features of this arrangement were that, if he thought she ridiculed him, an apology would increase the offense by being disbelieved; and if he thought she wanted him to woo her, it would read like additional evidence of her forwardness."

Commentary

Hardy briefly shows the new awareness of Bathsheba and Boldwood for each other, and thus gives a new twist to the plot.

We begin to realize that Boldwood is extraordinarily naive about women and probably would be impervious to most pursuit simply because he would not know it for what it was. But Bathsheba's bold "Marry me" is, if nothing else, direct. The frivolity of her gesture is lost on Boldwood, just as the possibility that a careless act might have tragic consequences was lost on Bathsheba.

CHAPTER 18

Summary

Boldwood gave the impression of being aristocratic. He lived in a home recessed from the road, with stables behind it. It was all overgrown with shrubbery. In the stables were fine, healthy horses; all was warmth, contentment, and plenty. Looking after the horses was almost a sacred ritual for Boldwood. "This place was his almonry and cloister in one."

Boldwood's "square-framed perpendicularity showed more fully now than in . . . the markethouse." He paced flatfootedly, his face bent downward. Except for "a few clear and thread-like horizontal lines," his face was smooth. "That stillness, which struck casual observers . . . may have been the perfect balance of enormous antagonistic forces—positives and negatives in fine adjustment. His equilibrium disturbed, he was in extremity at once." Had Bathsheba known the intensity of his nature, she might have been frightened.

It was spring, and one sensed the awakening of the countryside. Bathsheba was across the fields with Oak and Cainy. When Boldwood saw her, his face lit up "as the moon lights up a great tower." He resolved at once to cross the fields to speak to her.

Bathsheba blushed at Boldwood's approach. Gabriel, attuned to her moods, remembered that Boldwood had asked him to identify the handwriting on the valentine, and he suspected that Bathsheba might have been up to something. Finally Boldwood decided not to speak. Bathsheba, aware that she had caused a reaction in the farmer, resolved not to do such a thing again. "But a resolution to avoid an evil is seldom formed till the evil is so far advanced as to make avoidance impossible."

Commentary

Two characteristics of Hardy's writing are emphasized here —the careful sketching of forms, this time of animals, and the sound and olfactory effects as well as the visual ones. Hardy builds up an intensity of feeling. Boldwood is deeply involved with Bathsheba; she recognizes that she has done a foolhardy thing. Gabriel intuitively knows there will be complications.

CHAPTER 19

Summary

When Boldwood finally called on her, Bathsheba was not in. He had forgotten that, being a serious farmer, she might well need to be out-of-doors. Having put her on a pedestal, he found it difficult to see in her an everyday individual like himself. Their relationship was one of "visual familiarity, oral strangeness. The smaller human elements were kept out of sight; the pettinesses that enter so largely into all earthly living and doing were disguised by the accident of lover and loved one not being on visiting terms." Boldwood resolved to find her.

The sheep-washing pool in the blossoming meadow, full of the clearest water, made a pretty spectacle. Several farmhands stood there with Bathsheba, who was in an elegant new riding habit. Two men pushed the sheep into the pool, then Gabriel pushed them under as they swam and, as the heavy wool became saturated, hauled them out with a crutchlike device. Bathsheba bade Boldwood a constrained good-day, momentarily thinking he had come to watch the washing. She withdrew, but he followed her. She sensed his silent emotion. Then, without preamble, he proposed. He stated his age, his background, and declared his need of her.

Very formally, Bathsheba declined. He continued, regretting his inarticulateness, and said he would not have spoken, had he not hope. "You are too dignified for me to suit you sir," she said, and blurted out apologies for thoughtlessly sending the valentine. He insisted, however, that it was not thoughtlessness but instinct which promoted it. Again he entreated, until she begged him to stop, asking for time. "Then she turned away. Boldwood dropped his gaze to the ground, and stood long like a man who did not know where he was. Realities then returned to him like the pain of a wound received in an excitement which eclipses it, and he, too, then went on."

Commentary

Hardy's rendering of the sheep-washing portrays a particularly lovely bit of country life, a seemingly placid performance which contrasts with the intense emotion of Boldwood. In this highly unlikely situation, in the midst of something as earthy as washing sheep, the overwrought gentleman chooses to plead his suit. Bathsheba regrets her "wanton" and "thoughtless" act, is sympathetic toward Boldwood, and is frightened by the unanticipated consequences of her deed.

CHAPTER 20

Summary

Bathsheba, though not in love, nevertheless realized that Boldwood was an eligible bachelor. "He is so disinterested and kind to offer me all that I can desire," she thought. "Yet Farmer Boldwood," the author informs us, "whether by nature kind or the reverse to kind, did not exercise kindness here. The rarest offerings of the purest loves are but a self-indulgence, and no generosity at all." Bathsheba was not eager to be married, nor had the novelty of being a landowner begun to wear off. "Bathsheba's was an impulsive nature under a deliberative aspect. An Elizabeth in brain, and a Mary Stuart in spirit."

Next day, Bathsheba saw Gabriel grinding shears. Cainy Ball was turning the handle of Gabriel's grindstone, but Bathsheba sent him on an errand, offering to sharpen while Gabriel turned the stone. She did not do well, and Gabriel took her hands to show her the proper angle for holding the blades. Meanwhile, she attempted to find out about the men's comments on her meeting with Boldwood. Oak admitted the men had spoken of the prospect of a marriage. When she asked Gabriel to contradict them, he refused to lie for her. He told her that her conduct was unworthy of a thoughtful woman. Bathsheba became sarcastic, saying his attitude might be due to her refusal of him. To this, Gabriel replied that he had long since stopped thinking about the possibility of marrying her. He repeated that it was wrong for her to trifle with Boldwood. Angrily, Bathsheba dismissed Oak as of the end of the week.

Gabriel preferred going at once. " 'Go at once then, in Heaven's name!' said she, her eyes flashing at his, though never meeting them. 'Don't let me ever see your face any more.' " Gabriel agreed. "And he took his shears, and went away from her in placid dignity, as Moses left the presence of Pharaoh."

Commentary

Hardy has interpolated his own views on marriage motives and an intensive psychological study of Bathsheba; the chapter invites careful reading. Bathsheba resents Gabriel's frankness, after having sought it, and even more she resents his statement that he no longer wishes to marry her. The equanimity with which he accepts dismissal enrages her. We know that when Gabriel's helpfulness, on which she has come to rely, is no longer available, she will rue her rashness.

The minute detail with which Hardy draws his characters is exemplified in this passage: "It may have been a peculiarity— at any rate it was a fact—that when Bathsheba was swayed by an emotion of an earthy sort her lower lip trembled; when by a refined emotion, her upper or heavenward one. Her nether lip quivered now."

36

CHAPTER 21

Summary

Gabriel had been gone about twenty-four hours when, on Sunday, men came running to Bathsheba to report that many of her sheep had broken into a field of clover. " 'And they be getting blasted,' said Henery Fray. . . . 'And will all die as dead as nits, if they bain't got out and cured!' said Tall."

Bathsheba shouted at the men for not having gone directly to the fields to do something about it. Despite her velvet dress, she too ran to the fields. The animals were very ill. When she asked what to do, the men told her that the sheep had to be pierced to be relieved, and that only Oak knew how to perform this operation. Bathsheba was furious. She thought of Boldwood, but the men told her that some of his animals had been similarly affected by vetch the other day, and he had sent for Gabriel. Still Bathsheba refused to consider this. Suddenly a sheep fell dead, and Bathsheba sent a message ordering Oak to come.

The men waited until Laban Tall returned with word that Gabriel would not come unless properly asked. After another sheep died, Bathsheba wrote the request and added at the bottom: "Do not desert me, Gabriel!"

When Gabriel appeared, Bathsheba looked at him with gratitude but reproved him for his unkindness. He went at once to lance the animals. He did forty-nine successful operations. There was only one mishap. Four other sheep had died before his arrival. Fifty-seven sheep were saved.

" 'Gabriel, will you stay on with me?' she said, smiling winningly, and not troubling to bring her lips together again at the end, because there was going to be another smile soon.

" 'I will,' said Gabriel.

"And she smiled on him again."

Commentary

The chapter serves less to point up Bathsheba's strong-mindedness than as a picture of the vicissitudes of farm life and an appraisal of the constancy of duty on a farm. Gabriel's delay is a matter of discipline, to show Bathsheba that she is dependent on the skills of others and must deal fairly with them.

CHAPTER 22

Summary

"Gabriel lately, for the first time since his prostration by misfortune, had been independent in thought and vigorous in action to a marked extent. . . . But this incurable loitering beside Bathsheba Everdene stole his time ruinously."

On this first of June, Gabriel enjoyed the blossoming countryside and, in the ecclesiastical atmosphere suggested by the architecture of the huge and ancient barn, he participated in the ritual and pageantry of the centuries-old rite of sheep-shearing. Each man played his greater or lesser role in the service. In the background, women gathered the shorn fleeces. Bathsheba made sure that the men would shear closely yet give no wounds. Carelessness was reprimanded.

While Bathsheba watched, chattering constantly, Gabriel sheared a sheep in a surprisingly short time—twenty-three and one-half minutes. Cainy brought the tar pot. The initials B. E. were stamped on the newly shorn skin, and the panting animal leaped away, joining "the shirtless flock outside."

Unexpectedly, Boldwood appeared and talked to Bathsheba as Gabriel continued shearing. The girl left, reappearing in her new riding habit. Distracted, Gabriel cut a sheep. Bathsheba reproved him. Superficially unmoved, Gabriel medicated the wound. The other two went off to view Boldwood's Leicesters.

"That means matrimony," predicted one woman, beginning the gossip. Henery, still resentful that he had not been appointed bailiff, was most talkative. Gabriel brooded. All the others looked forward to the feasting which would crown the ritual of the shearing.

Commentary

Still another fine description of Wessex life is drawn here. The animation and motion are absorbing as we follow the careful work of the shearers.

Gabriel's tension rises when Boldwood appears. "Gabriel at this time of his life had outgrown the instinctive dislike which every Christian boy has for reading the Bible, perusing it now quite frequently, and he inwardly said, 'I find more bitter than death the woman whose heart is snares and nets!' This was mere exclamation—the froth of the storm. He adored Bathsheba just the same." Note that this quotation follows the indirect reference in the preceding chapter to a man's using distraction by a woman as an alibi for not making progress in his profession.

CHAPTER 23

Summary

"For the shearing-supper a long table was placed on the grass-plot beside the house, the end of the table being thrust over the sill of the wide parlour window and a foot or two into the room. Miss Everdene sat inside the window, facing down the table. She was thus at the head without mingling with the men."

Bathsheba was sparkling. She invited Gabriel to occupy the vacant seat at the opposite end of the table, only to ask him to move again when Boldwood appeared, apologizing for his lateness.

After supper, Coggan began singing folksongs. When it was Poorgrass's turn, he was a bit in his cups and stalled at first. Then he rendered a composition of his own. Young Coggan became convulsed with laughter, and his father had to send him off. Tranquility restored, others sang, and "the sun went down in an ochreous mist: but they sat and talked on, and grew as merry as the gods in Homer's heaven."

Suddenly Gabriel noticed that Boldwood was missing from the place of honor. As Liddy brought candles, he saw him within the parlor, sitting close to Bathsheba. The guests asked Bathsheba to sing "The Banks of Allan Water." After a moment's consideration, Bathsheba assented, beckoning to Gabriel "to accompany her on his flute." Boldwood sang the bass "in his customary profound voice." Bathsheba then wished everyone good night.

Boldwood closed the sash and the shutters but remained inside to propose once again. After some hesitation, Bathsheba said, "I have every reason to hope that at the end of the five or six weeks . . . that you say that you are going to be away from home, I shall be able to promise to be your wife." Boldwood withdrew with a serene smile. Bathsheba still had qualms: "To have brought all this about her ears was terrible; but after a while the situation was not without a fearful joy. The facility with which even the most timid women sometimes acquire a relish for the dreadful when that is amalgamated with a little triumph, is marvellous."

Commentary

Hardy offers still another lovely old country custom in his depiction of the farm supper: the crosscurrents of feeling; the power of song, effecting a momentary calm over ruffled spirits; the maintenance of individuality within the group—these are things that Hardy expresses very well.

A verse of the song Bathsheba sings foreshadows future developments in the plot:

> For his bride a soldier sought her,
>   And a winning tongue had he
> On the banks of Allan Water
>   None was gay as she!

At present, though, it appears that Bathsheba will ultimately accept Boldwood.

CHAPTER 24

Summary

Bathsheba was in the habit of inspecting the homestead before retiring. Almost always, Gabriel preceded her on this tour, "watching her affairs as carefully as any specially appointed officer of surveillance could have done; but this tender devotion was to a great extent unknown to his mistress, and as much as was known was somewhat thanklessly received. Women are never tired of bewailing man's fickleness in love, but they only seem to snub his constancy."

Bathsheba carried a dark lantern, lighting it to peer in corners. She heard the contented munching of animals as she made her return through a pitch-dark fir plantation. Suddenly she heard footsteps and almost immediately stumbled, for her skirt was caught. Recovering her balance, she was aware of the figure of a man seeking to pass her. He asked her to turn on her lantern. The light revealed a scarlet military jacket and also the fact that the soldier's spur had caught the braid trimming of Bathsheba's skirt. His attempts to free her were not very earnest, and finally Bathsheba herself completed the disentanglement.

Gallantly, the handsome soldier, who identified himself as Sergeant Troy, thanked her for the opportunity of seeing how lovely she was. His lavish compliments included the remark, "I wish it had been the knot of knots, which there's no untying!" Flattered and confused, Bathsheba ran to the house, where Liddy told her something of Troy's reputation as a dandy. Bathsheba now regretted having been rude when Troy had probably meant only to be kind. Boldwood suffered by comparison with the sergeant: "It was a fatal omission of Boldwood's that he had never once told her she was beautiful."

Commentary

Hardy has complicated the design in his pastoral tapestry once again. Bathsheba appears to have won a new admirer. In addition to the faithful, stable Gabriel, who has been dismissed as not good enough for her, and the enamored, troubled Boldwood, a man of property who is still under consideration although Bathsheba does not love him, is the charming Sergeant Troy, who has literally—and perhaps symbolically—snared her.

CHAPTER 25

Summary

"Idiosyncrasy and vicissitude had combined to stamp Sergeant Troy as an exceptional being. He was a man to whom memories were an incumbrance, and anticipations a superfluity. Simply feeling, considering, and caring for what was before his eyes, he was vulnerable only in the present. . . . With him the past was yesterday; the future, to-morrow; never, the day after."

Troy was "moderately truthful" to men, but lied to and flattered women. "He had been known to observe casually that in dealing with womankind the only alternative to flattery was cursing and swearing. There was no third method. 'Treat them fairly, and you are a lost man,' he would say."

Bathsheba was relieved by Boldwood's absence. She was surveying the haymaking in her fields when she noticed a red uniform behind a wagon. The sergeant had "come haymaking for pleasure; and nobody could deny that he was doing the mistress of the farm real knight-service by his voluntary contribution of his labour at a busy time." As soon as Bathsheba appeared, Troy put down his fork, gathered his riding crop, and came toward her. Bathsheba blushed and lowered her eyes.

Commentary

Sergeant Troy is an undeniably charming liar who gives no thought to the harm his words may cause. When we remember

Bathsheba's unthinking acts—her treatment of Oak, her valentine to Boldwood—we cannot help but feel some satisfaction that she has finally met her match—and more.

CHAPTER 26

Summary

Troy's first remark was an apology to Bathsheba for his brashness in their first encounter. He had inquired about her identity, he said, and should have known her to be the "Queen of the Corn-Market," as someone had characterized her. He explained his presence now by saying he had always helped in the fields in her uncle's day.

"I suppose I must thank you for that, Sergeant Troy," said Bathsheba indifferently. At Troy's hurt look, she explained that she did not wish to be obligated to him for anything. Undaunted, Troy continued his extravagant praises of Bathsheba's beauty until she admitted her confusion, seeing no basis for his flattery and at first denying that she merited it. But then she began to weaken. "Capitulation—that was the purport of [her] simple reply, guarded as it was—capitulation, unknown to herself. Never did a fragile tailless sentence convey a more perfect meaning. The careless sergeant smiled within himself, and probably too the devil smiled from a loop-hole in Tophet, for the moment was the turning-point of a career. Her tone and mien signified beyond mistake that the seed which was to lift the foundation had taken root in the chink: the remainder was a mere question of time and natural changes."

Sergeant Troy regretted that he could stay only a month, insisting that he had loved Bathsheba the instant he saw her. Disclaiming the possibility of such sudden feeling, she asked the time. Since she had no watch, Troy impulsively sought to bestow his own upon her. It bore the crest and motto of the earls of Severn and had been left to Troy by his natural father. Bewilderment and agitation lent Bathsheba's features an animation and beauty which moved Troy to see the truth in phrases he had used in jest. Suddenly he blurted out: "I did not mean you to accept it at first, for it was my one poor patent of nobility . . . but . . . I wish you would now."

Bathsheba again refused the watch, but Troy did exact her promise that he might continue to work in her fields. In complete consternation, "she retreated homeward, murmuring, 'O, what have I done! What does it mean! I wish I knew how much of it was true!'"

Commentary

This is an excellent study of the glib and suave soldier, proud of his presence, his uniform, and the adventurous elements in his background. Though Troy begins his pursuit of Bathsheba lightheartedly, she is completely taken in by him, revealing herself to be rather gullible and guileless in her confused responses. No doubt her own vanity helps to convince her that he is sincere. Troy, however, seems to have fallen into his own trap, now meaning in earnest what he had said in jest.

CHAPTER 27

Summary

The swarming of the bees was late that June. Bathsheba watched them finally gravitating toward one high branch of an unwieldy tree, forming a huge black mass. Since the farmhands were all haying, she decided to hive the bees alone. Wearing clothes that covered her completely, including gloves, hat, and a veil, she fetched a ladder and mounted it.

Troy appeared and offered his help, declaring how fortunate he was to be arriving at just the right moment. Bathsheba insisted that he don the protective hat, veil, and gloves. "He looked such an extraordinary object in this guise that, flurried as she was, she could not avoid laughing outright. It was the removal of yet another stake from the palisade of cold manners which had kept him off."

Troy brought the filled hive down, a cloud of bees trailing behind it. He remarked that holding the hive made his arm ache more than a week of sword exercises did. When Bathsheba said that she had never seen an exhibition of swordplay, he volunteered to give one for her, privately, that evening. Reconsidering her plan to bring Liddy with her, after Troy reacted to it coldly, Bathsheba agreed to come unaccompanied, "for a very short time."

" 'It will not take five minutes,' said Troy."

Commentary

This chapter contains lighthearted conversation and rare laughter. The ludicrous costuming of Troy adds to the merriment. Also, in this further encounter between Bathsheba and Troy and their plans for still another meeting, the pace of the plot is quickened.

CHAPTER 28

Summary

At eight o'clock that midsummer evening, Bathsheba appeared in the fern hollow amid the soft, green, shoulder-high fronds. She paused, changed her mind, and was halfway home again before she caught sight of a red coat approaching. She considered Troy's disappointment were she not to appear, and she ran back to the hollow. When she reached the verge of a pit in the midst of the ferns, she saw Troy standing at the bottom and looking toward her.

Troy's performance with the sword was precise and filled with bravado. It grew a bit frightening. He pretended the girl was the enemy and brandished his sword about her so realistically that she imagined herself run through. It was a dexterous feat. As a final tour-de-force, he said, "That outer loose lock of hair wants tidying. . . . Wait: I'll do it for you."

"An arc of silver shone on her right side; the sword had descended. The lock dropped to the ground." Next Troy speared a caterpillar which had settled upon Bathsheba's bosom. Only then did Troy admit that the sword was razor-sharp. "You have been within half an inch of being pared alive two hundred and ninety-five times."

Then the man stoped to pick up the lock of Bathsheba's hair. He tucked it inside his coat. Softly he announced that he had to leave. He disappeared, and, overcome by tumultuous emotion, "aflame to the very hollows of her feet," Bathsheba wept, feeling "like one who has sinned a great sin."

"The circumstances had been the gentle dip of Troy's mouth downwards upon her own. He had kissed her."

Commentary

Troy is so completely in command of his sword and so perfectly confident of his skill that he does not hesitate to risk Bathsheba's life for the sake of his performance. His actions have utterly overwhelmed Bathsheba: "She felt powerless to withstand or deny him."

We must not overlook Hardy's own showmanship. He creates a sensuous chapter, with the lush setting, textures, colors, and lighting all playing their parts. He does a masterful job of describing the flashing of lights and the lightning speed of Troy's every move. Hardy was interested in dramatics and here uses his sense of effective staging.

CHAPTER 29

Summary

"Bathsheba loved Troy in the way that only self-reliant women love when they abandon their self-reliance. When a strong woman recklessly throws away her strength she is worse than a weak woman who has never had any strength to throw away. One source of her inadequacy is the novelty of the occasion. She had never had practice in making the best of such a condition. Weakness is doubly weak by being new."

Bathsheba had talked of Boldwood to Liddy, but she spoke to no one of Troy. Gabriel, however, noticed and sorrowed over this new infatuation. He decided to talk with Bathsheba, basing his appeal on her unfairness to Boldwood.

Oak met Bathsheba one evening when she went for a walk. He spoke of bad characters in the neighborhood, wishing to imply that Troy was one of them. He said that in the absence of Boldwood, who would normally protect her, he thought it advisable to take on this role himself. Bathsheba assured him that no wedding with Boldwood was in prospect; she said she had given the farmer no answer.

Gabriel cited Troy's unworthiness. He considered him to be a man without conscience and on a downward course in life. Bathsheba countered his arguments. Oak begged her to be discreet: "Bathsheba, dear mistress, this I beg you to consider—that, both to keep yourself well honoured among the workfolk, and in common generosity to an honourable man who loves you as well as I, you should be more discreet in your bearing towards this soldier."

Again Bathsheba wanted to dismiss Oak for meddling, and again he agreed to go, but only if she were to hire a good bailiff. When she refused to do so, Gabriel refused to leave the farm. Then, "as a woman," she asked him to leave her alone. Gabriel saw her meet Troy but, not wishing to eavesdrop, he left.

Troy had told Bathsheba that he attended church secretly, entering by the side door. Gabriel, doubting Troy's truthfulness, checked this door; he found it overgrown with ivy and therefore impossible to enter.

Commentary

We admire Gabriel for his honesty, fairness, and courage in confronting Bathsheba with her dalliance with Troy. Oak is almost certain that she will not heed him, but he deems it his duty to speak. We understand his point of view when his lack of faith in Troy's veracity is corroborated.

CHAPTER 30

Summary

Despite her promise not to reject Boldwood before his return, Bathsheba could not wait. "The farewell words of Troy, who had accompanied her to her very door, still lingered in her ears. He had bidden her adieu for two days, which were, so he stated, to be spent in Bath visiting some friends. He had also kissed her a second time."

Restless and perturbed, Bathsheba impulsively wrote to Boldwood that she could not marry him. Taking the letter to the kitchen for one of the maids to mail, she overheard the servants gossiping about her latest romance. Furiously insisting that she hated Troy, but with the next breath defending him, she forbade their gossip. Alone with Liddy, Bathsheba confided her love, begging reassurance that all the stories circulating about Troy were not true. Eager to please her mistress, Liddy agreed with all her statements. Bathsheba turned on her: "Mind this, Lydia Smallbury, if you repeat anywhere a single word of what I have said to you inside this closed door, I'll never trust you, or love you, or have you with me a moment longer—not a moment!"

" 'I don't want to repeat anything,' said Liddy, with womanly dignity of a diminutive order; 'but I don't wish to stay with you. And, if you please, I'll go at the end of the harvest, or this week, or to-day . . . I don't see that I deserve to be put upon and stormed at for nothing!' "

Liddy's words led to a tearful reconciliation; she promised always to be Bathsheba's friend, shedding a few more tears "not from any particular necessity, but from an artistic sense of making herself in keeping with the remainder of the picture."

Commentary

Hardy's portrait of feminine frailty and women's weapons is not without humor. Bathsheba does not wish to think ill of Troy, does not want to believe the stories about him, and fights against the possibility of their truth.

Liddy envies her mistress her femininity and her conquests. She is also proud of her position and dignity. Both girls enjoy having a good cry. They agree that "God likes us to be good friends." Liddy assures her mistress that, while Bathsheba is a match for any man, she is not mannish. "O no, not mannish; but so almighty womanish that 'tis getting on that way sometimes. I wish I had half your failing that way. 'Tis a great protection to a poor maid in these illegit'mate days!"

CHAPTER 31

Summary

To avoid Boldwood at his return, Bathsheba planned to visit Liddy, who, granted a week's holiday, was visiting her sister. Bathsheba set out on foot and, after walking about two miles, saw coming toward her the very man she was seeking to evade. Boldwood was obviously disturbed by her letter of rejection and expressed his feeling for Bathsheba in these words: "You know what that feeling is. . . . A thing as strong as death. No dismissal by a hasty letter affects that." He pleaded with her, claiming to be beyond himself, as Bathsheba feared he indeed was. Referring to the valentine, he repeated that she must have had some feeling for him. Bathsheba tried to explain it away by saying, "You overrate my capacity for love."

Boldwood countered that he knew she was not the cold woman she claimed to be. "You have love enough, but it is turned to a new channel. I know where." Bathsheba delayed her reply but could not deny the accusation. Boldwood became unreasonably angry and launched into a long, distraught harangue. "Bathsheba, sweet, lost coquette, pardon me! I've been blaming you, threatening you, behaving like a churl to you, when he's the greatest sinner. He stole your dear heart away with his unfathomable lies! . . . I pray God he may not come into my sight, for I may be tempted beyond myself. . . . yes, keep him away from me."

With that, he slowly went on his way. Bathsheba, unable to comprehend "such astounding wells of fevered feeling in a still man," feared for Troy. Previously she had been in control of herself. "But now there was no reserve. In her distraction, instead of advancing further, she walked up and down, beating the air with her fingers, pressing her brow, and sobbing brokenly to herself." Copper clouds appeared in the sky, presaging inclement weather. Then the stars came out. Bathsheba saw nothing. "Her troubled spirit was far away with Troy."

Commentary

Boldwood, obviously overwrought, has been pushed to the point of potential violence. He bears little resemblance to the remote, dignified gentleman we first encountered at Bathsheba's house. Keep in mind the curse which Boldwood places on Troy: "May he ache, and wish, and curse, and yearn — as I do now!"

CHAPTER 32

Summary

"The village of Weatherbury was quiet as the graveyard in its midst, and the living were lying well-nigh as still as the dead. The church clock struck eleven. The air was so empty of other sounds that the whirr of the clock-work immediately before the strokes was distinct, and so was also the clock of the same at their close." Maryann, alone in the manorhouse, was startled by a stealthy footfall. She saw a gray figure enter the paddock; shortly thereafter, she heard the gig traveling down the road. Thinking that gypsies had stolen the wagon, she ran to Coggan's house, where Gabriel was again staying. The men found that Dainty was the horse which had been stolen. To pursue her, they would need light, quick horses; Gabriel decided to borrow Boldwood's.

They followed the hoofmarks, and were sure because of the shoeing on one foot that it was indeed Dainty. Finally, at a toll-gate, they caught up, only to discover that the "thief" was — Bathsheba!

Bathsheba explained that she had given up the trip to Liddy's for "an important matter." Then, unable to rouse Mary-ann, she had chalked a message on the coach-house door. She said that now that she had removed the stone from Dainty's shoe, she would be able to reach Bath by daylight. The men were sure she was miscalculating the distance, as in truth she was.

"Bathsheba's perturbed mediations by the roadside had ultimately evolved a conclusion that there were only two remedies for the present desperate state of affairs. The first was merely to keep Troy away from Weatherbury till Boldwood's indignation had cooled; the second, to listen to Oak's entreaties, and Boldwood's denunciations, and give up Troy altogether."

Following Troy to Bath insured another meeting with him, but this was something Bathsheba chose not to think about. The rest of her plan was to go from Bath to Yalbury, meet Liddy, and return with her.

Commentary

The deductions made by the men in tracing and identifying the "stolen" horse reveal native skills, as does their estimation of distances. Since both men are sufficiently convinced that Bathsheba's behavior is erratic, Gabriel easily enjoins Coggan to silence.

CHAPTER 33

Summary

After a week, Bathsheba had not returned. Maryann received a note that her mistress was detained. Another week elapsed, and the oat harvest began. As the men worked in the fields they saw a runner. Maryann, who was helping bind sheaves, had an uncomfortable premonition, for she had dropped the door key that morning and it had broken.

The runner proved to be Cainy Ball, on holiday because he had an inflammation on his finger and could not work. The men commented on the advantages of an occasional indisposition which afforded time to get other things done, things more to one's liking. Cainy, choking and coughing, exasperated everyone because he was unable to catch his breath sufficiently to deliver his message. They pounded him and gave him cider to drink. Finally, in spasms, he told of having been to Bath, where he had seen Bathsheba with a soldier. "And I think the sojer was Sergeant Troy. And they sat there together for more than half-an-hour, talking moving things, and she once was crying a'most to death. And when they came out her eyes were shining and she was as white as a lily; and they looked into one another's faces, as far gone friendly as a man and woman can be."

Gabriel, deeply affected, tried to question Cainy further, but the boy had nothing more to tell about Bathsheba, and wanted to talk only about the wonders of Bath. Coggan privately advised Oak, "Don't take on about her, Gabriel. What difference does it make whose sweetheart she is, since she can't be yours?"

" 'That's the very thing I say to myself,' said Gabriel."

Commentary

Realistically, Cainy blurts out the narrative between coughs and sneezes. In his discomfort and obtuseness, he arouses the curiosity of the listeners even more. After a long-winded recital of trivia about the town of Bath, he can offer no further morsel of excitement to climax his tale. The account is not without caricature and humor.

CHAPTER 34

Summary

That same evening at dusk Gabriel was leaning over Coggan's garden-gate, taking an up-and-down survey before retiring to rest." A carriage approached and from within came the voices of two women—Bathsheba and Liddy. "The exquisite relief of finding that she was here again, safe and sound, overpowered all reflection and Oak could only luxuriate in the sense of it. All grave reports were forgotten."

A half-hour later Boldwood walked to Bathsheba's, but Liddy, acting rather strangely, did not admit him. He left at once, feeling that he had not been forgiven. Walking through the village, he saw the carrier's van draw up and Troy's scarlet figure emerge. Troy had once before stayed at the carrier's house. Boldwood, making a sudden decision, hurried home and then quickly returned to meet Troy. As the sergeant came up the hill, Boldwood accosted him, introducing himself and telling Troy that he knew why Fanny had run away. When Troy declared that he was too poor to marry Fanny, Boldwood offered to settle a sum on her. Troy was still reluctant. Boldwood lost his calm and accused Troy of having ruined his chances with Bathsheba. Troy questioned this. Again Boldwood proffered money, assuring Troy that Bathsheba was only toying with him. Troy accepted fifty pounds. Boldwood promised him five hundred more pounds the day he married Fanny. Although Troy said that he thought Fanny too menial for him to marry, he accepted the offer.

Bathsheba approached, not seeing Boldwood, and Troy went to meet her. The astounded Boldwood overheard their loving conversation and Bathsheba's assurance that she had sent the servants away. Troy sent her home, telling her that he would join her as soon as he fetched his carpetbag. Then, arrogantly, he invited Boldwood to accompany him. The devastated farmer lunged at Troy, then realized that he was helpless: Troy was in the bargaining position. Boldwood now pleaded Bathsheba's cause, begging Troy to preserve her honor by marrying her and amazing Troy with the intensity of his infatuation. Troy accepted the remaining twenty-one pounds Boldwood had brought with him. Although Bathsheba was not to know of the financial arrangement, he wished Boldwood to come along to inform her of the marriage plan.

At the door, Troy asked that Boldwood wait outside. After a moment, he thrust a newspaper through the door and held a candle for Boldwood to read of the marriage of Troy and Bath-sheba in Bath. With derisive laughter and a moral lecture on Boldwood's being willing to believe the worst, Troy threw the money out toward the road and locked the door.

"Throughout the whole of that night Boldwood's dark form might have been seen walking about the hills and downs of Weatherbury like an unhappy Shade in the Mournful Fields by Acheron."

Commentary

Hardy does some very deft weaving of the plot threads in this chapter. He has built suspense and now must satisfy curiosity. Bathsheba has made her choice. In the process, the cruel, taunting Troy and the pitiful, baffled Boldwood are contrasted masterfully. We know from the violent reactions (which suggest the influence of the Greek tragedies) that more trouble must follow. Boldwood is so devastated that we know he will not be able to renounce Bathsheba. And Fanny's fate is still unresolved.

CHAPTER 35

Summary

Very early the next morning, Gabriel and Coggan were in the fields. They heard an upper casement window being opened. Troy leaned out. "She has married him!" said Coggan. As Gabriel failed to reply, Coggan, glancing at the averted face, said, "Good heavens above us, Oak, how white your face is; you look like a corpse!" The two men stood near the stile, "Gabriel listlessly staring at the ground. His mind sped into the future, and saw there enacted in years of leisure the scenes of repentance that would ensue from this work of haste." He mused over the reasons for all the mystery. Had Bathsheba somehow been entrapped?

As the men turned toward the house, Troy hailed them. Coggan replied and, after some urging, so did Oak. Troy commented on the gloom of the house, suggesting modernization. Gabriel defended it for its traditions. Troy preferred comfort. After this discussion, Troy suddenly asked Coggan whether there was any insanity in Boldwood's family. Coggan seemed vaguely to remember an old, disturbed uncle. Troy dismissed this information and announced his intention of being out in the fields after a few days. Then he threw them a half-crown so that they might drink to his health. Gabriel was angry, but Coggan caught the coin and urged Gabriel to restrain himself, for he was certain that Troy would buy his discharge from the army and become master of the farm. "Therefore 'tis well to say 'Friend' outwardly, though you say 'Troublehouse' within."

Boldwood appeared, reminding Coggan of Troy's inquiry. "Gabriel, for a minute, rose above his own grief in noticing Boldwood's. . . . The clash of discord between mood and matter here was forced painfully home to the heart; and, as in laughter there are more dreadful phases than in tears, so was there in the steadiness of this agonized man an expression deeper than a cry."

Commentary

Observe how quickly Troy takes over the reins. The reactions of Coggan and Oak are typical: Gabriel needs time for self-control, but Coggan seeks to serve his own interests by serving his new master. The stern pose of Boldwood after his earlier outbursts seems to indicate that he is trying to suppress his true feelings. Hardy's keen observation of many types of people manifests itself in the small but telling gestures, poses, and expressions of all the characters.

CHAPTER 36

Summary

Late August brought storm threats, and Oak worried for the eight exposed hayricks. Troy had designated the evening for the harvest supper and as Gabriel approached the barn, he heard music. The place was decorated with garlands, and fiddlers played for the dancing. The musicians asked Bathsheba to choose a tune. When she said it made no difference, they suggested "The Soldier's Joy." Flattered, Troy led the dance with her. He announced that he had left the army but would remain a soldier in spirit.

Gabriel tried to warn Troy about the hay, but Troy brushed him aside, saying there would be no rain. Besides, this was the wedding feast. Everyone would be served an extra-strong drink, he said. Bathsheba protested that the men had had enough. Troy overruled her and dismissed the women. Furiously, Bathsheba left.

For politeness's sake, Oak stayed a while. As he left, Troy cursed him for refusing a second round of grog. On the way home, Oak accidentally "kicked something which felt and sounded soft, leathery, and distended, like a boxing-glove." It was a toad. "Finding it uninjured, he placed it again among the grass." He knew this to be a warning of foul weather. Indoors, he found another warning: a garden slug had taken refuge in his home. He sat and thought for a while, finally deciding to rely on the instincts of the sheep. He found them "crowded close together. . . . all grouped in such a way that their tails, without a single exception, were toward that half of the horizon from which the storm threatened."

Gabriel, now certain there would be a storm, mentally calculated the potential loss of five wheat ricks and three of barley to be seven hundred and fifty pounds. Returning to the barn to get help to save Bathsheba such a great loss, he saw a peculiar spectacle. The entire male assemblage was sprawled grotesquely in every imaginable position. The central figure was the scarlet-coated sergeant.

Oak realized he would have to work alone. He fetched the key to the granary from Tall's house; rushing back, he found sail-cloth and tools. He covered all but two wheat ricks with the cloth, then thatched the barley.

Commentary

Hardy's depiction of the portents of the approaching storm is yet another example of his closeness to nature.

The contrasting pictures of the men before and after the revel are like a pair of companion canvases. Hardy uses his favorite motif of a red-clothed figure at the apex of the composition. In turn, these word paintings contrast with that of the struggling, solitary figure of Oak.

Gabriel cannot be thought of as merely thrifty and practical: "Such was the argument that Oak set outwardly before him. But man, even to himself is a palimpsest, having an ostensible writing, and another beneath the lines. It is possible that there was this golden legend under the utilitarian one: 'I will help to my last effort the woman I have loved so dearly.'"

CHAPTER 37

Summary

A series of flashes and rumblings signaled the closeness of the storm. After the second peal of thunder, a candle was lit in Bathsheba's room. The fourth flash of lightning struck Oak's ricking-rod, and he paused momentarily to improvise a lightning rod. The fifth flash brought Bathsheba into the fields. Once she learned that Troy was asleep, she tried to help stow the sheaves. When a flash frightened her, Gabriel steadied her. Another "dance of death" split trees, and the pair realized they had had a narrow escape. Gabriel told Bathsheba to leave, but she replied, "You are kinder than I deserve! I will stay and help you."

When Gabriel would not explain the absence of the other men, Bathsheba said slowly, "I know it all—all.... They are ... in a drunken sleep, and my husband among them." Bathsheba followed Gabriel to the barn and looked through the chinks: "All was in total darkness, as he had left it, and there still arose, as at the former time, the steady buzz of many snores." As Oak returned to his work, Bathsheba abruptly confessed the reason for her trip to Bath. She had intended to break off with Troy, but jealousy of a possible rival and her own distraction had led her to marry him instead.

The pair continued working in silence until Gabriel sent Bathsheba away because of her fatigue. He worked on, finally "disturbed . . . by a grating noise from the coach-house. It was the vane on the roof turning round, and this change in the wind was the signal for a disastrous rain."

Commentary

This chapter deserves careful reading for its appeal to the senses. The structure, punctuated by flashes of lightning, shows nature in anger, illuminating character, and calling for self-realization and truthfulness.

CHAPTER 38

Summary

"It was now five o'clock, and the dawn was promising to break in hues of drab and ash." The wind grew stronger and un-covered some wheat ricks, and Gabriel weighted them down with fence rails. He continued to cover the barley while the rain beat down heavily. He remembered that eight months earlier he had fought a fire in this same spot, for love of the same woman.

Two hours later, as Oak was wearily finished, wavering figures emerged from the barn. A scarlet one headed for the house. Not one of them remembered the ricks. On his way home, Gabriel met Boldwood, who remarked that Gabriel looked ill and asked the trouble. Oak explained that he had been working on the ricks, and Boldwood admitted having forgotten his. Once such an oversight would have been impossible for him. "Oak was just thinking that whatever he himself might have suffered . . . here was a man who had suffered more."

Boldwood preoccupied with what people thought, said that Bathsheba had not jilted him, that she had never promised him anything. He lamented his fate, his expression wild. Then he roused himself and resumed his reserve, saying, "Well good morning; I can trust you not to mention to others what has passed between us two here."

Commentary

Bathsheba and her three admirers again appear in the same chapter — Troy whistling and carefree; Boldwood suffering from deep emotional tension; and Gabriel remaining loyal to Bathsheba and the land and sympathizing with Boldwood.

CHAPTER 39

Summary

Bathsheba was riding up steep Yalbury Hill in the gig, with Troy walking alongside. He was no longer in uniform. They were discussing his gambling losses, which he blamed on a wet race-track. Bathsheba tearfully predicted the eventual forfeit of the farm if he continued his present rate of loss. He grumbled displeasure at her "chicken-hearted" wifely ways.

A woman appeared at the brow of the hill and, while Troy's back was to her, asked him whether he knew the closing time of the workhouse gates. Her voice startled him, but he did not turn. When she heard him reply, "she uttered an hysterical cry, and fell down." Troy ordered Bathsheba to leave.

Alone with the woman, Troy asked her why she had not written. She said that she had been afraid to. Troy gave her the little money he had with him, explaining that his wife kept him short. He told the woman to stay at the workhouse, Casterbridge Union-house, until Monday, when he would meet her on Gray's Bridge, give her as much money as he could obtain, and find lodgings for her.

When Troy caught up with Bathsheba, he admitted that he knew the woman, but not her name.

" 'I think you do.'

" 'Think if you will, and be—' The sentence was completed by a smart cut of the whip round Poppet's flank, which caused the animal to start forward at a wild pace. No more was said."

Commentary

We suspect at once that "the woman" is Fanny Robin—in fact, Troy lets the name slip. Otherwise Hardy maintains the term "the woman." Troy's concern for her is real. Fanny is another victim of his inability, or his refusal, to live by anything but impulse. Impulse dictated his marriage to Bathsheba, which now is obviously crumbling. His childish nature is further revealed by his complete disregard for the financial ruin which his gambling losses will eventually bring about.

CHAPTER 40

Summary

The woman continued on her slow way, stopping to rest from time to time and praying for strength. She counted the milestones to encourage herself to proceed. A carriage passing in the darkness lighted her face, "young in the groundwork, old in the finish; the general contours were flexuous and childlike, but the finer lineaments had begun to be sharp and thin." At a lone copsewood she paused. Groping, she selected two Y-shaped sticks and used them as crutches. These helped her to the last milestone, where she swayed, fell, lay for a while, then crawled and fell again.

A dog licked the woman's cheek. "In her reclining position she looked up to him just as . . . she had, when standing, looked up to a man." The animal, as homeless as she, withdrew a step, then returned, sensing her need. Using him as a prop, the woman

slowly moved ahead. They reached a shabby building, so overgrown with ivy that it had become one of the attractions of the
town. The woman managed to pull the bell before falling down.

A man emerged and went for help to get her into the building. The woman revived enough to ask for the dog. "'I stoned
him away,' said the man. The little procession then moved forward — the man in front bearing the light, two bony women next,
supporting between them the small and supple one. Thus they
entered the house and disappeared."

Commentary

Some critics find this chapter less effective than most — cit-
ing, for example, the interrupting discourse on the manufacturer
of a Swiss prosthetic device which is compared to the woman's
improvisation of a crutch. The agonies of Fanny's journey have
been called melodramatic. Animal lovers protest the use of the
dog, although it seems that Hardy's point was that at times animals have more humanity than people. Hardy's succinct descriptions remain effective, as in the description of the ivy-covered
almshouse to which the force of "Nature, as if offended, lent
a hand."

CHAPTER 41

Summary

Troy asked Bathsheba for money but would not say why he
needed it. Bathsheba commented that his mysterious manner
worried her. Troy responded: "Such strait-waistcoating as you
treat me to is not becoming in you at so early a date." He warned
her not to pry too far. Bathsheba said she felt that their romance
was already at an end. Troy said, "All romances end at marriage."
After more bickering, she gave him twenty pounds from her
household money. He opened the back of his watch, and she saw
a small coil of yellow hair. Troy admitted that it belonged to a
young girl he had once planned to marry.

Bathsheba was jealous, but Troy remained unmoved, saying prophetically, "I can't help how things fall out . . . upon my heart, women will be the death of me!" He left Bathsheba to her chagrin. "She had never taken kindly to the idea of marriage . . . as did the majority of women. . . . In the turmoil of her anxiety for her lover she had agreed to marry him; but the perception that had accompanied her happiest hours . . . was rather that of self-sacrifice than of promotion and honour."

Next morning, Bathsheba rode out to inspect the farm. When she returned for breakfast, she learned that Troy had gone to Casterbridge. She left on another tour of inspection, "finding herself preceded in forethought by Gabriel Oak, for whom she began to entertain the genuine friendship of a sister." She saw him across the fields, and saw also that Boldwood was approaching him. The two men talked earnestly, then called to Poorgrass and spoke with him. Later Poorgrass came toward her and "set down his barrow, and putting upon himself the refined aspect that a conversation with a lady required, spoke. . . . 'You'll never see Fanny Robin no more. . . . because she's dead in the Union.' "

Poorgrass speculated that the cause of death was a general weakness of constitution: "She . . . could stand no hardship, even when I knowed her, and 'a went like a candle-snoff, so 'tis said. . . . Mr. Boldwood is going to send a waggon at three this afternoon to fetch her home here and bury her.'

" 'Indeed I shall not let Mr. Boldwood do any such thing— I shall do it! Fanny was my uncle's servant . . . she belongs to me.' " Bathsheba arranged for a wagon to be filled with evergreens and flowers to cover the coffin.

Later, Bathsheba questioned Liddy about Fanny. Fanny's hair had been golden. Troy had said he knew the soldier who was Fanny's friend "as well as he knew himself." They had served in the same regiment, and "there wasn't a man in the regiment he liked better."

Commentary

This involved chapter has many undercurrents. Along with Bathsheba, we try to ascertain the facts. Boldwood, Oak, and Poorgrass are preoccupied and reluctant to talk with Bathsheba. They evade her questions. Liddy rambles on, suggesting things which Bathsheba is not yet willing to face, and so Bathsheba angrily silences her.

CHAPTER 42

Summary

The workhouse had a small rear door three or four feet from the ground. Here, at about three o'clock, a bright wagon containing flowers drew up. Joseph Poorgrass backed the wagon to the door, and a plain coffin was lifted into it. A man wrote on the coffin with chalk, then covered it with a worn black cloth, and someone handed Joseph a certificate. He placed the flowers over the coffin and drove off. A heavy mist was falling, and gray gloom and quiet enveloped the wagon.

Passing through Roy-Town, Joseph came to Buck's Head Inn, a mile and a half from his destination. With great relief, he stopped at the inn. There, to his delight, were "two copper-coloured discs, in the form of the countenances of Mr. Jan Coggan and Mr. Mark Clark. These owners of the most appreciative throats in the neighborhood, within the pale of respectability," hailed him as he entered. Joseph explained that his peaked look was caused by the load he was driving. They drank, and drank again. Joseph said he had to be at the churchyard at a quarter to five, but the men went on discussing life, death, and theology. Poorgrass grew less concerned with time.

As the clock struck six, Oak arrived. He reproved the men, but, with drunken logic, Coggan explained that all the hurrying in the world couldn't help a dead woman. Joseph was now singing. He denied being drunk but said his malady of a "multiplying eye" had caught up with him. Oak drove the wagon back, reflecting on the rumor that Fanny had run away to follow a soldier. Due to Oak's and Boldwood's tact, Troy had not been identified as the man, and Oak hoped the secret would be kept.

When Gabriel reached Bathsheba's house, it was too late for the burial, and so Bathsheba ordered the coffin brought into the house, for to leave it in the coach-house seemed unfeeling. Troy had not yet returned.

Oak and three other men carried the coffin in, Gabriel lingered on alone, overcome by the irony of it all, and looked again at the writing on the lid. The scrawl said simply, "Fanny Robin and child." He took his handkerchief and carefully rubbed out the last two words, leaving visible only the inscription "Fanny Robin."

Commentary

Even in death it seems that there can be no rest for Fanny. In her coffin, she still travels the roads of Wessex. Appropriately, it is Oak who comes to her aid in death, just as he once did in life; and, finally, her body is given lodging within a house.

Though their behavior seems rather callous, the men at the inn are merely accepting Fanny's death (as they have doubtless accepted many others) as the will of Nature. These people, instinctively close to Nature, accept the results of her actions without question.

CHAPTER 43

Summary

Bathsheba questioned Liddy again about Fanny. Liddy didn't know any more, but said that Maryann had heard tales. Bathsheba refused to believe what Liddy whispered to her, arguing that there was but one name on the coffin.

Feeling that she must draw strength from another to see her through what lay ahead, Bathsheba went to Oak's cottage.

Through the window she watched him close the book he had been reading and realized that he was about to retire. Unable to bring herself to ask him about the matter which troubled her, Bathsheba returned home. Standing near the coffin, she sobbed, "I hope, hope it is not true that there are two of you!" Finally she fetched a screwdriver and opened the coffin. "It was best to know the worst, and I know it now!" The tears came, "tears of a complicated origin." Unable to refrain from hating Fanny, Bathsheba knelt beside the coffin and prayed. When she arose, she was calmer.

The slamming door of the coach-house announced Troy's arrival. He asked what had happened, but Bathsheba would not tell him. The two approached the coffin. A candle illuminated the bodies. Overcome, Troy sank to his knees, then kissed Fanny's face. Bathsheba cried out to him. He pushed her away and told her, "This woman is more to me, dead as she is, than ever you were, or are, or can be." Turning to Fanny, he said, "In the sight of Heaven you are my very, very wife!"

Bathsheba turned and ran from the house.

Commentary

Intuitively, Bathsheba knew the truth and, impelled by guilt feelings caused by the initial surge of hatred and jealousy which she had felt, she showed her pity toward mother and child by placing flowers around their bodies. Troy's emotion and remorse reinforce her realization that her marriage is over.

The title which Hardy gave to this chapter, "Fanny's Revenge," suggests something of the Greek tragedies, as does the dramatic revelation of truth which the chapter contains. But it is not Fanny who is vengeful—it is fate.

CHAPTER 44

Summary

"Bathsheba went along the dark road, neither knowing nor caring about the direction or issue of her flight." Finally she sank down in a brake of ferns. At daybreak, unsure whether or not she had slept, she felt calmer. Eventually Liddy found her, and the two women decided to walk about until Fanny had been taken away. Liddy went back to the house to check, telling those who asked that her mistress was unwell so that people would assume Bathsheba was in her room.

When Liddy returned, Bathsheba lectured her, warning, "You'll find yourself in a fearful situation; but mind this, don't you flinch. Stand your ground, and be cut to pieces. That's what I'm going to do."

They re-entered the rear of the house, Bathsheba withdrawing into an unused attic. Liddy brought in a piece of carpet and laid a fire. From the window Bathsheba viewed the farm and saw the young men at play in the sunset. Suddenly they stopped. Liddy said, "I think 'twas because two men came just then from Casterbridge and began putting up a grand carved tombstone." The young men had gone to see whom the stone was for.

" 'Do you know?' Bathsheba asked.

" 'I don't,' said Liddy."

Commentary

Hardy does not use nature as mere setting: it is an integral part of his story. Bathsheba discovers before her a hollow in which there is a swamp: "The general aspect of the swamp was malignant. From its moist and poisonous coat seemed to be exhaled the essences of evil things in the earth. . . . Bathsheba arose with a tremor at the thought of having passed the night on the brink of so dismal a place." Thus Bathsheba's physical surroundings reflect the dark happenings in her life. She has been brought to the edge of an evil abyss, but she has not fallen into it.

CHAPTER 45

Summary

"When Troy's wife had left the house at the previous midnight his first act was to cover the dead from sight." He then went upstairs to wait for morning.

"Fate had dealt grimly with him through the last four-and-twenty hours." He had taken the twenty pounds from Bathsheba and another seven pounds ten which he was able to muster and had gone to meet Fanny. To his chagrin, she again failed to appear. He waited until the stroke of eleven — "in fact, at that moment she was being robed in her grave-clothes by two attendants at the Union poorhouse." Having watched the bridge and parapet until his patience ran out, Troy called for his gig and went to the racetrack, but he kept his vow not to wager. Leaving town at nine, he regretted not having inquired about Fanny. His return home was a shock.

In the morning he arose, indifferent to Bathsheba's whereabouts. He walked to the vacant grave, then hastened to Casterbridge, where he sought out the stonemason. He asked for the best stone they had for twenty-seven pounds. He paid for it and gave directions for the inscription. In the afternoon he returned and saw the stone placed in the cart which would take it to Weatherbury. Toward dusk he traveled homeward, carrying a heavy basket. In the course of his journey he met the mason's men returning from the graveyard. They assured him that the stone had been set.

At ten, Troy entered the cemetery and found the grave near the rear tower of the Weatherbury church where the land had recently been cleared of rubble to make room for new charity graves. Troy fetched a spade and lantern and read the inscription on the stone. Then he opened the basket and took out several bulbs. He had chosen a variety so that there would be blossoms from early spring until late fall. "Troy, in his prostration at this time, had no perception that in the futility of these romantic doings, dictated by a remorseful reaction from previous indifference, there was any element of absurdity."

Just as he was finishing the planting, he felt rain and his lantern candle sputtered out. He groped his way to the north porch of the church and there fell asleep.

Commentary

Troy's reversal to remorse is interesting. Where he had been callous and heedless, he is now precipitate in his contrition. Gravestone, planting—all must be done at once, and he spends every penny he has on them (although it should be remembered that this was the money he originally intended to give to Fanny). Nor is it surprising to have him remain in the churchyard, intent on completing his service to the departed as soon as he wakes.

CHAPTER 46

Summary

One of the ugly gargoyles of the church parapet jutted out over the area newly assigned for charity graves. This stony land had been uncared for, and as a heavy downpour developed, water gushed forth, falling upon the grave of Fanny Robin some seventy feet below. The carefully planted bulbs were washed away and floated off in the mud.

When he awoke, Troy was stunned into disbelief. "The planting of flowers on Fanny's grave had been perhaps but a species of elusion of the primary grief, and now it was as if his intention had been known and circumvented. Almost for the first time in his life Troy, as he stood by this dismantled grave, wished himself another man." Not informing anyone, left the the village.

Bathsheba remained imprisoned by her own choice. The night before, Liddy had noticed the light of Troy's lantern in the graveyard, and they both had watched it for a time, not knowing whose it was.

In the morning both women commented on the heavy rain and the noise of the water coming from the spouts. Liddy noted that the water used to merely spatter on the stones, but "this was like the boiling of a pot." Asking whether Bathsheba wished to see the gravesite, Liddy also volunteered the information that the master must have gone to Budmouth, for Laban had seen him on that road.

Bathsheba went to Fanny's corner of the churchyard. Here she saw the spattered tomb. Gabriel was standing nearby. He had already seen the inscription: "Erected by Francis Troy in Beloved Memory of Fanny Robin." He looked to see how Bathsheba would react to this. He himself was astonished, but Bathsheba was calm. She asked Gabriel to fill in the hole, and, picking up the plants, she carefully set back those which had been washed out. She requested Gabriel to ask the wardens to redirect the mouth of the gargoyle to a different angle. Before departing, she wiped the tomb clean.

Commentary

Providence is often hostile to man in Hardy's world. Troy wants to change, as his gesture toward Fanny shows, "but to find that Providence, far from helping him into a new course . . . actually jeered his first trembling and critical attempt in that kind, was more than nature could bear."

CHAPTER 47

Summary

"Troy wandered along towards the south. A composite feeling, made up of disgust with the, to him, humdrum tediousness of a farmer's life, gloomy images of her who lay in the churchyard, remorse, and a general averseness to his wife's society, impelled him to seek a home in any place on earth save Weatherbury."

Climbing a hill, he saw the sea. There was a small pool enclosed by the cliffs, and Troy was drawn to it for refreshment. He undressed and swam out between two projecting spires of rock, not knowing of a strong current there. He was carried out to sea and at that moment remembered hearing of danger in this area. He tried to direct his strokes toward shore but failed because of fatigue. Then a ship's boat appeared. Troy's vigor revived, and he hailed it and was rescued. The sailors were part of a brig's crew, coming ashore for sand. They lent him clothes and took him to their vessel.

Commentary

Seeking solitude seems appropriate for Troy at this time. That a boat should appear at the moment when he is drowning is the author's manipulation of the plot, but the action moves so swiftly that the reader is not inclined to pause and meditate on the amount of coincidence Hardy utilizes.

CHAPTER 48

Summary

Bathsheba accepted Troy's absence with a mixture of surprise and relief. Sooner or later he would return, and she feared only the loss of the farm and the poverty which that would bring. To all else she was indifferent: "Perceiving clearly that her mistake had been a fatal one, she accepted her position, and waited coldly for the end."

The next Saturday, when she went to market, a man sought her out to say that Troy had drowned. Bathsheba fainted. Boldwood saw her and caught her as she fell. He questioned the man and learned that a coastguardsman had found Troy's clothes on the shore. Boldwood's eyes flashed excitedly as he carried Bathsheba to the King's Arms Inn, where he arranged for a woman to look after her. He then went out to get further particulars, but none were forthcoming. When he offered to drive Bathsheba home, she declined, preferring to drive herself. Word had already reached the farm, and Liddy met Bathsheba.

A newspaper paragraph told how a physician had driven by the cliff and had seen a swimmer being carried off by the current. He doubted that even a strong swimmer could escape. This and the finding of Troy's clothing seemed to corroborate that Troy was dead. But when Liddy mentioned the need for mourning clothes, Bathsheba declined to wear them. She was convinced that Troy was still alive.

Late at night "Bathsheba took Troy's watch into her hand. . . . She opened the case as he had opened it before her a week ago. There was the little coil of pale hair which had been as the fuse to this great explosion.

" 'He was hers and she was his; they should be gone together,' she said. 'I am nothing to either of them, and why should I keep her hair?' " She held it to the fire but then pulled it back. " 'No — I'll not burn it — I'll keep it in memory of her, poor thing!' she added."

Commentary

Circumstantial evidence satisfies most people that Troy is dead, but something will not permit Bathsheba to accept their conclusions. She appears able to withstand all that has happened and continues to go about her duties, albeit somewhat mechanically. The fact that her sympathy for Fanny outweighs her resentment testifies that she has retained at least some emotional equilibrium.

CHAPTER 49

Summary

Autumn passed and winter came. "Bathsheba, having previously been living in a state of suspended feeling which was not suspense, now lived in a mood of quietude which was not precisely peacefulness." She kept the farm going, however, finally appointing Oak bailiff, a role he had, in fact, been filling anyway. Boldwood lost his crops through neglect; even the pigs rejected his rotted corn. He suggested that Gabriel administer his farm, as well as Bathsheba's, and Bathsheba languidly assented to this plan. "Gabriel's malignant star was assuredly setting fast."

Oak could now be seen "mounted on a strong cob, and daily trotting the length and breadth of about two thousand acres in a cheerful spirit of surveillance . . . the actual mistress of the one-half, and the master of the other, sitting in their respective homes in gloomy and sad seclusion." This led to talk that Oak was "feathering his nest fast." Actually, Bathsheba paid him a fixed wage, but Boldwood gave him a share of the profits. Gossips considered Oak miserly because he continued to live exactly as he had in the past.

Boldwood's devotion to Bathsheba was becoming a madness. Bathsheba's mourning—she had been prevailed upon to wear it—let him hope that there would be a time, however far off, when his waiting would be rewarded. Shortly, Bathsheba paid a two-month visit to an old aunt in Corcombe, and on her return, Boldwood questioned Liddy as to his prospects. She told him that Bathsheba had once spoken of the seven-year period before the legal declaration of Troy's death.

"Poor Boldwood had no more skill in finesse than a battering-ram, and he was uneasy with a sense of having made himself to appear stupid. . . . But he had, after all, lighted upon one fact by way of repayment. . . . though not without its sadness it was pertinent and real. In little more than six years from this time Bathsheba might certainly marry him." Meanwhile, late summer was approaching, bringing on the week of the Greenhill Fair.

Commentary

This transitional chapter serves to show a change in Bathsheba, the reward for Gabriel, and the birth of new hope for Boldwood. Hardy alludes to the biblical story of Jacob serving for Rachel and the importance of the sacred number seven. He was obviously very familiar with the Bible, and his works are liberally sprinkled with such references.

72

Note that the time has advanced from late autumn to the next summer.

CHAPTER 50

Summary

Greenhill, the summit of a hill with an ancient rampart, was an ideal fair site. There were permanent buildings and also tents. Shepherds who had traveled with their flocks for days thronged in. The colors identifying the owners of the sheep formed a pleasing pattern. A pony wagon for first-aid to the sheep wove in and out. The sheep of Gabriel's two employers were admired for their breeding, beauty, and grooming.

As the day wore on and the sheep were sold, the shepherds turned their attention to a huge tent which would house the Royal Hippodrome's performances. Bands were playing and the crowds were tremendous, with folks like Poorgrass and Coggan adding to the shoving. Two performers' dressing rooms were at the rear of the tent. In one was a young man—Sergeant Troy.

Troy had signed on with the ship which had rescued him and "ultimately worked his passage to the United States, where he made a precarious living . . . as Professor of Gymnastics, Sword Exercise, Fencing, and Pugilism. A few months were sufficient to give him a distaste for this kind of life. . . . There was ever present, too, the idea that he could claim a home and its comforts did he but choose to return to England." He often wondered whether Bathsheba thought him dead.

Back in England now, he was reluctant to return to her; he expected her to be vengeful. He fell in with a traveling circus and became a daring rider. Billed as "Mr. Francis, The Great Cosmopolitan Equestrian and Roughrider," he found himself at Greenhill. Here he played the highwayman in an old love story.

Boldwood asked Bathsheba whether her sheep had done well. All were sold. Save for an appointment with a dealer, she was ready to leave. She inquired whether Boldwood had seen the play "Turpin's Ride to York" and whether the story was authentic. He assured her that it was and politely offered to get her a seat for the performance. This "reserved seat" proved to be on a raised bench covered with red cloth in a conspicuous section of the tent, and Bathsheba was the only person sitting there. She sat self-consciously enthroned, her black skirts draped about her. Peeping from the dressing room, Troy saw her.

Troy explained to the show's manager that he could not go on because a creditor of his was in the audience. The manager, afraid to offend his leading man at this point, made a suggestion. "Go on with the piece and say nothing, doing what you can by a judicious wink now and then. . . . They'll never find out the speeches are omitted." Thus the "creditor" did not recognize him by his voice, and makeup and a beard disguised his appearance.

However, at the next performance Troy suspected that he had been recognized by his wife's former bailiff, Pennyways. Troy resolved to find the man and speak to him. When it was almost dark, he donned a thick beard and wandered about the grounds. Then he spied Bathsheba sitting in the refreshment tent. He found a point outside the tent where he could hear her, and he cut a small hole through the canvas so that he could see her. He saw Pennyways approach Bathsheba, who refused to listen to him. Pennyways then wrote her a note which said that her husband was alive. Impulsively, Troy reached under the edge of the canvas and snatched the note from Bathsheba's hand. Then he ran away. In the confusion, Troy found Pennyways, whispered with him, "and with a mutal glance of concurrence, the two men went into the night together."

Commentary

Hardy terms Greenhill the "Nijni Novgorod" of South Wessex; this refers to a town in Russia once famous for its annual fair.

Hardy's avowed purpose was to preserve all the culture and traditions of his countryside, and he put loving care into the planning of this elaborate chapter. One could argue that it contains too many coincidences, but it must be acknowledged that there are, as well, many colorful and realistic passages.

Troy is still impulsive and shrewd, but he lacks some of his former cockiness. He does not want Bathsheba to see him in his present circumstances. Although surprised at how attractive she still is to him, he wants to discover what he can about her financial situation before deciding whether or not to reveal that he is alive.

CHAPTER 51

Summary

Because Poorgrass had suffered a recurrence of his "multiplying eye," Oak was to drive Bathsheba home. He was still involved in Boldwood's business, however, and so when Boldwood offered to escort Bathsheba, she accepted, still somewhat alarmed by the incident in the tent. Riding beside her, Boldwood renewed his proposal.

He suggested that now there was no longer any reasonable doubt about Troy's death. Bathsheba objected: "From the first I have had a strange unaccountable feeling that he could not have perished." She did not want to remarry, but she did regret her treatment of Boldwood and wished she could make amends. Boldwood immediately asked her to repair the wrong by marrying him in six years, when Troy could legally be declared dead. When he persisted, she asked to delay her answer until Christmas.

Later, Bathsheba told Oak that she was afraid that outright refusal would cause Boldwood to go mad. Oak advised a conditional promise. Suggesting that there was no guarantee that they would all be alive in six years, she deferred to Oak's judgment. "She had spoken frankly, and neither asked nor expected any reply from Gabriel more satisfactory than she had obtained. Yet in . . . her complicated heart there existed at this minute a little pang of disappointment. . . . He might have just hinted at that old love of his. . . . it ruffled our heroine all the afternoon."

Commentary

Boldwood's obsession with Bathsheba is further revealed. Yet, for all the farmer's seeming unbalance, he is shrewd enough to play on Bathsheba's guilt about her treatment of him. This is probably the only effective weapon he has in his struggle to win her.

Oak maintains his surface calm, while Bathsheba, eternally feminine, is piqued when he does not attempt to win her himself.

CHAPTER 52

Summary

The story builds toward a focal point on Christmas Eve. The chapter is divided into seven parts:

1. Boldwood, surprisingly, had planned a Christmas party. Mistletoe, garlands, and decorations were brought in from the woods, and elaborate preparations were made.

2. Bathsheba was agitated and reluctant to go. She admitted to Liddy that she was the cause for the party. To avoid gossip, she would wear her widow's weeds.

3. Boldwood fussed over his newly tailored clothes. When Oak arrived to report on the day's work, Boldwood reminded him that he was expected at the party. "Make yourself merry. I am determined that neither expense nor trouble shall be spared." Gabriel replied that he might be late. He was glad to see Boldwood in better spirits. Boldwood asked whether women keep promises. Oak replied, "If it is not inconvenient to her she may." Boldwood, feverishly cheerful, commented that Oak had become quite cynical lately.

4. Troy was in a tavern in Casterbridge with Pennyways, who reminded him that his deceit was punishable by law. He could not answer Troy's question about Bathsheba's relationship with Boldwood. This was to be Bathsheba's first appearance at Boldwood's home. Pennyways still bore her a grudge. He told Troy that Oak was still the boss and that Bathsheba couldn't manage without him.

5. Bathsheba, though plainly dressed, looked very well. Liddy suggested it was because of her excitement. Bathsheba admitted that she was vacillating between feeling buoyant and feeling wretched. When Liddy joked about Boldwood's imminent proposal, Bathsheba gravely silenced her.

6. As Oak helped Boldwood tie his cravat, he urged him to be cautious and not to count on Bathsheba. Boldwood said he knew of Oak's love, and he wished to reward him for his decency. He would increase the extent of his partnership. When Oak had gone, Boldwood pulled out a small box and regarded a handsome ring. Hearing wheels in the distance, he put the box in his pocket and went to greet his guests.

7. While Troy was attiring himself in a high-collared greatcoat and traveling cap, Pennyways counseled against his going to Boldwood's party. Troy argued angrily, "There she is with plenty of money, and a house and farm . . . and here am I still living from hand to mouth — a needy adventurer." In addition, Troy knew he had been seen and recognized in town. Pennyways realized he would have to get back into Bathsheba's good graces in the event of a reconciliation, and so, as a first step, he suggested to Troy, "I sometimes think she likes you yet, and is a good woman at bottom." Troy announced that he would be at Boldwood's before nine.

Commentary

Hardy has kept strict account of the threads running through the novel and here arranges them so that they can be tucked into the complicated tapestry. Structurally, this chapter is carefully outlined in seven sections which indicate what must follow. Troy has a premonition of tragedy, but, characteristically, he shrugs it off and sends for more brandy. Boldwood is keyed up but confident. Bathsheba's feelings vacillate, and Oak is gloomy and apprehensive.

CHAPTER 53

Summary

A group of men congregated outside of Boldwood's house, watching the guests arrive and whispering rumors of Troy's reappearance. They were sure Bathsheba hadn't heard of it but weren't sure whether that was a good or bad omen. They sympathized with their mistress.

Boldwood came out. Not noticing the watchers, he leaned on the gate, murmuring, "I hope to God she'll come, or this night will be nothing but misery to me!" A few minutes later, wheels were heard; Boldwood went to welcome Bathsheba.

Tall, Smallbury, and Samway went to the malthouse. They saw Troy peeping in a window. "The men, after recognizing Troy's features, withdrew across the orchard as quietly as they had come. The air was big with Bathsheba's fortunes to-night: every word everywhere concerned her." The men were unnerved by Troy's return and decided that they should warn Bathsheba. Laban was chosen to tell her but was reluctant; he entered Boldwood's house and left again. He couldn't bring himself to ruin everything. The men decided they had better all join together.

Meanwhile, having stayed an hour and thus satisfied amenities, Bathsheba wished to leave. But before she could go, Boldwood found her and insisted on an answer to his proposal. Finally, she gave her promise: if she were truly a widow, she would not marry anyone, if not Boldwood. The man's restraint broke, and he told her of how he had suffered, of how much he loved her. Sobbing, Bathsheba finally agreed to marry him in six years. Boldwood gave her the ring. Bathsheba said it would be improper for her to wear it. When he persisted, she agreed to wear it just for the evening.

Bathsheba descended from the little parlor to find the party somehow deadened. As one of her men stepped forward to talk to her, there was a knock at the door. Someone wished to speak to Mrs. Troy. Boldwood asked the man in; he was one of the few who did not recognize Troy. Bathsheba sank down at the base of the staircase, staring. Still unaware, Boldwood invited the stranger to have a drink. Troy strode in, turning down his collar and laughing. The truth suddenly dawned on Boldwood.

Troy ordered Bathsheba to leave with him. She hesitated. Boldwood, in a strange voice, told her to go. Troy then pulled her roughly, and she screamed. There was a loud noise. Smoke filled the room.

When Bathsheba had cried out, Boldwood's face had changed. He had taken a gun from the rack and had shot and killed Troy. He then attempted to shoot himself but was prevented by Samway. Boldwood said, "There is another way for me to die." He kissed Bathsheba's hand, "put on his hat, opened the door, and went into the darkness, nobody thinking of preventing him."

Commentary

The action of this chapter is crowded and rapid. One event swiftly follows another, adding to the dramatic quality—as Hardy well knew, having been in his earlier years a playwright.

An atmosphere of inevitability surrounds the climax of the chapter. Once before Boldwood attempted to save Bathsheba from Troy, and when he found he was being tricked he had warned, "I'll punish you yet!" Since that time Boldwood's emotional instability has been made increasingly apparent. His determination to possess Bathsheba is that of a fanatic. Troy has changed little, and he is once again able to thwart Boldwood by trickery and deceit. Never a man of caution, he has ignored a premonition of disaster, and his dramatic gesture costs him his life. We may initially be shocked at Troy's murder, because the chapter has moved so quickly, but we are not really surprised by it once we pause to reflect.

CHAPTER 54

Summary

Boldwood, walking easily and steadily, arrived at the jail. He rang, said something to the porter in a low tone, and entered. "The door was closed behind him, and he walked the world no more."

When Gabriel heard of the catastrophe, he rushed to Boldwood's house, arriving some five minutes after Boldwood's departure. The scene was dreadful. Bathsheba sat on the floor beside the body, Troy's head pillowed in her lap. "With one hand she held her handkerchief to his breast . . . though scarcely a single drop of blood had flowed, and with the other she tightly clasped one of his. The household convulsion had made her herself again. . . . Deeds of endurance which seem ordinary in philosophy are rare in conduct, and Bathsheba was astonishing all . . . for her philosophy was her conduct."

She ordered Gabriel to ride for a surgeon. In town, Gabriel also stopped to notify the authorities and so learned of Boldwood's surrender. Meanwhile, Bathsheba had Troy moved home. Liddy admitted the doctor, telling him that Bathsheba had locked herself in the room with the body. She had left orders that the surgeon and Parson Thirdly were to be admitted.

The surgeon found Troy's body lit by candles and draped in white. Returning to Oak and the parson, the doctor remarked in a subdued voice, "It is all done. . . . this mere girl! She must have the nerve of a stoic!"

"The heart of a wife, merely," Bathsheba whispered behind him. Then, silently, she sank to the floor. She had a series of fainting fits that for a time seemed serious, but the surgeon attended her. Liddy was told to watch over her during the night. She heard her mistress moan, "O it is my fault—how can I live!"

Commentary

Bathsheba's display of strength reminds the surgeon of the ancient stoics; it is also reminiscent of the great women of Greek tragedy. Then, having done what was required of her, Bathsheba can yield to weakness (and Victorian tradition) and faint away. This was a common frailty in the women of Victorian times, both in literature and in life. Bathsheba's stern conscience, which continues to trouble her, is another typical Victorian characteristic.

CHAPTER 55

Summary

On a bleak day three months later, a number of people gathered on Yalbury Hill. The high sheriff waited in a carriage. Another carriage arrived carrying the judge of the circuit court; he switched carriages, trumpets flourished, and a procession went into town. Bathsheba's men discussed their hopes that the judge would be merciful to Boldwood.

Much had been learned of Boldwood's behavior. No one had guessed the extent of his derangement. The closets in his home were found to contain an expensive and elegant collection of ladies' clothes, muffs, and jewelry, all wrapped, labeled "Bathsheba Boldwood," and dated six years ahead. Boldwood had bought the things in Bath and elsewhere and had brought them to his home.

The group which gathered at the malthouse thoroughly discussed the question of Boldwood's odd behavior. Once the suggestion had been raised, it was simple to find examples of the farmer's oddity. "The conviction that Boldwood had not been morally responsible for his later acts now became general." But Gabriel arrived to announce the verdict: "Boldwood, as every one supposed he would do, had pleaded guilty, and had been sentenced to death."

A petition was sent to the home secretary, asking for reconsideration of the verdict because of Boldwood's state of mind. But not too many inhabitants of Casterbridge signed it. Shopkeepers resented Boldwood's patronage of other towns to purchase the finery for Bathsheba. A few merciful men prodded others into signing.

The reply to the petition had not arrived by the Friday preceding the day set for the execution. Coming from the jail where he had bidden farewell to Boldwood, Gabriel saw the scaffold being erected. Bathsheba was in bed, wasting away. She constantly asked whether the messenger had arrived with an answer to the petition. Gabriel too was worred. His "anxiety was great that Boldwood might be saved, even though in his conscience he felt that he ought to die; for there had been qualities in the farmer which Oak loved."

At last, late that night, a rider brought the answer they awaited. The sentence had been commuted to "confinement during Her Majesty's pleasure."

" 'Hurrah!' said Coggan, with a swelling heart. 'God's above the devil yet!' "

Commentary

In this chapter we learn most of the news through hearsay and the expression of the views of the townsfolk. Liddy, for example, tells us that Bathsheba's "sufferings have been dreadful," and that she fears for her mistress' sanity if Boldwood is executed. Oak, as always, remains steadfast.

CHAPTER 56

Summary

"Bathsheba revived with the spring. The utter prostration that had followed the low fever from which she had suffered diminished perceptibly when all uncertainty upon every subject had come to an end." In summer, she eventually attempted to walk to town. She passed the church and heard the choir practicing. Then she stood before Fanny Robin's grave and read the words which Troy had had inscribed. Beneath them was a new inscription: "In the same Grave lie The Remains of the aforesaid Francis Troy. . . ."

The children in the church were rehearsing a hymn, "Lead, Kindly Light." Bathsheba, recalling all that had happened, wept. Oak approached. He had been inside the church, singing with the choir.

Their talk was formal, Bathsheba addressing him as Mr. Oak. As they walked back, Gabriel spoke of his plans to leave England and go to California. He admitted that he had an option to buy Boldwood's farm, but he had decided merely to finish out his year as manager. Bathsheba was upset that Gabriel, whom she now considered an old friend, would no longer be there to help her. Gabriel answered that her very helplessness was another reason for his planned departure. From that day on, he avoided Bathsheba.

Fall and winter passed, and when Bathsheba finally received the long-expected letter of resignation from Oak, she wept bitterly. Then she donned her bonnet and went to his house. He did not realize it was she at first—then, apologetically, he admitted her. His bachelor quarters had no comforts, he said, for ladies.

Bathsheba asked if she had offended him. Gabriel explained that, on the contrary, he was leaving because there was gossip that he was waiting to buy Boldwood's farm just so that he would be rich enough to court Bathsheba.

"Bathsheba did not look quite so alarmed as if a cannon had been discharged by her ear, which was what Oak had expected. 'Marrying me! I didn't know it was that you meant. . . . Such a thing as that is too absurd—too soon—to think of, by far!'" Gabriel heard only the "absurd," not the "too soon," and their talk continued at cross purposes until Gabriel said that he wished he knew if she would let him court her. Bathsheba tearfully assured him that he would never know whether she would have him unless he asked. The two found release in laughter, finally throwing off the inhibitions and constraints of employer and employee. To Bathsheba's embarrassed remark that she had come courting him, Gabriel replied that it was his due for having long danced to her tune.

"They spoke very little of their mutual feeling; pretty phrases and warm expressions being probably unnecessary between such tried friends. . . . when the two who are thrown together begin first by knowing the rougher sides of each other's character, and not the best till further on."

Commentary

Hardy is now winding up the plot details swiftly and directly. It is in character that Bathsheba's first visit is to the churchyard, and that Gabriel's life is neatly ordered. Somewhat aloof since the tragedy, Gabriel no longer overtly aspires to win Bathsheba, but he does resign to protect her reputation. Hardy spares us a coy or saccharine close, ending rather with a bit of wise philosophy about the basis of a sound marriage.

CHAPTER 57

Summary

" 'The most private, secret, plainest wedding that it is possible to have.' Those had been Bathsheba's words to Oak one evening, some time after the events of the preceding chapter, and he meditated a full hour by the clock upon how to carry out her wishes to the letter."

There was the matter of the license. Oak met Coggan in town and admitted his plans but swore his friend to secrecy. Coggan delivered a message to the parish clerk, Laban Tall, telling him to meet the mistress next morning and to be wearing his best clothes. He told the clerk's curious wife, "Mind, het or wet, blow or snow, he must come. . . . 'Tis very particular indeed. The fact is, 'tis to witness her sign some law-work about taking shares wi' another farmer for a long span o' years. There, that's what 'tis, and now I've told 'ee, Mother Tall, in a way I shouldn't ha' done if I hadn't loved 'ee so hopelessly well." The next call at the vicar's excited no curiosity.

Bathsheba awakened before Liddy's call. As Liddy was brushing her mistress' hair, Bathsheba told the inquisitive girl that Oak was coming to dinner. Liddy guessed the purport and was excited.

Oak arrived with an umbrella, and, a short time later, swathed head to foot in greatcoats, he and Bathsheba, each under an umbrella, walked into town, like sensible people who were on a brief errand. In the church were Tall, Liddy, and the parson.

After the wedding, there was tea at Bathsheba's. Oak had decided to move in, since he did not as yet have appropriate furnishings in his house. "Just as Bathsheba was pouring out a cup of tea, their ears were greeted by the firing of a cannon, followed by what seemed like a tremendous blowing of trumpets in the front of the house. . . . Oak took up the light and went into the porch, followed by Bathsheba with a shawl over her head." A group of male figures set up a loud hurrah; there was another cannon shot, followed by a "hideous clang of music" from assorted ancient and venerable instruments. Oak said a warm, "Come in, souls, and have something to eat and drink wi' me and my wife." "Not to-night," was the unselfish reply. The men suggested that drinks be sent to Warren's, instead. Oak gladly accepted the suggestion.

Commenting on the ease with which Oak said "my wife," the friends withdrew, Oak laughing and Bathsheba smiling. As they moved away, Poorgrass had the last word: "And I wish him joy o' her. . . . since 'tis as 'tis, why, it might have been worse, and I feel my thanks accordingly."

Commentary

The simple close is both appropriate and artistic. We feel that this time things will be all right. Oak's manner contrasts with Troy's after his marriage, when he was so condescending toward the hired help. Though Oak and Bathsheba are the focal point, the scene is mellowed and subdued. There is a voluntary outgoing of affection toward the couple and a friendly understanding of the roles they all will play.

HARDY'S PHILOSOPHY AND IDEAS

Hardy is primarily a storyteller and should be viewed more as a chronicler of moods and deeds than as a philosopher. Yet a novel such as *Far from the Madding Crowd,* which raises many questions about society, religion, morals, and the contrast between a good life and its rewards, is bound to make the reader curious about the author who brings them up.

Hardy lived in an age of transition. The industrial revolution was in the process of destroying the agricultural life, and the subsequent shifting of population caused a disintegration of rural customs and traditions which had meant security, stability, and dignity for the people. It was a period when fundamental beliefs — religious, social, scientific, and political — were shaken to their core and brought in their stead the "ache of modernism." The new philosophies failed to satisfy the emotional needs of many people. As a young man, Hardy read Darwin's *Origin of the Species* and *Essays and Reviews* (the manifesto of a few churchmen who held radical theological opinions), both of which were to influence his views toward religion. He found it difficult, if not impossible, to reconcile the idea of a beneficent, omnipotent, and omniscient diety with the fact of omnipresent evil and the persistent tendency of circumstances toward unhappiness.

When one thinks of Hardy the novelist, that aspect of his work which comes to mind most readily is his frequent use of chance and circumstances in the development of his plots. But the reader must learn to view Hardy's stories in the light of the author's fatalistic outlook on life, for Hardy fluctuates between fatalism and determinism. Fatalism is a view of life which acknowledges that all action is controlled by the nature of things, or by a Fate which is a great, impersonal, primitive force existing through all eternity, absolutely independent of human wills and superior to any god created by man. Determinism, on the other hand, acknowledges that man's struggle against the will behind things is of no avail, that the laws of cause and effect are in operation—that is, the human will is not free and human beings have no control over their own destiny, try as they may. Hardy sees life in terms of action, in the doomed struggle against the circumstantial forces against happiness. Incident, for example, plays an important role in causing joy or pain, and often an act of indiscretion in early youth can wreck one's chances for happiness. In Hardy's novels, then, Fate appears as an artistic motif in a great variety of forms — chance and coincidence, nature, time, woman, and convention. None is Fate itself, but rather all of these are manifestations of the Immanent Will.

The use of chance and coincidence as a means of furthering the plot was a technique used by many Victorian authors but with Hardy it becomes something more than a mere device. Fateful incidents (overheard conversations and undelivered letters, for instance) are the forces working against mere man in his efforts to control his own destiny. In addition, Fate appears in the form of nature, endowing it with varying moods which affect the lives of the characters. Those who are most in harmony with their environment are usually the most contented; similarly, those who can appreciate the joys of nature can find solace in it. Yet nature can take on sinister aspects, becoming more of an actor than just a setting for the action.

Besides the importance of nature in Hardy's novels, one should consider the concept of time. There is tremendous importance placed on the moment, for time is a great series of moments. The joys of life are transitory and the moments of joy may be turned to bitterness by time. Woman, also, is used by Hardy as one of Fate's most potent instruments for opposing man's happiness. Closer to primitive feelings than man, woman is helpless in the hands of Fate and carries out Fate's work. In her search for love, the motivating passion of her life, woman becomes an agent in her own destiny. In short, one is, according to Hardy, powerless to change the workings of Fate, but those things which are contrived by man—social laws and convention, for example—and which work against him can be changed by man. Man is not hopelessly doomed.

ESSAY QUESTIONS

1. Show how Hardy indicated the passage of time, rarely using actual dates.

2. Discuss how the changing seasons are bound up with the story.

3. Discuss Hardy's use of biblical, literary, and artistic allusions.

4. Show in what ways Bathsheba's character changes and in what ways it remains the same.

5. Show how Victorian ideas of morality affect the lives of Fanny Robin; Sergeant Troy; Bathsheba.

BIBLIOGRAPHY

ABERCROMBIE, LASCELLES. *Thomas Hardy*. London: Martin Secker, 1912.

ALLEN, WALTER. *The English Novel*. New York: E. P. Dutton, 1954.

BLUNDEN, EDMUND. *Thomas Hardy*. New York: Macmillan, 1962.

BROWN, DOUGLAS. *Thomas Hardy*. London: Longmans, Green, 1954.

CECIL, DAVID. *Victorian Novelists*. Chicago: University of Chicago Press, 1958.

CHEW, SAMUEL C. *Thomas Hardy, Poet and Novelist*. New York: Russell & Russell, 1964.

Colby College Library. *A Century of Thomas Hardy*. Catalog of Exhibit, Waterville, 1940.

DAICHES, DAVID. *The Novel in the Modern World*. Chicago: University of Chicago Press, 1960.

DUFFIN, H. C. *Thomas Hardy*. London: Longmans, Green, 1916.

FRIEDMAN, ALAN. *The Turn of the Novel*. Oxford: Oxford University Press, 1966.

GUERARD, ALBERT J. *Thomas Hardy*. New York: New Directions, 1964.

HARDY, EVELYN. *Thomas Hardy*. New York: St. Martin's Press, 1955.

HARDY, FLORENCE EMILY. *The Life of Thomas Hardy*. New York: St. Martin's Press, 1962.

JOHNSON, LIONEL. *The Art of Thomas Hardy*. New York: Haskell House, 1969.

KARL, FREDERICK. *A Reader's Guide to the Nineteenth Century British Novel*. New York: Farrar, Straus & Giroux, 1964.

SAXELBY, F. OUTWIN. *A Thomas Hardy Dictionary*. New York: Humanities Press, 1962.

Great Expectations

GREAT EXPECTATIONS

NOTES

including
- *Life of the Author*
- *Brief Summary of the Novel*
- *List of Characters*
- *Summaries and Commentaries*
- *Critical Analysis*
- *Character Analyses*
- *Review Questions*
- *Selected Bibliography*
- Great Expectations *Genealogy*

by
Arnie Jacobson
University of Nebraska

REVISED EDITION

INCORPORATED

LINCOLN, NEBRASKA   68501

Editor

Gary Carey, M.A.
University of Colorado

Consulting Editor

James L. Roberts, Ph.D.
Department of English
University of Nebraska

ISBN 0-8220-0551-4
© Copyright 1979
by
C. K. Hillegass
All Rights Reserved
Printed in U.S.A.

1992 Printing

Cliffs Notes, Inc.   Lincoln, Nebraska

CONTENTS

Great Expectations Notes

LIFE OF THE AUTHOR

Charles Dickens was one of the most successful of English novelists. He was also one of the greatest. And he was certainly one of the least understood.

Precisely because he *was* so successful—in periodicals, in English book editions, and in American editions (which were largely pirated)—he became suspect to the captive force of critics. A man *that* successful couldn't really be *that* good. It bothered no one, except perhaps Dickens, that this was the same thing Elizabethan critics had said about Shakespeare. Like Sir Walter Scott before him, Dickens wrote out of a compulsion to succeed. He had, like Scott, taken on the support of a huge and expensive living establishment. Payment could come from only one place: his pen. But by 1860, the year in which *Great Expectations* was written, the till was beginning to run dry. Even his fantastic success as a public lecturer could not meet his expenses, and his latest book, *The Uncommercial Traveller*, a book of sketches, had only mediocre success. In addition, his magazine, *All the Year Round*, had begun to show a significant drop in sales. Drastic action was called for. This action resulted in *Great Expectations*.

It is no accident that in this time of crisis Dickens reached far back into his own experience and wrote a book about the young man he might have been. Although Pip, the youth in *Great Expectations*, was not completely Charles Dickens, as David Copperfield, his predecessor, had also not been, Dickens had, in the manner of all great artists, plunged into his own soul for the great book he needed, and the novel was an enormous success.

Charles John Huffam Dickens was born in 1812 at Landport, Portsea, which is on the southern coast of England; he was the second of eight children of an Admiralty clerk. At the time of his birth, his family was relatively well-to-do, but his father, like Mr. Micawber in *David Copperfield*, was incapable of managing his own financial affairs. In 1824 he was placed in a debtors' prison in London—symbolized by Newgate in *Great Expectations*—and young Charles was sent to work in a factory. Out of this experience came the roots of Dickens' strong sympathies for the underprivileged.

After his father had been released from prison as a result of receiving a legacy, Charles spent three years in school at

Hampstead. After a couple of years as a law clerk—an experience which also reflects itself in this novel—he entered the newspaper business. His success as a reporter was so spectacular that he abandoned a theatrical career on which he had half launched himself. He was a born actor, as his career as a dramatic reader of his own work testifies. His death in 1870 was a direct result of overstrain during his last lecture tour, ironically in America, a country he never liked and which he had written about in *American Notes* (1842) and *Martin Chuzzlewit* (1844).

In 1836, Dickens married Catherine Hogarth, from whom he was later divorced though her sister remained his companion thereafter; also in that year, he published *Sketches by Boz* and began publication of *The Posthumous Papers of the Pickwick Club*, his first great success. He was now launched as a successful writer, which he continued to be until he died, leaving *The Mystery of Edwin Drood*, his last novel, unfinished. There have been several attempts to complete this book, but none of them have been successful. Dickens took his last secret—how the book would end—to the grave with him.

The character of his work changed radically in his later years. It became deeper, more brooding, and less compromising. Even though he continued his practice of writing for serial publication, he had perfected the technique to the point where in *Great Expectations* the seams between installments are invisible. This later period began with *Bleak House* (1853) and includes the following other major novels: *Little Dorrit* (1857), *A Tale of Two Cities* (1859), *Great Expectations* (1861), and *Our Mutual Friend* (1865). *Our Mutual Friend*, his last completed full-length novel, shows a distinct falling off from *Great Expectations*, the high point of the series and of Dickens' canon.

A major advance in Dickens' work in this last period was his greatly increased sensitivity to language. The style which he had been developing through a long series of novels was now completely under his control; in *Great Expectations* it is one of the glories of the novel. His genius for fusing style, plot, and characterization made *Great Expectations* a masterpiece and Dickens one of the greatest writers who ever lived.

INTRODUCTION TO THE NOVEL

There is general agreement that *Great Expectations* is Dickens' best book. *David Copperfield*, to a considerable extent because of Mr. Micawber, remains a sentimental favorite; *A Tale of Two Cities* is widely used in schools because of its seeming simplicity; *Bleak*

House, a much less read but strong and somber book, has its advocates; and *A Christmas Carol* arrives promptly on schedule every Christmas. Yet it is always to *Great Expectations* that one returns if one wishes to reread Dickens and recapture the experience that one encounters in the presence of genius.

To explain why *Great Expectations* is Dickens' finest novel, it is necessary to study his plot structure, his style, and his thematic elements, which is done in the Critical Analysis section of these Notes. Of equal importance to an understanding of Dickens is a keen attention to his characters. With the exception of Faulkner, Dickens probably created more memorable characters than any other novelist in English literature; despite the handicap of writing for serial publication, he regularly constructed plots which keep the reader's attention to the end; he became the master of a unique personal style which was ideally suited to his purposes, which is immediately recognizable, and which has never been imitated; his imagination was prodigious; and he used all these gifts to present, in story after story, the ancient theme of the struggle between good and evil. We can add one more. Dickens' books are adhesive: they stick in the mind long after the reader has finished them. This is perhaps one of the best tests of a great writer.

As an example of Dickens' uncompromising skill as a novelist, consider the way in which he develops the book's basic irony: the fact that Pip's money and great expectations, and his illusory and aristocratic love both stem from the same source—Magwitch, his benefactor and Estella's father. This amazing coincidence violates nothing that has gone before; it is consistent with everything that has happened since the first chapter. Dickens carefully drops hints along the way, events which become significant only in retrospect, so that when the truth finally dawns on Pip (in Chapters 48 and 50) it is completely plausible. Futhermore, Dickens uses this—without comment—as a symbol of the thematic idea that wealth and position are corrupting and corrupt.

Great Expectations is a well-structured novel in another way. In the character of Pip, Dickens makes a serious effort to present the *ambivalence* of the problem of good and evil. Pip is not simply a young man of native goodness thrown on adversity but finally rising above it. He is a complicated mixture of good and bad—considerate and selfish, loving and callous, humble and ambitious, honest and self-deceiving. The core of Dickens' universal theme lies inside Pip himself, and the triumph of good comes about through Pip's self-discovery.

Even this is ambivalent. Pip's self-discovery is forced on him, primarily by Magwitch. In this murderer and lifelong criminal Pip discovers a genuine goodness which finally breaks through his wall of selfishness. Even at this point, however, he continues to act uncertainly. Having first refused to accept any more of the convict's money out of loathing for him, he continues to refuse out of what he considers nobility when loathing turns to love. The net result is that he deprives Magwitch of his one great wish in life, though he is considerate enough not to let him know it, and makes certain that all the money that the convict has worked so hard to amass for Pip's benefit will be confiscated by the courts.

In Pip's character development, the complexity of the struggle between good and evil is continuously demonstrated. Even in his triumph there is loss: he finds himself, but at a cost, not simply of money but in a crippling of his emotional life. He never marries, getting his family life indirectly through Herbert and Clara, and he finally achieves success through his own efforts, in partnership with Herbert and Clarriker in the counting house, but there is no evidence that he takes any great satisfaction in it.

There is genuine art at work here, as there is in the creation of the other characters, in the plot structure, and in the style. All of these elements are directly related to the developments within Pip, which are the core of the book. This is the fusion which, when applied to material of the magnitude and significance Dickens offers here, is the hallmark of a true work of art.

BRIEF SUMMARY OF THE NOVEL

Pip, an orphan, lives with his sister and her husband, Joe Gargery, the village blacksmith. One day on the marshes he meets an escaped convict who forces him to steal food and a file from the Gargerys. The convict is almost immediately recaptured. Pip is subsequently hired by Miss Havisham, a wealthy, elderly recluse, as a playmate for her beautiful, haughty, adopted daughter, Estella, with whom he immediately falls in love.

When Jaggers, a shrewd and powerful lawyer, tells him that money has been settled on him and that he has "great expectations," Pip assumes that Miss Havisham is his benefactor. In London, where Jaggers is his guardian, and Jaggers' assistant, Wemmick, becomes his friend, Pip learns gentlemanly manners from his roommate, Herbert Pocket, a relative of Miss Havisham's, and with Herbert's father he begins his education. He persuades himself that Miss Havisham is preparing him to marry Estella. Meanwhile, he neglects Joe, his earliest and best friend, and also Biddy, a girl who has helped him and the Gargerys; in short, he becomes somewhat of a snob.

One stormy evening when he is twenty-three, a weather-beaten stranger appears at his door. Pip recognizes him as "his convict" and is horrified to learn that this is his benefactor. Magwitch has been exiled to New South Wales, Australia, has made money, and has now returned to England, despite penalty of death, to see Pip. What has sustained him in the long years "down under" has been his determination to repay Pip's boyhood kindness by making him a gentleman. Revolted, Pip nevertheless feels obligated to help Magwitch. As a further blow, he learns that Estella is to marry Drummle, a boor.

On Wemmick's advice, Pip and Herbert move Magwitch to a house by the river. In quick succession, Pip saves Miss Havisham from fire, though she later dies; discovers that Magwitch is Estella's father; is almost murdered by Orlick, Joe's former assistant; and attempts to get Magwitch on a boat headed for the continent and safety.

Magwitch is captured but dies before his execution from injuries sustained in an underwater struggle with his old enemy, Compeyson, who brought about his capture. Pip, who has learned both love and humility from Magwitch, falls seriously ill and is nursed back to health by Joe. His false pride gone, Pip joins Herbert in business in India. Years later he again sees Estella, also educated by suffering. In the original ending they part friends; in the revised ending they will stay together.

LIST OF CHARACTERS

Pip (Philip Pirrip)

The narrator and chief character of the novel has been an orphan since infancy. His driving ambition is to better his station in life; unfortunately, Pip rejects his closest friends in order to achieve his social goals, and it is only after much heartbreak and disappointment that he realizes that good friends are far more valuable than wealth.

Miss Havisham

She is an eccentric lady who lives in semi-seclusion with her adopted daughter, Estella. Because she was deserted on her wedding day, she has reared Estella to take malicious revenge on the male sex.

Joe Gargery

As Pip's brother-in-law and father-figure, Joe is the most sympathetic of all the characters in this book. He is a hard worker, a loyal and gentle friend, and a highly moral man.

Abel Magwitch

Pip's benefactor, a convict, was deeply grateful when young Pip supplied him with food and a file after he attempted to escape. He worked many years in New South Wales, Australia, to amass enough money so that he could give the lad a better chance in life than he had.

Estella Havisham

As the adopted daughter of the bitter, eccentric Miss Havisham, she was brought up as an instrument of her benefactress' revenge on men. She is both beautiful and poised, and Pip is infatuated with these qualities, despite the fact that she openly scorns him.

Molly

Mr. Jaggers' housekeeper; the true mother of Estella by Magwitch.

Mr. Jaggers

The Old Bailey lawyer who defended Magwitch; he is commissioned by Magwitch to see that Pip is given an allowance at the proper time and made a gentleman, without Pip's knowledge of who his benefactor is. During this time, Jaggers acts as Pip's guardian.

Uncle Pumblechook

A pompous seed merchant; Joe's uncle. He is one of the sharpest expressions of Dickens' unrelenting scorn of humbug and hypocrisy.

John Wemmick

Mr. Jaggers' chief clerk has two life-styles: at the office, he is a piece of legal machinery, but at home he is an eccentric romantic, devising ever-new gadgets for his mini-castle home. He shows unusual patience and love for his deaf father, whom he calls the "Aged P."

Mr. Wopsle

He would have liked to be a clergyman, but since he was not of the right social class, he became a parish lay clerk until frustration lured him to small town theatrical stages.

Mrs. Joe

Joe's wife was more than twenty years old when Pip was born. She reared him "by hand," meaning basically that she hand-fed him as a baby, but as he grew older, she used a large and heavy hand to discipline him. Her temper proves her undoing when Orlick, her husband's apprentice, retaliates and almost murders her.

Biddy

Like Pip, Biddy is also an orphan. She is good-hearted, wise, and sympathetic to Pip's troubles. Early in the novel, she has a romantic crush on young Pip, but eventually she falls in love with and marries Joe Gargery.

Orlick

An employee of Joe Gargery and one of Pip's enemies. Orlick is broad-shouldered, strong and swarthy, and has a sharp, vicious temper. His attack on Mrs. Joe leaves her paralyzed and virtually speechless.

Compeyson

Miss Havisham's gentlemanly scoundrel-fiancé. He exploits her and her brother, then deserts her on her wedding day.

Herbert Pocket

Initially, Pip takes a dislike to this "pale young gentleman"; later, however, the two become close friends. Herbert is an amiable and frank person, easy to get along with, and a hard worker.

Bentley Drummle

Pip's rival for Estella's affections. A sturdy, heavy-set man, he is proud and chronically ill at ease. Estella marries him for his social position and wealth. Despite Drummle's unsympathetic qualities, he is highly instrumental in humanizing Estella.

Mr. Wopsle's Great-Aunt

She conducts the school and the store in which Biddy works.

Mr. Hubble

The wheelwright in Pip's village.

Mr. Trabb

The local tailor and undertaker.

Trabb's Boy

Pip's old enemy who nevertheless guides Herbert and Startop when Orlick is about to murder Pip.

Sarah Pocket, Georgiana Pocket, Mr. Raymond, and Mrs. Camilla

The toady relatives of Miss Havisham who have vain expectations.

Matthew Pocket

Herbert's father and the sole member of the family who will not condescend to flatter Miss Havisham; he is also an ineffectual father and a celebrated author and lecturer on family problems.

Mrs. Pocket

His wife; a studious reader of books on peerage.

Flopson and Millers

Nurses at the Pockets.

Mrs. Collier

A pretentious neighbor of the Pockets.

Startop

A former roomer at the Pockets, along with Pip and Drummle, who helps Pip and Herbert attempt Magwitch's escape.

The Avenger

A young, useless servant whom Pip, in his days as a professional gentleman, employs.

Bill Barley

An ex-purser; father of Herbert Pocket's fiancée and eventual wife.

Clara Barley

His devoted, sensible daughter, whom Herbert marries.

Mrs. Whimple

Landlady to the Barleys and friend and confidante of Herbert and Clara.

The Aged P.

John Wemmick's father.

Miss Skiffins

John Wemmick's bride.

Mr. Skiffins

Accountant and her brother; he arranges the business of Herbert's partnership with Clarriker.

Clarriker

A merchant.

SUMMARIES AND COMMENTARIES

CHAPTERS 1-6

Summary

Pip, a seven-year-old orphan whose real name is Philip Pirrip, lives with his sister, Mrs. Joe Gargery, wife of the village blacksmith. Their home is in the marsh country, down by the river and close to the sea. His parents, whom Pip has never seen, are buried in a graveyard in the marshes, along with five little brothers. Pip often visits the graves, his only momento of his family.

On one such visit, one bleak Christmas Eve, he is surprised by "a fearful man, all in coarse gray, with a great iron on his leg," who rises from among the graves. After turning Pip upside down to empty his pockets and finding only a piece of bread, the man quizzes him and finds out that Joe, Pip's guardian, is a blacksmith. He demands that early next morning, Pip bring him a file and some "wittles" (food) or he'll have Pip's "heart and liver out." To further terrify the boy, he adds that he has a young man with him who "has a secret way pecooliar to himself, of getting at a boy, and at his heart, and at his liver."

After swearing that he will be there, Pip flees in terror, and the man, hugging himself to keep warm, limps down toward the river, where a gibbet (gallows) stands outlined in the dusk.

Arriving home, Pip finds that his sister Georgiana, a stern woman with a heavy hand which she uses freely on both Pip and Joe, is out looking for him. "She made a grab at Tickler," Joe says, "and she ram-paged [rampaged] out." On returning, she freely applies Tickler, a wax-ended piece of cane, to Pip's behind; then, in her usual aggressive way, she serves Pip and Joe some bread and butter. Pip, mindful of his need to collect "wittles," slips his slice of bread down his pants leg. Joe, a good, gentle man, fears that Pip has swallowed it in one bite, whereupon Mrs. Joe drags Pip away for a dose of tar-water.

Since it is Christmas Eve, Pip has many chores to do, and as he finishes, he hears the sounds of large guns. He learns that this means that a convict has escaped from the Hulks, the prison ships lying just off the marshes. Another convict escaped yesterday, Joe says. Sent to bed, Pip is too frightened to sleep, and at dawn, he goes down to rob the pantry. It is well stocked because of the season, and he manages to steal bread, cheese, mincemeat, some brandy from a stone jug which he replenishes from a kitchen jug, a meat bone with very little on it, and "a beautiful round pork pie."

He appropriates a file from Joe's forge, adjacent to the kitchen, then runs for the marshes.

Racing through the misty morning, Pip sees the convict seated in the marshes with his back to him. Touching him on the shoulder, Pip finds, to his horror, that this is another man, dressed in similar clothing, complete with leg-iron. The man takes a futile swing at Pip and disappears in the mist. Convinced that he has seen the fearsome "young man" described by "his convict," Pip hurries on to the appointed place.

While "his convict" wolfs down the food, Pip asks apologetically whether he should not save some for the young man, whom he has just seen. The convict, much agitated, grasps Pip roughly. "Where?" he says. "Over there. . . . Didn't you hear the cannon last night?" Pip asks. "When a man's alone on these flats," the convict replies, "with a light head and a light stomach, perishing of cold and want, he hears nothin' all night but guns firing and voices calling."

Learning that the other man has a bruise on his left cheek, the convict shouts, "Show me the way he went. I'll pull him down, like a bloodhound." He grabs the file and begins to work frenziedly on his leg-iron. Pip, seeing that he is ignored, slips away for home.

Mrs. Joe's Christmas greeting to Pip is "And where the deuce ha' *you* been?" Pip, expecting the constable to arrive immediately, explains that he has been to hear the carols. He and Joe sit down to a breakfast of bread and milk. Mrs. Joe, having planned a superb dinner, has too much to do to bother with a decent breakfast for them. She is also too busy with cleaning to go to church, and so Joe and Pip represent the family. Joe is uncomfortable in his "holiday clothes," and Pip is in a torment of fear and remorse about his theft, particularly the pork pie.

The dinner guests arrive: Mr. Wopsle, the church clerk; Mr. Hubble, the wheelwright, and his wife; and Joe's Uncle Pumblechook, a well-to-do seed merchant in a nearby town. Uncle Pumblechook brings his perennial gift, a bottle of sherry and a bottle of port, and Mrs. Joe receives them with her usual deference to Pumblechook.

At dinner, Pip gets the worst servings, accompanied by sermons on his character by the entire company except for Joe, who tries to compensate by repeatedly giving him more gravy. As the climax of the dinner, Mrs. Joe goes out to get the pork pie. Pip, knowing that the pie has long since been devoured, rushes to the door—only to be met by a party of soldiers, one of whom holds out a pair of handcuffs.

Pip's secret dealings with the convict are safe, however; the sergeant merely wants the handcuffs repaired. When Joe is finished, he and the soldiers set off for the marshes in search of the convicts, accompanied by Mr. Wopsle and Pip, Mrs. Joe having given her permission out of curiosity to find out what happens. As they approach the Battery, where Pip had given his convict the "wittles" and the file, they hear several loud shouts and find the two convicts locked in a desperate struggle at the bottom of a ditch.

Pip's convict explains that he was dragging the other man, whom he obviously loathes, back to the Hulks. The second convict says he was being murdered. The sergeant replies that it makes little difference, and they set off for the landing-place. Pip's convict, to whom Pip has been able to give an indication that he was not responsible for the capture, announces that he stole food from Joe's house, including the pork pie which Mrs. Joe missed just as the soldiers arrived. Joe assures him that he is welcome to it. The boats then return the convicts to the Hulks.

Pip is miserable over not telling Joe about what he has done, but he is afraid of losing Joe's confidence and friendship. "In a word, I was too cowardly to do what I knew to be right, as I had been too cowardly to avoid doing what I knew to be wrong."

Joe carries the sleepy boy home on his back, and Pip gets the usual gruff reception from his sister and Mr. Pumblechook, who has an ingenious theory about how the convict got in the house and stole the pork pie.

Commentary

Dickens begins this novel boldly: a sad little orphan is confronted in a cemetery by an escaped convict; already on page two, we hear Pip cry, "Don't cut my throat, sir!" There are no long paragraphs of exposition, of setting, or character development, as other writers often used at that time. Dickens sketched in a few strokes, suggesting the desolation of the setting, gained our sympathy by having his main character a young orphan, and launched into his story.

He wrote this novel in monthly installments, for his own magazine, *All the Year Round*, and wanted to capture an audience. He did. From the first chapters, *Great Expectations* was a success and bolstered the magazine and Dickens' fame.

The novel is introduced as a remembrance, as a memoir, which adds authenticity to the story; it involves the reader through identification and creates curiosity as to the fate of young Pip, the orphan. Immediately, we feel sympathy for Pip because he has no parents and is standing before their graves; but, more important, Dickens makes us feel sympathy for Pip and Joe because both of them are, in a sense, victims or "prisoners" of Mrs. Joe's temper. Thus he creates a subtle parallel between Pip, a victim of misfortune and his sister's violence, and the escaped prisoner, another victim of circumstances—a figure of pity as well as horror.

Of particular importance in these first chapters is the emphasis which Dickens puts on the bond between Joe and Pip. Because both of them must yield and succumb to Mrs. Joe's fierceness, they form a special sensitiveness toward one another. Later, when Pip is tempted by ambition and the promise of "great expectations," he will, with much guilt, sever this bond with Joe, a "mere blacksmith."

Take note in this section of Dickens' plotting. The escaped convict needs a file to cut his leg-irons. Pip mentions that his brother-in-law is a blacksmith. Blacksmiths have files. This is coincidence, but a coincidence that is cleverly calculated by Dickens. From Pip's fear and his natural generosity, he aids the convict, an act which will affect Pip's whole future.

CHAPTERS 7-13

Summary

Pip, who is to be apprenticed to Joe when he is old enough, attends an evening school run by Mr. Wopsle's great-aunt, but unfortunately she sleeps through her own classes. One evening, about a year after the convict was recaptured, Pip shows Joe a badly misspelled letter which he has spent an hour or two working on. Joe is much impressed, although he can do no more than pick out the letters *J* and *O*, for Joe himself is illiterate. Pip then decides to secretly teach Joe to read.

Mrs. Joe arrives after a marketing trip with Uncle Pumblechook, and they announce that Pip has been asked to go and "play" at the house of Miss Havisham, a rich and grim woman who lives in seclusion in a large, dismal house in the town. Pip is vigorously scrubbed and dressed, then he sets off to spend the night with Uncle Pumblechook before going to Miss Havisham's. He is greatly puzzled about *why* he will play for her and *what* he will play.

After a breakfast at which Pumblechook examines Pip interminably on arithmetic, they set out for Miss Havisham's Satis House. At the locked gate, Pip is admitted by a condescending young girl who rudely turns Pumblechook away. Then, in a room where no daylight enters, Pip encounters Miss Havisham, a fantastic character dressed in a yellowed bridal gown which hangs loosely over her skeletal figure. She tells Pip that she has not seen the sun since before he was born, that she has a broken heart, and that she wishes him to "play" for her diversion. She then orders him to call Estella, the girl who admitted him, and directs them to play cards. As they begin the only game Pip knows, "Beggar My Neighbour," Pip realizes that everything in this room stopped all at once, a long time ago. Estella, disdainfully noting Pip's coarse hands and thick boots, ridicules him and "beggars" (defeats) him thoroughly.

Afterward, Miss Havisham tells Pip to come back in six days, and Estella leads him out and gives him bread and meat and beer "as insolently as if I were a dog in disgrace." As he leaves, Pip has a momentary vision of a figure much like Miss Havisham, hanging from a beam and desperately trying to call to him.

Arriving home, Pip is convinced that to describe things as he saw them would be misunderstood; thus, he launches into a wild series of improvisations, including stories about a black velvet coach, four immense dogs fighting over veal cutlets from a silver platter, and a game with flags. Pip's listeners are suitably impressed. Later, however, Pip sneaks out to the forge, tells Joe that it was all lies, and explains what really happened. Joe, though saddened, advises Pip not to say anything about it to his sister and to tell no more lies in the future. Pip then reflects upon what Estella has said: how "common" his boots and his hands are, and how "common" he himself is.

Next day, Pip decides to make himself "uncommon" and asks Biddy, also an orphan, to secretly help him with his learning. Later, when Pip joins Joe at the Three Jolly Bargemen, he meets a "secret-looking" stranger who asks him many questions and stirs his drink not with a spoon, but with a file—Joe's file. When they are leaving, he gives Pip a bright new shilling wrapped in paper. At home, Mrs. Joe discovers that the "wrapping" is two one-pound notes.

On his second visit to Miss Havisham's, Pip is taken into a large, dusty, once-handsome room. There, on a table covered with rotting cloth is a strange centerpiece, so overhung with cobwebs and spiders that it is impossible to tell what it was. In this room, Miss Havisham tells Pip, is the table where she will be laid out when she is dead; the cobwebbed centerpiece is her wedding cake. Pip then meets several of Miss Havisham's cousins, and he and Estella play cards, after which he has a brief scuffle with a bookish young man. Impressed and delighted, Estella lets Pip kiss her cheek before he leaves.

For the next eight or ten months, Pip returns to Miss Havisham's every other day at noon, pushing her around the rooms in a wheelchair, and playing cards with Estella, who is alternately indifferent, condescending, friendly, and hateful. Miss Havisham questions Pip about his life, but never offers aid in his education or money for his services. At home, speculations about his prospects are never-ending.

One day, Miss Havisham tells Pip to bring Joe to Satis House. It is time, she says, for Pip to become apprenticed to him. Uncomfortably dressed in his Sunday suit, Joe accompanies Pip to Miss Havisham's, and there she establishes the fact that Pip has shown no objection to apprenticeship and that the indenture papers are in order. She then gives Pip a bag containing twenty-five guineas, specifying that this is all he will get for his services. She tells Pip that he is not to come again: "Gargery is your master now."

At Pumblechook's, Joe lies about Miss Havisham's sending regards and money to Mrs. Joe and, after some teasing, he hands over the money. Pip is then formally indentured at Town Hall, and Mrs. Joe treats them all, as well as the Hubbles and Mr. Wopsle, to dinner at the Blue Boar—with Pip's money. Pip, kept awake during the festivities to "enjoy himself," falls asleep at last with the unhappy knowledge that once long ago he liked Joe's trade, but, unfortunately, "once was not now."

Commentary

These chapters show us in detail Pip's growing dislike of his "commonness." Pip should be, one might think, grateful that his sister has taken him in and provided him with food and clothing, but, we discover, Pip has a dreamer's spirit and drive. He is tempted, from the first, by Miss Havisham's rich if eccentric furnishings and by Estella's contemptuous behavior. There is a certain perverseness in Miss Havisham's enjoying Pip's discomfort as he plays cards with the haughty, sharp-tongued Estella, but, because of his feelings of inferiority, Pip is determined that he will learn to read and write and better himself. He is a fiercely determined boy, convinced that someday he will be Estella's cultural equal.

Besides providing us with Pip's growing ambitions and his expectations for a better life than that of a blacksmith, Dickens inserts a key scene in the Three Jolly Bargemen. We realize that Pip's encounter with the escaped convict will indeed have consequences which he—and we—cannot yet imagine. The file which Pip gave to the convict is used to stir a drink, and, in addition, Pip is given money. Earlier, Pip had a nightmare about the reappearance of the file; the dream has come true—and will appear again.

As these chapters end, Pip is alone in his bedroom, unable to sleep. He is miserable, aching for a better position in the world. He does not realize the sick dimensions of Miss Havisham's life, nor has he fathomed the cause and depth of Estella's snobbery. As he was a victim of Mrs. Joe's temper, he is now a victim of social class feelings.

CHAPTERS 14-17

Summary

Home life has never been pleasant for Pip, even though Joe has done his best to make it so, but now it seems "all coarse and common," thanks to Miss Havisham and Estella. Pip would like to run away but does not because Joe has always been good and loyal to him. His greatest fear is that Estella might see him at work and jeer at him.

One day, at his and Joe's favorite retreat down by the Battery, Pip broaches the idea of his paying Miss Havisham a visit (an excuse to see Estella). Joe is against it: when Miss Havisham dismissed Pip, she said that was *all*. Pip argues, and Joe finally acquiesces on the condition that it be merely an expression of gratitude which, if not well received, will not be repeated. For this purpose, Pip asks for a half-holiday.

Next day, Sarah Pocket, a Havisham cousin admits Pip to Satis House. Miss Havisham is alone, with everything unchanged. When Pip tells her he has come only to see how she is and thank her for her help, she invites him back on his birthday. Estella is abroad, she says, "educating for a lady." Shortly after, Pip meets Mr. Wopsle, and as they are going homeward in the misty night, they find the doors of the Jolly Bargemen wide open and the customers in a state of great commotion. Something dreadful has happened at Pip's house while Joe was out: someone, presumably a convict, has broken in, and somebody is injured. The somebody is Mrs. Joe, whom Pip finds lying senseless in front of the fire, felled by a tremendous blow on the back of her head, "destined never to be on the rampage again while she was the wife of Joe."

Found beside Mrs. Joe is a convict's leg-iron, which has clearly been filed off some time ago; both Joe and the people from the Hulks agree on this point. Guiltily, Pip thinks it must be "his convict's" leg-iron.

When Mrs. Joe recovers from the attack, her vision and hearing are impaired and her speech is unintelligible. Her writing, always bad, is a poor means of communication, but her temper is much improved. The problem she has left is the care of the household; the new one she has created is the need for somebody to care for her. Both are solved when Mr. Wopsle's great-aunt dies and Biddy becomes a member of the household. It is Biddy who deduces that a curious "T" which Mrs. Joe is constantly drawing might be a hammer and might refer to Orlick, a surly employee of Joe's. When Orlick is produced, however, Mrs. Joe is very friendly, almost subservient to him. The mystery remains.

Pip's life as an apprentice is disturbed only by his annual visits to Miss Havisham, who gives him a guinea each birthday and a glimpse into her "uncommon" world, enough to perpetuate his desire to better himself. Although these visits last only a few minutes, they are enough to keep him reminded of his discontent with his present life. Gradually, however, he becomes aware of Biddy. Her appearance has changed; she is now cleaner and fresher—not beautiful, but wholesome and sweet-tempered. She keeps pace with Pip in his studies, but she seems to learn everything he does without even trying. On a long Sunday walk on the marshes, Pip confides to her that he wants to become a gentleman because of Estella. Biddy (who secretly loves Pip) gives him the sensible advice that it's not worth changing his ways simply to spite Estella, and that if he has to change himself to win her, the girl is not worth winning.

Pip realizes that Biddy is a good woman and that Estella, at any given moment, might make him miserable. "If I could only get myself to fall in love with you—" he says to Biddy. "But you never will," she replies. On the way home, Joe's journeyman, Orlick, offers to walk along with them, and Biddy asks Pip to refuse, saying, "I am afraid he likes me." Pip does try to protect Biddy thereafter, but his thoughts roam. He is heavily discontent and is sustained only by the irrational hope that Miss Havisham will "make his fortune" when his apprenticeship is finished.

Commentary

Here we have, as it were, a framework for Pip's frustrations. Once, Joe's standards of living and his occupation were measurements of manhood for Pip. Now those standards have been scoffed at, ridiculed, and rejected by a girl whom Pip is infatuated with. Pip finds himself an "orphan" in a new world. He has no one to confide in, he has no mentor to guide him, and, most important, he has no money to realize his dreams of escaping what he has come to think of as "the common life." Estella is a cold siren, luring him, with the help of Miss Havisham, to another world.

Pip might have languished in his romantic imagination except for a single incident: some time ago, he helped an escaped convict. In Chapter 15, Dickens reintroduces the convict theme. The firing of guns at the Hulks announces that a prisoner has escaped, and a leg-iron is found next to Mrs. Joe, who has suffered a terrible blow on the back of her head.

Because of Mrs. Joe's "being silenced," Biddy comes to the household and soon begins to teach Pip to read and write, practical preparations for his future. The home life of Joe and Pip becomes more tranquil, but note that Pip is still dissatisfied by the day-in, day-out monotony of being ˋa blacksmith's apprentice. Here, Dickens presents an especially suspenseful struggle between Pip's personal ambition and his discontent.

It is here, too, that Orlick, a sinister figure, is introduced into the story; during these chapters, hostility will increase between Pip and Orlick until Orlick will attempt to murder Pip.

CHAPTERS 18-19

Summary

One evening during the fourth year of Pip's apprenticeship, a group which includes Joe and Pip is gathered around the fire at the Jolly Bargemen listening to Mr. Wopsle read a newspaper account of a particularly vivid murder. Mr. Wopsle plays every role, and all agree to the verdict: willful murder.

He is interrupted by an authoritative stranger who proceeds to demonstrate Wopsle's complete ignorance of judicial procedure. After disposing of Wopsle, the stranger asks for Joe and Pip. Pip recognizes him as a burly gentleman he met once on the stairs at Miss Havisham's. When they arrive home to talk, the stranger announces that his name is Jaggers.

After determining that Joe will not hold Pip to his apprenticeship if there is something better in store for the lad, Jaggers tells Pip that he is "a young gentleman of great expectations." There are conditions, but they are simple: he must move from his present surroundings, and he must always bear the name of Pip. The name of his benefactor is to remain secret until it is revealed to him, and Pip is to make no inquiries whatever about this. A substantial sum of money has already been lodged with Jaggers, whom Pip is to regard as his guardian. Does Pip agree? Pip does. "My dream was out," he thinks. "Miss Havisham was going to make my fortune on a grand scale."

Jaggers suggests, first off, that Pip should take as his tutor Matthew Pocket, the same Matthew whom Pip had heard reviled at Satis House. Pip is then given twenty guineas to buy new clothes and is told to be in London in a week. When Jaggers again suggests that Joe accept the compensation he is authorized to pay, Joe becomes belligerent and Pip has to intervene. Money, Joe says, can never compensate "for the loss of the little child—what come to the forge—and ever the best of friends!"

Intoxicated with his good fortune, Pip nevertheless feels gloomy and lonely. Joe and Biddy are happy for him, but feel a great sadness about his leaving. Pip consents to show his new clothes to them after he buys them but to no one else in the village; that would be a "coarse and common business."

Pip strolls over the marshes in a farewell reverie and is joined by Joe before they return home. Later, with a condescension he supposes to be generosity, Pip tells Biddy that he proposes to improve Joe's manners and that he would like to raise him into a higher sphere. When Biddy replies that Joe is proud and might want to stay in a place he "fills well and with respect," Pip chides her as being envious and showing a "bad side of human nature." But at the tailoring establishment of Mr. Trabb and at the hatter's, the bootmaker's, and the hosier's, he finds the obsequiousness overwhelming but pleasant—exactly what he desires. At Pumblechook's, he is treated to an elaborate meal and greeted with much servility and handshaking.

On Friday, dressed in his new clothes, he visits Miss Havisham, who admits to having heard of his good fortune from Jaggers. On his last night at home, a fine dinner is served, but Pip, Biddy, and Joe all are "low, and none the higher for pretending to be in spirits."

Next morning at five, Pip leaves alone, unwilling to be seen in his new clothes alongside Joe, although he does not fully admit this. Once on the coach, he feels remorse and considers going back for a better parting. But he doesn't, for "the mists had all solemnly risen now," he recalls, "and the world lay spread before me."

Commentary

Chapters 18 and 19 bring to a close the first stage of Pip's "great expectations." Mr. Jaggers explains the mysterious circumstances of Pip's fortune and the stipulations necessary for Pip to acquire it. Pip is now free from his apprenticeship to Joe, but he is not quite free from his feelings of guilt. The goodness of Joe and Biddy, who are left behind, sustains the struggle in Pip's mind, even as his great expectations are at last about to be fulfilled.

Pip's expectations dazzle him. He does not yet realize how Miss Havisham has toyed with him; he believes her to be his "good angel," the answer to his prayers. Nor does he perceive the true worth of Biddy, who has taught him much and who has come to take care of him and Joe; now she is left behind him, a piece of his unpleasant past. Someday, however, she will become more prominent in Pip's life.

Pip is not completely happy, but happy or not, the orphan youth, with a new suit of clothes and money in his pocket, sets out for London, eager to become a gentleman worthy of the fair, if cold, Estella.

CHAPTERS 20-22

Summary

Arriving in London at last, Pip is terrified by the city's immensity; certainly it is not a fabled heaven on earth. In particular, the streets are "rather ugly, crooked, narrow, and dirty." Pip discovers, however, a pleasant surprise: Mr. Jaggers is a great man, despite the fact that his establishment in the unsavory district of Smithfield is unprepossessing, especially his dreary private office, dominated by two dreadful plaster casts of swollen faces. While waiting, Pip walks outside. The surroundings, including the slaughterhouse, the market around the corner, and Newgate Prison, he finds "sickening." But Mr. Jaggers, whom Pip encounters returning from his morning trials, is masterful. He is surrounded by hopeful clients, all of them obviously depending on Jaggers to save someone from jail or hanging. He deals with them in an arrogant and incisive fashion, characteristically shaking his huge forefinger at them and having to do only with those who have already paid their bills.

At the office, he settles Pip's business quickly while he wolfs down a sandwich and nips from a pocket flask of sherry. Pip is to go to Barnard's Inn to room with a young Mr. Pocket until Monday, when they will go to the elder Pocket's home, where Pip is to study. Pip also learns of his allowance, which is very liberal, and is given cards for tradesmen where his credit will be excellent. This is an advantage to Pip and also a means whereby Jaggers can check on his expenditures. Jaggers' clerk, Wemmick, walks with Pip to the inn.

Barnard's Inn proves to be a shockingly dingy collection of rotting buildings, where a notice on the letter-box announces that "Mr. Pocket, Jun." will return shortly. Pip is depressed. Pocket arrives, half an hour later, laden with fruit from Covent Garden Market, bought for Pip's arrival to supplement the food which, on Mr. Jaggers' instructions, Pip will supply. Pip is startled to find that he recognizes young Pocket. He is the "pale young gentleman" whom Pip skirmished with at Miss Havisham's.

Pip feels immediate rapport with his new friend, Herbert Pocket, who nicknames him Handel, after "The Harmonious Blacksmith," a piece of music by Handel. From Herbert, Pip learns Miss Havisham's story, sandwiched in between his first lessons about table manners.

Miss Havisham, the daughter of a wealthy brewer, was a spoilt child whose mother died when Miss Havisham was a baby. Later her father secretly married his cook, who bore him a son who turned out altogether bad. After first disinheriting him, the father relented on his deathbed and left him well off. The lad quickly squandered his inheritance and Miss Havisham was not inclined to help him. Then one day a new suitor appeared among her many callers and, to everyone's surprise, Miss Havisham fell passionately in love with him. He was not, Herbert's father had averred, a "gentleman," and he got great sums of money out of her, including the purchase of the half-brother's share of the brewery at a ridiculous price. Herbert's father, in fact, incurred her wrath by questioning her actions and has not seen her since.

On the day set for the wedding, the groom did not show up; instead, he wrote a letter which was received at twenty minutes to nine. It is supposed that the fiancé and the half-brother shared in the scheme, dividing the profits. Thenceforth, Miss Havisham devoted herself to seclusion and to bringing up Estella to wreak vengeance on the male sex. Of Estella's parents, Herbert knows nothing, only that Miss Havisham adopted her.

When Herbert begins to talk about his own prospects in the insurance business, Pip soon senses that, as in their fight, his hopes exceed his capabilities. This impression is reinforced when Pip discovers that the grimy counting-house, which he visits next day, pays Herbert absolutely nothing. Herbert is simply "in it" for the experience of looking about and learning about shipping, merchants, and insuring.

That evening, when they visit Pip's tutor, Herbert's father, Pip finds a somewhat addled Mr. Pocket reading under a tree with seven little Pockets "tumbling up" instead of growing up, under the casual supervision of two nurses, Flopson and Millers. Mr. Pocket understandably proves to be a "gentleman with a rather perplexed expression of face."

Commentary

Chapter 20 shows Pip's arrival in London and his first introduction to that city, the site of his next years of development. Throughout these chapters, Pip will be beginning a new life. Since he has left his friends and "family," these chapters will show him meeting new people who will influence the next portion of his life.

The first person he meets is Wemmick, Mr. Jaggers' clerk, who is responsible for looking after the financial aspects of Pip's career. Wemmick will turn out to be one of Dickens' most delightful creations with his enigmatic life style—his private Walworth life and emotions and, juxtaposed, his business life with its opposite emotions. Wemmick will later prove to be most helpful when Pip needs him. He is also categorized by the importance which he places on "portable property."

Mr. Jaggers' personality is also further developed. As in the scene with Pip and Joe, when Mr. Jaggers reveals that Pip has great expectations, Mr. Jaggers seems to conduct his business mainly by bullying people around. Dickens writes that "he seemed to bully his very sandwich as he ate it." And this was apparently the technique that he used to tame Molly, who will turn out to be Estella's mother.

As soon as Pip finds out that he is to share quarters with Herbert Pocket, and discovers that Herbert is the same young man whom he fought at Miss Havisham's, this fact serves to strengthen his belief that she is his benefactress. In this novel filled with coincidences, however, this is not necessarily one of them, since Mr. Jaggers, as we later find out, does not know any suitable young people other than Herbert Pocket, whom he knows only through Miss Havisham. Miss Havisham's story, as far as Herbert knows it, only verifies what Pip might have, and the reader probably has, suspected. The reasons for her doting attentions to Estella, her admonitions to "beggar" Pip and "break their hearts" (meaning men), are now clarified. Who Estella is and where she comes from remains a mystery. But for the first time Pip has had a look at Satis House through a friend's knowledgeable eyes.

Herbert is open and frank with Pip, qualities which will later influence Pip to set Herbert up in the business world. From Herbert, he hears all about Miss Havisham's past and is able to see that, unlike the other relatives of Miss Havisham, Herbert is not mean, impolite, or vindictive. At the end of Chapter 22, Herbert takes Pip out to the Pocket home, where he is exposed to the entire Pocket family, which is "tumbling up." Many scholars feel that the Pocket family is based on Dickens' own family since Dickens' wife apparently had no more talent for running a household than does Mrs. Pocket.

CHAPTERS 23-26

Summary

Mrs. Pocket, obsessed with the idea of social position, has "grown up highly ornamental, but perfectly helpless and useless," her sole occupation being reading books about the nobility. Matthew Pocket, who distinguished himself at Harrow and Cambridge, became a Grinder on acquiring Mrs. Pocket but, tiring of dull blades, he decided to come to London, where he supported himself on a modest income, on literary compilations and corrections, on tutoring, and by running a boarding house. Pip's fellow boarders (he decides to have a room here in addition to his quarters with Herbert) are Bentley Drummle, a dull young fellow who is "next heir but one to a baronetcy," and Startop, a younger and more attractive young man.

At dinner that night the confusions of the household are manifest. The servants run the house, the children run rampant, Mrs. Pocket is in her usual state of abstraction, and Mr. Pocket periodically tries to lift himself out of his chair by his own hair.

Mr. Pocket, who knows more of the plans for Pip's future than Pip does, proves surprisingly serious, honest, and practical as a tutor and advisor. Pip visits Jaggers to gain permission to maintain his establishment with Herbert at Barnard's Inn, and he again comes into contact with Wemmick, the head clerk. From Wemmick, Pip gets a further sense of the efficiency of Jaggers' professional manners; he learns, for example, that the two plaster casts in the inner office are replicas of two celebrated clients after they were hanged, and he discovers further that the jewelry which Wemmick wears came as gifts from clients who were also hanged. Wemmick values this curious jewelry as his "portable property."

Wemmick warns Pip that when he dines with Mr. Jaggers he will see "a wild beast tamed"—his housekeeper, whom Pip should keep his eye on. He also extends an invitation for Pip to visit him at home at Walworth. They end the day by watching Mr. Jaggers in action in police court. Pip's chief impression is that everybody is afraid of Jaggers: "Which side he was on, I couldn't make out, for he seemed to me to be grinding the whole place in a mill."

Eventually, Pip writes a note to Wemmick accepting an invitation for dinner. While they walk to Walworth together, Wemmick outlines dinner: stewed steak (home preparation) and cold fowl (which will be tender because the master of the cook-shop was once a juryman for whom Jaggers had done a favor); because the fowl came as a present, it is definitely considered "portable property." Wemmick also reveals to Pip that Jaggers *never* locks his house at night and boasts that he'd "want to see the man who'll rob *me*."

Walworth is unusual. It resembles a castle, although it is the smallest house that Pip has ever seen, with imitation Gothic windows, a flagstaff, a moat four feet wide and two feet deep, a drawbridge, and a cannon which fires every night at nine o'clock

Greenwich time. In back are a pig, fowls, rabbits, and a small garden; in case of siege, Wemmick is prepared to hold out for a long time. Wemmick's father, the Aged Parent, is a clean, sprightly old man, very deaf, to whom his son is obviously devoted. They communicate by well-worn phrases and by nods, in which Pip actively participates. The main point of Wemmick's having the cannon is to give the Aged Parent something he can hear.

In the morning, as they return to the city, Wemmick retreats more and more into his hard, dry London self. When they arrive in their section, known as Little Britain, it is as if Wemmick's curious home and his Aged Parent had been "blown into space together."

One day Jaggers invites Pip, Herbert, Startop, and Drummle to dinner at his house in Soho, a stately but neglected house, of which he generally uses only the first floor. The lawyer takes a quick fancy to Drummle, whom he nicknames the Spider, and has him sit next to him. The dinner goes well, despite Drummle's temper and despite an episode in which Jaggers exposes a powerful scarred wrist of his housekeeper to prove that no man there is as strong as Molly. Pip later apologizes to Jaggers for Drummle's behavior, but Jaggers confides that he likes Drummle; he says that the fellow is "one of the true sort."

Commentary

In Chapter 23, we are introduced to two more young men who will influence Pip's life in one way or the other. Startop will later help him try to escape with Magwitch, and Drummle will later prove to be Pip's worst enemy and the source of great envy as Estella's husband.

Mrs. Pocket's pride in her ancestry should be contrasted with Pip's recent sense of pride and the pride which he will continue to develop until the end of the novel. Herbert apparently took after his father and not his mother. Also in contrast to Herbert are the other Pockets who come to visit Miss Havisham and who hate Pip with "the hatred of cupidity and disappointment."

Chapters 25 and 26 offer contrasting dinner parties. At Wemmick's house, everything is friendly and warm, if curious. Dickens takes great effort to make the reader see and appreciate the congenial relations between Wemmick and his father, often referred to as the "Aged P." Dickens is further developing the relationship between Pip and Wemmick so that Wemmick will be able to advise and help Pip later on.

In contrast to the warmth at Wemmick's house, we get an entirely different type of dinner at Mr. Jaggers' estate. His food is served by the mysterious Molly, whom Wemmick had earlier warned Pip about as being like a wild animal, tamed. Jaggers' exposing her wrist is his way of keeping her tame and keeping her under his control.

Jaggers' continued interest in the unpleasant Drummle must be accounted for as the latter's being a type that would attract the interest of an outstanding criminal lawyer. Note, here, that Jaggers warns Pip not to have much to do with the young man.

CHAPTERS 27-30

Summary

A letter from Biddy informs Pip that Joe is coming to town next day and will stop to see him at Barnard's Inn. Pip receives the news "with considerable disturbance, some mortification, and a keen sense of incongruity." In short, he is ashamed that someone might see the "common" blacksmith, especially Drummle, whom Pip despises.

Joe arrives, terribly self-conscious, and says that Mrs. Joe is no worse than before; Biddy is "ever right and ready"; all friends are the same except for Wopsle. He's "had a drop"—that is, he has left the church and has begun playacting on the stage. Joe sits down to tea and, to the accompaniment of many "Sirs," reveals that he has a message for Pip from Miss Havisham. Estella is home and would be glad to see him. On Biddy's advice, he has come to bring the message rather than having her write it. He readies himself to leave and refuses to return for dinner. "You and me is not two figures to be together in London," he says with simple dignity. When Pip can recover himself sufficiently, he goes out to look for Joe, but his old friend is gone.

Pip loses no time getting to see Estella; on the stagecoach next day, he finds himself in the company of two convicts who are being transported down to the Hulks. One of them, to his alarm, is the man who had used a file to stir his drink and had given Pip the two one-pound notes at the Jolly Bargemen; the convict, however, does not recognize Pip in his new gentleman's clothes. Waking from a doze, Pip hears the man talking about some money, and he learns that "his convict" had given the notes to this man with a request that he "find out that boy that had fed him and kep his secret." Pip gets out at the edge of town and goes to the Blue Boar, feeling that it would not be socially advisable for him to go to Joe's.

Convinced that Miss Havisham, who has adopted Estella and has "as good as adopted" him, intends for them to marry eventually, Pip goes to Satis House, where he is admitted by Orlick, now Miss Havisham's watchman. Pip finds Miss Havisham unchanged but Estella so grown-up and beautiful that at first he doesn't recognize her. As Pip and Estella walk together through the garden, she tells him that what was once fit company for him is not fit company now. He now feels certain that he should not visit Joe.

Back with Miss Havisham, Pip learns that Jaggers will come for dinner. Estella then leaves to dress, and Miss Havisham puts her arm around Pip's neck and says, "Love her, love her, love her." No matter how Estella hurts him, Pip is to love her. Jaggers enters, and Pip realizes that Miss Havisham, like everybody else, is afraid of him.

Jaggers and Pip talk, and Jaggers tells Pip that no one has seen Miss Havisham actually eat a meal since her dreadful wedding day. In answer to one of Pip's questions, Jaggers says that Estella's name is Havisham. After cards, Pip goes to bed and dreams of marrying her.

Next morning, Pip tells his guardian what he knows of Orlick's surly behavior as Miss Havisham's watchman, and Jaggers says that he will discharge the fellow from his post at once. Pip then takes a coach to London and there he immediately sends "a penitential codfish and barrel of oysters to Joe." He prepares to confide his feelings about Estella to Herbert, but it is not necessary; Herbert already knows and tries to dissuade him from his interest in the girl. The education she has had with Miss Havisham can lead only to trouble. Pip agrees but says he can't help it. Shortly thereafter, the two chaps discover a playbill Joe left announcing Mr. Wopsle's appearance in *Hamlet* that evening, and they set out to see the performance.

Commentary

Pip's false sense of pride and his ingratitude is brought to the forefront when he receives a letter from Biddy announcing the expected arrival of Joe for a visit. This news causes great consternation in Pip's mind and continues the conflict between the duty and love which he owes to Joe and his own "uncommon" personal ambitions. Pip admits that "if I could have kept him away by paying money, I certainly would have paid money." His fear is based on the anxiety caused by the possibility that Drummle, Pip's worst enemy, might catch a glimpse of the rustic Joe and therefore make Pip an object of ridicule. Thus, Pip realizes, "our worst weaknesses and meannesses are usually committed for the sake of the people whom we most despise."

In contrast to Pip's false pride is the simple dignity of Joe. Pip is so tense about Joe's visit that he makes Joe tense also. When they are alone, Joe is able to explain in simple language that carries with it a ring of true dignity the nature of their relationship—that if Pip ever wants to see him, he won't look nearly so foolish in his work clothes at the forge as he does in his suit here in London. Pip fails to recognize that Joe also has a sense of pride, and not false pride, in his own work.

The thought of Estella intensifies Pip's shame of his origin, and he cannot conceive of staying at Joe's and also visiting Estella; thus, he hypocritically deceives himself that it would be inconvenient for him to stay at Joe's. Along with the revival of the Estella theme is the re-emergence of the convict theme. The convict whom Pip had seen stirring his drink with the file is also on the carriage which carries Pip to meet Estella; Dickens is constantly reminding us of the interchange of these two ideas.

When Pip again sees Estella, he hardly recognizes the elegant and beautiful lady as being the same Estella whom he once played cards with. And whereas earlier, fear of Drummle prevented Pip from receiving Joe openly, now the elegance of Estella puts all notions of visiting Joe out of the question. The only connection between Joe's forge and Miss Havisham's Satis House is Orlick, Pip's evil nemesis; since he works as the gatekeeper there, Pip's part in getting Orlick fired will later be part of the reason that Orlick tries to murder Pip.

On his return to London, Pip confesses his love for Estella to Herbert and discovers that in addition to his being warned by Estella herself, Herbert also thinks that Estella is incapable of love. Thus we perceive that Dickens is building a contrast between three love affairs: Herbert confesses his love and intent to marry Clara, and we have heard of Wemmick's and Miss Skiffins's love for each other; only the last of the trio, Pip's love for Estella, is destined for sadness.

CHAPTERS 31-33

Summary

To call the production of *Hamlet*, in which Mr Wopsle stars, amateurish would be an unwarranted compliment. Nevertheless, despite the shabby character of the whole production and the jeers and jests from the audience which Pip and Herbert have to laugh at in spite of themselves, Pip "had a latent impression that there was something decidedly fine in Mr. Wopsle's elocution." After the performance, an emissary from Mr. Waldengarver (Wopsle's stage name) intercepts them and invites them to visit Wopsle backstage. The conversation between them and this messenger, who is the owner of the costumes which Pip and Herbert have been laughing at, consists entirely of how well Wopsle showed off the costumes.

A letter from Estella, with neither salutation nor regards, informs Pip that he is to meet her on the midday coach. Pip arrives at the coach-office almost five hours early, where he has the good fortune to encounter Wemmick, who invites him to visit Newgate prison with him. The experience is most unpleasant; Pip finds the prison a "frouzy, ugly, disorderly, depressing scene." Wemmick, however, walks "among the prisoners much as a gardener might walk among his plants." He is, Pip realizes, both highly popular and respected. At one point, Wemmick introduces Pip to a "Colonel," a counterfeiter who is shortly to be hanged; the evidence was too strong, and Jaggers has lost the case. The Colonel regrets he cannot afford a good ring to give Wemmick, but the latter suggests a brace of pigeons, certainly "portable property," as it were.

After a three-hour wait, during which Pip meditates on the role which prison and crime have played in his life, he suddenly sees Estella's beautiful face and her hand waving to him from a coach. She gives Pip a purse to pay the expenses for a carriage to Richmond, where she is to live, then for the second time, she lets Pip kiss her cheek, commenting all the time about their fates "being disposed of by others." The person with whom she will be staying, she says, is a well-placed lady who can introduce her to the right people, and Pip, she adds, has been given the freedom to visit her freely.

Commentary

These chapters do little or nothing to move the plot forward. Chapter 31, dealing with Mr. Wopsle (or Mr. Waldengarver, as he is known on the stage), is both a hilariously funny and, at the same time, a pathetic story of his bumbling failure.

Chapter 32 is a digression, the type of which is quite famous in the Dickens canon of writing. The digression was intended to call attention to the disgraceful conditions in London prisons. Dickens, who was very concerned with penal reforms, uses any available opportunity to draw attention to them. However, as an artist, Dickens also includes an implied contrast between the low and sordid conditions in the prison and the beauty, pride, and elegance of Estella; and there is also the later knowledge that Estella's origins are closely connected with Newgate prison, and that Pip's great expectations are also connected with prison life. Thus there is a certain irony connected with Pip's desire to protect Estella even from the knowledge of Newgate, thinking her too superior even to hear about this horrible place.

When Estella first arrives, and every time he meets her during this stage of his life, he is strangely haunted by some familiarity to someone else whom he has recently seen. It will be much later, however, before he is able to make the connection between Estella and Molly.

The only plot development in this section is that Estella, in being placed with Mrs. Brandley, will now be moving out into society, will meet the odious Drummle, and will cause Pip even more distress.

CHAPTERS 34-35

Summary

Pip's guilt about how he feels toward Joe and Biddy continues to bother him, but he remains bound to Estella, and contributing to his discomfort is the fact that he has fallen into debt and has led Herbert, who has no financial expectations, along with him.

One evening as Pip and Herbert are trying to organize their finances, a black-bordered letter arrives for Pip. It is from Trabb & Company, informing him that his sister has died and that his presence is requested at the funeral the following Monday.

Pip is troubled all week long by memories, somewhat softened by time, of a sister whom he has no reason to remember fondly. Later, he walks along the familiar streets of his childhood, still feeling the loss until he finds that Joe's house has been taken over temporarily by Mr. Trabb, the tailor, who doubles as undertaker. The mourners, of whom Joe is chief, are dressed stiffly in black, and Pumblechook, busy with sherry and food, is as obsequious as ever.

After the burial, Pip walks with Biddy awhile. Biddy is moving to Mrs. Hubble's and is hopeful of becoming a teacher in a newly finished school. Mrs. Joe died quietly, she says, her head on Joe's shoulder, saying "Joe," "Pardon," and, finally, "Pip." Orlick, now apparently working in the quarries, still seems to be shadowing her. Pip tells her he will often come down to see Joe, and he reproaches her angrily when she indicates doubts and insists on calling him "Mr. Pip." That night, he is restless and has trouble sleeping. He broods about Biddy's lack of faith in his character. Next morning, he leaves, promising to come back, but with an inner knowledge that Biddy is right; he probably will not.

Commentary

Chapter 34 shows Pip becoming accustomed to someday receiving "great expectations" and, as a result, he begins to go deeper and deeper in debt. He is beginning to squander his money, a perilous course, especially later when his expectations no longer exist. Then he will be in dire circumstances and will be faced with the dilemma of accepting money either from Magwitch, the convict, or from Miss Havisham, neither of whom is obligated to him.

Chapter 35, which presents the details of the funeral, gives a vivid picture of the social customs of the time connected with burial rites. Pip is troubled because he can feel so little sorrow over his sister's death. Even though his memories of Mrs. Joe are softened by her death, there was never any deep love between them, nothing to compare with the feelings between himself and Joe; consequently, true remorse is replaced by simple regret.

Still, however, Pip is very defensive about his relationship with Joe. His sense of superiority keeps him at a distance from both Joe and Biddy, and as he talks with Biddy about his intent to leave London and visit them more often, Biddy's remarks indicate her knowledge that Pip will probably not visit them. Pip knows that Biddy is correct, and we know that Pip will have to undergo a significant change before he recognizes the true worth of both Biddy and Joe.

CHAPTERS 36-39

Summary

On the day of Pip's "majority"—that is, his twenty-first birthday—he calls by invitation at Mr. Jaggers' office. There he receives congratulations, a banknote for five hundred pounds, and the information that this amount will hereafter be his yearly allowance, drawn quarterly, until his benefactor chooses to reveal himself. He is now in charge of his own financial affairs. At work, and feeling generous, he makes tentative inquiries to Wemmick about ways to help Herbert in his business career and discovers that this is a question which will have to be asked later to the "Walworth Wemmick" (the "private" self that lives in the curious castle cottage).

Arriving at Wemmick's castle, Pip finds the Union Jack flag flying and the drawbridge up. The Aged P. admits him quite peacefully and futilely attempts conversation until a sign pops out beside the fireplace chimney which says "John." Wemmick is home, and the Aged P., trailed by Pip, hurries out to lower the drawbridge and admit him. Wemmick is accompanied by Miss Skiffins, an angular maiden whose dress makes her look like a boy's kite. That she is a regular visitor is soon evidenced by another demonstration of the chimney signs, this one reading "Miss Skiffins."

While tea is being prepared, Pip tells Wemmick about his desire to anonymously help Herbert buy into a small partnership. Wemmick thinks this is a fine idea and says that he will help Pip. Before the week is out, he hears from Wemmick that a Mr. Skiffins, the angular lady's accountant-brother, has found a fine possibility. After much consultation, matters are arranged for Herbert to be employed by a young shipping-broker, keeping Pip's involvement secret. Herbert's joy over his unexpected "opening" at Clarriker's (the broker's) brings Pip his first feeling that his expectations have at last done some good.

After Pip's interminable visits to the house in Richmond where Estella is staying (during which he has not enjoyed "one hour's happiness in her society; and yet my mind all round the four-and-twenty hours was harping on the happiness of having her with me unto death"), he learns one day that he is to take Estella on a visit to Satis House. Miss Havisham's obsession with Estella's conquests, including Pip, is more intense than ever. Though he sees clearly that "Estella was set to wreak Miss Havisham's revenge" on him, he still believes that eventually she will be assigned to him permanently.

During the visit there, Pip hears the first sharp words that he has ever heard between Miss Havisham and Estella. The old lady accuses Estella of growing tired of her and pleads for love. Estella, perfectly composed, replies that she is only behaving as cold and hard as Miss Havisham trained her to be. Pip is given a place to sleep in Satis House for the first time. He sees and hears Miss Havisham walking about, ghostly and agitated.

Back in London, Pip dines at a fancy gentleman's club, and he and Drummle nearly come to blows after Drummle proposes a toast to a lady friend, Estella. Later observations at Richmond prove to Pip that Estella is deliberately encouraging Drummle's romantic attention. Pip protests, but Estella tells him candidly that she deceives and entraps everyone but Pip. Pip is unable to understand.

Pip becomes twenty-three, and one day as he is reading a book in the new quarters he shares with Herbert, he hears a footstep on the stair below. It is a muscular stranger about sixty years old, gray haired, browned by the sun, and roughly dressed. Once inside the apartment, he gazes around with obvious pleasure and holds out both hands to Pip. Pip recoils, not recognizing the man until the stranger abruptly takes out a file, wraps a handkerchief around his head, and hugs himself and shivers. Pip knows him: it's his convict.

The man tells him that Pip was generous to him on the marshes and he has never forgotten it. Pip holds him off, then thanks him loftily, pointing out that under his new circumstances he cannot be expected to renew a chance acquaintance of long ago. Yet the man stays for tea and explains that he has been living as a sheep farmer in New South Wales, Australia, and has done wonderfully well. When Pip condescendingly repays the two one-pound notes, the man burns them. Gradually, by revealing an intimate knowledge of the way Pip's money has come to him, the old stranger lets Pip realize that it was *he*, not Miss Havisham, who has been his benefactor. "Yes, Pip, dear boy," he says, "I've made a gentleman on you! It's me wot has done it!"

Overwhelmed by repugnance and disappointment, Pip asks desperately if there was no one else but the old convict involved. The answer is negative. Only the knowledge that the old man was making Pip a finer gentleman than any of the colonists who looked down at him has enabled him to bear up through a hard struggle.

Afterward, Pip sits dejected by the fire, his dreams about Miss Havisham and Estella shattered, his guilt about Joe intensified, and his worry about the convict's safety intensified by his fear and his dislike of him.

Commentary

Pip's basic nature is generous, as we see in Chapter 36, when he begins to receive the first of his "great expectations." He immediately wishes to help Herbert Pocket get started in business and his first action is with that in mind. But we should also remember that Pip's love for Estella has made him blind to the simple dignity of Joe and Biddy; only when he learns the full truth of Estella's parentage and the source of his own "great expectations" will he recognize the true worth of his old friends.

In contrast to Mr. Jaggers, who is always the same whether in business or at dinner, Wemmick gives Pip one opinion about investing "portable property" at the business office and will give another and completely different one when Pip calls upon him at Walworth. Thus, Chapter 37 continues to show Pip's basic generosity as the secret plot to help Herbert is initiated. Also, at Walworth, Wemmick is comically involved in his love skirmishes with Miss Skiffins—a contrast to the relationship between Pip and Estella.

In Chapter 38, the scene between Miss Havisham and Estella should have made it perfectly clear to Pip that Estella is incapable of any emotion or true feelings: her heart is made of stone. Actually

Pip does recognize part of this truth, but his love for Estella blinds him to the full truth: "I saw in this, that Estella was set to wreak Miss Havisham's revenge on men, and that she was not to be given to me until she had gratified it." This chapter also contains the beginning of the relationship between Estella and Drummle, Pip's worst enemy. Why Estella attaches herself to Drummle is a mystery to many people. Most critics suggest that Dickens had the end of the novel in mind and knew that Estella must be subdued and must suffer, and that it would take such a brute as Drummle to effect this change in Estella. In fact, Estella's most honest statement is that she does not lay any traps for Pip, and that she is honest and open only with Pip.

In Chapter 39, the first major crisis of the novel occurs with the revelation that Pip's benefactor is the convict whom he helped when he was a young lad. That all of his great expectations relied upon a convict, an unmentionable in society, and not from Miss Havisham, is the most dramatic situation that Pip has had to face. But, finally, many truths are clear to him. He now knows that he has been used by Miss Havisham as "a convenience, a sting for the greedy relations." He also realizes that Estella was never meant for him, and his connections with a convict further remove her from his world. And, in addition, he realizes with great remorse that he deserted Joe for this convict.

It is fortunate that Magwitch, the convict, is so completely engrossed in seeing Pip again as a gentleman that he is totally oblivious to the horror he creates in Pip. "The abhorrence in which I held the man, the dread I had of him, the repugnance with which I shrank from him, could not have been exceeded if he had been some terrible beast." Yet it is to Pip's credit that he has absolutely no thought of betraying this man and immediately accepts the burden of protecting the returned convict who, if caught, will be hanged. That the convict so loves Pip as to risk his own life in order to see him is an additional burden upon Pip. Thus ends the second stage of Pip's expectations.

CHAPTERS 40-42

Summary

When Abel Magwitch, as the convict reveals his name to be, awakens, Pip tells him about a mysterious man whom he saw crouched on the stairs. The stranger eluded him, however; Magwitch hopes that he is not known in London and that he was not followed. He faces certain death if he is caught, and since he was last tried here in London, the possibility of his being recognized certainly does exist. Pip then suggests that Magwitch pass as his "uncle," using his shipboard name of Provis. "Provis" agrees and gives Pip a thick pocketbook, railing against "every one, from the judge in his wig, to the colonist a-stirring up the dust." Pip, he says, is a better gentleman than all of them put together.

When Pip talks with Jaggers, the lawyer confirms that Magwitch is indeed Pip's sole benefactor. Pip's dreams about Miss Havisham's generosity have no foundation. Pip returns and tries to outfit the convict in new clothes with no luck: "Prisoner, Felon, and Bondsman" are written all over him. Herbert arrives, wins Magwitch's approval, and is sworn to secrecy on a greasy little black Testament.

After Magwitch is moved to safe quarters nearby, Pip and Herbert try to decide on a plan of action. Herbert understands Pip's repugnance for the convict and his reluctance to take any more money. Perhaps, he suggests, they should find out more about Magwitch.

Agreeing to tell the lads more about himself, Magwitch begins by saying that he has no idea where he was born or who his parents were. He has been in jail and out of jail over and over; a deserting soldier taught him to read and a "travelling Giant" taught him to write. He finally made connections with a man named Compeyson, who considered himself a bit of a gentleman and hired Magwitch to do his dirty work for him. Compeyson, who had "no more heart than an iron file," kept him busy "swindling, handwriting forging, stolen bank-note passing, and such-like." Slowly, Compeyson involved Magwitch deeper and deeper in his schemes, but Magwitch insists that he was careful never to involve his own wife—of whom we hear no more for the present.

Eventually Compeyson and Magwitch were tried together on a felony charge. Compeyson, however, looking like a perfect gentleman, was recommended for mercy. Compeyson was sentenced to seven years, Magwitch to fourteen. Magwitch swore then that someday he would smash in Compeyson's face, and at last, when he escaped the prison ship and Compeyson followed by the same route, he had his opportunity. Compeyson, Pip realizes, was the *second* convict on the marshes. For escaping, Compeyson was punished lightly but Magwitch was sentenced for life.

While Magwitch explains that he doesn't know whether Compeyson is dead, Herbert hands Pip a note scribbled on the cover of a book: "Young Havisham's name was Arthur. Compeyson is the man who professed to be Miss Havisham's lover."

Commentary

Pip is deeply troubled as to how to protect his "dreaded visitor." Immediately, suspicion is aroused when the door keeper confirms that another person came immediately after Magwitch arrived. Later we learn that Magwitch's every move has been observed since he left New South Wales.

What might have seemed to be too many coincidences at first are somewhat reduced by the fact that Magwitch once used Jaggers as his lawyer. Furthermore, the fact that Jaggers is one of the most famous lawyers of London would partly account for the coincidence that both Miss Havisham and Magwitch used him. However, since the requests of both Miss Havisham and Magwitch are idiosyncratic, it is understandable that both would seek the aid of one of London's most renowned lawyers, and one who is well versed in all types of activities.

When Pip goes to Jaggers for verification of who his benefactor really is, he is still hoping, albeit rather feebly, that Magwitch is *not* the one. Using very careful language so as not to implicate himself, Jaggers is able to confirm that Magwitch of New South Wales is indeed Pip's sole benefactor, and he convinces Pip that he has never given any indication that it was Miss Havisham. Everything was circumstantial evidence, not to be relied upon in a court of law.

In Chapter 42, however, coincidence might test the reader's credulity. As Magwitch tells about his past, the fact that he was once a partner with the man who betrayed Miss Havisham and that both Magwitch and Miss Havisham have been the victims of Compeyson will tend to test one's credulity. However, Magwitch's story creates suspense when the convict refers to a wife with whom he once had some trouble. This clue becomes more important later in tracing Estella's parentage. Further suspense is created by the rumor that Compeyson, Magwitch's enemy, is probably still at large in England and possibly in London.

CHAPTERS 43-44

Summary

Pip speculates on how much of "his shrinking from Provis might be traced to Estella," and to "the abyss between Estella in her pride and beauty, and the returned transport whom [he has] harbored," and decides to see Estella and Miss Havisham one last time before he leaves the country with Provis. Finding that Estella has gone to Satis House alone, Pip goes after her. Arriving at the Blue

Boar by coach, he finds Drummle at the inn; he is down visiting Estella and will dine with her that evening. Pip and Drummle indulge in a bit of childish arguing and pushing one another, then Drummle rides off, and Pip sets out for Satis House.

Miss Havisham seems taken aback at Pip's arrival; why has he come? Pip explains that he has found out at last who his patron is. Miss Havisham admits that she furthered his delusion that she was his benefactress, and asks, "Who am I, for God's sake, that I should be kind?" She states, "You made your own snares. *I* never made them." Pip asks nothing for himself but does ask that she continue the help he has begun for Herbert, which he can no longer continue for reasons which are somebody else's secret, not his. He then turns to Estella and tells her that he has always loved her; to his amazement, he learns that she is soon to be married to Drummle. He pleads eloquently that she "not let Miss Havisham lead you into this fatal step." Estella, calm as usual, explains that it is entirely her idea. Miss Havisham wants her to wait, but she is bored with the life she is leading.

Downhearted, Pip arrives at the porter's gate at his lodgings in London and is given a note in Wemmick's handwriting, which he reads by the porter's lantern: "Don't Go Home."

Commentary

In these chapters, Pip is trying to salvage what he can from his life. He is sorely disappointed that his benefactor for these many years has been a common convict, yet his pride is still with him, even though he recognizes the "abyss between Estella in her pride and beauty" and himself. This same pride earlier made him spurn Joe. But now he uses Joe as an excuse to go back to Miss Havisham's for a final farewell and to confront her with this new knowledge.

In this troubled state of mind, he is even more annoyed to discover that his only enemy (Drummle) is also staying at the inn. The scene between the two is amusing, but not very significant to the novel, except to make it more difficult for Pip to realize that his beloved Estella is giving herself to the scoundrel.

In his interview with Miss Havisham, it is to Pip's credit that he shows no rancor and no hatred after he realizes that he has been used by her. He is calm enough to confront his failing fortunes and try to get help so that Herbert's place in the Clarriker firm will be assured. Again, Pip's generous and thoughtful nature is emphasized as he makes a last effort to benefit a friend.

Pip's confession of the depth of his love for Estella has no effect on the young woman, who has continually warned Pip that she has no feelings. Surprisingly, however, Miss Havisham apparently feels the effect of Pip's deep, genuine words of adoration for Estella and begins to have remorse over her actions, thereby initiating a reversal in her character.

CHAPTERS 45-48

Summary

After spending a night hiding in a miserable inn, Pip hurries early next morning to Walworth, where Wemmick greets him cheerfully and tells him that he has learned that a certain person of not "uncolonial pursuits, and not unpossessed of portable property" has caused a stir by disappearing from his part of the world and that Pip's chambers in Garden Court are being watched. Pip also learns that Compeyson is living in London, and he deduces that Compeyson is involved.

Wemmick, meanwhile, has consulted Herbert and has advised him that Provis should be moved at once to the upper floor of the house in which Herbert's fiancée lives with her invalid father. The place is on the river so that it will be easy to get Provis aboard a ship when the time is ripe and Pip will be able to get regular news of his benefactor through Herbert. Time being short, Provis is already installed; Pip can visit him tonight before going home, but then must stay away. No attempt to get Provis out of the country should be made until things have quieted.

After a peaceful day with the Aged P., Pip sets out for Provis' new quarters. He has difficulty, however, finding Mill Pond Bank, which he knows only to be at Chink's Basin on the river, by the Old Green Copper Rope-Walk, in an area of ship repair yards. Finding the house at last, he is introduced to Herbert's fiancée, Clara, a charming dark-eyed girl of about twenty, obviously devoted to Herbert.

Provis, now lodged as "Campbell," is comfortably settled in two fresh and airy rooms. Pip finds him inexplicably softened. Omitting mention of Compeyson, he tells him what Wemmick has told him. Provis is agreeable to everything, including Pip's not changing his way of living at present, despite the funds in the thick pocketbook. Herbert suggests that Pip get a boat, which they can anchor at Temple stairs. Both of them being good oarsmen, they can make daily trips up and down the river until people are accustomed to seeing them. At the right time, they can take Provis to a ship themselves. Provis approves the scheme. Next day, Pip buys the boat and rowing begins.

Pip, having sent the unopened pocketbook back to Magwitch, has had to begin selling his jewelry. He broods over his last meeting with Estella, but his main worry is the possibility of Magwitch's capture. Weeks of inaction fret him.

One evening, after having rowed downriver and having seen the signal that all is well (a lowered blind), Pip is intercepted by Jaggers, who invites him to dinner, saying Wemmick will also be there. Wemmick, who is as dry and distant to Pip "as if there were twin Wemmicks and this was the wrong one," has a message from Miss Havisham. Pip is to come down on the "little matter of business" he had mentioned to her. Pip does so, and when Molly, the housekeeper, enters the room, Pip suddenly realizes who the nameless shadow is that has been haunting him. Molly's "hands were Estella's hands and her eyes were Estella's eyes." This woman is Estella's mother! As Pip and Wemmick leave, Pip asks about Molly's past history, and Wemmick tells him what he knows. Molly's case was the one which made Jaggers' reputation. It was a desperate case. She was accused of strangling to death an older and much bigger woman out of jealousy over a "tramping man." Jaggers demonstrated that the scratches on Molly's hands could have been caused by brambles, some of which were found embedded there. There was also talk that Molly had killed her own daughter as revenge against this same man, but Jaggers showed that this was not an issue in the trial. The jury gave in, and immediately after her acquittal, Molly went into Jaggers' service, where she has remained ever since.

Commentary

Essentially, these chapters begin to unravel the many complications that have been set up and therefore move the plot on towards its end. Having received the note from Wemmick, Pip goes the next day, and suspense is heightened by the knowledge that Compeyson is indeed in London.

Wemmick also strongly advises Pip to hang onto any "portable property." Both Wemmick and Pip know that if Magwitch is caught, *all* of his property goes to the state. Therefore, in Chapter 47, when Pip returns the money without touching a bit of it even though he is being hounded by creditors, even Pip cannot say whether he did it out of a true or false satisfaction or motive.

While dining at Jaggers', Pip is more convinced than ever that Molly, Jaggers' maid, is really Estella's mother, and upon further inquiry through Wemmick, he is now convinced that this is the truth.

CHAPTERS 49-51

Summary

Pip finds Miss Havisham brooding before the fire in a room across from her own. Although she fears that Pip "can never believe, now, that there is anything human" in her heart, she wishes to show him that she is not made of stone and that she genuinely wants to help Herbert. With difficulty, because her attention wanders, Pip explains the situation in detail. Nine hundred pounds is needed to complete the purchase of Herbert's partnership. After inquiring about Pip's happiness and desiring to help him too, she tells him that it is noble of him to say that he has causes of unhappiness that she knows nothing about; she then gives him a note to take to Jaggers for the money. Handing him the tablets on which she has written, she says, "My name is on the first leaf. If you can ever write under my name, 'I forgive her,' though ever so long after my broken heart is dust—pray do it!"

She then becomes emotional and tells Pip that for years she hoped to save Estella from her own fate, but finally she realizes that she "stole her [Estella's] heart away and put ice in its place." She doesn't know whose child Estella really is. Long ago she asked Jaggers to bring her a little girl to rear and love, and one night he brought the child she called Estella. Of this, Estella knows nothing, and Miss Havisham learned nothing more about Estella.

After parting from Miss Havisham, Pip walks around the place. Disturbed, he stops back to check on her and finds her ablaze; sitting too close to the fire, she ignited her flowing garments. Pip rolls on the floor with her, smothering the flames with his cloak and burning himself severely in the process. When the doctor arrives, he says that she is seriously burned, but that the real danger is nervous shock. She is treated on the table where her cobwebbed wedding cake has rested, the place where she had long before sworn she would be laid out in death one day. During the night she regularly repeats, "What have I done!" and "Take a pencil and write under my name, 'I forgive her,' " a sentence she continues to repeat as Pip kisses her goodbye before taking the early morning coach.

Herbert, who tends to Pip's burns, tells him that Provis has confided in him about the "missis" he spoke of (Chapter 42). She was tried for strangling another woman, a larger and older woman, and her acquittal was won by Jaggers. After the murder she swore to Magwitch that she would destroy her child and vanish until she was caught and tried. Provis believes that she carried out her threat. Compeyson knew the story and used it as a means of keeping his power over Magwitch. This is what "barbed the point of Provis' animosity" toward Compeyson. The girl would now be about Pip's age; Pip's appearance on the marshes when he was seven reminded the convict of his own little lost daughter. As Herbert tells the story, Pip realizes that the man they have in hiding down the river is Estella's father.

Next morning, Pip gives Jaggers the details of Miss Havisham's accident, and he reveals that Miss Havisham has told him all she knows about Estella. But Pip himself knows more about the mystery. He knows who Estella's mother and father are. Jaggers clearly does not know about the father, and he is, for the first time, genuinely startled when Pip says that it is "Provis—from New South Wales." When Jaggers, after Pip's full explanation, drops the subject and proposes to return to work, Pip makes a passionate appeal for more information. Jaggers then reveals that he took the baby to Miss Havisham because this is one child from the many he had seen growing up in a life of crime and poverty that he could save. It had been a secret until Pip got wind of it, and no one, he convinces Pip, particularly Estella, will be helped if the secret goes further. Jaggers and Wemmick then resume work on rather ill terms, which are alleviated only when they combine to throw out a perennially snivelling client.

Commentary

These chapters deal with the continued unraveling of the mystery surrounding Estella's parentage. Pip, for example, receives new information when he goes to visit Miss Havisham. When he first sees her, he is surprised by the tremendous change. She is no longer hard and cynical. Seeing Pip suffer so greatly has renewed all her own suffering and has caused her to realize all the suffering she has caused Pip. As an expression of her regret, she will fulfill Pip's request that Herbert Pocket be helped. Again, even though Pip is deeply in debt, he refuses any financial help from Miss Havisham for himself, and he freely forgives her for everything that she has done to him. Thus, in spite of the manner in which he has treated poor old Joe, Pip is rapidly rising in the estimation of the reader.

During the fire, Pip's attempt to rescue Miss Havisham causes serious burns, which will severely handicap his usefulness in helping

Magwitch to escape. Again, it is to Pip's credit that he takes great personal risks in order to save Miss Havisham. It is furthermore ironic that she is so severely burned because everything is so rotten with age that it crumbled and shredded in Pip's grasp.

With information gathered from Miss Havisham, then from Herbert's narration of Magwitch's wife and child, Pip is able to conclude the parentage of Estella and is able to confront, and for once confound, Jaggers with his discoveries. The only use he will ever make of the information is to delight Magwitch with it on Magwitch's death bed.

CHAPTERS 52-53

Summary

One Monday at breakfast, Pip receives the following letter from Wemmick: "Walworth. Burn this as soon as read. Early in the week, or say Wednesday, you might do what you know of, if you felt disposed to try it. Now burn." Pip and Herbert resolve to do it, and because Pip's arms were disabled by the burns, they take a friend of Pip's to row in place of him. They then study the schedules of all outbound ships in preparation for placing Magwitch aboard one. Pip also plans to go with his benefactor.

Then another note is placed in Pip's box: "If you are not afraid to come to the old marshes to-night or to-morrow night at nine, and to come to the little sluice-house by the limekiln, you had better come. If you want information regarding your Uncle Provis, you had much better come and tell no one and lose no time. You must come alone. Bring this with you." Bewildered, Pip takes the next coach down. Awaiting nighttime, he visits Satis House and is informed that Miss Havisham is "still very ill, though considered something better."

When Pip reaches the sluice-house, there is no answer to his knock. The door is open, so he enters, but he finds himself suddenly trapped by a noose thrown over him from behind and tied securely to a wall. When his assailant lights a candle, Pip sees that it is Orlick, who says that he lured Pip here to kill him. Pip cost him his job as a guard at Miss Havisham's and came between him and Biddy. Orlick means to kill him and then burn his body in the limekiln. Pip, his mind working "with inconceivable rapidity," fears the terrible death ahead of him, but dreads even more the fact that everyone will think that he deserted them, and that he will be "misremembered after death." Orlick, drinking steadily to get his courage up, tells Pip that he now works for Compeyson and that it was he who was hiding on the stairs the night of Magwitch's arrival.

As Orlick comes toward Pip with a stone-hammer in his hand, Pip gives a great shout, and figures burst in as Orlick, emerging "from a struggle of men," runs out into the night. Pip, who faints, revives to find Herbert beside him.

Since there is no time to pursue Orlick, they hurry back to London, treating Pip's painful arm all the way. After a half delirious day and night in bed, Pip wakens early to begin their great adventure.

Commentary

Pip's generosity is finally attested to as he completes the arrangements to have Herbert set up in business, at least as far as he can go at the present moment. To his credit also is his sincere desire to help the man who has been his benefactor. Consequently, Pip feels that it is necessary to check upon the mysterious letter that he receives. His loyalty emerges as a welcome and positive attribute.

On his way to the meeting place, in the marsh country, Pip seems to realize how unfair he has been to Joe and Biddy and he seems to be truly repentant. This might be termed as one of the turning points in his moral regeneration.

We should remember in this section that Orlick has been Pip's evil nemesis since childhood, and the scene, while having little to do at this time with the main plot, allows the reader to know that it definitely was Orlick who gave Mrs. Joe her fatal injury. Other than hearing that he was jailed later for breaking into Mr. Pumblechook's house, we hear no more of Orlick.

CHAPTERS 54-56

Summary

The young men start downriver at nine, when the tide changes. Pip carries a bag filled with "the few necessaries" he will need, come what may. After picking up Magwitch at Mill Pond stairs on schedule and finishing a hard row against the tide, they reach an inn that evening. It is a dirty place, but no one else is in the house.

During the night, Pip is awakened by a noise and sees two men peering into their boat. Next morning, they sight a steamer and are preparing to board it when a four-oared galley shoots out from the bank a little ways beyond them. As the two boats come alongside each other, the galley's steersman calls on them to surrender

Magwitch and drives his boat into theirs. He seizes Magwitch, and Magwitch pulls the cloak from the sitter beside the steersmen, revealing Compeyson. Pip's boat overturns right in the steamer's path. Taken aboard the galley, Pip finds Herbert and their friend, Startop, there; the two convicts are missing. Magwitch soon appears, swimming, and is taken aboard and manacled; he has a severe chest injury and a deep cut in his head. There is no sign of Compeyson.

Back at the inn, Pip gets permission to buy new clothes for Magwitch (whose possessions, including the pocket-book, are confiscated) and to accompany him back to London. "Now," Pip tells us, "my repugnance to him had all melted away, and in the hunted, wounded, shackled creature who held my hand in his, I only saw a man who had meant to be my benefactor, and who had felt affectionately, gratefully, and generously towards me with great constancy through a series of years. I only saw in him a much better man than I had been to Joe."

Magwitch is content to take his chances. "I've seen my boy," he says, "and he can be a gentleman without me." Pip, realizing that all Magwitch's possessions will be confiscated, also understands that Magwitch need never know this.

Despite Jaggers' aid in a hopeless case, Magwitch is indicted. But he remains in ignorance of the fact that Pip will not inherit his property.

Next Monday, Pip meets Wemmick for a morning walk. Wemmick is carrying a fishing rod and says he just likes to walk with it. In quick succession, Wemmick finds a church which he suggests they enter; white gloves in his pocket, which he suggests they put on; Miss Skiffins, whom he suggests marrying; the Aged P., who needs help to get his gloves on; a clergyman; and a ring. The Aged P., despite not hearing the clergyman, manages to give the bride away, and the party repairs to a nearby tavern for an excellent breakfast. "Now, Mr. Pip," Wemmick says, shouldering his fishing-rod, "let me ask you whether anybody would suppose this to be a wedding party!"

Pip regularly visits Magwitch in the prison infirmary. The convict is in great pain, having broken two ribs and suffered a punctured lung, but is uncomplaining. His trial is "very short and very clear": he is guilty. On the last day of the session, the judge picks Magwitch as a prime example of wickedness. Magwitch responds briefly but with dignity. "My Lord," he says, "I have received my sentence of Death from the Almighty, but I bow to yours."

On his last visit Pip finds his benefactor on his deathbed. As the old man is dying, Pip tells him that his daughter is alive. "She lived and found powerful friends. She is living now. She is a lady and very beautiful. And I love her!" Magwitch raises Pip's hand to his lips, and dies.

Commentary

These chapters wind up the complicated plot element of the novel. Dickens is famous for the intricacy of his plots and the major concern at the end of his novels is often the unraveling of all the complexities found in the novel. Thus we have the final attempted escape, the capture of Magwitch, Magwitch's final revenge on his enemy, and his death in prison.

Pip's change is further emphasized in these chapters. When he earlier expected "great expectations," he acted in an incorrigible manner towards Joe and Biddy. Now he has no hopes of great expectations from anyone, so his conduct will be motivated solely by his purer instincts. Thus we see why Dickens had Pip return the money. Had he kept Magwitch's money, he would have been obligated to remain by Magwitch's side. Now that he can expect absolutely nothing, the decision to remain by him redeems Pip in the reader's sight. And his view of Magwitch has also undergone a complete reversal. All of Magwitch's repugnance has disappeared and in "the hunted, wounded, shackled creature," Pip sees only a man who has "felt affectionately, gratefully, and generously" towards him "with a constancy through a series of years." Furthermore, he sees in the convict a loyalty that is sorely missing in his own relationship with Joe.

CHAPTERS 57-59

Summary

Pip, now seriously in debt, gives notice on his chambers and plans to sublet them until his lease runs out. However, he falls seriously ill. Two men come to arrest him for debt, but he is too sick to be moved. When he regains consciousness after weeks of delirium, he finds Joe taking care of him; Biddy sent him down as soon as they learned that Pip was ill.

As he grows stronger, Pip learns that Miss Havisham is dead. She left the bulk of her estate to Estella, but a codicil gives a "cool" four thousand pounds (the phraseology is Joe's) to Matthew Pocket because of Pip's "account of the said Matthew."

Pip's health returns, and Joe becomes more distant and formal, addressing Pip as "Sir" again. Then one morning Pip awakens and finds Joe gone and a letter on the table: "Not wishful to intrude I have departured fur you are well again dear Pip and will do better without Jo. P. S. Ever the best of friends." Inside the note is a receipt for the debt for which Pip had been arrested. Pip knows that he must return to the forge and talk with Joe. He also hopes he can persuade Biddy to marry his old friend.

Walking home slowly, still weakened, Pip is alarmed at not hearing Joe's hammer at the forge. The reason is soon apparent: this is Joe and Biddy's wedding day. Pip congratulates them both in the old kitchen and tells them he will never cease working until he repays Joe the money that kept him out of prison, but that this is only a fraction of his debt to them. He also hopes that they will have a child who "will sit in this chimney-corner, of a winter night, who may remind you of another little fellow gone out of it forever," and who will become a better man than he did.

Back in London, Pip sells everything and goes East to join Herbert, who soon returns to bring Clara back with him. When Pip finally works up to become the third partner, Clarriker tells Herbert how Pip bought his partnership. Their friendship undiminished, Pip begins to realize that the ineptitude he had seen long ago in Herbert had been in himself.

After eleven years, he revisits England and finds Joe and Biddy the same, but parents of a small son, whom they have named Pip, and a daughter. When Biddy asks whether Pip still frets for Estella, he replies that this has all gone by. Nevertheless, after dinner he walks over to the cleared space that was once Satis House. He has heard that Estella, having been cruelly used, separated from Drummle, who was subsequently killed in "an accident consequent on his ill-treatment of a horse." The stars are shining and as Pip looks where the old house was, he sees a solitary figure beside a desolate garden walk: it is Estella.

The Satis House property, the last thing she held on to, is about to be built on, she explains, and she has come to bid it good-bye. Suffering has taught her much. She begs that they may be friends, even if apart.

"I took her hand in mine," Pip concludes, "and we went out of the ruined place; and, as the morning mists had risen long ago when I first left the forge, so the evening mists were rising now, and in all the broad expanse of tranquil light they showed to me, I saw no shadow of another parting from her."

Commentary

The final chapters of most Victorian novels are usually devoted to tidying up the narrative's loose ends and informing the reader of the disposition of all of the characters. *Great Expectations* is no exception. After Joe again demonstrates his generous nature, a true reconciliation is effected between Pip and Joe and Biddy. After the years of unhappiness between Joe and Mrs. Joe, he has now made a good marriage with Biddy. Herbert and Clara are also married, and Pip, after eleven years in the East, returns to England, meets Estella at Satis House, and realizes that she has been disciplined by life and made into a worthier person. In the "standard edition" ending, Pip sees "the shadow of no parting from her." This ending was written at the suggestion of one of Dickens' friends as being more appropriate for the reading public. In the original ending, Pip meets Estella in London and sees that she is greatly changed. She left Drummle and, after his death, married a doctor. They exchange gentle words with each other and then part forever. Dickens described the change this way: "I have put in as pretty a little piece of writing as I could, and I have no doubt the story will be more acceptable through the alteration."

CRITICAL ANALYSIS

THEME

The basic theme of *Great Expectations* is that true goodness does not come from social station or wealth; it comes from inner worth. Joe and Biddy illustrate this; so does Abel Magwitch. Pip has to learn it the hard way. His salvation is that, for all his ignorance during the days when he is a gentleman with great expectations, he finally does learn. Estella learns the hard way too, in both of Dickens' endings for this novel. One of the virtues of the original ending, however, is that it shows Pip as having discovered that one of the prices of finding his own worth is giving up his illusions.

For Dickens, a necessary corollary to this basic theme was that wealth and position are corrupting. He has been severely criticized for hypocrisy about this view—a charge that a man who was writing a novel to save his own magazine and to preserve his comfortable existence as the squire of Gad's Hill obviously left himself open to. Despite his few early years of hardship, Dickens never personally turned his back on wealth and position. George Orwell, the author of *1984*, states the case very strongly; Dickens' real allegiance, he says, was to the "shabby genteel."

The trouble with this view is that it confuses the man with the book. Regardless of Dickens' personal habits, there is no doubt of what he was trying to say in *Great Expectations*. The good people are for the most part the working people and the rebels. Joe Gargery and Abel Magwitch, different as they are, both epitomize this. It is no accident that Compeyson, Magwitch's great enemy, passes for a gentleman while Magwitch is a "warmint."

It is very easy to oversimplify all this. In fact, critics have made a career of oversimplifying Dickens. There are ambiguities throughout the novel. Magwitch, convict and rebel that he is, spends—and loses—his life trying to make Pip a gentleman. Orlick, a journeyman blacksmith, is a villain. Herbert Pocket, poor but genteel, is a naturally good man. The point is that Dickens wrote about *people*, some of them good, some of them bad. It is also, however, important to understand the general drift of his sympathies without falling into the error of assuming that he wrote a tract rather than a novel.

This brings us back to the reasons for Dickens' success as a popular novelist. We have already noted that part of the reason was his enormous skill at characterization and plot structure. But this was only part of it. The other ingredient was his universal theme, exemplified in this novel as in all his others. Dickens was no social reformer, though much paper has been used up in analyzing him in these terms. He had passionate convictions about many social questions and a passionate hatred of such institutions as courts, jails, and the law in general. But these feelings stemmed from a much more fundamental point of view.

Dickens was a sentimental, complicated man with strong moral feelings which he frequently failed to live up to himself. His formal schooling was very limited, as was his knowledge of literature, the arts, and a considerable segment of English society—the upper classes. Note that during the whole of Pip's career in London learning to become a gentleman, we never see him actually engaged in any "gentlemanly" activities, unless the dinner with the Finches of the Grove, which is only a pretext for an encounter with Drummle, can be termed such. But what Dickens did know—the life of the common man in London, the plight of those who fall afoul of the law, and how life was for the ordinary man in the country villages—he knew accurately.

But his readers also understood something else. Stripped to its essentials, the moral structure of this private world could almost be described as a Victorian melodrama. It was Good versus Evil, the honest and loyal man against the selfish schemer. His audience reveled in this, just as today's American audiences revel nightly in cowboy, detective, and similar shows on television. And this is intended as no slur on Dickens. This antithesis is the basis of the greater part of literature. What matters is how it is treated. If in Dickens the lines were generally sharper, the opposites simpler and more clear cut, he nevertheless used this polarity as a vehicle for his characterization, his plot structure, and his style.

PLOT STRUCTURE

To understand Dickens' incredible skill at this complicated art, we must understand his method of composition. From the beginning, Dickens wrote for publication in periodicals for a very simple reason. This is where the quickest money was, and Dickens always, like many writers, needed quick money, "portable property," in Wemmick's favorite phrase. However, serialization in Dickens' time was utterly unlike the same thing today. The author would often end his narrative for the magazine upon what was called a "cliff-hanger"—that is, the end of a magazine episode would end in such a manner as to cause the reading public to anxiously await the next edition of the magazine to discover "what happened." For example, at the end of Chapter 4, when Mrs. Joe misses the pork pie and is wondering about its theft, there is a knock at the door and when Pip answers the door, he is confronted with a constable holding out a pair of handcuffs. The implication is that Pip has been discovered as the thief. The reader, however, must wait until the next edition of the magazine to discover what has happened. In this way the magazine was insured a continued circulation. Nowadays, an author often finishes a book first and then sells the serial rights. Dickens, in contrast, stayed just one jump ahead of his deadlines, so that most of the book would be in print before the final chapter had even been written.

In spite of this, his plot structure in this novel is impeccable. As has been noted in the comments on individual chapters, all the basic plot lines have been set out by the end of Chapter 11, and the principal characters have appeared on stage. This is a remarkable achievement for any author; for a man who was rushing serial chapters into print, it is truly incredible.

STYLE

There is no part of Dickens' art, especially in the later novels, that has been less appreciated than his ability as a stylist. This is better illustrated than simply commented on. A suitable example is this one from Chapter 45, where Pip is staying at Hummums after Wemmick's warning: "Don't Go Home."

"There was an inhospitable smell in the room of cold soot and hot dust; and, as I looked up into the corners of the tester over my head, I thought what a number of bluebottle flies from the butcher's, and earwigs from the market, and grubs from the country, must be holding on up there, lying by for next summer. This led me to speculate whether any of them ever tumbled down, and then I fancied that I felt light falls on my face—a disagreeable turn of thought, suggesting other and more objectionable approaches up my back. When I had lain awake a little while, those extraordinary voices with which silence teems began to make themselves audible. The closet whispered, the fireplace sighed, the little washing-stand ticked, and one guitar-string played occasionally in the chest of drawers. At about the same time, the eyes on the wall acquired a new expression, and in every one of those staring rounds I saw written, DON'T GO HOME."

The point about this kind of writing is not simply Dickens' marvelously precise use of words. The important thing is that Dickens transcends this precision. He manages to make the physical scene a part of the psychological experience of the person involved. Pip's inner fears and confusions are described in terms of the *furniture*. This goes beyond the standard novelistic technique of identifying a person's role and station by the kind of surroundings he chooses to have around him.

SOCIAL CRITICISM

So much has been written about Dickens as a social critic that one sometimes feels such commentators have forgotten that he was a novelist, not a reformer. He had, as we have earlier noted, passionate convictions about many social matters, and these constantly recur in his novels. But he had no interest in plunging himself into the committed and demanding life of the reformer. He was much more interested in writing, in acting and its offshoot, his readings, and in living the good life as the Squire of Gad's Hill. His social concerns were a part of his general moral concern, but only a part, and we misread him if we try to separate the social protest out from the whole. Fagin's mistreatment of Oliver in *Oliver Twist* and Mrs. Joe's mistreatment of Pip in *Great Expectations* are, in human terms, the same. It is people that Dickens is primarily interested in.

Consider the law and the penal system, Dickens' prime targets for social criticism in *Great Expectations*. Without question he gives them their come-uppance, even going out of his way (in Chapter 32) to get Pip inside Newgate, at the same time utilizing this diversion with his customary skill to juxtapose Estella with the life of crime Pip believes her to be so remote from. But what he is really interested in is the remarkable characters involved in this process—Jaggers, Wemmick, and Magwitch. It is not correct to call his social criticisms incidental, but they *are* secondary.

In passing, it is worth noting that Dickens was not really writing about his own day at all. By 1860, for example, the railroad age was well advanced in England, but in *Great Expectations* the standard means of travel is by coach.

CHARACTER ANALYSES

With the possible exceptions of Dostoevsky and Faulkner, there has been no writer of fiction in the Western world who had Dickens' genius for creating such an infinite variety of characters. Part of this, of course, is a result of the sheer bulk of his work, but primarily it is a tribute to his inventiveness. Characters sprang from Dickens' mind full-blown, like Athena from the brow of Zeus. One of the hardest jobs for a writer of a guide to Dickens' novels is to keep the discussion of characters within reasonable bounds. The problem is not merely that there are so many of them; it is that they are all so interesting.

It was this ability, plus his amazing aptitude for plot structure, which in part accounted for his enormous success as a popular novelist. The point that many of his critics have missed, however, is that all these people, no matter how briefly sketched, are *real*. They are generally outlined with very clear characteristics—Jaggers, for example, points with his great forefinger, buries his nose in his handkerchief, apparently equivocates, but moves ruthlessly to the end of whatever business he is about. Nevertheless, there is also a great subtlety in the depiction of Jaggers. His kindness to Estella, Molly, Miss Havisham, and Pip, for example, does not fit the stereotype Dickens first seems to have made of him.

As a result, Dickens put more enduring characters into the minds of English and American readers than any writer since Shakespeare. This alone would insure his greatness.

Pip (Philip Pirrip)

One of the most interesting things about Pip is that he is the only character in the novel of whom we have no physical description whatever. Dickens was a master of quick characterization through appearance, but we never learn what Pip looks like.

There is nothing accidental about this. What Dickens is interested in is Pip's *interior*. His concern is the changes that take place inside Pip. Dickens' usual habit is to give his characters sharply marked physical characteristics which reflect their moral attitudes. Generally they stay in character throughout. Pip does none of these things. He changes, radically: he moves from a frightened and selfish innocence, to the snobbery and pretense of being a manufactured gentleman, to the wisdom that the convict Magwitch's basic goodness finally forces on him.

The external facts of Pip's life are very simple, despite the series of dramatic episodes he participates in. An orphan who never saw his parents, for reasons which are not explained, he is raised "by hand" by his sister, Mrs. Joe Gargery, befriended by her husband, the village blacksmith, and begins his career by finding a convict, Abel Magwitch, on the marshes one morning when he has gone out to visit his parents' graves. This sets off a series of events which includes his association with Miss Havisham and his fascination by Estella, his great expectations, which he finally learns have been provided by Magwitch, and his eventual discovery, after Magwitch's capture and death, that his convict was one of the five genuinely good people he has ever known. The others are Biddy, Joe Gargery, Herbert Pocket, and John Wemmick. The point of the novel is that Pip himself finally becomes a good man.

Miss Havisham

We never learn her first name. She is the daughter of a wealthy brewer; her brother Arthur, a ne'er-do-well, has conspired with the book's villain, Compeyson, to swindle her through a fraudulent engagement. When Compeyson does not show up for the wedding, Miss Havisham stops all the clocks in the house at the precise time his letter of regret arrived, twenty minutes to nine, and spends the rest of her life in her yellowed bridal gown, wearing only one shoe because she had not yet put on the other at the time of the disaster, and educating Estella, her adopted daughter, to wreak her revenge on men.

At the time Pip first meets her, she is a gaunt, white-haired woman with wild eyes. She remains this to the end. She undergoes a superficial change, but, unlike Pip's, it is not a real one. What she discovers is remorse when she finds that she has made Estella into a girl with a heart of ice. But this too is in character. She has always been an utterly self-centered person, and her dismay about Estella reflects her realization of the fact that by making the girl unable to love, she has made her unable to love *her*. She is undoubtedly insane, and in a well-regulated modern world would have been committed long ago. Dickens' readers can be thankful that in Victorian England, eccentrics, as they were then called, were left alone as long as they stayed indoors. Miss Havisham did, and died there. But she remains one of the most enduring characters in the novel.

Joe Gargery

Joe is a rather incredible characterization. Any writer knows that it is much easier to depict bad people than good ones: bad people are generally more complicated and therefore more interesting. A standard critical commentary on Milton's *Paradise Lost*, for example, is that Lucifer is the most interesting character in the poem. Nevertheless, Joe, a rough giant who is unalloyed goodness, is one of the most alive characters Dickens ever created.

Joe grew up the son of a lovable but drunken father and had to quit school to support his mother. Until he married Biddy, he never learned to read or write. But he has great native intelligence, as well as formidable skills as a blacksmith. He considers himself simple, but his conversation, which Dickens renders impeccably, shows him to be just the opposite. He is whole-hearted, a considerably different thing. He submits to Mrs. Joe's rampages because he feels an obligation to be good to women, and because he would rather have her wrath fall on him than on Pip. He is, in his own words, "ever the best of friends" with Pip—a man to cherish.

Abel Magwitch

Magwitch, besides being central to the book, is also one of its most interesting characters. Unlike Joe, his image is ambiguous. Superficially he seems all bad. Most of his life he has been a prisoner or a convict; he is the latter throughout the novel. When Pip first encountered him on the marshes, he was "a fearful man, all in coarse gray, with a great iron on his leg." When Magwitch arrives in London years later, to inform Pip, in his new guise as "Provis," that he has been his benefactor, Pip finds him equally revolting and refuses, foolishly, to take anything from him.

Underneath, however, Abel Magwitch is a tender and generous man. The father of Estella, the husband of Molly (Jaggers' housekeeper), the enemy of Compeyson, and the creator of Pip's great expectations, Magwitch dies, denounced by the law (Chapter 56) but beloved by his foster son, Pip.

Estella Havisham

Estella has had a hard and undeserved time at the hands of critics. She becomes precisely what Miss Havisham educated her to be—a girl with a heart of ice. But she also, as she grows up, develops a basic honesty that is admirable. In contrast to her treatment of Pip as a child, when she had called him a common laboring-boy with coarse hands and thick boots, she tries to explain to him that emotion is something she is incapable of feeling. She says the same thing to Miss Havisham. The fact that neither of them understands her is evidence of their illusions, not her cruelty.

Estella is beautiful and intelligent, and she becomes a lady. She marries a boor, Drummle, out of malice aforethought. "Should I fling myself away," she tells Pip (Chapter 44) "on the man who would the soonest feel (if people do feel such things) that I took nothing to him?" That man would have been Pip, even though, he cannot understand it. But Estella's honesty, in these situations, is a part of her ironic heritage from her father, Abel Magwitch, a convict, and her mother, Molly, a murderess. What Dickens is trying to say through Estella is that a potentially good woman has been warped through a pseudo-aristocratic education grounded in hate.

Molly

We learn very little about Molly except the details of her crime: she murdered an older woman out of jealousy over Magwitch, and Jaggers got her off; she became Jaggers' housekeeper immediately afterwards, a wild beast whom the lawyer tamed; she is also Estella's mother. Her resemblance to Estella makes Pip eventually realize that she is indeed Estella's mother. Her chief physical characteristic is her immensely strong wrists.

Mr. Jaggers

In a novel full of strong characters, he is one of the strongest. He is burly, has a great forefinger which he is always aiming at people while he is making a point, often gestures with a large silk handkerchief which he employs any time he needs to stall, and he washes frequently with scented soap.

He is also perhaps the most intelligent man in the book. Jaggers is the epitome of the shrewd, arrogant, and careful lawyer. He never commits himself to anything, and he is apparently interested only in things which will make money for him. But he also saves Estella from a foredoomed criminal career, takes in Molly when the easiest thing would have been to forget about her, and treats Pip with a kindness which this young man is not at the time equipped to understand.

Dickens hated the courts and lawyers. His trouble with Jaggers was that he fell in love with his own creation. Undoubtedly he started out to make Jaggers a parody of all the parts of the law that he hated. But Jaggers got too big to be a parody and became a man in his own right—a transformation for which we should all be grateful.

Uncle Pumblechook

Of all the distasteful characters that Dickens ever created, Pumblechook is a good candidate for the top of the list. He is the classic humbug. Through him Dickens, again speaking for the underprivileged, is saying that the small-time operator who has hustled his way to success in a little business can be depended on to be untruthful. Pumblechook represents that subsection of the rising middle class that Dickens particularly detested. Pumblechook, a corn and seed merchant, thinks he has helped Pip achieve his great expectations and fawns over Pip, but runs him down to everyone when Pip does not show proper "gratitude." Actually, he had no hand in Pip's good fortune.

John Wemmick

He is one of the novel's genuinely good people. He, too, is carefully typed, but in two roles. The "London Wemmick" is absolutely precise, has a mouth like "a postbox," and follows the coldly businesslike methods he has learned from his master, Jaggers. The "Walworth Wemmick" is relaxed, gentle, and completely devoted to his father, the "Aged Parent." As his home, he has constructed an imitation castle with a moat a few feet wide, and a cannon, the Stinger, which Wemmick fires every night at precisely nine because it's the only thing the Aged can hear.

With Pip, Wemmick breaks the dichotomy of his existence to give him Walworth help in London. He also invites Pip to his marriage, in one of the most charming chapters of the book (Chapter 55). He is the source, unwittingly, of the misinformation that leads to Magwitch's capture.

Mr. Wopsle

While it is not correct to say that any of Dickens' characters has no function in the plot—he puts them all to work—Wopsle comes close. A former parish clerk with a fine voice and ambitions for the stage, Wopsle grows steadily in Dickens' mind all through the story. At first he is only a spear carrier: his function is to provide comic relief in the small society of Pip's unnamed village. Later, having become a London actor under the name of "Mr. Waldengarver," a mediocre Hamlet and buffoon, he serves as the means of alerting Pip to the fact that Compeyson is tailing him.

REVIEW QUESTIONS

1. How does the atmosphere and setting in the early chapters of the novel enhance the emotional states of the orphan and the convict?

2. How is Joe's profession as a blacksmith initially important to the plot?

3. How does Dickens suggest a measure of sympathy for Magwitch when we first encounter him?

4. Discuss the "victimization" theme, in regard to Magwitch, Joe, and Pip.

5. How would the novel change if Pip refused to help Magwitch?

6. Discuss the hostility between Magwitch and Compeyson.

7. How does Magwitch return Pip's goodness?

8. What is Magwitch's sentence after he is apprehended?

9. Why is Estella so cold to Pip?

10. Describe Miss Havisham and her house.

11. Why is Pip so fascinated by Estella?

12. What role does Matthew Pocket play in Pip's growing up?

13. Who is the "pale young gentleman" whom Pip meets and what particular quality does Pip discern about him?

14. Discuss Miss Havisham's relatives and her attitude towards them.

15. Why does Pip believe that Miss Havisham is probably his benefactor?

16. What is Orlick's role in the novel? Why are he and Pip antagonistic to one another?

60

17. Why does Biddy move into Mrs. Joe's household?

18. Why does Pip treat Joe so snobbishly?

19. What sort of lawyer is Jaggers? What is his relationship with Pip?

20. Describe Pip's first impression of London.

21. How does Dickens arouse and sustain our interest in Molly, Jaggers' housekeeper?

22. What is the function of Dickens' depiction of Newgate Prison in the novel?

23. What is the irony of Pip's thinking of Estella as superior to the Newgate setting?

24. Describe Pip's generosity in regard to Herbert Pocket; be specific.

25. What is Pip's reaction when he discovers the true identity of his benefactor?

26. Where and why in the narrative line does Dickens insert mention of Magwitch's "missis" and Compeyson?

27. How is Pip rescued from Orlick?

28. Describe Miss Havisham's last months.

29. How is she involved in Herbert's future?

30. What happens to Compeyson?

31. Discuss Pip's reconciliation with Joe and Biddy.

32. Which of Dickens' endings for *Great Expectations* do you prefer and why?

33. Discuss Dickens' use of either humor or irony in the novel.

34. What is the moral lesson of the novel?

35. What is your favorite episode in the novel? Find examples and details of style and characterization that make the episode effective.

SELECTED BIBLIOGRAPHY

Chesterton, Gilbert Keith. *Charles Dickens*. New York: Schocken Books, 1965.

Engel, Monroe. *The Maturity of Dickens*. Cambridge, Massachusetts: Harvard University Press, 1959.

Fielding, K. J. *Charles Dickens: A Critical Introduction*. New York: David McKay Co., 1958.

Forster, John. *The Life of Charles Dickens*, 2 vols. New York: E. P. Dutton, 1928.

Gissing, George. *Critical Studies of the Works of Charles Dickens*. New York, Greenberg, 1924.

House, Humphry. *The Dickens World*, 2nd ed. New York: Oxford University Press, 1960.

Huxley, Aldous. *Vulgarity in Literature*. London: Chatto and Windus, 1930.

Johnson, Edgar. *Charles Dickens: His Tragedy and Triumph*, 2 vols. New York: Simon and Schuster, 1953. (The standard biography).

Leacock, Stephen. *Charles Dickens: His Life and Work*. Garden City, New York: Doubleday, Doran, 1934.

Ley, J. W. T. *The Dickens Circle*. London: Chapman and Hall, 1919.

Miller, J. Hillis. *Charles Dickens: The World of His Novels*. Cambridge, Massachusetts: Harvard University Press, 1959.

Nisbet, Ada. *Dickens and Ellen Ternan*. Berkeley: University of California Press, 1952.

Orwell, George. *Dickens, Dali and Others*. New York: Harcourt, Brace, 1946.

Pearson, Hesketh. *Dickens: His Character, Comedy, and Career*. New York: Harper and Brothers, 1949.

Pope-Hennessy, Una. *Charles Dickens: 1812-1870*. London: Howell, Soskin, 1946.

Van Ghent, Dorothy. *The English Novel: Form and Function*. New York: Holt, Rinehart and Winston, 1953.

Wilson, Edmund. *The Wound and the Bow*. New York: Oxford University Press, 1947.

Great Expectations Genealogy

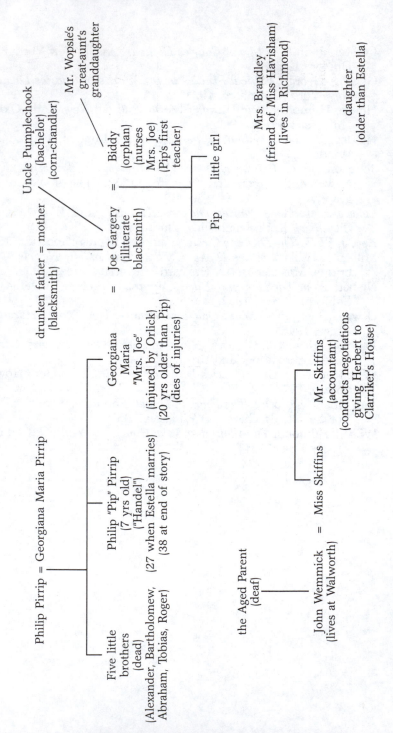

Great Expectations Genealogy

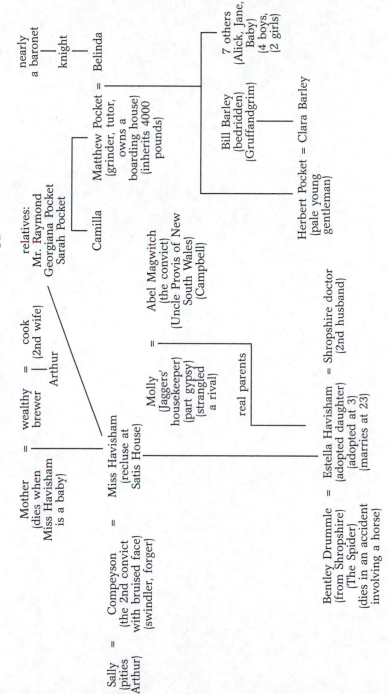

Hard Times

HARD TIMES

NOTES

including
- *Introduction*
- *Life of the Author*
- *Background Material*
- *Character Analyses*
- *Significance of Setting*
- *Summaries and Commentaries*
- *Dickens' Philosophy and Style*
- *Questions for Review*

by
Josephine J. Curton, Ph.D.
Department of English
Tallahassee Community College

INCORPORATED

LINCOLN, NEBRASKA   68501

Editor

Gary Carey, M.A.
University of Colorado

Consulting Editor

James L. Roberts, Ph.D.
Department of English
University of Nebraska

ISBN 0-8220-0578-6
© Copyright 1964
by
C. K. Hillegass
All Rights Reserved
Printed in U.S.A.

1992 Printing

Cliffs Notes, Inc.   Lincoln, Nebraska

CONTENTS

HARD TIMES

INTRODUCTION

When you read *Hard Times,* you may, at first, decide that its title is inappropriate to the story. The names of the characters, the exaggerated situations, and the satire make for delightful reading; however, it is not a novel for mere entertainment. It is a novel of protest; its voice is that of nineteenth-century English workers.

"Why," you may ask, "should I read a novel concerned with the problems of another era?" The answer is simple: from the literature of the past one learns how better to deal with the present.

These notes are not a substitute for reading *Hard Times;* they are only guides to your understanding of the novel. After all, who would wish to become a member of the school of *FACTS* and deprive himself of the adventure of reading and learning that there is *FANCY* in the world too?

ABOUT THE AUTHOR

The title of Charles Dickens' novel *Hard Times* is an apt designation of his early life and youth. Born February 7, 1812, the boy was one of eight children. His formal education was scanty, but as a child Charles spent much of his time reading and listening to the stories told by his grandmother. His reading included works by Daniel Defoe, Samuel Richardson, Henry Fielding, Oliver Goldsmith, and Tobias Smollett — all outstanding English novelists. Too, young Dickens frequently attended and enjoyed the theater with his uncle.

Charles' father, John Dickens, was a poor manager; consequently, after failing at many jobs, he was arrested and sent to debtor's prison at Marshalsea. All of the family furniture and possessions were sold and Charles went to work in a blackening warehouse. In this job he was treated as a drudge. His mother and family went to Marshalsea; however, Charles, feeling that living in debtors' prison was degrading, did not stay with them, but lived nearby. When the Insolvent Debtors Act resulted in John Dickens' discharge from prison, the family fared better than it had in a long time.

After his father's release, Charles went to school; then he began to work as a clerk for an attorney. Determined to raise his standard of living, he studied shorthand and became a court reporter. Later he began to work for the *Morning Chronicle*. His *Sketches by Boz* (1834-36), which appeared in the *Chronicle*, brought him fame. From this beginning he wrote many books, all of which utilized as characters his own family and people he met. He used for his themes and plots both the working conditions and the social conditions of his time. His Christmas stories, of which *A Christmas Carol* (1843) is most famous, were the only ones which did not describe the plight of his contemporaries. In 1867 he achieved the standard of living which he had set out to attain: he received one hundred thousand dollars for a lecture tour in America. After his return to England in 1870, he died suddenly at the dinner table. Medical men attributed his death to overexertion. Leaving behind a family of four children and a wife to mourn him, Charles Dickens — blackening house apprentice and poor lower middle-class boy — was buried in Westminster Abbey beside other great figures of English literature.

Dickens left behind a large number of much-loved novels, including *Oliver Twist* (1837-39), which satirized the conditions and institutions of the time; *The Old Curiosity Shop* (1840-41), one of the most widely known works in all literature; and *Martin Chuzzlewit* (1843-44), in which Dickens reported his impressions of America. Mrs. Roylance, an early landlady of the author's, appears in *Dombey and Son* (1846-48). *David Copperfield* (1849-50) drew heavily on the writer's own experiences. In *Bleak House* (1852-53) one sees reflected the sorrow that Dickens felt over the deaths of his sister and daughter. In *Hard Times* (1854) he skillfully combined many literary techniques to produce a great novel of social protest. His *Little Dorrit* (1855-57) describes the arrest and imprisonment of his own father. In *A Tale of Two Cities* (1859) a triangle love plot is developed against the background of the French Revolution. *Great Expectations* (1860-61) narrates the growing up of a boy under conditions of mystery and suspense. Dickens' last volume, *Life of Our Lord,* a book for children, was not published until 1934.

In all of his novels — those that appeared as serials in newspapers or magazines and those that were first printed as whole books — Dickens reveals his keen observation, his great understanding of human nature, and his varied techniques of style. True, his characters are sometimes exaggerated; however, the very exaggeration adds vitality and humor to the stories. As a novelist and a social critic, Dickens was a giant of his era; later generations have turned to his works for both amusement and instruction.

BACKGROUND MATERIAL FOR UNDERSTANDING *HARD TIMES*

Since Charles Dickens wrote of the conditions and the people of his time, it is worthwhile to understand the period in which he lived and worked.

No British sovereign since Queen Elizabeth I has exerted such a profound influence on an age as did Queen Victoria (1837-1901). She presided over the period rather than shaped it. The nineteenth century was an age of continual change and unparalleled expansion in almost every field of activity. Not only was it an era of reform, industrialization, achievement in science, government, literature, and world expansion but also a time when man struggled to assert his independence. Man, represented en masse as the laboring class, rose in power and prosperity and gave his voice to government.

There were great intellectual and spiritual disturbances both in society and within the individual. The literature of the period reflects the conflict between the advocates of the triumphant material prosperity of the country and those who felt it had been achieved by the exploitation of human beings at the expense of spiritual and esthetic values. In theory, men of the period committed themselves on the whole to a hard-headed utilitarianism, yet most of the literature is idealistic and romantic.

The prophets of the time deplored the inroads of science upon religious faith; but the Church of England was revivified by the Oxford Movement; evangelical Protestantism was never stronger and more active; and the Roman Catholic Church was becoming an increasingly powerful religious force in England.

Not even in politics were the issues clear-cut. The Whigs prepared the way for the great economic reform of the age, the repeal of the Corn Laws; but it was a Tory leader, Sir Robert Peel, who finally brought that repeal through Parliament.

This century, marked by the Industrial Revolution, was also a century of political and economic unrest in the world: America was torn by the strife of the Civil War; France was faced with the problem of recovery from the wars of Napoleon; and Germany was emerging as a great power.

The Industrial Revolution, though productive of much good, created deplorable living conditions in England. Overcrowding in the cities as a consequence of the population shift from rural to urban areas and the increase in the numbers of immigrants from poverty-stricken Ireland resulted in disease and hunger for thousands of the laboring class. But with the fall of Napoleon, the returning soldiers added not only to the growing numbers of workers but also to the hunger and misery. With the advent of the power loom came unemployment. A surplus labor supply caused wages to drop. Whole families, from the youngest to the oldest, had to enter the factories, the woolen mills, the coal mines, or the cotton mills in order to survive. Children were exploited by employers; for a pittance a day a nine-year-old worked twelve and fourteen hours in the mills, tied to the machines, or in the coal mines pulling carts to take the coal from the shafts. Their fingers were smaller and quicker than those of adults; thus, for picking out the briars and burrs from both cotton and wool, employers preferred to hire children.

Studies of the working and living conditions in England between 1800 and 1834 showed that 82 percent of the workers in the mills were between the ages of eleven and eighteen. Many of these studies proved that 62 percent of the workers in the fabric mills had tuberculosis. The factories were open, barnlike structures, not equipped with any system of heat and ventilation.

These studies, presented to Parliament, resulted in some attempt to bring about reforms in working conditions and to alleviate some of the dire poverty in England. In 1802 the Health Act was passed to provide two hours of instruction for all apprentices. In 1819 a child labor law was enacted which limited to eleven hours a day the working hours of children five to eleven years of age; however, this law was not enforced.

The first great "Victorian" reform antedated Queen Victoria by five years. Until 1832 the old Tudor list of boroughs was still in use. As a result, large towns of recent growth had no representation in Parliament, while some unpopulated localities retained theirs. In essence, the lords who controlled these boroughs (known as rotten boroughs in history) sold seats to the highest bidders. This political pattern was broken when the Reform Bill of 1832 abolished all boroughs with fewer than two thousand inhabitants and decreased by 50 percent the number of representatives admitted from towns with a population between two thousand and four thousand. Only after rioting and a threat of civil war did the House of Lords approve the Reform Bill. With this bill came a new type of Parliament —one with representatives from the rising middle class—and several other important reforms.

In 1833 the Emancipation Bill ended slavery in British colonies, with heavy compensation to the owners. Even though chattel slavery was abolished, industrial slavery continued. Also in 1833 came the first important Factory Law, one which prohibited the employment of children under the age of nine. Under this law children between the ages of nine and thirteen could not work for more than nine hours a day. Night work was prohibited for persons under twenty-one years of age and for all women. By 1849 subsequent legislation provided half day or alternate days of schooling for the factory children, thus cutting down the working hours of children fourteen or under.

The Poor Law of 1834 provided for workhouses; indigent persons, accustomed to living where they pleased, bitterly resented this law, which compelled them to live with their families in workhouses. In fact, the living conditions were so bad that these workhouses were named the "Bastilles of the Poor." Here the poor people, dependent upon the government dole, were subjected to the inhuman treatment of cruel supervisors; an example is Mr. Bumble in Dickens' *Oliver Twist*. If the people rejected this rule of body and soul, they had two alternatives as the machines took more jobs and the wages dropped — either steal or starve. Conditions in prisons were even more deplorable than in the workhouses. Debtors' prison, as revealed in Dickens' *David Copperfield,* was a penalty worse than death.

The undemocratic character of the Reform Bill of 1832, the unpopularity of the Poor Law, and the unhappy conditions of the laborers led to the Chartist Movement of the 1840's. The demands of the Chartist Movement were the abolition of property qualifications for members of Parliament, salaries for members of Parliament, annual election of Parliament, equal electoral districts, equal manhood suffrage, and voting by secret ballot. Chartism, the most formidable working-class movement England had ever seen, failed. The Chartists had no way to identify their cause with the interests of any influential class. Ultimately, though, most of the ends they sought were achieved through free discussion and legislative action.

In 1846 the Prime Minister, Sir Robert Peel, led the repeal of the Corn Laws of 1815. With the repeal of these laws, which were nothing more than protective tariffs in the interest of the landlords and farmers to prevent the importation of cheap foreign grain, came a period of free trade and a rapid increase in manufacture and commerce which gave the working class an opportunity to exist outside the workhouses.

As the country awoke to the degradation of the working classes, industrial reform proceeded gradually but inevitably, in spite of the advocates of laissez-faire and industrial freedom. The political life of the nineteenth century was tied up with its economic theories. The doctrine of laissez-faire (let alone), first projected by Adam

Smith's *Wealth of Nations,* was later elaborated upon by Jeremy Bentham and T. R. Malthus, whose doctrine of Utility was the principle of "the greatest happiness for the greatest number." In other words, this principle meant that the government should allow the economic situation to adjust itself naturally through the laws of supply and demand. With this system, a man at one extreme becomes a millionaire and at the other, a beggar. Thomas Carlyle called this system of economy "the dismal science." Dickens, influenced by Carlyle, castigated it again and again. The Utilitarians, however, helped bring about the repeal of the Corn Laws and to abolish cruel punishment. When Victoria became queen there were four hundred and thirty-eight offenses punishable by death. During her reign, the death penalty was limited to two offenses—murder and treason. With the softening of the penalties and the stressing of prevention and correction came a decrease in crime.

Even though writers of the period protested human degradation under modern industrialism, the main factor in improvement of conditions for labor was not outside sympathy but the initiative taken by the workers themselves. They learned that organized trade unions were more constructive to their welfare than riots and the destruction of machines, which had occurred during the Chartist Movement. Gradually the laboring classes won the right to help themselves. Trade unions were legalized in 1864; two workingmen candidates were elected to Parliament in 1874.

Karl Marx founded the first International Workingmen's Association in London in 1864; three years later he published *Das Kapital,* a book of modern communism. In 1884 the Fabian Society appeared, headed by Beatrice and Sidney Webb, George Bernard Shaw, and other upper middle-class intellectuals. The Fabians believed that socialism would come about gradually without violence.

Once the rights of the workers were recognized, education became of interest to Parliament. In 1870 the Elementary Education Bill provided education for all; in 1891 free common education for all became compulsory. Poet George Meredith and economist and philosopher John Stuart Mill worked for "female emancipation." From this period of change came such women as Florence Nightingale and Frances Powers.

Politics and economics do not make up the whole of a nation's life. In the nineteenth century both religion and science affected the thought and the literature of the period. In 1833, after the Reform Bill of 1832, a group of Oxford men, dissatisfied with the conditions of the Church of England, began the Oxford Movement with the purpose of bringing about in the Church a reformation which would increase spiritual power and emphasize and restore the Catholic doctrine and ritual. Begun by John Keble, the movement carried on its reforms primarily through a series of papers called *Tracts for the Times*. Chief among the reformers was John Henry Newman, a vicar of St. Mary's.

The second half of Queen Victoria's reign was one of prosperity and advancement in science. Inventions such as the steam engine, the telephone, telegraph, and the wireless made communication easier and simpler. Man became curious about and interested in the unknown. New scientific and philosophic research in the fields of geology and biology influenced the religious mind of England. A series of discoveries with respect to man's origin challenged accepted opinions regarding the universe and man's place in it. Sir Charles Lyell's *Principles of Geology* (1830-33) established a continuous history of life on this planet; Sir Frances Galton did pioneer work in the field of heredity; Charles Darwin's *Origin of Species* gave the world the theory of evolution. *The Origin of Species* maintained that all living creatures had developed through infinite differentiations from a single source. This one work had the most profound influence of all secular writings on the thinking of the period. Following its publication there were three schools of thought concerning man's origin: first, Darwin's evidence did not justify his conclusions; therefore, nothing had changed in man's religious beliefs regarding his origin and creation. Second, Darwin's evidence had left no room for God in the universe; therefore, everything had changed and thinking must change. Third, Darwin's theories simply reaffirmed the Biblical concepts; therefore, "evolution is just God's way of doing things."

The conflict between the theologians and the scientists raged not only throughout the remainder of the century but was inevitably reflected in the literature of the period. Poets of the era can be classified through their attitudes toward religion and science. Alfred Tennyson and Robert Browning stand as poets of faith, whereas Matthew Arnold and Arthur Hugh Clough represent the skeptics and the doubters. Later Victorian verse showed less of the conflict than the earlier.

Historians have called Charles Dickens the greatest of the Victorian novelists. His creative genius was surpassed only by that of Shakespeare. Many later novelists were to feel the influence of this writer, whose voice became the trumpet of protest against economic conditions of the age. George Bernard Shaw once said that *Little Dorrit* was as seditious a book as *Das Kapital*. Thus, according to critics, Dickens' *Hard Times* is a relentless indictment of the callous greed of the Victorian industrial society and its misapplied utilitarian philosophy.

CHARACTERIZATION

A. INTRODUCTION

In *Hard Times* Dickens placed villains, heroes, heroines, and bystanders who are representative of his times. Even though many of these characters have names which indicate their personalities or philosophies, they are not caricatures but people endowed with both good and bad human qualities. Shaped by both internal and external forces, they are like Shakespeare's characters—living, breathing beings who love, hate, sin, and repent. True to the class or caste system of nineteenth-century England, Dickens drew them from four groups: the fading aristocracy, the vulgar rising middle class, the downtrodden but struggling labor class, and the itinerant group, represented by the circus people.

B. MAJOR CHARACTERS

1. Representative of the fading aristocracy are Mrs. Sparsit and James Harthouse.

    a. Mrs. Sparsit, a pathetic, but scheming old lady, earns her living by pouring tea and attending to the other housekeeping duties for Mr. Josiah Bounderby, whom she despises. Sparing with words, she is literally a "sitter," first in Bounderby's home and later in his bank. She lends her respectability and culture to his crude, uneducated environment. Resentful of Bounderby and others who do not have the background that she has, she seemingly accepts Bounderby's philosophy of life. In direct discourse with him, she simpers and hedges; when he is not present, she scorns him and spits on his picture. Throughout the novel, Mrs. Sparsit connives and plans for her own advantage. Her role in the first book is one of waiting and watching; in the second book, she continues this role and enlists the aid of Bitzer, an aspirant to the middle class, to bring revenge upon Bounderby; in the last book she serves as informer and is rewarded by losing her position with Bounderby and by being compelled to live with a hated relative, Lady Scadgers.

b. James Harthouse, the second face of the aristocracy, is a young man who comes to Coketown because he is bored with life. He is employed to advance the interests of a political party. When introduced to Louisa, he becomes infatuated with her and seeks to arouse her love. Taking advantage of Bounderby's absences from home, he goes to see Louisa on various pretexts. When Louisa refuses to elope with him, he leaves Coketown for a foreign country. The only hurt he has received is a blow to his ego or vanity.

2. Characters of the middle class take many faces: the wealthy factory owner, the retired merchant who is a champion of facts, the "whelp," and the beautiful Louisa nurtured in facts. Just as the buildings of Coketown are all alike in shape, so are these people alike.

a. Josiah Bounderby, the wealthy middle-aged factory owner of Coketown, is a self-made man. Fabricating a story of his childhood, he has built himself a legend of the abandoned waif who has risen from the gutter to his present position. To add to his "self-made" station in life, this blustering, bragging bounder has told the story of his miserable childhood so long and so loud that he believes it himself. The story is simple: he says that after being abandoned by his mother, he was reared by a drunken grandmother, who took his shoes to buy liquor; he relates often and long how he was on his own as a mere child of seven and how he educated himself in the streets. In the final book, when his story is proved false by the appearance of his mother, who had not abandoned him but who had reared and educated him, he is revealed as a fraud who had, in reality, rejected his own mother. With this revelation and other events came his downfall and eventual death.

An opinionated man, he regards the workers in his factories as "Hands," for they are only that—not people to him. The only truth to him is his own version of truth.

In the first book, as a friend of Thomas Gradgrind, he is intent upon having Louisa, Gradgrind's older daughter, for his wife. In the conclusion of book one he succeeds —by taking Gradgrind's son into the bank—in marrying Louisa, who does not love him; for she has never been taught to love or dream, only to learn facts. True to braggart nature, Bounderby expands the story of his miserable rise to wealth by letting everyone know that he has married the daughter of a wealthy, respectable man.

Book two reveals him more fully as the bounder; however, he is a blind bounder—he does not know that his young wife has found a younger man to whom she is attracted. In the final book, when she leaves him and returns home, his ego cannot stand the blow. He does not change, even though almost everyone and everything around him changes.

b. Gradgrind is the father of five children whom he has reared to learn facts and to believe only in statistics. His wife, a semi-invalid, is simple-minded; although she does not understand his philosophy, she tries to do his bidding. As the book progresses, however, he begins to doubt his own teachings. Mr. Thomas Gradgrind represents the Utilitarian philosophy of the nineteenth century.

In the first book he takes into his home a young girl whose father, a circus clown, has abandoned her. He undertakes her education but fails, since she is the product of another environment. In this book he presents Bounderby's suit for marriage to Louisa and is pleased when she recognizes that wealth is important.

In the second book Gradgrind emerges as a father for the first time. He takes Louisa back into his home after she leaves Bounderby. Having lived with the foundling in his home, he has come to recognize that there are emotions such as love and compassion. When his daughter comes to him as a daughter looking for help and sanction, he reacts as a father.

In the last book Gradgrind abandons his philosophy of facts again to help Tom his wayward son to flee from England so that he will not be imprisoned for theft. Gradgrind also vows to clear the name of an accused worker. Here he learns — much to his regret — that Bitzer, one of his former students, has learned his lesson well; Bitzer refuses to help young Tom escape.

c. Tom Gradgrind, the son, is also a face of the middle class. Having been reared never to wonder, never to doubt facts, and never to entertain any vice or fancy, he rebels as a young man when he leaves his father's home, Stone Lodge, to work in Bounderby's bank. He uses Bounderby's affection for Louisa to gain money for gambling and drink. He urges Louisa to marry Bounderby, since it will be to his own benefit if she does.

Freed from the stringent rule of his father, Tom (whom Dickens has Harthouse name "the whelp") becomes a "man about town." He begins to smoke, to drink, and to gamble. When he becomes involved in gambling debts, he looks to Louisa for help. Finally she becomes weary of helping him and denies him further financial aid. Desperate for money to replace what he has taken from the bank funds, Tom stages a robbery and frames Stephen Blackpool. Just as he uses others, so is he used by James Harthouse, who has designs on Louisa.

At the last, Tom shows his complete degeneration of character. When he realizes that exposure is imminent, he runs away. The only redeeming feature of his character is that he truly loves his sister and ultimately regrets that he has brought her heartache. Escaping from England, he lives and dies a lonely life as an exile. In his last illness he writes to his sister asking her forgiveness and love.

d. Louisa Gradgrind Bounderby, a beautiful girl nurtured in the school of facts, reacts and performs in a manner in keeping with her training until she faces a situation for which her education has left her unprepared. A dutiful daughter, she obeys her father in all things—even to contracting a loveless marriage with Bounderby, a man twice her age. The only emotion that fills her barren life is her love for Tom, her younger brother. Still young when she realizes that her father's system of education has failed her, she begins to discover the warmth and compassion of life. Only after her emotional conflict with Harthouse does she start her complete re-education.

3. Dickens employs Biblical parallels to portray the characters of the struggling working class. Stephen Blackpool, an honest, hard-working power-loom weaver in Bounderby's factory and the first victim to the labor cause, is likened unto the Biblical Stephen, the first Christian martyr. Just as the Biblical Stephen was stoned by his own people, so is Stephen Blackpool shunned and despised by his own class. Even though he realizes that Bounderby and the other factory owners are abusing the workers and that something must be done to help them, he refuses to join the union. He

is perceptive enough to know that Slackbridge, the trade-union agitator, is a false prophet to the people.

Married to a woman who had left him years before the story opens, Stephen finds himself hopelessly in love with Rachael, also a worker in the factory. Rachael is likened unto the long-suffering woman of the same name in Biblical history. Stephen cannot marry his beloved because the laws of England are for the rich, not the penniless workman. When he goes to Bounderby for help to obtain a divorce from his drunken, degenerate wife, he is scorned and bullied until he speaks up, denying Bounderby's taunts. On another occasion he defends the workers against Bounderby's scathing remarks; consequently, he is fired and has to seek a job in another town. When Stephen learns that he is accused of theft, he starts back to Coketown to clear his name; however, he does not arrive there. He falls into an abandoned mine pit and is found and rescued minutes before his death. Although he is just one of the "Hands" to Bounderby and others of the middle class, Stephen Blackpool is a very sensitive, religious man who bears no enmity toward those who have hurt him.

4. The last social group that Dickens pictures is best represented by Cecilia "Sissy" Jupe, who is the antithesis of the scholars of Gradgrind's school. This group, the circus people whose endeavor is to make people happy, is scorned by the Gradgrinds and the Bounderbys of the world. Sissy, forsaken by her father, who believed that she would have a better life away from the circus, is a warm, loving individual who brings warmth and understanding to the Gradgrind home. Because of her influence, the younger girl, Jane Gradgrind, grows up to know love, to dream, and to wonder. In the conclusion of the book, Sissy can look forward to a life blessed by a husband and children. The handwriting on the wall foretells her happiness and Louisa's unhappiness.

C. MINOR CHARACTERS

Dickens used the minor characters for comic relief, for transition of plot, and for comparison and contrast.

1. Bitzer is a well-crammed student in Gradgrind's model school of Fact. He is the living contrast to the humble, loving, compassionate Sissy. Bitzer can best be characterized as the symbolic embodiment of the practical Gradgrindian philosophy: he is colorless, servile, mean; and he lives by self-interest.

2. Mr. M'Choakumchild, a teacher in Gradgrind's model school, is an advocate of the Gradgrind system. Dickens says that he might have been a better teacher had he known less.

3. Slackbridge, symbolized as the false prophet to the laboring class, is the trade-union agitator.

4. Mrs. Pegler is the mysterious woman who shows great interest in Mr. Bounderby. One meets her, usually, standing outside the Bounderby house, watching quietly.

5. Adam Smith Gradgrind and Malthus Gradgrind are Thomas Gradgrind's two youngest sons. Their names are in keeping with the economic concern of the book.

6. Members of the Sleary Circus, in addition to Mr. Sleary, are Emma Gordon, Kidderminster, who plays the role of cupid; Mr. E. W. B. Childers, and Josephine Sleary.

7. Unnamed characters are members of the "Hands" and the sick wife of Stephen Blackpool.

SIGNIFICANCE OF SETTING

Settings can be classified as scenic, essential, and symbolic. Scenic is self-explanatory; it is there, but it does not influence the story. Essential means that the story could not have happened any other place or at any other time. A symbolic setting is one which plays an important role in the philosophy of the book. Such a setting is Coketown, England. Coketown, with all its brick buildings and its conformity and sterility and the Educational System, is conspicuous as part of the setting. Dickens uses many symbols to convey the horror of the setting: Coketown is the brick jungle; the factories are the mad elephants; the death-bringing smoke is the serpent; the machinery is the monster. The sameness, the conformity, creates an atmosphere of horror. An ironic note in the setting is the paradoxical reference to the blazing furnaces as Fairy Palaces.

ANALYSIS OF STORY

Hard Times, a social protest novel of nineteenth-century England, is aptly titled. Not only does the working class, known as the "Hands," have a "hard time" in this novel; so do the other classes as well. Dickens divided the novel into three separate books, two of which, "Sowing" and "Reaping," exemplify the Biblical concept of "whatsoever a man soweth, that shall he also reap" (Galatians 6:7).

The third book, entitled "Garnering," Dickens paraphrased from the book of Ruth, in which Ruth garnered grain in the fields of Boaz. Each of his major characters sows, each reaps, and each garners what is left.

A. BOOK ONE: "SOWING"

Book One consists of sixteen chapters in which are sown not only the seeds of the plot but also the seeds of the characters. As these seeds are sown, so shall they be reaped.

Chapters 1, 2, and 3

These chapters, titled "The One Thing Needful," "Murdering the Innocent," and "A Loophole," give the seeds that Thomas Gradgrind sows. He sows the seeds of Fact, not Fancy; of sense, not sentimentality; of conformity, not curiosity. There is only proof, not poetry for him. His very description is one of fact: "square forefinger...square wall of a forehead...square coat...square legs, square shoulders...."

In the second chapter Thomas Gradgrind teaches a lesson as an example for the schoolmaster, Mr. M'Choakumchild, a man who chokes children with Facts. Thomas Gradgrind tries to fill the "little pitchers"—who are numbered, not named—with facts. Sissy Jupe, alone, is the only "little vessel" who cannot be filled with facts, such as the statistical description of a horse. She has lived too long among the "savages" of the circus to perform properly in this school. Here Bitzer, later to show how well he has learned his lesson, can recite all of the physical attributes of a horse.

In the third chapter some of the seeds that Thomas Gradgrind has sown appear not to have taken root. On his way home from his successful lesson to the children, he spies his own children, Louisa and Tom Jr., peeping through a hole at the circus people of Sleary's Horse-riding. Although he had sown seeds of Fact and seeds of not wondering, there was a loophole: his two children desired to learn more than what they had been taught in the "lecturing castle" or in Stone Lodge. At Stone Lodge each of the five little Gradgrinds has his cabinets of Facts which he must absorb. Gradgrind scolds his erring offspring, admonishing them by asking, "What would Mr. Bounderby say?" Here one sees that Gradgrind, though retired from the hardware business and a member of Parliament, is aware of the wealth and influence of the factory owner. The reader sees here, too, that Louisa, a girl of fifteen or sixteen, is protective toward her younger brother, Tom.

Chapter 4 — "Mr. Bounderby"

Chapter 4, "Mr. Bounderby," gives a portrait of this influential man. Described as a "Bully of Humility," he is rich: a banker, merchant, and manufacturer. Although he is forty-seven or forty-eight years of age, he looks older. His one marked physical characteristic is the enlarged vein in his temple. As usual, he is bragging that he is a "self-made man." The reader also meets Mrs. Gradgrind, a pathetic woman who understands little of the world in which she lives. As she listens to Mr. Bounderby's story, the reader can see that he has bored her many times before with his supposedly miserable birth and childhood—born in a ditch, he was abandoned by his mother to the not-so-tender mercies of a drunken grandmother who sold his shoes for liquor and who drank fourteen glasses of intoxicant before breakfast.

When Bounderby is told of Louisa and Tom's grave misdeed of spying on the circus, he accuses Sissy Jupe of corrupting the children of the town and says that she must be removed from the school. Very generously, he forgives Tom and Louisa. As Louisa accepts his kiss, the reader learns that she does not like him. She tells Tom that she would not feel the pain if he were to take a knife and cut out the spot on her cheek that Bounderby had kissed. Jane, the youngest Gradgrind, is pictured asleep, her tear-stained face bent over her slate of fractions.

Chapters 5 and 6

In these two chapters one gets a picture of Coketown and learns that Sissy Jupe's father has abandoned her. Chapter 5, "The Keynote," describes Coketown as a town of red brick sacred to Fact. It is a town in which all of the buildings are so much alike that one cannot distinguish the jail from the infirmary without reading the names of the two inscribed above the doors. It is a town blackened by the "serpent-like" smoke that billows endlessly into the air from the factory chimneys and settles in the lungs of the workers, a town with a black canal and a river that runs purple with industrial waste, a town of eighteen denominations housed in pious warehouses of red brick. Who belongs to these eighteen denominations is the mystery. The laboring classes do not belong, even though there are always petitions to the House of Commons for acts of Parliament to make the laboring classes religious by force. A Teetotal Society has tabular statements showing that people drink; chemists and druggists have tabular statements showing that those who do not drink take opium. Also in this chapter is an analogy between the conformity of the town and the conformity of the Gradgrinds and the other products of Fact.

Bounderby and Gradgrind, on their way to Pod's End, a shabby section of the town, to inform Sissy's father that he must remove her from school before she corrupts the other children, encounter Sissy being chased by Bitzer, the ideal student. They send Bitzer on his way and go with Sissy to see her father. Having gone for "nine oils" for her father's "hurts," Sissy tells the two men about her father's profession as a clown and about Merrylegs, his performing dog. Bounderby, in his usual manner, comments with a metallic laugh, "Merrylegs and nine oils. Pretty well this, for a self-made man."

Chapter 6, entitled "Sleary's Horsemanship," portrays the circus folk, who are in direct contrast to Bounderby and Gradgrind. In this chapter, one learns that Sissy's father, thinking that others will take better care of her than he can, has deserted her. In the Pegasus's Arms, the hotel of the circus people, Bounderby and Gradgrind exchange philosophy with Mr. Sleary, a stout, flabby man, the proprietor of the circus, and with Mr. E. W. B. Childers, and Kidderminster, performers in the circus. The ensuing conversation between the schools of Fact and Fancy reveals that there is little understanding between the two. When Bounderby states that the circus people do not know the value of time and that he has raised himself above such people, Kidderminster replies that Bounderby should lower himself. Sleary's philosophy is that of Dickens, "Make the betht of uth, not the wurtht." (Make the best of it [life], not the worst.)

When Sissy is convinced that her father has deserted her, she accepts Gradgrind's invitation to become a member of his household. Gradgrind's offer is motivated by Fact. Louisa will see what vulgar curiosity will lead to. Sleary encourages Sissy to accept the offer of the "Squire" (the name he has given Gradgrind). He says that she is too old to apprentice; however, he contends that there must be people in the world dedicated to amusing others.

Chapter 7 — "Mrs. Sparsit"
This chapter is one of character portrayal. Here the reader meets Mrs. Sparsit, a member of the ancient Powler stock. A widow left penniless by her spendthrift former husband, she serves as Bounderby's housekeeper. Depicted as a contrast to her employer, she does not contradict Bounderby to his face; however, she despises him for the uncouth person that he is. Here, too, the reader sees being planted the seeds of Bounderby's intentions of marrying

Louisa. He hopes that Sissy will not corrupt Louisa, but that Louisa will be good for Sissy. The chapter concludes with Sissy's being told that she is ignorant and must forget the stories of Fairies and Fancy that she has read to her father.

Chapter 8 – "Never Wonder"

"Never Wonder," the keynote of the Gradgrind educational system, is discussed by Louisa and Tom Gradgrind. Dickens' satire on the educational system is expounded through young Tom's dissatisfaction with his own education and Louisa's desire to do and to learn more. She feels that there is something missing—although she does not know what—or lacking in her life. Tom, calling himself a "donkey," vows to take revenge on his father and the whole educational system. He wishes that he could take gunpowder and blow up the doctrine of Facts. His revenge is that he will enjoy life when he leaves home. He has completed his "cramming" and will soon enter Bounderby's bank. Tom later reveals the secret of his future enjoyment: he tells his sister that, since Bounderby is so fond of her, she can make his life easier by playing up to Bounderby. As they gaze into the fire and "wonder," they are interrupted and scolded for their wondering by their mother, a pathetic woman who does not understand her logical husband. Her complete character can be summarized in one of her own comments: "I really *do* wish that I had never had a family, and then you would have known what it was to do without me!"

Chapter 9 – "Sissy's Progress"

Sissy's education in the Gradgrind home and in M'Choakum-child's school does not progress as rapidly as Mr. Gradgrind would desire. She—reared to wonder, to think, to love, and to believe in Fancy—cannot digest the volumes of Facts and figures given her. She cannot be categorized or catalogued. She cannot learn even the most elementary principles of Practical Economy. Even though Sissy cannot be educated into the ways of the Gradgrinds, she becomes a partial educator of Louisa and young Jane. When she talks with Louisa, she defends her runaway father; in doing so and in repeating some of the stories of the circus, she adds nourishment to the tiny seeds of doubt that have been implanted in Louisa's mind about the training she has received. Daily she inquires of Mr.

Gradgrind if a letter for her has arrived. She does not lose hope of hearing from or about her father. Gradually Sissy teaches Louisa the first lesson of compassion and understanding.

Chapters 10, 11, 12, and 13

Chapters 10, 11, 12, and 13 present a picture of the struggles, the desperation, and the momentary joys of the working class. Entitled "Stephen Blackpool," "No Way Out," "The Old Woman," and "Rachael," they are chapters of character representation, of Dickens' philosophy, and of symbolism.

The tenth chapter injects some of Dickens' philosophy into the character sketch of Stephen Blackpool, a power-loom weaver in the Bounderby mill. Representative of Dickens' picture of the Hands, Stephen, a man of integrity, is forty years of age. Even though he has been married for many years, his wife had left him long ago. In this chapter, the seeds of Stephen's discontent are revealed when he returns to his lonely apartment after walking his beloved Rachael home and finds that his drunken wife has returned. Through the words of Blackpool, the reader learns that Dickens believes the laws of England to be unfair to the poor workingman. On the other hand, Dickens lets Rachael, the woman whom Stephen loves, tell him that he should not be bitter toward the laws. When he realizes that the object of his misery has re-entered his life, he sinks into despair; tied to this disreputable creature, he can never marry Rachael.

The title of the eleventh chapter, "No Way Out," is significant in that it characterizes Stephen's hopeless marriage and the seemingly futile struggles of the working class. This chapter also contains imagery that adds to the tone of the story. Dickens satirizes the Industrial Revolution as he likens the roaring furnace to Fairy Palaces and the factories to elephants from which belch forth the serpents of death-giving smoke. The people must breathe this poison daily as they struggle with the monstrous machines in order to earn a pittance. Dickens also satirizes Malthus' system of determining the economy through arithmetic.

Further, one sees Stephen going to his employer to seek help with his marriage. Bounderby's title could well be "Bully of

Humanity" for the manner in which he deals with this worker. Stephen learns only one thing: the laws are truly for the benefit of the rich. If he leaves his drunken wife or if he harms her or if he marries Rachael or if he just lives with Rachael without the sanction of marriage, Stephen will be punished, for the laws are thus arranged; on the other hand, if he seeks a divorce, he cannot obtain one, for money is the only key that opens the doors of the courts of justice in England. As he leaves Bounderby's house, Stephen concludes that the laws of the land are a muddle. During the entire discussion Mrs. Sparsit listens and seems to agree with her boasting employer. Bounderby terminates the interview with his favorite comment: "I see traces of turtle soup, and venison, and gold spoon in this." In other words, he regards the Hands as people desiring the best of life without working for it.

The twelfth chapter, entitled "The Old Woman," introduces mystery into the novel. As Stephen departs from Bounderby's house, he encounters an old woman who asks eagerly about Bounderby. She seems to be entranced as she looks at Bounderby's house and the factory. Stephen, too dejected concerning his own affairs, answers her many questions but does not wonder as to her interest in his employer.

Again, through satire, Dickens censures the machine age by referring to the towering smoke pipes as Towers of Babel, speaking without being understood. At the end of his long day, Stephen turns his feet homeward, walking slowly, dreading to re-enter the small apartment where his wife lies in a drunken stupor.

In Chapter 13 Dickens enters the story again as he draws a portrait of Rachael, the thirty-five-year-old Hand, as a ministering angel. Through Stephen, Dickens expresses the thought that during the nineteenth century there was no equality among men except at birth and death. Stephen, on entering the apartment, finds his beloved Rachael seated by the bedside of his wife. She tells him that his landlady had summoned her to care for the sick woman. His love for Rachael fills him momentarily as he hears her refer to his wife as one of the sick and the lost, a sister who does not realize what she is doing. He and Rachael sit by the woman's bedside, watching over her while Rachael treats her injuries. As the night lengthens, Stephen falls into a troubled sleep and is wakened just in time to see his wife reach for one of the bottles of antiseptic. The seeds of his misery begin to grow as he watches stupor-like, knowing that if she drinks the poisonous preparation she will die. He seems to be dreaming of his own death, knowing that it would come before he had lived happily. As he watches the woman reach for the instrument of her own death, he sits unmoving. Perhaps the object of his miserable existence will be taken; although frightened at his thoughts, he cannot act as the distraught woman pours from the bottle. But Rachael awakens and seizes the deadly cup. Stephen bows in shame for what he almost let happen, blesses Rachael as an angel, and tells her that her act has saved him from complete destruction. She consoles him and leaves the apartment, knowing that he will not weaken again. To him she is the shining star that illuminates the night as compared to the heavy candle that dispels only a little of the darkness that shrouds the world.

Chapters 14, 15, and 16

These three chapters, "The Great Manufacturer," "Father and Daughter," and "Husband and Wife," complete the sowing of seeds for the major characters.

The first, "The Great Manufacturer," is a time-span chapter. Several years have passed since the previous one; Tom has gone to work in Bounderby's bank; Louisa has become a woman; Sissy has been adjudged hopeless as to her progress in education, but accepted because of her kindness and goodness. In the concluding pages of the chapter the seeds of marriage are sown. Here one sees, too, that young Tom's seeds of revenge are growing to maturity. Away from his father's house, he has learned and has come to like the ways of the world. He uses Louisa's love for him to encourage her to accept the proposal that he knows is forthcoming from Bounderby. The seeds of wonder are growing in Louisa; yet they have not been nourished enough to deter her from accepting only facts.

In the next chapter, "Father and Daughter," Mr. Gradgrind presents Bounderby's proposal of marriage to Louisa. When he does, Louisa asks him if he thinks that she loves Bounderby. His embarrassed answer is one that brings a second question to her lips. "What would you advise me to use in its stead?" (instead of love.) His answer is in keeping with his philosophy: "to consider the question simply as one of tangible Fact." Louisa accepts the proposal by stating that there is no other answer for her; she has had no experience of the heart to guide her; she has never been allowed to wonder or to question. The only one who shows any emotional reaction to Gradgrind's announcement of his daughter's betrothal to Bounderby is Sissy, who regards Louisa with pity mingled with wonder and sorrow.

In the final chapter of Book One Bounderby and Louisa are married. When Bounderby imparts to Mrs. Sparsit the news of his coming marriage, she wishes him happiness, but with condescension and compassion. She feels a pity for this aging man who is foolish enough to believe that a woman as young as Louisa can make him a satisfactory wife. When he announces to Mrs. Sparsit the forthcoming nuptials, Bounderby makes plans for her welfare. He offers her an apartment over the bank and her regular stipend for being a keeper of the bank. Mrs. Sparsit realizes that he is doing this only because of her former position with him. Being deposed from her position does not agree with the lady; nevertheless, she accepted the offer rather than eat the bread of dependency.

The courtship was not one of love but one of facts. Dresses were made, jewelry was ordered, all preparations went forward. A church wedding, naturally in the New Church, the only one of the eighteen that differed slightly in architecture, took place. Only once during the entire proceedings did Louisa lose her composure: that was upon parting from her brother, Tom, who was an inadequate support for the occasion. Her brother, whose whole concern in the matter was his own welfare, made light of her fears and sent her to the waiting Bounderby.

B. BOOK TWO – "REAPING"

Consisting of twelve chapters, the second book depicts the harvest – meager for some, abundant for others. Mr. Bounderby, having sowed seeds of unkindness, reaped an unhappy marriage and the loss of his wife; Mr. Gradgrind's seeds of logic and Fact led to disillusionment and destruction; Louisa Gradgrind Bounderby, sowed with the seeds of Fact, reaped unhappiness; for Tom, the seeds of dishonesty produced a harvest of loneliness and destruction; Stephen planted seeds of discontent and reaped ostracism by his kind. Each character reaped a harvest of his own making.

Chapter 1 — "Effects in the Bank"

Apparent immediately is Dickens' satire, setting the tone for this chapter and the entire book. It begins, "A sunny midsummer day. There was such a thing sometimes, even in Coketown." Even in Coketown, the rays of sunlight, or reforms, penetrated the smoke and the fog—mistreatment of the workers and the duping of the factory owners. Even in Coketown there had come a time when the laboring class united for self-preservation and education for their children. Not only the workers but also the entire town "seemed to be frying in oil": Bounderby, in the oil of Mrs. Sparsit's pity; young Tom, in the oil of her suspicions; Bitzer, in the oil of her disdain; Louisa, in the oil of destruction. Guardians of the bank by night and spies by the day, Mrs. Sparsit and Bitzer were ill-matched companions; nevertheless, they were bound together by Fact. Bitzer, grown from the brilliant student of Fact into a cold young man of self-interest, shared not only tasks in the bank with Mrs. Sparsit but also the desire to undermine the position of young Tom. In this chapter the reader learns that Mr. Gradgrind has reared a son who is an idler and a parasite.

Introduced in this chapter is another character who is going to be influential in helping Louisa reap unhappiness and in helping Bounderby gather the just harvest of his pretensions. By mistake he meets Mrs. Sparsit first and inquires about Louisa; Mrs. Sparsit's replies pique his interest.

Chapter 2 — "Mr. James Harthouse"

Introduced in Chapter 2 by name is the stranger of Chapter 1. James (Jem) Harthouse, a young man bored with all of his travels and education, comes to work in the service of Gradgrind's political party. Upon first meeting Bounderby, Harthouse is unimpressed by the "self-made man" story or by the pride of Bounderby — the smoke that is the "meat and drink" of Coketown. Here Dickens subtly lets the reader know that this "meat and drink" to Bounderby is the death and destruction of the workers.

Bounderby takes Mr. Harthouse home for dinner in order to meet Louisa. Harthouse is singularly struck by the bareness of the room that he enters, which, devoid of a woman's touch, is a symbol of the sterility of the life that exists there. Intrigued by Louisa's detachment and the withdrawn expression of her eyes, Harthouse decides that his next challenge is to arouse some response in those eyes. When introduced to Tom — whom he immediately nicknames the "whelp" because of the younger man's manners and attitude — Harthouse sees the first flicker of emotion in Louisa's face and realizes that she lavishes upon her brother all of the love of which she is capable. Carefully, by encouraging Tom's friendship, Harthouse plants the seeds that will win Louisa's confidence.

Chapter 3 — "The Whelp"

The seeds of Facts planted by Thomas Gradgrind in his son have become a harvest of deceit and hypocrisy. Flattered by Harthouse's interest, Tom reveals the circumstances of Louisa's marriage to Bounderby. Bragging that he was the only one who could influence her, Tom, while he drinks Harthouse's liquor and smokes his cigars, discusses Louisa's having never loved. Harthouse leads Tom on until he learns all that he wishes to know about Bounderby, Mrs. Sparsit, and Louisa. More and more Harthouse becomes enchanted by the prospect of the "chase." Dickens concludes the chapter by philosophizing that Tom is so ignorant that he does not realize the damage he has done.

Chapters 4, 5, and 6

The next three chapters, entitled "Men and Brothers," "Men and Masters," and "Fading Away," focus upon Stephen and his relationship with his fellow workers, his encounter with his employer, and his loss of employment.

In Chapter 4, Dickens pictures the workers seeking to lessen the burdens of their lives. The labor-union agitator, Slackbridge, is the supposed "saviour" for the workers as they make their voices of protest heard. Dickens shows that the labor leaders may be as corrupt as the employers; he depicts the laboring class grasping at straws and led by a Judas or a false prophet. Of the laboring group, Stephen is the only one who cannot agree with Slackbridge's ideas; consequently, Slackbridge uses him as an example and turns the other workers against Stephen. When Stephen announces his decision not to join the union, the workers are convinced that "private feeling must yield to the common cause." Ostracized by his fellow workers, Stephen walks alone, afraid even to see his beloved Rachael. At the conclusion of the chapter Bitzer comes to him and tells him that Bounderby wishes to see him.

In "Men and Masters" Stephen defends the workers against Bounderby, who calls them the "pests of the earth." Stephen says that he has not refused to join the union because of his loyalty to Bounderby but because he has made a promise. Although his own fellow workers distrust him, he is faithful to them and gives his reasons for needed reform, thus infuriating Bounderby, who dismisses him from his job in the factory. Dickens' philosophy is expressed in the conversation as Stephen tells Bounderby that men are not machines, that they do have souls. After Bounderby, who cannot bear to hear any truth except his own, fires him, Stephen leaves the large "brick castle" saying, "Heaven help us in this world." The discussion between Bounderby and Stephen has made a deep impression upon Louisa.

In the sixth chapter, "Fading Away," many threads of the plot appear. Upon leaving Bounderby's house, Stephen meets Rachael and the old woman whom he had met some time before standing outside Bounderby's house. The old woman questions Stephen carefully about Bounderby's wife. When she hears that Louisa is young and handsome, she seems delighted. Again, Stephen wonders little about the woman's curiosity concerning Bounderby. He tells Rachael he has been fired and that he plans to leave Coketown to seek employment elsewhere. He tries to make her understand that it would be better for her if she were not seen with him anymore. Later at his room, where he and Rachael are talking with the old woman, who calls herself Mrs. Pegler, Louisa and her brother Tom come to see Stephen. For the first time Louisa has come to the home of one of the workers. She knows well the facts of supply and demand, the percentage of pauperism and the percentage of crime, and the results of the changes in wheat prices; but she knows nothing of the workers who make up these statistics. Indeed, to her they have been just so many units producing a given amount of goods in a given amount of time and space. For the first time she realizes that these people are not mere statistics; they have pride; they struggle to exist. She learns, too, that if a worker is fired from his job, he will not be able to find another one in the same town.

As she talks with Stephen and Rachael, she feels compassion for them and offers Stephen money to help him find employment away from Coketown. When Stephen accepts two pounds from her, Louisa is impressed with his self-command.

Tom remains quiet while Louisa converses with Rachael and Stephen. When he sees his sister ready to depart, he asks Stephen to step out on the stairs with him while Louisa remains inside the room talking with Rachael. Tom persuades Stephen that he may be able to do something for the discharged worker during the few days remaining before his departure from Coketown in search of work. Tom hints strongly about a job as a light porter at the bank. Stephen wonders about, but does not question, the strange request made of him to wait outside the bank for a while each evening. Stephen agrees to grant the request. During his three days of fruitless waiting, Stephen is probably observed by Mrs. Sparsit and Bitzer. At the end of that period, having completed the work on his loom, Stephen takes leave of Rachael and departs from Coketown.

Dickens weaves into this chapter some third-person narration concerning the fate of the workers. He says, "Utilitarian economists, skeletons of schoolmasters, Commissioners of Fact, genteel and used-up infidels, gabblers of many little dog's-eared creeds, the poor you will have always with you." He urges these people to give the poor some consideration, lest they—when nothing is left except a bare existence—rise up and destroy their oppressors.

Chapter 7 — "Gunpowder"

Aptly named "Gunpowder," this chapter shows that three characters — Louisa, Tom, and Jem Harthouse — are figuratively sitting on kegs of explosives.

Harthouse, having performed his duties well, has gained the confidence of both Gradgrind and Bounderby. They are unaware of his objective: to make Louisa love him. His pursuit of Louisa is amusing to him, and he becomes a frequent caller at the Bounderby house. The reader learns that Bounderby, having foreclosed a mortgage on Nickits, who speculated too much, has moved his family into a country estate some fifteen miles from Coketown and accessible by railway. In the flower garden Bounderby has planted cabbages; in the house filled with elegant furnishings and beautiful paintings, Boundery has continued his barrack-like existence.

The day of Harthouse's triumph arrives at Bounderby's country home, when he broaches to Louisa the subject of Tom's gambling by saying he is interested in Tom's well-being. He convinces Louisa of his deep interest in Tom. While they are walking back to the house, they encounter Tom carving a girl's name in a tree. Tom, in a bad mood, is barely civil to his sister, who has refused him a hundred pounds. When Louisa goes into the house, Harthouse remains in the garden with Tom. Persuaded by Harthouse, Tom discusses his troubles with him. When Harthouse asks Tom how much money he needs, Tom replies by saying it is too late for money. Harthouse persuades Tom to apologize to Louisa for his rudeness. When Tom does apologize, Louisa believes that the change in him is due to Harthouse's influence; her smile is for Harthouse now.

Chapter 8 — "Explosion"

When gunpowder is set off, an explosion always follows. Accordingly, this chapter is well named. It has a twofold purpose: to relate the bank robbery and to show Louisa's growing fondness for Harthouse and her continued awakening to the realization that something is missing from her life.

The chapter opens with Harthouse smoking his pipe and musing over the happenings of the preceding night. Pleased with himself at the turn of events, he did not dwell long on the consequences of what could happen as a result of his relationship with Louisa. Here the reader sees Dickens drawing an analogy between Harthouse and the Devil. Harthouse departs early for a public occasion, at some distance from the Bounderby residence. When he returns to the Bounderby house at six, he is met by Bounderby, who informs him of the robbery at the bank. Whoever entered the bank did so with a false key; the key was later found in the street. One hundred and fifty pounds is the missing sum. At the Bounderby house are Bitzer, who is scolded for sleeping so soundly, and Mrs. Sparsit, who has come to stay because her nerves are too bad for her to remain in her apartment at the bank. Bounderby comments that even Louisa fainted when she learned of the robbery. The reader realizes almost immediately the identity of the thief, but Stephen Blackpool is suspected of the crime. Coming under suspicion as an accomplice is the old woman who is yet a mystery to all. When Harthouse inquires concerning Tom's whereabouts, Bounderby says he is helping the police.

As the evening progresses, Mrs. Sparsit obliges her employer by occasionally resorting to copious tears as she caters to Bounderby's whims — playing backgammon with him and preparing his sherry with lemon-peel and nutmeg — and watches Louisa and Harthouse, hoping for the worst.

Louisa lies sleepless waiting for Tom's return; she is concerned, for she suspects that he — not Blackpool — has forced open the safe and used the false key, if indeed it were used. An hour past midnight she hears Tom enter. After giving him time to prepare for bed, she goes to his upstairs room, hoping that he will confide in her. They discuss their visit with Blackpool and Rachael and agree not to tell anyone about it. Tom lies to Louisa, telling her that he had taken Stephen outside on the stairs that night to tell him what good fortune he had in getting her help. Troubled, Louisa leaves her brother, who weeps, unable to confide in her or anyone else.

Chapter 9 – "Hearing the Last of It"
"Hearing the Last of It" bears a dual meaning: the last of Louisa's determination to remain aloof from Harthouse and the last

of Mrs. Sparsit's scheme to be again the respected housekeeper in the Bounderby house. This dual meaning is incomplete until the final chapter of this book.

In spite of her "bad nerves," Mrs. Sparsit reassumes all of her duties as housekeeper and hostess in Bounderby's house. Even though she refers to Louisa as Miss Gradgrind, Bounderby takes no offense. He is pathetic in his acceptance of the old regime — his tea poured, a ready ear, a smooth-running household, and an obvious, agreeable admirer of his talents as a "self-made man."

The reader realizes that Mrs. Sparsit is aware of the dangerous alienation of husband and wife. She kisses Bounderby's hand when she is in his presence, but shakes her right-hand mitten at his picture in his absence and says, "Serve you right, you Noodle, and I am glad of it." Mrs. Sparsit's constant reference to Louisa as Miss Gradgrind lets the reader know also that no real marriage exists between the aging tyrant and the young woman just awakening to life.

Louisa is summoned home to see her gravely ill mother. Since her marriage, she has been home very few times. Now as she returns, she has no childhood memories to make her homecoming glad. Rather she goes with a heavy, hardened kind of sorrow to find her mother rapidly sinking. In those last minutes of Mrs. Gradgrind's life, Louisa lets the reader know how much Sissy has influenced her and the youngest Gradgrind child, Jane.

Chapters 10, 11, and 12

The final three chapters of this book are chapters of complete harvest: unhappiness for Louisa and the destruction of Gradgrind's philosophy and of Bounderby's pride.

Chapter 10, entitled "Mrs. Sparsit's Staircase," is one of symbolism. Not only is the "staircase" a staircase erected in Mrs. Sparsit's mind as symbolic of Louisa's eventual shame for the dark at the bottom, but it is also the staircase of destruction for many of the other characters.

After several weeks at the Bounderby home, Mrs. Sparsit returns to her apartment at the bank. On the eve of her departure,

Mr. Bounderby invites her to be a constant weekend guest at his home. Following this invitation, she and Mr. Bounderby discuss the bank robbery. Bounderby says that Rome was not built in a day and neither will the thief be discovered in such a short period of time. He adds that if Romulus and Remus could wait, so can he; for he and they have much in common: they had had a she-wolf for a nurse; he, a she-wolf for a grandmother. He makes reference not only to Tom's diligence at the bank but also to the old woman, who is under suspicion.

Constant companions, Louisa and Harthouse discuss the robbery. Louisa cannot believe that Stephen could rob the bank. Meanwhile Mrs. Sparsit watches the growing friendship between the two and does nothing to prevent the disaster she knows will come.

"Lower and Lower," the next chapter, depicts Mrs. Sparsit's watchful waiting for Louisa's complete descent into the black gulf at the bottom of the staircase. It also shows Gradgrind's unemotional acceptance of his wife's death; he hurries home, buries her in a business-like manner, and returns to his "dust-throwing" in Parliament.

Even though Mrs. Sparsit is not at the Bounderby country residence during the week, she manages to keep a close watch on Louisa through talk with Bounderby, Tom, and Harthouse. When Mrs. Sparsit learns that Bounderby is to be away for three or four days on business, she, inviting Tom to dinner, skillfully worms from him information concerning Louisa and Harthouse. When she learns that Harthouse is expected back the next afternoon from a hunting trip to Yorkshire and that he has asked Tom to meet him, Mrs. Sparsit gloats over Louisa's final descent. She first suspects, then learns, that Harthouse is using the ruse of Tom's meeting him to be alone with Louisa.

The next afternoon she goes out to the Bounderby country residence and looks for the pair. Hiding behind a tree in the woods, she hears Harthouse, who has returned by horseback, declare his love for Louisa and urge her to go away with him. A storm rises and the rain begins to fall in sheets. Afraid of discovery, Mrs. Sparsit is drenched as she watches Louisa leave Harthouse and go into the house. Much to her delight, Mrs. Sparsit sees Louisa, clothed in a cloak and hat, leave the house and go to the railroad station. Following her, Mrs. Sparsit — drenched, cold and sneezing — bursts into tears when, after the train arrives in Coketown, she realizes that she has lost Louisa.

The final chapter of this book, entitled "Down," is significant in that the reader sees Mr. Gradgrind's philosophy crumbling around him as his daughter, Louisa, falls in an insensible heap at his feet.

When the chapter opens the reader sees Mr. Gradgrind, home from Parliament, occupied in his usual pursuit — working with statistics, unmindful of the pouring rain and storm. He is startled as the door opens and Louisa enters. Fleeing to the house of her birth for refuge against the emotions which stir her and which she does not understand, she curses the day of her birth, challenges her father's philosophy to save her now, and explains to him why she married Bounderby. Although she tells her father of Harthouse's declaration of love and his desire that they elope, she assures him that she has not disgraced the family name. As he sees the crumbling of his dogma, he reacts as a father who loves his daughter. He holds her in his arms, not knowing how to comfort her. The book ends with her, the symbol of all his teachings, lying in an insensible heap at his feet.

C. BOOK THREE — "GARNERING"

Just as the Biblical Ruth garnered in the fields of Boaz picking up the wheat dropped by the reapers, so do the characters garner or pick up what the grim reapers of experience have left behind. Thomas Gradgrind, after realizing the failure of his system, tries to help his children to pick up the pieces of his and their shattered lives. Returning to bachelorhood, Bounderby, exposed as a fraud, garners a life of loneliness, dying perhaps in the streets of Coketown. As they sowed, as they reaped, so must they reassemble what is left.

Chapters 1, 2, and 3

The first three chapters — "Another Thing Needful," "Very Ridiculous," and "Very Decided" — primarily concern Louisa's fight for self-understanding. Here Thomas Gradgrind reverses the thing needed; he bears out Dickens' beliefs that people's emotions cannot be measured in statistics. In the first chapter of the novel the thing needed was a factual education, a concern of the head; in the first chapter of the final book of the novel, the thing needed is understanding and compassion, a concern of the heart. In this chapter, too, the reader learns that Jane Gradgrind, the younger daughter, is leading and will continue to lead a life quite different from that which her older sister has led. Facts mixed with Fancy, statistics mixed with compassion, love, and understanding will shape her life. Under the influence of Sissy, she will grow into another Sissy, but a better educated Sissy.

Even though Gradgrind blames himself for the unhappiness that has come to Louisa, she does not blame him. Rather, in the conclusion of the chapter, she—bewildered and lost with no consolation from her education of Facts—turns to Sissy, begging for help.

In the second chapter, the reader finds Sissy—modest, shy, gentle Sissy—taking into her own hands matters concerning Louisa. This chapter also depicts the ridiculous situation in which Harthouse finds himself. Harthouse, who spends an anxious and uneasy twenty-four hours after Louisa leaves him, is taken aback at the appearance of Sissy at his quarters. Although he argues with her, he bows to her command that he leave Coketown, never to see Louisa again. Had any person other than the innocent Sissy gone to him, he might have reacted differently.

After Sissy takes her leave of him, he writes three letters: one to his brother declaring his boredom with Coketown, one to Bounderby announcing his departure, and one to Gradgrind stating that he is leaving his position. Calling himself the "Great Pyramid of Failure," he proves himself to be a very shallow and selfish man: he is concerned only with what the "fellows" will think if they learn of his failure.

"Very Decided," the title of the third chapter, could describe Bounderby, Thomas Gradgrind, and Louisa.

Having lost Louisa in the dark and rain and being anxious to bear the tidings to Bounderby, Mrs. Sparsit goes to London and seeks him out at his hotel in St. James' Street. Although she has a sore throat from her drenching and is barely able to talk, Mrs. Sparsit relates the news of Louisa's supposed elopement and faints at the feet of the great "self-made man." Later she and Bounderby rush back to Coketown to inform Gradgrind of his daughter's disgrace. When Bounderby learns that Louisa is at Stone Lodge and that her father proposes to keep her for awhile, he becomes furious. He delivers his ultimatum: if Louisa has not returned to his house by noon the next day, he will send her clothing and conclude that she prefers to stay with her family. Should she decide not to return, he will no longer be responsible for her.

The reader learns from the conversation and manner of the two men that Gradgrind has undergone some change of philosophy. Bounderby becomes infuriated, probably because Gradgrind uses words almost identical to those spoken by Bounderby to Stephen in discussing Stephen's responsibilities toward his wife. He reacts in a manner in keeping with Josiah Bounderby, the "self-made man" of Coketown. According to Bounderby, the incompatibility is that of Loo Bounderby, who might have been better left Loo Gradgrind. True to his expected pattern, he comments that she wants "turtle soup and venison, with a gold spoon."

When Louisa does not return to Bounderby's house the next day, he sends her clothing and personal belongings to her, begins negotiations to sell the country house, returns to his town house in Coketown, and reassumes his life as a bachelor.

Chapters 4 and 5 — "Lost" and "Found"
The titles of these two chapters show the loss and the finding of many things: Bounderby's loss of his "miserable childhood" and the town's finding he has a mother; Louisa's loss of a husband and a belief in Facts and the finding of a loving friend and an understanding of others; and Gradgrind's loss of faith in his system and a finding of love and understanding for his family.

Bounderby does not let his broken marriage interfere with his business; indeed, he pursues the bank robbery with more vigor, offering twenty pounds for Stephen's apprehension. The boldly painted reward poster is read by those who can read and to those who cannot. Each person has his own ideas concerning the innocence or guilt of Stephen. To strengthen his position with the workers, Slackbridge capitalizes upon Stephen's "disgrace."

Bounderby brings Rachael and Tom to Louisa to confirm or to deny Rachael's story of Louisa and Tom's visit to Stephen's home that evening so long ago. Rachael, though she would rather not, believes that Louisa has had something to do with Stephen's being accused of the robbery. Tom is upset when Louisa admits their visit to Stephen's room and her offer of financial aid to Stephen.

When Rachael admits under questioning that she has had a letter from Stephen, who has taken an assumed name in order to obtain a job, Bounderby is positive that Stephen has done this in order to prevent discovery of the robbery. Rachael sends Stephen a letter asking him to return to Coketown to clear his name. When Stephen does not come at the end of the fourth day, Rachael tells Bounderby under what name and in which town Stephen is working. Messengers sent to bring Stephen back cannot find him. As the days pass, the people of the town are divided in their attitudes and beliefs concerning him and the robbery.

"Found," the title of Chapter 5, is symbolic of the events. Days pass; life goes on; Rachael finds a friend, Sissy, who shares her heartbreak and anxiety. Found is Bounderby's mother. The mysterious Mrs. Pegler, taken against her will before Bounderby by Mrs. Sparsit, refutes his story of a miserable childhood after Gradgrind scolds Mrs. Pegler for being an unnatural mother. Cutting a ridiculous figure, the "Bully of Humility" refuses to comment on Mrs. Pegler's story of his secure childhood, of his forsaking her, and of his pensioning her off on thirty pounds a year providing she would stay away from him.

Chapter 6—"The Starlight"

In her grief over Stephen's not returning, Rachael turns to Sissy for comfort and companionship. On a Sunday morning more than a week after Stephen's disappearance, she and Sissy are walking in the fields near Coketown. They find Stephen's hat and discover he had fallen into Old Hell Shaft, an abandoned mine shaft. When they summon help, the local villagers mobilize, rig up a windlass and bucket, and rescue him. His body broken and wasted from starvation, Stephen is hoisted from the shaft. He lives long enough to request that Gradgrind clear his name of robbery, thus implicating Tom, Gradgrind's son; to ask Louisa's forgiveness for believing that she had plotted to harm him; and to say that all men should learn to live together with understanding. Stephen dies quietly, his hand in Rachael's and his eyes gazing at the star that had been his source of comfort in his prison. The march back to Coketown is a funeral procession.

Chapter 7 — "Whelp-Hunting"

When Gradgrind realizes that his son is a thief, he retires to his room for twenty-four hours, not coming out even to eat or drink. Upon deciding to help his son, he learns from Sissy that she has sent him to Sleary's circus for refuge. The three journey separately to the circus—Gradgrind alone and Sissy and Louisa together. There they find Tom masquerading as a black-face comic. The ensuing conversation between Gradgrind and Sleary indicates that Gradgrind's system of education, shaped by the economic conditions of the time, has been destroyed. From Sleary they learn what has happened to the circus people and with him they plan Tom's escape. Tom is surly with his father and Louisa, heaping coals on the fire of Gradgrind's grief by referring to Facts—statistics which show that a certain percentage of people employed in positions of trust are dishonest. Gradgrind plans to send Tom to Liverpool and then abroad; however, Bitzer suddenly appears and interferes.

Chapters 8 and 9

Chapters 8 and 9 conclude the final book of the novel; entitled "Philosophical" and "Final," they complete Gradgrind's realization of the complete destruction of his system of education and serve as Dickens' prophecies of what is to come. When Bitzer stops Tom's escape, Gradgrind asks Bitzer if he has a heart. Bitzer replies, "The circulation, sir, couldn't be carried on without one. No man, sir, acquainted with the facts established by Harvey relating to the circulation of the blood can doubt that I have a heart." When Gradgrind, by asking him how much money he wants, tries to persuade

Bitzer not to return Tom to Bounderby, Bitzer reveals that his sole purpose is to gain a promotion to Tom's former job. In the course of the conversation Bitzer says that "...the whole social system is a question of self-interest." The reader learns here that Dickens believed the economic system of nineteenth-century England was based on self-interest. Though in front of Bitzer Mr. Sleary feigns indignation that Gradgrind wants him to help Tom—Gradgrind's thieving son—escape, he makes use of a dancing horse and a trained dog to harass Bitzer while Mr. Childers drives Tom to safety.

Sleary, telling Gradgrind that Signor Jupe's dog Merrylegs has returned to the circus, says that Jupe is surely dead. The circus people had agreed not to reveal Jupe's death to Sissy, his daughter. It seems a bit ironic that Sleary is the one to refute Bitzer's statement that the whole social system is based on self-interest, for the circus people and their understanding have shown that there is also love.

A sadder and wiser Gradgrind takes his leave of the circus people with Sleary's words ringing in his ears: "People mutht be amuthed. They can't be alwayth a-learning, nor yet they can't be alwayth a-working, they an't made for it. You *mutht* have uth, Thquire. Do the withe thing and the kind thing too, and make the betht of uth, not the wurtht!"

It seems significant, too, that the novel opens with the children in class and closes with them at a circus.

In "Final" the future is anticipated by Dickens. He foretells Mrs. Sparsit's lot with her complaining relative, Lady Scadgers, Mr. Bounderby's death in the streets of his smoke-filled town, Bitzer's rise in position, Sissy's happy marriage blessed with children, Gradgrind's being scorned by his former associates for his learning Hope, Faith, and Charity, and Tom's penitence and death thousands of miles away. Dickens also pictures Louisa—loved by Sissy's children and the children of others, but none of her own—seeking to understand and to help others. With hope for a brighter future for the children and the working classes of England, Dickens concludes his novel.

DICKENS' PHILOSOPHY AND STYLE

Charles Dickens, required to write *Hard Times* in twenty sections to be published over a period of five months, filled the novel with his own philosophy and symbolism. Dickens expounds his philosophy in two ways: through straight third-person exposition and through the voices of his characters. His approach to reality is allegorical in nature; his plot traces the effect of rational education on Gradgrind's two children. He presents two problems in the text of his novel; the most important one is that of the educational system and what divides the school of Facts and the circus school of Fancy. The conflicts of the two worlds of the schoolroom and the circus represent the adult attitudes toward life. While the schoolroom dehumanizes the little scholars, the circus, all fancy and love, restores humanity. The second problem deals with the economic relationships of labor and management. Here one sees that Dickens lets the educational system be dominated by, rather than serve, the economic system. His philosophy, expounded through his characters, is best summarized by Sleary, who says that men should make the best of life, not the worst of it.

His symbolism takes such forms as Coketown's being a brick jungle, strangled in sameness and smoke, the belching factories as elephants in this jungle, the smoke as treacherous snakes, and the children as little "vessels" which must be filled. His symbolism also becomes allegorical as he utilizes Biblical connotation in presenting the moral structure of the town and the people.

In addition to dialogue, straight narration, and description, Dickens employs understatement to convey through satire the social, economic, and educational problems and to propose solutions for these problems. His often tongue-in-cheek statements balance the horror of the scenery by the absurdity of humor, based on both character and theme.

STUDY QUESTIONS

1. Critics have called *Hard Times* an allegory. Would you agree with this statement? Prove your response by making direct reference to passages in the novel.

2. Characterize Mrs. Gradgrind; in what ways does she show that, being incapable of comprehending her husband's philosophy, she has withdrawn from the world?

3. Louisa was descending the allegorical staircase of shame. Were there others descending with her? Support your answer.

4. What analogy is drawn between Coketown and the Gradgrindian philosophy?

5. What are Mrs. Sparsit's reasons for not calling Louisa Mrs. Bounderby?

6. Explain what Dickens means by "Bounderby's absolute power."

7. Rachael and Stephen have been subjected to criticism by readers who say that they are almost too good to be true. At what points in the story do Rachael and Stephen refute this criticism?

8. What is Mrs. Sparsit's role in the novel?

9. Dickens, as we all know, is utilizing satire to agitate for better conditions in England. To what advantage does Kidderminster serve Dickens' purpose?

10. What motivated Louisa's visit to Stephen? What were the results of this visit?

11. What, according to Tom, was Louisa's method of escape?

12. Of what significance was the "Star Shining" to Stephen? What does this represent symbolically?

13. In the time of the Hebrew prophet Daniel, Belshazzar, last king of Babylon, saw the "handwriting on the wall," which foretold his destruction. How does Dickens utilize this analogy?

14. Why is it significant for the novel to open in the classroom of Facts and conclude in the circus of Fancy?

15. What hope does Dickens give concerning Gradgrind?

16. By clearing Stephen's name, Mr. Gradgrind realized that someone else would be implicated. Who was this person? How does Gradgrind react when he realizes the implications?

17. How does Bounderby's concept of smoke differ from that of the Hands?

18. What is the motive behind Mrs. Sparsit's spying on James Harthouse and Louisa Bounderby?

19. Bitzer states that the entire economic system is based on self-interest. Does his character prove his statement? What characters other than Bitzer would be examples of his statement?

20. How did Gradgrind react when he realized that his educational philosophy was a failure?

NOTES

NOTES

NOTES

Jane Eyre

JANE EYRE

NOTES

including
- *Life of the Author*
- *List of Characters*
- *Brief Synopsis*
- *Introduction to the Novel*
- *Critical Commentaries*
- *Character Analyses*
- *Essay: "Jane Eyre and the Victorian Era"*
- *Suggested Essay Topics*
- *Selected Bibliography*

by
Mary Ellen Snodgrass, M.A.
Former Chair, English Department
Hickory High School
Hickory, North Carolina

NEW EDITION

INCORPORATED

LINCOLN, NEBRASKA 68501

Editor	Consulting Editor
Gary Carey, M.A. *University of Colorado*	*James L. Roberts, Ph.D.* *Department of English* *University of Nebraska*

ISBN 0-8220-0672-3
© Copyright 1988
by
C. K. Hillegass
All Rights Reserved
Printed in U.S.A.

1992 Printing

Cliffs Notes, Inc.   Lincoln, Nebraska

CONTENTS

JANE EYRE
Notes

LIFE OF THE AUTHOR

Early Childhood and Education (1816–25) The third child of the Reverend Patrick Brontë, minister of the Church of England from County Down, Ireland, and Maria Branwell Brontë, Charlotte (1816–55) spent most of her life in and under the influence of the parsonage at Haworth, Yorkshire, in northern England. Her mother died of cancer in 1821 when Charlotte was five, leaving the six children – Maria, Elizabeth, Charlotte, Patrick Branwell, Emily Jane, and Anne – in the care of prim, pious Aunt Bess (Elizabeth Branwell, Mrs. Brontë's spinster sister) and their financially hard-pressed father.

In an effort to educate his children, Mr. Brontë took advantage of the Clergy Daughters' School at Cowan Bridge, where tuition was supplemented with donations. First, Maria and Elizabeth, then Charlotte and Emily, enrolled for training in history, geography, grammar, writing, arithmetic, and needlework. The strict code of behavior, coupled with poor hygiene, bad food, damp rooms, and regular walks in the cold, resulted in the deaths of first Maria, then Elizabeth from tuberculosis. As a result, Mr. Brontë brought Charlotte and Emily home; there, he attempted to educate Branwell in the classics, while Aunt Bess held classes in her room for the three girls.

Development of Talents (1825–31) The children suffered a saddened, lonely existence after their sisters' deaths. To entertain themselves, they took long walks on the windy moors and devoted themselves to the care of household pets, injured birds, and other wild animals. Adapting readily to independence and the pleasures of nature, they found entertainment and creative fulfillment from 1825 to 1831 in a series of writings which began in response to their father's gift of a box of toy soldiers. The tiny manuscripts – minutely hand-printed, covered with scrap paper, and stitched through the middle – were products of their joint creative skills, proof of the family's inherited love of literature, especially fantasy.

Growing from their parents' bookish leanings and, in particular, from Mr. Brontë's Celtic "gift of gab," the Brontës' literary skills took shape, resulting in a flair for narration and a fluency of style that led to the girls' eventual literary triumphs. However, Mr. Brontë's near-fatal bout with a lung disorder brought these quiet years to an end when he decided to enroll his children in school to guarantee their ability to support themselves in the event of his death. In January, 1831, twenty miles from Haworth in Mirfield, Charlotte entered Roe Head School—a pleasant, challenging institution which based its educational philosophy on respect for the student. During her two years there, she formed a lasting friendship with Ellen Nussey, who preserved over four hundred of Charlotte's letters and assisted biographers after Charlotte's death.

Charlotte, at first homesick and shy, received an unenthusiastic response from her classmates. Her four-foot, nine-inch body was thin and weak; her frizzy curls, sallow complexion, and old-fashioned clothes, along with a nearsighted squint and prominent Irish accent, set her apart from more graceful, well-favored girls. Gradually, however, the others perceived her keen academic abilities and honest, dutiful character. By the end of the first term, Charlotte had earned three prizes for scholarship. When she returned to Haworth in 1832, she had completed all the books at Roe Head and was offered a teaching position, which she declined, preferring to return home.

Advanced Training (1832–46) From 1832 to 1838, Charlotte busied herself by tutoring her sisters, drawing, walking on the moors, sewing, and reading. She wrote steadily in the imaginary vein of her childhood, producing a powerful, mature series of Byronic romances. One critic suggests that this absorption with fantasy freed her from the dreary, isolated life of a country parson's daughter, but at the same time it obscured harsher realities which later proved devastating not only for Charlotte but also for her brother and sisters. For a time, Charlotte returned to Roe Head and taught there, and she served as a governess at Stonegappe and Blake Hall. During this period, she rejected two offers of marriage from local clergymen.

Conceiving a plan to open a school at Haworth, Charlotte, at the age of twenty-six, journeyed to Brussels to increase her knowledge of foreign languages. At La Maison d'Education Les Jeunes Demoiselles, she experienced the great adventure of her life – increasing her cultural awareness of another country, and, perhaps more important, forming a one-sided romantic attachment to the married headmaster, Constantin Heger. For two years after her return to England, she wrote him poignant love letters, but received no encouragement. Her life was further marred by her brother's failure to establish himself in either art, writing, or teaching and his subsequent downhill slide into drunkenness, opium addiction, and reckless immorality.

The Creative Years (1846–55) In 1846, Charlotte, Emily, and Anne (under the masculine pseudonyms of Currer, Ellis, and Acton Bell) published at their own expense a collection of poems. Then, still fired with enthusiasm for writing, they each began a novel. Both Anne's *Agnes Grey* and Emily's *Wuthering Heights* found willing publishers, while Charlotte's account of her experiences in Brussels, *The Professor,* received only rejections. In 1847, she began *Jane Eyre,* which was immediately accepted by the firm of Smith, Elder, and Company. Public popularity and critical acclaim were followed by intense curiosity as to the identification of the notable Bells. In addition to recognition, Charlotte earned 300 pounds.

Despite the success of *Jane Eyre,* Charlotte's personal life met with unhappiness. Her brother, a pathetic figure of public ridicule and family dismay, died of consumption in 1848 and was quickly followed in death by both Emily and Anne. As Charlotte completed *Shirley,* her second novel, the sadness of loss affected her work. She traveled often to London, encountering both congenial support from her editors and friendship among the famous, including critic George Henry Lewes, novelist William Makepeace Thackeray, and biographer Elizabeth Gaskell. In 1850, Charlotte composed a memorial preface to honor her two sisters upon the second edition of their novels:

> I may sum up all by saying, that for strangers they were nothing, for superficial observers less than nothing; but for those who had known them all their lives in the intimacy of close relationship, they were genuinely good and truly great.

A series of illnesses ravaged Charlotte's slender frame over the last four years of her life. She suffered a liver infection in 1851 as she was completing *Villette,* her third novel. The following year, she accepted the proposal of the Reverend Arthur Bell Nicholls, her father's curate. They were married in June, 1854 (despite Reverend

Brontë's outbursts of jealousy and his refusal to attend the ceremony),
and they honeymooned in Ireland. Near Killarney, Charlotte was
thrown from a horse but appeared unhurt.

On a subsequent walk with her husband, she became ill after
being caught in the rain three miles from home. Her strength continued to fade, complicated by the normal sickness of early pregnancy,
and she died of tuberculosis on March 31, 1855, at the age of thirty-
nine. In 1860, *Cornhill* magazine published a fragment, *Emma,* which
Charlotte Brontë was writing at the time of her death. Reverend
Nicholls continued living in the parsonage at Haworth and cared for
his father-in-law until Patrick Brontë's death in 1861.

LIST OF CHARACTERS

Jane Eyre

Jane is the orphaned daughter of a poor parson and his disinherited wife. She lives at Gateshead Hall in the care of her sullen, moody,
and overly critical aunt, Sarah Gibson Reed, until she enrolls at
Lowood, a boarding school for poor, orphaned girls. There, Jane distinguishes herself in her classes and eventually takes a position as
governess to a little French girl, Adèle Varens, the ward of Edward
Fairfax Rochester, the master of Thornfield Hall. Jane and Rochester
develop a mutual admiration and love for each other. Their marriage
plans are interrupted, however, and Jane flees Thornfield. In the intervening year's separation before their eventual marriage, she establishes
her independence. The two finally find happiness together and produce a son.

Edward Fairfax Rochester

After Rowland, Edward's brother, receives the entire Rochester
family inheritance, Edward, the strong-willed second son of a wealthy
landowner, is tricked into marrying an insane woman whom he barely
knows. In anguish, Edward wanders throughout Europe looking for
release from his misery. His love for Jane Eyre rekindles hope, despite
the fact that his wife is secretly locked away in a third-story room
of Thornfield. Following the loss of his home to a terrible fire, the
death of his mad wife, and blindness and amputation of his left hand

after the fire, he is reunited with Jane at Ferndean, marries her, and eventually recovers sufficient vision in one eye to see their son.

Mrs. Alice Fairfax

Mrs. Fairfax is the housekeeper at Thornfield; she is also a distant relative of Rochester by marriage. She maintains the house during Rochester's frequent absences. Her motherly affection is a pleasant contrast to the hateful females whom Jane has known in girlhood, yet Mrs. Fairfax doubts the wisdom of Mr. Rochester's marrying Jane, a girl half his age, and she discourages the marriage. Ultimately, Mrs. Fairfax receives a generous pension and retires after Jane leaves Thornfield.

Blanche Ingram

The fashionably beautiful, haughty, and shallow daughter of the Dowager Lady Ingram; she uses her polish and glamour to lure Edward Rochester toward a proposal of marriage. However, her enthusiasm for Edward fades when he discloses that his fortune is not as large as she had thought it was.

Céline Varens

The French singer and dancer who was once Edward Rochester's pampered mistress until he broke off their affair after overhearing her ridicule him to a foppish admirer.

Adèle Varens

The French child of Céline Varens whom Edward Rochester refuses to claim as his daughter but rescues from neglect and installs at Thornfield as his ward. Her association with Jane Eyre, her governess and friend, brings happiness to both of them.

Sara Gibson Reed

The buxom, mean-spirited widow of Jane Eyre's uncle who torments Jane's early years by spoiling her own three children while downgrading and punishing Jane at every opportunity. Despite Jane's later attempt to make up for the past, Mrs. Reed rejects any reconciliation and, in her mid-forties, Mrs. Reed dies alone, unloved by her daughters.

John Reed

The fourteen-year-old darling of the Reed household who menaces and bullies Jane at every opportunity; he is adored and spoiled by his mother. In adulthood, he reduces his mother to poverty and despair by leading a dissipated life among rascals and ne'er-do-wells after being thrown out of school and failing when he tries to study law. After his mother refuses to give up Gateshead Hall to him, he threatens to kill either his mother or himself. At the age of twenty-three, he dies violently and is rumored to have killed himself.

Eliza Reed

The older daughter of the Reed household. She keeps chickens, hoards her egg and chicken money, and lends it to her mother at a high rate of interest, entering each transaction in a notebook. When Sara Reed lies on her deathbed, Eliza cold-heartedly ignores her mother and devotes herself to a nun-like existence of frequent church attendance, religious stitchery, gardening, and tidying her account book. After Mrs. Reed's death, she takes the veil at a convent in Lisle, France, and eventually rises to the position of Mother Superior, leaving her fortune to the nunnery.

Georgiana Reed

The vain, self-indulgent beauty of the Reed family; Jane is often compared unfavorably to Georgiana by the Reeds. Georgiana is "slim and fairy-like," possessing blue-eyed, flaxen-haired good looks and a flair for fashion. She accuses Eliza of sabotaging her plans to marry Lord Erwin Vere. After enduring the boredom of her sister's company while the two await Mrs. Reed's death, Georgiana returns to London and marries a wealthy man.

Helen Burns

The fourteen-year-old devout, sickly, motherless student from Deepden, Northumberland. She befriends Jane at Lowood and offers encouragement by word and example as the two girls endure the hardships of school life. Helen suffers constant harassment from Miss Scatcherd, but she is appreciated and loved by Miss Temple. On her deathbed, Helen anticipates contentment with God and a reunion with Jane in heaven.

Bessie Lee

The servant at Gateshead Hall who entertains the children with stories. She consoles Jane with treats from the kitchen when Jane is excluded from family festivities, and she visits Jane at Lowood and admires her accomplishments. Bessie marries Robert Leaven, the coachman, has three children, and continues working for the Reed family.

Miss Abbot

The servant at Gateshead who parrots Sarah Reed's criticisms and helps Bessie subdue Jane in the red-room.

Mr. Lloyd

The apothecary who treats Jane at Gateshead, listens to her life story, and decides that she should go to school.

Mr. Bates

The surgeon who treats students of Lowood during the epidemic.

Mr. Brocklehurst

The "straight, narrow, sable-clad" minister of Brocklebridge Church and son of Naomi Brocklehurst, founder of Lowood School; he interviews Jane at Gateshead. His grim, hypocritical evaluation of Jane's shortcomings follows her to Lowood, where he publicly labels her a liar. Attending to minute purchases with scrupulous attention in order to avoid waste, Mr. Brocklehurst serves as manager and treasurer of the school. He castigates Miss Temple for her generosity to students.

Maria Temple

The superintendent and music teacher of Lowood; she conducts herself with such grace, self-confidence, and purity that she becomes Jane's idol. She champions Jane and Helen, quietly treating them to her meager store of seedcake, and she encourages Helen's interest in French and Latin literature. After Miss Temple marries the Reverend Mr. Nasmyth and leaves Lowood, Jane realizes how much she misses Miss Temple.

Bertha Antoinetta Mason Rochester

Tall, dark, and majestic, the only daughter of a wealthy West Indies planter, she conceals the retardation and madness characteristic of her mother's side of the family and marries Edward Rochester, son of her father's business partner. She soon disintegrates into coarseness and perversity, however, and after four wretched years, Edward takes her to England, locks her away at Thornfield under the care of Grace Poole, and deserts her for long periods of time. She cleverly escapes from her keeper at intervals and causes mischief. Aware that Rochester plans to marry Jane, Bertha ignites Jane's bed, then leaps from the roof to her death.

Richard (Dick) Mason

A West Indies merchant and Bertha Mason's brother. He visits Thornfield and suffers biting and stabbing in the shoulder from his deranged sister. After he learns of Jane's engagement, he makes a second visit to Thornfield and halts the wedding by announcing Edward's intention to commit bigamy.

Grace Poole

An able, trustworthy, but eccentric employee in her late thirties. Her position at Thornfield remains a mystery until Rochester divulges the existence of his wife, whom Grace feeds and cares for. Grace's fondness for gin diminishes her dependability and gives Bertha occasional opportunities to wander throughout Thornfield and harm its residents.

Leah

A kitchen maid at Thornfield whose private conversation about

Grace Poole's high wages and difficult task indicates to Jane that the servants know a good deal about the mysterious night wanderer.

John and Mary

Rochester's servants who remain to take care of him at Ferndean after fire destroys Thornfield.

St. John (pronounced *sin' jin*) Rivers

The cold, priggish, and overly zealous minister of the parish at Morton. He serves as head of his family after his father's death, and he rescues Jane from starvation. He attempts to repress his passion for Rosamond Oliver, prepare himself for the mission fields of India, and force Jane to marry him and serve as his missionary assistant. Jane rejects him, and St. John remains unmarried, burying himself under his religious duties.

Diana and Mary Rivers

The benevolent, gentle, and scholarly sisters of St. John Rivers. These girls welcome Jane into their home and, ultimately, into their family. Diana's perceptive assessment of her brother's self-centered obsession with missionary work gives courage to Jane on the night that she struggles to free herself from St. John's domination.

Rosamond Oliver

A conceited and shallow daddy's girl who finances the girls school at Morton and uses it as an excuse to flirt with St. John Rivers. She befriends Jane and invites her to tea. Rosamond later becomes engaged to the grandson and heir to Sir Frederic Granby after a two-month courtship.

Mr. Oliver

The adoring father of Rosamond; he indulges his daughter's charities and admires Jane's portrait of Rosamond. He encourages Rosamond to marry St. John because of St. John's talents and because of his old, established family name.

Mr. Briggs

The solicitor who halts Rochester's marriage to Jane.

John Eyre

Jane's uncle; her father's brother. He is a self-made man who attempts to locate his niece (Jane) in order to leave her his fortune after his quarrel with St. John Rivers' father makes it impossible for him to leave his money to the Rivers children.

Hannah

The faithful, protective servant at Moor House for thirty years. At first, she rejects Jane—gives her a penny and shuts Moor House's door in her face. Later, after they become friends, Hannah assists Jane in establishing a comfortable home for Jane, St. John, Diana, and Mary.

Mary Ann Wilson

Jane's shrewd and witty schoolmate at Lowood.

Mother Bunches

The name which Rochester assumes when he disguises himself as a gypsy fortuneteller.

Mr. Carter

The surgeon who binds Richard Mason's shoulder wound, amputates Rochester's mangled hand, and keeps secret his knowledge of Bertha Mason Rochester.

Alice Wood

Jane's assistant, hired by Rosamond Oliver, at the Morton school for girls.

Madame Pierrot

The likeable, elderly French teacher at Lowood from Lisle, France.

Miss Gryce

Jane's roommate and fellow teacher at Lowood.

Miss Miller

The busy under-teacher of the smallest children at Lowood; she takes charge of Jane during her first night at the school.

Miss Scatcherd

The sharp-tongued, mean teacher of history and grammar at Lowood. She repeatedly punishes and humiliates Helen Burns.

Miss Smith

The overseer of sewing at Lowood.

The Host

The former butler of Edward Rochester's father and innkeeper of The Rochester Arms; he serves Jane's breakfast and fills her in on the events that led to the fire and to Rochester's injuries.

BRIEF SYNOPSIS

Orphaned when she is a small child, Jane Eyre endures the hateful treatment of her aunt, Sarah Reed, and the daily teasing and bullying of her cousins, John, Eliza, and Georgiana, at Gateshead Hall. Jane, who is often excluded from family activities, takes refuge in reading and drawing. Despite the occasional kindness of the maid, Bessie Lee, Jane reaches the limit of her silent tolerance when she is ten years old. Therefore, at the suggestion of the apothecary, Mr. Lloyd, Mrs. Reed arranges for Jane to be interviewed by an administrator of Lowood School.

Mr. Brocklehurst, a pious, overbearing minister and treasurer of the institution, agrees with Mrs. Reed that Jane is a sinful child and that she needs the rigors of a Christian boarding school, where part of her tuition will be paid by charitable donations. After Mr. Brocklehurst's departure, Jane feels deeply wronged. She has been humiliated and wrongfully accused of deceit. She confronts her aunt and stands

Jane's Genealogy

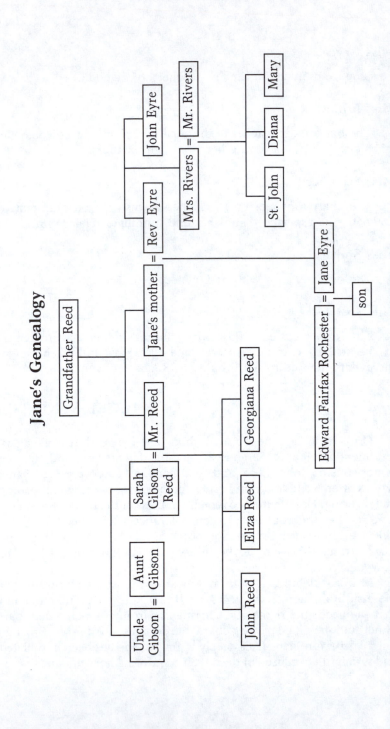

Rochester's Genealogy

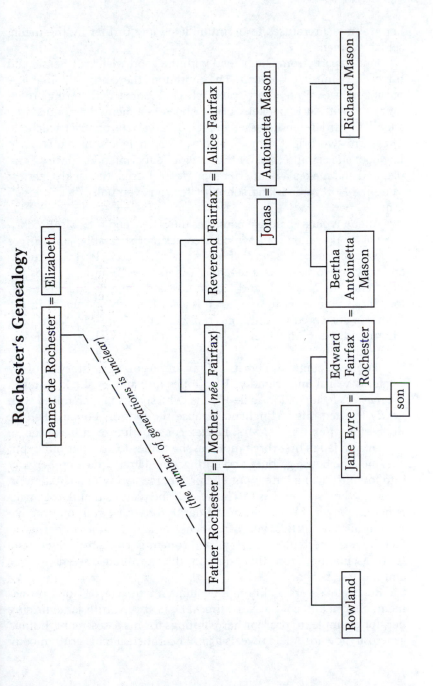

her ground; she refuses to be intimidated any further by the mean, selfish woman.

Jane departs from Gateshead with the good wishes of Bessie and travels fifty miles to Lowood. The conditions there are abominable – burnt porridge for breakfast, miserably cold rooms, unflattering brown uniforms with little pockets, crude shoes, regimented activities in a cheerless garden, and classes taught by a variety of strict teachers. There are two bright moments, however, in Jane's introduction to Lowood: she is impressed by the gracious superintendent, Miss Temple, and she makes a dear friend of Helen Burns, the sickly, almost saint-like Northumberland schoolmate who eventually dies in Jane's arms.

After a typhus epidemic paralyzes the school and robs Mr. Brocklehurst of his power, life at Lowood becomes more bearable. Jane thrives on academic successes, and, after six years, she completes her studies and serves two years as a teacher. When Miss Temple marries the Reverend Mr. Nasmyth and leaves Lowood, Jane decides that she, too, should move on to another position. Her advertisement in the *Herald* is answered by only one reply: a letter from Mrs. Fairfax of Thornfield, near Millcote, a sixteen-hour journey. Jane decides to accept the job.

Jane's welcome at Thornfield, an imposing three-story country estate, is warm and friendly. Her duties are simple: she is to teach the master's foster child, Adèle Varens, who speaks French mixed with newly learned bits of English. Because the master, Edward Fairfax Rochester, often travels, Mrs. Fairfax runs the house in his absence.

During Jane's first three months, she comes to love her pupil, but she finds the house gloomy and boring. One January day, on her way into town to mail a letter, Jane helps a horseman who has fallen on the ice. When she returns to Thornfield, she realizes that the stranger is her employer, Mr. Rochester, a darkly brooding and unattractive man in his late thirties; yet, Mr. Rochester is not without charm – in fact, he has a certain mysterious and romantic charisma which Jane finds fascinating. From this point on, the stern house seems livelier and more appealing.

Rochester's personality is a peculiar mixture of brusque refinement, charm, and coldness. At times, he is abrupt with Jane, forcing her, for example, to present her paintings for his assessment, but his generosity toward Adèle reveals a kind heart beneath his gruff, moody exterior. He tells Jane how his French mistress, opera dancer Céline Varens, deceived and ridiculed him and how he abandoned her. At her death, he rescued Adèle, Céline's daughter, whom he does not claim as his own, but, nevertheless, whom he brought to Thornfield, along with her French-speaking nursemaid, Sophie.

One night, Jane hears hands groping the walls outside her door and a crazed laugh. When she notices smoke coming from Rochester's room, Jane throws water on the fire and awakens her master. Rochester urges Jane to keep the matter a secret. He rushes upstairs to investigate, then leads Jane to believe that Grace Poole, a house servant, is at fault. His tender farewell to Jane leaves her sleepless. The following morning, Jane's flushed face and trembling hands are evidence of her growing love for Rochester.

Rochester, however, pursues a local beauty, Blanche Ingram, and he gives a houseparty for her and seven other guests. Richard Mason joins the gathering and is mysteriously assaulted during the night. Jane assists Rochester in tending to Mr. Mason's bleeding shoulder. Again, blame rests on the eccentric Grace Poole.

Jane leaves Thornfield briefly to visit her aunt, Sarah Reed, who is ill and calling for Jane. She offers her aunt an opportunity for reconciliation, but Mrs. Reed, as always, rejects Jane. She deeply resents the fact that long ago, she promised to obey her dying husband's request that she raise his niece, Jane. Mrs. Reed always resented Jane's presence at Gateshead. Before her death, Sarah Reed tells Jane that John Eyre, Jane's uncle in the West Indies, has been trying to locate her. Mrs. Reed admits that she discouraged him. Sarah Reed dies, unloved and unmourned by her selfish daughters.

On her return to Thornfield, Jane is happy to find Rochester at home. Without warning, he stops courting Blanche Ingram and proposes to Jane. She is overwhelmed and skeptical of his seriousness, but she accepts. Mrs. Fairfax objects to the match, noting the difference in their ages. Rochester spends lavishly on his future bride, buying her a new carriage and tempting her with bright-colored dress material. Jane, who is short and plain, rejects his extravagant choices and selects plain fabrics for her dresses. She sends a letter to her uncle announcing her upcoming marriage.

On her wedding day, Jane follows Rochester beyond the gate at Thornfield to the church. They see strangers walking among the tombs in the churchyard. Later, when the minister begins the ceremony,

Mr. Briggs, a solicitor, halts the wedding with news that Mr. Rochester is already married. In fact, Mr. Briggs says, Rochester's wife was recently seen in Rochester's house by her own brother (Richard Mason).

Rochester then escorts Jane, the minister, and the two men to the third floor of Thornfield where Bertha Mason Rochester, a raving madwoman, is locked away and guarded by Grace Poole. The solicitor explains that Richard Mason learned of Richard's plan to marry Jane from Jane's letter to her uncle, Mason's business associate. Jane, fearing that she will now be forced to be Rochester's mistress — and never his wife — flees from Thornfield, taking the morning coach as far as her money will allow.

Arriving at Whitcross with no money, Jane searches for work and eventually is reduced to begging for charity. Three days later, she collapses on the doorstep of Moor House, where the maid denies her entrance. However, the master of the house, St. John Rivers, a dedicated but cold-natured minister, rescues Jane from the rainy night. He extends the hospitality of his hearth and introduces Jane to his two studious sisters, Diana and Mary. After recuperating under the Rivers family's care, Jane forms a lasting friendship with them and accepts a job as schoolmistress of a newly opened local girls school.

One day, St. John discovers that Jane has inherited 20,000 pounds from her uncle, John Eyre, and, furthermore, that she is a cousin to the Rivers family — whom John Eyre excluded from his will. Jane gladly shares her inheritance equally with St. John and his sisters, then refurbishes Moor House as a home for her cousins. When St. John presses Jane to learn Hindustani so that she can accompany him to India as a missionary, she agrees to study the difficult language. St. John makes passionless proposals of marriage, but Jane is not impressed by the man. From far off, a distant voice seems to call her back to her former love, Rochester.

Clinging to her loving memories of Rochester, Jane decisively rejects St. John and returns to Thornfield. When the thirty-six-hour journey finally ends, Jane hurries to the manor and discovers only a burned-out shell. At The Rochester Arms, an inn, Jane orders breakfast and asks the innkeeper to tell her about the events of the past year. He describes in detail Rochester's interrupted plans to marry a governess, his futile search for the governess, and the tragic fire that was set by the mad Bertha Rochester, who plunged to her death from the roof despite her husband's attempts to rescue her. In the fire, Rochester suffered a mangled hand, which was later amputated, and he also was blinded.

Jane hires a chaise to take her to Ferndean, Rochester's current home, and she observes him from a distance as he blindly attempts to walk outdoors. He has obviously been changed by his terrible suffering, but his face still retains its forceful character.

Jane carries a tray to him, reveals her presence, and enjoys a poignant reunion with her love. When Rochester inquires about her year apart from him, Jane describes St. John Rivers and his proposals, but she emphasizes that St. John is incapable of feeling genuine love for her. Rochester realizes then that Jane is still willing to marry him. In three days, they marry and settle at Ferndean.

Ten years later, Jane tells us, she is content with her married life. Adèle visits during vacations from boarding school, and Rochester has recovered vision in one eye and is able to see their newborn son. Jane continues her friendship with Diana and Mary, both of whom have married, and she maintains a correspondence with St. John Rivers, who is showing the strain of his devotion to God's service in India.

INTRODUCTION TO THE NOVEL

Although *Jane Eyre* echoes the **romantic conventions** of the Victorian era and also recreates many incidents of Charlotte Brontë's own life, the book is neither a **stereotype** nor an **autobiography**. Rather, it has an energy and a singularity of purpose that sets it apart from novels of the period, which often chronicled the sufferings of young girls spurned in love. Jane Eyre's **first-person narration** of her life, from the age of ten through the first ten years of her marriage, details a strong, readily identifiable character, rich in individuality and determination and fortified by religious faith. Throughout her struggle for independence and love, the heroine never loses her sense of self, nor does she compromise her values.

In a variety of **settings**, Jane encounters a series of frustrations. From Gateshead Hall, where she suffers the humiliation of living as a penniless, unwelcome relative, Jane enrolls at Lowood School, educates herself and locates honest work. She is successful as a governess at Thornfield, and eventually she succeeds in endearing herself to its crusty, moody master. However, just as the reader experiences relief from the tensions of Jane's struggle to rise above poverty and dependence, her happiness and plans for the future plunge to new depths. Forcing herself to depart from the comforts of Thornfield and the security of Rochester's love, she travels as far as her bit of money will take her. She refuses to become Rochester's mistress, fearing that Rochester will cast her off, as he has his former mistresses.

The **theme** of belonging is prominent at this point in the story. At the Rivers' cottage, where Jane faints from hunger and exhaustion, she finds a different sense of security from the joys of marriage which she anticipated at Thornfield – an acceptance into a real family and success as a teacher of illiterate farmgirls. Then, an unforeseen inheritance sets her free of dependence on charity, enabling her to assume the role of benefactor to the Rivers girls, her newly discovered cousins. The boost to her self-image empowers Jane to resist St. John Rivers' bullying, demeaning proposal. She returns to Thornfield to find Rochester maimed, dependent, but still eager to marry her. The triumph of Jane's principles over temptations and trials results in a satisfying conclusion.

In retrospect, we can see that two literary movements of the nineteenth century – **romanticism** and the **gothic novel** – greatly influenced Charlotte Brontë's work. Writers of **romantic novels,** particularly Sir Walter Scott (Charlotte's favorite), emphasized freedom and the individual. The central factor of **romantic works** – the predominance of imagination over reason – is evident in Jane's struggle to control her growing passion for Rochester, a man who, by conventional wisdom, is socially and chronologically unsuited for her:

> When once more alone, I reviewed the information I had got; looked into my heart, examined its thoughts and feelings, and endeavoured to bring back with a strict hand such as had been staying through imagination's boundless and trackless waste, into the safe fold of common sense.
>
> Arraigned at my own bar, Memory having given her evidence of the hopes, wishes, sentiments I had been cherishing since last night – of the general state of mind in which I had indulged for nearly a fortnight past; Reason having come forward and told in her own quiet way, a plain, unvarnished tale, showing how I had rejected the real, and rapidly devoured the ideal; – I pronounced judgement to this effect: That

a greater fool than Jane Eyre had never breathed the breath of life: that a more fantastic idiot had never surfeited herself on sweet lies, and swallowed poison as if it were nectar. (Chapter 16)

Even as Jane struggles to remain objective about her position as governess at Thornfield, she is aware that romantic yearnings are luring her toward romantic foolishness.

The second influence, the **gothic novel,** often employs richly overstated scenes of mystery and horror to heighten the misadventures of a "maiden in distress," a woman who must rely on her wits and/or the intervention of mystic powers to aid her from succumbing to overwhelming odds. Jane, on several distinct occasions, finds herself in such circumstances. As she learns the layout of Thornfield, she hears a laugh "as tragic, as preternatural a laugh as any I ever heard; and, but that it was high noon, and that no circumstance of ghostliness accompanied the curious cachinnation; but that neither scene nor season favoured fear, I should have been superstitiously afraid." (Chapter 11)

This episode, coupled with other disjointed clues, fails to coalesce in Jane's mind until the day of her wedding, when Rochester reveals the whole story of Bertha's imprisonment. Although these mysterious, chilling elements build suspense, they never dominate the story, which emphasizes that such human frailties as pride, callousness, and greed very often cause human suffering.

In several scenes in which Jane is faced with **dilemmas,** she experiences telepathic communication—in particular, on the night that Rochester cries out for her from Ferndean:

I might have said, "Where is it?" for it did not seem in the room, nor in the house, nor in the garden; it did not come out of the air, nor from under the earth, nor from overhead. I had heard it— where, or whence, for ever impossible to know! And it was the voice of a human being—a known, loved, well-remembered voice—that of Edward Fairfax Rochester; and it spoke in pain and woe, wildly eerily, urgently. (Chapter 35)

However, Jane does not rely on mysticism or external intelligence to decide her fate. She never lacks the gumption to weigh her choices and decide for herself what is the most sensible course of action.

Other factors enhance the novel, highlighting it with memorable scenes and details. In addition to the suspense and mystery of Thornfield's secret, mad resident, Charlotte Brontë employs bizarre, unforeseen turns of **plot.** At one point, Rochester disguises himself as an aged female gypsy and tells the fortunes of his houseguests and Jane. Of Jane, he says:

> You are cold, because you are alone: no contact strikes the fire from you that is in you. You are sick, because the best of feelings, the highest and the sweetest given to man, keeps far away from you. You are silly, because, suffer as you may, you will not beckon it to approach, nor will you stir one step to meet it where it waits for you. (Chapter 19)

This unusual scenario enables Rochester to achieve two distinct goals — to discourage Blanche Ingram's hopes of marrying into a fortune and to encourage Jane to reach beyond the limits imposed by her brain for the rewards waiting in her heart.

To offset the grimness that permeates much of the novel, Brontë employs understated **humor.** For example, Mr. Brocklehurst, who attempts to intimidate Jane, reveals his own gullibility when he describes how his son chooses verses of a Psalm over a ginger-bread-nut and then is rewarded with "two nuts in recompense for his infant piety." (Chapter 4)

Later, as Brocklehurst harangues the students of Lowood on the subject of thrift and feminine modesty, he is interrupted by the arrival of his wife and daughters, "splendidly attired in velvet, silk, and furs." (Chapter 7)

Although Charlotte Brontë's sisters' experiences at the Cowan Bridge school serve as bitter prototypes for Brontë's exposés of boarding school life and the fraudulent piety of religious leaders, she inserts here a humorous touch of **incongruity,** giving us a wry smile as she contrasts the befurred ladies with the poor girls.

Coincidence, too, plays an important part in the plot. When Jane travels to the moors, using the last of her money for the journey, she wanders for three days, then collapses, by chance, on the doorstep of unknown relatives. In another instance of unlikely coincidence, Jane writes to her Uncle John in Madeira to announce her engagement to Rochester. By chance, his business associate is Richard Mason, Rochester's brother-in-law, and when Mason learns of Rochester's plans to marry Jane, he hurries to England and halts the wedding at the altar. These instances of coincidence, however, even though highly unlikely, do not detract from the overall worth of the novel.

Other stylistic details indicate that Charlotte Brontë understood the complex workings of fiction and could please an audience by the skillful incorporation of literary devices. The **symbolism** of the old horse-chestnut tree shattered by lightning in the Eden-like garden of Thornfield, which is the scene of Rochester's proposal of marriage, **foreshadows** the couple's doomed hopes for union.

In addition, the grave of Damer de Rochester serves as a grim backdrop as Rochester hurries Jane up the hill toward an illicit marriage; it reminds the reader that the past still intrudes, even though Rochester uses every means to lock it away.

Another device, the **pathetic fallacy** (parallel moods in nature to reflect the emotions of the characters), suggests that nature intervenes in Jane's life, preluding events and coloring the mood of the story. In one instance, Jane relishes the harvest scene during a spell of good weather as she joyfully anticipates her marriage. Later, during her first night on the moor, she says, "Nature seemed to me benign and good; I thought she loved me, outcast as I was. . . . To-night, at least, I would be her guest, as I was her child: my mother would lodge me without money and without price." (Chapter 28)

Despite the author's use of these standard literary devices, however, at no point in the narrative do they encumber the action, which never fails to move along toward its conclusion. From the first to the end, Brontë grips the reader's imagination with her powerful story.

Despite some Victorian disapproval of Jane's thinly veiled sexuality, the result of Charlotte Brontë's art was immediate, popular success. Her enthusiastic readers included Queen Victoria, who read *Jane Eyre* aloud to Prince Albert and approved both the spunk and moral fiber which undergird Jane's dauntless character.

In 1893, in an effort to preserve what little remained of Charlotte Brontë, her fans formed the Brontë Society and made the Haworth parsonage a museum where thousands of people still journey in order to experience their idol's environment. Recent times have proved *Jane Eyre* worthy of presentation on both screen and television, owing in part to its strong feminist **theme** as well as to its graphic scenarios.

SUMMARIES & CRITICAL COMMENTARIES

SECTION ONE

CHAPTER 1

Summary

Kept indoors on a raw November day, ten-year-old Jane (an orphan) feels painfully rejected by her aunt, Sarah Reed, who clusters her own three children about her. When Jane withdraws to the window seat of the breakfast room to enjoy a book on British birdlore, John Reed, fourteen years old, locates her peaceful nook and strikes her, sneering a reminder that she is a penniless, unwelcome relative. John throws the book that Jane was reading at her, and she falls against the door and cuts her head. Jane's aunt, cousins, and the servants, Bessie and Miss Abbot, blame Jane for the quarrel and take her upstairs to the red-room and lock her in.

Commentary

The desolation which Jane feels in this cold, hostile environment on this bitter November day is echoed by the passage that Jane reads in Bewick's *History of British Birds,* concerning a rock "standing up alone in a sea of billow and spray." This rock, defying the stormy sea, symbolizes Jane's own endurance against the tyranny of fourteen-year-old John Reed, an abusive, overweight mama's boy. From the beginning, Brontë develops the idea that Jane relies on inner reserves to bolster her during troubled times.

CHAPTER 2

Summary

Jane's resistance to authority reveals a new side of her personality. Jane feels that she is like any rebellious slave and must resist Bessie and Miss Abbot. But to spare herself the shame of being tied to the stool with Miss Abbot's garters, Jane promises to behave. The servants, doubtful of Jane's sanity, urge her to pray and repent; then they lock her in the sumptuous unused room where Mr. Reed died nine years previously.

Jane stares at her pale reflection in the mirror and notes that her cousin Georgiana, with her blonde good looks, would never be so mistreated. A surge of defiance fills Jane with the will to run away or starve herself to death. Then, sinking once more into her more accustomed state of depression, she thinks about the promise which Mr. Reed, on his deathbed, extracted from his wife—that she would bring up Jane as a member of the family. Clearly, Mrs. Reed has not kept this deathbed promise.

Suddenly, Jane is shaken by an imagined presence in the red-room. She screams and shakes the door, summoning the servants and her aunt. She begs for pity and forgiveness, but Mrs. Reed insists that Jane stay another hour in the red-room. After they leave, Jane faints.

Commentary

Here, Jane experiences the first of a series of ghostly visitations which precede important changes in her life. Although she believes that her mother's brother (Mr. Reed) would show kindness if he were still alive, Jane fears the "rushing of wings," which warns her of an unnatural presence. Out of the entire household at Gateshead Hall, only Bessie (the nursemaid) shows any sympathy for the orphaned girl. Mrs. Reed, a cold and suspicious woman, views Jane's actions as a compound of "virulent passions, mean spirit, and dangerous duplicity."

CHAPTER 3

Summary

Awakening in her own bed after midnight, Jane receives tender care from Bessie. Then she is examined by Mr. Lloyd, an apothecary. The following day, Bessie brings Jane a tart and offers her a copy of *Gulliver's Travels,* but Jane is unable to eat or read. As Bessie sews doll clothes for Georgiana, she sings a sad song about the plight of orphans. Mr. Lloyd returns and calls Jane a baby for crying over petty matters. He suggests that she might be happier in school and discusses the possibility with Mrs. Reed.

Jane accidentally learns about her family's history when she overhears a conversation between Miss Abbot and Bessie: Jane's father was a poor clergyman who married Jane's mother against the wishes of Grandfather Reed, who disinherited his daughter. A year after their marriage, both of Jane's parents died of typhus, leaving their tiny daughter alone in the world.

Commentary

Jane's silent tears are evidence of the deep sadness that envelopes her life. At the age of ten, she is unable to alter the daily pattern of abuse and neglect which she encounters at the hands of her aunt and cousins. Her hope that Mr. Lloyd may help her is dashed when he makes fun of her for crying. Even Bessie's show of kindness fails to comfort the forlorn child who sits wrapped in a shawl before the nurseryroom fire. When Mr. Lloyd weighs the alternatives to Jane's misery at Gateshead Hall, however, she truthfully admits that she prefers her present social level over the degradation of poverty.

Jane's position in the Reed household is only a little better than exile; even the servants look down on her. Miss Abbot characterizes Jane as a "little toad," a young Guy Fawkes who seems to be watching and plotting against the family. Miss Abbot agrees with Bessie that Jane would receive more sympathetic treatment if she possessed the appealing good looks of Georgiana.

CHAPTER 4

Summary

Jane waits nearly three months, hoping for a change. Ignored by the Reeds during the festive Christmas season, she grasps at crumbs of comfort – the love of her shabby doll and the infrequent kindness of Bessie. On January 15, a hasty summons to the breakfast-room fills Jane with foreboding.

Mr. Brocklehurst, who stands like a black pillar topped with a carved mask, interviews Jane about sin, hell, and the Bible. Jane parries with him, refusing to follow his reasoning. She confirms her aunt's worst suspicions about her by declaring the Psalms "uninteresting." At Mrs. Reed's insistance, Mr. Brocklehurst agrees to accept Jane at Lowood, a boarding school for girls. He also promises to be on his guard against Jane's worst fault – deceit.

Jane struggles with her feelings of helplessness until she and her aunt are alone. Refusing to be dismissed, Jane confronts her and accuses her of being bad – hardhearted and deceitful – and threatens to expose her to the residents of Lowood. Mrs. Reed, agitated and thrown off-guard, leaves the room. Glorying in her moment of victory, Jane savors her first taste of vengeance, which is like "aromatic wine."

She takes a short walk in a lonely part of the estate under a wintry sky. When Bessie scolds her for refusing to answer a summons for lunch, Jane presents a fearless front to the servant and convinces her not to scold, to be friendly until Jane leaves for school. Bessie confides that her own mother pities Jane's position in the Reed household, and then she rewards Jane with a special tea cake, an evening of enchanting tales, and some sweet songs.

Commentary

Jane's victory over intimidation extends beyond a moment's courage. She battles with the shallow Mr. Brocklehurst, refusing to be cornered by narrow, pious platitudes. Her confrontation with Mrs. Reed gives Jane a sense of self-confidence that she lacked in earlier battles. The final test, convincing Bessie to accept her as a friend, proves to Jane that inner resolve may be her best weapon.

The future, on the other hand, may hold greater challenges. Although she leaves behind Georgiana's vain primping and Eliza's greed, Jane appears to be entering a severe environment where young girls eat plain food, dress in humble attire, and follow a strict, spartan regimen. By Mr. Brocklehurst's own admission, he has "studied how best to modify in them the worldly sentiment of pride," which he overlooks in his own silk-clad daughters.

SECTION TWO

CHAPTER 5

Summary

On January 19, her last day at Gateshead Hall, Jane arises at 4:30 A.M., dresses, and sets out for the porter's lodge in the company of Bessie, her only well-wisher. After riding in a coach for fifty miles,

Jane arrives after dark at Lowood and is escorted by Miss Miller, a young under-teacher, to a large room where seventy-odd girls, from nine to twenty years old, are studying their lessons and whispering their repetitions. That night, Jane shares Miss Miller's bed, and, next day, Jane follows a full schedule, including doing her lessons from before dawn until five in the evening. During lunch break, Jane questions an older girl (Helen Burns) about the stone tablet which identifies Lowood as an "institution." The girl explains that all the residents at Lowood are orphans and that benevolent subscribers make up a portion of the tuition with donations.

For the most part, Jane keeps to herself, as is her custom, and evaluates her surroundings, noting the poor quality of the food, the kindness of the superintendent, Miss Temple, and the cruelty of Miss Scatcherd, who punishes Helen Burns by making her stand in the center of the room.

Commentary

This chapter reveals the dismal existence of poor, orphaned boarding students. Their uniforms, cheerless high-necked brown dresses and narrow tuckers with a workbag tied at the waist, are complemented by woolen stockings, brogans with buckles, and an uncurled hairstyle. A straw bonnet and gray cloak serve as covering for their visit to the garden, which the girls are expected to tend in season.

Jane's first day at Lowood begins before daylight with prayers and an hour's reading of Scripture; a breakfast of burned porridge, lessons in geography, grammar, history, writing, and arithmetic. Lunch is served in the garden, where bread and cheese make up the deficiencies of the morning meal. The four classes, taught by Misses Scatcherd, Miller, Pierrot, and Smith, resume. Dinner, consisting of a bad-smelling stew of potatoes and meat, interrupts the afternoon's work. Classes end at five; the students consume a mug of coffee and half a slice of brown bread and enjoy half an hour's recreation. They study, eat a snack of water and a piece of oatcake, say their prayers, and retire.

During the lunch break, Jane relies on her love of fanciful literature to guide her to a new friend, who sits on a stone bench reading Samuel Johnson's *Rasselas*. Although the book appears dull and lacks any mention of fairies or genii, Jane follows her instincts in allying herself with another loner who turns to literature to relieve the miseries of daily life.

CHAPTER 6

Summary

The weather turns so cold the next day that washing is suspended because the water in the pitchers is frozen, but the moaning wind and drifting snow delight Jane, who has no warm home to long for. She settles into the routine of Lowood, struggling with the fourth table's rote learning of difficult lessons and hemming two yards of muslin for Miss Smith while observing Miss Scatcherd's continued abuse and humiliation of Helen Burns, Jane's new acquaintance. Although Helen recites her history lesson better than the other students, Miss Scatcherd scolds her for having dirty nails and lashes Helen's neck a dozen times with a bundle of twigs as punishment.

Later, Jane joins Helen by the fireside and inquires about her stoic response to Miss Scatcherd's continual abuse. Helen acknowledges her weaknesses—carelessness and poor concentration—and explains how her thoughts too frequently tend to drift toward her home in Deepden, Northumberland. Rejecting any notion of rebellion against a teacher's authority, she tells Jane to learn from criticism and to thereby avoid punishment. Jane then pours out the painful injustice she suffered in the Reed household, but Helen remains firm in her belief that Jane should forget animosity and emulate Christ's example by loving her enemies. Helen, lost in her contemplation of eternity, drifts into a peaceful reverie until a monitor threatens to tattle if Helen does not straighten the contents of her drawer and fold her work.

Commentary

Here, Charlotte Brontë appears to be inserting the pious mouthings of a mature person into the conversations of young Helen Burns. Although Helen is only around thirteen, her advice to Jane far exceeds either the depth of logic or speech patterns of so young a girl. The ominous forebodings of Helen's delight in eternity, her inability to concentrate, and her insistent cough foreshadow an early death.

Helen serves as an obvious foil to Jane, whose discontent grows as she adds the many examples of deprivation that she sees at Lowood Institution to the miseries which she suffered at Gateshead Hall. Still filled with the audacity which enabled her to face Mrs. Reed, Jane appears to be preparing herself to do battle with even more injustice in her adult life.

CHAPTER 7

Summary

A fierce, raw winter engulfs the inmates at Lowood, who lack boots, gloves, and sufficient food. Struggling through the almost impassable road that leads to Brocklebridge Church, the girls and their teachers shiver through two services and a meager meal of cold meat and bread. Miss Temple, however, sets an example of the "stalwart soldier" on the march back to Lowood, where tea is highlighted by a whole slice of bread and a welcome smidgen of butter.

One afternoon in February, Mr. Brocklehurst, the treasurer and manager of Lowood, visits the school to assess how supplies are being used. Jane sinks down in her seat and hides her face with a slate to escape his notice. After berating Miss Temple for treating the girls to lunch as a replacement for their spoiled breakfast, he demands that the older girls' hair be cut to a more modest length.

Mr. Brocklehurst's attention is diverted when Jane drops her slate, breaking it into two pieces. He orders Jane to stand on a high stool for a half hour as punishment for being a liar (according to Mrs. Reed), and he warns the faculty and students to avoid such bad company. The kind reassurance of Miss Temple and a fleeting smile from Helen Burns sustain Jane through this ordeal.

Commentary

Charlotte Brontë's weekly two and a quarter-mile walk to the parish church of Tunstall, Lancaster, during her year at the Clergy Daughters' school serves as the model for Jane's unpleasant experiences at Brocklebridge. As the daughter of a clergyman of the Church of England, Miss Brontë was well acquainted with both meanness of spirit and excessive outpourings of fraudulent piety. She clearly delineates the character of Brocklehurst himself, who, from his introduction in Chapter 4, serves as a symbol of hypocrisy and insensitivity.

In particular, note that when Brocklehurst is railing against the loss of sewing needles, complaining about holes in stockings (which he examined as they dried on the line), and expounding the virtues of Christian martyrdom, he is interrupted by the arrival of his fashionably dressed wife and two daughters. Their ostrich plumes, ermine, beaver hats, and false French curls contrast with the cold, raw hands of the underdressed little girls who huddle on the back row before the fire, reminding the reader of the Brontë sisters' disastrous experiences in a similar boarding school.

CHAPTER 8

Summary

After five o'clock strikes and the girls go to the refectory for tea, Jane steps down from her stool. Almost immediately, her strength gives way to sobs. She lies on the floor, alone in a corner, fearful that all her progress at Lowood has been destroyed by Brocklehurst's cruel and unfair accusations. Helen brings Jane her portion of cake and bread and comforts her with common sense. She says that because the students distrust Brocklehurst, they will not accept his condemnation of Jane. Jane admits to Helen that she prefers death to a solitary, friendless life. Helen chides Jane for depending too much upon human love.

Miss Temple invites the two girls to her apartment, treats them to tea and some seed-cake, and Jane pours out her life story, receiving Miss Temple's sympathy and her promise to contact Mr. Lloyd for confirmation of Jane's innocence. Then turning her attention to Helen, Miss Temple engages the girl in a conversation about French and Latin authors. Helen's depth of learning and experience with literature amaze Jane.

The following day, Miss Scatcherd renews her perpetual harping on trivial matters and binds a piece of pasteboard with the word "Slattern" on it around Helen's forehead. About a week later, Miss Temple keeps her word to Jane and announces publicly that Jane has been falsely accused of being a liar. After being cleared, Jane begins to thrive at Lowood, adding basic French to her curriculum and creating mental images for future art sketches.

Commentary

Jane finds role models at Lowood who influence her behavior as an adult. From Helen and Miss Pierrot, she develops a love of French literature, which she incorporates into her later conversations with Adèle and Edward Rochester. With Miss Temple as an example, Jane begins to build trust in human kindness and generosity. Despite Miss Temple's obvious preference for Helen, Jane learns to love them both. In contrast to her earlier, love-starved existence at Gateshead Hall, Jane discovers hope and creative expression through sketching and foreign language skills.

CHAPTER 9

Summary

Spring thaw brings a loosening of discipline at Lowood. May is bright and serene, and Jane is able to go rambling in the outlying woods with a new friend, Mary Ann Wilson. They enjoy picnics and take pleasure in flowers, foliage, and herbs. Suddenly, however, the school atmosphere changes as a result of rampant typhus, which afflicts forty-five of the eighty girls. Some of the victims die and are hastily buried to lessen the threat of the epidemic. Miss Temple devotes her waking hours to the sick-room. After some pupils and staff members, notably Mr. Brocklehurst and his family, leave the premises until the contagion ends, control of supplies relaxes and servings of food increase.

One day, returning from an outing, Jane notices the pony of Mr. Bates, the surgeon, at the door and learns that Helen Burns is dying of consumption. Later, near eleven, when the others are asleep, Jane creeps down the hallway and joins Helen in her crib beside Miss Temple's empty bed. Briefly, Jane awakens as a nurse carries her back to her own bed, and she learns a day or two later that she was found clasping Helen, who had died during the night.

Commentary

This chapter contrasts the revival of spring in the hills around Lowood with the suffering of little girls who have weakened during the winter months from neglect and slow starvation and have fallen prey to typhus. Jane experiences a feeling of ambivalence – a joy in the freedom of the outdoors and, at the same time, an awareness of the death which comes to us all. She recoils from the notion of death, but she bravely faces contagion to visit Helen one last time. Despite her love for a worldly new friend (Mary Ann Wilson), she remains loyal to Helen. Jane hints that fifteen years later, when she is financially solvent, she pays for the stone marker that was placed over Helen's unmarked grave in the Brocklebridge churchyard. The stone proclaims in Latin, *Resurgam,* meaning "I shall rise again."

CHAPTER 10

Summary

Jane summarizes the next eight years of her life, emphasizing the reforms and alterations at Lowood as the typhus epidemic draws public attention to the neglect and deprivation of the inmates. A more significant change for Jane occurs after Miss Temple is married to the Reverend Mr. Nasmyth. Jane analyzes her feelings of loss not only of a friend and role model, but of a surrogate mother. Seized by a desire to meet new challenges in a more realistic setting, Jane searches for a "new servitude," but is at first stymied by her lack of experience.

Almost as if a mysterious voice speaks to her in the night, Jane is convinced that she must place an advertisement in the *Herald* for a governess' position. The single reply, signed by Mrs. Fairfax of Thornfield, Millcote, frees Jane after eight years in an institution— six as student and the last two as a teacher—but always under the firm rule of a superintendent and a governing board.

The night before Jane leaves, Bessie Lee (the Reeds' nursemaid) makes an unannounced visit and marvels at Jane's education and artistic accomplishments. Bessie narrates developments in the Reed family and reveals an important bit of news—a visitor, John Eyre, came to Gateshead Hall seven years earlier to locate his niece, but could not travel the fifty miles to Lowood because he had booked passage on a ship due to leave shortly for Madeira.

Commentary

Jane continues to evaluate her feelings and desires as she searches for relief from boredom, restlessness, and discontent. She correctly assesses her reliance on Miss Temple, who serves as a mother figure, but fails to note that she has always chosen older girls, such as Bessie Lee, Helen Burns, and Mary Ann Wilson, as confidantes, another indication of her need for a maternal presence in her life. Although Jane envisions herself in the continued role of a servant, she chooses freedom from institutionalization and looks forward to the bustle of Millcote, an industrial community seventy miles closer to London.

Bessie performs a useful service in this chapter: she offers an encapsulated version of the Reed family's problems, emphasizing Georgiana's thwarted elopement and Sarah Reed's dissatisfaction with her dissipated son. More important, however, is Bessie's assessment of Jane Eyre, whom she describes as "head and shoulders" shorter than Sarah Reed and lacking in physical attraction. She confides, however, that she never doubted Jane's academic excellence over Georgiana and Eliza Reed.

(Here and in following chapters, foreign words and phrases are translated for you, as is the one below)

- *en regle*   according to proper form

SECTION THREE

CHAPTER 11

Summary

The sixteen-hour ride to Millcote tires Jane, and by the time that she travels the additional six miles to Thornfield, it is nearly midnight. Despite its massive, imposing architecture, the house is inviting. Mrs. Fairfax greets Jane warmly and serves refreshments by the fireplace. Jane learns bits of information – that Mrs. Fairfax is the housekeeper, that eight-year-old Adèle Varens (the master's ward) will be her pupil, and that Mr. Rochester (the master of the manor) is away much of the time.

After a good night's sleep, Jane meets Adèle and her nurse, Sophie, who speaks only French. She learns that Adèle was born on the Continent, which she left only six months ago. During these months, Adèle has learned a bit of English, but she speaks mostly a hodgepodge of French and English which Mrs. Fairfax cannot understand. Adèle is delighted that her new governess speaks French. She tells Jane how her mother has "gone to the Holy Virgin" and how Mr. Rochester took her and Sophie from Madame Frederic's home to a boat which brought them to England.

After examining the library, which will serve as Adèle's classroom, Jane follows Mrs. Fairfax on a tour of the three-storied mansion, admiring the dark oak paneling, elegant furnishings, and spacious lawn. Standing near the staircase, Jane hears a distinct, haunting laugh. Mrs. Fairfax explains that Grace Poole, an eccentric seamstress, often laughs like that.

Commentary

Although Jane experiences a momentary feeling of estrangement when she arrives at the George Inn in Millcote, her fears are quieted by Mrs. Fairfax's welcome and the beauty of her surroundings. For the first time in her life, Jane is given a feminine room of her own. Her first act is to kneel down, thank God and beg for guidance.

Jane's initial impressions seem to promise better things – the congeniality of the housekeeper, the respect given Jane as governess, the richness and good taste displayed in the mansion, Adèle's talents and enthusiasm, and a brief description of Mr. Rochester's fair treatment of his staff. Jane's conversation with Mrs. Fairfax about ghosts, however, foreshadows Jane's further encounters with spirits – both living and dead.

- *bonne* nurse
- *C'est là ma gouvernante?* Is this the governess?
- *Mais oui, certainment.* Yes, certainly.
- *naivete* innocence
- *La Ligue des Rats: fable de La Fontaine* "The Plot of the Rats": a fable written by Jean de La Fontaine
- *Qu'avez-vous donc? lui dit un de ces rats; parlez!* "What do you have then?" says one of the rats, "Speak!"
- *Mesdames, vous êtes serviés! J'ai bien faim, moi!* Ladies, you are served! I am very hungry!

CHAPTER 12

Summary

Jane is successful in her new career and notes progress in Adèle, who gives up her spoiled ways and responds to Jane's discipline and instruction. Still, however, Jane contends with bouts of boredom, discontent, and restlessness during the confining winter months at Thornfield. She frequently continues to hear laughter and occasionally catches a glimpse of Grace Poole, often "bearing a pot of porter"—that is, dark brown beer. Grace also drinks gin, and the fact that she is probably an alcoholic will prove to be a pivotal matter later in the novel.

To alleviate the feeling of captivity, Jane volunteers to mail a letter for Mrs. Fairfax in Hay, a nearby village. On her way she encounters a black and white Newfoundland dog and hears a clatter as a horse and rider slip on a patch of ice. Jane assists the man, whom she perceives to be "past youth," not handsome, but broad-chested, with stern features. His injuries are confined to a sprain; with Jane's support, he remounts and continues on his way. Dreading the return to Thornfield, Jane arrives late and discovers that the horseman she aided is her employer, Mr. Rochester.

Commentary

Although her mind dredges up Bessie's tales of a forbidding animal spirit called a "Gytrash," Jane is unafraid of Pilot, Mr. Rochester's dog, but she is less successful in confronting and managing Rochester's horse. Her past experience with stern, demanding people and with her own lack of physical beauty enables her to face the fallen rider without fear and to offer her assistance. She comments that had he been young and handsome, she would have felt ill at ease. It is important to note that Jane provides support to a man who obviously outweighs her slight frame. Rochester's arrival is well-timed in that he serves as a break from the classroom routine and from the comfortable, if boring, isolation of Thornfield.

- *par parenthèse* by the way
- *Revenez bientôt, ma bonne amie, ma chère Mdlle. Jeanette.* Come back soon, my good friend, my dear Miss Jane.

CHAPTER 13

Summary

Ousted from the library, which is now used for master/tenant talks,

Jane and Adèle work upstairs and listen to the sounds below, where Mr. Rochester is awakening Thornfield to new life. After the day's business is concluded, Adèle, eager for a gift, hurries downstairs. Mrs. Fairfax invites Jane to take tea at six o'clock and instructs her to change to more formal attire. As Jane approaches the couch where Rochester rests his sprained foot, the master nods a cursory acknowledgment. Jane sits in silence while Mrs. Fairfax knits and Adèle pets Pilot.

After tea, Rochester asks pointed questions about Jane's past, her family, and her tenure at Lowood. His comments are gruff, discourteous, and unsympathetic. When Jane demonstrates her skill at the piano, Rochester offers a grudging compliment to her sparse talents. Her artwork, on the other hand, impresses him with its wild, romantic subject matter.

At nine o'clock, he dismisses all three females. Jane questions the housekeeper about the master's peculiarities. Mrs. Fairfax makes a guarded analysis of Rochester's behavior, which Jane has called "changeful and abrupt." She blames his brusqueness on "family troubles," which evolved from his brother Rowland's desire to corner all the family wealth.

Commentary

The soul of Thornfield is obviously its master, whose arrival restores the mansion to bustling activity. Despite his haughty moodiness, however, Rochester has won the hearts of both Mrs. Fairfax, who speaks no ill of her employer, and Adèle, who risks a harsh response and implores Rochester to reward her with a *cadeau* (a gift). Jane once again relies on past experience with antipathy as she adroitly parries Rochester's personal comments about her nun-like existence at Lowood. Rochester astutely notes that Jane is "tenacious of life." In view of Mrs. Fairfax's description of the master's own experiences, both Rochester and Jane appear to share that tenacity.

- *ami, Monsieur Edouard Fairfax* de *Rochester* friend, Mister Edward Fairfax of Rochester
- *Et cela doit signifier qu'il y aura là-dedans un cadeau pour moi, et peut-être pour vous aussi, mademoiselle. Monsieur a parlé de vous: il m'a demandé le nom de ma gouvernante, et si elle n'était pas une petite personne, assez mince et un peu pâle. J'ai dit qu'oui: car c'est vrai, n'est-ce*

pas, mademoiselle? And this must mean that there is a gift inside for me, and perhaps for you too, Miss. The gentleman has spoken about you: he asked me the name of my governess, and if she was not a small person, rather thin and a little pale. I said yes: because it is true, isn't it, Miss?

- *N'est-ce pas, monsieur, qu'il y a un cadeau pour Mademoiselle Eyre dans votre petit coffre?* Sir, isn't there a gift for Miss Eyre in your little trunk?

CHAPTER 14

Summary

After several days of being ignored, Jane and Adèle are summoned to spend the evening with Rochester, who admits his need for human communication. He gives Adèle the long-awaited box of presents, but he tells her to look at them in silence, inviting Mrs. Fairfax to keep her company. Focusing his attention on Jane, Rochester again notes her nun-like primness and asks her to comment on his own looks. Jane examines his dark hair and features and his massive chest and says that he is not handsome. Rochester tells her to speak freely. At first, she is silent. Then Rochester apologizes for his brusque behavior, blaming his cantankerousness on age. Jane, thinking him under the influence of wine, selects her words carefully, but does not back down from his intense questions.

Rochester admires Jane's spunk and "mentally shakes hands with" her for her honesty and boldness. They discuss sin, remorse, and reformation. Rochester ridicules Jane's simplistic belief in reformation, accusing her of being a "neophyte" – too young to know the difficulties he has faced since his twenty-first birthday when he, too, was an innocent like Jane. He says that he has abandoned the dissipation of his earlier years.

At nine o'clock, Jane, eager to end a conversation she no longer understands, rises to take Adèle to bed, but Rochester insists that they wait until Adèle tries on her new dress, stockings, and sandals. Entranced with her rose satin finery, Adèle cavorts about Jane, calling to mind Céline Varens' materialism. Rochester describes Adèle as a "French floweret" whom he is rearing as a penance for the sins of his youth.

Commentary

Rochester openly displays his self-indulgent nature to Jane, commanding her to sit in the place he has selected for her so that he will not have to move his head. He does not like conversation with old women and children. He rationalizes his foul temper and arrogance with hints of past immorality which festers like "a rusty nail" and poisons his natural generosity. On the other hand, he is concerned that he has wounded Jane by his sharp, authoritarian tone.

Jane reminds Rochester that a master should not worry about a servant's feelings, but she in no way grovels before his authority. Her cool, common sense response to his outrageous behavior meets with his approval—he is simultaneously irritated by Jane's saucy responses and attracted to her self-confidence and moral convictions. It is obvious to the reader that Rochester has more than an employer's interest in Jane.

- *petit coffre*   little chest
- *Ma boîte! ma boîte!*   My box! my box!
- *tiens-toi tranquille, enfant; comprends-tu?*   keep quiet child; do you understand?
- *Oh, ciel! Que c'est beau!*   Oh, heaven! This is so beautiful!
- *tête-à-tête*   in private conversation
- *nonnette*   nun
- *et j'y tiens*   and I firmly believe it
- *Il faut que je l'essaie! et à l'instant même!*   I must try it on! and this very minute!
- *Est-ce que ma robe va bien? et mes souliers? et mes bas? Tenez, je crois que je vais danser!*   Does my dress look good and my shoes? and my stockings? Wait, I believe I am going to dance!
- *chasséed*   made a hopping step
- *Monsieur, je vous remercie mille fois de votre bonté. C'est comme cela que maman faisait, n'est-ce pas, monsieur?*   Sir, I thank you a thousand times for your generosity. Mother did it like this, didn't she, Sir?

42

CHAPTER 15

Summary

While walking in the garden with Jane and Adèle, Rochester tells Jane the story of his "great love" for Adèle's mother, a French opera-dancer. He says that he was innocent when he met her, and that it was his fault that he believed her flattery and succumbed to the age-old self-deception that blinds a lover to the truth. One night, however, Céline arrived home with a young viscount and mocked Rochester's "deformities"; Rochester overheard the entire conversation and ended his affair with Céline, although he left a generous settlement to help her reestablish herself elsewhere. In the Bois de Boulogne, he took satisfaction in a duel with her lover, whom he wounded in the arm. Céline abandoned her six-month-old daughter, and Rochester rescued the child and brought her home to Thornfield, although he is fairly sure that he is not Adèle's father.

Rochester fears that his sordid story will sour Jane on her little pupil, but Jane insists that she can now identify more readily with this "lonely little orphan" who needs a friend. Rochester's confession now helps explain his dark moods and unpredictable harshness; Jane believes that he is predominantly decent. Rochester alters his usual pattern and stays home for eight weeks.

At two o'clock one morning, Jane hears a laugh and the sound of fingers sweeping past the panels of her door. At first, she thinks that Pilot is wandering down the hall. But when she hears a door open and close, Jane investigates and finds smoke pouring out of Rochester's open door and fire threatening to engulf his bed. She uses several basins of water to put out the flames, and then, with difficulty, she awakens Rochester from a deep sleep.

Rochester wraps Jane in his cloak and leaves her while he investigates the cause of the fire. Upon his return, he accepts Jane's suggestion that Grace Poole set the fire, and he urges Jane to keep the whole affair secret. Rochester is reluctant to let go of Jane's hand; he calls her "my cherished preserver," a good spirit whom he has never doubted would bring him good luck. The remainder of Jane's night is restless; her sleep is torn by joyous if troubled thoughts.

Commentary

More and more, Rochester reveals his growing love for Jane. For example, he interrupts his account of Céline's unfaithfulness to comment on Jane's inexperience with love and its accompanying jealousies. Although he says that it is inappropriate for him to confess the story of his mistress to so sheltered and inexperienced a person as Jane, he marvels that Jane's response to him is completely the opposite of Céline's. With painful honesty, he describes the humiliation which he felt when he overheard Céline's conversation with a brainless young lover, ridiculing and insulting Rochester. His basically good nature, however, prevented him from seeking revenge on Céline; instead, he provides for her and for the daughter whom she said was his.

Jane, too, reveals strength of character through her sympathy for Adèle. In an attempt to establish closer ties between Rochester and Adèle, she searches the child's face for a resemblance to Rochester, but finds none. Reflecting over the events of the day, Jane ponders Rochester's mixed love for Thornfield, his short-lived affair with the French opera-dancer, and the recent warming of his attitude toward her. Later, in her dreams, her frustrated attempts to escape turbulent waters and reach a distant shore foreshadow the difficulties which she will encounter in loving Edward Rochester.

- *grande passion*   great love
- *taille d'athlète*   stature of an athlete
- *croquant*   devouring
- *voiture*   carriage
- *Mon ange*   my angel
- *porte cochère*   carriage entrance
- *roué*   womanizer
- *vicomte*   viscount
- *beauté mâle*   masculine beauty
- *fillette*   little girl
- *hâuteur*   arrogance

CHAPTER 16

Summary

Jane spends the next day in turmoil, dreading to see Rochester, yet longing to hear his voice again. By accident, she encounters Grace Poole sewing rings for new curtains to replace those destroyed in the fire. Like the other servants, Grace believes that Mr. Rochester fell asleep while reading and that his candle ignited the curtains and bedclothes. At the end of their conversation, Grace tells Jane to bolt her door in the future.

At dinner, Jane continues to puzzle over Grace Poole's position in the house and Mr. Rochester's failure to press charges against her. Adèle notices Jane's flushed cheeks and trembling hands, and Mrs. Fairfax laments Jane's lack of appetitite. She tells Jane about Mr. Rochester's departure for the Leas, the home of Mr. Eshton, ten miles from Millcote, for a week-long house party. She describes in detail the looks and talents of Blanche Ingram, a twenty-five-year-old beauty whom Mr. Rochester admires. In the privacy of her room, Jane castigates herself for daydreaming about Mr. Rochester. As an exercise in self-discipline, she forces herself to sketch a self-portrait and to create an imaginary portrait of Blanche Ingram on ivory as a contrast to her own plainness.

Commentary

Jane's application of logic to the mystery of Grace Poole fails to produce a sensible answer to Rochester's request for secrecy and to his continued tolerance of a potentially dangerous person in his household. In addition, the master's absence delays Jane's asking him a number of pertinent questions.

At this point, Jane admits to herself that she is attracted to Edward Rochester, whom she delights in alternately "vexing and soothing." Her frank self-evaluation, however, pulls her back to the reality that she is plain, impoverished, and lowly. In contrast to Blanche Ingram, whom she has never seen in person but vividly imagines from Mrs. Fairfax's description, Jane is certain that she runs a poor second.

One aspect of Jane's quandary is the matter of social class. Jane ranks higher than Leah, John, the cook, Sophie, and even Mrs. Fairfax, but she is still an employee. Despite Rochester's attentiveness, it is unlikely that a governess could aspire to the position of lady of the manor. Mrs. Fairfax further deflates Jane's hopes by noting that Blanche, seven years Jane's senior, is far too young for a forty-year-old man.

- *Qu' avez-vous, mademoiselle? . . . Vos doigts tremblent comme la feuille, et vos joues sont rouges: mais, rouges comme des cerises!* What is it, Miss? . . . your fingers tremble like a leaf, and your cheeks are as red as cherries!
- *ignis-fatuus* a light that sometimes appears over marshy ground, often attributable to the combination of gas from decomposed organic matter; sometimes referred to as a will-o'-the-wisp.

CHAPTER 17

Summary

Despite sensible reminders to herself that she is socially inferior to Rochester, Jane longs for his return during the two weeks that he is away from Thornfield; she even considers advertising for another position. Then, a letter arrives near the end of March, announcing Mr. Rochester's return and a house party for the "fine people at the Leas." Mrs. Fairfax, Jane, and the servants fill the intervening three days with cleaning, polishing, and cooking to ready the hall for several weeks of entertainment. By accident, Jane overhears Leah telling one of the charwomen that Grace Poole receives more than five times Leah's pay. A sudden halt in their conversation warns Jane that she is being excluded from information about Grace—a "mystery," she calls it, and a mystery which is common knowledge to the rest of the staff.

Adèle, temporarily freed from schoolwork, is thrilled at the arrival of eight ladies and five gentlemen, and she pleads to join the party. Jane slips downstairs by a back entrance to get food for Adèle, Sophie, and herself; she and Adèle watch the festivities from the gallery. When Jane and Adèle are summoned to the drawing-room, Jane retires to a secluded window-seat and concentrates on her knitting. She observes Blanche Ingram's dark, majestic beauty, her sarcasm, and her haughtiness, and she admits to herself that Rochester probably does admire Blanche. Jane ponders her own sense of emotional kinship with Rochester, whom she never intended to fall in love with.

Blanche seats herself at the piano and commands Rochester to sing a solo. Jane stays until the end of the song before slipping out the side door. When she stops to tie her shoe in the hallway, Rochester approaches and inquires about her depressed state. Although he orders her to return to the drawingroom and to be present as long as the guests remain at Thornfield, he sees tears in her eyes and relents, stopping short of uttering an endearment lest the servants overhear.

Commentary

Charlotte Brontë contrasts Adèle's liveliness and her love of decoration, company, and attention with Jane's apprehensive curiosity concerning Rochester's behavior in the presence of the regal and talented Blanche Ingram. Both Jane and Adèle look forward to a closer view of the guests, but Adèle appears not to notice Lady Ingram and Blanche's deliberately cruel dissection of past governesses. Only Jane sees the fine ladies for what they are – arrogant, self-centered, willful, and rude.

When Jane describes the guests, she dwells on height, which is, to her, an important trait. Although Jane does not verbalize the contrast to her own diminuitive size, her references to "taller and more elegant in figure," "the loftiest stature of woman," "a fine soldierly man," and "length of limb" attest to her belief that a tall frame is essential to beauty. However, it is not stature that attracts her to Rochester but a face "full of interest . . . an influence that quite mastered me." Jane believes that she understands the "language of his [Rochester's] countenance and movements," even though there are great differences in social rank and wealth between them.

- *passées*   out of style
- *Elles changent de toilettes.*   The women are changing their outfits.
- *Chez maman, . . . quand il y avait du monde, je le suivais partout, au salon et à leurs chambres; souvent je regardais les femmes de chambre coiffer et habiller les dames, et c'était si amusant: comme cela on apprend.*   In my mother's house, when there was company, I followed them everywhere – to the drawing-room and to their rooms; often I watched the chambermaids arrange their hair and dress the ladies, and it was very entertaining: I learned to imitate them.

- *Mais oui, mademoiselle: voilà cinq ou six heures que nous n'avons pas mangé.* Oh, yes, ma'am: it has been five or six hours since we last ate.
- *et alors quel dommage!* and then too bad!
- *Est-ce que je ne puis pas prendre une seule de ces fleurs magnifiques, mademoiselle? Seulement pour completer ma toilette.* Can I not take even one of these splendid flowers, ma'am? Only to complete my outfit.
- *minois chiffone* darling, pretty face
- *Bon jour, mesdames* Good day, ladies
- *père noble de théâtre* great patriarch of the theatre
- *Tant pis!* So much the worst! (and even worse that *that!*)
- *charivari* clatter
- *la belle passion* beautiful passion
- *Au reste* Besides
- *Signoir Eduardo* Mr. Edward
- *con spirito* with spirit
- *Gardez-vous en bien!* Take care!

CHAPTER 18

Summary

The guests organize a game of charades, which Jane declines to join and observes at a distance. Rochester and Blanche enact first a wedding and then a man and woman at a well; Rochester concludes with a scene of a prisoner in chains. Colonel Dent's team guesses correctly — Bridewell, an English prison. As Rochester's teammates seat themselves in the semicircle, Jane turns her attention from the actors to the spectators.

Although she is certain that Rochester intends to marry Blanche, Jane is aware that Rochester does not love his intended, whose behavior reveals that she is a shallow, unoriginal woman — one completely without warmth. Jane surmises that Rochester, in the style of gentry, courts Miss Ingram for political reasons and because of her social rank and connections. In contrast to Miss Ingram's conceited flirtations, Jane fantasizes how she would like to challenge Rochester's prickly exterior in order to find his true nature beneath.

One day while Mr. Rochester attends to business in Millcote, his absence dampens the exuberance of the group. But a post-chaise arrives, and Adèle announces her guardian's return. Then she realizes that it is not Rochester, but a stranger. Blanche Ingram, temporarily elated, leaps to the window; disappointed by Adèle's mistake, she calls the child a "tiresome monkey." Jane takes an immediate dislike to the "unsettled and inanimate" appearance of the man. Mr. Mason, who claims to be an old friend of Rochester, complains of the cold. Having just arrived in England from the West Indies, he demands more coal for the fire.

Sam, the footman, whispers to Mr. Eshton about old Mother Bunches, a troublesome old gypsy woman, who refuses to leave until she is allowed to tell the fortunes of "the quality." Blanche overrules Lady Ingram's rejection of the gypsy and insists on having the first private session. After fifteen minutes, Blanche returns, refuses to reveal the results of the fortune-telling, and sits scowling at a novel which she is obviously not reading. Mary Ingram and Amy and Louisa Eshton venture to hear their fortunes read and return in high spirits, much impressed with the gypsy's astonishing knowledge about many details of their personal lives.

Sam indicates that the gypsy will not leave until she has seen the last "young single lady" in the room and offers to wait outside until Jane's fortune is told. Jane, spurred by curiosity, goes willingly to the library for her turn, unafraid of the dark-skinned old woman. The guests, pressing the girls for details of their experience, fail to notice when Jane leaves to go and listen to the old gypsy.

Commentary

This chapter contains pivotal material which will influence the remainder of the novel. Mason, who immediately repels Jane with his vacant stare and sallow complexion, will play an important part in her evolving romance with Rochester. Likewise, the appearance of a "gypsy," who seems to have affronted Miss Ingram in some unknown way, builds suspense as Jane fearlessly approaches her turn for a glimpse into the future.

An important aspect of this chapter is Jane's curious attitude toward her rival. Despite Blanche's Diana-like stature, entrancing conversation, and musical talents, Jane declares that she herself is nearly free of jealous thoughts. In their place is a kind of "sour grapes" pity for Blanche, who possesses a "heart barren by nature" and a lack of "tenderness and truth." Jane, hopelessly in love with her master and obligated to watch his courtship of a woman who is in many respects Jane's social superior, appears to be convincing herself that she need not envy a rival so lacking in character.

- *Voilà Monsieur Rochester, qui revient!*   Look, it's Mr. Rochester who is returning!
- *surtout*   overcoat
- *le cas*   an occasion

CHAPTER 19

Summary

The fortuneteller, who sits in the chimney corner reading from a little black book and muttering to herself, looks directly into Jane's eyes. Jane, after warming her hands by the fireside, claims to lack faith in the gypsy's skills, but pays a shilling and listens attentively to her words. The old woman implies that Jane has been nourishing secret longings while sitting in the drawing-room. Jane admits to a desire to save her money and set up a school, but refuses to reveal her inmost thoughts.

Gradually, Jane sinks into a dream-like state, wondering about the gypsy's keen knowledge of matters close to Jane's heart. After the gypsy explains how she crushed Blanche Ingram's hopes for wealth through marriage to Rochester, Jane interrupts the old woman's rambling about Rochester's fortune and urges her to return to Jane's fortune. The gypsy, describing Jane's future as "doubtful," presses her to "stretch out [her] hand" for the happiness that Chance has in store. She encourages Jane to stop denying herself laughter and enjoyment, which Jane's intelligence and independence overrule.

As the voice of the gypsy slips into the familiar tones of Mr. Rochester's voice, Jane recognizes his ring. Rochester removes his disguise and begs Jane's forgiveness for the charade. Jane agrees that the disguise was unfair and admits suspecting Grace Poole of posing as the gypsy. Rochester encourages Jane to describe his guests' reactions to their "fortunes." Begging permission to retire as the hour nears eleven, Jane indicates that Mr. Mason awaits Rochester. Rochester pales, leans against Jane, and asks her to fetch him a glass of wine.

Alarmed, Jane brings the wine and offers her strength and loyalty to her employer, who hints that the houseguests may someday scorn or shun him. As Rochester directs, Jane summons Mr. Mason, shows him to the library, and retires to her room. Later that night, she relaxes as she hears Rochester cheerfully conducting Mason to his room.

Commentary

Rochester comes close to disclosing his love for Jane. His admission that Blanche is attracted to his money indicates that he is not deceived by her flirtations. He urges Jane to listen to her heart instead of to her brain and to display her inner beauty and charm. Note his words, uttered as if he were Jane, just prior to this point when he can no longer continue playacting: ". . . my harvest must be in smiles, in endearments, in sweet− . . ."

Rochester's desire to escape to a quiet island with his "little friend" prepares the reader for a revelation of his worries, although the nature of his fears and his terrible anxiety remains secret for seven more chapters. It is sufficient for the moment that he rely on Jane as a "ministrant spirit," the devoted, loving comforter in whom he eventually entrusts his life.

- *diablerie*   witchcraft
- *ad infinitum*   endlessly

CHAPTER 20

Summary

Later that night, as Jane reaches to draw her curtain and shut out the brilliant moonlight, she is startled by a shrill, savage cry and the sounds of a struggle in the third-story room above her own. Three times, a voice calls for help.

Rochester soothes the fears of his guests, claiming that a servant has had a nightmare, and hurries upstairs. Jane dresses and waits for her master's summons, which come an hour later. She fetches a sponge and smelling salts and, assuring Rochester that she is prepared for the sight of blood, she offers him her hand, which is "warm and steady."

From an adjacent room, Jane hears inexplicable snarling laughter and Grace Poole's distinctive cackle. Richard Mason sits in a chair; one arm and one side are soaked in blood. Jane holds a candle as Rochester sponges blood that oozes from the bandages. He gives Jane instructions on tending to Mason's wound for "perhaps two hours," and he warns Mason "at the peril of [his] life" not to speak to Jane. Rochester then hurries out of the room and locks the door behind him.

Alarmed by the bestial sounds from the next room and fearing for Mason's life, Jane dutifully attends to the tasks. As day approaches, Rochester returns with Carter, the surgeon, who notes teethmarks in Mason's shoulder and quickly dresses the wound. Rochester chastises Mason for attempting to talk alone with "her." Jane locates a shirt and cloak in Rochester's room for Mason, and then Rochester administers twelve drops of cordial in a glass of water. Mason revives, pleads with Rochester to take care of "her," and departs in a carriage to the surgeon's house. Rochester comments that he wishes that there were "an end of all this."

Afterward, Rochester and Jane enjoy a few moments of peace in the garden as the sun rises. He makes veiled, fearful comments about Mason, and Jane assures him that he is safe if Mason is no more a threat than she herself is. Rochester then poses a hypothetical case about a wild, undisciplined boy who makes "a capital error" while living in a foreign land and spends twenty years in self-imposed exile before returning home. There, he encounters a stranger whose good qualities encourage him to renounce sensual pleasures and to devote himself to a life "more worthy of an immortal being," even though "custom" impedes his choice. Jane replies that reformation depends not on human approval but on a higher power.

Rochester shifts to a sarcastic tone and asks Jane if marriage to Blanche Ingram will regenerate him. Pacing up and down the walk, he stops before Jane, asking if she curses him for disturbing her sleep. When Jane replies in the negative, he urges her to sit up with him on the night before his marriage. He describes Blanche as "a rare one," tall and buxom with hair like "the ladies of Carthage." Catching sight of Dent and Lynn in the stables, he urges Jane to return through the wicket and strides off to tell his guests that Mason set off before sunrise.

Commentary

Both mystery and suspense build in this chapter as Jane ponders the bloodcurdling shriek, the dog-like snarling sounds, the bite on Mason's shoulder, Rochester's insistence on Mason's silence, Mason's power to terrify Rochester, and Rochester's promise to continue caring for an unnamed woman. Rochester compounds Jane's puzzlement by hinting at past errors in judgment and dissipation in foreign places as well as societal disapproval of his new acquaintance, the "gentle, gracious, genial stranger." His abrupt change of tone and renewed interest in Blanche Ingram suggest that he is tempted to choose a loveless marriage as an easy way out of his quandary.

Rochester's description of Thornfield Hall as a "mere dungeon" filled with slime, cobwebs, sordid slate, refuse chips, and scaly bark prepares the reader for its destruction. In order to free himself from the past, Rochester must find contentment in nature, which he describes as "real, sweet, and pure." He casts himself in the role of a shepherd, guarding his "pet lamb" from the "wolf's den" nearby. As in earlier episodes, Jane has proven herself worthy of trust in difficult times. Her discretion and stability strengthen Rochester when he contemplates the consequences of his worldly, restless ways.

CHAPTER 21

Summary

Over a week-long period, a recurring dream about an infant seems to warn Jane that trouble is at hand. Then, one afternoon, Robert Leaven, Bessie's husband (the coachman at Gateshead), arrives with news that John Reed (the child who was such a bully) has died, possibly by suicide, and that Sarah Reed has suffered a stroke and is calling for Jane. Interrupting Rochester's game of billiards with Miss Ingram, Jane asks for one or two weeks' leave from her duties to visit her aunt. Rochester is surprised to learn that Jane has family ties, and Jane explains that she never spoke of them before because her relatives cast her aside. Rochester discourages her from making the hundred-mile journey to visit a woman who could die at any moment, but Jane insists on obeying her aunt's wishes. Rochester offers Jane fifty pounds, then reduces the amount to ten pounds after she reminds him that her salary is only fifteen pounds per year.

Jane's subsequent questions about Rochester's wedding plans result in a discussion of Jane and Adèle's futures. Rochester agrees to send Adèle to a school before his bride comes to Thornfield, and Jane, dreading to think of life in the same house with Blanche Ingram, offers to advertise for a new position. Rochester insists on finding one for her. Then they bid each other farewell, with Rochester hinting that he would like a less formal relationship with Jane.

In her nine years' absence from the Reed home, Jane has grown more self-assured, and she is able to face the family crisis with confidence. At five P.M. on the first of May, she arrives at Gateshead and greets Bessie, who is nursing her third child in the kitchen of the lodge. After catching up on each other's news, Jane goes to the main house and receives an unencouraging greeting from the Reed girls, Eliza and Georgiana. Ignoring her cousins' discouragement of her visit, Jane boldly follows Bessie upstairs to the once-dreaded room of chastisement and stoops to kiss her dying aunt. Jane realizes that her aunt has not changed, because almost immediately, Mrs. Reed reveals her hatred for Jane's mother, Mr. Reed's favorite sister, and, talking wildly, she wishes Jane had died at Lowood during the typhus epidemic.

Occupying herself with sketching during the next ten days, Jane tolerates the discourtesy of her cousins and impresses them with a freehand sketch of Rochester. The girls then sit for quick pencil portraits of themselves. For the most part, we learn, Eliza spends her days attending to a strict schedule of religious study, needlework, writing in her diary, working in the kitchen garden, and regulating her accounts; in addition, she attends church services at every opportunity. In contrast, Georgiana, plump, lazy, and self-centered, lies on the sofa and complains about boredom, impatient to return to the gaiety of London. In desperation at her sister's vain, indolent behavior, Eliza self-righteously promises to part company with Georgiana as soon as their mother is buried. Georgiana retorts that Eliza is jealous and that she deliberately ruined Georgiana's chance of marrying Lord Edwin Vere.

One rainy afternoon, Jane slips secretly upstairs to visit her aunt; the situation brings back memories of the dying Helen Burns. Rousing herself, Mrs. Reed unburdens herself of two regrettable offenses against Jane—breaking her promise to Mr. Reed, when he was dying, to treat Jane as her own child, and, also, lying to Jane's uncle, John Eyre, that Jane died at Lowood. She then gives Jane John Eyre's letter, written three years earlier, asking for Jane's address so that he could adopt her and name her as his heir. Jane offers Mrs. Reed forgiveness but it is too late for the bitter, dying woman to change. She lapses into a stupor and dies alone at midnight.

Commentary

Because both her daughters have little sympathy for her, Mrs. Reed's imminent death seems especially dire and bleak. Seemingly, she grieves herself into an early grave over her dissipated, spendthrift son, whose gambling debts have brought hard times to Gateshead Hall; sadly, she dies without learning of his own death.

Mrs. Reed's daughters waste little effort in comforting their dying mother: Eliza busies herself with selfish concerns and narrow self-righteousness; Georgiana thinks only of London social life and her prospects for a rich husband. Despite the Reed children's callousness, however, the reader wastes little pity on Mrs. Reed—especially after she rejects Jane's generous offer to reconcile their differences.

In contrast to this bitter, dying woman, it is obvious to us now that John Reed, Jane's maternal uncle, had a tender, loving heart toward his niece, whom he took in infancy after the death of both her parents. All is not totally lost, though: the mention of John Eyre, Jane's paternal uncle in Madeira, West Indies, raises some hope that Jane may yet find a secure home and a loving relative.

CHAPTER 22

Summary

A month later, Jane returns to Thornfield, having stayed at Gateshead until Georgiana left for her uncle's home in London and Eliza departed for a convent in Lisle, France, where she planned to convert to Catholicism and become a nun. Jane comments that Eliza eventually reaches the position of Mother Superior of the nunnery; Georgiana marries a wealthy "worn-out man of fashion." Jane also tells us that Mrs. Fairfax wrote to Jane while she was at the Reeds, assuring her that the houseparty had ended and telling her that Mr. Rochester had left for London—probably to buy a carriage in anticipation of his forthcoming marriage.

After a grueling return trip, which is broken into two fifty-mile segments, Jane decides to walk from Millcote to Thornfield; it is a pleasant June evening, and she welcomes the opportuniity to observe the activities of the haymakers. She experiences a buoyant sense of gladness as she approaches Thornfield.

Unexpectedly, Mr. Rochester, who is sitting on a narrow stone stile and writing in a book, catches sight of Jane before she can take another route. He calls out to her and teases her about playing a trick; he says that she should have sent for a carriage.

Jane, appreciative of Rochester's warm welcome, experiences a feeling of "home." Rochester speaks of Blanche Ingram and asks Jane for a charm to make him handsome. Jane replies that the change "would be past the power of magic," and she silently notes that "a loving eye" is sufficient. Rochester's rare smile feels like sunshine. He makes room for Jane to cross the stile, and, on impulse, Jane thanks him for his kindness and tells him, "Wherever you are is my home—my only home."

At Thornfield, Adèle is wild with happiness, and Mrs. Fairfax, Sophie, and Leah add to Jane's feeling of welcome. Meanwhile, Jane ignores an inner voice that warns her of a coming separation, and, later, settling next to Mrs. Fairfax, she snuggles Adèle to her other side and says a silent prayer for their continued life together. Rochester sees them grouped together and takes pleasure in the tableau.

For the next two weeks, Jane asks for information about the wedding, but Mrs. Fairfax has no news to share. Likewise, Rochester gives no definite answers about a possible date and makes no visits to Ingram Park, a twenty-mile horseback ride from Thornfield. He sees Jane more frequently and continues to be kind, inspiring great love in Jane.

Commentary

Here, Jane's description of her secret fears parallels the image of death and children in her recurrent dream as she says, "And then I strangled a new-born agony." The insecurity that encroaches on her feelings of warmth and happiness is a constant internal reminder that future contentment is still unsure. While there are no outward signs of wedding preparations, Jane nurtures her love for Rochester and prays for more time to bask in the love and acceptance of the first real family she has ever known.

56

In an unprecedented moment of honesty, Brontë depicts the fragility of Jane's hopes when Jane allows her expectations to exceed reality. Jane accedes to Rochester's earlier request that she follow her heart rather than her head and renders herself truly vulnerable. Her impulsive expression of gratitude at the stile is out of character with her more guarded remarks in earlier encounters. There are too many unexplained mysteries at Thornfield for Jane to have reached the end of her trials.

- *ignis-fatuus* a will-o'-the-wisp
- *bon soir* good evening
- *prête à croquer sa petite maman Anglaise* ready to devour her little English mother

CHAPTER 23

Summary

Fair weather prevails in the countryside after the haymaking is completed. On a splendid midsummer's evening, Jane walks through the garden toward the orchard, aware of Rochester's nearness by the scent of his cigar. She attempts to slip away secretly, but he calls her to examine a large moth which reminds him of a West Indies moth. Jane is embarrassed to be walking with her employer in the shadowy orchard so late in the evening but finds no evil in Rochester's mind. She decides that the evil exists only in her mind.

Rochester introduces serious thoughts into their conversation, noting Jane's attachment to Thornfield and to Adèle and Mrs. Fairfax. He considers the necessity of a new position for Jane before his marriage and, at the suggestion of Lady Ingram, proposes that Jane go to Bitternutt Lodge in Connaught, Ireland, to educate the five daughters of Mrs. Dionysius O'Gall. When Jane considers the distance and the sea which would separate her from Rochester, she bursts into tears.

Rochester seats Jane beside him on the bench beneath a large horse-chestnut tree. He describes the sense of kinship that he feels with Jane—as though a string were connected under his left ribs to a similar place on her body. He fears that a break in the connection would cause him inward bleeding. Again, Jane breaks into sobs, recounting her delight in life at Thornfield, where she is treated fairly and encouraged by "an original, a vigorous, an expanded mind." To Jane, departure from Rochester and from Thornfield will be like death.

Rochester, defying custom and convention, embraces Jane, kisses her and proposes marriage. Jane, incredulous, pulls away from his grip and searches his face in the moonlight; he accuses her of torturing him. At length, she agrees to marry him and calls him "Dear Edward." He makes a savage declaration that God has sanctioned his choice; he rejects the world's judgment and defies public opinion.

A vivid crash of thunder and lightning suddenly sends them back toward the house at midnight. They are drenched, and as Rochester helps Jane out of her wet outer garments, he murmurs endearments, and kisses her repeatedly. Meanwhile, Mrs. Fairfax watches, "pale, grave, and amazed."

Commentary

This chapter contains a noteworthy example of the pathetic fallacy—nature reflecting human emotion. Beginning with "a band of Italian days" which come "like a flock of glorious passenger birds, and lighted to rest them on the cliffs of Albion," the perfection of midsummer echoes Jane's blissful return to Thornfield, where she feels acceptance, contentment, and love. As she wanders in Rochester's Eden-like garden and enjoys the early evening, the eastern sky charms her with its "fine deep blue, and its own modest gem, a rising and solitary star . . ."

Nature provides the setting for Rochester's proposal. At the foot of an old, familiar horse-chestnut tree, he clasps Jane to him and fiercely professes his love. An abrupt change in the weather, however, disrupts their intimate confessions. Before they can make more definite plans for the future, thunder and lightning, wind and rain force them to hurry into the house. Symbolically, they are dampened, and they are spared the fiery clash that sends lightning through the old, enormous horse-chestnut tree, splitting half of it away. Nature's violent display preludes the coming tragedy and separation.

58

CHAPTER 24

Summary

The next morning, Jane feels transformed. She wonders if Rochester's proposal was a dream. She is so happy that her mirrored reflection seems prettier and her clothing more becoming. This inner joy prompts her to donate her last three or four shillings to a beggar woman and child at the door. Mrs. Fairfax offers a quiet, cool, good-morning greeting, and Rochester embraces and kisses Jane. He reminds her that she will be Jane Rochester in four weeks' time, and Jane pales with giddiness. With a hint of fear, she declares it all to be "a fairy tale—a daydream."

Rochester says that he has already written and requested his London banker to send the Rochesters' heirloom family jewelry so that he might pour them into Jane's lap and dress her in splendor. Jane rejects any notion of beauty or glamor, claiming she would look like a costumed ape if she were dressed in satin and lace. Rochester, however, continues his extravagant promises to Jane: a lengthy trip to Paris, Rome, Naples, Florence, Venice, and Vienna, all of which he visited during his ten years of escape from unhappiness, but which he can now enjoy in the company of his "angel."

Jane declares that she will continue to be herself and predicts that Rochester will cool toward her after six months or less. Rochester vows that he will prove his ability to love a woman who is both "tender and true." Then Jane asks a favor, and Rochester promises her anything. Her request is for an answer that will satisfy her curiosity.

At first, Rochester is alarmed, but the question—about his pretense of love for Blanche Ingram—does not prove threatening. He explains that he hoped to inspire jealousy in Jane by courting Miss Ingram. Jane fears for Miss Ingram's hurt feelings and accuses Rochester of eccentricity.

Jane then makes a second request—that Rochester explain to Mrs. Fairfax his intention to marry Jane. While Jane dresses for an excursion to Millcote in the new carriage, Rochester speaks briefly with Mrs. Fairfax, who makes an effort to congratulate Jane, but continues to worry about the differences in their social position and age. Tears come to Jane's eyes, causing Mrs. Fairfax to apologize and to remind Jane that "all is not gold that glitters." Adèle dashes in and interrupts their discussion; Rochester has refused to include her in the trip, but he relents when Jane appears unhappy with his decision.

On the trip into Millcote, Rochester entertains Adèle with a fanciful tale about his taking Jane on a trip to the moon. At the silk warehouse, he instructs Jane to choose half a dozen dresses; she selects only two—a black satin and a pearl-gray silk, rather than the pink and amethyst fabrics that Rochester prefers. On the way home, Jane plans to write a letter to her uncle in Madeira, hoping to gain for herself a small amount of financial independence by becoming John Eyre's adopted daughter and legatee. She defends her rejection of extravagance by reminding Rochester of the manner in which he spoiled Céline Varens, and she says that she will continue her role as a hired governess until the wedding.

Overruling her objections, Rochester insists that Jane dine with him. She wards off excessive intimacy by encouraging Rochester to sing for her. His romantic love song sparks a harsh response in Jane, who declares herself "naturally hard—very flinty." Although Rochester grimaces at Jane's rejection of his lovemaking, Mrs. Fairfax relaxes her anxiety and approves of Jane's behavior. Jane admits, however, that keeping her lover at bay is difficult because he has become an idol and the center of her life.

Commentary

Charlotte Brontë employs many allusions in this chapter. Jane persists in seeing herself as an unglamorous "Quakerish governess," Rochester accuses her of witchery, and she herself recalls the women who seduced Hercules and Samson. When Rochester offers Jane half his estate, she labels him King Ahasuerus, husband of Queen Esther, a brave Jewess, in the Old Testament. Rochester commands Jane not to "turn out a downright Eve" after she requests to be admitted to the secrets of his heart.

In Rochester's tale of the moon, he explains to Adèle how he will gather manna, the food eaten by the children of Israel, to keep Jane from starvation. Then he abandons biblical allusions and enters the realm of fairyland, explaining to Adèle how he met Jane in a field after her return from Millcote. Jane, he insists, is a fairy and possesses a magic ring, a talisman to "remove all difficulties."

Later, as they return to Thornfield from their shopping trip, Rochester's comparison of himself to a Grand Turk with a seraglio (a

60

harem) irritates Jane, causing her to retort that if he were to do so, she would become a missionary and inflame his harem to mutiny, and then she would refuse to cut the despot's bonds until he signed a charter freeing all the slaves of the harem.

- *sans mademoiselle?* without Miss?
- *Oh, qu'elle y sera mal—peu comfortable!* Oh, how bad it will be for her there—scarcely comfortable!
- *un vrai menteur* a genuine liar
- *contes de fée* fairy tales
- *du reste, il n'y avait pas de fées, et quand même il y en avait* however, there were no fairies and since likewise there were none there . . .
- *pour me donner une countenance* for me to give myself an air
- *tête-à-tête* intimate conversation

CHAPTER 25

Summary

The day before her wedding, Jane's trunks are packed, but she cannot bring herself to label them with cards proclaiming her as "Mrs. Rochester." She closes the closet door on her wedding garments and, feeling feverish, goes outdoors into the wind. She ponders a strange event, which she plans to disclose to Rochester when he returns from a two-day business call at a small estate thirty miles from Thornfield. Wandering down the laurel walk, Jane approaches the blackened horse-chestnut tree, now split into two dying halves. The windy, over-cast evening gives her a small glimpse of a blood-red moon. In the distance, Jane hears a melancholy wail.

Returning to the house with apples from the orchard, Jane readies the house for Rochester's return. Restless and impatient after the clock strikes ten, she wipes a tear from her eye and ponders aloud the un-named event of the previous night, which she interprets as a "warning of disaster." Unable to contain herself longer, she walks down the road a quarter of a mile and meets Rochester on horseback. He helps her mount before him, kisses her, and notes her feverish state.

Jane changes her wet clothes and joins Rochester for their last dinner at Thornfield before their honeymoon in Europe. She is unable to eat, but she keeps her promise to stay up with Rochester the night before his wedding. He worries aloud at her bright cheeks and glittering eyes, and asks if she fears that he will not be a good husband. When Jane replies in the negative, he demands an explanation for her strange behavior.

Jane narrates the events of the previous night. At sunset, Sophie had called her upstairs to examine her wedding dress. Jane found a present from Rochester – a veil sent from London, which she doubts can mask her lower-class status. Wishing Rochester were at home, Jane wandered the house, tried to sleep, and dreamed that she was carrying a feeble, crying child, wandering a road and attempting to overtake Rochester. Rochester interrupts, but Jane insists on telling the rest. In the second part of her dream, Thornfield has been reduced to a crumbling, shell-like facade. As Jane tried to catch a last glimpse of Rochester, who galloped away toward a distant country, she sat on a ledge, braced against the wind, and leaned forward for a final look. The wall crumbled, Jane dropped the child, fell, and then awakened.

She opened her eyes on candlelight and a dark form emerging from the closet. A woman, tall, thick, and dark, wearing a straight, white garment, took Jane's veil, placed it on her own head, and turned toward the mirror. Jane saw a ghastly face – with red eyes, savage expression, and purple lips. It reminded her of a vampire. The creature tore the veil in half, flung it on the floor, and trampled it. When it thrust the candle into Jane's face, Jane fainted for the second time in her life. Jane ends her narrative with a plea – "tell me who and what that woman was."

Rochester, embracing Jane, calls the event half-dream and half-reality. He blames Jane's mental state for the apparition and rejoices that only the veil was harmed. He surmises that the woman was probably Grace Poole, and he promises to explain all "a year and a day" after their marriage. Long after one o'clock, Jane goes to bed with Adèle in the nursery, promising to be ready by eight the next morning. The wind is calm; the night is serene and lovely. Jane, however, is unable to sleep. She clasps Adèle, who seems to epitomize Jane's past life.

Commentary

Jane has demonstrated throughout the novel her belief in omens, visions, and prophetic dreams. The foreshadowing in Jane's dream is a very real representation of the actual events to come – the separation from Rochester is about to take place; the feeble, crying child, mentioned earlier as a symbol of sorrow, suggests Jane's frail hopes for the future; and the crumbling walls of Thornfield prefigure its pathetic remains after a fire destroys the structure. This dream, which has plagued her with dread during a time when she should have been enjoying blissful expectations, reduces Jane to nervous agitation and plays havoc with her hopes for happiness.

This chapter is well stocked with omens – the wraith-like wedding clothes, the dying tree, the red moon and raging wind, the distant wail, the furrowed face that reminds Jane of a "foul German spectre," the torn veil, and Jane's lapse into unconsciousness. Charlotte Brontë is preparing the reader for Chapter 26, the climax of the novel, when Jane learns the truth about her lover and the mysterious events that have plagued her since her arrival at Thornfield.

• *(D.V.)* *Deo Volente*   God willing

CHAPTER 26

Summary

At seven o'clock, Sophie comes to dress Jane and insists that she look at herself in the mirror. The robed figure in the glass seems almost like a stranger to Jane. Rochester, declaring Jane the "pride of his life," gives her ten minutes to eat breakfast before clasping her hand in an iron grip and grimly walking to the church, which lies just beyond the gate. Jane can concentrate on nothing but his face. At the church-yard gate, Rochester halts to let Jane catch her breath. She sees two strangers walking among the headstones. They disappear at the rear of the church.

As the bride and groom approach the altar, the two figures re-appear inside the church near the Rochester tombs. At the altar stands Mr. Wood, the clergyman, who asks if either bride or groom knows of any impediment to their marriage. A voice declares the existence of an impediment. Rochester stubbornly urges the minister to proceed. Then Mr. Briggs, a London attorney, insists that Rochester married Bertha Antoinetta Mason in Jamaica fifteen years earlier. Rochester does not deny the marriage, but he asserts that there is no proof that his first wife is alive. Richard Mason declares that he saw Bertha Rochester in April at Thornfield Hall.

After a ten-minute pause, Rochester admits that he planned to commit bigamy because he had been deceived into marrying a mad-woman who came from a family of "idiots and maniacs"; he commands the wedding party to follow him. Brusquely dismissing his servants, he strides to the room on the third floor; there Grace Poole guards Bertha, his insane wife, who grovels on all fours, hidden beneath a mane of "dark, grizzled hair." Grace warns Rochester to beware; he stands his ground and forces Bertha into a chair, binds her, and introduces his wife to the assembled onlookers. He urges them to compare the snarling lunatic to Jane before sending them all away.

Briggs surprises Jane by explaining that her letter to John Eyre alerted Richard Mason, her uncle's business associate, of the impending bigamous marriage. Briggs advises Jane to remain in England to await news of her uncle, who is suffering from a fatal illness. Jane returns to her room, mechanically removes her wedding dress, and puts on her ordinary clothes. Her head resting on her arms, she is overwhelmed with thoughts, but she cannot recall her real identity. Once more alone and desolate, she feels cheated by Rochester, whom she once trusted. She blames herself for being blind and weak, remembers the words to a prayer that her lips cannot utter, and lies helplessly as torrents of anguish rush over her.

Commentary

After rising to the pinnacle of her hopes and dreams, Jane is once more flung downward to the depths of despair. In the same imagery as her prophetic dream, her faith in Rochester is again compared to a "suffering child in a cold cradle." She stops short of hating him for deceiving her and finds fault with her own conduct. She assumes that he will reject her and order her to leave Thornfield at once. At the end of the chapter, Jane pictures herself lying in a "dried-up bed of a great river." Lacking the strength to save herself, she yields to the sudden, surging flood waters. Words fail her as she sinks into a "deep mire."

CHAPTER 27

Summary

Near sunset, Jane comes to her senses and asks herself, "What am I to do?" A voice urges her to rely on inner strength and leave Thornfield. Jane realizes that she is hungry and stumbles out the door, falling into Rochester's waiting arms. He is perturbed that she has remained so long in her room without uttering a sound, and he begs for her forgiveness, which she silently, but freely gives. He carries her to the library, warms her by the fire, and offers her food and wine. When Jane rejects his kiss, Rochester paces furiously about the room.

He explains his plans to send Adèle to school and to care for Bertha at Thornfield. Jane, assuming that Rochester plans to live alone, misunderstands his desire to make her his mistress. When she gives way to tears, he accuses her of loving only his station. Jane vows that she loves him, but that she must leave Thornfield. Rochester implores her to live with him in the south of France. She fears that he will lose respect for her if she becomes his mistress. When he warns her of a raging passion within him and asks her to take his throbbing wrist, she shouts out, "God help me!"

Seeking to reason with her, Rochester explains how his father, wishing to keep his property in one piece, bequeathed everything to Rochester's brother, Rowland, and, so that Rochester would not be penniless, he arranged a marriage for Rochester with a wealthy woman in the West Indies. Both families – the Rochesters and the Masons – kept Rochester from learning about the Mason family's inclination toward madness and idiocy. Rochester, however, immediately realized that his bride – "coarse and trite, perverse and imbecile" – was unsuitable. His family kept the marriage a secret, but after four years, unable to end his marriage legally, Rochester considered shooting himself. Instead, he decided to leave and live in Europe. Following a nightmarish voyage to England, he installed Bertha in a secret apartment at Thornfield with Grace Poole as her keeper. He then set out for the Continent to find an ideal wife for himself, one who would be intellectual, faithful, and loving.

Rochester admits to Jane that he has had three mistresses. He abandoned all of them and returned to Thornfield in despair, and there he found Jane, "my genius for good or evil," waiting in Hay Lane. Jane, moved by his tender description of their meeting, wrestles with her conscience and maintains her intent to leave. When Rochester throws himself on the sofa and weeps, she returns to comfort him, then hurries to her room.

After a short rest, during which she dreams that her mother's voice urges her to leave, she packs a parcel with linen and jewelry, a purse with twenty shillings, her shawl, and straw bonnet, and tiptoes past Rochester's door, through which she can hear him sighing and pacing the room. Taking a road in the opposite direction from Millcote, she struggles along, weeping wildly. She is painfully tempted to return, but seemingly, "God [leads her] on." She pays a coachman to take her as far as her money will allow.

Commentary

Jane's reliance on God remains firm in difficult times. She advises Rochester to avoid vice and to trust himself to a higher power. However, he lacks her deep religious faith and can only fight himself and his urge to overpower her and force her to be his mistress. The contrast of the two strong-willed characters prepares the reader for the change which takes place in the last segment of the novel, in which Jane and Rochester trade roles. Jane continues to rely on her better instincts and ultimately returns to a weakened, dependent Rochester — one who needs the same protection and care that he once pledged to devote to her.

• *gräfinnen*   countesses

SECTION FOUR

CHAPTER 28

Summary

After two days' travel, Jane arrives at Whitcross — not a town, merely a whitewashed marker, a crossroads in a north-midland shire surrounded by vast moors and distant mountains. She turns to nature, eating berries as well as the last of her bread. Then she says her prayers and falls asleep in the deep heather. During the night, she awakens and prays for Rochester.

Next morning, Jane wishes that she had died during the night. She follows a road to a village, requests information about employment from a shopkeeper, but finds her prospects bleak. Jane disdains to beg and walks on beyond the village. A farmer cuts her a slice of bread, and a little girl gives her some congealed porridge that was about to be thrown into a pig trough.

After dark, Jane wanders in the rain toward a distant light and, through a small latticed window, she observes two young ladies, Diana and Mary, translating German while Hannah, their housekeeper, looks on. At ten o'clock, they worry that their brother is out so late. They discuss the recent death of their father. Jane knocks at the door and begs for food and lodging. The housekeeper promises Jane a piece of bread and gives her a penny, but decides to lock the door, leaving Jane outside in the rainy night.

At this moment, the man of the house, St. John, returns, overrules Hannah, and takes Jane inside and to the fireside, where Diana feeds her milk-soaked bread. Jane gives her name as Jane Elliott and begs to be asked no more questions until her strength returns. St. John and his sisters, Mary and Diana, wonder how they can help Jane. They decide to give her a room for the night. Jane thanks God and sleeps.

Commentary

In this chapter, Charlotte Brontë characterizes the plight of the homeless who are spurned for being in the way and suspected of criminal intent, even by people who think of themselves as Christian. Although Jane assumes an optimistic outlook and initially undertakes a life in the "breast of the hill" under stars which assure her that God is infinite, omnipotent, and omnipresent, she quickly succumbs to despair when the warm July weather gives way to a cold and damp rain. Constant rejection and suspicion from local people undermine her self-confidence. Ultimately, she is reduced to begging. Had not St. John offered her a refuge from the rain, Jane might have met her death in a less-than-idyllic fashion.

- *ignis-fatuus* a light that sometimes appear over marshy ground, often attributable to the combination of gas from decomposed organic matter

- *Da trat hervor Einer, anzusehen wie sie Sternen Nacht.* Only one person came forward, to be watched like a crystal clear night.
- *Ich wäge die Gedanken in der Schale meines Zornes und die Werke mit dem Gewichte meines Grimms.* I weigh my thought on a small scale, my temper and behavior with weights the size of my outburst.
- *Deutsch* German
- *bairn* child
- *alias* a false, or assumed name

CHAPTER 29

Summary

For three days, Jane lies on her bed like a stone, barely aware of the people who take care of her. Diana and Mary surmise that Jane would have died on their doorstep if they had not taken her in; they also determine by her accent that she has had some education. St. John looks in only once and comments that Jane is — and always will be — plain. Diana tries to defend Jane by remarking that she is ill, but St. John adheres to his first assessment of her looks.

On the fourth day, Jane struggles to dress in her own clothes, which have been cleaned and straightened. With slow determination, she creeps down the stairs to the kitchen and sits with Hannah. Hannah implies that Jane is a beggar because she has neither home nor money. Jane, making herself useful by stemming gooseberries, answers questions about her education and past employment and learns that the house is called Marsh End, or Moor House, that St. John Rivers is a parson, and that the family's father died of a stroke three weeks ago. Jane comments that Hannah's thirty years as the Rivers' family servant prove that she must be an honest and faithful employee.

Hannah, who was at first cold to Jane, responds to the compliment and asks pardon for rejecting Jane at the door. Jane reminds her that poverty is not a crime. The two women become friends. Hannah explains that the children take after their mother, who was also an avid reader. Diana, Mary, and St. John return from a walk to Morton and serve tea in the simple, yet serviceable parlor. St. John, a handsome man in his late twenties, with classic features, studies Jane but says little. Jane, declining to explain where she worked after leaving Lowood, answers questions about her age and marital status. She acknowledges that her name is an alias and asks for support only until she can find whatever work is available.

Commentary

Charlotte Brontë quickly reveals the distinct personalities of the Rivers household. Hannah, suspicious and protective of the "bairns" whom she has helped to raise, speaks in the north-country dialect characteristic of Scottish influence. Mary is kind, yet less demonstrative of her concern for others. St. John, the fair-haired and blue-eyed brother, receives his sisters' respect. He yields to the obvious dominance of Diana, the kindest and most outgoing of the three, who does not hesitate to chastise her brother for his crustiness toward Jane. The three are ambitious – both girls are studying to become governesses, and St. John serves as parson to the small parish in Morton.

CHAPTER 30

Summary

In a few days, Jane sufficiently recovers her health so that she can help out about the house and also walk outdoors. Much to her satisfaction, she discovers a mutual love of reading and an appreciation of home and nature in Diana and Mary. Jane particularly admires Diana, the natural leader of the family, who is both attractive and physically vigorous. The girls, more accomplished than Jane in academic learning, share their books and ideas; Diana even offers to teach German to Jane. Jane, in turn, gives Mary art instruction.

St. John, who is often absent from home, seems more complex. Although he devotes himself to his parish and visits the poor and sick whatever the weather, he seems to take no real joy in his work and seems to function only out of a sense of duty. When Jane hears one of his sermons, she is moved by his calm, earnest zeal. At its conclusion, however, she detects a strange bitterness in St. John, as though his life has always been tinged with disappointment. She concludes that he has yet to find peace in God.

At the end of a month, Diana and Mary prepare to leave Moor House and return to jobs as governesses in a large city in southern England. Cautiously, Jane asks St. John about the employment he promised to find her. He tells her that plans have been made: he will return to the parsonage at Morton, taking Hannah with him. Moor House will be closed.

After repeated proddings, he unveils his plans for Jane: he will open a school at Morton for local girls, and she will be its mistress if the offer is agreeable. Although he warns her that the simple tastes and abilities of local people will not be challenging, she will have her own furnished cottage adjacent to the school. An orphan from the workhouse will assist her, and she will receive thirty pounds a year in salary. Jane, eager for a refuge and independence, accepts this proposal and wants to open the school the following week. St. John is aware of Jane's inner drive and her need for human involvement; he describes her as "impassioned" and predicts that neither she nor he would long be satisfied in menial, unstimulating work.

As time for parting approaches, Diana and Mary are sad and quiet, anticipating their separation from brother and home. Diana weeps for her brother, who conceals strong urges in order to devote himself to simple parish duties. More sadness afflicts the family when St. John receives a letter announcing their Uncle John's death. Diana explains to Jane that he was their mother's brother, who quarreled with their father over a speculative business proposition that brought financial ruin to their father. Their uncle pursued more profitable undertakings, made a fortune of twenty thousand pounds, and bequeathed it all to another relative, leaving only thirty guineas for St. John, Diana, and Mary. The subject is dropped, and Jane departs the next day for Morton. The family goes their separate ways, and the old house is locked up.

Commentary

Brontë no doubt speaks from experience when she depicts the enigma of St. John Rivers – a man who dedicates himself to Christian teachings and works tirelessly for the good of his parishioners, but who reaps no satisfaction from his efforts. Jane correctly explains his fault – he has found no peace with God. His sermons, the products of narrow Calvinistic doctrines, lack "consolatory gentleness." Jane is able to commiserate by comparing his gloominess to her own concealed regret at losing Rochester.

When St. John hesitates to offer Jane the job of schoolmistress to local girls, he reveals his oversight of two important traits in Jane:

her strength of character and her need for security. Although he makes a fair estimation of her cultural accomplishments and her liking for human companionship, he does not perceive the effect which Lowood has had upon her feelings of security and independence, both of which are satisfied by the job in Morton. In Jane's mind, the job of teacher is far more suitable than a position as governess in a wealthy home where she would be treated like a servant. Brontë emphasizes a governess' frustration in an environment where haughty family members rate the job on a par with the cook or waiting-woman.

CHAPTER 31

Summary

Jane's home, she tells us, is a "cottage." It consists of a single furnished room with an overhead sleeping chamber; it is spare but certainly adequate. The little orphan girl, whom she was promised as a helper, serves ably as a handmaid. On the evening of her first day of class, Jane reflects on her twenty students, only three of whom can read. None can write or do mathematics. All of them speak with such a heavy local dialect that teacher and students have difficulty understanding each other. Some are unwilling to learn; others try hard. Jane commits herself to developing the best traits in the latter group. As she evaluates her personal reaction, Jane discerns feelings of degradation and loneliness. She hopes that, in time, gratification will displace her disgust at the village children's ignorance and coarseness.

Debating her original choice to leave her beloved Rochester and Thornfield, Jane reconfirms that decision: she does prefer, she tells herself, the honest profession of schoolmistress to a shameful life in France as Rochester's mistress, a life in which she would have been a "slave in a fool's paradise at Marseilles." However, even though she believes that God has guided her choice, Jane finds herself weeping. She turns her gaze from the lonely expanse of moor and leans against the doorframe.

At this moment, St. John arrives, bringing art supplies which Diana and Mary left for Jane. He tries to comprehend Jane's depression and urges her to turn from "forbidden fruit" toward the path which God has shown. Comparing his own former misery only a year ago, he describes his doubts about entering the ministry. Despite his desire for a literary life, he yielded to a heavenly call and resolved to be a missionary. Even when his father objected, St. John persevered in his aim. Ultimately, he hopes to leave Europe and go to a mission in the East.

Jane and St. John are so deeply engrossed in conversation that they fail to notice the approach of Rosamond Oliver, benefactress of the school, whose physical perfection Jane freely acknowledges. Rosamond asks Jane about the school, her cottage, and her orphaned assistant, little Alice Wood, all of which Rosamond provided. She invites St. John to visit her father at Vale Hall. Although he refuses, the flush on his face indicates his attraction toward Miss Oliver. As she leaves, taking a path down the field, St. John strides away in the opposite direction. Jane agrees with Diana that St. John is "inexorable as death."

Commentary

As Rochester once observed, Jane's head is often in conflict with her heart. Her mind finds much to approve in the first day at school. She does her best to enumerate the good points of her job as schoolmistress, but her tears are proof of her heartfelt desolation. Although she now has independence and security, a lonely life among ignorant, unimaginative village children, far from Rochester and her new friends, Diana and Mary, is less than fulfilling. In addition, St. John's stilted, stiff-necked sermonette on resoluteness is equally ineffective in relieving her depressed mood. The arrival of Rosamond, a flirtatious member of the gentry, provides a temporary diversion as Jane turns her attention to St. John's denial of his own deeply felt, personal desires.

CHAPTER 32

Summary

During the fall months, Jane develops an appreciation for her students and their skills. With success in the classroom comes respect from community members, who invite Jane into their homes. Although their regard is to her like "sitting in sunshine," her nights are agitated by unsettling dreams of Rochester. Often she awakens, trembling and saddened, but she is still able to carry out her duties each morning at nine o'clock.

Rosamond Oliver frequently visits the classroom while St. John is teaching the catechism. She realizes her power over him by his flushed face. St. John, however, refuses to acknowledge and declare his love for Rosamond. Thwarted in her flirtations, Rosamond pouts. Despite her frivolous nature, Jane likes and admires Rosamond and draws a sketch of her. The following day, Mr. Oliver visits and asks Jane to finish the portrait. He insists that Jane take tea at Vale Hall. Mr. Oliver speaks openly of his admiration for St. John Rivers, whom he would welcome as a son-in-law because of his worthy family name and talents.

On the fifth of November, a holiday from school, Jane completes the miniature of Rosamond. When St. John arrives and stares at the picture, Jane offers to make him a copy to take with him to some far-off missionary post in the East. She boldly questions him about his feelings for Rosamond, which St. John does not hide. Jane encourages his love for Rosamond by revealing Rosamond's regard for him. Placing his watch on the desk, St. John allows himself fifteen minutes in which to fantasize about Rosamond.

At the end of the time period, he halts his daydreams, reminding Jane that he is devoted to his profession and that he realizes Rosamond would be an unsuitable wife for a missionary. He stresses that he is a "cold, hard man," bound by the philosophies of Christianity. Before he leaves, he notices a scrap piece of paper on Jane's desk. Snatching it up, he stares at Jane, tears a strip from the edge, and departs. Jane, unable to explain his odd behavior, ponders the mystery but soon dismisses it from her mind.

Commentary

Both Jane and St. John suffer from unrequited love. At night, Jane pursues her dreams of marriage to Rochester; when day approaches, she forces herself to concentrate on her job. St. John is likewise consumed by fantasies of marriage to Rosamond. However, when he allows himself to imagine life at Vale Hall, far from the martyred life of a missionary, he hardens his heart, forcing his reason to control all physical urges. While both characters repress their true emotions, St. John appears to do more damage to his psyche by denying himself human weaknesses. Jane suffers and sheds her tears without wrenching her heart from a normal response to passion and fulfillment.

- *lusus naturae*   freak of nature
- *Cui bono?*   To what good?

CHAPTER 33

Summary

Snow makes the moors impassable the following day; Jane sits by the hearth and reads *Marmion.* St. John interrupts her and asks to have a talk with her. His peculiar state of excitement causes Jane to wonder momentarily about his sanity. She pities him because of his gaunt features and his lonely life at the parsonage. At first he is silent, but Jane's insistent questions cause him to take out a notebook and a letter. As the clock strikes eight, he begins his narration about the daughter of a poor curate whose parents die and leave her to rich maternal relatives. It is obviously Jane's life story.

When St. John reaches the name of Rochester, Jane interrupts. But St. John continues, describing the situation which aborted Jane's marriage and caused her to flee Thornfield. He concludes by saying that a Mr. Briggs, a lawyer, is seeking Jane about an urgent matter. Jane, failing to comprehend the significance of the search, questions St. John at length about Rochester's well-being. Because the letter came from Alice Fairfax, he can give Jane no information to calm her fears. When St. John surmises that Rochester must have been an evil man, Jane rebukes him warmly.

He then produces the slip of paper which he tore from Jane's art supplies. The inscription, "Jane Eyre," explains how he made the connection between Jane and "the missing Jane Eyre." He explains that her uncle, John Eyre of Madeira, has died and left her a legacy. Jane feels a great loss at the death of her single relative, but the announcement of the amount of her legacy—twenty thousand pounds—produces a different emotion. Jane becomes extremely excited and stops St. John from leaving until he explains his association with Mr. Briggs. At first he claims that ministers are often called in to locate missing people. Unsatisfied with his answer, Jane stands her ground and forces him to admit that he is Jane's cousin.

St. John misinterprets Jane's immense joy. Jane, however, is thrilled to have a "family" at last. St. John, however, assumes that she is excited merely because she has received an inheritance. Aloud, Jane thinks about how she can share the wealth four ways—five thousand pounds each for Diana, Mary, St. John, and herself. She suggests that the money may even induce St. John to marry Miss Oliver. She herself resolves to live at Moor House. Because St. John misunderstands her pleasure, Jane explains how "delicious" it feels to be able to repay kindness and to have a home of her own. She rejects his suggestion that she might marry.

Jane and St. John part on a happy note. She is pleased to have him for a "brother." He admits that she has always been "agreeable," and he looks forward to having a third "sister." Jane plans to keep the Morton School open until a substitute administrator can be found. The legal matters concerning the inheritance are carried out, and St. John, Diana, Mary, and Jane share John Eyre's inheritance.

Commentary

Here, St. John reveals how little he understands human nature, including his own. Although he has dedicated himself to the ministry, he possesses hardly any notion of the needs that motivate other people. He is surprised that Jane's first reaction to the letter is sadness at the death of her Uncle John, whom she never met, but whom she has treasured as her only living family member. St. John is further dumbfounded when she offers to give away three-fourths of her money to the Rivers family—only minutes after receiving it. Her joyous affirmation of a "family" is a vivid contrast to St. John's stuffy declaration of love for his sisters, whom he loves out of "respect for their worth, and admiration of their talents." St. John's stern, Calvinistic outlook, it seems, has blinded him to normal human instincts in other people and in himself.

CHAPTER 34

Summary

As Christmas approaches, Morton School is closed, the legal matters are settled, and Jane turns her attention to Moor House, which she plans to clean and redecorate. St. John gives her two months in which to enjoy domestic happiness before turning to less worldly endeavors. Jane proves him wrong. She and Hannah work hard to clean, polish, and renew the old house before Diana and Mary come home for the holidays. St. John inspects their work, but takes no pleasure in the changes. Jane remarks to herself that St. John is correct in choosing a missionary's life; he would never make a good husband. "This parlor is not his sphere," Jane reflects.

In contrast, Diana and Mary are thrilled at the renovation of Moor House; they embrace their new cousin. In contrast, St. John offers a cool, contained greeting to each of them, and then he returns to his window seat in the parlor to read. When a local boy requests the parson's assistance for his dying mother, St. John sets out across the moors at nine in the evening for a four-mile journey that occupies him until midnight. He returns hungry but pleased with his pastoral visit. During Christmas week, the girls throw themselves wholeheartedly into conversation and holiday fun while St. John continues to withdraw into his parish duties, visiting the sick and the poor.

St. John makes definite plans to depart from England the following year. And then, "serene as glass," he announces Rosamond Oliver's wedding plans to someone else. Jane feels sympathy for him, but St. John is "again frozen over" and shows little need for her compassion. He begins to exercise firm control over Jane's time and behavior, urging her to leave off her study of German and to practice Hindustani with him. Jane recognizes his despotic power over her, yet she complies with his wishes. In May, when Jane's letters to Mr. Briggs and Mrs. Fairfax bring no news of Rochester, she is reduced to tears. St. John invites Jane for a walk.

He reminds her that his departure is six weeks away and encourages her to "enlist under the same banner." Jane shows little enthusiasm for the task. St. John elucidates his plan—he wants Jane to be his wife and helper. During fifteen minutes of consideration, Jane realizes that she could easily die in India and that St. John would never grieve for her because he does not love her. She would be to him what a good weapon is to a soldier. She answers him with a tentative "Yes"—she would go to India, but as his sister, not as his wife.

Their discussion becomes more heated when Jane vows to give her heart to God because St. John rejects it. Stung by her sarcasm, St. John remains adamant. He rejects her offer because of the implied impropriety: a thirty-year-old man cannot travel with an unmarried nineteen-year-old girl. Jane scorns both him and his notion of love, which she terms "counterfeit sentiment." She apologizes for her outburst. They end their argument with St. John's offering Jane two weeks to reconsider his offer. He warns her that a rejection of his proposal is tantamount to a rejection of God.

St. John returns to the house in silence. That night, he kisses his sisters and ignores Jane. She is hurt by the deliberate omission. Diana urges her to follow him into the passage. Jane runs after St. John to say good-night, but his icy cordiality gives her no comfort.

Commentary

St. John's assessment of Jane's good qualities reveals much about his own personality. He admits that he has studied her for ten months and has used "sundry tests" to determine her worth. He admires Jane for her strong constitution and for her willingness to work. He notes that she is "docile, diligent, disinterested, faithful, constant, and courageous; very gentle, and very heroic," a list of characteristics that might apply equally well to Carlo, his dog.

In addition, Jane has been punctual, upright, and tactful in the classroom. When the legacy came her way, she immediately shared it with her cousins, revealing "a soul that revelled in the flame and excitement of sacrifice." In their private studies, Jane has shown perseverance and tireless energy. In short, Jane has met his every test.

At no time does St. John mention the quality which Jane possesses in greatest quantity—heart. Having shut himself off from his own humanity, St. John has no need for love and therefore assigns it no value on his list of requirements for a "helpmeet." As Jane evaluates their relationship, she is torn by her appreciation of a new-found brother and her desire for a love like the one she knew with Rochester. St. John's unsuitability is obvious. Jane rejects the idea of becoming a martyr to St. John's idealism. She chooses to counter him rather than acquiesce to his proposal.

- *paysannes* peasant women
- *Bäuerinnen* peasant women
- *beau-ideal* perfect type
- *carte blanche* full authority

CHAPTER 35

Summary

St. John punishes Jane by delaying his departure for Cambridge, continuing their morning studies, and showing more kindness to his sisters, in contrast to his hard-heartedness toward Jane. The evening before he is to leave, Jane addresses the unspoken issue between them by disclosing her unhappiness at his anger. He evades her directness. Jane pursues the matter, at which point St. John expresses shock that she is not going to accompany him to India. She explains that a loveless marriage would kill her, and again she promises to accompany him as a helper. He then offers to find her a place with a married couple so that she can keep her promise. Jane realizes that she is being manipulated, and she counters his claim that she made a formal promise. When Jane admits that she must first settle a personal matter, an indirect reference to Rochester, St. John accuses her of cherishing an interest that is "lawless and unconsecrated."

Diana watches them from the parlor window. She extracts from Jane the whole story and confirms Jane's decision that missionary work in India would lead her to an early death because St. John would force his relentless servitude on her. Jane feels herself too plain to marry so handsome a man, especially one who values her only as "a useful tool." Both Diana and Jane agree that St. John is a good, but misguided man.

At supper, St. John maintains his usual courtesy. At evening prayers, he reads from Revelation 21, in which unbelievers are condemned to the fires of hell. He follows the reading with an emotional prayer for "wanderers from the fold." When Diana and Mary retire, St. John again urges Jane to change her mind. Jane realizes that he speaks with the voice of a pastor, not a lover. He draws her into a gentle embrace, and Jane begins to weaken. But suddenly she hears a voice, crying her name. Jane recognizes the voice as Rochester's, and she hurries into the garden. All she finds is midnight loneliness. She returns to her room, locks herself in, and prays to God, thankful for her rescue from St. John.

Commentary

Charlotte Brontë creates a powerful portrait in this chapter of the unscrupulous manipulator who employs religion as a means of psychological torture. St. John's use of Jane's vulnerability, love, and gratitude is villainous. He is cunning, and his devotion to religious duties is no excuse for emotional blackmail. In particular, his charismatic reading of scripture and his fervent prayer sways Jane closer toward submission. Jane is saved only at the last, climactic moment by genuine human love, in the form of the disembodied voice of Rochester.

CHAPTER 36

Summary

Jane arises at dawn on the first day of June, a rainy Tuesday, and she waits until St. John departs before leaving her room. He slides a note under her door, urging her to "watch and pray" in hopes that she will have changed her mind by the time he returns from Cambridge. At breakfast she announces her intention to leave for at least four days so that she can ease her concern over a "friend."

Diana and Mary make no comment. At 3 P.M., Jane takes the coach to Whitcross; by Thursday, a day and a half later, she begins to recognize the green and pastoral scenery near Millcote. At The Rochester Arms, Jane hears an inner voice urging her to ask for information. Before obeying, she walks up the path toward Thornfield. There, she is dismayed to find a blackened ruin. Only a shell-like wall remains. Jane realizes now why her letters went unanswered.

The host at the inn identifies himself as old Mr. Rochester's butler, and he tells Jane about the events that destroyed Thornfield. It was Bertha, Rochester's mad wife, he says, who set fire to the room adjacent to her chambers as well as to the bed which Jane once slept in. Actually, only a few lives were endangered because Rochester had shut himself in like a hermit after searching in vain for the missing governess. Mrs. Fairfax had retired from her post as housekeeper, Adèle was attending boarding school, and Rochester managed to lead the remaining servants to safety.

On the night of the fire, the host at the inn remembers seeing Rochester trying to save Bertha. She had climbed to the roof and, within moments, leaped to her death onto the pavement below. On his way out of the flaming building, Rochester was trapped by a falling staircase. He lost an eye, and his left hand had to be amputated. The other eye became inflamed and, eventually, Rochester became totally blind. Afterward, he moved to Ferndean, his isolated manor-house thirty miles away. He lives there now with two old servants. Jane immediately engages a chaise, telling the driver that she will double the rate if he can deliver her to Ferndean before dark.

Commentary

In this chapter, Charlotte Brontë builds suspense by introducing the long-winded innkeeper. His announcement that he worked for the "late" Mr. Rochester shocks Jane. Does he mean her beloved Rochester? She drops all pretense of the impersonal questioner with a single gasp. The host, unaware that he is addressing the missing governess, continues his rambling tale, explaining that the "late" Mr. Rochester is not Edward Rochester, but Edward's father.

Another purpose of the innkeeper's story is our chance to hear the tragic revelation from an outsider's point of view. The host, who worked at Thornfield when Rochester was a child, knows the family well, and he interprets the events with knowledge, not mere rumor. He is also aware of Grace Poole's fondness for drink, a fact which explains how Bertha escaped detection on the night she caused Thornfield's destruction. The fact that he witnessed the terrible fire makes his telling more believable.

The host edges his chair closer to Jane before disclosing the existence of a "lunatic" in the house. Jane tries to extract information about Rochester, but the host insists on a digression in which he describes the abortive wedding and the scandal over Rochester's attempted bigamy. He justifies Rochester's fascination for the small-statured governess as an aberration common to middle-aged men who fall in love with young girls.

The host implies that Bertha, although mad, knew Jane's status in the household and planned to kill her out of jealousy. Jane wastes no emotion on Bertha's malice; she devotes her attention to any scrap of fact concerning Rochester. The host satisfies Jane somewhat by describing Rochester's anguish and loneliness after the governess mysteriously departed. He compliments Rochester for being a man of courage and will, free of such common masculine vices as drinking and gambling. In the host's opinion, Rochester was truly heroic in his efforts to save his demented wife.

CHAPTER 37

Summary

Just before dark, Jane alights from the chaise and walks the last mile on foot. The undergrowth hinders her progress, and, for awhile, Jane fears that she has taken a wrong turn. She eventually spies the house, which appears deserted. She hears the pattering rain on the forest leaves. Then the door opens and Rochester exits, stretching out his hand to feel the air for rain. His physique has not changed, but his face looks "desperate and brooding." His dealings with John, his servant, reveal Rochester's short temper. He uses his hands to feel the way; frustrated in his efforts to walk alone outdoors, he returns to the house.

Jane enters and greets John's wife. She sends John to fetch her trunk and, in response to Rochester's summons for candles, Jane offers to carry him a tray containing a glass of water and candles. Her trembling hands and Pilot's exuberant welcome, however, cause her to spill half the water. Rochester at first thinks she is only a disembodied voice. Then he draws her to him, overjoyed that she is real. Jane explains that her uncle's will has made her an independent woman. She has returned to care for him. Rochester fears that, owing to his handicaps, they will have to share a father/daughter relationship.

Jane combs Rochester's tangled hair and examines his mutilated arm and the scars left by the fire. She urges him to eat supper in order to recover his spirits. In comparison to the stiff, loveless arrangement proposed by St. John, she feels at peace in her relationship with Rochester. When he begins to question her about the past year, Jane softens the truth of her sufferings and asks to be excused from lengthy explanations until she has rested. Rochester confesses to Jane that he fears that she will desert him because of his scars. She teases him by remarking that he has always been ugly. Rochester is pleased to encounter her old sense of humor.

The next morning is bright and sunny, and Jane and Rochester sit near a tree stump. Jane sits on his knee as she answers all his questions about her year with the Rivers family. Then, jealously, he urges her to get off his knee and return to St. John, her "Apollo." Jane contrasts her feelings for the two men—St. John is admirable but coldhearted; Rochester is her real love. A tear slides down his face. He proposes their immediate marriage, and Jane accepts.

Rochester apologizes for leading Jane to believe that she would have been forced into an illicit relationship. He regrets that she ran away without money and says that he would have given her half his fortune if she had asked for it. He discloses a low point in his life four days earlier, between eleven and twelve on Monday evening, when he had called her name and heard her answer. Jane keeps secret her own experience on that same night. Rochester vows that he has established a closer relationship with God and that he intends to lead a pure life.

Commentary

After the stilted, self-serving speeches of St. John, Rochester's blunt, energetic wooing is a relief to both Jane and the reader. He has softened somewhat because of his dependence upon servants and his guilt at driving Jane from Thornfield. Yet, he retains his former lusty pride, his determination to have what he wants, and his unabashed adoration of Jane. In Jane's eyes, however, Rochester is a caged eagle, still in possession of the flash and spirit that first attracted her to him.

In contrast to his rival, St. John is also proud and driven to satisfy his wants. The difference between the two men lies in St. John's denial of passion. Rochester, ten years older than St. John, has wasted years searching for a meaningful life. He has experienced the dissipations of the flesh and has renounced them in favor of a true relationship based on mutual trust and respect. St. John represses his manhood, even when he so obviously yearns for Rosamond. His selection of Jane results from a need—Jane would be a means to an end in his idealistic plan to serve as a missionary in India.

- *faux air*   false appearance
- *Jeune encore*   Still young

CHAPTER 38

Summary

Ten years later, Jane describes her marriage and life with Rochester. They are enjoying a lasting satisfaction in each other's company. The Rivers girls, Diana and Mary, communicate their approval, and St. John writes at regular intervals, but he never mentions Jane's marriage. Adèle, who was, for a time, pale and thin from the severity of the school she attended, came to Ferndean. After attempting to nurse Rochester and tutor Adèle, Jane decided to find a school close by that would meet Adèle's special needs. Adèle, Jane says, lost her "French defects" and grew up to be a well-mannered and moral young woman.

After two years, Rochester sensed the return of sight in one of his eyes. He consulted a London doctor and eventually regained his vision. By the time his son was born, Rochester was able to see the child, who resembled his father. Diana married a sea captain and Mary, a clergyman. St. John has pursued his missionary efforts in India until he has now worn himself out. Jane fears that he will soon die, but she comforts herself with the knowledge that St. John will go to a sure reward.

Commentary

This pious conclusion is typical of Victorian literature. Charlotte Brontë, ever the minister's daughter, reaches an unexpected justification of all matters — Bertha comes to a violent end as a result of deception and trickery; Adèle, blameless for her mother's sins, serves as a comfort and a friend to Jane; Alice Fairfax retires after long years of faithful service at Thornfield; Diana and Mary find worthy husbands. St. John, devoted servant of God, gets what he asks for — a life of self-denial and hardship. Rochester finds peace in a fuller knowledge of the Almighty, whom he wronged by willful disregard for Christian virtues. His punishment is the loss of his stately home, his youth, and the use of one eye and one hand, but his reward is a proper and loving wife, one who accepts him for his strength of character, a comfortable home at Ferndean, and a son.

Jane has metamorphosed from the frustrated, lonely orphan among unfeeling relatives to an independent, self-confident woman. Through her humbling, trying experiences, she has become a whole person. Her reward for perseverance is financial security — not lavish, but adequate; a son; and the love and devotion of an adoring husband.

• *She'll happen do better for him nor ony o' t' grand ladies. . . . If she ben't one o' th' handsomest, she noan faâl, and varry good-natured; and i' his een she's fair beautiful, onybody may see that.* She'll probably do better for him than any of the grand ladies. . . . If she isn't one of the handsomest, she is not ugly, and very good-natured; and in his eyes she's quite beautiful, anybody may see that.

CHARACTER ANALYSES

JANE EYRE

From the beginning, Jane Eyre demonstrates a strong need to be herself – to exercise her artistic talents, to take responsibility for her own actions, and to follow the dictates of a mature, developed sense of morality. While she lives with the Reeds and endures their daily assaults to her self-esteem, Jane tries to retain all of the individuality that she can and retreats into reading and drawing; they become her refuge throughout her life. As her unhappiness grows, Jane surprises herself one day and confronts Mrs. Reed with a clearly stated list of complaints: "I am not deceitful: if I were, I should say I loved you; but I declare I do not love you: I dislike you the worst of anybody in the world except John Reed: and this book about the liar, you may give to your girl, Georgiana, for it is she who tells lies, and not I." (Chapter 4) As Jane reflects on the scene twenty years later, she realizes that the result of a youthful outburst of truth is remorse. Yet, at the time, the ten-year-old orphan realizes a bonus from her outburst – a newfound power over others. She stands her ground and refuses to be walked over.

At Lowood, Jane's patience with insensitivity and hardship is tested to the limit, climaxing in a terrible loss, the pathetic death of Helen Burns. Helen characterizes the paradox of Jane's weakness-turned-strength when she accuses Jane of caring too much about human relationships and of lacking self-control: ". . . you think too much of the love of human beings; you are too impulsive, too vehement." (Chapter 8) These qualities, which trouble the thoughtful and other-worldly Helen, prove to be great sources of strength for Jane, who refuses to retreat into piety and submission. For Jane, life is to be lived – in intellectual pursuits and in human society.

Despite Helen's advice to Jane that she must endure the bad meals, cold walks, unbecoming uniform, and surly teachers with stoic patience and a faith in God's goodness, Jane will have none of it. Her inner sense of justice holds firm: ". . . I could not comprehend this doctrine of endurance; and still less could I understand or sympathize with the forbearance she expressed for her chastiser." (Chapter 6) Despite their different outlooks, however, Jane remembers Helen's advice and rewards her fifteen years later with "a gray marble tablet . . . inscribed with her name, and the word *'Resurgam.'*" (Chapter 9)

After acquiring sufficient education, Jane recognizes the appropriate time to move on. She is proud of her initiative, and she is justly rewarded with a job at Thornfield; yet her feelings about the move are mixed: "It is a very strange sensation to inexperienced youth to feel itself quite alone in the world. . . . The charm of adventure sweetens that sensation, the glow of pride warms it: but then the throb of fear disturbs it . . ." (Chapter 11) Day by day, Jane learns to control her apprehension and to face the challenges of a governess' job, overcoming one obstacle at a time – meeting the staff, learning the master's expectations, overcoming Adèle's faults, and coping with boredom.

Jane's unforeseen first meeting with Rochester in Hay Lane sets the tone of their relationship: she is self-reliant, dutiful, and compassionate. She briefly explains her connection with Thornfield, masters her fear of the stranger's horse, leads him to his master, and shoulders the stranger's weight until he can remount. At her first formal meeting with Rochester, he acknowledges her inner strength with a single perceptive comment – in reference to her eight years at Lowood, he declares, ". . . you must be tenacious of life." (Chapter 13) Indeed, Jane does hold tight to life, braving the poverty and neglect of her past and daring to hope for better things for herself.

At first, Jane hesitates to acknowledge her growing feelings of affection for Rochester. Although their mutual trust and admiration for each other is developing, the progress of their love for one another has its peaks and valleys, as is evident when Rochester devotes weeks to courting Blanche and, later, when Mr. Briggs halts Jane and Rochester's wedding. The night that Edward proposes beneath the enormous horse-chestnut tree, Jane allows her low self-esteem to boil to the surface: "Do you think because I am poor, obscure, plain, and little, I am soulless and heartless? You think wrong!" (Chapter 23) This and other references to her social inferiority and small, petite frame reveal the remnants of her childhood attitudes, based on years as "poor relation" at Gateshead and her status of employee at Thornfield. Jane is unable to see herself as Rochester's wife, as lady of the manor and wife of a cultured gentleman. Even during the month of their engagement, Jane rejects lavish finery and continues to choose sedate colors for her outfits.

The eventual evolution of Jane Eyre into a whole woman comes about after her experiences on the moors. There, she gains three necessary adjuncts to self-confidence and fulfillment – success in her school, acceptance from the Rivers family, and financial independence. After she breaks free from St. John's tyranny, Jane is ready to return to Rochester and assume the role of his wife and his equal. It is a new Jane who takes charge at Ferndean and reassures Rochester that she is an "independent woman now." (Chapter 37)

Wisely, she assesses the damage the fire has done to his body and to his ego, and she carefully avoids patronizing him and overprotecting him. She returns to the witty joking of their early days, teasing Rochester that he has been "metamorphosed into a lion." (Chapter 37) Rochester's gift to Jane after his second proposal of marriage symbolizes their new relationship. He offers Jane his watch, which he can no longer see, and he tells her to fasten it to her belt. Now in control of her life, Jane marries Rochester. She summarizes their happiness: "All my confidence is bestowed on him, all his confidence is devoted to me; we are precisely suited in character – perfect concord is the result." (Chapter 38)

EDWARD FAIRFAX ROCHESTER

Rochester's physical appearance, as well as his personality, is an appropriate foil to Jane's. His dark, rough face, square-cut body, and grim features complement his decisive nature. Beneath his gruff, cantankerous exterior, however, lies a fearful heart which counts the wasted years as a husband to a madwoman. Rochester longs for the soft, feminine comforts of a wife. From the time of his marriage, Rochester has felt cheated of a normal life. His father's decision to establish Edward in a pre-arranged marriage was based on monetary gain, not emotional satisfaction. Edward pays the penalty for his father's interference. He wanders across the continent of Europe, searching for love. He finds only empty relationships with a series of mistresses, restless discontent, and shame for his dissipation.

Edward is not devoid of generosity or compassion. He chooses to support the young child, Adèle Varens, despite his belief that she is not his child. He treats her to pretty outfits that suit her Parisian flair, and he finances the type of education proper to the daughters of gentry. Other evidences of kindness are the testimony of Mrs. Fairfax as to his liberal nature, the costly veil which he buys for Jane, and his heroic attempt to save Bertha from the fire. These are diametrical facets to Rochester's grumpy, gruff exterior. Throughout Rochester's relationship with Jane, his moods swing from harsh, bitter outbursts to outpourings of paternal warmth and protective vigilance. He is likewise loyal to Pilot and Mesrour, his brother-in-law (Dick Mason), his faithful employees, and his mad wife.

The crux of Rochester's contradictory personality lives in his underlying need to be rid of an unfair burden (his mad wife) and the need to cleanse himself of the shame of a misspent, dissipated life, which he pursued in violation of nineteenth-century standards of gentlemanly conduct. Once Bertha is dead, however, and Rochester is free to begin anew, he is able to confess his sins and establish a closer relationship with God. Invigorated by Jane's quiet faith and determination, Rochester partially overcomes his handicaps and greets his just reward—an infant son, whom he is able to see after the sight returns to one of his eyes. Although he has been grievously punished for his intended crime of bigamy, Rochester faces the remaining years of his life with hope.

ST. JOHN RIVERS

As restless as Edward Rochester but lacking his rival's lusty enjoyment of life, St. John Rivers confines himself to a narrow life and an even narrower philosophy. As the only son of the Rivers family, he protects his two sisters. As clergyman to the rural parish of Morton, he throws himself into religious work, visiting the sick and dying and establishing a school for the daughters of poor farmers. His few free evenings are spent in intellectual pursuits, including the study of Hindustani, which he hopes to utilize in the missions of India.

Ostensibly, St. John follows the precepts of Christianity—that is, he rescues Jane from certain death, he shares his home with her, and he finds work suited to her talents. Yet he lacks the humanistic spark—an absence which Jane recognizes from his sterile sermons. He is not a whole, living man. Because St. John denies his humanity, walls away his heart from Rosamond Oliver, devotes his energies and talents in zealous servitude to his church, and pledges himself to marry

Jane, a woman he will never love, he loses the reader's sympathy. St. John becomes a religious robot, going through the motions of saving souls, but losing his own in the process.

The reader cannot dismiss St. John's importance to Jane. Even after she resists his charismatic appeal and flees to Rochester, her former love, thoughts of St. John remain alive. Jane describes St. John's qualities to Rochester—his handsome, classic profile, his polished manners, and his profound scholarship. Before Rochester can misconstrue her admiration as love, however, Jane explains the other side of St. John—his cold, severe authoritarianism and his formidable will. In fact, the last paragraphs of the novel are devoted to St. John, whom Jane suspects will soon die in service to God. She reassures herself in the belief that St. John will reap a sure reward when "the good and faithful servant has been called at length into the joy of his Lord." (Chapter 38)

CRITICAL ESSAY

JANE EYRE AND THE VICTORIAN ERA

Charlotte Brontë reflects the influence of Victorian mores in her writing. Her characters respect high standards of decency and moral conduct, as exemplified by Mrs. Fairfax's disapproval of Jane's engagement to a man old enough to be her father, St. John's rejection of Jane's offer to travel with him as an unmarried associate, and Jane's refusal to become Rochester's mistress. At Ferndean, Rochester regrets that he failed to make clear his intentions after the wedding, when Jane assumed she would be coerced into a sinful, degraded life and fled Thornfield without money or belongings. The overall tone of the novel supports the nineteenth-century emphasis on propriety and careful, prudent behavior, particularly as it applies to male/female relationships.

A second aspect of Victorian literature, respect for the family, is obvious in several instances. On the night of Jane's return from her visit to Gateshead, Rochester takes pleasure in the warm family grouping near his hearth, where Mrs. Fairfax works at her knitting, Jane sits nearby, and Adèle nestles close to Jane. Rochester even refers to Jane as Mrs. Fairfax's "adopted daughter" and as Adèle's "petite maman Anglaise." (Chapter 22) In another instance, after Jane receives her inheritance, she sets about establishing a comfortable home for Diana and Mary, the first real family that Jane has ever known. Brontë makes a strong case for the contentment of a loving family which, in contrast to the Reed household, accepts and nurtures its individual members.

Another worthy theme, the workings of justice, a subject which profoundly influenced both Charles Dickens and George Eliot, also colors Brontë's philosophy. Her characters pay for their sins – the bully, John Reed, dies a sordid, violent death; Sarah Reed rejects Jane's forgiveness for her early unfairness and dies alone; Bertha entraps Rochester into marriage and suffers her own entrapment in insanity; Mr. Brocklehurst neglects the sanitation and standard of living at Lowood and subsequently loses control of the institution when an epidemic reduces its enrollment. Most profound of all punishments is Edward Rochester's loss of eyes and hand, home and prospective wife. Although he violates the laws of God and man by seeking a second wife, his chastisement seems excessive. Yet Brontë justifies his suffering as a necessary awakening, after which he renews his acquaintance with God, marries, and recovers partial vision.

The negative side of Victorianism – prissy self-righteousness and hypocrisy – never impinges on Jane Eyre's behavior. Charlotte Brontë declares her liberation from the fussier aspects of her age. Yet her creation of a sensual, rounded female character who is in touch with her sexuality and completely comfortable with it seems somewhat surprising, given the author's background. That an unmarried woman, living in her father's household and meeting the rigid standards expected of a parson's daughter, could devise so womanly a character as Jane is indeed refreshing.

SUGGESTED ESSAY TOPICS

1. Contrast Sarah Reed and Bertha Mason in terms of their vindictive urges. How does each woman bring about her own destruction?

2. Contrast the talents and interests of St. John Rivers and Edward Rochester. What reason(s) would Rochester have to be jealous of St. John?

3. Describe several instances in which Edward Rochester demonstrates his dependence on Jane. How does she respond to his needs?

4. Explain why Jane feels gratitude toward Mr. Reed, Miss Temple, Bessie Lee, Mrs. Fairfax, and Diana and Mary Rivers.

5. Contrast Jane Eyre and Blanche Ingram in terms of their physical characteristics and their attitudes toward Rochester. Why does Edward respond to Jane and abandon his courtship of Blanche?

6. In what respect is Rochester as much a prisoner as Bertha Mason? Why was life especially hard for second sons of wealthy parents?

7. Explain how Jane can have faith in God yet deplore the sanctimonious preachings of Mr. Brocklehurst and St. John Rivers.

8. Using either one of Jane's dreams or one of her early paintings, analyze what frustrates the main character. What symbols are prominent? What do they foreshadow?

9. Describe how the ballad in Chapter 3 foreshadows Jane's unhappy life. How does Helen Burns demonstrate a similar attitude toward God and His mercy?

10. Using examples of past conversations and actions, predict the kind of marriage Jane and Rochester will have.

11. Analyze the effect which wealth and position have on Rosamond Oliver, the Dowager Lady Ingram, or Blanche Ingram. How does the inheritance of twenty thousand pounds affect Jane?

12. State Jane Eyre's personal code of conduct. Cite examples which prove that she is true to her philosophy. Would her code seem old fashioned by today's standards?

13. Explain the irony of Jane's letter to her Uncle John, announcing her engagement to Edward Rochester. How does the letter lead to a resolution of the mystery of Grace Poole and the mysterious laugh?

14. Compare the discomforts of Lowood with the misery of Jane's life at Gateshead Hall. Why does Jane conclude, "I would not now have exchanged Lowood with all its privations for Gateshead and its daily luxuries"?

15. In her biography *The Life of Charlotte Brontë*, Elizabeth Gaskell makes the following observation about the moors of Yorkshire:

> "Grand, from the ideas of solitude and loneliness which they suggest or oppressive from the feeling which they give of being pent-up by some monotonous and illimitable barrier, according to the mood of mind in which the spectator may be."

Employ the meaning of this quotation to explain Jane's response to nature in the garden at Gateshead Hall, in the forest near Lowood, in the fields and gardens surrounding Thornfield, and on the moors near Morton.

16. Defend or refute the judgment of Robert Southey, the Poet Laureate of England, who warned Charlotte Brontë, "The day dreams in which you habitually indulge are likely to induce a distempered state of mind and, in proportion as all the ordinary uses of the world seem to you flat and unprofitable, you will be unfitted for them without becoming fitted for anything else."

17. Compare two mystical moments in Jane's life when voices lead her in the right direction. Whose voice gives her the courage to resist St. John Rivers?

18. Discuss the theme of pride as it affects the three major characters—St. John Rivers, Edward Rochester, and Jane Eyre.

19. What is the effect of multiple losses on Edward Rochester? How does he cope with blindness? with the destruction of Thornfield? with the disappearance of Jane Eyre?

20. What important information does Jane learn from the host at The Rochester Arms? How does it affect her desire to find Rochester? Why does the host feel free to assess Edward Rochester's actions?

21. Explain Brontë's use of bird imagery throughout the novel, such as Rochester's use of a dove to describe Jane and her vision of Rochester as an eagle.

22. Explain how Mother Bunches evaluates Jane's personality. What does she emphasize as Jane's strong points? What would she change?

23. Discuss the implications of the names "Thornfield" and "Ferndean." What other proper nouns contain an implied meaning?

SELECTED BIBLIOGRAPHY

BENTLEY, PHYLLIS. *The Brontës and Their World.* London, 1947.

CECIL, LORD DAVID. *Early Victorian Novelists.* London, 1934.

EVANS, BARBARA, and GARETH LLOYD. *The Scribner Companion to the Brontës.* New York, 1982.

EWBANK, INGA-STINA. *Their Proper Sphere: A Study of the Brontë Sisters as Early-Victorian Female Novelists.* London, 1966.

GASKELL, ELIZABETH CLEGHORN. *The Life of Charlotte Brontë.* London, 1960. First published 1857.

GERIN, WINIFRED. *Charlotte Brontë: The Evolution of a Genius.* London, 1967.

HANSON, LAWRENCE, and ELIZABETH M. HANSON. *The Four Brontës.* London, 1949.

HINKLEY, LAURA L. *Charlotte and Emily.* New York, 1945.

MANLEY, SEON, and SUSAN BELCHER. "The Moor Was Mightier Than the Men: The Brooding Brontës," *O, Those Extraordinary Women!* New York, 1972.

MARTIN, ROBERT B. *The Accents of Persuasion: Charlotte Brontë's Novels.* London, 1966.

MAURAT, CHARLOTTE. *The Brontës' Secret.* Translated from the French by Margaret Meldrum. New York, 1967.

PETERS, MARGOT. *Unquiet Soul.* Garden City, New York, 1975.

RATCHFORD, FANNIE E. *The Brontë's Web of Childhood.* New York, 1941.

SPARK, MURIEL, ed. *The Brontë Letters.* London, 1954.

WISE, THOMAS J., and JOHN A. SYMINGTON, eds. *The Brontës: Their Lives, Friendships and Correspondence.* 4 vols. Oxford, 1932.

NOTES

NOTES

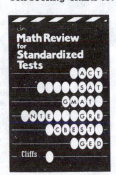

Jude the Obscure

JUDE THE OBSCURE

NOTES

including
- *Hardy's Life and Career*
- *Brief Synopsis*
- *List of Characters*
- *Chapter Summaries and Commentaries*
- *Analyses of Main Characters*
- *Critical Analysis of the Novel*
- *Review Questions and Theme Topics*
- *Selected Bibliography*

by
Frank H. Thompson, Jr., M.A.
University of Nebraska

Cliffs Notes

INCORPORATED

LINCOLN, NEBRASKA 68501

Editor

Gary Carey, M.A.
University of Colorado

Consulting Editor

James L. Roberts, Ph.D.
Department of English
University of Nebraska

Cliffs Notes, Inc.   Lincoln, Nebraska

CONTENTS

Jude the Obscure

HARDY'S LIFE AND CAREER

Born on June 2, 1840, in Upper Bockhampton, not far from Dorchester, in Dorsetshire, Thomas Hardy was the son of Thomas Hardy, a master mason or building contractor, and Jemima Hand, a woman of some literary interests. Hardy's formal education consisted of only some eight years in local schools, but by the end of this period he had on his own read a good deal in English, French, and Latin, just as later in London he made his own rather careful study of painting and English poetry. He was also interested in music and learned to play the violin. At the age of sixteen he was apprenticed to an architect in Dorchester and remained in that profession, later in London and then again in Dorchester, for almost twenty years.

He began to write poetry during this time, but none of it was published. His first novel, *The Poor Man and the Lady,* written in 1867-68, was never published, and the manuscript did not survive except insofar as Hardy used parts of it in other books. His first published novel was *Desperate Remedies* in 1871; the first novel which came out in serial form before publication as a book, an arrangement he was to follow for the rest of his novels, was *A Pair of Blue Eyes* in 1873; his real fame as a novelist, along with sufficient income to enable him to abandon architecture for good, came with *Far from the Madding Crowd* in 1874. On September 17, 1874, Hardy married Emma Lavinia Gifford.

From this time on Hardy devoted his full time to writing, continuing to publish novels regularly until his last in 1895, *Jude the Obscure.* Among these are some of the best of his so-called Wessex novels (Hardy was, incidentally, the first to refer to Dorset as Wessex): *The Return of the Native,* 1878; *The Mayor of Casterbridge,* 1886; *The Woodlanders,* 1887; *Tess of the D'Urbervilles,* 1891; in addition to *Jude.* To this list of best should be added the earlier *Far from the Madding Crowd.* In writing most of his novels,

Hardy meticulously worked out the details of time and geography he wanted to use; almost every novel is, therefore, located in a carefully mapped out area of Wessex and covers a specified period of time. *Jude the Obscure,* for example, covers the period 1855-74 and is set principally in Fawley, Oxford, and Salisbury (called in the novel Marygreen, Christminster, and Melchester). *Tess* sold more rapidly than any of his other novels, and *Jude* was probably more vehemently denounced. During this period of time Hardy also published his first poems as well as short stories. On June 29, 1885, he moved into a house he had built in Dorchester and lived there for the rest of his life.

On November 27, 1912, Mrs. Hardy died, a woman with whom he had become increasingly incompatible; and on February 10, 1914, he married Florence Emily Dugdale, a woman whom he had referred to for several years previously as his assistant and who was about forty years younger than he. After the appearance of *Jude* Hardy devoted his attention entirely to poetry and drama, publishing a number of books of poems, including one which he prepared just before his death. He also wrote and published an epic drama on the Napoleonic era, *The Dynasts,* which appeared in three parts with a total of nineteen acts. He was given a number of honors, including an honorary degree from Oxford, which he had criticized so severely in *Jude.* The success of *Tess* had made possible a good income from his writing for the rest of his life, and when he died he left an estate of nearly half a million dollars. He died on January 11, 1928, and a few days later was buried in Westminster Abbey.

BRIEF SYNOPSIS

Jude Fawley, an eleven-year-old boy, wants to follow the example of his teacher Mr. Phillotson, who leaves Marygreen for Christminster to take a university degree and to be ordained. Jude is being raised by his great-aunt, whom he helps in her bakery. He studies very hard on his own to prepare for the move, and to provide a means by which he can support himself at the university, he learns the trade of ecclesiastical stonework. He meets, desires, and marries Arabella Donn, who deceives him into marriage by making him think he has got her pregnant. They do not get along at all, and eventually Arabella leaves him to go with her family to Australia.

Though delayed, Jude does get to Christminster, partly because of his aspirations but also partly because of the presence there of his cousin Sue Bridehead. He meets and falls in love with her, though the fact of his being married causes him to feel guilty. Sue will not return his love, and when he realizes that Phillotson, under whom she is now teaching, is interested in Sue, Jude is in despair. This plus the fact that he has made no headway on getting into the university and realizes he never will causes him to give up that part of his dream and leave Christminster.

At Melchester he intends to pursue theological study and eventually enter the church at a lower level. Sue is there at a training college and is to marry Phillotson when she finishes, but she flees the school when punished for staying out all night with Jude. Jude is puzzled by Sue because her ideas are different from his and she will not return the feeling he has for her.

Shortly after he tells her he is married, she announces her marriage to Phillotson and asks Jude to give her away. He sees Arabella again, who is back from abroad, spends the night with her, and learns that she married in Australia. When he next encounters Sue, she tells him perhaps she shouldn't have married, and Jude vows to go on seeing her in spite of his aim to discipline himself to get into the church.

When Jude's aunt dies, Sue comes to Marygreen for the funeral, and there she admits to him she is unhappy and can't give herself to Phillotson. The kiss Jude and Sue exchange when she leaves for Shaston causes him to think he has reached the point where he is no longer fit for the church; therefore, he burns his theological books and will profess nothing.

Sue asks Phillotson to let her live apart from him, preferably with Jude, but he only allows her to live apart in the house until an instance of her repugnance to him causes him to decide to let her go. Sue goes to Jude and they travel to Aldbrickham, but she will not yet allow intimacy. Phillotson is dismissed from his job at Shaston when Sue never returns, and after seeing her later and not being able to get her back he decides to divorce her to give her complete freedom.

After living together a year at Aldbrickham Jude and Sue have still not consummated their relationship, and though they repeatedly plan to be married they never go through with it. Only when Arabella appears and seems to threaten her hold on Jude does Sue allow intimacy. Arabella marries Cartlett, her Australian husband, again and sends to Jude her and Jude's son, Little Father Time.

When opinion turns against Jude and Sue and he loses a job because of their reputation, they decide to leave Aldbrickham, and they live in many places as Jude works where he can find employment in anything other than ecclesiastical work, which he decides to give up. They now have two children of their own and another on the way. Having seen Sue in Kennetbridge, Arabella, whose husband has died, revives her interest in Jude, and when she encounters Phillotson, who is now in Marygreen, she tells him he was wrong to let Sue go. Jude, now ill and not working regularly, wants to return to Christminster.

They do return to Christminster, arriving on a holiday, and Jude is upset by his return to the city that has meant so much to him and gives a speech to a street crowd in an attempt to explain what his life has meant. Despairing talk by Sue triggers off a reaction in Little Father Time, and he hangs the other two children and himself. And the child Sue is carrying is born dead. Jude and Sue have reached the point where their views of life have about reversed, Jude becoming secular and Sue religious; and when Phillotson writes to ask Sue to come back to him, she agrees, thinking of it as a penance.

Sue returns to Phillotson at Marygreen and marries him again, though she still finds him repugnant. Arabella comes to Jude, and by persistent scheming she gets him to marry her once more. They get along about as before, and though ill Jude goes to see Sue and they declare their love for each other. As a further penance, Sue then gives herself to Phillotson. Jude learns of this, and on the holiday the following year, while Arabella is out enjoying the festivities, Jude dies. Only Arabella and Mrs. Edlin are present to stand watch by his coffin.

LIST OF CHARACTERS

Jude Fawley
A young man of obscure origins who aspires to a university education and a place in the church and who learns the trade of ecclesiastical stonework to help him realize his goals.

Sue Bridehead
Jude's cousin, an intelligent, unconventional young woman whom Jude loves and lives with but who is twice married to Phillotson.

Arabella Donn
A sensually attractive young woman whom Jude marries twice and who in between is married to Cartlett.

Richard Phillotson
Jude's former teacher who has the same aspirations as his pupil.

Little Father Time (Jude)
The son of Jude and Arabella.

Drusilla Fawley
Jude's great-aunt, who raises Jude.

Physician Vilbert
A quack doctor of local reputation.

Mrs. Edlin
A widow who looks after Drusilla Fawley before she dies and who is a friend to Jude and Sue.

Mr. Donn
Arabella's father, a pig farmer and later owner of a pork shop.

Anny
A girl friend of Arabella's.

Cartlett
Arabella's "Australian husband."

George Gillingham
A teacher friend of Phillotson's.

Tinker Taylor
A "decayed church-ironmonger" and drinking companion of Jude's.

Chapter Summaries and Commentaries

PART FIRST

CHAPTERS 1-2

Summary

The schoolmaster, Mr. Phillotson, is preparing to leave the village of Marygreen in Wessex. He is bound for Christminster, where he intends to take a university degree and then be ordained. He is helped in his preparation by Jude Fawley, an eleven-year-old boy who has been his student and who admires him. Phillotson has given the boy a book as a farewell gift, and the schoolmaster tells Jude to look him up if he ever comes to Christminster. After Phillotson leaves, Jude stands thinking of the schoolmaster at the old well, to which he has come originally to draw water for his great-aunt and which is one of few old parts of the village still remaining, the rest having been replaced by more modern structures, most notably the church.

Returning to the house with water from the well, Jude hears his great-aunt, Drusilla Fawley, who runs a bakery in the house, in conversation with some friends. When he enters the room, his aunt explains to her friends the circumstances of Jude's life that brought him into her care a year before. She describes him as bookish, like his cousin Sue, and tells him that he should never marry, since the Fawleys are unlucky in matrimony. Jude goes off to his job in Farmer Troutham's cornfields, where he is supposed to scare off the rooks with a noisemaker. Depressed by the ugliness of the fields and sympathetic with the birds' hunger, he soon gives up his noisemaking and happily watches the birds eat. He is caught by Troutham, reprimanded, and punished for deserting his duties, and dismissed from his job. His aunt is annoyed by his now having nothing to occupy him and wonders aloud why he didn't go off with the schoolteacher to Christminster. Jude asks her about this city but is told he'll never be able to have anything to do with it. Jude leaves, reflecting on the difficulties of growing up and the incomprehensibility of life. He decides to see Christminster and starts off, his direction necessarily taking him back through Farmer Troutham's fields.

Commentary

The use of a series of short scenes to develop the plot is typical of Hardy's narrative technique and is exemplified in the opening chapters. The last of these four or five scenes, in fact, is continued into Chapter 3; this too occurs several times in the novel. There are very few scenes which could be called long; the longest, perhaps, occurs when Sue comes to Jude's lodgings after fleeing from the training school in Melchester (Part Third, Chapters 3-5). In the present chapters, the plot moves smoothly from one scene to another, from Phillotson's loading his luggage to Jude's climbing up toward the ridge-track; in many cases, however, the transitions are abrupt and sometimes awkward.

These scenes serve to foreshadow a number of things that will occur later in the novel. Jude's admiration for Phillotson will shortly become a desire to emulate his teacher's ambitions and follow him to Christminster. Jude's inability to hurt any living creature, as Hardy explicitly points out, may cause him to suffer as he goes through life. Jude does not understand "nature's logic" and in reflecting on life thinks: "All around you there seemed to be something glaring, garish, rattling, and the noises and glares hit upon the little cell called your life, and shook it, and warped it." This too is full of suggestion as to what Jude's life will show.

The setting for this novel is, of course, Hardy's Wessex, which he invented and used in a series of novels. Several aspects of that "landscape" are of interest here. Marygreen, it is said, is changing: few of the old structures are still in existence; an outstanding example of the new is the church, which is of "modern Gothic design." The well at which Jude stands is one of few old things left in the village.

Some of the characters in the novel are used as a part of this local landscape and reflect its history and customs. Aunt Drusilla is one of these, with her talk about Jude's family and her foreboding comment that the Fawleys are luckless in marriage, both Jude and his cousin Sue having been victims of that bad luck.

Above all, what is strongly suggested in these opening scenes is the coming of the new and the dying out of the old, the effects of which go to form the theme of the novel. It is the spirit of the modern that makes itself felt in this place and on these characters. Its effects will be widespread, as suggested here, ranging all the way from Jude's desire to better himself to large questions about the nature of the universe and the power that governs it.

CHAPTERS 3-4

Summary

At first when Jude reaches a high point outside of town, the "ridge-track," he cannot see Christminster; nor can he see it from the roof of a barn nearby, locally called the Brown House. He waits patiently, prays for the visibility to improve, and finally just before sunset does see light reflected from buildings in the city. Frequently thereafter he comes to this high place to look, occasionally at night. On one such occasion he encounters a man driving a wagon who talks to him about Christminster, describing it as a place of learning, religion, and beautiful music. After listening to the carter's account, all secondhand, Jude decides this is the place that may satisfy his need for a foundation. He calls Christminster "a city of light."

Walking home after the occasion of his conversation with the carter, Jude encounters Physician Vilbert, a quack doctor of local reputation. After seeking confirmation of his exalted view of Christminster from the man, Jude says he wants to learn Latin and Greek and offers to advertise Vilbert's pills if the physician will get grammars of the two languages for him. The man agrees, and Jude works hard for two weeks to get orders for him. When they meet again as arranged, Jude has orders for him, the physician has forgotten the books, and the boy realizes the man has no interest in his aspirations. When Phillotson sends for the piano he has left behind, stored with Jude's aunt, Jude encloses in the packing case a request for the grammars. When they eventually arrive, Jude discovers to his dismay that there is no rule or secret by which the words of his own language can be changed into those of Latin or Greek. Appalled by the labor of learning a language word by word and amazed at what prodigious intellects the learned men of Christminster must have, Jude throws the books aside and wishes he had never seen a book and had never been born.

Commentary

Hardy uses a series of major and minor symbols to help convey the meaning of his novel. Certainly one of the major ones is Christminster. In these chapters Jude is to be seen making Christminster into a symbol of all that is good and meaningful in his life. He looks at it from a distance both in the daytime and at night. He wonders where in the lights of the city Phillotson may be. He inquires of everyone he meets about life in that place: workmen, a carter, a quack doctor. From the common talk about it that they repeat to him he forms an idea of it as a "city of light." He even puts himself to the task of learning Latin and Greek on his own in order to be accepted there, and the grammars he finally gets come from a lucky inhabitant of that place, Phillotson.

Considering his age, Jude is likely to have fixed the meaning of Christminster to him forever in his mind. And that meaning, in turn, will affect his own life at every step, as it will affect the lives of others who come into contact with him.

CHAPTER 5

Summary

During the next few years Jude tries to educate himself by reading Latin and some Greek with the use of a dictionary. This study takes place as he drives the bakery wagon for his aunt's expanding business, paying more attention to his reading than to where he is going or with whom he is supposed to do business. One day when he is sixteen he stops near the Brown House, kneels by the side of the road, and reads aloud a poem he has been reading in honor of the then setting sun and rising moon. This pagan impulse causes Jude to wonder if he as a future minister hasn't spent too much time on secular works. He then takes up the study of the New Testament in Greek and eventually theological works.

In order to make possible his future move to Christminster, Jude decides he must have a trade to support himself. He chooses ecclesiastical stonework because of his interest in medieval art and also because of the fact that his cousin Sue's father had been an ecclesiastical metalworker. Apprenticing himself in the nearby town of Alfredston, he begins to learn his trade. At the age of nineteen Jude is living in the town during the week and returning to Marygreen every Saturday evening.

Commentary

This is an instance of a transition chapter. Its purpose is to span the time from Jude's decision to go to Christminster to that point at which he has learned as much as he can on his own but is not quite ready financially. Some six or seven years pass, during which, as shown in summary, he studies constantly on his own and begins to learn a trade in order to support himself. There is only one brief scene, but it is presented descriptively rather than dramatically.

Jude's choice of occupation is one of many ironies in the novel. It is established in the very first chapter that even in a small village like Marygreen the old style of church is being replaced. His deliberate choice of ecclesiastical stonework in medieval Gothic style, therefore, will limit his opportunity to work, though of course he doesn't realize it. The fact that he chooses this craft partly because he likes medieval art and culture will be later, when his views change, one of the reasons for which he will give up working on churches.

CHAPTERS 6-8

Summary

One weekend as he walks home from Alfredston, Jude makes an accounting of what he has accomplished to the age of nineteen. He believes he has some fluency in Latin and Greek, both Homeric and Biblical; he has studied some mathematics, theology, and history. What he does not yet know he will learn at Christminster, where books and instruction await him. As soon as he saves more money he will be off. He dreams of getting his D.D. and becoming a bishop or perhaps an archdeacon. He is brought back to reality by being hit on the ear by something, and he realizes that on the other side of the hedge is a pig farm and he hears girls' voices. After a bantering conversation as to who threw the pig's offal at him, Jude asks one of the three girls if she wants to meet him. They do meet on a plank bridge across the stream alongside which the girls have been working; the girl is Arabella Donn. Jude finds her attractive, aware of girls as such for the first time. Arabella easily maneuvers Jude into calling on her the next day, a Sunday. When he walks off again, his single-minded concentration on getting to Christminster fades before the onrush of new emotions.

On Sunday afternoon, which he has set aside to read in his new Greek Testament, Jude easily convinces himself to keep his date with Arabella. In going for a walk they pass the Brown House, from which eminence Jude has often looked out at Christminster. Walking farther than intended, they stop at an inn for tea, sitting in a room on the wall of which is a picture of Samson and Delilah. Unable to get tea, they settle for beer, and Jude is surprised at Arabella's knowledge of its ingredients. They then walk to Arabella's house in the dark, several times stopping to kiss, Jude finally holding her close as they walk. As he walks home later, Jude is impatient of the fact that he must wait a whole week to see her again. Next day, Arabella declares to her two girl friends she wants to marry Jude, and they tease her because she says she doesn't know how to make sure she gets him. One of them whispers to her, and she obviously has told Arabella to let Jude get her pregnant.

Passing the Donn farm one weekend on his way home from Alfredston, Jude encounters Arabella chasing some newly acquired pigs which have got out of the sty. Giving up the chase of the last one, they lie down on a hilltop, and when Arabella can't get Jude to caress her as she wishes she pretends to be affronted and goes off home. When the next day, Sunday, Arabella hears talk of Jude's going to Christminster, she decides to get him to make love to her, in short, to carry out the plan suggested by her girl friends. She arranges to get her parents out of the house that evening, and when she and Jude are alone in the house she teases him with a cochin's egg she is carrying in her bosom to hatch, an old custom, she says. Exciting Jude by removing it and replacing it several times, Arabella gets him to pursue her. She disappears upstairs and Jude follows her. Obviously they make love.

Commentary

Now that Jude thinks he is about ready for Christminster, it is dramatically as well as thematically the time to introduce the first of a series of conflicts that by the end of the novel changes his life and his hopes radically. It is appropriate that the first should be occasioned by a woman.

At the beginning of the scene in Chapter 6 Jude is walking home from work, mentally adding up his accomplishments of the past few years, estimating how close he is to Christminster and what rewards it will bring. At the end of the scene he realizes he is putting aside his ambitions but can think only of the "fresh and wild pleasure" which Arabella promises. In between he is introduced to sex. Hardy makes it clear that Arabella is attractive but not unusually beautiful, that she deliberately attracts his attention, and that when they meet she flirts with him. In short, she does what any other girl might do. Her effect on Jude comes from an awakening in him over which, it is said, he has no control.

This coming to awareness of sex conflicts, of course, with the aspirations Christminster represents; but it is also the introduction into his life of a desire or need which he will try always to satisfy, with consequent effects on other areas of his life.

The use of the minor symbol of Samson and Delilah, appearing in this section first and then several times later in the novel, is appropriate to the idea Hardy is trying to convey by introducing Arabella into Jude's life. Here the symbol appears in the form of a picture on the wall of an inn; elsewhere, it appears in other forms, for instance, in a description of Jude as Arabella looks at him.

CHAPTER 9

Summary

Two months later, Arabella tells Jude she is pregnant, and though he has said it is time for him to leave for Christminster he promises to marry her, speaking of his aspirations as impossible dreams. They marry and go to live in a cottage alongside the road between the Brown House and Marygreen. Jude quickly discovers several things about his wife: that she wears false hair, that she was once a barmaid, that the dimples in her cheeks are artificially produced. After admitting to one of her friends that she isn't pregnant at all, Arabella is apprehensive about telling Jude. When she does, he sees how unnecessary the marriage is; Arabella is complacent in her legal status. He wonders to himself about the justice of a society that causes an individual to have to forego his highest aspirations.

Commentary

When Jude finds out that Arabella is not pregnant, some very disturbing thoughts pass through his mind: "He was inclined to inquire what he had done, or she lost, for that matter, that he deserved to be caught in a gin which would cripple him, if not her also, for the rest of a lifetime?" Later, of course, he discovers that she deliberately enticed him to make love to her so that she could claim to be pregnant. Hardy already has had Jude as a boy wonder what it is that noisily seems to warp one's life.

What comes out here, as elsewhere, is part of Hardy's theme in the novel: Jude's beliefs, conventionally Christian as they are, cannot account for what is happening to him. Something blind or malign is operating to undermine his dream. In short, the old explanations do not seem to account for life. By the end of the novel Jude will be shown in a self-admitted "chaos of principles." Here, he is just becoming aware of the disparity between what he has been taught to believe and what the circumstances of his life confront him with.

CHAPTERS 10-11

Summary

When the pig killer doesn't come to kill the pig Jude and Arabella have been fattening, Jude is forced to do the job. He wants to kill it quickly so as to be merciful, but Arabella insists it should slowly bleed to death so that the meat will be better. Jude sticks the pig deeply and it bleeds quickly, much to Arabella's disgust and anger. Coming home from work that day, he overhears Arabella's girl friend tell another girl she put Arabella up to tricking Jude. When he confronts Arabella with this, she makes light of it, saying many girls work the same deception. But Jude insists she was wrong to so trap him into a marriage satisfactory to neither of them.

When the next morning, a Sunday, in the course of her work with the pig's fat Arabella tosses some of Jude's books aside, he gets angry at her. She leaves the house and, disheveled, walks up and down the road in front, lamenting her ill-treatment and accusing Jude of being like his father and his father's sister in their relationship to their spouses. When Jude goes to his aunt to ask her about this, she tells him his parents couldn't get along and separated, his mother later drowning herself. His father's sister couldn't get along with her husband and eventually left him, taking her daughter Sue with her.

In despair Jude walks out onto the ice of a pond as if to drown himself, but the ice doesn't break. He decides to do something more suitable to his degraded state and goes to get drunk. Coming home later, he discovers Arabella has gone, leaving him a note that she will not return. In a few days she writes to say she wants no more of him and she is going with her family to Australia. Jude replies that he has no objection and sends her money as well as his household goods for her to include in the auction the family is going to have.

Later, in a secondhand store he discovers among the goods from the sale that the dealer has bought a photograph he gave Arabella. This puts an end to whatever feeling he may yet have for her. On a stroll one evening he comes to the place on the ridge-track from which he has so often looked for Christminster and realizes that though much has happened he has still not achieved his ambitions. These ambitions are reawakened by his seeing on the back of a milestone nearby an inscription he carved to symbolize his goal in life. He decides to go to Christminster as soon as his apprenticeship has ended.

Commentary

Several aspects of the setting are made use of in these chapters. The Brown House on the ridge-track was important earlier as marking the spot from which Jude first looked out at Christminster. Now, it is revealed that he inscribed a symbol of his aspirations on the back of a nearby milestone. Jude also learns that his parents separated in this very same location, and his aunt hints too that a gallows which once stood here is somehow connected with the history of the family (much later in the novel, Jude hears this tale from Mrs. Edlin).

It is said that Arabella's deception of Jude is a common practice in the locality if a girl wants to make sure she gets the man she chooses to marry her. Above all, there is the killing of the pig, a commonplace practice certainly but one which is used here to reveal important differences between Jude and Arabella. To her the killing of the pig is an ordinary action to be done in a businesslike way. To Jude it is an occasion for scruples. As a person who is said to be unable to hurt any living thing, he is forced into being the one who kills the pig. He doesn't want to do it and tries to kill it quickly, contrary to the best local practice. His desire not to let the pig suffer is reflected later in the novel when he mercifully puts an end to a rabbit caught in a trap. And he himself, near the end of his life, wishes someone would dispatch him as he killed the pig.

The vivid details of this last scene, incidentally, were found disgusting by many of Hardy's contemporary readers, the contention being, apparently, that realism can be carried too far.

PART SECOND

CHAPTER 1

Summary

Three years later, his apprenticeship ended, Jude is on his way to Christminster. Not only have his old aspirations caused him to come; but he has seen a photograph of his cousin Sue Bridehead and has been told by his aunt that the girl lives in the city. He arrives at sunset, finds himself lodgings in an inexpensive suburb nicknamed Beersheba, and goes to look over the city. He has read and thought so much about it that as he wanders among the ancient colleges he seems to encounter the ghosts of the famous men associated with them. Back in his lodgings, before he falls asleep he seems to hear these men speak to him in words that he has read.

Commentary

For Jude Christminster is as much a dream when he is actually there as when he viewed it from the ridge-track outside Marygreen. It is significant that his first contact with the place is at night, a time when it is easier for him to make the physical facts conform to his idea. He studies the buildings of the colleges with great care and soon seems to encounter the ghosts of the great men of the past who were associated with Christminster. Even when he returns to his lodgings, their words fill his head before he goes to sleep.

Jude has finally got to Christminster, but it is a Christminster of his imagination, one that very likely never existed at all.

CHAPTERS 2-3

Summary

Jude's first concern is a job, though his working is to be done only as a way of supporting himself until he can enter the university. He goes to apply to a stonemason recommended by his employer in Alfredston. While there, he notices that the workmen are doing only copying and patching, not realizing that medieval building is coming to an end. He decides, while waiting to hear about the job, not to look up either Sue or Phillotson as yet. Now actually in Christminster he sees how really far away he is from realizing his dream, but he takes the job when offered and sets to work studying late into the night, as before not knowing what the best way is to go about it. By means of word from his aunt he comes upon Sue working in an ecclesiastical warehouse; though he is struck by her appearance and the work she is doing he doesn't speak to her. Nor does he when he sees her on the street. He decides he must think of Sue only as a relative for several reasons: he is married; it is not good for cousins to fall in love; and the family's bad luck in marriage would be even worse with a blood relative.

Though Jude sees Sue at a church service, at the moment feeling repentant of his sensual interest in Arabella, he does not reveal himself to her because he isn't sure of his motives for wanting to know her. Earlier than this incident, while on an afternoon's holiday Sue has bought plaster reproductions of statues of Venus and Apollo. Once home with them — she lives where she works — she doesn't know how to conceal them from the very pious woman who is both her employer and landlady. When the lady sees them wrapped in a corner of her room, Sue refers to them as saints. Alone in her room later, she places the figures on a chest of drawers in front of a print of a crucifixion, from time to time looking up at them from her copy of Gibbon. In another part of the city Jude is earnestly reading his Greek Testament.

Commentary

Here Hardy uses contrasting scenes to show the difference between Jude's impression of Sue and Sue as she actually is. Jude sees her first at work and remarks on what a "sweet, saintly, Christian business" she is in. On another occasion he sees her in church and concludes she is no doubt "steeped body and soul in church sentiment." But another scene shows her admiring and buying plaster reproductions of statues of Venus and Apollo and reading Edward Gibbon's *Decline and Fall of the Roman Empire*.

These scenes also help to indicate the differences in beliefs between Jude and Sue which go to make up part of the structure of the novel. That structure can be described as embodied in the reversals of belief in Jude and Sue, the changing marital relationships, and the slow, inevitable defeat of both. Jude's conventional beliefs are partly revealed in the authors he quotes from in the last chapter, as well as in his reverence for Christminster, the old university. Sue is shown to admire pagan statuary and to read the agnostic Gibbon, even as in a different part of the city Jude is poring over his New Testament in Greek.

These scenes also reveal part of the changes in Jude's emotional life. Arabella has left him; though he was attracted to her first of all as an object of sexual desire she proved to be incompatible in other ways. But the desire is aroused and always waiting to be satisfied. He is in love with Sue even before he meets her, though he is still married to Arabella. When he sees Sue he makes her into a saint, but beneath this veneer of interest he himself is aware that he wants her as a woman.

CHAPTER 4

Summary

Once more Jude has the opportunity to reveal himself to Sue but does not, still troubled by the legitimacy of his interest in her. He wants to pray to be delivered from temptation, but his every desire is precisely to be so tempted. Finally, it occurs that Sue looks him up at work, he is not there at the time, she sends him a note, he replies immediately when she says she may leave Christminster that he will meet her the same evening, and they do meet. Phillotson is mentioned in conversation, and Jude discovers he is still but a schoolmaster in Lumsdon just outside the city.

Jude and Sue walk out to call on Phillotson, and at first he does not remember Jude. Jude tells the older man that he is determined to follow his example, but Phillotson has given up his aspirations now except for the possibility of entering the church as a licentiate. Later as they walk back to the city, Sue explains why she plans to leave Christminster: her employer has seen her pagan statues and they have quarreled. Jude suggests she return to teaching, since Phillotson has said he needs help. Sue is interested, Jude convinces Phillotson to hire her if she is really interested, and Sue accepts the job.

Commentary

The scene in which Jude and Sue meet is used as a sharp contrast with that in which he and Arabella met. Sue does not scheme to meet him, she does not flirt with him, and during the whole time there is no element of sexual tension at all. As Jude himself sees, Sue acts more like a friend toward him than a woman. His feelings for her are more those of love than desire. Unlike Arabella, Sue is sensitive to place, does not want to meet on a "gloomy and inauspicious" spot. Arabella did not mind at all where they met, getting up from her work with the pigs' chitterlings to go to the plank bridge.

From the very beginning Jude is in no doubt about what Arabella represents to him. With Sue it is a different matter. From a distance she is a saint; when they meet he loves her more than ever; eventually, however, he will desire her too. Arabella represents no puzzle, but Sue will be an exasperating mystery to him for the rest of his life.

CHAPTER 5

Summary

Phillotson's interest in Sue quickly becomes more than that of a master in a new teacher. Though he is impressed by her ability as a teacher, he is also attracted to her as a person. On the occasion of their taking the pupils to Christminster to see a model of Jerusalem, Sue questions the authenticity of the reproduction and remarks, to Phillotson's surprise, that Jerusalem was certainly not first-rate by comparison with other ancient cities. They encounter Jude at the exhibition, and when Phillotson mentions Sue's criticizing the model Jude says he understands what she means.

A few days later a school inspector visits the school to observe Sue at work, and she is so upset that Phillotson has to look after her, assuring her with more than professional interest that she is the best teacher he's ever had. When Jude comes to visit them at Lumsdon, at their request, he observes their coming out of the vicarage together and Sue's not objecting to Phillotson's putting his arm around her waist. Jude returns to the city without calling on them, appalled at what he has been responsible for.

Commentary

Not only is the reader aware of the irony of Jude's introducing Sue to Phillotson, but Jude himself realizes it. He has gone out of his way to get Sue a job under Phillotson for entirely selfish reasons: he does not want her to leave Christminster, or the area close by. He wants to keep her near him. But when he goes to Lumsdon to visit her and sees Sue allow Phillotson to put his arm around her waist, he realizes that he has been the means by which the two are put into daily contact.

In the many ironies which occur in the novel, sometimes only the reader is aware of the disparity between what is intended and what happens. At other times, however, the characters themselves also recognize this difference, invariably, of course, when it is too late to change anything. They, therefore, are made to suffer doubly.

CHAPTERS 6-7

Summary

The following Sunday Jude goes to Marygreen to visit his aunt, who is ill. When he reveals he has been seeing Sue the old woman warns him off, and both she and her companion, who looks after her, recall incidents revealing the fact that people in the town thought of Sue as a unique, sometimes unconventional, child. The fact that some of the villagers he meets remind him by their questions of his as yet unaccomplished purpose in going to Christminster causes Jude to take stock of himself.

Practically, he has gotten nowhere; he decides to write to several masters in the colleges for advice. While waiting for replies, he learns that Phillotson is moving to a new school and wonders what this means. Realizing that he will be able to get into the university neither by qualifying for a scholarship nor by buying his way in, Jude considers how he has been seduced by the glamor of Christminster. From a high building he surveys the ancient university which it is not his destiny to be a part of, and he thinks how easily he could have given up his ambitions with Sue as a companion. After drinking at an inn, he goes home, to discover a letter of rejection from one of the masters he has written to. Again, he goes to a bar, later thinking as he walks alone that the real history of the city is in the streets among the common folk, not in the ancient buildings of the colleges. On a wall of the college whose master replied to his letter he scornfully scrawls a verse from Job.

The next day, despairing of both his ambitions and his relationship with Sue, Jude spends the day drinking in a tavern, meeting some of the habitués and loudly leading the criticism of all aspects of university life. Challenged to repeat the Creed in Latin, Jude does so, with the help of drinks the others buy. Disgusted with himself and longing for Sue, he makes his way to Lumsdon and raps on her window. She takes him in and listens to him berate himself as wicked; she insists he get some sleep and promises him breakfast in the morning.

Once awake in the morning, however, Jude is ashamed to face Sue and sneaks away, deciding he will leave Christminster. Discovering he has been dismissed by his employer, he packs his belongings and walks to Marygreen. Once there, he realizes that the ignominy into which he fell with Arabella is not nearly so deep as the abyss in which he now finds himself. Talking of this to the new clergyman who has called on his aunt, he says he is less sad over his inability to get into the university than he is over his losing the chance to get into the church.

Commentary

Hardy represents Jude's sense of failure at Christminster in two ways: from the heights and from the depths, as it were. Jude goes to a place from which he can view the whole city and contemplates the buildings of the colleges from which he is to be excluded. This is the real Christminster he is looking at, but it is the ideal one which has brought him here and from which he feels shut out.

He then descends to the streets and the taverns. Here he drinks, and here it is that he has an opportunity to display his learning, reciting the Creed in Latin for his drinking companions. This recitation is echoed in the last part of the novel when he addresses a street crowd in Christminster, some of whom are now in this scene at the tavern.

As a kind of anticlimax, Jude rushes to Sue in despair, though she can do nothing for him and he leaves again, ashamed. He has been undone again, even as he was by his marriage to Arabella. Later, Jude is to think that women have time and again frustrated his hopes. Hardy suggests throughout that this is but the outward appearance of a cause that is more universal and deeply disturbing.

PART THIRD
CHAPTERS 1-2

Summary

Jude believes that his original plan may have come more from ambition than a desire to serve and that his entering the church as a licentiate will enable him both to do good and to purge himself of sin. He does nothing about his new idea until he hears from Sue that she is going to Melchester to a training college, and he decides to go there, work and study, and eventually enter the theological college. He will be near Sue, whom he will learn to love as a friend, and will be realizing his new plan. Upon an urgent letter from Sue, now at Melchester and lonely and sorry that she let Phillotson persuade her to come, Jude leaves Marygreen for Melchester.

When Jude calls on Sue at the college, he finds her changed in appearance and manner but not in any other way. Determined finally to tell her of his marriage to Arabella, Jude is equally determined to discover the nature of her relationship to Phillotson. After talking about everything else, Sue finally tells Jude she has promised to marry Phillotson at the end of her two years of training. Jude is upset but resolute in his desire to keep seeing her no matter what, certain that his late night visit to her at Lumsdon precipitated her engagement. Jude finds work and lodgings and sets out on his theological study.

During an afternoon together, Jude and Sue visit an old castle, an example of Corinthian rather than Gothic architecture, at Sue's insistence. And they look at the paintings there, Jude preferring religious pictures, Sue secular. At Jude's suggestion they go for a long walk, planning to take a different train back to Melchester; but they discover too late they will not be able to make it. Forced to stay overnight with a shepherd, they disagree over Sue's remark that she likes such a rustic life, Jude insisting she is really a city person. They return the next day, and of course Sue has overstayed her leave. Before she leaves him at the college she gives him a new photograph of herself.

Commentary

It is both thematically and dramatically appropriate that after Jude's failure at Christminster he should discover upon meeting Sue again that she is engaged to Phillotson. Failure follows hard upon failure, and Jude's realization that his running to Sue in despair over his having to give up his Christminster dream hastened the engagement makes it no less easy to take. When by chance he is put in the position of staying out overnight with her, he is further reminded that he cannot have what he wants. In short, Hardy is using the scenes here to trace the early stages of Jude's defeat, the frustration of whatever hopes he has.

CHAPTERS 3-5

Summary

At the training college the previous evening there is a good deal of talk about Sue and her young man. The year before a student was seduced by a young man who claimed to be the girl's cousin, so there is some doubt about the fact that Jude is supposed to be Sue's cousin. After Sue does come in the next morning, the girls learn she has been severely punished, and they make a protest, only to learn that inquiries made have revealed Sue has no cousin. That evening they learn that Sue has gone, presumably climbing out of a back window and crossing a river. Sue turns up at Jude's lodgings wet and asking for help. He gives her a suit of his clothes until hers can dry, and after taking some brandy she falls asleep.

When Sue awakens, she and Jude talk through much of the night, the conversation beginning with what Sue has read and why. She says her unusual taste in books came from a Christminster undergraduate with whom she had a "friendly intimacy." She looked upon the two of them as intellectual companions and after she had agreed to live with him in London was surprised that he meant as a mistress. They did live together, and the young man accused her of cruelty in not yielding to him. When Jude says he believes her as innocent as she is unconventional, she replies she has never had a lover and is proud of it, though he says that not all women are like her.

Sue refuses to pray with Jude, his usual evening custom, and goes on to criticize both the religious and intellectual life of Christminster, pointing out that Jude is the very kind of person for whom the colleges were founded. Jude says he can do without Christminster and prefers something "higher"; Sue retorts that she wants something "broader, truer." After Jude says his prayers Sue speaks of the new New Testament she made for herself by rearranging the books into chronological order and decries the attempt to falsify or misrepresent the contents of the Bible. She promises not to disturb his convictions but says she hoped when she met him that he might be the man whom she had always wanted to "ennoble" to "high aims" but he is too traditional. Jude wishes he could see her as other than a woman because she would make a fascinating companion.

In the morning Sue, uncertain as to what she will do and what Phillotson will think, decides to visit a friend near Shaston until her disgrace has been forgotten. Before she leaves, Jude wants to tell her that he has been married and that he loves her, but she guesses the latter and says he mustn't love her. But as soon as she reaches Shaston she writes him, telling him that she has been cruel and that he may love her if he wishes. Not hearing from her for several days, Jude goes to Shaston, to discover she has not written him because of the reason for her not being readmitted to the training college: it is said she has been intimate with Jude. Sue accuses him of mistreating her by not revealing that he loves her, and though he realizes he is even more to blame because he is married he still doesn't tell her about Arabella. He is puzzled by her annoyance at his saying that of course she can't care about him because of Phillotson. And he is both puzzled and pleased the next day when she writes to ask forgiveness for the way she treated him when he called on her as well as to tell him she would like to see him when she comes to Melchester.

Commentary

Though Hardy's handling of point of view is conventional for his time, it is noteworthy that the first part of Chapter 3 is not told from the point of view of any of the main characters, a practice which he follows in most of the novel. Much of the time, of course, the point of view is appropriately centered in Jude.

Bringing Jude and Sue together, after she flees the training college, enables Hardy further to develop the difference in their views of the world, a difference established earlier in the novel. It is true that Jude and Sue are, in a sense, counterparts, as Jude remarks; they are both sensitive and thoughtful. But Jude is still the conventional Christian in belief, though these beliefs have been little consolation to him in his times of crisis, and Sue is an agnostic, complaining of the way the Bible is falsified. Sue will not join Jude in his prayers, refusing to be a hypocrite, as she puts it. And she explains the way in which she has rearranged her New Testament in chronological order.

She is also critical of the Christminster Jude so much admires. She says that "intellect at Christminster is new wine in old bottles" and that Jude, unable to enter academic life, is the very kind of man for whom the colleges were founded. She professes a freedom of thought which cannot be confined by a university and which she implies she engaged in with her undergraduate friend.

These are the views which will undergo a reversal during the course of the novel, a reversal which is part of the structure of the novel. In this reversal Jude will learn from Sue, who will in turn seem to repudiate what she has taught him. Especially will Jude come to scorn the religious beliefs he once held. Both will increasingly feel their lives manipulated by some force which they cannot explain.

The changes in Jude especially will demonstrate the theme of the novel. Both he and Sue are, of course, caught in the changes which bring into being the modern spirit, one of questioning and doubt.

CHAPTERS 6-7

Summary

In his new position at Shaston Phillotson, though pursuing his work at the school as well as his interest in antiquities, thinks mostly of Sue: saving money to support his future marriage, rereading her letters, looking at photographs of her. Though for a while he has honored Sue's desire that he not visit her frequently at the training college in Melchester, he grows impatient and pays her a visit only to discover she has been expelled. Entering the nearby cathedral, he encounters Jude and from him discovers the truth about the alleged scandal as well as something of Jude's feelings for Sue.

When Jude meets Sue, finding her evasive about whether she has seen Phillotson, he tells her of his marriage to Arabella. Sue is angry because he has thought of himself first in concealing his marriage and has caused her to allow him to love her, and she asks him how he can reconcile this with his religious beliefs. To Jude's insistence that his marriage is the only obstacle between them, she names several, among which is that she would have to love him. As a reason for not telling her of Arabella, Jude mentions the family's lucklessness in marriage, which momentarily frightens them both. They part, pretending they can still be friends.

When Sue writes to Jude that she is going to marry Phillotson soon, Jude wonders if his revealing his marriage to Arabella has hastened her decision, as he feels his visiting her drunk hurried her engagement. Even more upsetting is a second letter asking Jude to give her away at the ceremony, with its mention of him as her nearest "married relation." At Jude's suggestion Sue comes to stay with him so as to marry from his house, and their behavior toward each other is strained. Certain that she is making a mistake in marrying Phillotson, Jude allows Sue to go into the church a few hours before the wedding to see the place where she is to be married, an odd request that she herself acknowledges is characteristic of her. This and, later, the wedding are painful to Jude, and he wonders if she has willfully wanted him to be present. After the wedding and a meal at Jude's lodgings, when the newly married couple are ready to leave Sue hurries back into the house for her handkerchief. She looks at Jude as if to speak but says nothing and hurries out.

Commentary

Jude is here shown to believe that his telling Sue about his marriage to Arabella has helped to hasten Sue's decision to marry Phillotson, just as earlier he believed that his going to her in despair precipitated her engagement. Even if Jude is wrong in both cases, he believes that he is the unwitting cause. Or, perhaps, it strengthens his growing conviction that some inimical power rules his life and makes his best intentions produce results that undermine him.

In his handling of narrative, Hardy uses two devices here. He has Sue and Jude walk arm in arm down the aisle of the church in which she is to marry Phillotson as a kind of ironical comment on the fact that he is not the one who is really marrying her and as a foreshadowing of the fact that though they try many times to marry they never actually will. Hardy also uses here, and elsewhere, letters between Sue and Jude especially to show the difference between Sue in person and Sue as she writes. Even Jude comments on this difference, remarking that she is nicer in her letters than she is in person.

The treatment of Phillotson in the first part of Chapter 6 is an instance of static analysis of a character, which is used only infrequently in the novel. He is shown in his new situation at Shaston, his interests and habits are catalogued, and his personal appearance at this point is described. Part of the reason for the inclusion of this section is, of course, to show what sort of man Sue is shortly to marry. More often than not, however, Hardy uses scenes and contacts between characters to develop his characterizations.

CHAPTERS 8-9

Summary

With Sue gone, Jude finds Melchester oppressive. News that his aunt is ill and an offer from his former employer at Christminster give him excuse to leave. Finding his aunt very ill indeed, he writes to Sue, suggesting she come and offering to meet her on his way back from Christminster. He finds it a city of ghosts and decides not to return there, but before leaving to meet Sue he goes into a tavern, the one where he recited the Creed, for a drink to relieve his depressed feelings. There he encounters Arabella, back from Australia, working as a barmaid. He agrees to meet her later, though it means missing the train and his meeting with Sue. When Jude has no ideas as to arrangements for their separation, at Arabella's suggestion they go to Aldbrickham and spend the night, giving themselves time, according to her, to decide what to do.

Back in Christminster the next day, Arabella tells Jude she married again in Australia and when he is angry about this says she will go back to the other man if Jude won't have her. No sooner has he left Arabella than he encounters Sue, who has come to look for him, thinking he may have started drinking as the result of being in the city where so many of his hopes have been disappointed. They return to Marygreen together, and Jude tries unsuccessfully to find out about her marriage, convinced she is unhappy. But she will say nothing but good of Phillotson, and she is offended, later, when Aunt Drusilla makes derogatory remarks about marriage and about Phillotson as a husband. Out of her hearing, Sue admits to Jude she may have made a mistake but will not discuss the subject further. In the days after her departure Jude tries to discipline himself not to think of his love for her. While still at Marygreen, Jude gets a letter from Arabella announcing that she is joining her second husband in London and will help him run a tavern.

Commentary

In his return to Christminster and in going back to Marygreen with Sue, Jude encounters the past wherever he walks. In Christminster he comes upon the place where Sue once worked, his old lodgings, the stone yard, and finally the tavern where he recited the Creed in Latin. He and Sue pass the Brown House, the house where he and Arabella lived, and the field where he worked as a boy. Each is a reminder to him of some part of his life, and most have more than a single association attached to them.

It is in the tavern in Christminster that Jude encounters Arabella unexpectedly. Hardy has often been criticized for excessive use of coincidence in his handling of plot, and not one but two instances occur here. He meets Arabella, back from Australia, and soon after leaving her the next day comes upon Sue, whom he expects to be in Marygreen. It is true that both encounters occur at dramatically right times: Arabella after Sue's wedding; Sue after he has spent the night with Arabella. However, the appearances in both cases come about as the result of Hardy's desire to demonstrate something in the relationships among the characters rather than the necessities of the plot.

CHAPTER 10

Summary

Back at Melchester, Jude tries to fight against the temptation to visit Sue at Shaston and tries desperately to pursue his study for the ministry. Enlarging his interest in sacred music and eventually joining a choir in a village church nearby, he is greatly moved by a new hymn and thinks that the composer of it must be the kind of man who would understand his own perplexing state of mind. Jude seeks out the composer but discovers he is interested only in money. Coming home from this trip, he discovers Sue has relented and asked him to visit on that very day. Abandoning his attempt to discipline his feelings for her, he writes to arrange to visit as soon as possible.

Commentary

Jude's impulsive visit to the composer turns into another irony. The man who Jude thinks would be best equipped to understand and sympathize with him turns out to be a kind of businessman. He is interested only in money, not the beauty of his music. Jude is an increasingly lonely man, and this attempt to break out of his loneliness comes to nothing, as all such attempts will. It is a part of what is happening to him. Slowly straying away from his old beliefs, he finds himself without any context for his actions and thoughts. Sue is no help here: she is too self-centered, and all she can offer is questions, not answers. All men are like Jude, so Hardy seems to suggest — modern men, at least.

PART FOURTH

CHAPTERS 1-2

Summary

When Jude visits Sue at Shaston, he sits playing his favorite hymn while waiting for her to come in. Her being moved by it causes him to say that at heart they are alike, but Sue counters by saying they are, however, not alike "at head." When they argue over whether they can still be friends, Jude calls her a flirt; she replies by saying that some women can't be satisfied with loving and being loved by only one man. She calls him a Joseph, a Don Quixote, a St. Stephen, and speaks of herself as a woman full of conflicting feelings. Leaving her and wandering about the town while waiting for his train, Jude finally finds his way back to Sue's house, and from the dark sees her inside take out a photograph and clasp it to her bosom but can't be sure if it's his. He knows that he will go see her again, no matter what resolves he makes.

Though Sue writes to say he mustn't come to see her and Jude replies to agree, he does notify her when his aunt dies, expecting Sue to come to Marygreen for the funeral. She does come, and after the funeral she brings up the subject of unhappy marriages and the reasons for them, particularly mentioning a woman's "fastidiousness." When Jude tries to apply her remarks personally, she insists she is not unhappy. Purposely, Jude tells her that he has seen Arabella and he may go back to her because of the way Sue has acted toward him. Sue finally does admit she is unhappy but blames it on her own wickedness, though she says that "what tortures [her] so much is the necessity of being responsive to this man whenever he wishes, good as he is morally." Later, when Jude goes outside to put out of its suffering a rabbit caught in a trap, he finds that Sue has been unable to sleep. She says that with his religious beliefs he must think it a sin for her to tell him her troubles, but Jude replies that he will forego all his beliefs if she will let him help her.

Commentary

Jude and Sue are brought together, first at Shaston and then by the aunt's death at Marygreen, in order to make possible a criticism of the institution of marriage. The essential point is that marriage as a social institution is unresponsive to the needs of the individual, and Sue is the spokesman for this view, not only on the basis of her fairly brief experience with Phillotson, but also on the basis of her ideas. She speaks here for the new woman whose "love of being loved is insatiable," as is her "love of loving." She assumes more freedom than, perhaps, she knows what to do with, and her sense of being free is in conflict with what society demands. What it demands is, of course, commitment or contract until death. As a character Sue, naturally, is trying to justify her attitude toward Phillotson as well as Jude, neither of whom is able to make her out. Jude's response, finally, is his willingness to give up his old notions of marriage, not because they are wrong, but because he will do anything for Sue.

This consideration of marriage is continued in the next two chapters in Sue's comments to Phillotson and Phillotson's to Gillingham. Of the four characters, only Gillingham maintains the conventional view steadfastly. Even Phillotson changes sufficiently to allow Sue to leave him, although he says it is against his principles. In short, the old is giving way to the new, though even Sue, the most outspoken, keeps referring perfunctorily to the fact that she must be wicked to act toward her husband as she does. She prefers the idea of freedom to the idea of sin, but the old habits of thought and the old terminology still persist.

CHAPTERS 3-4

Summary

When Sue leaves, she and Jude kiss passionately; reflecting on it, Jude sees it as a sign of his alienation from the ministry, an indication of his being unfit to profess the conventional beliefs. He thinks of the fact that Arabella hindered his aspirations to knowledge and now Sue has interfered with his desire to enter the church. He therefore burns all his theological works, so as not to leave himself in a hypocritical position. Sue berates herself for being weak but when she sees Phillotson again tells him of Jude's holding her hand, not his kissing her. That night she sleeps apart from her husband and the next day asks if she can live away from him. She tells him that she married him because she could not think of anything else to do and was frightened by the scandal at the training college. She argues that "domestic laws should be made according to temperaments," when Phillotson says her request is irregular. When he asks what she means by living away from him, she says she meant living with Jude, not necessarily as his wife, but in any way she chooses. In a series of notes exchanged between their classrooms as they teach, Phillotson agrees only to letting her live apart from him in the house.

When one night Phillotson mistakenly enters Sue's room, she leaps out of the window and slightly injures herself, later explaining to her husband that her action was caused by a dream, an explanation he doesn't believe. Phillotson goes to see his teacher friend Gillingham, in a nearby town, to have someone to talk to. Admitting that Jude and Sue "seem to be one person split in two," he tells his friend that he has decided to let Sue go, her jumping out the window being the final sign of her unwillingness to stay with him. Against Gillingham's arguments, Phillotson can only say that his instinct tells him to set Sue free, though it is opposed to all he believes in. He tells Sue of his decision, and on the day she is to leave they discuss only practical matters. After Sue leaves, Gillingham comes to call.

Commentary

Hardy is quite right: the kiss Jude and Sue exchange before she leaves Marygreen is a turning point for him. Very quickly, Jude is shown deciding he must give up a career in the church, and he burns his theological works in the garden of his aunt's house. Returning to Phillotson, Sue sleeps apart from him, asks to live away from him, and very soon is allowed to leave him to go to Jude.

It is a turning point in those relationships which embody the structure of the novel. Jude is giving up any hope for a career: "he was as unfit, obviously, by nature, as he had been by social position, to fill the part of a propounder of accredited dogma." And even if he says that he will no longer profess anything although he may believe as before, it is obvious he is reaching the point where he doubts too much to believe as he did. Sue's instruction plus what she means to him has reached a ready pupil. Since he is willing to give up so much for her, to let his emotional life take precedence over his dream of a career, he is ready for her to come to him.

Though Sue believes as she has from the start, perhaps because she does, she is ready to give up a marriage that she has never believed in. That she is ready for a different relationship than that she has had with Jude before is another matter, but giving up on Phillotson, in a sense she has no one but Jude. The radical change in her beliefs comes later.

An interesting aspect of Hardy's narrative method here is the way he shows the deteriorating relationship between Sue and Phillotson. Sue debates with her husband, almost formally, with references to authorities. Their discussion finally collapses into a series of notes exchanged between their classrooms. Their communication is really no communication at all, and it becomes ludicrous.

CHAPTER 5

Summary

Jude meets Sue at Melchester and they go on to Aldbrickham. He tells her Arabella has written to ask him to divorce her so she can remarry her Australian husband; Jude is therefore free. When he tells Sue he has reserved a room for them at a hotel, she protests she can't be intimate with him yet and tries to defend herself by saying she hasn't the courage of her convictions. Angry, Jude says she is incapable of "real love," but she replies that she has trusted Jude "to set [her] wishes above [his] gratification." When Jude says that in spite of her views she is as conventional as anyone, she mentions again a woman's love of being loved and the way this can lead her into unfortunate situations. Needing to find a different hotel, Jude unwittingly takes her to the inn where he spent the night with Arabella, and Sue finds this out from a maid. Though Sue was then supposedly happy with Phillotson and Jude legally married to Arabella, Sue is angry, and Jude complains that she expects too much of him. She is pacified only when she learns that at the time he didn't know Arabella was married to another man. She asks him to repeat some lines from Shelley to flatter her, but when he can't recall them she does so herself.

Commentary

When Sue meets Jude and they go off to Aldbrickham, coincidence puts them in the same inn as the one in which he and Arabella spent a night after Sue's marriage. Even the room Sue has is the same one Jude and Arabella used. Again, it suits Hardy's purposes to have the relationship between Jude and Arabella in the background of this first night after Sue has left Phillotson to come to Jude. But the manipulation of the plot to put the two in this particular place is a little too obvious.

Jude and Sue take separate rooms at the inn, and there is a symbolism of separate rooms running throughout the novel. Sue and her undergraduate live together in London but in separate rooms. When Jude and Sue are on an outing during the time she is in the training college in Melchester, they sleep separately at the shepherd's cottage when they must stay away overnight, though the shepherd first takes them for a married couple. Before Sue comes to Jude, she manifests her repugnance toward Phillotson by insisting they sleep in separate rooms. It is significant, indeed, that now that Sue has fled from her husband she requires of Jude that he sleep apart from her. She tries to justify this demand by arguments that she has used before, and Jude complains as before that she is incapable of "real love." After a year of living together, they will still be found in separate rooms.

In the present scene this symbolic separation is set against the memory of Jude's having shared the room with Arabella. Sue shows that this memory strikes her forcefully and, in a way, is a kind of pressure on her to allow the intimacy Jude wants. Arabella's actual presence later in the novel does, of course, force her to yield to him.

CHAPTER 6

Summary

When Sue does not return to Phillotson and he does not hesitate to tell the school authorities why, he is asked to resign, refuses to do so, and is dismissed. In the public meeting he calls to defend himself, most townspeople are against him, but some few are for him. The scuffle that results turns the meeting into a bad farce. Owing to Gillingham's telling her that he is ill, Sue comes to see Phillotson; he asks her to come back but she will not. He learns for the first time that Jude has been married. Later, he tells Gillingham that for Sue's sake he is going to divorce her, as Jude is divorcing Arabella.

Commentary

The "farcical yet melancholy" scene of the public meeting that Phillotson insists on calling is the only one of its kind in the novel. It occupies only one paragraph, and it is described rather than presented dramatically. But it does have a kind of appropriateness in showing to what a decent man like Phillotson has been reduced.

What the slapstick quality of the scene helps to show is the irony in the fact that with the best of intentions Phillotson has brought about all the difficulties he now finds himself in. He decided to let Sue go though it was against his beliefs; he insists on being honest about why she never returns; he goes out of his way to call a meeting in which to try to defend what he has done. What he now suffers is what Gillingham predicted that he would: public ignominy and scorn. Even worse, the whole thing has collapsed into low comedy. Like Jude, Phillotson is unable to hurt anyone, and again like Jude, with the best will in the world he usually succeeds in hurting himself. In spite of what has happened, he predictably decides he will divorce Sue and give her complete freedom.

PART FIFTH

CHAPTER 1

Summary

A year later at Aldbrickham, Jude and Sue are still living as they were. With Phillotson's divorce from Sue now final, they both are free, Jude's divorce from Arabella having become final some time before. When Jude brings up the subject of their marrying, Sue says she would rather they go on as lovers and avoid the oppressive effects of marriage, though Jude objects that most people marry as a matter of course. Again, he complains of her lack of "animal passion" and her seeming inability to love him, but she still wants to dictate the terms of their relationship and Jude acquiesces. With some assistance from Sue, Jude is doing work on headstones, "a lower class of handicraft" than his cathedral work previously.

Commentary

In addition to using frequently a series of short scenes to develop his narrative, Hardy sometimes falls into awkwardness when it is necessary to indicate a passage of time. This chapter begins: "How Gillingham's doubts were disposed of will most quickly appear by passing over the series of dreary months and incidents that followed the events of the last chapter, and coming on to a Sunday in the February of the year following." It is hardly a felicitous transition. In fact, this sentence might well be omitted, and the chapter open with the paragraph that follows.

In the conversation which occurs in this chapter, which presents briefly the state of the relationship established between Jude and Sue since they have been living together, Sue complains that Jude is "too sermony" in the way he speaks. The same might be said about other conversation in the novel. At times Jude and Sue especially seem to make speeches to each other rather than converse.

CHAPTERS 2-3

Summary

When Arabella calls on Jude and Sue, he discovers she is not married; she tells him that she has something important to discuss with him. When Sue urges him not to go out with Arabella because she isn't his wife, Jude replies that neither is Sue. When he returns soon, not having found Arabella in the street, Sue again implores him not to go to her. Though Jude admits his weaknesses, he is bitter about denying himself for nothing. Faced with a choice, Sue gives in to Jude, saying she will marry him, will allow the intimacy he has so strongly desired; and Jude does not go out looking for Arabella.

The next morning Jude talks of starting arrangements for their marriage, and Sue goes to see Arabella. She quickly sees that Sue possesses Jude in a way she didn't yesterday and says her visit probably helped it along. She receives a telegram from her Australian husband in which he agrees to marry her, a circumstance she has brought about by telling him Jude might take her back. Arabella tells Sue that she will write to Jude about the important matter she came to discuss.

Though Jude and Sue start out to the parish clerk's, they decide to delay putting up the banns for their marriage, Sue saying Arabella's remarks about matrimony have reminded her of the oppressiveness of such an obligation. Arabella's letter arrives, announcing that she is married to Cartlett and that she wants Jude to look after their son, born soon after her arrival in Australia. Jude is willing to look after the child, whether or not it actually is his, and Sue agrees, suggesting maybe they should now marry. The boy arrives by himself from London, sent on by Arabella after he leaves the ship from Australia, and comes to Jude and Sue. Sue says she sees Jude in the boy and allows him to call her mother.

Commentary

With Sue's giving herself to Jude, they are now "married," though they will never be joined in any ceremony recognized by society. This "marriage" is significant in several ways for the structure of the novel. Jude has strayed far from the conventional beliefs he held at the beginning of the novel, largely through the influence of Sue. And though each has been married to another, they are legally free and are living together as husband and wife. The relationship is not exactly what either one has wanted, but they are together.

That Sue's giving herself to Jude is brought about by Arabella's presence is an irony even Arabella is conscious of. In a sense, Sue is made to compete with Arabella at her own level or, to put it fairly, at the level at which any woman must compete for a man. Though she does so unwillingly, Sue wants to keep Jude from Arabella. The further irony is, of course, that even with this concession on Sue's part Arabella will eventually win, in a sense.

That this and other events in the novel may be brought about by some threatening power that controls man's destiny is symbolized in the appearance of Jude's child, Little Father Time. He makes his appearance as "Age masquerading as Juvenility," and everything about him suggests that he is meant to be more than a child. In fact, there is never much about him that suggests he is a child. That he should appear soon after Sue gives herself to Jude, an important event in the novel, is certainly no coincidence.

Jude's allusion to Job, "Let the day perish wherein I was born," is one of several throughout the novel. Jude remarks here that some day his son may find himself saying this; but, of course, it is Jude himself who repeats this very passage from Job before he dies. The symbol of Job is an appropriate one for Jude: he suffers much, and it is never given to him to know why.

CHAPTER 4

Summary

The morning after the boy arrives, Jude and Sue discover he is called Little Father Time because, as he says, he looks so old. Jude and Sue give notice of their wedding and invite Mrs. Edlin, the widow who took care of his aunt, to come. The night before they are to marry, Mrs. Edlin tells a tale about a man hanged near the Brown House, a man who may have been an ancestor of Sue and Jude. The next day they go to marry at the registry office, but after watching other couples, first Sue and then Jude decide the setting is too sordid. They go to a parish church to watch a wedding, but they agree they can't go through with a ceremony like that they both experienced before. They decide that the compulsion of marriage is not for such as they, and Sue says, "If we are happy as we are, what does it matter to anybody?"

Commentary

These scenes make clear that Jude and Sue will never submit their relationship to the forms of society. In the registry office and in a church they watch others marry, just as before Sue's marriage to Phillotson they walk down the aisle of the church in a pretense of marriage. More important is the reason for their not going through with marriage. Sue says it is as if "a tragic doom" guided the destiny of their family in this respect. The idea that something outside their lives frustrates everything they do will come into their thoughts more and more, and of course is symbolized in the figure of Little Father Time. It has been in the background from the beginning of the novel but comes to the fore in this living symbol.

This idea is echoed in the tale Mrs. Edlin tells of the man hanged near the Brown House. Mrs. Edlin, who in her person and in her sense of family history is very much a part of the Wessex landscape, is used here to illustrate the idea of the doomed family.

CHAPTER 5

Summary

At the agricultural show at Stoke-Barehills Arabella, arriving with her husband, sees Jude, Sue, and the boy and follows after them, commenting on them to Cartlett. Leaving him to go his own way, Arabella encounters a girl friend and then Physician Vilbert. They follow Jude and Sue to the art department, where the couple view a model of one of the Christminster colleges they have made. Arabella jokingly buys a "love-philtre" from Vilbert and then goes off to join her husband. Meanwhile at the pavilion of flowers Sue ecstatically admires the roses, and she and Jude agree they are happy, though conscious of the gloomy face of Little Father Time beside them.

Commentary

The scenes at the agricultural show are used primarily to show Jude and Sue as seen through Arabella's eyes. Arabella is never far away from them and never gives up her desire to get Jude back; though she married Cartlett, it was only a way of providing for herself at the time. She is shrewd enough to see what others do not, and Jude and Sue themselves are unable to: "I am inclined to think that she don't care for him quite so much as he does for her." Of course, this observation is colored by the fact that she wants to believe that she can get Jude back; nevertheless, what she sees is true.

The way in which Little Father Time is used as a symbol is shown at the end of this chapter. Sue has been admiring some roses, and she and Jude have agreed that they are happy. They are, however, concerned about the fact that the child is not enjoying himself. The boy understands this and says, "I should like the flowers very much, if I didn't keep on thinking they'd be all withered in a few days." It is impossible to believe that a child his age would say this. And it demonstrates why this particular symbol fails. It is too obvious, and the child is made to represent more significance than he is naturally capable of doing. A symbol like that of Christminster, on the other hand, does not suffer from these shortcomings.

CHAPTER 6

Summary

To stop the talk about them, Jude and Sue go off to London for a few days as if to marry, but the talk continues and Jude thinks they should move to where they are unknown. Several incidents confirm this idea: Jude loses a job at a church when, because of Sue's presence there, he is recognized and the rumors about them are repeated; Little Father Time is taunted at school by other boys; Jude feels pressured to resign from the committee governing an artisans' improvement society he belongs to. Since they plan to live in lodgings instead of a house and also since they need money, Jude auctions off most of their household effects. They aren't sure where they'll go, but not to London, and since Jude is dissatisfied with church work he isn't sure what he'll do. Sue is upset by the sale of her pet pigeons, turns them loose later at the shop of the poulterer who bought them, and remarks bitterly, "O why should Nature's law be mutual butchery!"

Commentary

Jude and Sue are shown to suffer one setback after another: people are uncivil to them; Little Father Time is harassed at school; Jude's work diminishes; he loses a job at a church when Sue is recognized; he resigns from the committee of a workmen's educational society he belongs to under unspoken pressure from other members. They decide to move to where they are not known, and since they must take lodgings instead of a house they auction their household goods. The implication is that all this is happening to them because of that malign power that operates to frustrate man's hopes. Or it may be that society retaliates against those who violate the rules it sets down. But the former is more strongly suggested.

As Sue says, it is "droll" and ironical that she and Jude should be working to restore the Ten Commandments in the church. Neither in belief nor in action do they subscribe to the meaning of these rules.

CHAPTERS 7-8

Summary

Two and a half years pass, and Jude and Sue are living at Kennetbridge, not far from Marygreen, Jude having worked in many places over the years and still unchanged in his refusal to work on churches. During the time of the spring fair, Arabella comes with her friend Anny for the dedication of a new chapel and encounters Sue, who is selling cakes and gingerbreads at a stall. Arabella tells Sue her husband is dead and questions her about her life. She says that she is married, that she has two children (she is pregnant with a third), that Jude has lost his pride, is ill, and bakes cakes because he can do the work indoors. The fact that the cakes are in shapes reminiscent of buildings at Christminster causes both women to agree that Jude still thinks of the city as his ideal. Arabella tells Sue that since her husband's death she has found religion, and she has come from Alfredston, where she lives with her friend, for the dedication.

On her way home from Kennetbridge Arabella tells her friend Anny that she wishes she had Jude back, that he is more hers than Sue's, and that she won't be a hypocrite any longer about religion. Along the way, they meet Phillotson, now teaching at Marygreen again, and Arabella identifies herself, this being the first time they have met since Arabella was his pupil. Telling him where Sue now is, Arabella criticizes Phillotson for letting her go, pointing out that Sue was never initimate with Jude before the divorce. She lectures him on how he should treat a wife.

In Kennetbridge, when Sue returns to their lodgings, she tells Jude she has sold all the cakes and has seen Arabella. Jude takes Arabella's living near as a good enough reason for moving on and to Sue's surprise says he wants to return to Christminster, which he loves even though he knows it despises men like him. Accordingly, in a few weeks they go.

Commentary

Jude and Sue are reduced to living off the sale of the cakes and gingerbreads Jude bakes. The fact that they are made in the shapes of buildings at Christminster not only reveals that it is a "fixed vision" with him, as Sue says, but foreshadows his return there. Having aimlessly gone from one town to another for several years in pursuit of work, Jude will finally return to the place of his youthful dream as if to die there.

Arabella's meeting with Phillotson, coincidental though it may be, makes the final connection among the main characters, since they are the only two who have never met in recent years. Here and later, she reports to Phillotson on the state of the relationship between Sue and Jude; her motives are, of course, selfish.

PART SIXTH

CHAPTERS 1-2

Summary

Jude has planned it so they arrive on Remembrance Day (anniversary of founding of the university), and instead of looking for lodgings he wants to view the festivities. But when he sees young men from the colleges, he feels it will be "Humiliation Day" for him. He passes the building from which he looked out over the colleges and decided he would never achieve his academic ambitions, and he is recognized by several men with whom he drank and who now remind him of his failure. He addresses a speech to them and the crowd, in which he discusses his attempt to succeed and the reasons for failure, ending with the declaration that "there is something wrong somewhere in our social formulas." In their wanderings through the crowds Sue has spotted Phillotson, an indication to her that he must live somewhere near. They have a difficult time finding lodgings for the whole family, finally settling for rooms for Sue and the children only. When the landlady discovers Sue is not married, she tells her husband and informs Sue she must leave the next day. With Little Father Time she looks unsuccessfully for another place but decides not to worry Jude with the problem until the next day.

In the bare rooms from which Sue can see some of the colleges, a proximity Jude has insisted on, Sue talks to Little Father Time before they go to bed. The boy is sure the family's plight is caused by the children and can't understand why children are born at all, though Sue explains to him it is a law of nature. When she tells him she is pregnant with another child, he says she has done it on purpose to bring the family to further ruin. The next morning, without looking in on the children she goes to find Jude and tells him of their problem about lodgings. When they return to Sue's lodgings to prepare breakfast for the children, she goes into their room, to discover all three are dead. Jude and Sue decide, when they think about it later, that Little Father Time awakened to find Sue gone, hanged the two younger children first and then hanged himself. The note he left seems to confirm this.

To comfort Sue, Jude repeats the doctor's observation that Little Father Time is one of a new generation of children with a preternatural wisdom and sense of defeat. Sue, not relieved, speaks of a fate that has ruled their lives inexorably, says that in dealing with the boy she should have been wiser, and remembers with dismay that once she asserted they should enjoy the instincts nature gave them. Jude agrees that a fate rules and that they can do nothing about their destiny. Jude doesn't allow Sue to attend the funeral; however, when he returns from it he discovers she is gone and finds her at the grave, insisting the gravedigger stop filling in the grave so she can look at her dead children. Jude takes her home, puts her to bed, and calls the doctor; her baby is prematurely born dead.

Commentary

The two important scenes here embody the theme of the novel rather directly. Jude's speech to the street crowd is his second public performance, the other being his recitation in a tavern of the Creed in Latin. Here he tries to explain his life. He asserts that his failure is a failure of circumstances (poverty), not will; but later he remarks, "I was, perhaps, after all, a paltry victim to the spirit of mental and social restlessness, that makes so many unhappy in these days!" But Sue will not allow this and says he "struggled nobly to acquire knowledge." After admitting he is in "a chaos of principles" now, he ends by remarking that something is wrong with society. In short, Jude acknowledges that he has been caught in changes he doesn't understand and has ended not knowing what to believe in.

That "something external" to them, as Sue puts it with Jude agreeing by reference to a line from *Agamemnon,* should have shaped their destiny is vividly suggested in the melodramatic scene of the children's death. Suddenly, Little Father Time and the other two are gone, and Sue's child is born dead. Without reason, as far as Jude and Sue can see, this last blow is dealt them.

The scene is one of those sensational, melodramatic incidents for the use of which in his novels critics have often taken Hardy to task. Perhaps such scenes can be justified on the basis of the fact that most of his novels were first serialized in magazines and he needed to maintain reader interest from month to month. Whatever the reason for their inclusion, here the scene is impossible to believe, not the least of the reasons for which is the note Little Father Time leaves, "Done because we are too menny." Further, the scene is inconsistent with the kind of reality Hardy depicts everywhere else in the novel.

The unreality of the scene is increased because the chief actor in it is Little Father Time. It is appropriate to his symbolic meaning that he should be the one to hang the two children before, of course, taking his own life. As one critic has pointed out, Little Father Time as a symbol is unnecessary because what he stands for is already illustrated in Jude's own life.

It is of course significant that these scenes occur in Christminster, Jude's symbol of all that is good in life.

CHAPTERS 3-4

Summary

During her convalescence Sue says she is beaten and must conform, and Jude asserts he belongs to "that vast band of men shunned by the virtuous—the men called seducers." She still feels she belongs to Phillotson. Jude is aware of the fact that he and Sue are going in opposite directions: she is returning to the conventional ideas she taught Jude to abandon. She insists that now she must practice "self-renunciation," but Jude argues that she has only acted out of natural instincts. She has been attending church frequently, Jude finds out, and does not want to be criticized for doing so. She doesn't want to go through the marriage ceremony with him because she feels she is still married to Phillotson. When Arabella calls, having come to Christminster to look at her son's grave, Sue insists that she is not Jude's wife. After Sue mysteriously leaves, Arabella says she is living at Alfredson with her father, now back from Australia. Jude looks for Sue, finally discovering her in church. She tells him that Arabella's child killing hers is a judgment on her. They disagree over whether she is his wife, Jude arguing that their marriage was made by nature, Sue that it was not made in heaven as hers to Phillotson was.

Jude cannot understand how Sue can have changed so, but she is convinced she has seen the light at last. She doesn't want him to return to their lodgings, but he does anyway. A conversation ensues in which each tries to take the blame for the relationship between them: Jude says he shouldn't have forced her into intimacy, though he still complains she hasn't felt for him what he feels for her; she admits she tried to attract him and through envy of Arabella gave herself to him in order to hold him. She insists they part, though Jude tries to convince her that he needs her as a defense against his weaknesses. She tells him that they must separate not because she dislikes him but because her conscience says it's right, and she suggests they can still be friends as they used to be.

After seeing Jude and Sue in Christminster on Remembrance Day, Phillotson reads of the death of the children in a newspaper while in Alfredston. Encountering Arabella there, he learns from her that Jude and Sue aren't living together, that they have never married, that Sue considers herself Phillotson's wife, and that Little Father Time was really Arabella's child. He decides to ask Sue to return to him, realizing what positive effects it might have on other aspects of his life, and writes her a letter. In Christminster Sue calls on Jude to tell him she has decided to return to Phillotson, to remarry him, and she suggests Jude go back to Arabella. Jude cannot understand this extreme penance on Sue's part. She purposely walks with him to the cemetery so they can say goodbye over the graves of the children.

Commentary

Jude and Sue are shown in the scenes here to have reached the point at which their beliefs have reversed. The structure of the novel is such that the next step is for them to dissolve their relationship, with Sue the instigator. Sue now talks about the necessity of "self-renunciation" and the feeling that she still belongs to Phillotson. Jude argues that she was simply following her natural instincts in coming to him and that theirs is "Nature's own marriage." But Sue answers that it was not made in heaven, as was hers with Phillotson. The change in Sue is shown further in her attending church almost daily and in her conviction that Arabella's child killing hers was a judgment on her.

It is not surprising, then, that she accepts Phillotson's offer to return to him and remarry. It will be the right thing to do and will serve as a penance for her sins. She even suggests that Jude make things right by returning to Arabella.

CHAPTER 5

Summary

Sue goes to Marygreen and Phillotson's house, and when Phillotson greets her with a kiss she shrinks from him. The wedding is to be the next day, and she is to stay with Mrs. Edlin. When Sue refuses to wear an attractive nightgown, indeed destroys it, Mrs.

Edlin tells her she still loves Jude and shouldn't marry Phillotson. Phillotson discusses his reasons for wanting to marry Sue with Gillingham and says so much about the way a man should govern a wife that his friend wonders if he will not be too hard on Sue. Mrs. Edlin embarrasses Phillotson by coming to tell him that Sue is forcing herself to marry him and he shouldn't go through with it, but Gillingham assures him he is right to marry her. Phillotson and Sue are married in the church the next morning, and afterward at home he tells her he will respect her "personal privacy" as he did before.

Commentary

Every detail in these scenes shows Sue is forcing herself to re-marry Phillotson as a penance: she shrinks from his kiss; she is startled by seeing the marriage license; she destroys a nightgown she bought for Jude's sake and insists on wearing a plain one; she cries; she wants the marriage performed quickly.

Here and in the previous section Phillotson is shown to be acting on the basis of expediency in taking Sue back. He has decided it might improve his standing in the community and in his profession, and to Gillingham he mouths conventional advice about how a husband should govern his wife. In short, his motives for taking her back are less admirable than those for letting her go. Of course, he has suffered a good deal from allowing her to leave him for Jude.

CHAPTERS 6-7

Summary

In Christminster Arabella comes to Jude's lodgings, saying she has nowhere to go and asking him to take her in. Eventually he does give her a place to sleep, and when she asks him if he knows of the wedding, he is irritable about the subject. Another day, she offers to find out if the wedding actually took place when she goes to Alfredston. Upon her return she tells Jude that Sue and Phillotson are married, that Sue burned her good nightgown to forget Jude, that Sue thought Phillotson her only husband, and that she feels that way with respect to Jude. While Jude goes to a tavern to drink, Arabella arranges with her father, now living in the city, to bring Jude there that night. Finding Jude, Arabella encourages him in his drinking and later guides him to her father's house, Jude drunk enough not to be sure where he is.

The next day Arabella arranges with her father to keep Jude in the house until she can get him to marry her, one means of which is a sufficient supply of liquor. She brings his things from his lodgings so he can have no reason to go back there, and has her father give a party to entertain Jude and, supposedly, to advertise his pork shop. After the party, which includes some of Jude's former drinking companions, has been going on a long time, Arabella says it's time for Jude to carry out his promise to marry her; and when Jude says he doesn't remember any promise her father questions his honor. Saying he has never acted dishonorably to anyone, Jude goes off with Arabella and her father to be married. Upon their return Arabella triumphantly describes the wedding, and Jude says he has acted honorably and also done what Sue suggested.

Commentary

Both Jude and Sue have remarried; they have conformed. But the scenes depicting both ceremonies make clear that they are honoring the letter and not the spirit of the institution. As Jude says later, when they remarried he was "gin-drunk" and she was "creed-drunk." Or as he bitterly says here about his remarrying of Arabella, "It is true religion!"

The ceremonies are rather similar. They are held at a time when no one will pay much attention to what is going on. In each case, the officiating clergyman congratulates the couple on having done the right thing and says they ought to be forgiven now.

The marital relationships have come full circle now. Jude and Sue are back with the partners they began with, but for each it is a defeat.

CHAPTERS 8-9
Summary

Jude and Arabella are as incompatible now as they were the first time they were married, she complaining about his always being ill and he wishing he were dead. When Jude asks her to write to Sue for him, inviting her to visit, Arabella insults Sue, and he is violent with her but admits he couldn't kill her. Convinced that Arabella has never mailed the letter she wrote, Jude goes to Marygreen in spite of his ill health. When Sue congratulates him for marrying Arabella, he bitterly attacks the way she has changed and tells her she isn't worth loving. She tells him she has not given herself to Phillotson and she loves him; they embrace passionately. When he suggests they run away together, she tells him to leave. He does, passing for the last time the fields where he chased rooks and the ridge-track near the Brown House where so much has happened, even stopping to feel at the back of the milestone the carving he made there. He is back in Christminster late at night.

Arabella awaits Jude at the station, and he tells her he has accomplished the only two things he now wants: to see Sue and to die. As she takes him home past the walls of the colleges, he thinks he sees the eminent men of the past as he did when he first came to Christminster, but now they seem to laugh at him.

At Marygreen Sue tells Mrs. Edlin that Jude has been there, that she still loves him, and that she must now perform the most severe penance, going to Phillotson's bed. Though she asks Mrs. Edlin to stay overnight in the house because she is afraid, she goes to Phillotson, wakes him, and asks him to allow her to come in. She confesses Jude visited and they kissed, but she swears on a New Testament she will never see him again. Phillotson forgives her, and though she at first shrinks from his touch she does take his kiss without reaction.

Commentary

In both Marygreen and Christminster, Jude encounters for the last time those features of the setting that have been meaningful to him: the field where he scared rooks, the Brown House, the milestone; the buildings of the colleges, the ghosts of the great men of the past, who now seem to be laughing at him. He himself seems to be conscious of a farewell.

Jude's desire to run away with Sue and her decision to go to Phillotson's bed measure the extremes of the reversals in belief which have occurred in the two characters. This plus the change in marital relationships shows the structure of the novel moving to its completion. Neither character is as he was in the beginning, and both are seen to go down to defeat.

That they should declare their love for each other after their remarriages makes for a large irony in the novel. Jude's taunt, "Sue, Sue, you are not worth a man's love!" forces Sue momentarily to forget the penance she is determined to make. But it is too late for anything to change. The inexplicable power that has guided their lives so far, hinted at so often in the novel, makes their declarations merely acts of desperation.

CHAPTER 10
Summary

Jude often muses on "the defeat of his early aims" and thinks of the possible changes in the colleges to benefit people like himself. Though he tells Arabella he doesn't want Sue to know about him, when Mrs. Edlin calls he asks about Sue and is startled to discover she is now sharing her husband's bed. He talks about the best days of the relationship between Sue and himself and the ways in which each of them changed. Physician Vilbert, who has been attending Jude at Arabella's request, calls, but Jude's insults cause him to leave. On his way out he meets Arabella, who gives him wine with some of the quack doctor's own "love-philter" in it. From her allowing him to kiss her and from what she says, it is evident that Arabella is keeping an eye out for the time when Jude will be dead.

Commentary

As these brief scenes show, Jude has only the past; to Arabella belong the present and future. Jude is still trying to justify or understand the meaning of his life, this time to Mrs. Edlin: "Our ideas were fifty years too soon to be any good to us. And so the resistance they met with brought reaction in her, and recklessness and ruin on me!" This remark, of course, echoes what he said earlier in his speech to the street crowd.

Meanwhile, Arabella is flirting with Physician Vilbert. When Jude's gone, she'll need someone to take care of her, and she has to take what she can get now.

CHAPTER 11

Summary

On Remembrance Day Arabella, impatient to be off to the festivities, leaves Jude asleep and alone. He awakens, asks for water,
recognizes what holiday it is, and repeats some verses from Job.
Later, Arabella breaks away long enough to look in on Jude, who
she discovers is dead. She rejoins the holiday, eventually meeting
Physician Vilbert. She does finally leave him to see about arrangements for Jude's funeral. Two days later, only Arabella and Mrs.
Edlin stand by Jude's coffin; the sounds of the holiday come from
outside. Mrs. Edlin doesn't know if Sue will come to the funeral
but asserts that Sue has said she's found peace. Arabella says that
Jude didn't want Sue sent for and did not forgive her and that Sue
will never find peace until she is dead like Jude.

Commentary

In the city which is the symbol of his hopes Jude dies, and his
death comes on Remembrance Day, which is particularly meaningful to him. His last words are some verses from Job, that symbol
that has been used frequently in the novel: "Let the day perish
wherein I was born...." Jude has earlier wondered if his own son
wouldn't one day repeat these very verses.

There is, of course, irony everywhere in these closing scenes.
Certainly there is in the fact that Jude should die in Christminster.
Certainly too, there is in the fact that Arabella should have the last
word in the novel. About Sue she says, "She's never found peace
since she left his arms, and never will again till she's as he is now!"
In a way, only Arabella of the four principal characters survives.
Jude is dead; Sue is doing penance for what she thinks of as her sins
and, according to Mrs. Edlin, has aged greatly; Phillotson, devoid
of hope, is back at Marygreen where he began, living with a wife
whom he requires to swear loyalty to him on a New Testament.

Ironically too, Arabella has been the least ambitious of all the
main characters. The others have been caught up in the spirit of
the times and for reasons that seem inexplicable and out of their
control have been defeated in their attempts to realize their aspirations.

ANALYSES OF MAIN CHARACTERS

JUDE FAWLEY

Jude is obscure in that he comes from uncertain origins, struggles largely unnoticed to realize his aspirations, and dies without having made any mark on the world. He is also obscure in the sense of being ambiguous: he is divided internally, and the conflicts range all the way from that between sexual desire and knowledge to that between two different views of the world. Jude is, therefore, struggling both with the world and with himself.

He is not well equipped to win. Though he is intelligent enough and determined, he tries to force his way to the knowledge he wants. Though well-intentioned and goodhearted, he often acts impulsively on the basis of too little objective evidence. Though he is unable to hurt an animal or another human being, he shows very little concern for himself and his own survival, often needlessly sacrificing his own good. He never learns, as Phillotson finally does perhaps too late, to calculate how to get what he wants. In short, he is more human than divine, as Hardy points out.

He is obsessed with ideals. Very early he makes Christminster into an ideal of the intellectual life, and his admitted failure there does not dim the luster with which it shines in his imagination to the very end of his life. He searches for the ideal woman who will be both lover and companion, and though he finds passion without intellectual interests in Arabella and wide interests but frigidity in Sue he maintains the latter as his ideal to his deathbed. Recognizing the Christminster holiday just before he dies, Jude says, "And I here. And Sue defiled!"

Jude is reconciled to his fate before he dies only in the sense that he recognizes what it is. In a conversation with Mrs. Edlin he says that perhaps he and Sue were ahead of their time in the way they wanted to live. He does not regret the struggle he has made; at the least, as he lies ill he tries to puzzle out the meaning of his life. At the very end, however, like Job he wonders why he was born. But then so perhaps does every man, Hardy seems to imply.

SUE BRIDEHEAD

It is easy for the modern reader to dislike Sue, even, as D. H. Lawrence did, to make her into the villain of the book. (Lawrence thought Sue represented everything that was wrong with modern women.) Jude, as well as Hardy, obviously sees her as charming, lively, intelligent, interesting, and attractive in the way that an adolescent girl is. But it is impossible not to see other sides to her personality: she is self-centered, wanting more than she is willing to give; she is intelligent but her knowledge is fashionable and her use of it is shallow; she is outspoken but afraid to suit her actions to her words; she wants to love and be loved but is morbidly afraid of her emotions and desires.

In short, she is something less than the ideal Jude sees in her; like him she is human. She is also a nineteenth-century woman who has given herself more freedom than she knows how to handle. She wants to believe that she is free to establish a new sort of relationship to men, even as she demands freedom to examine new ideas. But at the end she finds herself in the role of sinner performing penance for her misconduct. As Jude says, they were perhaps ahead of their time.

If she is not an ideal, she is the means by which Jude encounters a different view of life, one which he comes to adopt even as she flees from it. She is also one of the means by which Jude's hopes are frustrated and he is made to undergo suffering and defeat. But it is a frustration which he invites or which is given him by a power neither he nor Sue understands or seems to control.

ARABELLA DONN

Arabella is the least complex of the main characters; she is also the least ambitious, though what she wants she pursues with determination and enterprise. What she is after is simple enough: a man who will satisfy her and who will provide the comforts and some of the luxuries of life. She is attractive in an overblown way, good-humored, practical, uneducated of course but shrewd, cunning, and tenacious. She is common in her tastes and interests. She is capable of understanding a good deal in the emotional life of other people, especially women, as shown on several occasions with Sue.

Arabella never quite finds what she wants either. Jude's ambitions put her off when they are first married, but after him Cartlett is obviously a poor substitute, though she doesn't complain. She wants Jude again and gets him, but she isn't satisfied, since he is past the point of being much good to her.

That she is enterprising is demonstrated everywhere in the novel; she has a self-interest that amounts to an instinct for survival, rather than the self-interest of a Sue that is the same as pride. And, of course, she does survive intact in a way the others don't. Though at the end of the novel she is standing by Jude's coffin, Vilbert awaits her somewhere in the city. Life goes on, in short.

RICHARD PHILLOTSON

Phillotson is eminently the respectable man. Though he fails to achieve the same goals Jude pursues, his bearing and view of things do not change much. Even when Arabella encounters him on the road to Alfredston, now down on his luck and teaching at Marygreen because it's the only place that will have him, this air of respectability remains. It must be this which Sue can't stand about him, the respectability plus the legal right to make love to her.

Sue's opinion of him does not make him any less decent. He is like Jude in many ways: he is goodhearted and honorable; he allows instinct to overrule reason; he is too accommodating for his own good; he is intelligent. Like Jude he is ill-equipped to get what he wants in life and soon resigns himself to mediocrity. However, unlike Jude he no longer is dazzled by ideals, perhaps because he is older. Maybe too late he learns to act on the basis of calculation, estimating that Sue's return will be worth the benefits it may bring.

Phillotson, in short, is a man whom it is easy neither to like nor to dislike; he goes largely unnoticed.

CRITICAL ANALYSIS

THEME

In no other novel by Hardy is theme so important. And his theme here may be stated briefly as follows: man is becoming aware that his life is governed by old ideas and old institutions and he desires to break out of these obsolete forms. This modern spirit causes him to question old beliefs and institutions and to seek new ones, to give up what is known and tried for the unknown and new, and hence to experience loneliness and frustration as he searches on his own. Specifically in the novel, Hardy depicts characters who raise questions about such things as religious beliefs, social classes, the conventions of marriage, and elite educational institutions and who feel in the absence of the old certainties that the universe may be governed by a mysterious, possibly malign power. Some critics have suggested that Hardy had in mind when he wrote the novel Matthew Arnold's comments on the coming of the modern spirit.

POINT OF VIEW

The most noteworthy thing about Hardy's use of point of view is that it is conventional for his time. He uses a shifting third person point of view which is usually centered in Jude but sometimes is moved to one of the other main characters. Historically, then, Hardy makes no use of the development of point of view as a technique carried out by his contemporary Henry James.

SETTING

Though in this novel Hardy makes less significant use of his Wessex landscape, as well as its customs, superstitions, humor, and human types, than he does in other novels, it is of some importance. Almost all the characters are deeply rooted in and responsive to place, as shown, for example, in Jude's sense of all that has happened on the ridge-track near the Brown House outside Marygreen. Characters like Drusilla Fawley or Mrs. Edlin are very much a product of the area, the aunt with her references to family history, the widow with her comments about marriage. But Hardy's desire to work out his theme seems to override most of this local reference.

PLOT

Hardy's narrative technique has often been criticized. He characteristically uses a succession of short scenes to move the plot forward instead of longer scenes developed in detail. Sometimes his transitions are awkward, especially in the way in which he summarizes the passage of time. He relies frequently on coincidence to bring together characters he wants to have meet. And now and again he indulges in a sensational, melodramatic scene.

Such shortcomings are to be found in this novel, but in Hardy's defense it should be said that he can develop a scene skillfully, he does use contrasting scenes with good effect in forwarding the plot, and he is capable of foreshadowing events in the novel with competence. It may be that his weaknesses in narrative technique come in part from the demands of serial publication; it may also be that he had less interest in this aspect of fiction than he did in others.

STRUCTURE

The structure of the novel might be described as the reversals of belief in Jude and Sue and their changing marital relationships as they both go down to defeat. In the beginning Sue's view of things is secular and rationalist, expressed, for example, in her sympathy with ancient rather than medieval culture, her scorn of conventional religious belief, her buying of pagan statuary, her reading of Gibbon. Jude's beliefs are, at first, conventionally Christian, as his desire to be ordained, his reading of standard authors, and his love of medieval culture and architecture show. By the end of the novel Sue has reverted to conventional beliefs, as evidenced by her concern for the sanctity of marriage and her desire to perform penances for her sins. On the other hand, Jude no longer professes his old beliefs and finds himself, as he says in his speech to the street crowd in Christminster, in "a chaos of principles."

This change in beliefs is closely paralleled by their marital relationships. At first, they are separated by marriage to other people as they are apart in belief. As Jude's ideas change, they are legally freed by divorce, and they come to live together and to be "married," in fact, if not in name. When Sue returns to conventional Christian beliefs, they separate and remarry their first spouses.

Jude's death as a failure in Christminster and Sue's forcing herself to go to Phillotson's bed are striking signs of their defeat in life. This defeat is mirrored as well in Phillotson, who at Mary-green has fallen to the bottom professionally and who stiffly requires Sue to swear loyalty to him on a New Testament, and to a lesser extent in Arabella, who though she loses Jude does not lose her vitality.

In these changes and defeat Hardy has embodied the theme of his novel: Jude and Sue have been caught up in the modern spirit, have struggled to break free of the old ways, and have suffered and failed. It is this that justifies Hardy's description of the novel, in his preface to it, as a "tragedy of unfulfilled aims."

SYMBOLISM

The symbolism in the novel helps to work out the theme. Such a minor symbol as the repeated allusion to Samson and Delilah reinforces the way Jude's emotional life undermines the realization of his ambitions. Two symbols of major importance are Christ-minster and the character of Little Father Time. They are useful to discuss, since the first is an instance of a successful symbol and the second an unsuccessful one.

Jude's idea of Christminster permeates not only his thinking but the whole novel. From his first view of it on the horizon to his hearing the sounds of the holiday there coming in his window as he lies on his deathbed, Christminster represents to him all that is desirable in life. It is by this ideal that he measures everything. He encounters evidence in abundance that it is not in fact what he thinks it is in his imagination, but he will not take heed. It finally represents to him literally all that he has left in life. Of course, other characters as well are affected by Jude's idea of the place. It is a successful symbol because it is capable of representing what it is supposed to and it does not call attention to itself as a literary device.

Little Father Time, however, is a different matter. The boy's appearance, his persistent gloom, his oracular tone, his inability ever to respond to anything as a child—all of these call attention to the fact that he is supposed to represent something. And Hardy makes the child carry more meaning than he is naturally able to. He is fate, of course, but also blighted hopes, failure, change, etc.

IRONY

The use of irony is of course commonplace in fiction, and a number of effective instances of it in Hardy's novel are to be found. In some of the instances the reader but not the character recognizes the irony; in others, both the reader and the character are aware of it. An example of the first is Jude's occupational choice of ecclesiastical stonework in medieval Gothic style in a time when medievalism in architecture is dying out or the way Arabella alienates Jude by the deception she has used to get him to marry her the first time. An example of the second is Jude's dying in Christminster, the city that has symbolized all his hopes, or the way Arabella's calling on Jude in Aldbrickham in order to reawaken his interest in her helps bring about Sue's giving herself to him.

Irony is particularly appropriate in a novel of tragic intent, in which events do not work out the way the characters expect. Certainly it is appropriate in a novel which has the kind of theme this one does. Struggling to break free of the old, the characters experience the old sufferings and failure nonetheless.

STYLE

Critics have often noted the faults in Hardy's style, and perhaps this is to be expected in a writer who was largely self-educated. Such writers can express themselves in striking and original ways, but their lack of formal education sometimes causes them to fall into awkwardness and excess. Shakespeare was, by Hardy's own admission, the greatest literary influence on him, but certainly not in the area of style. Several instances of lapses in Hardy's style might be pointed out, but one will serve to illustrate what is meant. Phillotson says to Arabella when they meet many years after she has been a student of his, "I should hardly recognize in your present portly self the slim school child no doubt you were then." It is inconceivable that anyone would talk in this way, not even the schoolmaster Phillotson. In Hardy's defense it should be said, however, that there are passages in the novel in which his style serves him quite well.

QUOTATIONS

In the novel Hardy uses a great many quotations from his reading: at the head of each part, in the narrative, and in the conversations and thoughts of the characters. Many of these are from either the Bible or Shakespeare, but they range over the whole of English literature as well. His practice here is typical of what he did in other novels. The sources of most of the quotations are given or are obvious; the others are identified in the appendices to the book by Carl Weber listed in the bibliography.

REVIEW QUESTIONS AND THEME TOPICS

1. In what specific ways are Jude and Sue counterparts? Take into account their personalities, their interests, the way they respond to things in life. (See Part Third, Chapter 3, and Phillotson's comments in Part Fourth, Chapter 4.)

2. How has Hardy contrasted Sue and Arabella? Consider what is said or shown about their appearance, manner, speech, interests, etc.

3. Compare Jude and Phillotson in their role as "husband" to Sue (Jude, of course, is never legally married to her). What do they require of her? How do they act toward her? What do they allow her to do?

4. Examine the relationship between Phillotson and Gillingham. What purpose in the novel does the latter serve in his role of friend to Phillotson? (See, for example, Part Fourth, Chapter 4, and Part Sixth, Chapter 5.)

5. Take another minor character like Anny. In relation to Arabella, what purpose does she serve in the novel? (See, for example, Part First, Chapter 9, and Part Fifth, Chapters 5, 8.)

6. Contrast the books that Jude and Sue read or have read. What do these reveal about the differences between them? (See, for example, Part First, Chapter 6, and Part Third, Chapter 4.)

7. Examine what is revealed about Sue's childhood in Marygreen. Does this help in any way to explain what Sue is as an adult? (See Part Second, Chapter 6.)

8. Look at the comments on marriage in the conversation of the characters, especially Jude and Sue. What questions about the conventions of that institution are raised? (See, for example, Part Fourth, Chapters 2-4.)

9. Examine the comments on Christminster in the conversation of the characters, especially Sue. What questions about the nature and value of that educational institution are raised? (See, for example, Part Third, Chapter 4.)

10. Look at the comments on fate made by Jude and Sue in the last part of the novel. In what way are they a questioning of conventional Christian beliefs? (See, for example, Part Sixth, Chapters 2-3.)

11. Suppose the novel were told entirely from the point of view of, say, Phillotson. In what ways would this change the nature and effect of the story?

12. For Jude the ridge-track near the Brown House outside Marygreen is a place full of significance for his life. Catalogue all the things that have happened to him here.

13. Mrs. Edlin may be thought of as a kind of local historian. List the reminiscences or anecdotes she relates in this role.

14. Study the first five paragraphs of Part Fifth, Chapter 7. This is a transitional passage summarizing the events occurring in the life of Jude and Sue for two and a half years. Is it effective? If not, explain. For example, has anything important been left out?

15. Is it a coincidence that Jude, Sue, Little Father Time, Arabella, Cartlett, Anny, and Vilbert all happen to be at the agricultural show in Stoke-Barehills at the same time? Or does the coming together of the characters grow naturally and necessarily out of the movement of the plot? (See Part Fifth, Chapter 5.)

16. It has been said that the death of the children is a sensational, melodramatic scene. What details of the scene support this contention? (See Part Sixth, Chapter 2.)

17. Take a brief scene like that in which Arabella gets Jude to make love to her. What is Hardy trying to show in this scene, and by what means does he accomplish his purpose? (See Part First, Chapter 8.)

18. Examine the scene in which Jude and Sue go on an outing during her stay at the training college in Melchester. What events, character relationships, or aspects of the characters are foreshadowed during the course of this scene? (See Part Third, Chapter 2.)

19. Is it true that Jude and Sue experience exact reversals in their beliefs? For example, at the end of the novel does Jude believe precisely what Sue did at the beginning? If not, explain. (See, for example, Part Sixth, Chapters 1, 3.)

20. To what extent do Phillotson's beliefs change during the course of the novel? If there is any change, describe it in detail. (See, for example, Part Sixth, Chapters 4-5.)

21. Hardy said that his novel was a "tragedy of unfulfilled aims." Discuss the aims that go unfulfilled, specifically among the main characters.

22. Explain the meaning of the allusion to Samson and Delilah; then, do the same for another minor symbol in the novel. (Samson and Delilah first appears in Part First, Chapter 7.)

23. Discuss the ways in which Jude's idea of Christminster affects other characters in the novel, particularly Sue and Arabella.

24. It has been said that the major symbol of Little Father Time is a failure. Document the reasons for this failure in detail. (See, for example, Part Fifth, Chapters 3-5, and Part Sixth, Chapter 2.)

25. Several instances of the use of irony which only the reader is aware of have been given; find additional examples.

26. Several instances of the use of irony which both the reader and the character are aware of have been given; find additional examples.

27. Try to justify the idea that in a tragic novel like this the use of irony is appropriate; support what you say by the use of instances of irony in the novel.

28. Find other examples, in addition to the one already given, of lapses in Hardy's style in the novel. Try to explain what is wrong with each example.

29. Find a passage in the novel in which Hardy's style is adequate to the occasion, and try to explain what is effective in his use of language.

30. Critics have said that this is the most modern of Hardy's novels. What twentieth-century novel does it seem similar to, even if only in part, and why?

SELECTED BIBLIOGRAPHY

Abercrombie, Lascelles. *Thomas Hardy: A Critical Study*. New York, 1912. An early analysis of Hardy's work as well as a summary of his attitudes.

Beach, Joseph Warren. *The Technique of Thomas Hardy*. Chicago, 1922. A study of the "structural art" of Hardy's novels, major and minor.

Guerard, Albert J. *Thomas Hardy: The Novels and Stories*. Cambridge, Mass., 1949. A study of Hardy's novels whose main purpose is "to describe the content and accomplishment of his novels in the simplest possible terms."

_____ (ed.). *Hardy: A Collection of Critical Essays*. Englewood Cliffs, N.J., 1963, Essays on Hardy's art, his major novels, his characters, and his poetry by such writers as D. H. Lawrence, John Holloway, Albert Guerard, Dorothy Van Ghent, and Samuel Hynes.

Hardy, Florence E. *The Early Life of Thomas Hardy*. London, 1928. A biography by Hardy's second wife, which was probably planned and partly written by Hardy himself.

____. *The Later Years of Thomas Hardy*. London, 1930. See Hardy, above.

Rutland, William. *Thomas Hardy: A Study of His Writings and Their Background*. Oxford, 1938. A study of the intellectual background of Hardy's thought and writing.

The Southern Review (Thomas Hardy Centennial Issue), Vol. VI (Summer 1940). Essays on various aspects of Hardy's fiction and poetry by such writers as R. P. Blackmur, F. R. Leavis, Arthur Mizener. John Crowe Ransom, and Allen Tate; those by Donald Davidson, Morton Dauwen Zabel, Delmore Schwartz, and W. H. Auden are reprinted in the collection edited by Guerard (listed above).

Weber, Carl J. *Hardy of Wessex: His Life and Literary Career*. New York, 1940. A study of Hardy's life and career, a second edition of which appeared in 1965, making use of recent scholarship and additional information from letters.

Webster, Harvey C. *On a Darkling Plain*. Chicago, 1947. A study of "the evolution of Hardy's thought and its effect upon his art."

NOTES

NOTES

NOTES

NOTES

NOTES

The Mayor of Casterbridge

THE MAYOR
OF CASTERBRIDGE

NOTES

including
- *Life and Background of the Author*
- *Introduction to the Novel*
- *Brief Summary of the Novel*
- *Chapter Summaries and Commentaries*
- *Literary Analysis*
- *Character Summations*

by
David C. Gild, Ph.D.
Yale University

REVISED EDITION

INCORPORATED

LINCOLN, NEBRASKA   68501

Editor

Gary Carey, M.A.
University of Colorado

Consulting Editor

James L. Roberts, Ph.D.
Department of English
University of Nebraska

Cliffs Notes, Inc.   Lincoln, Nebraska

CONTENTS

INTRODUCTION

Thomas Hardy was born June 2, 1840, in the village of Upper Bockhampton, about three miles from the town of Dorchester in Southwestern England. The impressions of his early youth—the people, the events, the surrounding countryside—became part of the subject matter of his "Wessex" novels and stories. The town of Casterbridge itself, for example, is modeled after Dorchester.

Hardy's father was a builder and stone mason and was by no means wealthy. His mother loved reading, and under her care young Thomas was given an ample introduction to the classics, folk songs, ballads, and local stories and legends. Music was also a common feature of the Hardy household. Thomas's father taught him to play the violin, for he himself was violinist in the church choir and often played at parties, weddings, and festivals. Music was a great love throughout Thomas Hardy's life and often figures in his writing. At least three important scenes in *The Mayor of Casterbridge* involve music.

Early Education and Architectural Apprenticeship

Hardy did not study at a university. His formal education consisted of a year in a village school at Lower Bockhampton and additional private schooling in Dorchester during which he learned French and German. When he was sixteen, his father apprenticed him to a Dorchester architect, John Hicks, where he was taught architectural drawing for the restoration of churches and old houses. Indeed, this association taught him much of local family histories and folklore. When the day's work was completed, Thomas usually undertook advanced Latin studies and the task of teaching himself Greek.

In 1862 Hardy went to London as a draftsman and worked in the office of A. W. Blomfield, an architect. During this time he won a number of prizes for essays, and he began to steep himself in architectural and art studies, classic literature, contemporary poetry, and fiction. In 1867 he returned to Dorchester to a better position as a church-restorer with his former master, and began to write more steadily.

The Years as a Novelist (1867–1895)

From this time on, Hardy wrote poetry and novels, though he dedicated himself chiefly to the novel form until 1895. At first Hardy published anonymously, but as interest grew in his work, he began to write under his own name. His novels were published for the most part in serial form in well-known magazines both in England and America. His major novels are: *Under the Greenwood Tree* (1872), *Far from the Madding Crowd* (1874), *The Return of the Native* (1878), *The Mayor of Casterbridge* (1886), *The Woodlanders* (1887), *Tess of the D'Urbervilles* (1891), and *Jude the Obscure* (1895). His works were highly acclaimed (the success of *Far from the Madding Crowd* enabled him to give up architecture and to marry), but he also encountered literary hostility. *Jude the Obscure* received such harsh criticism that Hardy gave up the writing of novels entirely.

The Years as a Poet (1895–1928)

Hardy retired to his house in Dorchester and there turned to poetry almost exclusively. Before his death he completed over 800 poems and a long epic drama, *The Dynasts* (1908). His first marriage was not a happy one, but in 1914, two years after the death of his first wife, he married a second time. The remaining supremely happy years of his life were spent in matrimonial devotion and reticent tranquility.

The last two decades of Hardy's life were increasingly full of honors. With Meredith's death in 1909, he became undisputed holder of the title of greatest living man of letters, and in 1910 he was awarded the Order of Merit. His house, Max Gate, became a literary shrine, and there he received many visitors from all over the English-speaking world. He continued to publish poetry well into the nineteen-twenties, even though he was then over eighty. He died at the age of 87 on January 11, 1928.

The Mayor of Casterbridge and Hardy's Background

On every page of Hardy's Wessex novels is displayed the influence of Hardy's upbringing, regional background, and architectural studies. His characters are often primitive—as is the case in *The Mayor of Casterbridge*—and exhibit all the passions, hates, loves, and jealousies that rustic life seems to inspire. Yet these characters are at all times real, for they are based on people he had grown up with, people he had heard about in legends and ballads, people whose tragic histories he had unearthed during his early architectural apprenticeship. There are also long, well-wrought, descriptive passages of the surrounding countryside, the buildings, the roads, the commerce, and the amusements that make up the environment of Caster-bridge. It is Hardy's naturalness in handling this particular environment, which he called "Wessex," that puts us at our ease and infuses the work with a life and a reality all its own.

Hardy's philosophy dramatizes the human condition as a struggle between man and man, and between man and his fate. Usually it is fate—or the arbitrary forces of the universe—that wins. Fate is all-powerful, and in its blindness human suffering is of no importance. This malevolence of fate certainly seems at times to be demonstrated in *The Mayor of Casterbridge*. Yet the victim of fate, Henchard, is also the greatest offender against morality, which would indicate purpose in the suffering he endures. Moreover, the novel ends on a note of hope because of Henchard's strength of will and his determination to undergo suffering and deprivation in order to expiate his sins. It is this element which makes the book a unique outgrowth of Hardy's philosophy.

Whether or not Hardy's pessimism seems valid, one should remember that during his lifetime, Darwin's *The Origin of Species* undermined the prevailing concept of the divine descent of man; the "higher criticism" recreated Biblical figures as humans, not divinities; science reversed prevailing opinions and superstitions; and life in general grew faster, harsher, less concerned with beauty and art, and more preoccupied with practical economics. Hardy, as a product of his age, was profoundly affected by the violent changes and forces which seemed to toss man about like a rag doll. It was natural that the events of his age should have created in him a deep pessimism, but it was also an exemplary virtue of his spirit that in one of his finest works, *The Mayor of Casterbridge,* he posed the solution of the dilemma: man will overcome because he has the nobility and strength to endure.

Brief Summary of the Novel

In a fit of drunken irritation, Michael Henchard, a young, unemployed hay-trusser, sells his wife Susan and his infant daughter Elizabeth-Jane to a sailor during a fair in the village of Weydon-Priors. Eighteen years later, Susan and Elizabeth-Jane return to seek him out but are told by the "furmity woman," the old hag whose concoction had made Henchard drunk at the fair, that he has moved to the distant town of Casterbridge. The sailor has been reported lost at sea.

Susan and Elizabeth-Jane, the latter innocent of the shameful sale eighteen years before, reach Casterbridge, where they discover that Henchard has become the mayor and one of the wealthiest businessmen in the area. Henchard, out of a sense of guilt, courts Susan in a respectable manner and soon after remarries her, hoping that one day he will be able to acknowledge Elizabeth-Jane as his daughter.

Concurrently with Susan's return, Henchard hires Donald Farfrae, a young Scotsman, as his business manager. After a short while, Susan dies, and Henchard learns that his own daughter had died many years earlier and that Elizabeth-Jane is really the illegitimate daughter of Newson, the sailor, Susan's second "husband."

Lucetta Templeman, a young woman from Jersey with whom Henchard has had a romantic involvement, comes to Casterbridge with the intention of marrying Henchard. She meets Farfrae, however, and the two are deeply attracted. Henchard, deeply disturbed by Farfrae's prestige in the town, has dismissed him, and Farfrae sets up his own rival business. Shortly after, Farfrae and Lucetta are married.

Henchard's fortunes continue their decline while Farfrae's

advance. When Henchard's successor as mayor dies suddenly, Farfrae becomes Mayor. Henchard's ruin is almost completed when the "furmity woman" is arrested as a vagrant in Casterbridge and reveals the transaction two decades earlier when Henchard sold his wife. Then, by a combination of bad luck and mismanagement, Henchard goes bankrupt and is forced to make his living as an employee of Farfrae's.

Lucetta, now at the height of her fortunes, has staked everything on keeping her past relationship with Henchard a secret. Her old love letters to him, however, find their way into the hands of Henchard's vengeful ex-employee, Jopp, who reveals them to the worst element in the town. They organize a "skimmity ride," in which Henchard and Lucetta are paraded in effigy through the streets. The shock of the scandal kills Lucetta.

Now an almost broken man, Henchard moves to the poorest quarters, where his life is made tolerable only by Elizabeth-Jane's kindness and concern. Even his comfort in her affection is threatened, however, when Newson, the sailor, returns in search of his daughter. Henchard's lie to Newson that Elizabeth-Jane has died is eventually discovered, and Elizabeth-Jane, his last source of comfort, turns against him.

Farfrae, after a period as a widower, renews his interest in Elizabeth-Jane. They are married and Henchard, when he comes to deliver a wedding gift, finds Newson enjoying his position as the bride's father. Heartbroken, Henchard leaves and shortly afterwards dies in an abandoned hut, attended only by the humblest and simplest of his former workmen. The novel closes when Farfrae and Elizabeth-Jane find the place where he has died and read his terrible will of complete renunciation.

CHAPTER 1

SYNOPSIS: A WIFE IS SOLD

Michael Henchard, an unemployed hay-trusser "of fine figure, swarthy and stern in aspect," his wife Susan, and their little child Elizabeth-Jane are wearily approaching the Wessex village of Weydon-Priors at the end of a late-summer day in the year 1826. When she looks at the child, Susan is pretty, but her face often has "the hard, half-apathetic expression" of one who expects the worst. They learn from a passer-by that there is no employment in the village. A fair is still in progress, and once the trio has arrived Michael attempts to enter a refreshment tent which advertises "Good Home-brewed Beer, Ale, and Cyder." However, Susan persuades him to enter the booth where "furmity" is sold, since the food is nourishing even if repulsive in appearance.

In the tent Michael pays the furmity woman, "a haggish creature of about fifty," to spike his basin of furmity with large dosages of rum. He quickly finishes a number of well-laced portions and, in a "quarrelsome" mood, begins to bewail the fact that he has ruined his life by marrying too young.

As the liquor takes hold, Michael offers his young wife for sale to the highest bidder. Susan, who has experienced his outrageous displays before, swears that if Michael persists, she will take the child and go with the highest bidder. She ignores the advice of "a buxom staylace dealer" and stands up for the bidding. Michael continues the bidding with renewed vigor and raises the price to five guineas for wife and child. The staylace dealer rebukes him to no effect. Before long, a sailor offers to meet Michael's terms. With the appearance of "real cash the jovial frivolity of the scene departed," and the crowd of listeners "waited with parting lips." Michael accepts the sailor's offer, pocketing the money with an air of finality. Susan and Elizabeth-Jane leave with the sailor, but before they depart she turns to Michael and, sobbing bitterly, flings her wedding ring in his face. The staylace vendor says: "I glory in the woman's sperrit." The shocked spectators—who until now had thought it all a joke—quickly depart, leaving Michael to his own conscience. Within a few moments he falls into a drunken slumber. The furmity woman closes up shop, and Michael is left in the dark, snoring loudly.

DISCUSSION

The physical surroundings in this chapter serve to reinforce the dramatic movement of the unpleasant events. The road toward Weydon-Priors is barren, the leaves on the trees are dull green, and powdered dust covers the road and shrubbery. There is no employment in this village, and, as Michael and Susan learn from a passing stranger, "Pulling down is more the nater of Weydon. . . ."

As we gather soon enough, Michael is portrayed as one given over to fits of despondent self-pity, violent outbursts, and irrevocable spur-of-the-moment decisions. Michael has too much of a liking for strong drink: he at first wants to enter the tent where beer and ale are sold; he is not satisfied with one or two bowls of spiked furmity; he becomes boisterous from the effects; after he has sold his wife, he falls into a stupor. Hardy is, of course, showing that at this point the flaw in Michael's character is aggravated by his liking for drink, which leads him to commit an outrageous act that haunts him for years and finally proves to be his downfall.

Why does Susan go with the sailor? First of all, Hardy has shown that the couple's marital relationship is not healthy, and from his opening descriptions we can easily imagine the silent, endless day's journey passed in an "atmosphere of stale familiarity." Also, it must be remembered that in the early part of the nineteenth century women often had no trades by which they could support themselves in a decent manner. Women were usually completely dependent upon their husbands for their sustenance. Susan realizes all these things. Furthermore, aside from the emotional justification she has for leaving—that is, being sold like a common streetwalker to the highest bidder—she also realizes that Michael has disclaimed all responsibility toward her and the child. Under these circumstances, Susan's choice is understandable.

Hardy lets the reader know in the first sentence that the novel will be laid in Wessex. "Wessex" is an ancient name for the West Saxon kingdom of the Middle Ages, which Hardy revived as a term for the region in which he set most of his novels and stories. (Unlike "Essex," "Sussex," and "Middlesex," it is a term no longer used geographically.) Wessex comprises Dorsetshire and parts of other western English counties, which have a number of local features exploited to great effect by Hardy.

By the time he published *The Mayor of Casterbridge,* Hardy had built a considerable following for his Wessex novels and tales: the reader could expect colorful dialogue, faithfully reproduced; a certain half-humorous, half-crabbed character in the natives; a good deal of poetic treatment of both town and country. The region was large enough not to be too confining for a novelist handling important themes, but small enough to impart color and character to setting.

fustian coarse cotton

thimble-riggers tricksters, conjurers. The expression may refer to the trick of trying to guess under which of three thimbles a pea is hidden. The hand of the "thimble-rigger" was, of course, faster than the eye of the spectator.

Weydon-Priors a village in upper Wessex, probably the fictitious name for Weyhill in northwest Hampshire

begad By God! A slightly toned down oath

'vation salvation

be-right truly; by-right

rheumy sniffling, runny-nose. The word refers to having a cold.

'od shortened from the exclamation, "God!," so as to avoid profanity

keacorn dialect for throat

QUESTION

How do you account for the fact that an incident as improbable-sounding and melodramatic as the sale of a wife seems believable and gripping rather than far-fetched?

CHAPTER 2

SYNOPSIS: THE OATH

Upon awakening the next morning, Michael finds Susan's

wedding ring on the floor and the sailor's money in his pocket. He now understands that the preceding night's events are not a dream, and "in silent thought" walks away from the village into the country. At first he wonders if his name is known.

He is angry with Susan, but, as the consequences of his conduct become clearer, he realizes that Susan's simplicity of mind and sober character will require her to live up to the bargain. He recalls her previous threat to take him at his word. He decides to search for his wife and child and, when he finds them, try to live with his shame. But first he goes to a church and swears an oath before the altar that he will not touch strong drink "for the space of twenty-one years—a year for every year that I have lived." He begins the search for his wife and child, but no one has any recollection of having seen them. His search lasts for months until, having carried his quest to a seaport, he learns that "persons answering somewhat to his description had emigrated a little time before." He abandons his search and journeys southwestward, not stopping until he reaches the town of Casterbridge in a distant part of Wessex.

DISCUSSION

Michael's pride and determination are shown in this chapter. He is willing to search for his wife and live with the shame he has brought upon himself, but his pride will not let him reveal that shame to others, even though such a revelation would certainly help him in his quest. Furthermore, he feels relief that he did not state his name during the transaction. His vow to stop drinking arouses our interest in his future conduct.

It is interesting that Hardy says of Henchard: "there was something fetichistic in this man's beliefs." Hardy has often been accused of fetichism, in the sense of not being satisfied with scientific explanations. The conflict between Hardy's verbal acceptance of the scientific attitude and his love of the supernatural is discussed by Baker, pp. 25–26. (See bibliography.)

With this chapter we reach the end of what is, in effect, the prelude to the major story of *The Mayor of Casterbridge*. As in the prologue to a Greek drama, and in the first scene or two of modern plays, the seeds of the dramatic conflict to follow are planted, and their growth is now about to be witnessed.

"the Seven Sleepers had a dog" referring to a portion found in the *Koran:* Seven sleepers in a cave, and their dog the eighth

sacrarium the sanctuary, or the place before the altar

strook struck

QUESTION

Does Henchard's failure to find his wife suggest that the sale of his wife is a closed chapter or will diminish in importance?

CHAPTER 3

SYNOPSIS: SUSAN AND ELIZABETH-JANE EIGHTEEN YEARS AFTER

It is approximately eighteen years later. Susan Henchard, her face less round and her hair thinner, who now calls herself "Mrs. Newson," is again walking along the dusty road into Weydon-Priors. She walks hand in hand with her daughter, Elizabeth-Jane, young, "well-formed," pretty, and vivacious. The two women are dressed in black, and we learn that Richard Newson, Susan's "husband" who bought her many years ago, has been lost at sea. "Mrs. Newson" is in quest of a "relation," as she has told Elizabeth-Jane, whose name is Michael Henchard, whom she had last seen at the fair in Weydon-Priors. However, she has not told Elizabeth-Jane of her true relationship to Henchard, the hay-trusser.

On the fairgrounds, whose trade has considerably diminished with the passage of time, Susan comes upon the "furmity woman." The furmity woman, now an old crone "tentless" and "dirty," barely able to make a living, does not recognize Susan. Over Elizabeth-Jane's protest, Susan asks her about Michael Henchard. At first the hag does not recollect the shameful event. However, upon reflection she recalls that a man who had figured in such an event had returned about a year after the sale. He left word with her that if a woman were to ask for him, the furmity woman should tell her that he has gone to Casterbridge. Elizabeth-Jane and Susan find lodging for the night before setting out for Casterbridge.

DISCUSSION

This short chapter, which depicts Susan's determination to locate her real husband, serves to explain the long passage of time and to raise two rather interesting problems. There must be a definite need for Susan to find Henchard, else under the circumstances she would never want to see him again. Also, we wonder what kind of complication will arise if she does find him. Perhaps he has remarried.

Elizabeth-Jane says to her mother: "Don't speak to her—it isn't respectable!" when Susan approaches the furmity woman, Mrs. Goodenough. This would indicate that Elizabeth-Jane might be excessively concerned about propriety.

QUESTION

Does Susan's rather uninteresting character lead you to expect exciting developments if she does find Henchard?

CHAPTER 4

SYNOPSIS: HENCHARD'S NAME IS OVERHEARD

A flashback reveals the events of Susan's life as Mrs. Newson. "A hundred times she had been upon the point of telling" Elizabeth-Jane about the past, but it had become "too fearful a thing to contemplate." We learn that the family had emigrated to Canada. We also see that during the eighteen years of their "marriage," Susan's simple nature was manifested by her absolute belief that their relationship was legal and binding. Thus, she and her new husband dwelled together humbly and peacefully for about twelve years in Canada. When Elizabeth-Jane was about twelve, the family returned to England and took up residence at Falmouth, a fishing town in South Cornwall. For a time Newson worked on the docks; he then acquired work in the Newfoundland trade which caused him to make seasonal trips at sea.

Susan's peace of mind is destroyed when, after confiding in a friend, she learns that her relationship with Newson is

not a valid one. She finally tells him that their relationship cannot be maintained. The next season Newson is reported lost
during a trip to Newfoundland. This news, though painful, is
almost a relief to Susan.

Because she has seen Elizabeth-Jane's desire to learn and
advance herself, Susan decides to seek out Henchard's help. She
fears that without aid the girl, who has "the raw materials of
beauty" and a fine mind, will be ruined by endless years of
poverty.

Having arrived at Casterbridge, the women hear Henchard's name mentioned by two passing men, but Susan persuades her daughter not to seek him out—"He may be in the
workhouse, or in the stocks . . ." They also learn from a gossip
that the agricultural town is suffering from a shortage of decent
bread, since the "corn-factor" had sold poor wheat to the millers
and bakers.

DISCUSSION

This chapter, by means of flashback, brings us up-to-date
concerning the intervening years of Susan and Elizabeth-Jane's
lives. It also reinforces our understanding of Susan's naive
belief in the validity of her second "marriage." Furthermore,
we are shown that Elizabeth-Jane is endowed with beauty and
intelligence, and that for the encouragement of her daughter's
promise only is Susan willing to seek Henchard's aid. Hardy
heightens suspense by having Henchard's name mentioned but
without the disclosure of details.

Hardy's intimate knowledge of Dorchester (the town after
which Casterbridge is modeled) is revealed in the highly detailed description of its streets and layout, its proximity to the
countryside, and "the agricultural and pastoral character of
the people." His use of concrete detail is a constant feature of
Hardy's realism, contributing greatly to his wonderful "atmosphere," although it is sometimes excessive, in the critic Robert B.
Heilman's view.

carkings disturbing, worrisome, vexing. This usage is archaic.
butter-firkins a firkin is a wooden vessel for holding butter or lard. Its capacity is usually the equiv-alent of one-fourth of a barrel. A butter-firkin is also termed as a unit of measurement approxi-mating 55 or 56 pounds.
seed-lips baskets for seeds
manna-food the food which God supplied to the Children of

Israel during their wanderings in the desert

swipes weak beer

growed wheat underdeveloped, poor wheat which looks developed to the untrained eye

plim blown up, swollen

corn-factor a factor is a commission merchant. In Scotland the meaning may be applied to a managing agent of an estate.

QUESTION

How would you compare Elizabeth-Jane with Susan from the standpoint of interest and dramatic potential?

CHAPTER 5

SYNOPSIS: THE MAYOR OF CASTERBRIDGE

The town band is playing merrily in front of the King's Arms, Casterbridge's chief hotel. A dinner is being held inside for all the town dignitaries and well-to-do citizens, although the windows are left open so the lesser folk can hear. Susan and Elizabeth-Jane are attracted to the gathering in front of the hotel. There they learn that Michael Henchard is the Mayor of Casterbridge. At forty, he is a dynamic, commanding figure, with "a rich complexion, . . . a flashing black eye, and dark, bushy brows and hair." A townsman among the group of spectators informs them that Henchard is also a wealthy businessman, the corn-factor who had sold bad wheat. A surprising note is interjected when the news is given that the Mayor is a complete teetotaler. Rumor has it that a long time ago the Mayor took a "gospel oath" to abstain from alcoholic beverages for many years, and that only two years remain until the oath expires. He gives the impression of a man with "no pity for weakness."

Elizabeth-Jane is eager and excited at learning of the prosperity and high status of her "relation," but Susan is despondent and frightened of meeting Henchard. Elizabeth-Jane discovers by talking to a few villagers that Henchard is thought to be a widower. The feast proceeds merrily inside the hotel until a member of a group of lesser merchants sitting at the farther end of the room asks if Henchard will replace the poor wheat he has sold them with wholesome wheat. The query is echoed among the onlookers ouside. Henchard is visibly upset by the demand, and answers: "If anybody will tell me how to turn grown wheat into wholesome wheat I'll take it back with pleasure. But it can't be done." Previous to this Henchard had informed the assembly that he, too, had been taken in when he bought the wheat. In order to minimize the chances of the recurrence of such a mistake, Henchard has advertised for a competent manager of the corn department. The matter is then dropped.

DISCUSSION

It is easy for us to understand Susan's consternation. She does not see in Michael Henchard a kind and forgiving personality. She is intimidated, too, by his power and affluence: "He overpowers me!" And thus she is left in despair.

Hardy introduces two elements of suspense in this chapter. What will happen when Henchard's oath of abstinence expires in two years? And what kind of manager will he hire? As he does so often, Hardy provides a commentary on the action by presenting the talk of the villagers—his "Wessex" types.

In England the term "corn" means wheat. What Americans call corn is termed "maize" by the English.

fall   a veil attached to the hat which women wore as a custom of modesty when walking in public

'a   he

rummers   a tall stemless glass for drinking

"shaken a little to-year"   disturbed or bothered this year

list   a strip, or streak

QUESTION

Why does it not seem improbable that Henchard, whom we last saw as a drunken, unemployed farm worker, should now be the dominant figure in a prosperous town?

CHAPTER 6

SYNOPSIS: HENCHARD FOLLOWS THE STRANGER

As the festivities proceed within the King's Arms Hotel,

a handsome stranger "of a fair countenance, bright-eyed, and slight in build," stops before the hotel, his attention arrested by the discussion about corn. After hearing Henchard's closing words on the subject, he hastily scribbles a note and instructs a waiter to deliver it to the Mayor. Having also asked the waiter about a less expensive hotel, he immediately leaves for the Three Mariners Inn. During all this time, Elizabeth-Jane has watched the young man's actions, and after his departure suggests to her mother that they, too, look for a lodging at the Three Mariners. Susan agrees and they also leave.

Henchard is given the note and upon reading it becomes evidently interested in its contents. He learns from the waiter that a young Scotsman sent the note and that he has gone to the Three Mariners. Henchard leaves the dinner-party—where most of the members have become tipsy—and walks to the inn.

DISCUSSION

This chapter may be considered as the beginning of the complex plot movements of the novel. It is interesting because a number of chance happenings occur which create the initial impetus of the events to follow: by chance a handsome Scotsman passes by the hotel and hears the discussion concerning corn; Elizabeth-Jane has traveled a great distance to listen to the same discussion and by chance to notice the young Scotsman; the three strangers go to the same inn, and Henchard, leaving the dinner-party to seek out the young Scotsman, by chance just misses his wife and Elizabeth-Jane. *If* Henchard had come upon Susan five minutes earlier, he might never have gone to the Three Mariners and the story would have been drastically altered. But this is only one of many chance "if's" the reader will encounter within the movement of the plot.

The Three Mariners is lovingly described, illustrating Hardy's recurrent fascination with the old, quaint, "native" aspects of Wessex.

mullioned a vertical dividing strip in an opening or a window. The sense of the passage is that the vertical strips on the windows should be perpendicular to the ground, but they are not. Thus, the building looks quaintly out of kilter.

yard of clay a long clay pipe

ruddy polls ruddy—reddish, healthy glow; poll—top or back of the head. Hence, shiny bald heads visible through the shutters of the Inn.

QUESTION

What function does the Three Mariners Inn serve in the story apart from local color?

CHAPTER 7

SYNOPSIS: A CONVERSATION BETWEEN HENCHARD AND FARFRAE IS OVERHEARD

Despite the modesty of their accommodations at the Three Mariners, Susan believes that they are "too good for us." Elizabeth-Jane is pleased at their "respectability," however. Unknown to her mother, she offers to defray some of the expense by working as a servingmaid in the busy bar. During these duties she is required to bring the young Scotsman's meal to his quarters. She does so, and while serving the meal takes the chance to study his handsome bearing. She also notices that the young man's room is directly beside the one she shares with her mother.

When Elizabeth-Jane finally returns to the room with their own meal, Susan motions her to remain silent. Michael Henchard is in the room next door with the young Scotsman, whose name they learn is Donald Farfrae. Because of the thinness of the walls, their entire conversation is audible next door.

It is learned that Donald Farfrae's note to Henchard contained information on how to restore grown wheat to wholesome second quality. Henchard is sure, as a result, that the young man is the one who answered his advertisement for a corn-manager, but Farfrae assures him that is not so. Farfrae, being kind and generous, demonstrates the procedure to Henchard free-of-charge. Henchard is astounded by Farfrae's ability and immediately offers him the position of corn-manager, plus a commission. However, Farfrae is just passing through on his way to Bristol where he plans to take ship to the New World: "I wish I could stay—sincerely I would like to," he replied. "But no—it cannet be! . . . I want to see the warrld." Showing bitter disappointment, Henchard must make do with this reply despite his liberal offer and persistent pleas. Farfrae offers Henchard a glass of ale, which is refused. Henchard states his reason for refusing: "When I was a young man I went in for that sort of thing too strong—far too strong—and was well-nigh ruined by it! I did a deed on account of it which I shall be ashamed of to my dying day."

DISCUSSION

We see that Henchard is a lonely man and has been looking for another employee who would be of value to him in his business and as a friend. Hardy is careful to convince the reader of Henchard's friendly attraction to the younger man who is temperamentally and physically the opposite of Henchard. We also see that Henchard is continually hounded by his youthful deed. There is a hint that Henchard is still the same, however, in the ease with which he forgets the prior claim to the corn-manager's job of the applicant named "Jipp" or "Jopp."

QUESTION

What is the importance of Henchard's offering the corn-manager's job to a man who is not the one expecting it?

CHAPTER 8

SYNOPSIS: FARFRAE SINGS AT THE THREE MARINERS

Elizabeth-Jane goes to remove Farfrae's supper tray, leaving Susan in their room, her face "strangely bright since Henchard's avowal of shame." Farfrae joins the patrons on the ground floor of the Three Mariners and before long is charming them with a plaintive Scotch ballad. Elizabeth-Jane, having cleared away Farfrae's dinner dishes, as well as her own, watches Donald from an inconspicuous spot. Farfrae is engaged in conversation by the townspeople, and because of his own trusting and higher nature refuses to accept the townspeople's belittling of Casterbridge. By popular acclaim he is required to sing some more songs, after which he takes his leave to retire.

Elizabeth-Jane, who has just turned down Farfrae's bedding upon the request of the landlady, passes him on the stairs. She is embarrassed and does not look at him. Farfrae, however, is drawn to her and sings a ditty apparently intended for her.

Before retiring, Elizabeth-Jane tells her mother about Farfrae. It is obvious that the similar, serious nature of their characters appeals to her and that she is attracted to him. When Susan speaks of Henchard as "he," Elizabeth-Jane assumes that "he" is Farfrae.

Outside the inn Henchard paces back and forth, disturbed because Farfrae has rejected his offer. He hears Farfrae's singing and says to himself: "To be sure, to be sure, how that fellow does draw me, . . . I suppose 'tis because I'm so lonely. I'd have given him a third share in the business to have stayed!"

DISCUSSION

Farfrae shows himself to be an appealing and charming young man. The townspeople take to him immediately since he is a man of creative ability as well as charm, and such men are not to be found in Casterbridge. Also, the scene between Elizabeth-Jane and Farfrae, though still strangers, serves the purpose of showing them drawing ever closer. Henchard's remarks, on the other hand, display his interest in Farfrae and foreshadow his reliance upon him in personal and business matters.

The scene in the inn is again a distinctively Hardyan touch of Wessex local color. The charm of the rustics comes through in their dialect and poetic speech-rhythms, but there is an undertone of sourness and ill humor in these characters also.

danged damned (used as an expletive)

lammigers lame people

wheel ventilator a fan which revolves by the action of the wind

Gallows Hill a reference to the English Civil War incident in the seventeenth century which resulted in the sentencing to death of about 300 people

ballet ballad

bruckle not trustworthy

Botany Bay penal colony in Australia

chiney china, dishes

chine a ridge or strip of wood; refers to such a strip on the bottom of a cask, on which the workman turns the cask, thus moving it without tipping it over

gaberlunzie wandering beggar

QUESTION

Does Farfrae's immediate popularity among the townspeople hint at anything that might develop later in the story?

CHAPTER 9

SYNOPSIS: FARFRAE TAKES THE JOB

The next morning, Donald Farfrae meets Henchard and together they walk to the end of town. Elizabeth-Jane sees the two men walking away and is sad and hurt at Donald's departure—he has seen her but has neither spoken nor smiled. Susan, bolstered by Henchard's quickness to like a complete stranger, his loneliness, and his avowed shame for his past behavior, sends Elizabeth-Jane to him with a note. Elizabeth-Jane is told to introduce herself and inform Henchard that a distant relative of his—her mother, the widow of a sailor—has arrived in Casterbridge. Elizabeth-Jane is instructed to bring back word when Henchard will meet with Susan. If Henchard refuses to see her, Susan and Elizabeth-Jane will leave town immediately.

As she walks to Henchard's place of business, Elizabeth-Jane is introduced to the bustling life of early morning Casterbridge. When she finally enters Henchard's business office she is shocked speechless to see Donald Farfrae at work. Donald does not seem to recognize her and tells her that Mr. Henchard is busy but will be with her soon. We learn from a brief flashback that Farfrae has accepted Henchard's last-minute, urgent plea to stay and name his own price.

DISCUSSION

A number of relevant incidents occur in this chapter. By sending Elizabeth-Jane to Henchard, Susan begins a restoration of her former relationship with Henchard. Elizabeth-Jane, in order to get to Henchard's place of business, must take a short walk through the town. Thus the reader is given a tour of the quaint surroundings and bustling commercial life of the town, and remains aware that Henchard is at the top of the seemingly endless business activity. Finally, Farfrae is persuaded to stay, and the hint of a relationship between him and Elizabeth-Jane is given.

Suspense is also created when the author deftly interposes the walk through the town to mask the discussion between Henchard and Farfrae and delay the actual meeting between Henchard and Elizabeth-Jane.

Hardy is almost lyrical in his appreciation of Casterbridge on market-day, when its closeness to the country is most pronounced, "differing from the many manufacturing towns which are as foreign bodies set down . . . in a green world with which they have nothing in common."

kerb curb

chassez-déchassez *chassé,* a quick set of gliding, sideward movements in dancing, always led by the same foot; from the French, *chasser.* Hence, *chassez-déchassez,* a French dance from right to left

terpsichorean figures Terpsichore, Greek Muse of the dance; figures in dance positions

netting fish-seines making fishing nets; also, fixing or repairing the nets

amaze amazement

Flemish ladders ladders whose sides become narrower toward the top

staddles a raised frame, or a platform used for stacking hay or straw to avoid contamination from moisture or vermin

QUESTION

Why has the question of Farfrae's employment suddenly assumed an importance equal to that of Susan's quest for Henchard?

CHAPTER 10

SYNOPSIS: HENCHARD "BUYS SUSAN BACK"

While Elizabeth-Jane is waiting for Henchard, Joshua Jopp, the applicant for the position of manager of the corn department, arrives as Henchard enters the room. Henchard informs him abruptly that the position is filled and dismisses him. Jopp leaves, "his mouth twitched with anger, and . . . bitter disappointment . . . written in his face everywhere."

Elizabeth-Jane reveals herself as the daughter of his "relative," Susan, to Henchard, who is shocked. He understands when Elizabeth-Jane refers to her family name as "Newson" that Susan has not revealed the truth to her child. They go indoors and after a few questions concerning the newcomer's past life, Henchard writes a note to Susan and places five guineas in it. He is visibly moved by Elizabeth-Jane's appearance and instructs her to deliver the note personally. Elizabeth-Jane leaves, touched by Henchard's concern. Henchard suddenly suspects that the pair might be impostors, but quickly changes his mind when he reflects upon Elizabeth-Jane's demeanor.

Upon her return Elizabeth-Jane is required to describe to her mother in explicit detail the meeting with Henchard. Susan reads the note which instructs her to tell Elizabeth-Jane nothing and to meet him at eight o'clock that night at the Ring on the Budmouth road. She finds the five guineas enclosed, and though nothing was said of the money in the note, the amount would suggest that Henchard was buying her back again.

DISCUSSION

The suspense of the last chapter is relieved by Henchard's kind treatment of Elizabeth-Jane. It is also significant to Susan that Henchard has enclosed five guineas in the note, the same amount which he received from Newson. He is, in effect, symbolically buying her back.

However, two elements of suspense enter the story here. Note that Henchard has created a potential enemy by his abrupt treatment of Joshua Jopp. Also, frightened of the shame which could be heaped upon him if the truth were known, Henchard arranges a secret meeting with Susan that night in a lonely spot outside of town. This is the beginning of the secretiveness that will surround their reunion. As will be seen in the next chapter, the place of the meeting will significantly add to the mystery.

Henchard's tactfulness in asking about Susan's poverty is in character. Several times in the novel he shows great consideration for people who are in need.

rouge-et-noir from the French: red and black. See the previous description of Henchard as Elizabeth-Jane entered Henchard's office.

Family Bible, *Josephus,* ***Whole Duty of Man*** three works considered indispensable in every respectable household. The Family Bible was a large Bible which usually contained a page in the front for recording marriages, births, deaths; Josephus Flavius (A.D. 37–100?), Jewish historian and statesman. His *History of the Jewish War* and other work shed much valuable light upon the occurrences of the Bible; *Whole Duty of Man,* 1658, of anonymous origin. A book of devotions.

QUESTION

What clues as to future developments can you perceive in Henchard's brief note?

CHAPTER 11

SYNOPSIS: A MEETING AT THE RING

Henchard meets Susan in the ruins of an old Roman amphitheatre outside of town. The amphitheatre is very large and dark, and due to the gloomy superstitions connected with its grim history almost no one comes there except for "appointments of a furtive kind." It is for this reason—so no one will know of his meeting with Susan—that Henchard arranges for the interview in such a forbidding place as "the Ring."

Henchard's first words to Susan are: "I don't drink, . . . You hear, Susan?—I don't drink now—I haven't since that night." During their discussion, Henchard learns that Susan had considered her alliance with Newson a binding one. She tells Henchard that if she had not thought that way, her life would have been "very wicked." Henchard says that he knows this and feels her to be an "innocent woman." He proposes that she and Elizabeth-Jane rent a house on High Street; after a courtship Susan and Michael will be remarried.

It is most important to Henchard that Elizabeth-Jane remain in complete ignorance of the past. When Susan and Henchard are remarried, Elizabeth-Jane will live with them as Henchard's step-daughter. He considers this to be the best way of fooling the town. Of course he will pay all their expenses. Susan agrees. As she is leaving, Henchard asks: "But just one word. Do you forgive me, Susan?" Susan murmurs something indistinctly and Henchard replies: "Never mind—all in good time, . . . Judge me by my future works—good-bye!"

DISCUSSION

Hardy takes great care in describing the Roman amphitheatre and its unsavory history. He certainly does want the reader to feel the darkness and the gloom of the surroundings in order to emphasize the mystery of the events. Such melancholy settings are common in Hardy's work, and serve to underscore his fancy for the grotesque. This particular setting also reveals his awareness of the Roman element in Wessex.

As Susan leaves, it appears that Henchard has indeed repented and that all will soon be well.

the Ring referring to Maumbury Rings in Dorchester, which served as the public gallows for the first half of the 18th century. Its history goes back many centuries. Under the Romans it was an arena for gladiatorial and wild beast displays. There is a certain unwholesome aura surrounding the Ring due to its history.

Jotuns giants in Norse mythology

rub o't rub of it: a problem, hindrance, doubt

aeolian modulations Aeolus, in Greek mythology, was god of the winds. The aeolian harp was a stringed instrument constructed to produce musical sounds when exposed to the action of the wind.

***must* start genteel** must begin in a manner appropriate to a well-bred person

QUESTION

Does Henchard's plan for "courting" Susan again seem to you as "natural and easy" as he says?

CHAPTER 12

SYNOPSIS: HENCHARD TELLS FARFRAE OF HIS PAST

Henchard returns home to find Donald Farfrae working late over the books. He brings Donald into his home and they have dinner together. After dinner, as they sit beside the fire, Henchard reveals his past to his new-found friend. Donald agrees that Henchard should try to make amends to Susan. However, Henchard further reveals that during his years as a lonely "widower" he had established a relationship with a young woman on the island of Jersey, who had once nursed him through a long illness. Their affair had become known, causing the young woman to suffer much from the scandal. Henchard, after hearing of her sufferings in her letters, proposed marriage to her if she would take the chance that Susan would not return. She readily agreed to this, but now Henchard realizes that his first duty is to Susan and that he cannot marry the other woman. Because she is in bad financial straits, he wishes to help her as best he can. Donald agrees to write a kindly letter to the young lady since Henchard would probably do a bad job of it. Yet Donald thinks that Henchard should tell Elizabeth-Jane that she is his daughter; Henchard cannot agree to that. Henchard mails the letter with a check, and as he returns home speaks aloud to himself: "Can it be that it will go off so easily! . . . Poor thing—God knows! Now then, to make amends to Susan!"

DISCUSSION

Hardy remains true to the character he has established for Henchard. Henchard is still the mercurial man he always was. He has known Donald Farfrae for only one day, yet he tells him what he has told no other living man. Henchard rationalizes that he is lonely. Since Donald is the only man he is genuinely fond of, it is fitting that he reveal himself to his friend. The reader knows, though, that it is really Henchard's characteristic spur-of-the-moment trait that causes him to talk of his past. Farfrae changes his plan to eat alone "gracefully," but he has already seen that Henchard's impulsiveness can mean inconvenience.

With the introduction of the young woman in Jersey, a new complication is brought into the story. Indeed, the mere fact that Henchard confides in Farfrae is another plot twist which at first does not seem too important. Hardy does not attempt to show the reunion with Susan in an optimistic light. Even Henchard's last remarks foreshadow some difficulties.

espaliers trellises or stakes on which small fruit trees or plants are trained to grow in a flattened-out state

"like Job, I could curse the day that gave me birth." from the *Book of Job,* in which Job, in the midst of his suffering, actually curses the day of his birth

sequestrated taken over for the purpose of settling claims

mun Scotch and British dialect: must

QUESTION

What implications do you detect in Henchard's revelation to Farfrae that he has had an affair with a young woman on the island of Jersey?

CHAPTER 13

SYNOPSIS: THE "MARRIAGE"

Michael Henchard installs Susan and Elizabeth-Jane in a cottage located in the western part of Casterbridge. The cottage is pleasant and well furnished. Henchard has even acquired a servant for Susan, to help create an aura of respectability.

As soon as Elizabeth-Jane and Susan are established in the cottage, Henchard calls upon them and stays for tea. Henchard pursues his courtship for a respectable period of time. It gives him some pleasure that Elizabeth-Jane has accepted the events and knows nothing of the truth, but Susan feels regretful at having deceived her child. One day Henchard asks Susan to name the day of their marriage. Susan fears that she is causing him too much trouble. Indeed, she had never planned on anything so elaborate as a remarriage. Henchard is resolved to make amends to Susan, provide a comfortable home for Elizabeth-Jane, and demean himself by marrying a woman who in the eyes of the town would seem to be beneath his status. He tells her that since he has acquired an excellent new business manager, he will have more time to devote to his family in the future.

The townspeople begin to talk about the upcoming marriage, and "Mrs. Newson" is nicknamed "The Ghost," because of her fragile, pale appearance. On a drizzly day in November, Susan and Henchard are remarried. The townspeople waiting outside the church comment upon Henchard's foolishness in marrying a woman so far beneath him. Christopher Coney makes a remark typical of the town's feelings: " 'Tis five-and-forty years since I had my settlement in this here town," said Coney; "but daze me if ever I see a man wait so long before to take so little!" He and the other rustics expatiate humorously on the disparity.

DISCUSSION

The culmination of Henchard's dogged attempts to make amends to Susan is realized in their marriage. However, the chapter is written to give the reader a feeling of malaise. Susan does not think it at all humorous that Elizabeth-Jane has been deceived by them, and in her futile way almost asks Henchard to drop the idea of marriage. However, because Henchard is still a man of stubborn will, he insists upon going through with it. The rain adds to the oppressiveness.

The townspeople also help to give the reader a sense of uneasiness about the proceedings. It has to be admitted that Hardy may be exaggerating somewhat the townspeople's ability to observe so much of hidden history from the appearance of the couple, but the mere mention of the word "bluebeardy" with its associations of cruelty and ruthlessness is enough to create the feeling of impending trouble.

There is a good deal of Hardy's earthy poetry in the villagers' comments. The reader will appreciate the author's artfulness by reading some of this aloud, especially Mrs. Cuxsom's wonderful passage, beginning: "And dostn't mind how mother would sing."

'en dialect for "him"

zilver-snuffers silver snuffers; a snuffer is a scissors-like instrument used for clipping the wick of a candle

cow-barton a cow-yard

"She'll wish her cake dough . . ." She'll wish she hadn't done it

twanking whining; in this sense weak and helpless

jumps or night-rail jumps would be equal to corset-stays, and a night-rail equivalent to a night-gown

small table ninepenny cheap drinks

QUESTION

Is Nance Mockridge's remark about Susan, "She'll wish her cake dough afore she's done of him," just village chatter?

CHAPTER 14

SYNOPSIS: ELIZABETH-JANE AND FARFRAE ARE BROUGHT TOGETHER

Susan and Elizabeth-Jane fit almost inconspicuously into Henchard's large house. Henchard is most kind to Susan, and her life begins to acquire the melancholy contentment of a late Indian summer. Elizabeth-Jane, however, finds her life growing more and more pleasurable. She no longer suffers from economic distress, and all that she sees is hers for the asking. But, due to her serious nature, Elizabeth-Jane does not allow her newly acquired position to alter her sober tastes and thoughtful respectability. Moreover, she still has "that field-mouse fear of the coulter of destiny," believing it would be "tempting Providence" if she were "too gay." As times passes, she begins to develop into a physically mature and beautiful young lady.

Henchard notices Elizabeth-Jane's light hair and asks Susan if she hadn't once assured him that it would become dark. Alarmed, Susan jerks his foot, and he admits to having nearly disclosed their secret.

One day Henchard asks Susan if Elizabeth-Jane, of whom he has grown extremely fond, would consider changing her name to Henchard. Susan seems reluctant to allow it, but submits to his will and informs Elizabeth-Jane. Henchard tells Elizabeth-Jane that she need not change her name from Newson to Henchard to please him only. Upon hearing this from Henchard, Elizabeth-Jane decides to retain her own name and nothing more is said of the matter.

Elizabeth-Jane notices that Henchard has a great deal of affection and respect for Donald Farfrae, and is seen with him continually. Farfrae's quiet humor sometimes arouses "a perfect cannonade of laughter" from Henchard. Under Farfrae's expert guidance, Henchard's business is modernized in accordance with the finest business procedures and thrives most successfully. Farfrae begins to find Henchard's "tigerish affection" a bit confining and suggests that his use as "a second pair of eyes" is being wasted if both employer and employee are always in the same place. Henchard explosively rejects the idea.

One day Elizabeth-Jane receives a note requesting her to come immediately to a granary on Durnover Hill. She goes there and, as she is waiting, Donald Farfrae arrives. Too shy to meet him there alone, Elizabeth-Jane hides. As the rain falls, Donald waits patiently until Elizabeth-Jane reveals her presence by accidentally dislodging some wheat husks. After Donald acknowledges her presence, they both realize that someone else has sent them the identical letter. Donald believes that someone has played a trick upon them and that Elizabeth-Jane should not mention it in the future. He helps her remove the wheat husks from her clothing before she departs. It is obvious that he is affected by her beauty.

DISCUSSION

A number of hints are scattered throughout this chapter that something unexpected may occur. Henchard distinctly remembers that Elizabeth-Jane's hair promised to be black when she was a child. Susan, of course, informs him that it is natural for the color to change with maturity. Susan is also reluctant to agree to Henchard's request that Elizabeth-Jane change her name to his. Furthermore, we find that Henchard is growing ever more fond of Elizabeth-Jane. With the trick played on Donald and Elizabeth-Jane—which results in Donald's acquiring an added interest in Elizabeth-Jane—it becomes obvious that fate, or someone, wants to bring them together.

Donald's mild chafing at Henchard's possessiveness, and the latter's continued "poor opinion" of Donald's physical smallness also hint at possible conflicts to come.

Martinmas summer late or Indian summer; that is, Susan's life became more bearable in her later years

spencer a bodice

viva voce by voice, oral; that is, Henchard kept almost no business books or records (Italian)

winnowing machine a machine used to separate grain from the chaff

victorine a scarf worn over neck and shoulders

QUESTION

Who do you think is the author of the notes?

CHAPTER 15

SYNOPSIS: HENCHARD AND DONALD QUARREL

Elizabeth-Jane begins experimenting with fine clothing and before long realizes that she is considered the town beauty. Donald Farfrae becomes even more interested in her as time passes. She balances her exhilaration by reflecting sadly on her own intellectual shortcomings.

One morning, vexed out of all patience by the continual tardiness of Abel Whittle, one of his workers, Henchard goes to Whittle's cottage, routs him out of bed, and forces him to go to work without his britches. Whittle is mortified but must go through with it since he needs the employment. Donald sees the embarrassing spectacle, reverses Henchard's orders, and tells Whittle to go home and get his britches. When Henchard hears of this, he and Donald quarrel in front of the men. Donald threatens to quit but gets his way.

As time goes by, Henchard is bothered by Farfrae's popularity among the workers and townspeople. He learns one day from a boy that the people prefer Farfrae's business judgment to his own and consider Donald his superior in every way. While going to estimate the value of some hay, Henchard meets Donald, who has been summoned to the same task. Henchard accuses Donald of indiscriminately hurting his feelings. Donald sincerely denies that such a thing could be. Henchard parts from his friend on good terms once again, but now always thinks of him "with a dim dread."

DISCUSSION

This chapter demonstrates not only Elizabeth-Jane's increasing awareness that she is a mature, beautiful woman but also her essential lack of vanity and giddiness. It also shows that Donald has acquired more than a passing interest in her. (Henchard, of course, does not suspect that Donald secretly admires Elizabeth-Jane.) After the quarrel, Henchard treats Donald more formally, and his overbearing friendship diminishes to a more courteous but distant relationship. As time passes, Henchard regrets having told Donald about his life. His regret is intensified when he learns the townspeople prefer Donald to him. Even though the quarrel is mended, Henchard still feels a "dim dread" concerning Farfrae.

the prophet Baruch in the *Apocrypha*. The sense is that Elizabeth-Jane was not considered a truly great beauty adulated by all.

Rochefoucauld French author whose philosophy states that human conduct is motivated by selfishness

fretted my gizzard worried

diment diamond

sotto voce under one's breath, in a low voice (Italian)

scantling a little bit, a tiny piece

QUESTION

What is the significance of the disclosure that "Henchard had kept Abel's old mother in coals and snuff all the previous winter"?

CHAPTER 16

SYNOPSIS: DONALD'S DISMISSAL

On the occasion of the "celebration of a national event," Donald borrows a number of rick-cloths from Henchard for an entertainment. Spurred on by Donald's initiative, Henchard decides to provide an elaborate outdoor entertainment complete with food and games. He is sure that everyone will come to his festivities since they are free, and Donald plans to "charge admission at the rate of so much a head."

On the day of the holiday a heavy rain ruins the turnout at Henchard's free festivities. He orders the games and tables removed and later goes into Casterbridge where he sees all the people flocking to a dance. Ingeniously, Donald has used the rick-cloths as a large tent between some trees within the town. Henchard hears the gay music and notices the warmth of the surroundings and the abandon of the dancers. Even Susan and Elizabeth-Jane have come to the dance which is, in the eyes of the people, an unqualified success far exceeding the efforts of the Mayor. Donald is the center of the proceedings, and even Elizabeth-Jane dances with him. Henchard overhears the cruel remarks of the townspeople and, goaded by the taunts and jests of other town officials, states that Donald's term as manager is drawing to a close. Donald quietly corroborates the declaration. Henchard goes home that night, satisfied that he is protecting his hard-won reputation. The next morning he deeply regrets his rash statement. He soon becomes aware that Donald plans "to take him at his word."

DISCUSSION

Once again Hardy places the reader within the mind of Henchard. We see the total failure of Henchard's plans, and for a moment it appears that everything is going wrong for him. Through Henchard's eyes we see Donald's unqualified success with the townspeople, and for a fleeting second we feel the jealousy Henchard feels. It is no surprise that Henchard acts the way he does, especially since we have listened with him to the ugly remarks and jests of the townspeople. In this chapter and in Chapter 15, Hardy has cleverly shifted the emphasis away from the Susan-Henchard-Elizabeth-Jane development and concentrated on the Henchard-Farfrae relationship.

Correggio famous Italian artist (1494–1534)

stunpoll stone head

"Miss M'Leod of Ayr" a tune that Hardy knew when a child

skipping on the small skipping in small "skips"

randy Scotch dialect: boisterous, fun-loving. The sense is that

Donald's character is one that loves merry-making, as opposed to Henchard's more staid personality.

"Jack's as good as his master" a proverb. The meaning is that the servant has become as good as the employer.

QUESTION

What do you make of the fact that Farfrae is firmer and more competent than the other victims of Henchard's impulsiveness?

CHAPTER 17

SYNOPSIS: DONALD GOES INTO BUSINESS

Elizabeth-Jane is covered with shame when someone hints that "she had not been quite in her place" in dancing with such pleasure in "a mixed throng." Donald accompanies Elizabeth-Jane to her home after she has left the dance. He reveals the break between Henchard and himself and states that he would ask her something special if only he were richer. Elizabeth-Jane asks him not to leave Casterbridge. She hurries home and thinks intensely about him.

Donald soon makes the break complete by purchasing his own hay and corn business. However, since he feels that Henchard has been very kind to him, he decides not to compete with him commercially. He is sure that there is ample business for both of them. He even turns away his first customer, a man who had dealt with Henchard within the last three months. Henchard now holds no affection for Donald and considers him an enemy, but his abuse of Donald finds little sympathy in the town council. He immediately forbids Elizabeth-Jane to have any further relationship with Donald and in a crisp letter informs Donald of his step-daughter's promise to obey his request.

Donald's business prospers, and though he had not attempted to come into competition with Henchard, he is forced "to close with Henchard in mortal commercial combat" when Henchard begins a price war. Before long, to add to Henchard's bitterness, Donald is given an official business stall at the market. He cannot bear to hear Farfrae's name mentioned at home.

DISCUSSION

This chapter brings the Henchard-Farfrae relationship to a complete break. Though Donald still has friendly feelings toward Henchard, Henchard considers him an enemy and forces him to engage in highly commercial competition. We also see that Henchard's friends and council members are not impressed with his statement that he will meet Donald's competition head-on. Apparently he has caused each one of them some pain in the past. This is probably the strongest hint so far that Henchard's fluctuating temperament has not earned him one friend. There are also two slight hints that Susan had wanted Elizabeth-Jane and Donald to get to know each other better.

This chapter contains the statement: "Character is Fate, said Novalis," one of the most widely discussed comments Hardy ever made in his novels. It appears to conflict with Hardy's emphasis on chance and impersonal forces as factors in man's fate, but it is certainly consistent with the character of Henchard throughout.

voot   foot
wo'th a varden   worth a farthing
sniff and snaff   haven't agreed to more than accepting his gentlemanly attentions (especially in regard to matrimonial plans), would be the sense of the expression
modus vivendi   working arrangement; a way of living (Latin)

Novalis   Baron Friedrich von Hardenburg (1772–1801) whose pen-name was Novalis; poet and novelist
Faust   the main character in Goethe's monumental drama
Bellerophon   character in Greek legends who killed his brother and fled from the society of mankind

QUESTION

What is the ethical implication of Hardy's phrase for Henchard as a Faust-like being "who had quitted the ways of vulgar men without light to guide him on a better way"?

CHAPTER 18

SYNOPSIS: SUSAN'S DEATH

Elizabeth-Jane's fears for her mother are confirmed. Susan becomes seriously ill, too weak to leave her room. Henchard gets the town's "richest, busiest doctor," but Elizabeth-Jane now fears the worst.

Henchard receives a letter from Jersey in which the young lady who had nursed him absolves him of any share in her troubles. She asks only that he meet her and return her letters which, though she only hints at it, could be compromising to her one day. The letter is signed, "Lucetta." Henchard brings the letters, but Lucetta does not arrive.

Susan, sensing her imminent death, writes a letter addressed to "Mr. Michael Henchard. Not to be opened till Elizabeth-Jane's wedding-day." As Elizabeth-Jane sits up with her mother one night, Susan confesses that it was she that sent the notes to Donald and her daughter: "It was not to make fools of you—it was done to bring you together. 'Twas I did it. . . . I—wanted you to marry Mr. Farfrae. . . . Well, I had a reason. 'Twill out one day. I wish it could have been in my time! But there—nothing is as you wish it! Henchard hates him."

Susan dies quietly one Sunday morning. The reader learns of her death through Donald's concern.

DISCUSSION

In this chapter Hardy ends Susan's struggle with life. However, he introduces new material which will create suspense and compensate for the loss of one of the characters. Lucetta makes an intriguing entry by sending Henchard a letter, then failing to meet him at the time and place proposed. Susan, prompted by some thought which we as yet do not know, writes a mysterious letter to Henchard with instructions to delay its opening until Elizabeth-Jane's wedding. Furthermore, utilizing Henchard's characteristic practicality, Hardy allows Henchard to think of marrying Lucetta after Susan's death. This is another grotesque touch whose enormity is only surpassed by the discussion of the townspeople at the end of the chapter. The theme of man's inability to cope with arbitrary causes is propounded succinctly as Elizabeth-Jane sits by her mother, ruminating over her own life. Elizabeth-Jane continues to grow in richness of character—she is now "the subtle-souled girl."

The village characters, despite their ghoulish humors, add interest and amusement with their running commentary in Hardy's unique rustic style.

doxology the character means "theology," but even then 'theology" would not be the appropriate word.

varnished for 'natomies skeleton bones sold, varnished, and used in colleges or schools for the study of anatomy

QUESTION

What can you tell about Lucetta's character from the style and content of her letter to Henchard?

CHAPTER 19

SYNOPSIS: HENCHARD READS SUSAN'S LETTER

Three weeks after Susan's funeral, prompted by loneliness and bothered by Elizabeth-Jane's inability to accept him as her father, Henchard impulsively reveals to Elizabeth-Jane that he is her real father. However, he hides from her the complete truth by telling her that Susan had thought him dead and had remarried. Elizabeth-Jane is confused at first. Henchard asks her if she will now consent to change her name to his. She agrees, and the letter is written and sent to the *Casterbridge Chronicle*. Henchard leaves her to find documentary proof of his marriage to Susan, but as he is rummaging through his papers, Susan's poorly sealed letter falls open before him. He reads the letter. It is Susan's revelations that Elizabeth-Jane is *not* his child, but Newson's. Henchard's little girl had died three months after he sold his wife.

Henchard's plans for happiness are now blasted. All that night he walks alone through the dismal northeastern part of town, where the jail and gallows are, meditating on the fate he has brought upon himself. He feels that he must continue along the path he has started rather than face abiding humiliation. When he greets Elizabeth-Jane at breakfast, she tells him that she has accepted him as her true father. But there is no joy for him in these long-awaited words: "His reinstation of her mother had been chiefly for the girl's sake, and the fruition of the whole scheme was such dust and ashes as this."

DISCUSSION

Fate seems to be closing in upon Henchard. Everything he does appears to be destined to failure. His elaborate scheme to remarry Susan and regain his child has almost succeeded, but if he had not been prompted by paternal, possessive feelings toward Elizabeth-Jane, he would not have searched for proof to show her. Thus, he would not have found Susan's letter of confession. It becomes apparent even to Henchard that some blind, dooming fate has structured the events of his life in a series of false leads toward happiness, only to dash them at the last moment.

pier-glass mirror
rosette an ornament resembling a badge similar to a rose
Prester John in mythology, a king who was punished by the gods. He was condemned to have his food snatched from him by harpies, half-woman,

half-birdlike creatures who acted as the gods' avengers.
Schwarzwasser black-water. It is also the name of a river in Poland. (German)
weir an obstruction or dam placed in a stream to divert or raise the waters

QUESTION

In the light of what you already know about Henchard, how do you expect the revelation in Susan's letter to affect his future attitude toward Elizabeth-Jane?

CHAPTER 20

SYNOPSIS: ELIZABETH-JANE MEETS A CHARMING STRANGER

Henchard becomes cold toward Elizabeth-Jane and critical of her lapses into country dialect, her bold handwriting, and her kindness to servants. His behavior to her worsens when the servant Nance Mockridge defiantly tells him Elizabeth-Jane had once worked as a waitress in a pub. The revelation that she had served at the Three Mariners is a bitter blow, and its bitterness is compounded by the news that he is not going to be chosen as an alderman at the end of his mayoralty, but that Donald Farfrae is to be offered a council seat. He begins to leave Elizabeth-Jane alone most of the time, preferring to have his meals with the farmers at the hotel. Henchard finally realizes that Farfrae could take Elizabeth-Jane off his hands, so he writes a letter to him stating that he may continue his courtship of Elizabeth-Jane.

Elizabeth-Jane is miserable, "a dumb, deep-feeling, great-eyed creature," and feels that Henchard disdains her because of her lack of education. Unknown to Henchard, she spends her empty hours patiently studying and reading. Between the intervals of study she visits her mother's grave. One morning as she stands before her mother's grave she meets a charming lady. The stranger's way are so disarming and sympathetic that Elizabeth-Jane reveals her past and her present unhappiness. The listener is kind, but "her anxiety not to condemn Henchard while siding with Elizabeth" is "curious." The newcomer informs Elizabeth-Jane that she will become a resident of Casterbridge at High-Place Hall and that she would like the unhappy girl to stay with her as a companion. Elizabeth-Jane quickly assents and joyfully contemplates her new position.

DISCUSSION

The plot movement has slowed momentarily, but much attention is given to Henchard's growing dislike of Elizabeth-Jane. The reader now feels the keenest sympathy for her. She, too, suffers from an arbitrary fate that uncannily destroys one's happiness and security. However, the arrival of the pretty stranger at this point introduces a new note in the story and provides a momentary hope for Elizabeth-Jane. We are now so aware of Hardy's practice of involving every new character in the action that we look forward to the events precipitated by the introduction of Elizabeth-Jane's new friend.

The reader should notice the breadth of Hardy's knowledge of history, art, and folklore, as his allusions here reveal.

jowned jolted. The expression would seem to mean, "Damn it, so am I", or "Be damned, so am I!"

Princess Ida in Tennyson's poem, *The Princess*

wimbling boring a hole, or piercing as with a wimble

the Constantines Emperors of Rome, father and son. Constantine the Great moved the capital of the Roman Empire from Rome to Byzantium, whose name was changed to Constantinople. Constantine II ruled for a short time after his father's death.

Karnac In Brittany: Carnac. Over two miles of parallel monoliths.

Austerlitz in 1805, the battle in which Napoleon defeated the Russians and the Austrians

leery tired

QUESTION

Does Elizabeth-Jane's decision to be the pretty stranger's companion indicate that her life will be comparatively happy from this point on?

CHAPTER 21

SYNOPSIS: ELIZABETH-JANE MOVES TO HIGH-PLACE HALL

Elizabeth-Jane, "almost with a lover's feeling," stealthily visits High-Place Hall, the chief town topic now that word is out of a new resident there. She is impressed by the easy but rather secret access the house has from many directions. Despite the fact that the appearance of the house suggests intrigue, she is anxious to move there immediately. Henchard also visits the house, but Elizabeth-Jane hides when she hears footsteps. Thus, neither of them is conscious of the other's identity.

After Henchard's return home, she realizes that his harshness has turned to "absolute indifference." She asks if she might leave his home to take employment which will advance her knowledge and manners. He readily agrees and is somewhat relieved that she is going. Elizabeth-Jane once again meets the stranger at the churchyard and learns her name is Miss Templeman. It is decided that Elizabeth-Jane will move into High-Place Hall that very evening, although Miss Templeman wonders if it might not be better to avoid mentioning High-Place Hall to Henchard. Henchard, upon learning of Elizabeth-Jane's immediate departure, tries at the last minute to persuade her to remain. Elizabeth-Jane tells him that she will not be far and that if he should need her she will return immediately. Henchard is surprised when he learns of her destination.

DISCUSSION

This chapter completes the work of the last two—that is, stripping Henchard of his remaining affectionate ties to others. The fact that Elizabeth-Jane cannot be dissuaded from leaving shows that she is acquiring an independent character. The reader assumes that the pretty stranger who takes such an interest in Elizabeth-Jane is Lucetta. This inference, coupled with the grotesque descriptions of High-Place Hall and Henchard's clandestine visit there, hints to the reader that new directions, possibly unpleasant, will be taken soon.

Hardy's professional interest in architecture is again evident in the description of High-Place Hall. His reasons for placing it so near the center of town rather than on the outskirts will become clear.

QUESTION

What parallels in his previous conduct can you name for Henchard's belated request for Elizabeth-Jane to stay?

CHAPTER 22

SYNOPSIS: LUCETTA WAITS FOR HENCHARD'S CALL

Henchard had gone to High-Place Hall the same evening as Elizabeth-Jane because he received a letter from Lucetta informing him of her new residence. However, Henchard learns that a Miss Templeman is the only resident, not a Miss Le Sueur (the name by which Henchard had known Lucetta in Jersey). Henchard receives another note from Lucetta informing him that she has taken the name of Templeman—from a recently deceased aunt—in order to keep her real identity secret. Henchard also learns that Lucetta has received a large inheritance from the aunt, and he immediately feels that now would be a proper time to pursue his marriage plans. He is amused that Lucetta has invited Elizabeth-Jane to be her companion since this will give him a reason to visit High-Place Hall. Henchard immediately goes to see Lucetta, but is told she is engaged. This annoys him, and he decides to punish her by delaying his next visit.

A few days pass and Henchard has not yet visited Lucetta. Elizabeth-Jane and Lucetta have become quite friendly, though Elizabeth-Jane now surmises that she is the less flighty of the two. Lucetta discloses her Jersey background even though she had resolved not to do so. Lucetta feels that Henchard will not come since he does not want to see Elizabeth-Jane. She therefore sends Elizabeth-Jane on some errands, writes a note to Henchard inviting him to come immediately, and awaits his arrival. A visitor is finally shown into her drawing room, but to Lucetta's surprise the man is not Henchard.

DISCUSSION

Some interesting developments occur in this chapter. Hardy shows that the clever deception which Henchard had practiced in order to marry Susan is being repeated in variation by Lucetta. Furthermore, the reader begins to doubt Henchard's ability to hold any affectionate ties since the question of love does not enter much into his consideration of marriage to Lucetta. He seems to be thinking of it primarily as a commercial alliance, although his sentiments "gathered around Lucetta before they had grown dry."

Lucetta's room overlooking the market has already become an important vantage point and a center of interest.

mon ami étourderie *mon ami,* my friend; *étourderie,* lack of concern — thoughtless action; thoughtlessness (French)

carrefour crossroads, open square (French)

gibbous rounded, seemingly hunch-backed

Titian famous Venetian artist (1477–1576)

netting making netting, the groundwork for delicate embroidery

cyma-recta an architectural term: a curved profile partly concave and partly convex, the convex part nearest the wall (often referring to a curved molding)

QUESTION

Why does Lucetta emerge as an interesting character in spite of Hardy's partly stock account of her as the typically flighty Frenchwoman?

CHAPTER 23

SYNOPSIS: A MUTUAL ATTRACTION

The visitor is Donald Farfrae, "fair, fresh, and slenderly handsome," come to call upon Elizabeth-Jane after receiving permission to court her. At first Lucetta and Donald are embarrassed, but a mutual attraction takes hold, and they pass the time flirting with each other. Overhearing a business transaction from the window and upset by the conditions, Donald goes down to the market for a moment to hire a young man who had been faced with abandoning his sweetheart in order to retain a position. Lucetta is impressed by Donald's romantic and humane spirit. He leaves, but only after they decide that he should visit again: "Farfrae was shown out, it having entirely escaped him that he had called to see Elizabeth." About three minutes after Donald's departure Henchard arrives. Lucetta, infatuated with her new-found acquaintance, sends word that since she has a headache she won't detain him. Henchard leaves, and Lucetta resolves to keep Elizabeth-Jane with her as a "watchdog to keep her father off."

DISCUSSION

Lucetta and Donald become infatuated with each other. Of course Lucetta does not know of Elizabeth-Jane's feelings toward Donald. Even though Donald tells her that he has come to visit Elizabeth-Jane, Lucetta does not end the interview immediately but prolongs it into an emotional flirtation. Though she states emphatically that she is not a *coquette,* we learn by this behavior that she is. Lucetta several times mentions "love" and "lovers" in her conversation with Donald. She is also flighty and deceptive—witness her decision to keep Elizabeth-Jane to fend off Henchard immediately after packing her off so as to encourage Henchard. She is filled with fluctuating emotions: "Her emotions rose, fell, undulated, filled her with wild surmise at their suddenness." Yet it would be unfair to judge her critically since our chief point of reference is Elizabeth-Jane's rather quiet, innocent, melancholy character. With her refusal to admit Henchard, Lucetta appears to have ended all possibility of their marriage.

Hardy often adds pleasing strokes of humor, as when Lucetta invites Donald to sit down: "He hesitated, looked at the chair, thought there was no danger in it (though there was), and sat down." The passage quietly reminds us of Farfrae's cautious nature in sizing up what is probably a spindly "French" chair, and adds a pleasant touch of ambiguity with "though there was."

kerseymere fine wool woven so that diagonal lines appear on the material
St. Helier large town in Jersey
waggon-tilts the canvas cover- ings of wagons
Dan Cupid Roman god of love. "Dan" is applied humorously to mean "Sir"

QUESTION

How would you project the changes that will occur in the lives of the main characters as a result of Lucetta's and Donald's mutual attraction?

CHAPTER 24

SYNOPSIS: LUCETTA TELLS ELIZABETH-JANE A STORY

Lucetta and Elizabeth-Jane now pass the days of the week in anxious anticipation of Saturday's market when they might be able to catch a glimpse of Farfrae from their window. A new seeding machine called a horse-drill is brought to town and Lucetta—wearing her beautiful new dress "of a deep cherry color" from London—suggests that they go to see the machine. While examining the drill, they meet Michael Henchard, whom Elizabeth-Jane immediately introduces to Lucetta. Michael gruffly criticizes the machine's function and departs quickly. Before he leaves, Elizabeth-Jane overhears him state under his breath to Lucetta: "You refused to see me!" Elizabeth-Jane reflects upon the incident but appears not to realize that a relationship exists between Lucetta and Henchard.

They meet Donald as he examines the new machine. It was upon his recommendation that the modern piece of farm equipment has been purchased. He explains to the two ladies that the machine will revolutionize farming. It becomes obvious to

Elizabeth-Jane that Donald and Lucetta have grown fond of each other.

A few days later, desiring to get advice about her own rather difficult position, Lucetta reveals her past to Elizabeth-Jane, but tells the story as if it had happened to another woman. Her main question is what should the other "she" do now that "she" has grown fond of a second man. Elizabeth-Jane refuses to answer so delicate a question. However, she knows that Lucetta had been referring to herself.

DISCUSSION

The plot becomes more involved. Farfrae is advancing in Lucetta's favor while Henchard declines. Though Elizabeth-Jane does not know of a relationship between Lucetta and Henchard, she is saddened by the interest in each other that Donald and Lucetta already show. Not only has fate taken away most of Michael Henchard's happiness, but it also appears that chance and blind circumstance are plotting to do a similarly thorough job on Elizabeth-Jane's life. Yet we admire increasingly the uncomplaining girl and respect her silent stoicism.

The seed-drill accents the differences between Henchard and Farfrae. Henchard's stubborn conservatism evokes sympathy, but progress is clearly on Farfrae's side.

QUESTION

What can you discern in the episode of the horse-drill about Hardy's attitudes toward technological progress?

CHAPTER 25

SYNOPSIS: LUCETTA CHOOSES DONALD

Both Donald and Henchard call upon Lucetta. Lucetta insists that Elizabeth-Jane be present when Donald calls. During these visits Elizabeth-Jane sees only too plainly that Donald's old passion for her has disappeared and that he is now in love with Lucetta. At these times she remains in the room until she can conveniently excuse herself.

Michael, having grown more possessive of Lucetta now that she has become inaccessible, visits her and proposes marriage. Lucetta puts off the decision, and Michael half-realizes that he has been rejected. Though he may suspect a rival, he does not as yet know of Donald. Elizabeth-Jane accepts Donald's rejection of her since she considers Lucetta far more desirable. However, as the days pass she cannot really understand Henchard's complete unconcern for her welfare. After all, she has never to her knowledge caused him any grief. Out of long experience with "the wreck of each day's wishes," Elizabeth-Jane becomes reconciled to being rejected by the two men in her life who have come to symbolize her happiness.

DISCUSSION

Though much occurs in this chapter concerning Donald and Henchard, most of the events are seen as they affect Elizabeth-Jane and appear to her understanding. In this manner Hardy emphasizes his theme of blind fate when he talks of Elizabeth-Jane's stoicism: "She had learnt the lesson of renunciation . . ."

QUESTION

Are your sympathies with or against Lucetta's cry: "I won't be a slave to the past—I'll love where I choose"?

CHAPTER 26

SYNOPSIS: HENCHARD HIRES AND FIRES JOPP

Henchard's faint suspicion that his rival might be Donald abates when the latter shows his ignorance that the lady in Henchard's past is Lucetta. But not long after, Henchard divines the rivalry when he and Donald are having tea with Lucetta. Elizabeth-Jane, who is witness to the awkward threesome, watches them and begins to feel that they are all behaving like fools. With "vitalized antagonism" toward Donald, Henchard hires Jopp, the man who had originally applied for the position

of manager, and instructs him to try every honest way of forcing Farfrae out of business. Jopp is only too willing since he
nurses a bitter grudge against Farfrae as the man who replaced
him. Henchard, unaware that "characters deteriorate in time of
need," quiets Elizabeth-Jane's distrust of Jopp "with a sharp
rebuff."

Henchard consults a local weather diviner named Mr.
Fall. He pays him for reading the future and predicting a very
wet harvest season. As a result of this less-than-reliable information, Henchard speculates heavily upon rainy harvest weather.
However, the weather changes and the harvest promises to be
a glorious one. Prices go down and Henchard has to sell his
speculative purchases at a great loss in order to meet current
obligations. He is forced to mortgage much of his property and
corn-holdings to the bank. Furious at Jopp for not advising
against the speculation, Henchard dismisses him. Jopp bitterly
vows vengeance against Henchard.

DISCUSSION

As the rivalry between Henchard and Donald grows more
keen, Hardy plants another seed of possible destruction. Jopp
is aware that Lucetta comes from Jersey and that Henchard had
often done business there. Fate and chance now will bear heavily
upon every continuing chapter. Hardy describes how directly
the well-being of the farmers depends upon fluctuations of the
weather. The great difference between Henchard and Farfrae
is thrown into bold relief when Henchard visits the soothsayer
for a prediction. It becomes clear that Henchard lives in the
past and Donald is the man of the future. Henchard's visit to
Mr. Fall recalls the statement in Chapter 2 that "there was
something fetichistic in this man's beliefs."

pis aller the last resource
  (French)
Alastor a deity of revenge
water-tights boots
bell-board a table or board on
  which were placed small bells
  that were rung at the appropriate time by a number of
  ringers. (Thus, the tune depended on each ringer; hence,
  Casterbridge depended on the

surrounding villages and ham-
  lets for its commerce.)
the evil scrofula. A toad-bag
  contained the legs of frogs, and
  was worn around the neck. This
  superstition held that the toad-
  bag was a cure for scrofula
  (sometimes called "the king's
  evil").
dungmixen dung-heap, dunghill

QUESTION

Why does Hardy have Henchard visit Mr. Fall rather than simply guessing wrong about the weather himself?

CHAPTER 27

SYNOPSIS: HENCHARD FORCES LUCETTA TO CONSENT

Farfrae begins buying grain now that promise of a fair harvest has driven prices down. The weather quickly turns damp, and it is clear that Farfrae has once again been shrewd.

An accident occurs beneath Lucetta's window, involving Henchard's and Donald's hay wagons. Lucetta and Elizabeth-Jane both side with Donald's driver. Henchard is brought to the scene where he gives instructions to Constable Stubberd. The constable tells him that there is only one case pending in the town court, that of a disorderly old woman. Henchard tells him that he will hear the case in the absence from town of Mayor Chalkfield.

After setting things right for the moment, Henchard attempts to call on Lucetta, who has returned home. She sends word that she has "an engagement to go out."

Henchard decides to wait in the shadows in order to learn if Donald might be her caller. Donald arrives at nine o'clock, and together he and Lucetta walk to the fields where the townsmen are reaping by moonlight. Henchard decides to follow them. The couple take a twisting route and soon double back upon Henchard who is forced to hide. From hiding he hears them declare their love for each other. He leaves and returns to Lucetta's home. Without knocking he enters the house and waits for her. Upon her return he threatens to reveal the past if she refuses to marry him. With Elizabeth-Jane as a witness, Lucetta agrees to the marriage. Lucetta faints, and Elizabeth-Jane upbraids Henchard for forcing her, for Lucetta "cannot bear much." Henchard leaves, and Elizabeth-Jane remains baffled by the strong hold he has over Lucetta.

DISCUSSION

Donald's business prosperity rankles morbidly in Henchard's mind. Hardy again emphasizes Henchard's "fetishism" by showing him wondering if someone has placed a curse on him. Henchard even believes that Donald will soon become mayor. We see that Henchard's brutal threat of blackmail against Lucetta is not a result of his desire to marry her, but of an unholy wish to beat Farfrae, to hurt him, to take something away from him. As usual, there is no love motivating Henchard's behavior.

zwailing swaying, shifting the wagon

gawk-hammer way awkward, ridiculous

"you would have zeed me!" you would have *seen* me

thill horse the horse which is harnessed between the shafts of

dand the word "dandy" is left uncompleted

giddying in a rotating or whirling fashion

no'thern a dialect word; wandering in mind, or incoherent

QUESTION

Is Henchard's insistence that Lucetta marry him motivated partly, entirely, or not at all by the question of honor in keeping a promise?

CHAPTER 28

SYNOPSIS: THE JUDGE IS JUDGED

Henchard, being a magistrate, is required to preside in the case of the old woman accused of creating an obscene nuisance.

In court Henchard fails to recognize the old crone, although she looks faintly familiar. However, after the arresting officer gives his story, the old woman tells the court that twenty years ago she witnessed the sale of a wife. She then points to Henchard and declares that he is the man who sold his wife. She concludes by saying that he has no right to sit in judgment over her. Henchard recognizes the furmity woman and is shocked. However, he agrees with her, corroborates the story, and leaves his place of judgment.

Her servant tells Lucetta of the furmity woman's story. Lucetta, who had always believed that Henchard's wife had been presumed dead, is taken aback. She decides that she must leave Casterbridge and vacation for a few days at Port-Bredy. Henchard calls upon her a number of times only to learn that she has left town. When he calls a few days later he learns that she has returned, but has gone for a walk on the turnpike road toward Port-Bredy.

DISCUSSION

Henchard's past has finally caught up with him. The turn of events is somewhat unexpected. Even more unexpected is Henchard's complete corroboration of the furmity woman's story. Despite all his shortcomings, Henchard must be respected for a rough kind of moral virtue. It would have been easy for him to deny the furmity woman's story, since she wasn't believed in the first place. However, the ironic justice becomes plain to him, and since we have become acquainted with his quick starts and sudden decisions, his confession is not unnatural.

Shallow and Silence in Shakespeare's *King Henry IV*, Part II. They are comic characters and serve as country justices of the peace.

ashlar a roughhewn square block of stone

Hannah Dominy from Latin *Anno Domine* (A.D., in the year of our Lord). A slight bit of satirizing of the rather ignorant type of justice of the peace. The word "instinct" which precedes the corruption of the legal phrase should be "instance."

wambling weaving, wobbling

turmit-hit turnip-head, turnip-top, idiot

"you son of a bee," "dee me if I haint" the constable does not want to swear in court.

larry commotion or disturbance

QUESTION

What are some of the reasons the author has the furmity woman unmask Henchard while he is sitting as judge rather than in the street or at home?

CHAPTER 29

SYNOPSIS: LUCETTA'S REVELATION

Lucetta is a mile out of town on the road to Port-Bredy waiting for Donald. Elizabeth-Jane comes to meet her when suddenly they are confronted by a ferocious bull. The enraged animal pursues them into a barn where they are forced to flee from his maddened charging. Henchard arrives, subdues the bull, and rescues them. He takes the hysterical Lucetta home.

Elizabeth-Jane, who had returned to the barn to retrieve Lucetta's muff, encounters Donald Farfrae in his carriage. She explains the events. Donald appears very upset by the news, but decides that he had better not seek out Lucetta for fear of intruding upon the two. He drops Elizabeth-Jane off and returns to his house, where his things are being packed for a move.

Henchard, meanwhile, has accompanied Lucetta to town. He informs her that he is willing to release her from an immediate marriage. She states that she would like to repay him with a large amount of cash in the same manner as he had been of financial assistance to her in the past. He refuses to take money, but asks her instead to say they will soon be married to a Mr. Grower, one of his heaviest creditors. Grower will then not press Henchard for immediate cash. He will then have sufficient time to raise the money. Lucetta cannot do this. She explains that when she learned that Henchard had sold his first wife, she feared to put her safety in his hands. She tells him that she and Donald Farfrae were married this week in Port-Bredy, and that Mr. Grower had been a witness to it.

Henchard is infuriated since he feels that she has broken her word. Lucetta tells him that her promise had been made under compulsion and before she had heard how he sold his first wife. She begs him not to tell Donald of the past. Henchard rages at her and once again threatens to tell the world of their past intimacy.

DISCUSSION

The chance appearance of the furmity woman has resulted in Lucetta's marriage to Farfrae. We are aware of Henchard's hold over Lucetta, and we are sure that he will take advantage of it in his rage. This chapter reveals Hardy's minute, but architectural structuring of the novel. All things fall into place, though the reader may feel somewhat pressed by the chance occurrence of so many events. Though the furmity woman may have come to Casterbridge by chance, it must be remembered that if Henchard had not committed an enormity years ago, the chance arrival of the furmity woman would not have mattered in the least. Thus we see that a man is never free of his past; he can set his own fate in motion and afterward have not the slightest control over it.

Yahoo in *Gulliver's Travels,* by Swift. An animal that looks like man, but behaves like a dumb, vicious beast

the Thames Tunnel completed in 1843. Hardy might be referring to toys that represented the tunnel. He might also be referring to the stereoscope, a viewing device that represented pictures in seemingly three-di-

mensional perspective.

Gurth's collar a swineherd in Scott's *Ivanhoe* who wore a brass ring around his neck, which could only be filed through to free him of the collar.

a pensioner of Farfrae's wife to be put on relief by Farfrae's wife, or to be financially dependent on Farfrae's wife

QUESTION

Do you think Henchard will stand by his threat to reveal his former relations with Lucetta?

CHAPTER 30

SYNOPSIS: ELIZABETH-JANE LEAVES HIGH-PLACE HALL

Donald arranges to have his belongings moved to Lucetta's home. When he arrives Lucetta informs him that she would like Elizabeth-Jane to remain and Donald consents. Elizabeth-Jane tells Lucetta that she fully understands the implications of the story she had been told of another woman's past, and that her father figures in Lucetta's life. She feels strongly that Lucetta should, out of propriety, marry Henchard. Lucetta says that her promise to Henchard was made under constraint. She reveals her marriage to Donald. Even though Elizabeth-Jane has decided immediately that she must leave the house because of her feelings toward Donald, she tells Lucetta that she will decide upon the issue later.

That night Elizabeth-Jane removes her belongings to a residence across the street from Henchard. She leaves a note explaining her move for Lucetta and returns to her new room to consider her prospects. The villagers have by now heard of the marriage and are busy conjecturing whether Donald will stay in business or live off his wife.

DISCUSSION

Elizabeth-Jane is a stickler for propriety, is, "indeed, almost vicious" in her condemnation of any form of waywardness. It is not hard to understand this, since the confusing events of her past life might appear to her to be the results of a neglect of the legal and social mores. Hardy, however, is guilty of forced logic in showing her disapproval of Lucetta's choosing Farfrae over Henchard. His rather weak account of Elizabeth-Jane as a homebody who never listens to gossip cannot make convincing her ignorance of the furmity woman's revelation and Henchard's corroboration.

"John Gilpin" a ballad by William Cowper (1731–1800)

Nathan tones the prophet Nathan was damning in his onslaught against King David's marriage to Bath-Sheba

Ovid famous Latin poet (43 B.C.–18 A.D.). The line is from his *Metamorphoses:* "Though I approve of the better things I see, I follow after the worse."

QUESTION

Compared with the other characters, how would you view Elizabeth-Jane's character and personality as they might lead to a happy and satisfying life?

CHAPTER 31

SYNOPSIS: HENCHARD'S BANKRUPTCY

After the furmity woman's revelation, Henchard's fortunes and esteem diminish rapidly. One of his heavy debtors fails and bad judgment by one of his employees causes a serious financial loss. Bankruptcy proceedings are instituted against Henchard in which his creditors take possession of all his property. He is at his lowest point: "The black hair and whiskers were the same as ever, but a film of ash was over the rest." At the proceedings, Henchard offers his remaining property, the loose change in his money-bag, and his gold watch. The creditors refuse to take these last remaining possessions, but instead praise him for his extraordinary honesty in giving over all his worldly goods. Much affected, Henchard leaves, sells his watch for the first offer, and brings the cash to one of his minor creditors.

Henchard moves to Jopp's cottage by Priory Mill. Elizabeth-Jane, moved to compassion by his terrible downfall, attempts to see him. However, Henchard is at home to no one, including Elizabeth-Jane. After an unsuccessful attempt to see her stepfather, Elizabeth-Jane passes by Henchard's former place of business. She learns that Donald Farfrae has bought the property and taken over all of Henchard's employees. Though the salary is slightly lower, the men are happy with Farfrae's working conditions. Furthermore, whereas Henchard's business had been conducted by rule-of-thumb procedures, Donald has instituted sound business techniques and modern innovations.

DISCUSSION

Henchard's rapid decline in fortune and prestige is as complete as Donald Farfrae's rise. Elizabeth-Jane is more alone now than she has ever been. All the elements have conspired to reverse the positions of the characters, and Farfrae has won out completely, even in love.

An odd note is sounded by the curious alliance that Henchard maintains with Jopp. There is certainly no friendship between the two men, since Henchard blamed Jopp for allowing him to speculate on the weather, and Jopp despises Henchard for dismissing him. The one connective would be their mutual hatred for Donald Farfrae. One gets the feeling that Jopp has taken in Henchard for the purpose of taunting him with his failure, and that Henchard is using Jopp as a scourge. Given Henchard's compulsion to do the self-destructive thing, there is an ironic justice in his identification with the village's most conspicuous failure.

One of the creditors is a "reserved young man named Boldwood." Boldwood is an important character in Hardy's much earlier novel, *Far from the Madding Crowd*.

QUESTION

What elements of Henchard's character come to the fore in the bankruptcy episodes?

CHAPTER 32

SYNOPSIS: FARFRAE HIRES HENCHARD

Henchard begins to haunt one of the town's bridges which has become known for its attraction to failures and suicides. One afternoon Jopp encounters him on the bridge and states that Donald and Lucetta have purchased Henchard's old house and are moving in. He also tells him that the man who bought Henchard's best furniture at the auction was in reality bidding for Donald Farfrae. Jopp departs well satisfied that he has wounded Henchard. Henchard's bitterness is increased at the vagaries of fortune. Donald Farfrae arrives in a gig to see Henchard. He repeats the rumor that Henchard is planning to emigrate and asks him to remain in Casterbridge, just as Henchard had once asked him to stay. Donald generously offers Henchard lodging within the same house that he and Lucetta have just purchased. Henchard visualizes this arrangement with repugnance and refuses outright. Donald then offers to give back to Henchard all the furniture which might hold sentimental value for him. For a moment Henchard is struck by Donald's magnanimity and says, "I—sometimes think I've wronged 'ee!"

Later Elizabeth-Jane hears that Henchard is confined to his room with a cold. She immediately goes to him and, after a preliminary refusal by Henchard, administers to him and sets his room in comfortable order. Due to Elizabeth-Jane's repeated visits and tender care, Henchard regains his strength and a more cheerful outlook. Judging that hard work never hurt a young man—Henchard is not much over forty—he applies to Farfrae as a day-laborer. Farfrae employs him, but is careful to relay instructions and orders through a third person. And thus Henchard who once worked as a hay-trusser dressed in clean, bright clothes appears in the yards he used to own; now he wears "the remains of an old blue cloth suit of his gentlemanly times, a rusty silk hat, and a once black satin stock, soiled and shabby."

The days go by and Henchard watches Donald and Lucetta. His old jealousy and hatred return, especially when he hears that Farfrae may be chosen mayor in a few years.

One day Elizabeth-Jane hears a villager say that "Michael Henchard have busted out drinking" again. The twenty-one year "gospel oath" has come to an end. Elizabeth-Jane immediately sets out to find him.

DISCUSSION

Whereas in the last chapter all of Henchard's property had been auctioned off and Donald had purchased Henchard's former place of business, this chapter is necessary to complete the reversal of fortune. Donald purchases Henchard's house and furniture. Only one more point need be added to furnish the final irony. Henchard himself answers fate's call and takes employment as a day-laborer in Donald's business. It would appear now that Henchard can go no lower; with the hint of Donald's likelihood of becoming mayor, it seems that he can go no higher. The close proximity of Henchard to the newly married couple is what begins to work upon his mind. It is evident that it lies within Henchard's character to wreak some kind of new havoc now that he has begun to drink again.

QUESTION

What other conditions besides his drinking now repeat Henchard's position when we first met him twenty years earlier?

CHAPTER 33

SYNOPSIS: HENCHARD'S RESENTMENT IS INFLAMED

One Sunday Henchard takes part in the after-church discussion and song-fest which the townspeople and the choir members hold at the Three Mariners. He sees Donald and Lucetta leaving church, and under the influence of drink, forces the members of the choir to sing one of the *Psalms,* which contains a curse against the man of "ill-got riches." When Farfrae passes, Henchard tells the dismayed company that the curse was meant for him. Elizabeth-Jane arrives and takes Henchard home. While walking with him she hears Henchard make veiled threats against Donald. She resolves to warn Donald as soon as it becomes necessary.

Henchard's misery is intensified by the pitying looks he gets from Abel Whittle. Elizabeth-Jane offers to help Henchard in Abel's place. Her reason for helping is to observe Henchard and Donald when they come face to face. One day Lucetta accompanies Donald into the yard, but wanders away and accidentally confronts Henchard. Henchard bitterly feigns servility to Lucetta. The next morning Henchard receives a note from Lucetta which asks him to behave with less bitterness toward her if they should meet again. Henchard realizes that this letter places Lucetta in a compromising position, but he destroys it rather than use it against her.

Elizabeth-Jane begins to bring Henchard tea in order to keep him away from stronger drink. One day she arrives to find Henchard and Donald standing near the open door on the top floor of the corn building. Elizabeth-Jane sees Henchard make a furtive gesture as if he intended to push Donald out the opening to his death. This so frightens her that she resolves to inform Donald of her stepfather's mental state.

DISCUSSION

This chapter shows Henchard becoming more and more bold in his threats against Farfrae as a result of his heavy drinking. As time passes, Donald begins to look upon Henchard as an ordinary worker. Of course this is a hint that such an attitude will have its effect upon Henchard. The one implausible element in the chapter is Lucetta's ignorance of Henchard's employment. Even though Donald has taken pains to ignore the new relationship between Henchard and himself, in a town which seems to thrive upon gossip it would appear strange that such a newsworthy item as Henchard's ironic employment had not reached Lucetta's ears. Even stranger is the fact that Donald has not informed her.

The loft is a vivid and appropriate setting for the incident Elizabeth-Jane spies when bringing tea.

Stonehenge a famous monument dating back to prehistoric times, consisting of stone pillars placed in a circular fashion

"We've let back our strings. . . ." We've loosened the strings (on the instruments).

rantipole rubbish rough or boisterous language or verses sung to accompany a procession which contains an acted out scene of a man beating his wife (the *rantipole ride*)

trap a trap-door

QUESTION

What can be said to justify Henchard's bitter sarcasm when he encounters Lucetta?

CHAPTER 34

SYNOPSIS: HENCHARD READS TO FARFRAE

Elizabeth-Jane meets Farfrae early one morning and warns him that Henchard may try "to do something—that would injure you." Donald makes light of the warning, but later receives a similar warning from the town clerk. We learn that Donald had offered the first fifty pounds if the town council would underwrite the remainder of the costs to install Henchard in a seed shop. Because of the disconcerting information Donald has to review the plans, and he cancels the negotiations with the owner of the seed shop. The disappointed owner tells Henchard that the council had planned to give him a new start but that Donald had ruined it.

Donald confides to Lucetta that he is upset because of Henchard's enmity. She suggests that they sell out and move away. Donald gives the thought consideration. At that moment Alderman Vatt arrives with the news that Mayor Chalkfield has died. He tells Donald that the Council would like to elect him mayor. Because it is the town's wish, Donald says he will accept the office if it is bestowed upon him. It seems that now, despite Lucetta's fears and his own worry over Henchard, he must stay because destiny requires it.

Lucetta meets Henchard by accident in the market-place. "Imprudence incarnate," she asks him once again to return her old letters. Henchard says he does not have them, but that he will consider her request. Next evening the town bell announces a new mayor. Henchard has remembered that the letters are among papers in the safe of his former house and arranges with Donald to come and retrieve them. Fortified with drink, Henchard arrives at Mayor Farfrae's home quite late. He gets the letters and morbidly reads their contents to Farfrae. This grotesque conduct seems to give Henchard pleasure, since at this point he holds the future happiness of Lucetta and Donald in his hand. However, he cannot bring himself to reveal to Donald that Lucetta had written the letters: "His quality was such that he could have annihilated them both in the heat of action; but to accomplish the deed by oral poison was beyond the nerve of his enmity."

DISCUSSION

Henchard's bitterness now takes concrete form. The misunderstanding of the seed shop incident inflames him, and Farfrae's election as Mayor adds still more to his enmity. When Lucetta imprudently asks Henchard for the letters, she unwittingly opens another means whereby Henchard can indulge his own self-pity and still flirt somewhat sadistically with the idea of revealing to Donald both the contents of the letters and the name of their author.

With his election as Mayor of Casterbridge, Farfrae now owns everything Henchard had owned when they met.

QUESTION

What would Farfrae's reaction be if he learned of the relationship between Henchard and Lucetta in the past?

CHAPTER 35

SYNOPSIS: HENCHARD AND LUCETTA AT THE RING

In a flashback we learn that Lucetta has overheard Michael reading the letters to her husband. She fears he has revealed all, but when Farfrae retires that night she learns "to her joyous amazement" that he knows nothing of her past. The next morning she writes to Henchard and asks to meet him at the Ring. She decides to present herself humbly and to beg for the return of her letters.

At sunset she meets Henchard at the Ring. The surroundings are gloomy, as usual, but the area brings to Henchard's mind his meeting with Susan, another woman whom he had wronged. This realization causes his heart to melt, and when he sees Lucetta so plainly dressed and so miserable, he relents. He feels that she has stupidly placed herself in a very compromising position by meeting him. He therefore loses all interest in her and promises that her letters will be returned the next morning.

DISCUSSION

Lucetta is shown to be losing her youthful beauty. Apparently the strain and suspense which Henchard has caused have begun to take their toll. By having Henchard promise to return the letters, Hardy is absolving him of any further intentions of destroying the marriage. However, the letters seem far too important to be dropped so suddenly.

Henchard appears in a generous light when he takes pity on Lucetta. His feeling that she is "very small deer to hunt" reveals that largeness of outlook that contributes so much to his stature as tragic hero.

QUESTION

What story developments do you expect from Henchard's promise to return Lucetta's letters?

CHAPTER 36

SYNOPSIS: JOPP OPENS THE LETTERS

Lucetta returns home to find Jopp waiting for her. He asks her to put in a few good words with Donald about employing him. She replies that she knows nothing about him, and that it is not her custom to interfere in her husband's business. Lucetta ends the interview abruptly for fear that Donald will miss her.

Jopp returns to his cottage, and Henchard asks him to deliver a parcel to Mrs. Farfrae. Jopp states that he will do it. After Henchard retires, Jopp begins to think about the connection between Henchard and Lucetta. Because Jopp had come from Jersey, he knows that Henchard had once courted her. His bitterness at Lucetta for refusing to speak to Farfrae intensifies his curiosity, so Jopp opens the package and finds the letters.

While on his way to deliver the package, Jopp encounters Mother Cuxsom and Nance Mockridge, who invite him to an inn called Peter's Finger in Mixen Lane, a place of evil repute near Casterbridge. At the gathering, when the furmity woman asks Jopp what the parcel contains, his bitterness at Lucetta comes out and he reveals the contents. Jopp proceeds to read the letters to the assembled company. Soon afterward a stranger appears on his way to Casterbridge. He hears the rogues in the tavern discussing a "skimmity-ride," and learns that it is a lower-class form of making fun of a married couple when the wife has not been altogether faithful. Since the stranger will be residing in Casterbridge for a while, and desiring some kind of entertainment, he gives the assembly of thieves and poachers a gold sovereign to cover the initial cost of the old custom. The townspeople begin to plan the skimmity-ride.

The next morning Jopp delivers the parcel to Lucetta, who burns the letters immediately.

DISCUSSION

The "Peter's Finger" episode is unusual in that the villagers become participants in the action rather than commentators merely. Hence the emphasis on them is not just the addition of local color or explanation but is an important new plot development as well.

dogs   the iron bars on which the logs are placed in a fireplace

Adulam   haven for people with troubles and difficulties

lifeholders, copy-holders   lifeholders held a lifetime lease to their homes and land. Copyholders did not own original legal deeds.

Ashton . . . Ravenswood   characters in Scott's *Bride of Lammermoor*. Ashton sees Ravenswood disappear (having sunk into quicksand).

swingels   part of a flail

oven-pyle   chips of wood for lighting a fire

skimmity-ride   skimmington-ride: a rowdy procession which is intended to make fun of a man whose wife is shrewish or unfaithful.

get it in train   to get it started

QUESTION

What is the significance of the appearance of the stranger in Mixen Lane?

CHAPTER 37

SYNOPSIS: HENCHARD GREETS THE ROYAL VISITOR

The town receives word that a royal personage will pass through Casterbridge in the near future. Mayor Farfrae and the council arrange for an elaborate reception. Henchard comes to the council meeting and asks to participate in the reception. Donald, with the concurrence of the council, refuses, whereupon Henchard makes plans to welcome the royal visitor by himself.

The royal visitor is escorted into the packed, spruced-up town by Donald and the members of the council. Lucetta indignantly tells some ladies looking on that Henchard had little or nothing to do with Donald's success. By this time, she doesn't like to be reminded that Henchard exists. Suddenly Henchard steps into the space before the Town Hall, waving a Union Jack (the British flag) and stretches out his arm to welcome the esteemed guest. Because it is Farfrae's duty as mayor to maintain decorum and safety for the visitor, he grabs Henchard by the collar and shoves him roughly into the crowd. The spectators, especially Lucetta and Elizabeth-Jane, are shocked by Henchard's low behavior. The royal personage, however, pretends "not to have noticed anything unusual."

The reader learns that the skimmity-ride will take place that night. Jopp confirms the plans and is now acting as a prime mover in the attempt to humiliate the Mayor. But two of the townspeople decide to write to the concerned parties and warn them of the impending demonstration.

DISCUSSION

It appears that Henchard, despite all common sense, still refuses to remain in his place. His character is as mercurial as it ever was, and the request he makes to the town council comes from a deep sense of the loss of his position, esteem, and wealth. He has always been subject to fits of rancor and bitterness, but with the resumption of his drinking these spells become more intense. Henchard's intrusion comes as a surprise to the reader, but Donald's rough treatment of him is con-

sidered justified by everyone in the crowd. The leader knows
that the public insult will only feed Henchard's fierce bitterness.

fête carillonnée   a celebration
complete with the pealing of
bells (French)

Royal unicorn   part of the Royal
emblem, or coat-of-arms of
Great Britain.

Calpurnia's cheek was pale   in
Shakespeare's *Julius Caesar*,
Brutus remarks that the cheek
of Caesar's wife—Calpurnia—
is pale. The reference is that

Farfrae (equivalent to a Caesar
among the crowd) has his
Brutus.

go snacks wi'en   go snacks with
him; to eat at his table; to live
with him

hontish   high-handed, haughty

to see that lady toppered   to see
that lady brought low—brought
to shame

QUESTION

What will be the effect on Lucetta of a skimmity-ride
involving her and Henchard at this point in her fortunes?

CHAPTER 38

SYNOPSIS: A DEADLY WRESTLING MATCH

Henchard, as maddened by Lucetta's scorn as Farfrae's
humiliating shove, resolves to wrestle Donald to the death. He
leaves a message for Donald to meet him in the corn storage
building and immediately goes there himself. Henchard knows
he is stronger than Donald, so he ties his left arm to his body,
rendering it useless in combat. Donald arrives later and Henchard calls him up to the loft. Michael faces him squarely and
says that Donald has snubbed him at work and disgraced him
in public. Now it is time to finish the wrestling match which
was begun that afternoon in front of the townspeople: " 'You
may be the one to cool first,' said Henchard grimly. 'Now this
is the case. Here be we, in this four-square loft, to finish out
that little wrestle you began this morning. There's the door,
forty foot above ground. One of us two puts the other out by
that door—the master stays inside. If he likes he may go down
afterwards and give the alarm that the other has fallen out by
accident—or he may tell the truth—that's his business. As the
strongest man I've tied one arm to take no advantage of 'ee.
D'ye understand? Then here's at 'ee.' "

Donald is no match against Henchard's strength, and soon he is half-out the open doorway with Henchard ready to hurl him to his death. But Henchard cannot commit the ultimate act of violence. He frees Donald and lies in a corner. The "woman-liness" of his posture "sat tragically on the figure of so stern a piece of virility." Donald departs, and Henchard overhears Donald tell Whittle that he has been unexpectedly summoned to Weatherbury, thus causing him to cancel his intended plans of *traveling toward Budmouth*. Henchard is overcome by re-morse and the desire to see Donald and seek his pardon. But Donald is out of town, and Henchard returns to his customary place on the bridge. From there he hears jumbled noises and rhythmical confusion coming from the town. So great is his con-sternation, he is not even curious about the unexplained noise.

DISCUSSION

Elizabeth-Jane's fears have become a reality. Michael Hen-chard has attempted to kill Donald Farfrae. But he is not a murderer, and it is his affection for the younger man that prevents him from snuffing out Donald's life. His physical su-periority has not amounted to a victory, but a lowering of his opinion of himself.

It should be noted that only Whittle and Henchard know of Donald's change of destination when he leaves town.

Weltlust enjoyment or love of worldly pleasure (German)

"And here's a hand . . . thine" from Robert Burns's well-known song, "Auld Lang Syne." "Fiere" means friend or companion, and

"gie's" is a dialect contraction for "give us."

forward stripling upstart young-ster

to close with Henchard to en-gage Henchard in combat

QUESTION

What do you expect Farfrae's future attitude toward Henchard to be?

CHAPTER 39

SYNOPSIS: THE SKIMMITY-RIDE

Though Donald's men have sent him a note asking him to go to Weatherbury as a pretext to spare him the sight of the skimmity-ride, they have taken no protective measures for Lucetta, since they believe she had carried on an illicit affair with Henchard. That evening the skimmity-ride is conveyed in a wild procession past Lucetta's house just as she is feeling most secure.

Elizabeth-Jane, aware of the vulgar display, rushes to Lucetta's house and begs her not to look. Lucetta, however, has heard two maids gossiping outside and cannot be restrained from observing the shame the townspeople wish to cast upon her. She goes to the window. There she gazes on the procession of the ignorant revellers accompanying a donkey upon whose back are the effigies of Henchard and herself tied together back to back by the elbows. The implication that the vulgar display reveals is only too clear to Lucetta. Driven to distraction by the fear her husband will see it and grow to hate her, she falls into an epileptic fit. The doctor is summoned, and since Lucetta is pregnant he fears her condition is highly critical. A man is immediately dispatched to bring Donald home from his supposed journey along the Budmouth Road. He has gone off to Weatherbury instead.

The feeble town constables are urged on by Mr. Grower, the witness at the Farfraes' wedding, to apprehend the perpetrators of the unlawful procession, but they are unable to discover who has taken part. They meet Jopp, but he claims to have seen nothing, and they finally go to the infamous Peter's Finger Inn in Mixen Lane, but there they discover only a quiet gathering. The reader knows that the members of the group at the inn had taken part in the skimmity-ride, but since they give false witness and establish alibis for each other, the constables are powerless to apprehend them.

DISCUSSION

The skimmington-ride has done more evil than its perpetrators had intended. Despite the good-hearted Elizabeth-Jane's efforts to hide the display from Lucetta, Lucetta sees the procession. It is strange that Hardy attributes the seizure to epilepsy. Though epilepsy may occur at unpredictable times, the disease is such that the sufferer usually has a history of seizures. Yet no mention has been made of such a history of sickness in Lucetta's past.

it mid be   it might be
cleavers . . . rams'-horns Old
  musical instruments or noise-
  makers; a "croud" would be a
  fiddle and "humstrums" would
be cranked instruments similar
  to a hurdy-gurdy
Comus   a masque by Milton
was with child an old form of
  saying "was pregnant"

QUESTION

How would you judge Jopp's part in the cruel skimmity-
ride by comparison with Henchard's misdeeds?

CHAPTER 40

SYNOPSIS: THE DEATH OF LUCETTA

Henchard is unable to sleep due to his consternation at
having fought with Donald. He makes his way into Casterbridge
and there sees the skimmington-ride. He immediately understands its meaning and the possible consequences. He goes
directly to Donald's house, learns of Lucetta's illness, and tries
to inform the inhabitants of Donald's true whereabouts. However, because of his recent unspeakable behavior, no one will
believe him. He therefore sets out at a fast run to intercept
Donald, knowing Lucetta's life could depend on her husband's
presence.

He finally meets Donald at a lonely road-crossing. But,
when Henchard tells Donald of his wife's sickness, Donald
refuses to believe him. He feels that Henchard may have set a
trap for him in order to finish what he had not done previously.
"The very agitation and abruptness of Henchard" make Farfrae
even more suspicious. He leaves toward his destination with
Michael Henchard running after the gig, begging him to return.

Henchard returns and despairingly curses himself "like a
less scrupulous Job." Throughout the night he makes inquiries
about Lucetta's condition. Donald returns and that night stays
beside his wife. During Donald's vigil, Lucetta informs him of
her past relationship with Henchard. The extent of the information she imparts to Donald remains "Farfrae's secret alone."

Henchard has gone to his lodgings and there thinks of
Elizabeth-Jane as his only comfort: "she seemed to him as a pin-

point of light." Jopp informs him that "a kind of traveller, or sea-captain of some sort" had called on Henchard. Henchard dismisses the information and that night, unable to sleep, paces to and fro before Donald's house. At dawn Michael learns that Lucetta has died.

DISCUSSION

This chapter is indeed a sad one. Hardy is bitterly denouncing man's evil treatment of his brother. One sentence in particular reinforces this judgment: "He went across, the sparrows in his way scarcely flying up from the road-litter, so little did they believe in human aggression at so early a time."

The introduction of a sea-captain creates a new pause for thought. Since Hardy seldom introduces a character unless there is an organic part for him to play in the unfolding plot, the reader assumes that the sea-captain will have some effect on the future action.

a less scrupulous Job the biblical character Job, who only lived to do right, cursed the day of his birth when he was punished by God for no apparent reason. Hence, Henchard, not quite as conscientious in his desire to do good, also curses himself as Job did.

well-be-doing a man who is well off, doing well

Lucifer the planet Venus when it appears as the morning star

QUESTION

Who do you think the sea-captain is?

CHAPTER 41

SYNOPSIS: HENCHARD LIES TO THE CAPTAIN

Elizabeth-Jane visits Henchard on the morning of Lucetta's death. There Henchard, moved to genuine love for his stepdaughter, offers to prepare breakfast while she refreshes herself with sleep. He waits for her "as if it were an honor to have her in his house." While Elizabeth-Jane sleeps, Captain Newson, the sailor who had figured so prominently in Henchard's life, arrives. When he identifies himself, "Henchard's face and eyes seemed to die." Newson informs Henchard that, in order to be kind to Susan who had found their relationship untenable, he had arranged the story of his loss at sea. He is now wealthy, and has returned to claim his daughter. Impulsively, fearing that Elizabeth-Jane will leave him, Henchard tells Newson that Elizabeth-Jane had died more than a year before. Newson is terribly dejected and, taking Henchard's word at face value, leaves Casterbridge immediately. Elizabeth-Jane awakens but Henchard is afraid to ask her to stay for he is sure Newson will return and claim Elizabeth-Jane himself. He goes to Ten Hatches—the name of the junction where the river runs deep —and contemplates suicide. Suddenly he sees his exact image floating in the water. He has a superstitous change of heart and returns home to find Elizabeth-Jane awaiting him. He takes her to Ten Hatches where she discovers that the image he has seen is the effigy used in the skimmington-ride, thrown into the river by the revellers in order to destroy the evidence. Elizabeth-Jane quickly guesses Henchard's plans and asks to be allowed to live with him and take care of his needs. Henchard readily assents, and from that moment on becomes a new man. In his new cheerfulness he says that "it seems that even I be in Somebody's hand!"

DISCUSSION

The sea-captain who had looked for Henchard in the last chapter turns out to be Newson. Henchard is barely able to find a grain of happiness before it is threatened and wrenched from him. He is still impetuous, and the information he gives Newson of Elizabeth-Jane's death can only result in his utter estrangement from her if she should learn of it. He knows this, yet his reason for lying is prompted by love, an emotion which is, to say the least, alien to Henchard's temperament. The effect of Elizabeth-Jane's concern and care is like a medication upon Henchard. He finds a momentary belief in a Supreme Power, changes in outlook, and is, for the moment, rejuvenated. As the book nears its close, a false happiness is being built upon a foundation of lies. Hardy's penchant for the grotesque is shown once again in the appearance of the effigy at the moment of Henchard's thoughts of suicide.

Hardy's belief in the power of music is shown in the passage where Henchard's despair is deepest: "If he could have

summoned music to his aid, his existence might even now have
been borne.''

QUESTION

Do you believe in Henchard's optimistic remark at the end
of the chapter?

CHAPTER 42

SYNOPSIS: FARFRAE AND ELIZABETH-JANE MEET AGAIN

About a year passes. Farfrae, not knowing of Jopp's malevolence, puts aside any plans to punish the perpetrators of the
skimmity-ride. Henchard now owns a small seed shop purchased
for him by the town council. Together he and Elizabeth-Jane
begin to make a respectable living for themselves. However,
even though Henchard has come to disregard the eventuality of
Newson's return, he now fears that Donald Farfrae will wish
to marry Elizabeth-Jane, thus robbing him of the only creature
close to him. He has seen many newly-bought books in Elizabeth-Jane's modest room and wonders how she has been able
to buy them.

Farfrae, in time, has come to believe that Lucetta's secret
would have come out sooner or later, and if she had lived their
chances for happiness would probably not have been so great.

Donald and Elizabeth-Jane begin to meet, accidentally at
first. Donald continues to give her presents of books, and soon
their old love grows anew. Henchard spies on them, burning
with a kind of possessive jealousy. His suspicions are justified
when he sees Donald kissing Elizabeth-Jane, and for a fleeting
moment he considers telling Donald of his stepdaughter's illegitimate birth. But he cannot quite bring himself to do it and
exclaims: "Why should I still be subject to these visitations of
the devil . . . ?"

DISCUSSION

Farfrae is now depicted by Hardy as a rather prim and
somewhat unforgiving man. Though he has shown forgiveness

to Henchard and an understanding of humanity in the past, his rueful thoughts about Lucetta seem to give him almost a puritanical air. This tends to give more weight to Henchard's thought that Farfrae might drop Elizabeth-Jane if he knew of her birth, however.

Juno's bird peacock

Argus eyes mythological figure with one hundred eyes. When Argus was killed the eyes were placed on the tail of Juno's

sacred peacock.

solicitus timor a worrisome fear (Latin)

locus standi accepted or recognized standing (Latin)

QUESTION

Why does Farfrae, who has never been unkind or unfair, seem like a lesser man than Henchard, who has been inconsiderate, untruthful, and even dishonorable throughout the story?

CHAPTER 43

SYNOPSIS: HENCHARD LEAVES CASTERBRIDGE

Henchard realizes that the town is filled with gossip about Donald and Elizabeth-Jane. The "philosophic party" among the rustics are the only ones entirely pleased at the thought of their marriage. Henchard begins to worry about the life he will lead once the two are married. One day he goes to spy with a telescope on Donald and Elizabeth-Jane, but discovers Newson waiting instead of the two lovers. Henchard returns and Elizabeth-Jane tells him of a letter she has received requesting her to meet a stranger on the Budmouth Road or at Farfrae's house in the evening. Henchard realizes that the stranger is Newson come to claim his daughter. Michael immediately says to her "as if he did not care about her" that he is leaving Casterbridge. Despite her pleas, Henchard will not reconsider and at dusk he leaves town, once more as an itinerant hay-trusser. She accompanies him a short distance and sadly bids him farewell. As she is returning to Casterbridge, Donald meets her and brings her to his home where she is reunited with Newson. After Newson informs her that Henchard had lied about her death, Elizabeth-Jane's feelings toward Henchard grow cold and bitter. She and Donald actually turn against Michael so strongly that Newson takes his part. However, the past is put aside for the moment and preparations for the wedding are begun.

DISCUSSION

One wonders how Newson had discovered Farfrae and Elizabeth-Jane. Hardy leaves out this incident possibly to prevent the inclusion of another chance occurrence. Yet Hardy may have skipped over these details to bring the climactic moment to a faster resolution and to make a number of points. The focus remains of Henchard and his emotional suffering. Because Henchard has learned to sacrifice for love and is truly suffering in expiation for his sins, the sympathy shifts directly upon him, and the reader begins to experience a more intense pity for the one-time esteemed Mayor of Casterbridge.

éclat distinction or brilliance (French)

Mai Dun a large fortress of the ancient Britons

via road, path (Latin)

Cain in *Genesis:* for killing his brother Abel, Cain was branded (Mark of Cain) and cursed by God to wander among men, and to be shunned by them.

schiedam gin (named after the town in Holland where it had been made)

QUESTION

What does Newson's response to Henchard's lie about Elizabeth-Jane reveal about his character?

CHAPTER 44

SYNOPSIS: HENCHARD BRINGS A WEDDING GIFT

Dressed as he was when he first came to Casterbridge, Henchard makes his way for six days to Weydon-Priors. There he re-enacts in his mind the events of his original rash deed and the consequences of it. He is unable to shake off his constant thoughts of Elizabeth-Jane. Finally he obtains work as a hay-trusser at a place about fifty miles by direct road from Casterbridge. As the days pass he comes to think of the possibility that Newson might not have come to reclaim his daughter. He decides that he may have acted rashly and determines to go to her wedding after surmising from the talk of travelers that its date is St. Martin's Day. Two days before the wedding he leaves on foot for Casterbridge, determined not to arrive until evening of the wedding-day.

Henchard stops at the town of Shottsford to purchase new clothes for himself and a gift of a goldfinch in a cage for Elizabeth-Jane. Henchard arrives after the wedding and waits outside town for dark to fall. That evening Farfrae's house is filled with music and gaiety. Henchard inquires after Mr. and Mrs. Farfrae at the back entrance of the house and momentarily deposits the goldfinch beneath a bush. While waiting for Elizabeth-Jane, he sees her and Donald dancing gaily. Suddenly he is aware of a new partner dancing with Elizabeth-Jane. He recognizes Newson, and Henchard's hopes are dashed. However, before he has a chance to leave, Elizabeth-Jane comes out. Her first surprised remark: "Oh—it is—Mr. Henchard!" Henchard is stung by the formality of the way she has addressed him and pleads for her to keep a little love in her heart. But Elizabeth-Jane cannot forgive him and accuses him of deceit. Henchard does not even attempt to defend himself, but apologizes for having caused her discomfort at his appearance: "I have done wrong in coming to 'ee—I see my error. But it is only for once, so forgive it. I'll never trouble 'ee again, Elizabeth-Jane—no, not to my dying day! Good-night. Good-bye!" With this Henchard leaves Elizabeth-Jane forever.

DISCUSSION

This chapter is the last to depict Henchard's dogged attempts to find love and affection. It was, of course, self-delusion on his part to persuade himself that Newson had not returned to claim Elizabeth-Jane. Throughout the book Michael Henchard is wrong in all his choices and all his plans. Yet, in the last few chapters one thought refuses to leave him. He believes that despite his persistent attempts to show Elizabeth-Jane deep and abiding love, she will not forgive him when Newson reclaims her. In this one instance—irony of ironies—he is absolutely right.

quickset hawthorn hedges
of aught besides of anything
  else, also
pixy-ring a fairy-ring. A term
  given to the area or ring on the
  meadow where a different type
  of grass is growing

pari passu at the same speed
  (Latin)
Martin's Day November 11th
sequestration seclusion
Samson shorn from *Judges*. A
  strong man who has been robbed
  of his strength

QUESTION

Why does this chapter seem sadder than the many others
in which Henchard has suffered misfortune?

CHAPTER 45

SYNOPSIS: AN OBSCURE DESTINY

It is about a month after the night of the wedding reception. Elizabeth-Jane has grown somewhat accustomed to her
new position. Newson has gone to live at Budmouth in sight
of the sea. A maid tells Elizabeth-Jane that they now know who
had abandoned the birdcage near the back entrance. One week
after her marriage Elizabeth-Jane had found the birdcage and
the starved goldfinch. She had been terribly upset by the discovery. The servant informs her that it was the "farmer's man
who called on the evening of the wedding." Elizabeth-Jane
realizes that Henchard had brought her a gift and feels anguish
at her harshness to him. She and Donald set out to find him,
and even though they travel a great distance in search of the
man who had apparently "sunk into the earth," their efforts
are fruitless. However, a good many miles from Casterbridge
they discover Abel Whittle entering a cottage which is "of
humble dwellings surely the humblest." They learn from Abel
that Michael has died within the half-hour. Abel had followed
Michael the night of the wedding reception and had taken care
of him during his sickness, because Henchard had been kind
to his mother when she was alive. He shows Elizabeth-Jane
Henchard's crudely written but deeply moving will. Michael
Henchard's last requests are that no formal ceremonies accompany his burial and that Elizabeth-Jane not be informed of his
death. Though Elizabeth-Jane now feels deep sorrow at having

been unkind to Michael, she nevertheless respects his strong determination and abides by the rude testament. She devotes the rest of her life to her husband and to the needs of the less fortunate.

DISCUSSION

This chapter shows Michael Henchard as a tragic figure. The reader understands that all Michael's sins have been expiated, not by his death, but through his suffering. His suffering, of course, is the direct result of his rash behavior as a young man. Yet there is an ennobling quality about his last actions, since they are motivated by love of another human being. His love and kindness toward Elizabeth-Jane are mirrored in Abel Whittle's tender care and devotion.

The symbolism of the starved goldfinch is quite effective since Henchard, himself, becomes sick and is unable to take nourishment. Furthermore, an added subtextual symbol is evident in the fact that Henchard, too, is starved to death for want of Elizabeth-Jane's love.

antipodean absences absences on the other side of the world. Probably the phrase refers to Australian penal colonies.

assize town a town where civil and criminal cases are tried by jury

Minerva-eyes . . . face the sense is that Elizabeth-Jane has acquired wisdom, and that she imparts the spirit of wisdom in her movements.

Diana Multimammia many-breasted Diana. The sense is that the burial-mounds appeared to be the many breasts.

Capharnaum from *Matthew;* place of darkness

QUESTION

How would you analyze each term of Henchard's will?

CRITICAL ANALYSIS

STRUCTURE

The Mayor of Casterbridge is one of Thomas Hardy's most unified works. Never for a moment is Michael Henchard out of our minds. Even when whole chapters are devoted to Donald Farfrae, Lucetta Templeman, Elizabeth-Jane, or some of the minor characters, Michael Henchard's strength of character lingers on each page like bass notes of impending doom. And indeed, this is how it should be, for Hardy subtitled his novel *A Story of a Man of Character*.

Hardy does not attempt to qualify Henchard's "character" as good or bad. His structure rests on the effect of Henchard's character upon his own life and the lives of others. It is certainly this element more than others that makes the novel stand out amidst the many Victorian novels whose important characters are less powerfully conceived than Henchard or all too easily disappear early and return from obscurity two hundred pages later. Susan's ruined life is a direct result of Henchard's rashness; by extension, Elizabeth-Jane owes her very existence to Henchard's folly; Donald Farfrae receives his start from Henchard, and indeed Henchard's wild speculations and superstitious nature only help to advance Farfrae; and Lucetta's death is a direct outcome of her past relationship with Henchard. Hardy did not require us to like Michael Henchard; however, he has so structured the novel that we cannot forget him. Henchard *is* the novel.

How is it, then, that the other characters in the novel keep our attention? In the case of Donald and Elizabeth-Jane, the reader knows they will marry before the end of the novel. Concerning Lucetta, the reader is thoroughly aware that she will not marry Henchard. It is only the pitfalls and vicissitudes of their lives that provide interest and suspense. Thus our interest in these characters is aroused in direct proportion to the catalytic effect that Henchard's character and behavior have in motivating their actions.

Throughout the novel is felt the influence of *King Lear,* Shakespeare's massive tragedy. One recalls that Lear rashly disowns his true and loving daughter, falls from the heights of regality into suffering and madness, and is briefly reconciled with her before his death. The realization of this structural parallel strengthens our knowledge that the unity of the work is predicated on Henchard's character. After all, his rashness precipitates the events which, once started, move unrelentingly on.

The first two chapters of the novel and the very last serve as a frame for the core of the novel's story. The opening chapters display the unhappy events that initiate the tale, and the last chapter rounds them off, thus bringing the plot full circle. That is, Henchard enters the novel impoverished and miserable, but young, vigorous, and still master of his own fate. In the last chapter he departs from the novel—and from this world—more impoverished, more wretched, barely in his middle-age, master of nothing. If the novel had begun with Henchard already established as mayor, the sale of his wife, if pulled out of the closet of obscurity as an old family skeleton, would make the story preposterous.

It was apparently not completely possible for Hardy to escape some of the seemingly melodramatic, and at times forced, incidents which abound in the fiction of his era. Henchard speculates wildly in order to destroy Farfrae, and the weather changes; the "furmity woman" shows up and causes Michael's complete downfall; Newson returns from the dead and destroys the ex-mayor's only chance for happiness.

Nevertheless, though these untoward events may seem heavily weighted on the side of the novelist's plot development, none of them is really incredible. Even Henchard cannot control the weather. What person would not remember the face of the man who sold his wife to the highest bidder (and since the "furmity woman" is a vagabond type, she could easily turn up in Casterbridge as well as anywhere else)? Is it not natural for Newson to attempt to reclaim his own child in order to bestow his fortune upon her as his heir? These events are justified, although the modern reader may be disturbed by the machinations behind them.

In this vein there are also at least four overheard conversations: Lucetta overhears Henchard reading her letters, and she naturally fears that Donald will surmise her past history; Henchard, earlier, hides behind a stack of wheat and listens to Donald and Lucetta's passionate conversation; Donald and Lucetta listen intently to the two parting lovers in the market, thus uniting their spirits in a romantic bond; and finally, Henchard, once again from hiding, overhears Donald addressing Elizabeth-Jane in tender words and knows the meeting has ended with a kiss. If the reader has assumed that these overheard conversations are melodramatic tricks, let him also note that such tricks are more melodramatic if the listener *accidentally* overhears. However, in these cases, each of the listeners *purposely* eavesdrops.

The comparative abundance of coincidences, returns from the past, secret letters, and the like, should not lead the reader to think that Hardy has mismanaged his realism. There are many realistic elements in the novel (modern critics tend to think that Hardy's realism of dialogue, precise descriptions of buildings and countryside, etc., are false criteria of his excellence), but the importance of *The Mayor of Casterbridge* is now generally assumed to lie outside its fidelity to the canons of painstaking realism, either of setting or incident. One critic sees in the sequence of events the working out of a scheme of retribution by an outraged moral order in the universe. Another sees in Henchard an astonishingly perceptive treatment of the character unconsciously bent on his own destruction, in this anticipating the findings of modern psychology. In either event, mere plausibility of structure appears of negligible importance.

POINT OF VIEW AND STYLE

Hardy's narrative style is that of the *omniscient* or *ubiquitous* narrator. This gives him a point of view that allows him to comment upon the vagaries of nature, to place himself in the mind of a character in order to give us reasons and motives, and to philosophize or describe the background to clarify whatever point he wishes to make. In short, Hardy knows all and is everywhere in *The Mayor of Casterbridge,* although we learn only what he wants us to know. When we have finished the novel, our thoughts about it are to some extent what Hardy wants us to think.

Hardy's actual writing style is usually clear and is often extremely well wrought. If an occasional awkward sentence or overly long descriptive passage comes to light, perhaps we should reflect upon the conventions of the era in which he wrote. The comparative infrequency of his lapses from clarity and economy may serve as a lesson for the student in "blue-penciling" or revision.

The opening pages of the novel display Hardy's ability to write admirable prose which delineates the personae, the background, and the circumstances from an omniscient narrator's point of view.

In the first two or three pages of the book we are treated to some excellent description, especially perhaps that of Susan's face. We also learn that the couple is unhappily married, the man is discontented, they are poor and somewhat shabby, and that Susan's philosophy toward life is rather pessimistic. Furthermore, the dry dust, the barren countryside, and the "blackened-green stage of colour" of the vegetation lend an oppressive air to the scene as a prelude to the dark events to come. Hardy reveals his somber mastery of setting, mood, and character throughout the novel, and the reader rarely has to search for clarity.

Hardy's ability with dialogue is evident on two levels. The dialogue reflects his characters' social position while it adds to our knowledge of their personalities. A passage from Chapter 9 will illustrate this.

"Now I am not the man to let a cause be lost for want of a word. And before ye are gone for ever I'll speak. Once more, will ye stay? There it is, flat and plain. You can see that it isn't all selfishness that makes me press 'ee; for my business is not quite so scientific as to require an intellect entirely out of the common. Others would do for the place without doubt. Some selfishness perhaps there is, but there is more; it isn't for me to repeat what. Come bide with me—and name your own terms. I'll agree to 'em willingly and 'ithout a word gainsaying; for, hang it, Farfrae, I like thee well!"

This example shows Henchard's very blunt character. Not a word is wasted, and he comes directly to the point. He uses countrified expressions but does not speak like the lower-class townspeople. Furthermore, the impetuous nature of his character is shown in both speeches by his vehement attempt to hire Farfrae because he likes him and to press upon Donald his immediate friendship, without the normal preliminaries, by insisting that he come to breakfast.

Farfrae's kind and fair disposition is amply brought out by a number of his speeches, although he is almost never given a very long speech. Farfrae's reasonableness and sweetness become somewhat cloying in the light of the struggles and transformation which Henchard is undergoing. Nevertheless, his unwillingness to commit an act of blatant vengeance or meanness, and his Scottish economy of speech are distinctly brought forth in these passages from Chapter 34.

"About that little seedsman's shop," he said; "the shop overlooking the churchyard, which is to let. It is not for myself I want it, but for our unlucky fellow-townsman Henchard. It would be a new beginning for him, if a small one; and I have told the Council that I would head a private subscription among them to set him up in it—that I would be fifty pounds, if they would make up the other fifty among them."

"But I cannet discharge a man who was once a good friend to me? How can I forget that when I came here 'twas he enabled me to make a footing for mysel'? No, no. As long as I've a day's wark to offer he shall do it if he chooses. 'Tis not I who will deny him such a little as that. But I'll drop the idea of establishing him in a shop till I can think more about it."

The letters of Lucetta Templeman are quite as revealing as most of her speeches. The reader wonders why she would be so reckless as to write such candid letters to Henchard. Her candor bespeaks a certain naïveté or trust on her part, but it also shows an element of abandon which Hardy carefully traces to her *French* background. The letters and her bantering with Farfrae show a certain sophisticated ability to play with words in a teasing manner. To Hardy—though not to us today—this is enough to characterize Lucetta with what was to the English mind French sensuality or even licentiousness. The following passages from Chapter 23 catch her character brilliantly.

"I mean all you Scotchmen," she added in hasty correction. "So free from Southern extremes. We common people are all one way or the other—warm or cold, passionate or frigid. You have both temperatures going on in you at the same time."

"It is very hard," she said with strong feelings. "Lovers ought not to be parted like that! Oh, if I had my wish, I'd let people live and love at their pleasure!"

"It is kind-hearted of you, indeed," said Lucetta. "For my part, I have resolved that all my servants shall have lovers if they want them! Do make the same resolve!"

Through her speech, Hardy shows the gradual change that takes place in Elizabeth-Jane through the years. At first she has a somewhat natural bent toward good times and playfulness, although she never appears giddy. As her sorrows increase, she turns more and more to study and reflection. At the end of the novel the reader finds Elizabeth-Jane characterized somewhat as a melancholy, kind, matronly woman whose speech seems highly studied and affected, even when her words are deeply emotional:

She flushed up, and gently drew her hand away. "I could have loved you always—I would have, gladly," said she. "But how can I when I know you have deceived me so—so bitterly deceived me! You persuaded me that my father was not my father—allowed me to live on in ignorance of the truth for years; and then when he, my warm-hearted real father, came to find me, cruelly sent him away with a wicked invention of my death, which nearly broke his heart. O how can I love as I once did a man who has served us like this!"

As far as the lower-class types are concerned, Hardy has characterized them as mischievous knaves who often speak in vulgar terms. Yet, they have a vigorous life of their own, and Hardy has revealed with enormous skill the picturesque qualities that can only be found in authentic folk dialect.

Another aspect of Hardy's over-all style is his fondness for Gothic atmosphere—that is, secret meetings or plots or incidents occurring in gloomy or melancholy surroundings. The opening chapter of the book has this quality to it, as does Henchard's meeting with Susan at the Ring, and his discovery of the "skimmity-ride" figure in the water. With little difficulty the student can probably recall at least two more incidents or surroundings that indicate a *Gothic* treatment.

In its wealth of realistic detail, Hardy's descriptive style created his Wessex world with such conviction and thoroughness that he became the model for dozens of other regional novelists. His realism is not now appreciated as much as his more tragic, universal qualities, but it contributes substantially in *The Mayor of Casterbridge* to the total tragic effect. Henchard is considered by at least one critic to be the only genuinely successful attempt at a tragic hero in the modern novel. But Henchard is so embedded in the real world of grain dealing, furmity, seed lips, stout breakfasts, and hay bales as to have for the modern reader an affinity with his own experience that other romantic heroes, enveloped in myth and legend, do not. As tragic hero he is of a stature comparable with theirs, but he comes to us, as it were, in the homely corduroy of a hay-trusser rather than in cape or toga. In part because of Hardy's Wessex realism, Henchard is a tragic hero we can touch.

THEME

The theme of *The Mayor of Casterbridge* appears to be the arbitrary and almost always malign workings of the universe and blind chance upon the destinies of men. Such evil, unrelenting machinations bring pain and suffering upon the characters in the novel, and there is no escape except in a day-to-day acceptance of life.

Much has been written concerning Hardy's famous pessimism. However, in *The Mayor of Casterbridge,* despite the workings of blind fate, the occurrences of chance, and the vagaries of a hostile natural environment, Michael Henchard is still responsible for his own fate. If he had not sold his wife in a fit of drunken self-pity, the painful events would not have ensued. If he had not overspeculated in order to ruin Farfrae, it would not have mattered if it rained, or snowed, or hailed. Certainly in his many years as corn-factor and leading businessman he had come through other natural disasters. It is only in this one case that he lets his keen sense of rivalry and lust for revenge cause him to speculate recklessly.

Nor is Hardy indifferent to man's senseless cruelty to his brother. He structures the events so that even Elizabeth-Jane has become too prim and unrelenting in her firm stand on Lucetta and Henchard. He is unsparing in his portrayal of the lower-class townspeople for their cruel and vicious "skimmity-ride." And, in Henchard's case, since he is the focal point of the novel, Hardy is saying that wickedness and evil will return to the perpetrator in full cycle, in like measure. He is indeed saying that the evil which man does will not only live after him, but it—evil, not fate—will dog man's steps until poetic justice has been satisfied.

One last word. Let the reader observe Henchard's behavior after Elizabeth-Jane has come to dwell with him, and the motivations for that behavior. Though Henchard's actions are somewhat tempered with the base emotion of jealousy—which is only human—all that he does is motivated by love of Elizabeth-Jane. He lies to Newson because he doesn't want to lose Elizabeth-Jane; he leaves Casterbridge because he cannot bear Elizabeth-Jane's scorn; he returns to show his love and to be forgiven; he departs forever so as not to cause his foster-daughter pain and embarrassment; and finally, he writes a will whose requirements will blot out his existence from the eyes of men, especially from Elizabeth-Jane whom he does not wish to hurt. There is nobility in Henchard because he willingly takes upon himself suffering as an expiation for the sins of his life. He carries his suffering and his love for Elizabeth-Jane in silence. And when man can rise to stature and nobility as Henchard does at the end of *The Mayor of Casterbridge*, then the dominant chord Hardy has struck swells to a bold theme of hope for mankind.

CHARACTER SKETCHES

Michael Henchard

Michael Henchard is a strong man with great energy. He has fine points in his character, but they are contrasted sharply with other less admirable qualities. Thus, he will try to make up for what he has done to Susan, but he will still remain rash and impetuous in his dealings with people. He is honest and upright, so much so that he insists on binding one of his arms when fighting Farfrae, and he refuses to hide one cent of his property from the administrators of his bankrupt business. Even the administrators praise his honesty. He is generous and kind to Abel Whittle's mother. Donald Farfrae owes much to Henchard's giving him a start. These are but a few instances of Henchard's honesty and generosity.

But the darker side of Henchard's character is even more evident. He has no compunction in punishing Abel Whittle too severely for lateness, and the quality of his kindness and friendship to Farfrae becomes overbearing and possessive. His pride is noteworthy, but often it grows into hideous egoism. Thus, his pride refuses to let him reveal his past to Elizabeth-Jane, and at the end of the novel he cannot bring himself to tell her the true account of his lie to Newson. Again, it is his pride which prompts the rivalry and jealousy he feels toward Donald Farfrae. But, despite obvious flaws in his character, Henchard has the ability to love deeply. He achieves the strength to take silently upon himself the suffering caused by his own sins, and it is this will to endure the wrath of the heavens that gives him great stature.

Susan

Hardy purposely drew Susan as a vague character. Before the end of the third chapter it becomes clear that she has suffered an outrage not to be endured. If her character were outlined more definitely, Hardy would be running the risk of displacing the focus from Henchard to Susan and give her a more assertive part in the plot. Thus it is unnecessary to speculate on what her life would have been like if Henchard had not auctioned her off. It is clear, however, that her simple nature lends her an innocence and trust that almost surpass the bounds of credibility. She believes pessimistically that the events of her life have been structured by an unkind fate, and she does not look to mankind for assistance.

Elizabeth-Jane

Elizabeth-Jane, tempered in poverty and the loss of her father, Newson, and her mother, resigns herself to study and self-betterment. Her beauty begins to flower with the more wholesome diet and relatively relaxed atmosphere of living in a wealthy home. She senses something improper in Susan and Henchard's past relationship, and almost unconsciously she strives to emulate a conservative, formal, correct social relationship with others. However, despite the melancholy aura which surrounds her, Elizabeth-Jane is able to love deeply and sincerely. In fact, she has observed so much of life around her with such an understanding eye that she cannot remain bitter in any way. Even when she renounces Henchard for lying to her about Newson—an understandable action considering her deep love for Newson—she cannot long remain bitter and sets out to find him. Her tribute to Henchard's memory is in honoring his last wishes since she knows that he was a man of indomitable will. She dedicates the rest of her life to kindness, humanity, and learning, and her soul becomes more beautiful as she advances through life.

Donald Farfrae

Donald Farfrae is a young Scotsman, leaner and frailer than Henchard. However, what he lacks in physical strength, he more than makes up for in charm, wit, and good humor. Donald has a mind for mechanical things and business. But, whereas Henchard has no penchant for creative endeavors, Donald has cultivated a pleasant singing voice and knows how to give an entertainment that will appeal to others. The most pronounced contrast between Henchard's and Donald's characters is that Donald cannot truly harbor a grudge or wish to be vengeful. He is prudent in his philosophy and social outlook, and one feels that he and Elizabeth-Jane are manifestly suited to each other.

Lucetta Templeman (Le Sueur)

In Victorian times, Lucetta would have been considered a reckless libertine. Today we would call her a rather flighty, flirtatious, indiscreet young lady. There is not much depth to Lucetta's character once we place her beside Elizabeth-Jane. She writes compromising letters to Henchard and takes her married life in her hands when she meets him secretly at the Ring. But she does not think of these things until it is too late. She is preoccupied with clothing, comfort, fashions, and sophisticated light banter. She is quick to deny Donald's former connection with Henchard during the disturbance of the royal visitor, and her rather snobbish attitude turns Jopp into a bitter enemy who plots her downfall. In short, the lack of depth in her personality is shown in Donald's own thoughts when he realizes, after her death, that he would not have been happy with her.

Newson

Newson, if we are to accept the statements of Susan and Elizabeth-Jane, is a kind, jovial man. We are given a demonstration of his kindness—or forgiving nature—when he refuses to chastise Henchard for lying to him. His trusting nature is shown again when he takes Henchard's word at face value and departs without even visiting the cemetery. Yet he is thoughtful of others. The story of his loss at sea is a kindly deception by which he will give Susan the freedom to return to Henchard.

Jopp

Jopp is a dark character who possesses no wit, business sense, or honor. What is clearest about his character is his ability to harbor a grudge and to take joy in seeing an enemy suffer. His function in the novel is at once to serve as a villain and a catalyst for villainous behavior.

Abel Whittle

At first singled out for his extreme simplicity, Abel Whittle becomes more the faithful follower than the scatterbrain as the story develops. From the clownish bumpkin of the trousers episode he becomes in his fidelity to the dying Henchard a figure comparable to Lear's Fool. His care for Henchard is an ironic instance of the completeness of Henchard's fall, for Abel, the lowliest character in the book, is Henchard's last tie to humanity.

Minor Characters

There are a number of rustics who not only provide atmosphere but act something like a chorus in Greek drama. Through Mrs. Cuxsom, Nance Mockridge, Christopher Coney, and Solomon Longways, the reader gets a feeling of the community, not only as it is but how it feels. These characters are partly individualized, Nance being low and spiteful, and Solomon, like his Biblical namesake, aspiring toward a judicious outlook on events.

NOTES

This is the TITLE INDEX, indexing the over 200 titles available by Series, by Library and by Volume Number for both the BASIC LIBRARY SERIES and the AUTHORS LIBRARY SERIES.

TITLE	SERIES	LIBRARY	Vol
Absalom, Absalom!	Basic	American Lit	4
	Authors	Faulkner	3
Adonais (in Keats & Shelley)	Basic	English Lit	1
Aeneid, The	Basic	Classics	1
Aeschylus' Oresteia (in Agamemnon)	Basic	Classics	1
Agamemnon	Basic	Classics	1
Alice in Wonderland	Basic	English Lit	3
All That Fall (in Waiting for Godot)	Basic	European Lit	1
All the King's Men	Basic	American Lit	6
All Quiet on the Western Front	Basic	European Lit	2
All's Well That Ends Well	Basic	Shakespeare	1
	Authors	Shakespeare	8
American, The	Basic	American Lit	2
	Authors	James	6
American Tragedy, An	Basic	American Lit	3
Animal Farm	Basic	English Lit	5
Anna Karenina	Basic	European Lit	3
Antigone (in Oedipus Trilogy)	Basic	Classics	1
Antony and Cleopatra	Basic	Shakespeare	2
	Authors	Shakespeare	9
Apology (in Plato's Euthyphro....)	Basic	Classics	1
Aristotle's Ethics	Basic	Classics	1
Arms and the Man (in Shaw's Pygmalion....)	Basic	English Lit	6
	Authors	Shaw	11
"Artificial Nigger, The" (in O'Connor's Short Stories)	Basic	American Lit	7
As I Lay Dying	Basic	American Lit	4
	Authors	Faulkner	3
Assistant, The	Basic	American Lit	6
As You Like It	Basic	Shakespeare	1
	Authors	Shakespeare	8
Autobiography of Benjamin Franklin	Basic	American Lit	1
Autobiography of Malcolm X, The	Basic	American Lit	6
	Special	Black Studies	
Awakening, The	Basic	American Lit	2
Babbitt	Basic	American Lit	3
	Authors	Lewis	7
"Bear, The" (in Go Down, Moses)	Basic	American Lit	4
	Authors	Faulkner	3
Bear, The	Basic	American Lit	4
	Authors	Faulkner	3
Bell Jar, The	Basic	American Lit	6
Beowulf	Basic	Classics	3
Billy Budd	Basic	American Lit	1
Birds, The (in Lysistrata....)	Basic	Classics	1

TITLE	SERIES	LIBRARY	Vol
Doctor Faustus	Basic	Classics	3
Doll's House, A (in Ibsen's Plays I)	Basic	European Lit	4
Don Quixote	Basic	Classics	3
Dr. Jekyll and Mr. Hyde	Basic	English Lit	3
Dracula	Basic	English Lit	3
Dune	Basic	American Lit	6
Electra (in Euripides' Electra & Medea)	Basic	Classics	1
Emerson's Essays	Basic	American Lit	1
Emily Dickinson: Selected Poems	Basic	American Lit	2
Emma	Basic	English Lit	1
Endgame (in Waiting for Godot)	Basic	European Lit	1
Enemy of the People, An (in Ibsen's Plays II)	Basic	European Lit	4
Ethan Frome	Basic	American Lit	3
Eumenides (in Agamemnon)	Basic	Classics	1
Euripides' Electra	Basic	Classics	1
Euripides' Medea	Basic	Classics	1
Euthyphro (in Plato's Euthyphro....)	Basic	Classics	1
Eve of St. Agnes, The (in Keats & Shelley)	Basic	English Lit	1
"Everything That Rises Must Converge" (in O'Connor's Short Stories)	Basic	American Lit	7
Faerie Queene, The	Basic	Classics	4
"Fall of the House of Usher, The" (in Poe's Short Stories)	Basic	American Lit	1
Far from the Madding Crowd	Basic	English Lit	3
	Authors	Hardy	4
Farewell to Arms, A	Basic	American Lit	4
	Authors	Hemingway	5
Fathers and Sons	Basic	European Lit	3
Faust, Pt. I and Pt. II	Basic	European Lit	2
"Fire and the Hearth, The" (in Go Down, Moses)	Basic	American Lit	4
Flies, The (in No Exit & The Flies)	Basic	European Lit	1
For Whom the Bell Tolls	Basic	American Lit	4
	Authors	Hemingway	5
"Four Quartets, The" (in T.S. Eliot's Major Poems and Plays)	Basic	English Lit	6
Frankenstein	Basic	English Lit	1
French Lieutenant's Woman, The	Basic	English Lit	5
Frogs, The (in Lysistrata....)	Basic	Classics	1
Ghosts (in Ibsen's Plays II)	Basic	European Lit	4
Giants in the Earth	Basic	European Lit	4
Glass Menagerie, The	Basic	American Lit	6
Go Down, Moses	Basic	American Lit	4
	Authors	Faulkner	3
Good Country People (in O'Connor's Short Stories)	Basic	American Lit	7
Good Earth, The	Basic	American Lit	4
Good Man is Hard to Find, A (in O'Connor's Short Stories)	Basic	American Lit	7
Grapes of Wrath, The	Basic	American Lit	4
	Authors	Steinbeck	12

TITLE	SERIES	LIBRARY	Vol
Tender is the Night	Basic	American Lit	5
Tess of the D'Urbervilles	Basic	English Lit	4
	Authors	Hardy	4
Three Musketeers, The	Basic	European Lit	1
To Kill a Mockingbird	Basic	American Lit	7
Tom Jones	Basic	English Lit	2
Tom Sawyer	Basic	American Lit	2
	Authors	Twain	13
Treasure Island	Basic	English Lit	4
Trial, The	Basic	European Lit	2
Tristram Shandy	Basic	English Lit	2
Troilus and Cressida	Basic	Shakespeare	1
	Authors	Shakespeare	8
Turn of the Screw, The (in Daisy Miller....)	Basic	American Lit	2
	Authors	James	6
Twelfth Night	Basic	Shakespeare	1
	Authors	Shakespeare	8
Two Gentlemen of Verona, The (in Comedy of Errors...)	Basic	Shakespeare	1
	Authors	Shakespeare	8
Typee (in Billy Budd & Typee)	Basic	American Lit	1
Ulysses	Basic	English Lit	6
Uncle Tom's Cabin	Basic	American Lit	2
Unvanquished, The	Basic	American Lit	5
	Authors	Faulkner	3
Utopia	Basic	Classics	4
Vanity Fair	Basic	English Lit	4
Vonnegut's Major Works	Basic	American Lit	7
Waiting for Godot	Basic	European Lit	1
Walden	Basic	American Lit	1
Walden Two	Basic	American Lit	7
War and Peace	Basic	European Lit	3
"Was" (in Go Down, Moses)	Basic	American Lit	4
"Waste Land, The" (in T.S. Eliot's Major Poems and Plays)	Basic	English Lit	6
White Fang (in Call of the Wild & White Fang)	Basic	American Lit	3
Who's Afraid of Virginia Woolf?	Basic	American Lit	7
Wild Duck, The (in Ibsen's Plays II)	Basic	European Lit	4
Winesburg, Ohio	Basic	American Lit	3
Winter's Tale, The	Basic	Shakespeare	1
	Authors	Shakespeare	8
Wuthering Heights	Basic	English Lit	4

This is the AUTHOR INDEX, listing the over 200 titles available by author and indexing them by Series, by Library and by Volume Number for both the BASIC LIBRARY SERIES and the AUTHORS LIBRARY SERIES.

AUTHOR	TITLE(S)	SERIES	LIBRARY	Vol
Aeschylus	Agamemnon, The Choephori, & The Eumenides	Basic	Classics	1
Albee, Edward	Who's Afraid of Virginia Woolf?	Basic	American Lit	7
Anderson, Sherwood	Winesburg, Ohio	Basic	American Lit	3
Aristophanes	Lysistrata * The Birds * Clouds * The Frogs	Basic	Classics	1
Aristotle	Aristotle's Ethics	Basic	Classics	1
Austen, Jane	Emma	Basic	English Lit	1
	Pride and Prejudice	Basic	English Lit	2
Beckett, Samuel	Waiting for Godot	Basic	European Lit	1
Beowulf	Beowulf	Basic	Classics	3
Beyle, Henri	see Stendhal			
Bronte, Charlotte	Jane Eyre	Basic	English Lit	3
Bronte, Emily	Wuthering Heights	Basic	English Lit	4
Brown, Claude	Manchild in the Promised Land	Basic	American Lit	7
	Manchild in the Promised Land	Special	Black Studies	
Buck, Pearl	The Good Earth	Basic	American Lit	4
Bunyan, John	The Pilgrim's Progress	Basic	English Lit	2
Camus, Albert	The Plague * The Stranger	Basic	European Lit	1
Carroll, Lewis	Alice in Wonderland	Basic	English Lit	3
Cather, Willa	My Antonia	Basic	American Lit	3
Cervantes, Miguel de	Don Quixote	Basic	Classics	3
Chaucer, Geoffrey	The Canterbury Tales	Basic	Classics	3
Chopin, Kate	The Awakening	Basic	American Lit	2
Clark, Walter	The Ox-Bow Incident	Basic	American Lit	7
Conrad, Joseph	Heart of Darkness & The Secret Sharer * Lord Jim	Basic	English Lit	5
Cooper, James F.	The Deerslayer * The Last of the Mohicans	Basic	American Lit	1
Crane, Stephen	The Red Badge of Courage	Basic	American Lit	2
Dante	Divine Comedy I: Inferno * Divine Comedy II: Purgatorio * Divine Comedy III: Paradiso	Basic	Classsics	3
Defoe, Daniel	Moll Flanders	Basic	English Lit	1
	Robinson Crusoe	Basic	English Lit	2
Dickens, Charles	Bleak House * David Copperfield * Great Expectations * Hard Times	Basic	English Lit	3
	Oliver Twist * A Tale of Two Cities	Basic	English Lit	4
	Bleak House * David Copperfield * Great Expectations * Hard Times * Oliver Twist * A Tale of Two Cities	Authors	Dickens	1

AUTHOR	TITLE(S)	SERIES	LIBRARY	Vol
Dickinson, Emily	Emily Dickinson: Selected Poems	Basic	American Lit	2
Dostoevsky, Feodor	The Brothers Karamazov * Crime and Punishment * Notes from the Underground	Basic	European Lit	3
	The Brothers Karamazov * Crime and Punishment * Notes from the Underground	Authors	Dostoevsky	2
Dreiser, Theodore	An American Tragedy * Sister Carrie	Basic	American Lit	3
Dumas, Alexandre	The Count of Monte Cristo * The Three Musketeers	Basic	European Lit	1
Eliot, George	Middlemarch * The Mill on the Floss * Silas Marner	Basic	English Lit	4
Eliot, T.S.	T.S. Eliot's Major Poets and Plays: "The Wasteland," "The Love Song of J. Alfred Prufrock," & Other Works	Basic	English Lit	6
Ellison, Ralph	The Invisible Man	Basic	American Lit	7
	The Invisible Man	Special	Black Studies	
Emerson, Ralph Waldo	Emerson's Essays	Basic	American Lit	1
Euripides	Electra * Medea	Basic	Classics	1
Faulkner, William	Absalom, Absalom! * As I Lay Dying * The Bear * Go Down, Moses * Light in August	Basic	American Lit	4
	The Sound and the Fury * The Unvanquished	Basic	American Lit	5
	Absalom, Absalom! * As I Lay Dying * The Bear * Go Down, Moses * Light in August The Sound and the Fury * The Unvanquished	Authors	Faulkner	3
Fielding, Henry	Joseph Andrews	Basic	English Lit	1
	Tom Jones	Basic	English Lit	2
Fitzgerald, F. Scott	The Great Gatsby	Basic	American Lit	4
	Tender is the Night	Basic	American Lit	5
Flaubert, Gustave	Madame Bovary	Basic	European Lit	1
Forster, E.M.	A Passage to India	Basic	English Lit	6
Fowles, John	The French Lieutenant's Woman	Basic	English Lit	5
Frank, Anne	The Diary of Anne Frank	Basic	European Lit	2
Franklin, Benjamin	The Autobiography of Benjamin Franklin	Basic	American Lit	1
Gawain Poet	Sir Gawain and the Green Night	Basic	Classics	4
Goethe, Johann Wolfgang von	Faust - Parts I & II	Basic	European Lit	2
Golding, William	Lord of the Flies	Basic	English Lit	5
Greene, Graham	The Power and the Glory	Basic	English Lit	6
Griffin, John H.	Black Like Me	Basic	American Lit	6
	Black Like Me	Special	Black Studies	

AUTHOR	TITLE(S)	SERIES	LIBRARY	Vol
Haley, Alex	The Autobiography of Malcolm X	Basic	American Lit	6
	The Autobiography of Malcolm X	Special	Black Studies	
see also Little, Malcolm				
Hardy, Thomas	Far from the Madding Crowd * Jude the Obscure * The Mayor of Casterbridge	Basic	English Lit	3
	The Return of the Native * Tess of the D'Urbervilles	Basic	English Lit	4
	Far from the Madding Crowd * Jude the Obscure * The Mayor of Casterbridge The Return of the Native * Tess of the D'Urbervilles	Authors	Hardy	4
Hawthorne, Nathaniel	The House of the Seven Gables* The Scarlet Letter	Basic	American Lit	1
Heller, Joseph	Catch-22	Basic	American Lit	6
Hemingway, Ernest	A Farewell to Arms * For Whom the Bell Tolls	Basic	American Lit	4
	The Old Man and the Sea	Basic	American Lit	7
	The Sun Also Rises	Basic	American Lit	5
	A Farewell to Arms * For Whom the Bell Tolls The Old Man and the Sea The Sun Also Rises	Authors	Hemingway	5
Herbert, Frank	Dune & Other Works	Basic	American Lit	6
Hesse, Herman	Demian * Steppenwolf & Siddhartha	Basic	European Lit	2
Hilton, James	Lost Horizon	Basic	English Lit	5
Homer	The Iliad * The Odyssey	Basic	Classics	1
Hugo, Victor	Les Miserables	Basic	European Lit	1
Huxley, Aldous	Brave New World & Brave New World Revisited	Basic	English Lit	5
Ibsen, Henrik	Ibsen's Plays I: A Doll's House & Hedda Gabler * Ibsen's Plays II: Ghosts, An Enemy of the People, & The Wild Duck	Basic	European Lit	4
James, Henry	The American * Daisy Miller & The Turn of the Screw * The Portrait of a Lady	Basic	American Lit	2
	The American * Daisy Miller & The Turn of the Screw * The Portrait of a Lady	Authors	James	6
Joyce, James	A Portrait of the Artist as a Young Man * Ulysses	Basic	English Lit	6
Kafka, Franz	Kafka's Short Stories * The Trial	Basic	European Lit	2
Keats & Shelley	Keats & Shelley	Basic	English Lit	1
Kesey, Ken	One Flew Over the Cuckoo's Nest	Basic	American Lit	7

AUTHOR	TITLE(S)	SERIES	LIBRARY	Vol
Knowles, John	A Separate Peace	Basic	American Lit	7
Lawrence, D.H.	Sons and Lovers	Basic	English Lit	6
Lee, Harper	To Kill a Mockingbird	Basic	American Lit	7
Lewis, Sinclair	Babbit * Main Street	Basic	American Lit	3
	Babbit * Main Street	Authors	Lewis	7
Little, Malcolm	The Autobiography of Malcolm X	Basic	American Lit	6
	The Autobiography of Malcolm X	Special	Black Studies	
see also Haley, Alex				
London, Jack	Call of the Wild & White Fang	Basic	American Lit	3
Machiavelli, Niccolo	The Prince	Basic	Classics	4
Malamud, Bernard	The Assistant	Basic	American Lit	6
Malcolm X	see Little, Malcolm			
Malory, Thomas	Le Morte d'Arthur	Basic	Classics	4
Marlowe, Christopher	Doctor Faustus	Basic	Classics	3
Marquez, Gabriel Garcia	One Hundred Years of Solitude	Basic	American Lit	6
Maugham, Somerset	Of Human Bondage	Basic	English Lit	6
Melville, Herman	Billy Budd & Typee * Moby Dick	Basic	American Lit	1
Miller, Arthur	The Crucible * Death of a Salesman	Basic	American Lit	6
Milton, John	Paradise Lost	Basic	English Lit	2
Moliere, Jean Baptiste	Tartuffe, Misanthrope & Bourgeois Gentleman	Basic	European Lit	1
More, Thomas	Utopia	Basic	Classics	4
O'Connor, Flannery	O'Connor's Short Stories	Basic	American Lit	7
Orwell, George	Animal Farm	Basic	English Lit	5
	Nineteen Eighty-Four	Basic	English Lit	6
Paton, Alan	Cry, The Beloved Country	Basic	English Lit	5
Plath, Sylvia	The Bell Jar	Basic	American Lit	6
Plato	Plato's Euthyphro, Apology, Crito & Phaedo * Plato's The Republic	Basic	Classics	1
Poe, Edgar Allen	Poe's Short Stories	Basic	American Lit	1
Remarque, Erich	All Quiet on the Western Front	Basic	European Lit	2
Rolvaag, Ole	Giants in the Earth	Basic	European Lit	4
Rostand, Edmond	Cyrano de Bergerac	Basic	European Lit	1
Salinger, J.D.	The Catcher in the Rye	Basic	American Lit	6
Sartre, Jean Paul	No Exit & The Flies	Basic	European Lit	1
Scott, Walter	Ivanhoe	Basic	English Lit	1
Shaefer, Jack	Shane	Basic	American Lit	7
Shakespeare, William	All's Well that Ends Well & The Merry Wives of Windsor * As You Like It * The Comedy of Errors, Love's Labour's Lost, & The Two Gentlemen of Verona * Measure for Measure * The Merchant of Venice * Midsummer Night's Dream *	Basic	Shakespeare	1

AUTHOR	TITLE(S)	SERIES	LIBRARY	Vol
Shakespeare, William	Much Ado About Nothing * The Taming of the Shrew * The Tempest * Troilus and Cressida * Twelfth Night * The Winter's Tale	Basic	Shakespeare	1
	All's Well that Ends Well & The Merry Wives of Windsor * As You Like It * The Comedy of Errors, Love's Labour's Lost, & The Two Gentlemen of Verona * Measure for Measure * The Merchant of Venice * Midsummer Night's Dream * Much Ado About Nothing * The Taming of the Shrew * The Tempest * Troilus and Cressida * Twelfth Night * The Winter's Tale	Authors	Shakespeare	8
	Antony and Cleopatra * Hamlet * Julius Caesar * King Lear * Macbeth * Othello * Romeo and Juliet	Basic	Shakeapeare	2
	Antony and Cleopatra * Hamlet * Julius Caesar * King Lear * Macbeth * Othello * Romeo and Juliet	Authors	Shakespeare	9
	Henry IV Part 1 * Henry IV Part 2 * Henry V * Henry VI Parts 1,2,3 * Richard II * Richard III * Shakespeare's Sonnets	Basic	Shakespeare	3
	Henry IV Part 1 * Henry IV Part 2 * Henry V * Henry VI Parts 1,2,3 * Richard II * Richard III * Shakespeare's Sonnets	Authors	Shakespeare	10
Shaw, George Bernard	Man and Superman & Caesar and Cleopatra * Pygmalion & Arms and the Man	Basic	English Lit	6
	Man and Superman & Caesar and Cleopatra * Pygmalion & Arms and the Man	Authors	Shaw	11
Shelley, Mary	Frankenstein	Basic	English Lit	1
Sinclair, Upton	The Jungle	Basic	American Lit	3
Skinner, B.F.	Walden Two	Basic	American Lit	7
Solzhenitsyn, Aleksandr	One Day in the Life of Ivan Denisovich	Basic	European Lit	3
Sophocles	The Oedipus Trilogy	Basic	Classics	1
Spenser, Edmund	The Faerie Queen	Basic	Classics	4

AUTHOR	TITLE(S)	SERIES	LIBRARY	Vol
Steinbeck, John	The Grapes of Wrath *	Basic	American Lit	4
	Of Mice and Men * The Pearl * The Red Pony	Basic	American Lit	5
	The Grapes of Wrath * Of Mice and Men * The Pearl * The Red Pony	Authors	Steinbeck	12
Stendhal	The Red and the Black	Basic	European Lit	1
Sterne, Lawrence	Tristram Shandy	Basic	English Lit	2
Stevenson, Robert	Dr. Jekyll and Mr. Hyde *	Basic	English Lit	3
Louis	Treasure Island & Kidnapped	Basic	English Lit	4
Stoker, Bram	Dracula	Basic	English Lit	3
Stowe, Harriet Beecher	Uncle Tom's Cabin	Basic	American Lit	2
Swift, Jonathan	Gulliver's Travels	Basic	English Lit	1
Thackeray, William Makepeace	Vanity Fair	Basic	English Lit	4
Thoreau, Henry David	Walden	Basic	American Lit	1
Tolkien, J.R.R.	The Lord of the Rings & The Hobbit	Basic	English Lit	5
Tolstoy, Leo	Anna Karenina * War and Peace	Basic	European Lit	3
Turgenev, Ivan Sergeyevich	Fathers and Sons	Basic	European Lit	3
Twain, Mark	A Connecticut Yankee * Huckleberry Finn * The Prince and the Pauper * Tom Sawyer	Basic	American Lit	2
	A Connecticut Yankee * Huckleberry Finn * The Prince and the Pauper * Tom Sawyer	Authors	Twain	13
Virgil	The Aeneid	Basic	Classics	1
Voltaire, Francois	Candide	Basic	European Lit	2
Vonnegut, Kurt	Vonnegut's Major Works	Basic	American Lit	7
Walker, Alice	The Color Purple	Basic	American Lit	7
	The Color Purple	Special	Black Studies	
Warren, Robert Penn	All the King's Men	Basic	American Lit	6
West, Nathanael	Miss Lonelyhearts & The Day of the Locust	Basic	American Lit	5
Wharton, Edith	Ethan Frome	Basic	American Lit	3
Whitman, Walt	Leaves of Grass	Basic	American Lit	1
Wilder, Thornton	Our Town	Basic	American Lit	5
Williams, Tennessee	The Glass Menagerie & A Streetcar Named Desire	Basic	American Lit	6
Woolf, Virginia	Mrs. Dalloway	Basic	English Lit	5
Wordsworth, William	The Prelude	Basic	English Lit	2
Wright, Richard	Black Boy	Basic	American Lit	4
	Native Son	Basic	American Lit	5
	Black Boy	Special	Black Studies	
	Native Son	Special	Black Studies	

BASIC LIBRARY (24-0)

THE SHAKESPEARE LIBRARY: 3 Volumes, 26 Titles (25-9)
    V. 1 - The Comedies 12 titles (00-3)
    V. 2 - The Tragedies, 7 titles (01-1)
    V. 3 - The Histories; The Sonnets, 7 titles (02-X)
THE CLASSICS LIBRARY: 4 Volumes, 27 Titles (26-7)
    V. 1 - Greek & Roman Classics, 11 titles (03-8)
    V. 2 - Greek & Roman Classics, 2 titles (04-6)
    V. 3 - Early Christian/European Classics, 7 titles (05-4)
    V. 4 - Early Christian/European Classics, 7 titles (06-2)
ENGLISH LITERATURE LIBRARY: 6 Volumes, 55 Titles (29-1)
    V. 1 - 17th Century & Romantic Period Classics, 7 titles (07-0)
    V. 2 - 17th Century & Romantic Period Classics, 7 titles (08-9)
    V. 3 - Victorian Age, 11 titles (09-7)
    V. 4 - Victorian Age, 10 titles (10-0)
    V. 5 - 20th Century, 10 titles (11-9)
    V. 6 - 20th Century, 10 titles (12-7)
AMERICAN LITERATURE LIBRARY: 7 Volumes, 77 Titles (33-X)
    V. 1 - Early U.S. & Romantic Period, 11 titles (13-5)
    V. 2 - Civil War to 1900, 11 titles (14-3)
    V. 3 - Early 20th Century, 9 titles (15-1)
    V. 4 - The Jazz Age to W.W.II, 11 titles (16-X)
    V. 5 - The Jazz Age to W.W.II, 10 titles (17-8)
    V. 6 - Post-War American Literature, 13 titles (18-6)
    V. 7 - Post-War American Literature, 12 titles (19-4)
EUROPEAN LITERATURE LIBRARY: 4 Volumes, 29 Titles (36-4)
    V. 1 - French Literature, 12 titles (20-8)
    V. 2 - German Literature, 7 titles (21-6)
    V. 3 - Russian Literature, 7 titles (22-4)
    V. 4 - Scandinavian Literature, 3 titles (23-2)

AUTHORS LIBRARY (65-8)

    V. 1 - **Charles Dickens** Library, 6 titles (66-6)
    V. 2 - **Feodor Dostoevsky** Library, 3 titles (67-4)
    V. 3 - **William Faulkner** Library, 7 titles (68-2)
    V. 4 - **Thomas Hardy** Library, 5 titles (69-0)
    V. 5 - **Ernest Hemingway** Library, 4 titles (70-4)
    V. 6 - **Henry James** Library, 3 titles (71-2)
    V. 7 - **Sinclair Lewis** Library, 2 titles (72-0)
    V. 8 - **Shakespeare** Library, Part 1 - The Comedies, 12 titles (73-9)
    V. 9 - **Shakespeare** Library, Part 2 - The Tragedies, 7 titles (74-7)
    V. 10 - **Shakespeare** Library, Part 3 - The Histories; Sonnets, 7 titles (75-5)
    V. 11 - **George Bernard Shaw** Library, 2 titles (76-3)
    V. 12 - **John Steinbeck** Library, 4 titles (77-1)
    V. 13 - **Mark Twain** Library, 4 titles (78-X)

SPECIAL LIBRARY

Black Studies Volume, 7 titles (90-9)

Moonbeam Publications ISBN Prefix: 0-931013-

CLIFFS NOTES
HARDBOUND LITERARY LIBRARIES
INDEX OF LIBRARIES

This is the INDEX OF LIBRARIES, listing the volumes and the individual titles within the volumes for both the BASIC LIBRARY SERIES (24 Volumes, starting below) and the AUTHORS LIBRARY SERIES (13 Volumes, see Page 6).

BASIC LIBRARY SERIES (24 Volumes)

THE SHAKESPEARE LIBRARY: 3 Volumes, 26 Titles

Vol 1 - The Comedies (12 titles)
*All's Well that Ends Well & The Merry
    Wives of Windsor*
As You Like It
*The Comedy of Errors, Love's Labour's
    Lost, & The Two Gentlemen of Verona*
Measure for Measure
The Merchant of Venice
A Midsummer Night's Dream
Much Ado About Nothing
The Taming of the Shrew
The Tempest
Troilus and Cressida
Twelfth Night
The Winter's Tale

Vol 2 - The Tragedies (7 titles)
Antony and Cleopatra
Hamlet
Julius Caesar
King Lear
Macbeth
Othello
Romeo and Juliet

Vol 3 - The Histories; The Sonnets (7 titles)
Henry IV Part 1
Henry IV Part 2
Henry V
Henry VI Parts 1,2,3
Richard II
Richard III
Shakespeare's Sonnets

THE CLASSICS LIBRARY: 4 Volumes, 27 Titles

Vol 1 - Greek & Roman Classics Part 1 (11 titles)

The Aeneid
Agamemnon
Aristotle's Ethics
Euripides' Electra & Medea
The Iliad
Lysistrata & Other Comedies
Mythology
The Odyssey
Oedipus Trilogy
Plato's Euthyphro, Apology, Crito & Phaedo
Plato's The Republic

Vol 2 - Greek & Roman Classics Part 2 (2 titles)

Greek Classics
Roman Classics

Vol 3 - Early Christian/European Classics Part 1 (7 titles)

Beowulf
Canterbury Tales
Divine Comedy - I. Inferno
Divine Comedy - II. Purgatorio
Divine Comedy - III. Paradiso
Doctor Faustus
Don Quixote

Vol 4 - Early Christian/European Classics Part 2 (7 titles)

The Faerie Queene
Le Morte D'Arthur
New Testament
Old Testament
The Prince
Sir Gawain and the Green Knight
Utopia

ENGLISH LITERATURE LIBRARY: 6 Volumes, 55 Titles

Vol 1 - 17th Century & Romantic Period Classics
Part 1 (7 titles)
Emma
Frankenstein
Gulliver's Travels
Ivanhoe
Joseph Andrews
Keats & Shelley
Moll Flanders

Vol 2 - 17th Century & Romantic Period Classics
Part 2 (7 titles)
Paradise Lost
Pilgrim's Progress
The Prelude
Pride and Prejudice
Robinson Crusoe
Tom Jones
Tristram Shandy

Vol 3 - Victorian Age Part 1 (11 titles)
Alice in Wonderland
Bleak House
David Copperfield
Dr. Jekyll and Mr. Hyde
Dracula
Far from the Madding Crowd
Great Expectations
Hard Times
Jane Eyre
Jude the Obscure
The Mayor of Casterbridge

Vol 4 - Victorian Age Part 2 (10 titles)
Middlemarch
The Mill on the Floss
Oliver Twist
The Return of the Native
Silas Marner
A Tale of Two Cities
Tess of the D'Urbervilles
Treasure Island & Kidnapped
Vanity Fair
Wuthering Heights

ENGLISH LITERATURE LIBRARY (cont'd)

Vol 5 - 20th Century Part 1 (10 titles)

Animal Farm
Brave New World
Cry, The Beloved Country
The French Lieutenant's Woman
Heart of Darkness & The Secret Sharer
Lord Jim
Lord of the Flies
The Lord of the Rings
Lost Horizon
Mrs. Dalloway

Vol 6 - 20th Century Part 2 (10 titles)

Nineteen Eighty-Four
Of Human Bondage
A Passage to India
A Portrait of the Artist as a Young Man
The Power and the Glory
Shaw's Man and Superman & Caesar and Cleopatra
Shaw's Pygmalion & Arms and the Man
Sons and Lovers
T.S. Eliot's Major Poems and Plays
Ulysses

AMERICAN LITERATURE LIBRARY: 7 Volumes, 77 Titles

Vol 1 - Early U.S. & Romantic Period (11 titles)

Autobiography of Ben Franklin
Billy Budd & Typee
The Deerslayer
Emerson's Essays
The House of Seven Gables
The Last of the Mohicans
Leaves of Grass
Moby Dick
Poe's Short Stories
The Scarlet Letter
Walden

<u>INDEX OF LIBRARIES (cont'd)</u>
<u>BASIC LIBRARY SERIES</u>

AMERICAN LITERATURE LIBRARY (cont'd)

Vol 2 - Civil War to 1900 (11 titles)

The American
The Awakening
A Connecticut Yankee in King Arthur's Court
Daisy Miller & The Turn of the Screw
Emily Dickinson: Selected Poems
Huckleberry Finn
The Portrait of a Lady
The Prince and the Pauper
Red Badge of Courage
Tom Sawyer
Uncle Tom's Cabin

Vol 3 - Early 20th Century (9 titles)

An American Tragedy
Babbitt
Call of the Wild & White Fang
Ethan Frome
The Jungle
Main Street
My Antonia
Sister Carrie
Winesburg, Ohio

Vol 4 - The Jazz Age to W.W.II Part 1 (11 titles)

Absalom, Absalom!
As I Lay Dying
The Bear
Black Boy
A Farewell to Arms
For Whom the Bell Tolls
Go Down, Moses
The Good Earth
The Grapes of Wrath
The Great Gatsby
Light in August

AMERICAN LITERATURE LIBRARY (cont'd)

Vol 5 - The Jazz Age to W.W.II Part 2 (10 titles)

Miss Lonelyhearts & The Day of the Locust
Native Son
Of Mice and Men
Our Town
The Pearl
The Red Pony
The Sound and the Fury
The Sun Also Rises
Tender is the Night
Unvanquished

Vol 6 - Post-War American Literature Part 1 (13 titles)

100 Years of Solitude
All the King's Men
The Assistant
The Autobiography of Malcolm X
The Bell Jar
Black Like Me
Catch-22
The Catcher in the Rye
The Color Purple
The Crucible
Death of a Salesman
Dune and Other Works
The Glass Menagerie & A Streetcar Named Desire

Vol 7 - Post-War American Literature Part 2 (12 titles)

The Invisible Man
Manchild in the Promised Land
O'Connor's Short Stories
The Old Man and the Sea
One Flew Over the Cuckoo's Nest
The Ox-Bow Incident
A Separate Peace
Shane
To Kill a Mockingbird
Vonnegut's Major Works
Walden Two
Who's Afraid of Virginia Woolf?

EUROPEAN LITERATURE LIBRARY: 4 Volumes, 29 Titles

Vol 1 - French Literature (12 titles)
Candide
The Count of Monte Cristo
Cyrano de Bergerac
Les Miserables
Madame Bovary
No Exit & The Flies
The Plague
The Red and the Black
The Stranger
Tartuffe, Misanthrope & Bourgeois Gentlemen
The Three Musketeers
Waiting for Godot

Vol 2 - German Literature (7 titles)
All Quiet on the Western Front
Demian
The Diary of Anne Frank
Faust Pt. I & Pt. II
Kafka's Short Stories
Steppenwolf & Siddhartha
The Trial

Vol 3 - Russian Literature (7 titles)
Anna Karenina
The Brothers Karamozov
Crime and Punishment
Fathers and Sons
Notes from the Underground
One Day in the Life of Ivan Denisovich
War and Peace

Vol 4 - Scandinavian Literature (3 titles)
Giants in the Earth
Ibsen's Plays I: A Doll's House & Hedda Gabler
Ibsen's Plays II: Ghosts, An Enemy of the People & The Wild Duck

AUTHORS LIBRARY

Vol 1 -Charles Dickens Library (6 titles)
Bleak House
David Copperfield
Great Expectations
Hard Times
Oliver Twist
A Tale of Two Cities

Vol 2 - Feodor Dostoevsky Library (3 titles)
The Brothers Karamazov
Crime and Punishment
Notes from the Underground

Vol 3 - William Faulkner Library (7 titles)
Absalom, Absalom!
As I Lay Dying
The Bear
Go Down, Moses
Light in August
The Sound and the Fury
The Unvanquished

Vol 4 - Thomas Hardy Library (5 titles)
Far from the Madding Crowd
Jude the Obscure
The Major of Casterbridge
The Return of the Native
Tess of the D'Urbervilles

Vol 5 - Ernest Hemingway Library (4 titles)
A Farewell to Arms
For Whom the Bell Tolls
The Old Man and the Sea
The Sun Also Rises

Vol 6 - Henry James Library (3 titles)
The American
Daisy Miller & The Turn of the Screw
The Portrait of a Lady

Vol 7 - Sinclair Lewis Library (2 titles)
*Babbitt * Main Street*

Black Studies Volume (7 titles)

The Autobiography of Malcolm X
Black Boy
Black Like Me
The Color Purple
The Invisible Man
Manchild in the Promised Land
Native Son